ANTHROPOLOGY AS ETHICS

Nondualism and the Conduct of Sacrifice

T. M. S. Evens

Berghahn Books
NEW YORK • OXFORD

Published in 2008 by
Berghahn Books

www.berghahnbooks.com

Library of Congress Cataloging-in-Publication Data

Evens, T. M. S.
    Anthropology as ethics : nondualism and the conduct of sacrifice /
by T. M. S. Evens.
    p. cm.
Includes bibliographical references and index.
ISBN 978-1-84545-224-7 (hardcover : alk. paper)
    1. Ethics. 2. Dualism. 3. Sacrifice. 4. Anthropology—Philosophy. I. Title.

BJ1031.E94 2007
301.01—dc22

                                                            2006100541

British Library Cataloguing in Publication Data

A catalogue record for this book is available from
the British Library.

Printed in the United States on acid-free paper

For Susan, my beloved—we grow old together.

CONTENTS

Preface   ix

Acknowledgments   xvii

Organization and Key Usages   xix

Introduction: Nondualism, Ontology, and Anthropology   1

PART I The Ethnographic Self: The Socio-political Pathology of Modernity   15

1. Anthropology and the Synthetic a Priori: Wittgenstein and Merleau-Ponty   17
2. Blind Faith and the Binding of Isaac—the Akedah   47
3. Excursus I: Sacrifice as Human Existence   76
4. Counter-Sacrifice and Instrumental Reason—the Holocaust   83
5. Bourdieu's Anti-dualism and "Generalized Materialism"   107
6. Habermas's Anti-dualism and "Communicative Rationality"   131

PART II The Ethnographic Other: The Ethical Openness of Archaic Understanding   151

7. Technological Efficacy, Mythic Rationality, and Non-contradiction   153
8. Epistemic Efficacy, Mythic Rationality, and Non-contradiction   162
9. Contradiction and Choice among the Dinka and in Genesis   176
10. Contradiction in Azande Oracular Practice and in Psychotherapeutic Interaction   197

PART III From Mythic to Value-Rationality: Toward Ethical Gain   215

11. Epistemic and Ethical Gain   217
12. Transcending Dualism and Amplifying Choice   241

13. Excursus II: What Good, Ethics?   256
14. Anthropology and the Generative Primacy of Moral Order   273

Conclusion: Emancipatory Selfhood and Value-Rationality   294

Notes   301

References   364

Index   376

PREFACE

I

The problem set that serves to guide my work centers on the basic anthropological question of what makes human beings tick. For me, that question is posed best in terms of *how* humans do what they do rather than *why*. By formulating the question in this way, I bracket the matter of motivation, putting it aside. I thus wittingly pre-judge the answer to my question and highlight the irony of asking what makes human beings tick. If motivation, in the causal sense of the term, is a secondary consideration only, then specifically human conduct is in the end incomprehensible in terms of one thing or part moving another. Rather, it must be grasped 'holistically', as self-movement of a peculiar kind, the kind in which, oxymoronically, 'free will' remains tied to external agency. The movement that concerns me, then, belongs at bottom not to a clock but to a kind of self.

Logically, such movement, where cause and effect are both different from and identical to each other, is exemplarily paradoxical. This circumstance obliges the anthropologist to investigate basic self-identifying, which is to say, the meanings imprisoned in our actions. Such lived or tacit meanings implicate self-identifying because they disclose the sense of our selves—personal, social, and cultural—as this sense, exhibiting a hopeless ambiguity, is both determinate of and given in action. Insofar as it is determining, the sense of self is understood *to effect* the action; insofar as it is given, the sense of self is seen as *informed by* the action. In either case, though, to reintroduce the paradox, the sense of self is only imperfectly distinguishable from the action and therefore always imperfect or open to one degree or another. But given its intrinsically purposeful nature, the sense of self is what gives meaning to and makes immediate sense of the action.

In view of the focus on self-identity as it is imprisoned in action, my approach is, I suppose, an anthropology of practice. This approach pictures practice, though, as a matter of ethics before anything else, including power and aesthetics. It features the manner in which the self conducts itself toward the 'other', that is, toward that which fundamentally enables the self. In effect, although I neither doubt the ultimate primacy of the other and the historical and contingent nature of our existence, nor fail to keep this primacy in observant account, for purposes of grasping what makes us tick as humans, I privilege the constitutionally limited or ambiguous way in which we, both individually and collectively, create ourselves and discharge our inescapable responsibility. In other words, in measured reaction to the essential but also, in serious part, befogging thrust of social science as science, to the mechanical move to explain, whether through causal or motivational relations, social phenomena, I want to bring into prominent account the relative bearing of the inexplicable moment of responsible or human agency on these phenomena. If personhood marks the intersection of self and other, of constituting and constituted activity, then I aim to highlight the element of personal agency that somehow emerges on that ecliptic plane, where the creative moment corresponding to the uttering or thinking of 'I' results in, to evoke Durkheim's singular insight, an act of moral being.

By 'ethics' I intend primarily not the scholastic department of philosophy that goes by that name, but the creative and paradoxically natural conduct whereby humans together determine their own good, thus informing themselves and their world, both wittingly and not, with second nature or value. By taking ethics and 'otherness' in tandem, I suggest that anthropology is by its very nature ethics, for otherness is one notion without which anthropological inquiry makes little if any sense.

Regarding anthropology as ethics does not mean that empirical research is not also necessary to the anthropological enterprise. On the contrary, in part what makes anthropology unique as ethics is its empirical discipline. But once the primarily ethical nature of anthropology is well and truly registered, 'empiricism' cannot abide. That is to say, although the 'facts' must be gathered, they never speak for themselves, and whosoever speaks for them always betrays value judgments and ethical determinations. There is, of course, nothing new about the observation that facts demand interpretation, and that interpretation necessarily conveys a particular and therefore value-laden point of view. What is new here is that I take this observation to entail not simply that as social scientists we need to be reflexive, but that we need to rethink the ontological presuppositions of our science.

As it is essentially paradoxical and ambiguous, self-movement demands that the anthropologist revise the received notion of reality in Western thought. That notion not only fails to admit of ambiguity; it positively disallows it. The ontological change I propose, then, is radical. I contend that the only way in which we can satisfactorily address the defining empirical problems of anthropology at their core is by rethinking the very gestalt that serves as the ontological scaffolding on which these problems have been determined.

An ontology that portrays reality as basically ambiguous is markedly out of keeping with 'ontology' in the strict sense, which denotes a determinate and entitative reality and is the final target of all postmodernist criticism. But a reality that is fundamentally ambiguous does not break down finally into things in themselves, entities with absolute boundaries. As a result, neither intellectualism nor empiricism, neither idealism nor materialism, can serve in the end to make such a reality perspicuous. These standard theoretical offerings are predicated on the received acceptation of ontology and are therefore ill equipped to entertain ambiguity that is basic.

By the defining empirical problems of anthropology I intend the problems keyed to otherness, whatever their institutional bearing (magic, religion, polity, social organization, etc.). Closely tied to the question of otherness are the consequential problems of today's social theory, problems turning on the antinomies of the relative and the absolute, or of the particular and the universal, and of subject and object, or self and other. For example, in light of the genocidal events and massively destructive military conflagrations of the twentieth as well as the twenty-first century, and of the question of power that arises in their connection, postmodernism has set out to deconstruct the precepts of a universal reason and self-transparent self or subjectivity.

By embracing reality as basically ambiguous, the antinomies implicated by these dire social problems get redefined as nondualisms, such that their principles are both opposed to and continuous with each other. As a result, the principles are neutralized neither by an idealist nor a materialist reconcilement. Instead of abstract logical oppositions, they reappear as profound tensions or vital dynamics. It is a key understanding of the argument of this book that human existence is virtually indistinguishable from these tensions. For anthropological purposes, rather than thinking of humans as a particular kind of physical or even socio-cultural being, a positive object or sheer subject, it is fruitful to consider humans in terms of a constitutionally ambiguous force, the dynamic of which is reflexive. Such a dynamic implicitly identifies itself as a difference between self and other as well as between the relative and the absolute. Put another way, being human amounts to the situational and reflexive negotiation of these and related differences. Given this picture of the human condition, conflict and violence remain endemic. But by contrast to the picture in which self and other are simply opposed to each other, absolute conflict, the kind characterizing the total exclusionism displayed by genocidal activity, becomes logically inconceivable and ethically insane.

There is no proving this picture of human existence. The change of ontology I propose is a matter of conversion, not proof. Nondualism redescribes reality; it does not explain it. Nevertheless, I can offer three good reasons for making the change. First, nondualism offers a practical disciplinary advantage: it allows for a fresh approach to empirical anthropological problems that remain intractable, despite powerful attempts to resolve them. In the present book, I address in particular the abiding anthropological problem of rationality—what used to be called the problem of primitive mentality. Second, nondualism offers a phenomenological advantage: it captures an experiential side of our existence that science cannot acknowledge without exposing the constitutional positivism of the scientific perspective as ultimately a pretense. In this volume, that side of our existence is disclosed in terms of sacrifice and our fundamental otherness to ourselves. Third, nondualism offers an ethical advantage: by allowing genuine value and discretionary activity as givens in any human universe, it revitalizes the ameliorative and irenic force of ethics. In this connection, the present work propounds anthropology as an ethics and projects a selfdom whose boundaries are perceived to connect no less than to separate. Given such an anthropology and selfdom, anchored in paradox and nondualism, and despite the very real efficacy of scientific practice, the world is projected as basically and truly enchanted. I mean by 'enchantment' precisely what Weber had in mind when he set out his famous thesis about rationalization and the disenchantment of the world.

II

From the standpoint of method, the anthropology and selfdom I intend call for a strenuous reflexivity. This method instructs one to doubt or throw into question what one 'knows'. Deploying it, Descartes found, famously, that he was left with his self alone—his "I think" or *cogito*. Some 325 years later, using the same method, albeit differently, Foucault discerned to the contrary that it is above all the self that misleads and imprisons, and that therefore needs to be undone. Unfortunately, although he catches his philosophical forefather in a flagrant act of self-deception, once it is seen (as Foucault himself came to see, or so I argue in chapters 11–12) that in the theorized absence of some agentially significant sort of selfhood there is nothing to remediate by his own sort of doubt, Foucault's revision also turns out to be less than coherent. What indeed is liberated, we may ask, when one's self is exposed as preponderantly a seductive systemic illusion created by the often demonic (but also productive) and always ubiquitous magician to which Foucault gave the name of power?

As against these two intellectual giants, it seems to me that when it is practiced unfailingly, reflexivity always leaves us in limbo, ever between self and other, such that the self is fixed only in its movement of becoming other to itself. This movement marks an eternal return that reiterates—with a peculiar twist—the essential and dynamic ambiguity of the other. Accordingly, both self and other are reaffirmed as they are cleared away: the other is reaffirmed as 'other' or what is irreducible to the self, and the self is reaffirmed as ever under construction (or, what amounts to almost the same thing, deconstruction), in view of its necessary, paradoxical foundation in the other. Whereas the wholly other, being nowhere in particular, is essentially homeless, the self, although positively defined in terms of indwelling or identity, can never quite go home again, because the security of its home has always already been breached as a condition of its being. The peculiar twist mentioned just above in relation to the Nietzschean notion of eternal return consists in the responsibility imposed on the self in the face of its at once limiting but enabling otherness. As a result of this condition of indebtedness, which arises together with reflexivity, the self-other tension and its attendant world of human existence are from their inception matters of ethics.

Using the method of doubt, Descartes—driven by philosophy in the identitarian sense given it by Plato, the sense in which 'to know' is always to know a thing in itself (an identity)—sought to arrive at indubitable knowledge or, more exactly, self-certitude. Certain knowledge and self-certain selfhood stand (and fall) together, since the *cogito* is implicit in the very idea of certain knowledge: how can the predicate be fixed and certain if its subject—that which *knows*—does not enjoy self-certitude? Foucault, however, having seen, felt, and documented the oppression of such an 'enlightened' epistemological regime (and, tellingly, echoing the Judeo-Christian God's punishing 'critique' of the First Couple for having fallen headlong for the Serpent's fascinating projection of their very own godlike selves), deployed the same method to expose the Cartesian or self-certain self as a pretense of power. The object of the present methodological exercise in reflexivity is neither exactly to secure nor to debunk the self. The object is, rather, in what I take to be the defining spirit of anthropology, to journey intellectually in search of otherness as it is found in both the other and the self. The idea is to make intelligible, with disciplinary rigor and purposefulness, what is ultimately irreducible to the self.

On the face of it, this endeavor—to make intelligible what is by definition unintelligible, or to reduce the irreducible—would seem self-defeating. But the appearance of unqualified contradiction here is a function of presupposing intelligibility to be nothing but a question of what has before now given the Occidental self its principal bearings, namely, reason in the strict sense. Once we set this formal presupposition aside, it becomes possible to conceive of the process of anthropological translation in terms other than strictly reductionistic ones. The terms I have in mind picture translation as, in a loose sense of the word, dialectical: the particulars of the other are indeed bent to fit those of the self, but not without the latter themselves suffering significant deformation in the process. The anthropologist must attend not only to the negative possibility of *ethno*centrism, but also to the positive possibility of *ec*centrism: having done what he can to decenter himself (his *self*), the anthropologist opens himself to redefinition in terms of the other. Intelligibility, then, is wrought by virtue of a distinctly creative act, in which the reduction of the other by the self-preserving self is ultimately neutralized rather than finalized. It is neutralized because the self preserves itself only by becoming other to itself, thereby preserving both itself and the other for otherness.

Accordingly, making the other intelligible need not be, and at bottom is not, a question of reducing the other by appealing to reason or any other cognitive medium as a common ground, but rather of *fashioning* a common ground. The possibility of this immensely creative but utterly quotidian activity certainly has much to do with what obtains beforehand in the way of suppositions and presuppositions—and these, as the hermeneuts tell us, are prejudicial by nature. In view of the history of imperialist enterprise, inasmuch as this enterprise proceeded under the principle of enlightenment, it cannot be doubted that the presumption of reason—though still not, as I argue in this book, without its great and undeniable merits—has wrought damages of horrific impact and colossal proportions. Suppositions and presuppositions make a powerful difference.

More fundamentally, though, the dialectical possibility of generating a common ground does not rest with these pre-existing notions and attitudes, whether or not they comport reason. Instead, it rests with the ontological primacy of self-and-other as an essential tension. Considered as a tension rather than sheer opposition, the self-other relationship shows itself also in terms of continuity. Put another way, by virtue of this relationship people always already, in practice, enjoy a common ground. But in this form, the common ground does not exactly pre-exist: it obtains as a moving dynamic, something ever in the making. In which case, of course, it can never be fixed beforehand, and, for this reason, always goes to affirm abiding otherness. A firm and immovable common ground bespeaks only the selfsame or identity and renders otherness impossible. But otherness abides, and because it does, we never do arrive at the common ground—we only travel in its direction.

As the academic study of humankind, the profession of anthropology uniquely specializes in this mode of travel. Conceived of as a universalizing but intrinsically non-culminant journeying toward the other, anthropological translation carries definite methodological implications. It implies that the traditional goal of capturing ethnographically a specimen other-culture indulges a monographic idolatry, a disciplinary devotion to written presentations of social and cultural orders as if these orders were basically fixed and decided. But if the common ground is in fact always on the move, then such monographs present false pictures of ethnic realities. For not only is the ground ever shifting beneath the seven-league feet of the professional anthropologist, but also the ethnic realities themselves are ceaselessly engaged in the building of their own social and cultural common grounds.

This criticism of previous anthropological practice is hardly new, although the discipline is still straining to come to terms with it. In this connection, the sense of anthropological translation proposed here definitely does not imply that anthropology should, in view of such epistemological conceit, abandon the study of others in favor of self-study alone or even preponderantly. This now familiar remedial strategy, although impressively grounded in the fear of reducing the other to ourselves or, with Orientalism, to our counter-selves, serves to reinforce the dualism of self and other. It thus ironically also promotes the understanding of the self as absolute. What is more, the fact that the ethnic realities we study are never really fixed but are themselves always under self-construction and deconstruction suggests that the transformation of definition they suffer at the hands of the ethnographer is not in itself an imposition. The picture of ethnography as inherently intrusive or worse betrays a critical and evidently hard-to-dispel misunderstanding of the studied realities as utterly self-contained, if not culturally, at least in their capacity for self-determination. But the ethnographic interaction is no different in principle from the social interactions that take place from 'within'. To be sure, the ethnographic interaction dramatizes the self-other and internal-external axes of social interaction, and for this reason is peculiar and carries special risks. But these are relative matters, for the tensions of self-and-other and internal-and-external constitute axes around which any social interaction revolves. The question that needs to be asked in respect to ethnographic 'authority', then, is not how we obviate this authority, but rather what form it should take and what the moral tenor of the definitional transformations it brings about should be.

If we are to understand the other, we must initiate a respectful process of give and take in which we need to be prepared to offer ourselves up, on behalf of our intellectual project, to otherness—not to resist but instead to enhance the way in which we are always already open to the other in spite of our*selves*. One consults the other and, once so informed, modifies oneself accordingly, validating the other's otherness. When doing so, however, to make an absolutely critical caveat, one need always bear in mind that the anthropological (as distinct from theological or even zoological) other is, while peculiarly representative of otherness per se, also a self or egoity in its own right and therefore subject to the same ethical accountability and critical scrutiny that one owes to one's own self. The fact that self-and-other constitutes an axis of direction rather than a dichotomy proper, and that the anthropologist is therefore constantly burdened with the task of forging the distinction between what is self and what is other about the other, only goes to show the inescapable way in which anthropology, even at its most empirical, is ethics.

Not only where but also how one draws the line between selfness and otherness marks the degree to which one is open to difference, and in the absence of such openness, ethics, considered in terms of the question of what is owing to the other, is effectively drained of meaning. To be sure, in the face of the various 'isms' that, on the basis of corporal difference (race) or some kind of categorical affiliation (nation, for instance), find it all too easy to make a hard and fast distinction between self and other, one might well ask why the difference is not given in absolute terms but in fact always remains a relative matter. I address this question in chapter 11, where, analyzing phenomenologically, I suggest that emergent consciousness, with a dialectical and immensely consequential cunning, appropriates to itself the kind of absolute boundary Descartes posited for things that extend in space, thus in principle sealing itself against otherness and constructing the self-other relationship as a dualism.

The principal methodological implication of the sort of translation I propose here, then, in focused accordance with the hallowed proscription on ethnocentrism, is that the anthropologist prepare herself in a disciplined manner to sacrifice her understanding of self and world on behalf of the other's otherness, but by no means in the interest of sheer relativism or the wholesale approbation of all that the other is and does. This discipline takes the form of ontological and phenomenological reflexivity, such that, in virtue specifically of the ethnographic interaction, whether on the ground or in the reading, one deconstructs one's own sense of self and reality. But such self-deconstruction does not take itself as its own end. Instead, its object is to create a substantial void in the anthropologist's second nature, which, since this nature too abhors a vacuum, and in virtue of the ethnographic consultation, fills itself with an*other*—a *re*constructed— sense of self and reality. In result, a fresh common ground is shaped, on the strength of which we will not have done the impossible and changed places with the other, but, in a way that ultimately defies rational determination, we will have made the other's point of view our own, including, very likely, a coefficient of contempt for ourselves.

III

The present work began as a short concluding section to an earlier monograph, *Two Kinds of Rationality* (1995). That study is highly theoretical but directly anchored in my ethnographic field research of an Israeli kibbutz. In what was to be an afterword, I set out to address even broader problems raised by the book's analysis. In order, though, to facilitate publication of *Two Kinds of Rationality*, I was persuaded to detach the projected afterword, allowing it to grow into its own book—the present one. Nevertheless, there remains an important, umbilical attachment between the two volumes. The ethnography of the kibbutz (as well as my career-long reworking of Evans-Pritchard's Nuer ethnography) stands to the present exercise as a conceptual provider, an instructor of ideas, as well as an empirical case study. For this reason, taken together the two works enact the kind of anthropology I extol below, an anthropology as ethics: the other or the ethnographic community is virtually consulted by the self or the anthropologist, thus identifying the other, not only as an object of inquiry and even criticism, but also as an anthropologically insightful agent in its own right. It seems to me that under the influence of postmodernism and its standard operating procedure of reflexivity, it has perhaps become too easy to claim something of the sort. But anyone who reads *Two Kinds of Rationality* will find that my anthropological approach has been substantially as well as critically informed by certain ideas on which I found the kibbutz to rest. These ideas bear on the nature of the creative capacity for generation, and in the final chapter of this volume (chap. 14), I find it edifying to revisit them.

My project is patently anthropological, yet it also stands at a tangent to the ontological presuppositions on which the discipline has characteristically been predicated. Indeed, by seeking to redefine decidedly what it means to be human—away from the received understanding and toward the idea of essential ambiguity and an irreducible dynamic—I am trying to undermine anthropology as we know it. In my view, despite many sincere, significant, and impelling proclamations more or less to the contrary, the received understanding remains at bottom static and dualist. By 'at bottom' I do not have in mind ethnographic practice, so much of which is admirable in purpose and splendid in accomplishment; rather, I refer to the epistemic plane in which the ontological presuppositions rest, presuppositions that in decisive part arose with modern science itself. It is easy to pay lip service to the sort of radical shift of definitions I propose. But if the redefinition is to be material, then the 'study of man' will have to change accordingly. It will have to become, above all, a peculiar kind of ethics, the kind bent on learning systematically—and in this broad sense, scientifically—about the other by also learning *from* the other.

My ontological contention about ethics and dualism is large, and its concomitant views about the nature of the human sciences are, in spirit, unusually philosophical for many orthodox anthropological frameworks. Traditional approaches aside, in a significant sense my project does not always fit comfortably even into certain of the prevailing avant-garde anthropological turns of the day. Its movement to at once embrace the political but vigorously refuse what I see as political reductionism in the discipline's adoption of the very same movement possibly puts the project in a kind of anthropological no man's land. But I nonetheless hope that my thesis of ontological conversion and the attendant ideas set out in this volume are worth pondering. By critically embracing the ontological enterprise that all social science really *is* (but is so hard pressed by constitutional scientistic pretension to deny), I hope here at least to have opened a view to a different way of conceiving of anthropology. I hope also to have shown that this way lends itself to argument and reason, and that it bears substantial disciplinary and interdisciplinary promise.

ACKNOWLEDGMENTS

This book has been many years in the writing, and a great many more in the thinking. Over these years I have benefited from comments (the less than appreciative ones included) of a number of readers. John Caputo, whose work I admire, very kindly agreed to read my interpretation of the biblical story of Abraham's 'binding' of Isaac (my chap. 2), although my request to do so came to him out of the blue. Christopher Browning expertly commented on my analysis of the Holocaust (chap. 4), and John McGowan did the same for my critique of Habermas (chap. 6). I feel very fortunate to have as university colleagues these two superb scholars. My departmental colleagues, Arturo Escobar and Peter Redfield, provided thoughtful commentary on my chapters on Foucault (chaps. 11 and 12) and rationality (chaps. 7 and 8), respectively. My old and very dear friend, Jeffrey Obler, a gifted intellectual and teacher, whose recent passing I deeply mourn, carefully read my chapter on the Holocaust (chap. 4), as well as the two excurses on ethics and Derrida (chaps. 3 and 13).

Given the long gestation of this book, earlier versions of many of the chapters have had a number of readers who, in various capacities, provided me with valuable commentary. In this connection, I wish to thank especially my brilliant (now deceased) teacher Mike (M. G.) Smith, my friends Craig Calhoun and Nancy Scheper-Hughes, and my friend and student Steven Klein. What has become the concluding section of chapter 14 sharply benefited from a close, critical reading by my good friend Lee Schlesinger, on whose provocative and perspicacious commentary one can always count. I must also mention the late Godfrey Lienhardt, who upon my request took the time to comment caringly on what is now the chapter on the Dinka (chap. 9), and Steven Lukes, who, in his capacity as a member of a journal editorial board, furnished exceptionally useful comments on what has become the chapter on the Azande (chap. 10). Because previous versions of chapters 5, 8, 9, and 10 have appeared as journal articles,[1] I have, in respect of these chapters, benefited from anonymous reviews submitted by readers for the journals.

Earlier renderings of some of the chapters were presented to the Equipe de Recherche d'Anthropologie Sociale of the Ecole des Hautes Etudes en Sciences Sociales. I remain eternally grateful to Louis Dumont, Daniel de Coppet, and Jean Claude Galey for inviting me to their *seminaire*. Daniel and his wife, the anthropologist Cécile Barraud, were a wonderfully warm and gracious host and hostess during my stay in Paris, and I was terribly saddened to learn of Daniel's sudden death. I need also thank the following institutions, where I delivered prior versions of a number of these chapters: the Centre for the Study of the Social Sciences, Calcutta; Vishva Bharati University, Santineketan; the Research Colloquium of the Department of Sociology, at the University of Delhi; the Department of Anthropology, University College, London; and my own Department of Anthropology at the University of North Carolina at Chapel Hill. In addition, I am grateful to my university's Institute of Arts and Humanities, where during my tenure as a Chapman Fellow, I wrote a substantial portion of my interpretation of the story of Abraham and Isaac (chap. 2). I also wish to thank the many students in my long-standing seminar, "Phenomenology and Anthropology," who in recent years were forced to read and comment on certain of the chapters of this book, as well as the many more undergraduates who found my course lectures on some of the topics in this book provocative enough to press me to try, and try again, to clarify my ideas.

Lee Diener deserves special thanks for taking on the tedious task of checking my textual references against my bibliography, while she herself was about to deliver a (highly original) project of her own.

Don Handelman and Bruce Kapferer read and commented on a number of the early chapters of this book. I am warmly indebted to both of these outstanding thinkers. My friendship with them runs deep and goes back to our days as fellow graduate students at Manchester University. Were it not for their unstinting encouragement and advice, I cannot help but wonder if this project would ever have seen publication.

I owe a huge debt of gratitude to Christopher Roberts, who magnanimously and scrupulously read critically and in its entirety the penultimate draft of this book. His comments and insights, even when they expressed doubts about my ideas, were invaluable: immensely perceptive, richly knowledgeable, and ever constructive. Indeed, they were so incisive and thoughtfully put that in responding to them, I often found myself employing his vocabulary and phraseology. Although I have credited him specifically in some of the notes, the impact of his close and critical reading greatly exceeds these citations. My argumentation remains involved, but I believe that his comments have helped me immeasurably to bring greater clarity to what I have done here.

Carie Hersh and Tim Elfenbein produced the index between them, and I am obliged to them for their thoughtful, painstaking labors. I am also indebted to Marion Berghahn for her independence and willingness to publish a work that sits squarely between anthropology proper and philosophical deliberation. Finally, I remain grateful to Shawn Kendrick for her splendid copy-editorial work. It is my belief that her conscientious, engaged, and intelligent reading; her clear eye for problems of grammar, consistency, and usage; and, above all, her concern that the interested reader be able to comprehend the text have helped to make a highly complex argument more accessible than it would otherwise be. Needless to say, for the final result, the eminent intellectual inspirations all the same, and whatever the defects, I must take responsibility.

ORGANIZATION AND KEY USAGES

Organization

Because this book tries to do many things at once, putting forward numerous topics and intertwined strands of thought, it is imperative to clarify at the outset the dual nature of its structure. From one perspective, the book's chapters tend separately to present diverse topics of analysis. Thus, the chapters respectively lay out arguments about Kant's philosophical notion of the synthetic a priori as reinterpreted by Wittgenstein and Merleau-Ponty, the Akedah or binding of Isaac, the Holocaust, Pierre Bourdieu's idea of practice, Habermas's notion of communicative rationality, Foucault's understanding of selfhood, Charles Taylor's of Foucault as well as of scientific rationality, Derrida's of ethics and the Akedah, the genesis stories of the Hebrew Bible and the Dinka, Zande oracular practice as opposed to psychotherapeutic interaction, the classical anthropological question of primitive mentality in relation to the logical law of non-contradiction, the force of ethics, and the question of ethnographic authority. In light of this wide array of topics, the chapters constitute a rhizomorphic rather than tree-like structure. Nevertheless, they do not make a motley, for each finds its ultimate sense in a critical rethinking of basic categories of anthropological thought—most particularly the self-other relation—in light of ontological nondualism. One way of reading this book, then, is as an assemblage of essays, each of which is meant to show the anthropological advantage and credibility of embracing nondualism when conceiving reality.

However, the premise of the critical importance of ontology for doing anthropology provides a second, no less substantial organizing principle, one that allows the chapters to read in meaningful sequence instead of mere assemblage. The principle of which I speak consists of the question of the relation between dualism and nondualism with respect to ethics. This principle organizes the book into three broad discursive steps: first, a critique of dualism and modernity (part 1: "The Ethnographic Self"); second, a comparative examination of nondualism in the context of so-called primitive society (part 2: "The Ethnographic Other"); and, third, a commentary on nondualism in relation to the unfulfilled promise of modernity (part 3: "From Mythic to Value-Rationality"). This tripartite structure features the central argument that arises out of the ontological premise and from which the book takes its title. The claim for the anthropological superiority of nondualism blurs but does not remove the distinction between self and other, subject and object, theory and practice, and structure and process. In doing so, it follows a phenomenological approach and theory of practice, in which, respectively, existential experience and process are featured analytically. Based on this theory and approach, the diacritical human experience is identified as confrontation with the question of relative indebtedness as between self and other. This confrontation makes a chronic and unavoidable lived experience that projects human existence as fundamentally an ethical dynamic of sacrifice and affords an unconventional sense of rationality. Sacrifice, ethics, and rationality, then, compose the thematic burden of the book's other structure, disposing a general linear argument (the topical variety of chapters notwithstanding) in which these themes are discussed for the most part in relation first to dualism, then to nondualism, and finally to a promise of modernity. Here, in the dependence on the thesis of nondualism, this structure of the book intersects directly with the other, rhizomorphic structure.

Key Usages

Nondualism

This book aims to expose ontological dualism as no less perilous for humankind than it is instrumentally powerful. It is argued that dualism promotes performative contradictions, which in turn foster a felt need to reduce one of the poles of whatever particular dualism is at stake—say, the real and the ideal—to the other, thus eradicating one of the poles altogether. But the book also explores and extols a different, nondualist way of seeing the world. In arriving at nondualism, I have been influenced by a myriad of thinkers and writings. I expect, though, that no work has shaped my thinking (and reading) more enduringly and directly than the phenomenological philosophies of Maurice Merleau-Ponty and Emmanuel Levinas and the anthropologies of Evans-Pritchard, Louis Dumont (especially in his Hegelian revision of the notion of hierarchy), Pierre Bourdieu, and—in its situationalism and its conjecture that the principles underlying any given social order basically conflict with each other—the Manchester School. By dualism I intend a (Cartesian) relationship of mutual exclusion, such that things are differentiated one from another in absolute terms. By nondualism, however, I do not have in mind monism or oneness, a state of being that, logically, can issue only from the kind of boundary that dualism defines—an immaculate boundary. Instead, I use this term to denote basic ambiguity or between-ness, an ontologically dynamic state in which boundaries connect as they separate and a thing is always also other than what it is. For the analyst, the challenge offered by this ontology is how to exploit the language of concepts, the analyst's principal tool, to describe a reality of this kind. In order to do its work of clarification, conceptual language depends on the logical law of non-contradiction and, in this sense, is significantly predisposed to exclude from consideration a reality in which nondualism is the order of the day. The analyst is therefore obliged to do his best to employ the logic of conceptuality in such a way that at critical points it disrupts its own epistemological certainty and thus, chiastically, manages to reflect (on) what this logic is not.

Other

In this work, notably inspired by Emmanuel Levinas, I make frequent use of 'other', 'otherness', and 'Other'. The line drawn between these usages is rather nebulous and context dependent, since each usage conveys what cannot be or has not been reduced to the self. Generally speaking, 'the other' refers to other subjectivities, whereas by 'otherness' I have in mind what appears as different or inimical or mysterious (to the self), and can include phenomena such as natural disasters and death. When capitalized, 'Other' can evoke the numinous; but I use it principally to suggest simply the essence of what is different or otherwise. Whereas the other constitutes an-other *self* and therefore, in at least this respect, can be assimilated to one's own self, the Other cannot—it is ontologically other, to the point that it is ultimately irreducible, an alterity that stays undisclosed to quotidian human understanding. As regards the concept 'self', because of its centrality to the book's argument(s), this notion is developed throughout and therefore is scarcely in need of comment here. At this point of commencement, suffice it to say that my usage of 'self' is more or less in line with some of what passes for postmodern thinking on the 'subject', and that for me 'self' does not denote self-contained subjectivity but rather a peculiarly human and existential modality of fundamental ambiguity, in which the self remains, as a condition of its being, always other to itself. It thus describes a necessary sacrificial dynamic of becoming, a back-and-forth movement through which the self makes itself both by standing against the other and by alienating itself on behalf of the other. Put another way, every human being is the very movement through which the differentiation of self and other is made manifest.

Ethics

The word 'ethics' comes from the Greek *ethos*, for 'moral character', 'habit', and 'custom', the last-mentioned concept in particular communicating the profoundly socio-cultural nature of ethics. I use the word here to refer in the first place to the process of deciding the good or the valuable or the desirable (by contrast to the desired). This is basically in line with the Greek usage, right up through Kant. However, departing from the Kantian understanding, which emphatically makes autonomy a condition of ethics, I follow Levinas in construing the ethical capacitation of humans as primarily a matter of heteronomy: instead of the self constructing itself from scratch, it becomes self-responsible or ethical only *in response* to the other's entreaty. By 'getting in one's face', the other virtually 'elects' one—thus occasioning the ethical situation—to decide what is owing to the self and what to the other. Plainly, the Levinasian understanding, which informs the Greek with the Hebrew, consists with the social in a broad but fundamental way that arguably is lost to the Kantian theory. In the Hebrew tradition, it is the Other that 'gets in one's face'.

It follows from the emphasis on ethics as 'deciding the good', that having to choose, in accordance with the ordinary Western acceptation of 'morality', between predetermined good and evil is simply one manifestation of ethics, and it is by no means the most elementary. Ironically, despite its understood invocation of principle, in practice such global predetermination of the good amounts to a commandingly instrumental manifestation. In fact, in my conception, precisely when the options are fixed beforehand as absolute, thus forestalling creative decision-making, the ethical process is, in a very substantial sense, undercut. In connection with this ultimately negative or self-defeating ethicality, whereby the fundamentally creative and processual impetus of ethics tends to be rendered as having been brought to completion, I speak of 'moralism'. Still, since reproduction may be regarded as production once removed, the selecting of an encoded option still presents ethics as such. Therefore, under my usage, 'morality' remains a term of ethics, which is why at times, depending on context, I employ this word to convey the idea of ethics, for example, when I speak of 'moral selection' by contrast to 'natural selection'.

In another departure from received philosophical usage, 'ethics', as I employ it, is not at bottom confined to one kind of decision-making; instead, it amounts to the quotidian and diacritically human conduct of deciding anything at all. This is in the spirit (but not, I think, the letter) of Levinas's thesis of ethics as the defining attribute of being human. Needless to say, most everyday decisions are scarcely of great moment. But even a decision, say, as to whether or not to take a cup of coffee in the morning has the potential to bring to the fore the decision's essentially ethical character. If, for example, one is concerned about the conditions of coffee field laborers or the effects of caffeine on an unborn child, then this choice of breakfast beverages is suddenly seen as belonging directly to the sphere of moral concern, for the economically exploited and the welfare of the fetus, respectively. Every decision, mutatis mutandis, is ethically charged in this way.

Explicitly instrumental decisions, which are classically regarded as separate and distinct from moral ones, are also essentially matters of ethics—and not just because they can have ethical consequences. The differentiating of a decision as merely instrumental is already an act of ethics, an understanding implicit in the (Nietzschean) postmodernist critique of rationality. Constructing, on the basis of instrumental rationality, a category of decisions that stand outside the realm of ethics is just a deceptive way of doing ethics by taking for granted the good of instrumentality or, more incisively, instrumentality as the good. Put another way, the inauguration of a clean, dualistic distinction between means and ends marks an ethical decision of immense moment implicitly made on the basis of instrumentality. Indeed, in the economizing of ethics, this distinction goes a step beyond moralism: instead of curtailing the ethical process by determining the bad and the good beforehand, this distinction precludes altogether an immense category of decisions from the very idea of ethicality. Instrumentality is of course unavoidable, and I certainly do not mean to suggest that it may be taken simply to define the bad. I leave that to the moralists. Rather, I am arguing that the sheer distinction between means and ends is, although epistemologically powerful, existentially deceptive and ethically insidious.

A principal thrust of my usage is that ethics enjoys a fundamental primacy over determinacy. Because all of our decisions ultimately rest on our decided agential capacity, in the end all must be a question of ethics. It is important to be clear, though, that this critical (Levinasian) thesis of ethical priority does not mean that the realization of the good is inexorable. Although I describe ethics as *the* human condition, when 'ontology' is taken in the strict sense—the deterministic sense in which it tells not only *what* but also *that* something is—the force of ethics is not exactly ontological. Obviously, an ethical injunction against theft, for example, does not hold that in reality nobody robs and steals. Rather, the priority of ethics means that human existence is always informed by discretion. Of course, the measure of choice being fundamentally limited, since the idea of wholly unconstrained choice is specious (absent worldly constraint or delimitation, what would there be to choose between?), discretion itself betrays existential necessity. But this very necessity is one key meaning of my thesis of the primacy of ethics, for, paradoxically, it virtually condemns us to conduct ourselves in terms of meanings and values. In turn, it entails yet a second key aspect of ethics: human existence is necessarily mediatory. By virtue of our finite capacity to determine our own good or ends, we are, to an exemplary degree, our own medium.

In effect, then, the force of ethics is not a question of the power of being but of our ability to determine our own worth, which is to say, to mediate our lives in terms of value qua value. On the basis of this ability (and taking direction from Levinas), we might reformulate the second meaning of the primacy of ethics as follows: because it enables us to take advantage of the mediatory possibility of the good, ethics is better, not more powerful, than ontic necessity (R. Cohen 1986). To speak in terms of 'better' evokes the ordinary meaning of ethics as a matter of relative good and evil. I mention this here because it explains the paradox of why—regardless of the truth of the other meaning of the primacy of ethics (that one's conduct cannot help but describe ethical process)—it remains possible to conduct oneself unethically, that is, to choose against ethicality. Choices of this kind enfeeble the human capacity for self-mediation.

Power

The exhortation 'to speak truth to power' distinguishes the sense of power I stress here. It opposes what is 'right' (in the sense of fair, or just, or good, all of which are, like 'right', enabling and relatively open terms) to what can simply be imposed without regard to what is right. In Nietzschean usage, 'power' signifies both sides of this opposition: the side of right as well as the side of might. Here I identify the right in terms of the concern to preserve and enhance humankind's capacity to make and remake itself continuously, which, apart perhaps from my insistence on this capacity's dependence on the other, I believe is similar to what Nietzsche had in mind by the positive, life-affirming side of power. More often than not, it is easier to spot what threatens rather than what fosters this side. From my perspective, which means to advance onto-epistemological nondualism, Nietzsche's purposely ambiguous usage—which has come to inform the theories of some of the most influential and celebrated thinkers of our age, such as Foucault and Bourdieu—is importantly salutary, since it brings into relief the fundamentally relative nature of power, the way in which the two sides of power help to define each other. Nevertheless, since I find that when it is used in this double-sided way, 'power' tends (perhaps because in the context of political economy, the relatively negative side has been so presumptive an acceptation) to reduce, and in this sense corrupt, the positive side, I prefer to use different terms for the two sides. I thus refer to the two sides as 'power' and 'ethics', respectively, the latter term serving as not only the opposed but also the inclusive rubric. By seeing power as both a counterpart to and a form of ethics, I make room for the relativistic nature of power while calling attention to the primacy of the positive side, which primacy is a question of power as a function of discretion, and of discretion or the principle of negative freedom as the pre-eminently distinguishing mark of being human.

Value-as-Such

I use 'value' loosely to mean end or good. By 'value-as-such' I am propounding a narrower meaning, in order to point to what it is about value that distinguishes the desirable from the merely desired. This usage follows from nondualism and the conception of ethics by reference to human existence as fundamentally a creative or mediatory dynamic. I do not intend by it value in itself, as if value could obtain without an element of practicality; rather, I am presenting the idea of a value that does not inherently lend itself to instrumental reduction. Put another way, value-as-such remains a relative usage, but one whose own relativity is itself relativized. Judging any given value is situationally dependent, but every such judgment is itself necessarily predicated on the idea of value, in the sense in which value is opposed to fact. Some values display this sense so representatively as to reaffirm critically the very idea of value. For example, because the value of 'turn the other cheek' transcends, *eo ipso*, the demonstrative economic function of reciprocity (in this instance, revenge), it veritably creates value-as-such. By contrast, the values of, say, racism and slavery, lending themselves as they do to economization and dehumanization, tend, paradoxically, to undermine or even deny the idea of value. I do not mean to suggest that any given value is in practice immune to all attempts to instrumentalize it, for depending on how it is deployed, it can always have its measure as value qua value vitiated. The rhetoric of values can serve well to conceal and justify instrumental conduct. Thus, a value such as 'freedom'—which surely is construable as a value-as-such—can be used to justify all sorts of perfectly instrumental and ethically vile practices (such as, for example, torturing human beings in order to extract information). Even so, I propose that inasmuch as a value-as-such logically is based on its own opposition to the instrumental, it differs significantly from values whose internal logic directly cultivates reduction to instrumentality. And for this reason, in my view, values-as-such, although hardly foolproof, may be regarded as crucial components and conditions of social arrangements and practices that furnish the interpretative and rhetorical resources to resist virulent instrumentalization.

INTRODUCTION
Nondualism, Ontology, and Anthropology

The crisis of modern man ... can be put in these terms. Reason triumphant through science has destroyed the faith in revelation, without, however, replacing revelation in the office of guiding our ultimate choices. Reason disqualified *itself* from that office ... precisely when it installed itself ... as sole authority in matters of truth. Its abdication in that native province is the corollary of its triumph in other spheres: its success there is predicated upon that redefinition of the possible objects and methods of knowledge that leaves whole ranges of other objects outside its domain. This situation is reflected in the failure of contemporary philosophy to offer an ethical theory, i.e., to validate ethical norms as part of our universe of knowledge.

— Hans Jonas, *Philosophical Essays*

Ontology and Anthropology

I offer here ontological reflections for the practice of anthropology. These reflections center around two key theses: first, that when it is seen from the ontological perspective of nondualism instead of dualism, the distinctively human condition is, above and beyond all else, a condition of choice and a question of 'ethics'; and, second, that in its defining and intrinsically revolutionary quest to understand others or otherness, to break the bonds of the self, anthropology has been profoundly hampered (if also epistemologically motivated) by its logico-philosophical foundations in Western dualism.

In effect, I want to demonstrate the limits of ontological dualism and explore the intelligibility of nondualism. In dualism, the distinction between, say, subject and object is complete. In nondualism, the distinction is neither negated nor finally subsumed (as it is in monism); rather, it is preserved as ambiguous or imperfect, such that subject and object are still seen as distinct from each other, but only relatively so.[1] Put another way, whereas dualism determines absolute boundaries alone, the boundaries predicated by nondualism both separate and connect, such that the distinctions these boundaries make are essentially fuzzy. As a result, the distinctions are definitively situational ('now you see them, now you don't'), depending on whether it is the boundary's power to cut or to bond that emerges as relevant in any given context. Put still another way, by making entitativity relative rather than absolute, nondualism betrays the oxymoron of an 'ontology' in which all 'things', because they somehow participate in one another, both are and are not.

Jerusalem, writes Derrida (1995: 70), is "a holy place, but also a place that is in dispute, radically and rabidly, fought over by all the monotheisms, by all the religions of the unique and transcendent God, of the absolute other." Here, in an apparently unbreakable nutshell, we see the trouble with dualism, as it spawns both monism and pluralism. We have three absolute, monotheistic religions, each declaring itself the one and only 'One', yet all three are also implicated, by force of vital circumstance, in the hope of co-existing together, pluralistically. But how can this hope make any sense if the definitive monism of these religions determines boundaries without any real give to speak of, including, at least at the end of the day, in relation to temporal authority? No wonder that Derrida speaks here of "wild-eyed ecumenism" (ibid.). The projected pluralistic order would have to be secured by a superordinate authority, which, for obvious reasons, can only be temporal. This possibility is predicated on the supposition that by subjecting the religious differences to a controlling institutional force—a sovereign political order—they can be retained and allayed at the same time. The trouble is that from the standpoint of the absolutism of these monotheisms (an absolutism so absolute that it occasions "radical and rabid" conflict), there really is no principled room for a higher sovereign force. Only where boundaries are reconceived as essentially relative, such that they always connect as they separate, does there seem to be any real hope for enduring community. But of course, this understanding of boundaries is nondualist and flies in the face of the absolutism at issue. By contrast to pluralism, nondualism promises community in which 'identity' is fundamentally relative rather than absolute and is therefore incapable of serving as a sine qua non of communal inclusion.

My method of inquiry is both phenomenological and anthropological. With phenomenology, I focus on tacit knowledge and experiential understanding. In this connection, I am especially concerned with the deep senses of self—and therewith of other—promoted by dualism and nondualism considered not as forms of logic as such but of social existence. Nondualism, which refuses to rend logic from existence, recommends just such an analytical strategy. I mean thus to avoid intellectualism or the presumption (perhaps the sorest affliction of social science) that most if not all human acts are behavioral conversions of prior programmatic predications, and position myself to grasp how dualism and nondualism actually move people. For within one's deepest—which is to say, one's most comprehensive, implicit, and absorbing—sense of self, act and idea may be virtually indistinguishable from each other.

Because tacit knowledge and experiential understanding run deep, they are ordinarily not open to reflection. Giving an anthropological turn to the phenomenologist's techniques for overcoming this difficulty, I try to bring to the surface critical presuppositions of Western thought and reason. I do so in two key ways: first, by taking up cases from 'home', that is, cases focused on the profound problematicity of Western dualism or so disturbingly extreme as to present the Western self as anthropologically other to itself; and, second, by plumbing Western thought and reason directly in view of the ethnographic fact of cultures—so-called other cultures—not readily intelligible in the usual terms of this reason and thought. In so doing, determinedly going beyond phenomenology to ethics, my aim is not simply to open to question fundamentals of Western selfhood, but to rethink these fundamentals by critically taking instruction from the ethnographic other as well as from the otherness in ourselves.

What makes the following study anthropologically novel as well as radical, then, is its explicitly ontological charge. Indeed, this charge recasts the discipline, not simply because it opens to question anthropology's deepest philosophical presuppositions and directly draws inspiration from certain philosophical literature, but because at the same time it (along with the philosophically anomalous sense of ethics I propose) derives from straightforward, empirical anthropological deliberations, thus making of our discipline a co-equal partner in a philosophically received enterprise. The revisions of self and reason I intend entail nothing less significant than a reconceiving of reality, from terms of dualism to terms of nondualism. One object of embracing reality as essentially uncertain and ambiguous is to re-emphasize the human condition as a condition of discretion and responsibility, and thereby to refocus and revitalize ethics as the (foundationless) foundation of social existence. Because it is keyed to uncertainty and process, this sense of ethics not only goes beyond but also throws into question the fixed morality of what I have earlier called moralism.

Another object of addressing the very nature of reality is to acknowledge the ethnographic enterprise as ontological at its very core. The claim is that the most fundamental problems of anthropological research may well yield to inquiry, but not simply by virtue of empirical analysis, however vital and necessary such analysis is. At bottom, these problems want explicit ontological deliberation. Such defining ethnographic problems as what is the nature of kinship? or how can there be order in a society without government? or, as is germane to the present work, what is the sense of magico-religious presumption? are problems of otherness, and they require for their resolution nothing less radical than ontological conversion. Going beyond phenomenological prescription to ethical act, the idea is not simply to bracket or suspend our received notion of reality (thus exercising the so-called phenomenological epoché) but to change it. By doing so, one hopes to affect, even if only in a small way and the long term, reality itself. The object is to disrupt the rigid pre-epistemological propositions—the material or practical a priori understandings—through which 'reality' is made to appear for us and against which nothing in our world seems normally to speak. Put another way, one wants to change the notion of reality so that it affords the opportunity for new modes of practice in the common project of social life. Underlying this ambition is that ideas can be powerful, and as those of (to select august figures) Plato or Descartes or Darwin or Freud or Marx demonstrate, there are none more so than ideas that bear roundly on the nature of reality.

Empirical research is a positively crucial condition of ethnographic inquiry. But that hardly means that that is all there is to the practice of ethnography: the discipline's pronounced turn in recent decades to sophisticated questions of interpretation theory plainly suggests otherwise. This turn, which focuses on the beholder's share in the determining of what there is, constitutes a distinct caution against the 'empiricism' that tends to lurk beneath the general idea of empirical research—that all knowledge is synthetic in nature, a matter of sensory perception, or that the facts speak for themselves. What is striking about the hermeneutic turn in anthropology, though, is that while it has occasioned an acute awareness that there is no such thing as an unbiased ethnographic perspective, it has only rarely grasped that the biases the ethnographer brings with her necessarily comport a taken-for-granted picture of what there is—that is, an implicit ontology. Instead, correlative to the disciplinary rise in importance of such *topoi* as women's and post-colonialist studies, emphatically the tendency has been to take the biases as primarily political in nature, as matters of power. It would seem that in reaction to the realization that the effort to maintain sheer ethnographic objectivity and impartiality is naive, the anthropologist, rotating dualistically, has been inclined on the whole to expressly politicize the discipline. This shift appears to have turned on an undeniably attractive logic to the effect that if implicit political bias is unavoidable, then one may as well assume, with all due deliberation, an explicit political position.

The resulting positions, the bulk of which move to empower and dignify the relatively powerless, are, surely, splendid and salutary in themselves. Nevertheless, and notwithstanding the consideration that perfect objectivity is indeed a chimera, insofar as it saps the life from the consideration that without the bias of relative objectivity ethnographic practice per se has no 'scientific' warrant, this politicization may itself be naive. It takes very little reflection to see what we all experience on a day-to-day basis anyway—that although there can be no observed in which the observer is not participant, the 'distance' between observer and observed is patently relative and varies precisely with the nature of the perspective the observer takes. And while it cannot afford the observer a view from nowhere, 'objectivity' can be efficaciously assumed as one such perspective. The critical point is that if when adduced on behalf of a political position ethnography (qua ethnography rather than pure political discourse or power play) is to serve effectively, it must take scrupulous care not to impugn its own relative objectivity, for its special force in relation to political argument must rest with its comparatively objective determinations.

But here what I particularly want to bring out about this politicizing movement is that, ironically, it seems not to have alerted the discipline substantially enough to the problem of empiricism as an implicit and obstructive dogma underlying ethnographic interpretation. Indeed, arguably the emphasis on 'power' as the defining concept of this anthropological turn continues, at least tacitly, to lend support to this dogma. To see this, one need only consider that 'power' is itself an inherent bias, one that carries with it a picture of reality consistent with the positivist idea of objectivity from which such empiricism takes flight. The empiricist dogma that all knowledge is reducible to brute facts, that is, to immediate experience, presupposes the 'clean' differentiation of an object world. In turn, on this positivistic conception of the world, 'power' is afforded a driving phenomenological purchase: since for its operation power requires an object, an ontology of absolute objectivity is likely to breed an epistemology of absolute power. For a full-blown example decidedly telling in respect to the rise of modernity, we can cite Baconian empiricism, according to which, on Horkheimer and Adorno's interpretation ([1972] 1998: 4; my italics), "What men want to learn from nature is how to use it in order *wholly* to dominate it and other men." Bacon aside, the point is that empiricism consists with power. In view of the arresting degree to which anthropology's politicizing turn has been informed by Foucault's work, I should add that if we take technology in the wide sense to include all techniques of domination, productive as well as repressive, then empiricism does so whether we are talking about power in a Weberian or a Foucauldian sense. For in line with Horkheimer and Adorno, Foucault's thesis of anonymous power that produces a subjectivity for the purpose of subjection implicates—inasmuch as the subject's subjectivity then consists in treating itself as an object—the enclosure of the subjective by the objective.

There is, then, reason to think that the relatively recent and conspicuous interpretive turn in anthropology, with its strong political character, has not confronted directly the shadowy but suffuse presumption of empiricism that has characterized ethnographic anthropology's rise as a social 'science' and has helped to eclipse from view the absolutely critical extent to which ethnographic inquiry is also and always an exercise in metaphysics.[2] It is notable that the ontological implications of Foucault's notion of power were not seen as such by anthropologists. (Given his anti-metaphysical proclivity, though, the great French thinker must take some blame for this oversight.) In conceiving of power in terms of production as well as repression, he had in mind the creation of the real. Although his work tended to concentrate on the constraining force of the reality thus produced, he also took this constituting function to mean that power must be seen in a positive as well as negative light. This supplementary understanding of power points directly to the importance of ontology for anthropology, to the way in which humans in their relations to things and to one another (including the ethnographic interaction) participate in the creation of reality. Because it seems not simply to blur but virtually to eradicate the distinction between ethics and power, I am loath to use the term 'power' in this universalistic (Nietzschean) way. Nevertheless, the usage plainly and forcefully suggests that at the end of the day, anthropology is—whether its practitioners know it or not and despite its quite proper credentials as social science—ontology, and that therefore ontological preconceptions, both those of the studied and the student, should be an explicit and pivotal concern of anthropological inquiry.

As they are constructed through experience, these preconceptions plainly are historical. Yet precisely because they are *pre*conceptions, they serve also to constitute reality. As synthetic a priori, they mark a zone of ambiguity between theory and practice, or between mental act and bodily action, and therefore, under most quotidian circumstances, their hosts are in no position to tell them from reality, including the reality of the hosts themselves. They are innocently enacted in the 'natural' course of everyday life. If this is correct, then it suggests that it is to our great advantage to seek to isolate and identify these ontological preconceptions, which betray themselves in their own existential and discursive practice (where 'betray' means both, on the one hand, 'deliver' or 'construct', and, on the other, 'disrupt'). And since the anthropologist's ontological preconceptions are critical to his professional inquiry, it is in his direct, professional interest to do the same for his own, taking advantage of the disruption offered by ethnographic confrontation to jar his reflexive insight and rethink reality. It is a central contention of this book that of anthropology's synthetic a priori, dualism remains one of the most, if not *the* most, stubborn and comprehensive, and that it has worked and continues to work to restrict profoundly—at the heart of the discipline's defining purpose—the anthropologist's ability to plumb the reality of other cultures.

Obviously, an anthropology rooted in ontological dualism is at an elemental disadvantage when facing an alien culture in which the real is projected as basically ambiguous, for such a reality cannot be neatly factored into things that simply stand outside to one another. Instead, an ambiguous reality presents entities as concretely participant of one another and therefore only relatively self-contained or identifiable. In order to capture the characteristic human dynamic of such a reality, I deploy the notion of 'primordial choice' (cf. Evens 1995). This notion is predicated directly on a reality the most diacritical feature of which is ambiguity. Under this ontological condition, reality may be seen as finally somehow giving rise to itself, presenting an open-ended causality not subject to analysis that pursues a cause-effect regression. This is so because basic ambiguity does not finally allow for things that are utterly separate and distinct, things that thereby lend themselves to the logical canons of identity, non-contradiction, and the excluded middle. Instead, basic ambiguity amounts to imperfect holism, and imperfect holism entails a causal dynamic in which, paralogically, the effect both issues from and is continuous with the cause. Inasmuch as cause and effect participate in each other, it cannot be otherwise.

Such causality amounts to a kind of self-generation, wherein what *is* both does and does not give rise to itself or is at once self-contained as well as other to itself, and therewith open to its other. Among humans, this fundamentally opaque causal process is so pronounced that it effects a reflexivity indistinguishable from what we, in the West, are accustomed to call 'choosing'. The openness of ontological ambiguity manifests itself consummately as, to make here a fruitful distinction, not *natural* selection but *moral* selection. Whereas in natural selection there is indeterminacy but no witting agent to speak of, in moral selection the self that is distinguished, not as a given but as a phenomenal function of the process of selection itself, continues to select with at least tacit intentionality. Still, the evident agency of moral selection is fundamentally imperfect. In the West, we are inclined to epitomize choice in terms of explicit intentionality and wholly autonomous selection. In fact, though, notwithstanding Kant's metaphysic of morals, choice as such is always necessarily to some critical extent heteronomous as well as autonomous. Put another way, to emphasize the paralogical nature of moral selection, heteronomy serves as an enabling condition of autonomous choice.[3]

By 'primordial choice', then, I do not intend choice that is perfectly witting, individual, and free, as if it springs from a self-transparent or noumenal or transcendental or absolute self. Still, as befits self-generation, to a notable extent a primordial choice also resists reduction simply to determination by what is other. It is characterized thus by a fundamental indeterminacy and is therefore also creative. Indeed, such a choice is so wonderfully creative that it tends to found a self-identity as well as the particular social and cultural world—the 'second nature'—that inevitably corresponds to any such purposeful identity. Hence, for example, as one differentiates oneself as either male or female, one distinguishes the world as dualistically gendered; or as one delineates oneself as a *cogito*, an 'I think', one identifies the world as divided pristinely between the subjective and the objective. The capacity of such choices to create worlds is relative and limited to be sure, but it is also plain and consequential.

Although primordial choice always presupposes essential ambiguity, paradoxically such a choice, if it is sufficiently oblivious to its own constant heteronomy, can project the self as complete unto itself and the corresponding world as given to immaculate boundaries between one thing and another. This picture of things is paradoxical because if immaculate rather than fuzzy boundaries are the rule, the primordial choice that issued in these boundaries becomes logically inconceivable. Primordial choice is intelligible only in a nondualistic world. Of course, if one takes for granted formal, classical logic and its law of bivalence, then by definition primordial choice is paradoxical in its own right. But precisely because nondualism does not take such logic for granted, proceeding instead according to a 'logic' of ambiguity, primordial choice remains a conceivable proposition. A logic of ambiguity allows for the possibility and functionally specific use of formal logic but ultimately does not admit of an absolute boundary between logic and practice.

Indeed, if choice is to be meaningful as such, which is to say, creative or originary, then the relevant options must themselves be essentially indeterminate as to their relative merits. These merits receive their determination, in part, by virtue of the choice itself, giving the choice its creational due. In a certain sense, a choice between alternatives the relative merits of which are perfectly fixed and decisive is no choice at all. Under this circumstance, even should one choose the non-meritorious or inferior option, the choice can issue only in the 'same', in which case it denies its own creative capacity, the capacity in view of which one can truthfully say that because of one's choice, things have indeed become otherwise. A choice that denies this amounts to a difference that makes no difference.

It must follow, then, however strange it is to say so about a social setting critically defined by 'free market' consumerism, the modern world, because it is thematically predicated on dualism, tends to deny, in the deep sense of the term, choice. Put another way, the modern world inclines to reduce choice—the essence of which is a relative indistinction or perplexity as between options—to the availability of a multiplicity of options defined in terms of certainty, on the model of, I venture, material delineation. To take a morally charged example, underlying the politically acrimonious debate on abortion in the United States is the implicit accusation by the 'pro-life' supporters that the 'pro-choice' side has equated abortion to shopping-mall selection, as if the decision to miscarry a fetus were simply an arbitrary question of, say, whether or not to buy a certain blouse or color of lipstick. In effect, the charge is homicidal reductionism. On the other hand, ironically, by failing to see that the elector of abortion may well be—and ultimately always is—caught between the vital and therefore equally absolute obligations of soulful life on the one hand and the life of one's soul on the other, the pro-life camp, by denying that something like abortion ought to be elective, takes the life out of choice and as a result dehumanizes human or soulful existence. Neither side of the debate seems to grasp very well the sense of choice in which what is at stake is, rather than simply 'the right to choose', the creative capacity that is critical to the very meaning of human life. If they did, they would find common ground and be logically compelled to acknowledge that the decision about abortion is an inherently creative matter involving the effort, a definitively ethical enterprise, to hold on to, at one and the same time, the two horns of a vital dilemma.

As the example of the abortion debate might suggest, dualism and nondualism basically describe here contrasting modes of self-other relations rather than ideal schemes of reasoning. Indeed, since I have defined the self-other relationship as an essential tension, dualism and nondualism may be construed as models of and for relatively comprehensive forms of conflict. Whereas dualism tends to make conflict absolute, in the end promoting total violence, as in ethnocide and genocide, nondualism pictures conflict as relative and is therefore superior for irenic purposes. More precisely, nondualism gives implicit force to the primacy of otherness, thematizes the way in which self and other are interdependent as well as opposed, and holds open the possibility of a rationality based on value rather than power.

I want to promote here the reassessment of Western reason and agency, not simply in the abstract, as an ethical exhortation, but also through the concrete means open to me by training—professional anthropology. I aim to demonstrate the merits of nondualism for empirical study in anthropology, and by doing so foster, in practical application, the reassessment of which I speak. Since it is forged in the study of otherness, the anthropological perspective is in principle revolutionary. It is perhaps nowhere more so than in relation to the anthropological problem of rationality (the philosophical problem of 'other minds' reformulated in terms of 'other cultures'), from the study of which I have taken instruction in nondualism. Nondualism, which could hardly be more 'other' from the standpoint of received Western thought, has much to offer to the pressing critique of modernity set out in postmodernism. That critique pertains directly to the problems of difference and power in society, and therefore bears sharply on questions of dominance, aggression, violence, and peaceful co-existence. In response to these questions, nondualism has practical implications for the formal organization of conflict and difference in society. In my work on the kibbutz and on the Nuer, I have tried to bear out this claim (e.g., Evens 1984, 1985, 1989a, 1995). What I dwell on in the present book is the broader implication of nondualism for the nature of human nature: by redefining this nature in terms of self-identifying at the behest of the other, nondualism serves to re-create human nature as a matter of responsibility for self and other. In other words, it re-creates it as a matter of ethics.

By 'ethics' (as well as by 'moral selection', since I see 'moral' as a term of ethics) I intend the dynamic of self-formation, wherein humans make their way by constantly running an optative course between self-interest and other-regard. In so doing, they tend to establish moralities or codes of good and bad, and by this token identify themselves as responsible agents and thus as human. By this definition, then, which is critical to understand at the outset, ethics is not above all the considered practice of conforming to a predetermined moral standard. Instead, it is the tensile, existential, and creative conduct whereby humans ceaselessly construct and reconstruct such standards as well as, in doing so, their very humanity. I am not particularly talking about the science of morals or the department of study concerned with the principles of moral duty, but rather about distinctively human conduct and its study in general. I conjecture that insofar as this redefinition of ethics takes root—insofar as its slow assimilation creates a predisposition, a habitus—we are, by virtue of the resultant understanding of ourselves as vitally and existentially always beyond or other to ourselves, more likely to conduct ourselves vis-à-vis one another with tolerance and reason instead of hatred and force. We will do so, precisely by virtue of our self-identification as peculiarly ethical creatures, a definitively open and dynamic self-identity that therewith ultimately encompasses political or economic or aesthetic or religious or familial being.

My argument is not about applying anthropology for purposes of utopian engineering, then, but about reshaping anthropology in a way that allows it to assume its intrinsic ethical charge as a profoundly human science peculiarly centered on self-other relations. Although no one will mistake it for 'working in the trenches', the anthropological thesis of nondualism is much more than a theoretical offering—it is patently interventionist. As a redefinition of human nature, it is a very practical measure, a concrete way of furthering self-responsible and other-regarding choice in human affairs.

Ethics, Sacrifice, and the Ethnographic Self

Being acutely inclined to ontological dualism, Western thought has characteristically projected reality as cleanly divisible between principles that are mutually exclusive. As a result, in this onto-epistemological tradition, the peculiar character that human actions bear has been pre-eminently construed in terms of a sheer and principled opposition between subject and object. The inevitable correlate has been the prevalence of a sense of self that derives its meaningfulness from its capacity to exclude the other as such, whether by incorporation or, more simply, by elimination. Disallowing otherness, dualism undermines the definition of the human condition in terms of ethics and therewith the fundamental ethical quality of social interaction. This remains true notwithstanding the pronounced differentiation of ethics qua ethics in Western thought (as in, exemplarily, Kant's philosophy). For in the absence of others and otherness, responsibility cannot really signify. It is the chief burden of this study to show that when it is seen from the perspective of nondualism, a perspective that embraces the logical scandal of self and other (or of subject and object) as only imperfectly distinguishable from each other, the peculiarly human condition turns out to be primarily ethics.

Instead of the usual ethnographic starting point of the ethnographic other as such, I choose to begin this study, in part 1, with the ethnographic self. I do so in order to expose the otherness presupposed by this self, thus moving always from self to other, even when I am *self*-occupied. Hence, each of the cases I examine in connection to Western thought and practice—whether the philosophic notion of the synthetic a priori, the Hebrew tradition of sacrifice, the Holocaust, Bourdieu's theory of practice, or Habermas's reconstruction of rationality—furnishes peculiarly and paradoxically an 'inside' site that flows into and promotes disclosure of its own 'outside', thus facilitating betrayal of the self's otherness to itself. Put another way, these 'at home' cases are uniquely distinguished by the magnitude to which they disarm the Western self, opening it and its defining dualism to fundamental question. This is self-evident in my discussion of the philosophical notion of the synthetic a priori, which I see as another name for nondualism and take as bearing sharply on my idea of primordial choice. It is also apparent in my critiques of Bourdieu's and Habermas's respective attempts to overcome dualism. Regarding my choice of the Akedah, the biblical story of Abraham's murderous sacrificial conduct towards his beloved son Isaac, and of the Holocaust as telling cases for my argument, I need to say more by way of introduction here.

More than any other event in the twentieth century, the Holocaust has informed recent Western social thought. For Popper, Arendt, Adorno, Habermas, Lyotard, Foucault, Derrida, Levinas, and a host of other celebrated thinkers, the Holocaust has served as a constant backdrop to the development of key ideas about human social order. In order to penetrate their imposing social theories—open and closed societies (Popper), totalitarianism and banalized evil (Arendt), the dialectical destructiveness of Enlightenment thought (Adorno), communicative or pragmatic rationality versus rationality proper (Habermas), the exclusionism and totalism of modernity (Lyotard), the powerful and insidious terrorism of the Occidental self (Foucault), the driving illusion of intellectual foundations (Derrida), and ethics or other-regard as the fundamental condition of human social existence (Levinas)—it is necessary to grasp that each of these thinkers was moved profoundly by an effort to understand how, in the midst of civilization, Nazi Germany could have perpetrated mass murder on a scale that lends itself to description in transcendental terms.

Because the Holocaust marks a watershed in the development of Western reason and displays human nature at its extremes, it lends itself markedly to the sort of root anthropological investigation I wish to conduct here. My interpretation focuses on the fundamental way in which the 'logic' and execution of the Holocaust depended on a dualistic picture of the world. By referring the logic of the Holocaust to the existential plane on which self-identity is forged, I position myself to construct a paradigm of human existence as a nondualistic, relational dynamic of self-and-other.

I build this paradigm in terms of sacrifice, a conduct well studied by anthropologists in its ritual forms. As I see it, an approach I initially develop here in my reading of the Akedah, sacrifice centers on the tension between self-interest and other-regard. It thus can serve representatively to describe the fundamentally ethical condition of being human. Whatever the specific cultural context, in order for the self to emerge, sacrifice of the other must occur. Indeed, by definition (drawing on, as will become clear in later chapters, Levinas's radical redefinition of subjectivity), selfhood always signifies displacement of otherness. However, since self can neither appear nor sustain itself outside of its differentiation from other, it is always and indispensably owing to the latter. Put another way, the self is 'bound' both by self-interest and (given that selfhood is inherently characterized by discretion) obligation to the cause of preserving the other. But this condition is acutely paradoxical, for it is only by virtue of abnegation that the self can manage the preservation of the other.

This picture of sacrifice and selfhood thus describes a fundamental human dilemma. The self, in all its vitality, both bodily and morally, is caught between other- and self-sacrifice. The dilemma can be lived, producing the temporal dynamic of conventional act and meaning we call 'human history', but it cannot be 'successfully' resolved. Because the dilemma describes the very dynamic of human existence, final resolution would spell the end of human history. It would be homicidal.

Whereas the Akedah tells the story of an aborted resolution of this kind, National Socialism, prompted and enabled by the dualism of Western reason, managed such a resolution—a 'final solution'—to an unprecedented degree. It is a terrifying irony that under Hitler's regime, the self-identification of Nazi men and women as 'human', which is to say, their master or primordial choice of how to live the dilemma of self-and-other, came to depend for its meaningfulness on the industrial perpetration of absolute violence and perfect exclusion. As Goldhagen, among others, has pointed out, existing Holocaust interpretation often fails to clarify how abstract explanatory categories—such as 'rationalism', 'capitalism', 'modernism', 'bureaucracy', or 'instrumentalism'—might motivate people to perform such violent acts. But although it comports a logic of hatred and may be a critical feature of genocide, even anti-Semitism seems to suppose a 'motivational' dynamic that runs deeper than sentiment (however strongly felt) and dogmatic conviction, if it is to account for eliminationism of mythical proportions and ambition. What one wants to know is how a pathology such as anti-Semitism can become the keystone of the arch of one's self-identity as human, that is, of one's humanity.

Given its existential import and gravity, its matchless capacity to represent the action through which the human sense of self is produced vis-à-vis the other, the idea of sacrifice can show how something so abstract as, say, formal rationality, that is, rationality consistent with logic proper, might move ordinary men and women to organized, absolute violence. For taken as a name for the continuous process of becoming human (as it is in the biblical story of Abraham's 'binding' of Isaac), sacrifice bears on the constitution of basic self-identity. By 'basic self-identity' I mean identity that is a matter of convention (and in this broad, loose sense, choice) and yet is existentially so indistinguishable from its host that its enactment veritably *is* the host's nature. In effect, basic self-identity is bodily, and thus no less necessary and a priori than it is contingent and arbitrary. The uniquely human challenge is to make it also 'good' by virtue of both reason and ethics—to ensure that its contingent character is not, contrary to all reason, merely arbitrary, and that on the side of ethics, this character fosters humaneness and the possibility of continuing self-other creation.

Rationality, Ethics, and the Ethnographic Other

The task I have set myself, that is, forging a nondualist ontology and an anthropology as ethics, is intimately tied to the question of rationality. Indeed, the critical emphasis on dualism (and nondualism) marks my enterprise as a study in both rationality and human agency. Although it finds roots in both its Greek and Judeo-Christian heritage, modern Western dualism received its baptismal formulation in Descartes' philosophy of consciousness, in which agency and selfhood are defined in terms of rationality. For Descartes' onto-epistemology, rationality was founded in the certitude of mathematics as well as in opposition to matter-as-mechanism. As one result, rationality, human agency, and selfhood have been pre-eminently conceived in terms of the efficient and calculated manipulation of matter by mind, or, put another way, of what is other by what is self.

Here, in stark contrast, I construe rationality primarily by reference to—as against self-evidence, absolute knowledge, and instrumentality—action and argumentation anchored in the consideration of the essential uncertainty of ethical choice. And I understand human agency not as self-transparent subjectivity but as selfhood, the autonomy of which knowingly and paradoxically depends on its own fundamental heteronomy, such that the self is always becoming other to itself.

My effort to rethink rationality in nondualistic terms pivots critically on the special research province of anthropology. Given its conspicuous and diagnostic focus on the study of magic, ritual, and politico-economic orders that are likely to appear to the modern Western observer as irrational, anthropology has had an abiding interest in the problem of rationality. Arguably, finding rationality in the mentation and enterprise of tribal and archaic peoples has defined the chief problem axis around which the discipline turns. From the perspective of dualism and instrumental efficacy, so-called primitive thought, or, if you like, atheoretical understanding, looks relatively uncritical or 'closed' and appears to define a separate and distinct mentality. From the perspective of nondualism and ethics, however, as I aim to show, this kind of thinking, for all its genuine limitations, enjoys a certain critical openness, and although it is hardly the same as or even a modal equivalent of 'modern' thought, it is fundamentally continuous with it.

The openness I have in mind corresponds to an implicit apprehension of the basic ambiguity of the world, an ambiguity that is understood as revelatory of the operation of discretion. Accordingly, instead of irrationality or even arationality, I speak here of

mythic rationality. Mythic rationality is nondualistic, and it enjoys a certain fundamental superiority over its instrumental counterpart. In this connection, it is important to see that this rationality, as nondualistic, does not exclude instrumental success.
Instead, it precludes the precept 'the end justifies the means', grasping the means in
virtue of not simply their outcome, but their capacity to bear the end in their own
doing. In effect, as befits nondualism, the means are not separate and distinct from
the end, but rather, in significant part, indistinct from it. In this light, the superiority
I claim for mythic rationality over instrumentalism proper has to do not with efficient
technological control and the powerful sort of truth that accompanies this control, but
with ethics and other-regard.

My aim, though, is revisionary, not primitivist, and I do not rest my argument with
the concept of mythic rationality. By presuming that discretion and otherness are given
rather than derived or contrived features of the world, mythic rationality entertains ethical openness implicitly. But as is an anthropological commonplace, this rationality, by
virtue of a pronounced naiveté or relative lack of reflexivity, is also unduly restricted in
the degree of choice it allows. It should follow that choice and ethical openness can be
amplified by strong reflexivity and, since such reflexivity is a principled condition of the
emergence of rationality as such, by rationality in the strict sense.

Strong reflexivity is, however, double-edged. On the one hand, epistemologically it
admits and even seems to encourage the appearance of a radical split between body and
mind: reflecting on itself, the self projects itself as an object or something bodily while it
differentiates itself implicitly, by virtue of the act of reflection, as a subject or something
mindful. As one overpoweringly consequential result of this dualistic differentiation
of the self as either body or mind—either creature or creator—strong reflexivity can
produce the illusion of choice and agency as utterly autonomous and complete. Such
idealist illusions amount to images of omnipotence and are bound to promote the
instrumentalization of the other. Put another way, radical reflexivity's predisposition
to mind-body dualism can lead to the pursuit of a perfect—in postmodernist cant, a
'totalizing'—resolution of the ethical tension between self and other. Such a resolution
is indeed final, amounting to the extermination of the very tension that constitutes the
possibility of human existence. Therefore, left largely unchecked (as it was to an incred-
ible degree in the case of Nazi Germany), the pursuit of such a resolution is bound to
result in the catastrophic destruction of both the other and, given the vital dependence
of the self on the other, the self. In other words, it results in genocide, ethnocide, homicide, and suicide. I expect that although here I take up the case of the Holocaust alone,
wherever ethnic or racial or political tensions manifest themselves genocidally (including, these days, non-Western and so-called Third World settings), dualism is informing
and boundaries are being defined in absolute terms.

On the other hand, the amplification of choice holds out the possibility of a self that
is especially aware of its own final indefinition, a self so acutely and steadfastly alert to
its ultimate indebtedness to the other, to its own otherness, that it mindfully seeks to
sustain its selfhood as a uniquely creative or experimental, rather than exclusive, force.
It does so by offering, in moderation but substantively, to ensure the other's due. In
terms of my paradigm of sacrifice, such a self does not seek self-completion by making
a total sacrifice, one that would free the self once and for all from its dependence on
the other. Nor does it close itself down, terrorizing itself with penitential visions, in

punishment for its imperfection. Instead, it proceeds by pursuing a continuous course of give-and-take between self and other, a course directed to realizing the self's, and therefore the other's, creative potential. Put so as to highlight the paradox of this ethical process, the potential can be kindled by, and only by, the self embracing the way in which it is always already other to itself.

The peoples of classic ethnography, traditional peoples thematically characterized by mythic rationality and for whom ritual sacrifice tends to be a routine part of everyday life, epitomize a nondualistic mode of human existence. But the point I am making now is that by informing archaic nondualism and mythic rationality with the acute reflexivity of developed reason, it is possible to do significantly more to realize the (defining) ethical vitality of human existence. For just as Western reason, by amplifying autonomous choice, can lead to the exclusion of the other and otherness altogether, so too can it expand the inherent ethical horizons of mythic rationality. It can do so by allowing for the acutely conscious choosing of the otherness that is taken for granted in mythic rationality. Paradoxically, it amplifies choice and autonomy by deliberatively acknowledging that both are fundamentally limited and other-informed. It thus promises to revise mythic rationality into reason that is essentially tempered, as a primary move, by the ethical considerations of choice and other-regard.

Adapting Max Weber's concept to my purposes, I call this form of reason value-rationality.[4] Value-rationality constitutes an important condition of the attenuation not only of the massively destructive violence characterizing settings informed in one way or another by modernity (including Third World settings), but also of the kind of insidious violence—witchcraft, sorcery, feud, bloody ritual, and the like—characterizing societies that anthropologists have traditionally studied. Of course, in view of the fact that all such violence is prosecuted in the name of one value or another, value-rationality is not a panacea. But without it, there is no hope at all. It is clear that instrumental rationality, wherein whatever counts is reduced to an object, makes nonsense of the very idea of value as intrinsic worth or significance. My point is not that we may regard any particular value as ahistorical, but rather that for humans, value, in the sense of the capacity to make and entertain particular values, is indeed a given. There is no being human without it. Put another way, the value of Value, whether we discern it or not, transcends its own particularity. Therefore, the particular 'value' of instrumental rationality not withstanding, it is vital to bear this consideration in mind by affording Value an ultimate primacy when deciding what we ought to do. In so doing, we oblige ourselves to adjudicate competing values by thoughtful appeal to a value that at once defines and exceeds us (Value), and therewith serves to open us to the value of otherness and other values. The burden of my study is to show that the probability of raising human consciousness (by digging ever deeper, to the specific nature of the groundlessness of all of our grounds) or changing our habits of thought to deliberatively embrace value-rationality can be decisively increased through the considered cultivation of a nondualist ontology. In effect, then, although matters are patently not so simple as to suggest (with the nineteenth-century evolutionists) that what comes first does not also remain fundamental and that moderns are the culmination of evolutionary progress, I will argue for the existence and possibility of epistemic and ethical advance.

Value-rationality is rational because it is non-arbitrary. And it is non-arbitrary because it is founded on a certain judgment of the good, namely, the possibility of setting ends.

This good is at once necessary and universal, in the sense that humanity as such cannot appear without it; to put it another way, in being human one always begins by manifesting this good. Nevertheless, as it ensures no end but the basically ambiguous one of having ends, it leaves one substantially free to arrive at one's own ends—or, better, to take Rousseau's famous dictum (but without the contractarian predicate), it forces one to be free. As a result, it necessarily describes a self, although one whose selfhood or autonomy is virtually defined by its heteronomy. And as the truth of this universal good affords to this self a crucial role in selecting ends, it continues to define an authentic, responsible human agency.

My effort to rethink rationality is thus critically tied to the hoary anthropological problem of rationality—the problem of why 'other' peoples adhere routinely, as a cultural practice, to apparently irrational conceptions of how things work. I intend to offer yet another solution to this problem, one keyed as roundly as possible to nondualism. The most prominent anthropological approaches to the problem of rationality, although enlightening in important ways, strike me as too tied to the Cartesian ontological predication of mutually exclusive entities and forces that act on one another through external relations only. As a result, these approaches cannot in the end do justice to the anthropological problem of rationality. The sociologism of structural-functionalism, the intellectualism of structuralism proper, the aestheticism of anthropological hermeneuticism, the (usual) materialism of practice theory, and the politicism of post-structuralism, all constitute perspectives that tend to leave Western reason unrevised in essence—even as they relativize or disparage it. It is precisely the dualist posit of immaculate boundaries between one thing and another that has informed the stark differentiation of such sociological categories as social utility, cognitive structure, aesthetics, practice, politics, and so forth. The same posit has also secured rationality in the strict sense of the term, constraining the apperception of much atheoretical thought as irrational. For atheoretical thought seems to presuppose a world in which the relations between one thing and another are, by jarring contrast to the received Western ontology, always basically ambiguous, always internal as well as external. For this reason, the anthropological problem of rationality has most notoriously presented itself in terms of atheoretical thought's apparent indifference to contradictions. Obviously, since it is predicated on basic ambiguity, nondualism is bound to put such thought in a fresh light. In the following chapters, I argue that from the perspective of nondualism, thought of this kind enjoys a certain primacy in relation to rationality proper, yet is also subject to progressive development precisely by means of the latter.

PART I

THE ETHNOGRAPHIC SELF
The Socio-political Pathology of Modernity

Part 1 argues that dualism constitutes the central principle on which reason qua reason ultimately depends, and that as a consequence reason of this received sort—the rationality peculiarly associated with the Enlightenment and invented by the ancient Greeks—disposes an exclusionism so final as to allow and even cultivate, when it informs political relations, the likes of the Holocaust. In order to bring into relief the phenomenological and existential bearing of this abstract thesis about rationality, I tie it to the conduct of sacrifice in general and Judeo-Christian mythic tradition in particular. Arguing that being human is fundamentally construable as a conduct of sacrifice, I describe the Holocaust as a ritualistic attempt to achieve a form of sacrifice prohibited by but gravitative in the sacrificial logic of Judeo-Christianity—namely, perfect sacrifice. Such a sacrifice is indistinguishable from counter-sacrifice, in that it constitutes an endeavor to establish a self-identity so closed and exclusive that further sacrifice to and on behalf of the other would be obviated. In as much as sacrifice, in my description, is a condition for being human, a defining component of the structural dynamic of human existence, perfect or final sacrifice must be, logically speaking, definitively inhuman (which, of course, only humans can be). It follows that any homicidal enterprise it promotes cannot but also be suicidal, and that the Judeo-Christian logic of sacrifice bears innately the seeds of its own destruction. Finally, in order to help clarify the character of my argument about rationality, I look appreciatively but also critically at the practical reason of both Bourdieu and Habermas. The object of these critiques is twofold: first, to clarify by contrast the difference made by rethinking 'practice' and 'rationality' with explicit reference to ontology, and, second, in line with the reflexive aim running throughout the earlier chapters, to bring out still more the extreme tenacity of dualism as a scaffolding of Western thought.

The Chapters

Chapter 1, the first of the six chapters in part 1, clarifies the critical importance of ontology for anthropology by looking closely at the Kantian notion of the 'synthetic a priori', as this notion is revised in the work of two major twentieth-century philosophers,

Wittgenstein and Maurice Merleau-Ponty. The chapter shows that the synthetic a priori amounts to an intellectually profound attempt to conceptualize ontological ambiguity or nondualism, and for this reason furnishes rich insight into the nature of culture and the peculiar character of human existence.

The next two chapters, 2 and 3, by showing how human existence per se can be described as the conduct of sacrifice, demonstrate the critical lived significance of the philosophical conceptual opposition between dualism and nondualism as well as the notion of ontological ambiguity. In chapter 2, I offer an intensive interpretation of the Akedah, the biblical story of Abraham's 'binding' (for sacrifice) of his beloved son Isaac. Contrasting the Akedah to Nuer sacrifice, and bouncing off Derrida's profound interpretation of Kierkegaard's reading, I argue that the story's logic of blind faith—not the only logic to the story, but the one on which Kierkegaard dwells—reveals, rather than a transcending and self-evident good, a dualistic and lethal principle of self-perfection. In chapter 3, the first of two excurses (both provoked by Derrida's piercing meditations), I contend that the Akedah's lesson of murderous abnegation offers a description of human life as essentially a sacrificial dynamic. In light of my argument about perfect sacrifice, chapter 4 takes up the case of the Holocaust. After analyzing the logical contribution of 'rationalization' to the realization of the Nazi death camps, I offer a phenomenological analysis of how something so abstract as rationality qua rationality could help to induce people to commit mass murder routinely, on an industrial scale. I find that the basic and most comprehensive self-identity fostered by Nazism pivots dualistically on a principle of self-perfection, making it especially receptive to a rationality defined in dualistic or absolute terms. In result, this existential, and hence 'naturally' impelling, self-identity inverts the vital purpose of sacrifice, constituting what I think of as a counter-sacrificial form and logic, whereby the object is simply—to the complete exclusion of abnegation or 'giving'—the total obliteration of the other.

Chapters 5 and 6 examine two exceedingly powerful and progressive but nonetheless insufficient social theoretical attempts to remedy the dualism that conditions such lethal sacrificial conduct. In chapter 5, I take up Pierre Bourdieu's theory of practice. Through close analysis of certain critical elements of Bourdieu's sociology, I show that his remedial notion of practice is keyed to terms of power rather than ethics, and that as a consequence it fails to overcome dualistic representation. In chapter 6, I perform a similar exercise, only now with 'rationality', as this concept is importantly reconstructed by Jürgen Habermas. Habermas takes rationality well beyond considerations of power, yet I show that his treatment of mythological thought as simply closed suggests that his progressive concept of rationality remains still informed by the dualist and instrumentalist one.

Chapter 1

ANTHROPOLOGY AND THE SYNTHETIC A PRIORI

Wittgenstein and Merleau-Ponty

And Hashem ['the Name', a translation of the Tetragrammaton] God formed out of the ground every beast of the field and every bird of the sky, and brought them to the man to see what he would call each one; and whatever the man would call to a living soul is its name.

— Genesis 2:19

"Whatever the man would call to a living soul is its name." Invert the verse and explain it as follows: Any living soul to which man would give a name, that name is its name forever.

— Rashi, *Commentary on the Torah.* Vol. 1: *Bereishis/Genesis*

Without inverting the verse, "call to" appears to be used in the sense of summoning; the verse would be saying, "Whatever living soul man would summon is its name." [A variant reading of Rashi (1995), given in a footnote in the same edition of Rashi's commentary on Genesis from which the two above quotes are drawn.]

Kant's Notion of the Synthetic a Priori

Before I develop and flesh out the implications and entailments of the ideas expressed in the introduction, I wish to do more to bring into relief their ontological purport. I can do this by putting them in a language more familiar to the expression of universals, namely, philosophy. There is no shortage today of postmodernist critiques maintaining that this (basically Greek) language is essentially culture-bound and, insofar as it continues to present itself as otherwise, has come to its end. However, the endeavor to express in philosophical terms the ontological reflections in question here—nondualist reflections—serves to bring out a self-deconstructive side of philosophy, a side that is, with reference to the strict sense of 'ontology', de-ontologizing. In this light, the presupposition of foundations or universals, a key diagnostic of philosophy, is not so much abolished as radically revised, such that foundations become, paradoxically, at once both relative and essential—or, more exactly, not only essentially relative but also relatively essential. My notion of 'primordial choice', as explained in the introduction, is meant to capture this paradoxical sense of foundations, as well as to suggest that foundations of the kind necessarily describe human existence as ethics. I also anticipate here the arguments of part 2 by directly linking this revised ontology of foundations (that are not foundations) to the traditional anthropological fare of magico-religious thought.

The philosophical notion proper of the a priori lacks a prominent professional anthropological genealogy. Nevertheless, it should serve well here to give my anthropological ideas philosophical expression. Although it is a Scholastic term that emerged from certain ideas of Aristotle, in recent centuries it is most critically associated with the thought of Kant and his 'Copernican revolution', in which he denied the obvious: not, as Copernicus had already done, that the universe has the earth as its center, but, in a limited yet deep sense restoring to humans the centrality of place of which Copernicus had deprived them, that the world, as *we* find it, stands utterly outside of our experience of it.[1]

The term 'a priori' literally translates as 'from what is prior', as opposed to a posteriori or 'from what is posterior'. Initially, the terms related directly to the idea of causality, since to know something from what comes before it is to know it by its cause. For Kant, however, who was concerned with the conditions of knowing, the term had to do with whether one's knowledge was based on experience or not. For to know something from what comes after the fact is to know it inductively, from the facts themselves. The critical Kantian distinction, then, obtained between a posteriori truths, or knowledge derived empirically, and a priori truths, or knowledge derived otherwise.

Obviously, at least in Western thought, insofar as it is defined as non-empirical, a priori knowledge appears to be a question of reason in Hume's sense of the relations of ideas. As such, it would seem to be logically necessary and universal, in contrast to a posteriori knowledge, which is contingent or relative and particular. For Kant, however, who was chiefly concerned to put metaphysical knowledge on a sound footing, it could not do to reduce the a priori thus to a matter of ordinary reason. He saw that humans cannot help making important and far-reaching judgments that present themselves as necessarily and universally true but are nevertheless not simply a matter of formal logical connection.

Judgments based on a relation of identity between subject and predicate, in which it would be self-contradictory to deny the truth of the predicate (as in, say, 'all bodies are extended'), Kant called analytic; judgments that do not enjoy this sheer logical independence, but are, instead, matters of fact, he spoke of as synthetic. Kant observed, however, that there are critical judgments that cut across the usual classifications, amounting to knowledge that is neither exactly learned by experience nor derived from formal logic as such, knowledge that is, as he said, both a priori and synthetic. The privileged philosophical site of such judgments is the *Meno*, in which Plato takes up the problem of how it is possible to inquire into the nature of something if one does not know what it is. In response to this problem, Plato has Socrates argue (to Meno) that because the soul is immortal and has had a previous existence, it recalls what it had learned before; arithmetic and geometry are given as examples of such knowledge. Kant, too, draws on these examples, arguing that the truths of mathematics and geometry—for example, the sum of the angles of any triangle is 180 degrees—are, although neither given in the concept of a triangle nor produced simply on the basis of knowing, a priori or universally necessary. But in addressing the question of how we come to have such synthetic a priori knowledge, even though he invokes a sense of prior knowledge from experience, Kant departs from the Platonic belief in rebirth and from Platonic metaphysics, since the latter's idealism posits a supersensible reality without regard to the subject's point of view. For Kant, the connection between the concept of a triangle and the truths about its angles consists in intuitive forms and transcendental logic. That is, he found his answer in pure reason, the reason of necessary and universal categories rather than the reason of particular ideas. Acknowledging that any world presupposes a subjective point of view, he sought to determine the logical conditions of the very possibility of a point a view and of experiential knowledge. Consequently, while Kant tended to exemplify synthetic a priori knowledge by referring to arithmetic and geometry, natural science, and metaphysics, following his conception of transcendental logic, most if not all of our most fundamental understandings about the world must ultimately be keyed to knowledge of this kind.

As knowledge that lies somehow between apparently mutually exclusive onto-epistemological categories, Kant's synthetic a priori plainly turns in the direction of nondualism. Such a turning is implicit in his revolutionary understanding that far from being wholly independent of us, the external world conforms to the categorical structures of mind, or, in other words, that that world is given form by us. Nevertheless, for all its revolutionary force, Kant's synthetic a priori not only falls short of nondualism, but also managed to put dualism on a more sophisticated intellectual footing than had previously been the case. Although he aims to critique reason, his deductive appeal to transcendental logic rather than to experience (in this word's dynamic sense of 'practice') leaves reason, in the last instance, in command.

Kant argued that although synthetic a priori truths are not analytically—and thus tautologically—necessary, they must be the case if human life is to be thinkable. In other words, asking himself what are the conceptual categories necessary to conceive of the human world, he deduced certain constituting concepts. Thus, he found that although spatio-temporal concepts such as, for example, 'object' and 'cause' are neither, strictly speaking, analytic nor empirically learned, they are presupposed in all human experience. As such, they and their like are necessary and universal, presenting themselves as the categorical begetters of human existence.

Plainly, Kant's notion of the synthetic a priori runs contrary to Hume's skepticism, according to which our knowledge of the external world can never really be rationally justified. Hume's skepticism followed naturally from his coupling of radical empiricism with ontological dualism, a combination that guarantees that what we know by experience to be the case can be established psychologically but not logically. Nevertheless, Kant's notion served in at least two crucial ways to reinforce rather than refute ontological dualism. One way concerns the fact that Kant, in an important sense, and despite his anti-Cartesianism, embraced the Cartesian *cogito* or 'I think' (Heidegger 1978: 45, 367). In Kant's argument, the self is rendered as, although emphatically not, as in Descartes' discourse, a 'thinking stuff' or substance, certainly timeless—something akin to a transcendental ego. "There can be in us," Kant writes (quoted in Walsh 1967: 312),

> no items of knowledge ... without that unity of consciousness which precedes all data of intuitions, and by relation to which representation of objects is alone possible. This pure original unchangeable consciousness I shall name *transcendental apperception* ... [U]nity of consciousness would be impossible if the mind in knowledge of the manifold could not become conscious of the identity of function whereby it synthetically combines it in one knowledge. The original and necessary consciousness of the identity of the self is thus at the same time a consciousness of an equally necessary unity of the synthesis of all appearances according to concepts, that is, according to rules.

In other words, subjectivity is still presented by Kant as ontologically utterly distinct from the objective world. Indeed, for Kant, the subject is not part of the 'real' world. Instead, it obtains in the transcendental logic (the realm of the ideal) that makes it possible to experience a world at all. To be sure, Kant's depiction of consciousness as active rather than passive serves, in a significant way, to link the subject to the object. But that dialectical linkage is predicated on a logically formal and complete distinction between form and content, by virtue of which what we give to the world is not empirical substance but shape alone. ("The identification of the a priori with the formal is the fundamental error of Kant," observed Scheler [cited in Dufrenne 1966: 57].) As a consequence, the linking remains no less ontologically problematical than in the philosophy of Descartes, who found it necessary to appeal to divine omnipotence to account for the obvious fact that he never met a mind and then a body but always the twain as one. It is not surprising, then, that Kant concluded—ironically deepening Hume's empiricist skepticism by refuting it with idealism—that things in themselves, unconditioned things, or, as he called them, 'noumena' (by contrast to phenomena, or things that may be known by their worldly appearance) were indeed inaccessible to human knowing.[2]

A second way in which Kant's synthetic a priori promoted rather than undermined dualism is this. Correlative to his preservation of an absolute distinction between subject and object, that is, between an inside or mental world and an outside or physical one, is the consideration that his argument continues to predicate a reason that is autonomous and pure. Although by definition it is not analytic, the synthetic a priori is nonetheless conceptual before it is experiential. Indeed, even while it moves to criticize reason by referring it to the evidence of experience, Kant's synthetic a priori proposes that that evidence is not exactly given but intellectually constituted. As Burke puts it (1969: 191), for Kant "experience derives its appearance from the nature of consciousness (the 'I think', or 'transcendental synthesis of apperception')." That is to say, instead of starting with human experience (in the mediatory middle, so to speak), he starts with reason qua reason (transcendental or not), arguing that the human world is begotten conceptually (categorically). Thus, he ends up with such universals as 'cause' and 'object', that is, with relative but determinate notions that he universalizes, rather than with 'universals' that are basically—and paradoxically—conditioned or not specifiable outside of their particular manifestations.[3]

At this juncture, I can make explicit that the philosophical notion of the a priori is connectable to anthropology at the very core of the latter's scholarly enterprise. As the notion of the a priori directly implicates the idea of universals, so it bears squarely on the question of cultural relativism. Indeed, the deployment of this philosophical notion has powerful implications for anthropological inquiry, from—to sum up broadly the direction of this inquiry—nineteenth-century evolutionism to twentieth-century relativism.

Since empirical statements can always be refuted by further observation, their truth (what indeed it is usual to call synthetic truth) is essentially contingent. But in a manifest sense, so is the truth of analytic statements, since it is dependent on the truth of the other such statements that go to make up the particular system of logic by which truth of this nominal—or, if you like, pure—kind is defined. Moreover, the truth of analytic statements may be regarded as finally necessary or a priori rather than contingent or a posteriori only when the system of logic from which they derive is itself necessarily universal rather than particular (as Kant [1963], in line with his transcendental idealism, professed is in fact the case with classical Western logic [see also Evens 1983]).

Obviously, then, since neither synthetic nor analytic knowledge in itself can support a claim to the epistemic superiority of one culture over another, both are compatible with cultural relativism as opposed to (the Enlightenment idea of) progressive cultural evolutionism. Kant's synthetic a priori, however, which, by virtue of the so-called transcendental deduction, makes some specific concepts both necessary and universal, certainly can offer such support. This helps explain why Kant paid virtually no attention to the role of culture and society in his philosophy of reason and knowledge. To be sure, in picturing consciousness as active rather than passive, Kant made room for cultural activity. By insisting, though, that the synthetic a priori is universal in the received sense (the sense defined by dualism or absolute division between the universal and the particular), and hence according to the epistemological principle of certainty rather than that of basic ambiguity, he could not take advantage of this ethnological opportunity. On the contrary, by defining humanity primarily in terms of reason—a reason whose purity had been critically cut, but only to be further and sublimely rarefied by transcendental distillation—Kant made it possible to conclude (and here I anticipate the interpretation of the Holocaust in chapter 4), whatever his own opinions in such matters, that any peoples who could be shown to fall short of such reason were backward, inferior, or less than human.

Toward True Synthetic a Priori:
Wittgenstein and Merleau-Ponty

Wittgenstein

It seems ironic that in his critique of metaphysics, Kant, in the thrall of reason, failed to follow to its logical conclusion the implication of his own Copernican revolutionary thesis, for if it is the case that all knowledge presupposes a point of view, then his 'transcendental logic' cannot escape this circumstance. Even if Kant's 'categories' serve as preconditions of empirical knowledge, they too are a form of knowledge and therefore cannot but entail a point of view. The truth of Kant's usage of 'transcendental' (that is, its metalogical status) notwithstanding, unless Kant is claiming that this point of view is no less than God's, it must be characterized, as with all points of view, as particular and therefore as less than autonomous.

During his lifetime, Kant did not escape criticism of this kind. Most notably, Johann Georg Hamann, a compatriot of Kant and fellow inhabitant of the city of Königsberg, developed a substantial critique in reaction to Kant's critique of reason, one that had an enormous influence on both eighteenth- and nineteenth-century thinkers (Beiser 1987: chap. 1). But I wish to focus on the twentieth century, when the idea of the synthetic a priori was subjected to further extensive revision, entailing fundamental rather than formal confusion of the a priori and the synthetic. Thus, for example, Saul Kripke (1980), in his brilliant *Naming and Necessity*, differentiates necessity from analyticity by arguing that referents are fixed by names rather than descriptions. In other words, for Kripke, a spade is a spade because it has been so called (or, as he says, "rigidly designated"), this name being passed on from one speaker to another, rather than because a spade fits a certain criterial description (the description could be variable or even wrong). Here, as in the biblical book of Genesis, the identity of a thing originates with its name, resulting in a truth that is a posteriori but also quite necessary (a spade is indeed a spade, no matter if, say, under changed circumstances, it is no longer found to be black). If a truth is both necessary and dependent upon concrete evidence for its warrant, a matter of sensory perception and yet inevitable, it would seem to play loose with the difference between the a priori and the a posteriori.

Again, for example, Harvard philosopher W. V. O. Quine (1953) argues, in his well-known essay, "Two Dogmas of Empiricism," for a gradualistic rather than dualistic distinction between the analytic and the synthetic. As he sees it, from the point of view of pragmatism, every system of logic in the end must give way at its edges to the lessons of experience, making its analyticity distinctly relative. If Quine is right, then there is—in the final instance—no logically necessary a priori but only a synthetic one.

In another place (Evens 1983), writing on the efficacy of the Nuer incest prohibition, I drew on Quine's argument about epistemological gradualism as between logic and experience, in order to propose a nondualist solution to the so-called anthropological problem of primitive mentality. My solution centered on a notion of half-logic, predicated on the ontological thesis of basic ambiguity, and capacitated therefore to endorse, in a subtle but forthright way, the apparently magical possibility of a rule or convention that enjoys the force of nature. Here, however, in order to ground my ideas directly in a phenomenological theory of perception, it is fitting to appeal to the thought of M. Merleau-Ponty and Ludwig Wittgenstein, both giants of twentieth-century philosophy. Their work readily lends itself to discussion in terms that leave no doubt as to the essential relevance of the idea of the a priori to professional anthropology.

At one point in his career, Ludwig Wittgenstein asked his student and friend, M. O'C. Drury, to read to him from J. G. Frazer's *The Golden Bough*. They read only from the first volume, not getting very far because of the profusion of Wittgenstein's critical remarks. His commentary, soon developed by him in writing, was eventually published as "Remarks on Frazer's *Golden Bough*." In this terse essay, Wittgenstein (1971) offers scathing criticism of Frazer's anthropological understanding of magical and religious practices among so-called primitives, and in doing so he sets out his own conception of how such practices might best be understood. His argument is, in my opinion, not only anthropologically rich and progressive, but also importantly revealing as to the way in which he came to think of the nature of the a priori in human life.

Basically, Wittgenstein argues that Frazer's understanding of magic and religion as a kind of foolishness is itself foolish, as it attributes to such practices a rational and instrumental objective that they do not entertain and fails to grasp their essentially expressive nature. In effect, Wittgenstein sets up a dualism of the instrumental and the expressive. However, in the course of his argumentation he makes points that are critically inconsistent with and transcend this dualism.

As Wittgenstein sees it, Frazer grasps magical and religious acts as mistakes, since such acts have no basis in the world of empirical fact. Wittgenstein objects (1971: 31): "There is a mistake only if magic is presented as science." "If the adoption of a child is carried out by the mother pulling the child from beneath her clothes," Wittgenstein goes on (ibid.), "then it is crazy to think there is an *error* in this and that she believes she has borne the child." Such acts, he holds, are not intended instrumentally, and we therefore need to "distinguish between magical operations and those operations which rest on a false over-simplified notion of things and processes" (ibid.). "The same savage who, apparently in order to kill his enemy, sticks his knife through a picture of him, really does build his hut of wood and cuts his arrow with skill and not in effigy," observes Wittgenstein (ibid.), as Malinowski similarly observed in his studies of magical usage among the Trobrianders.

How, then, as Wittgenstein sees it, should we understand magical acts? As essentially expressive (1971: 31):

> And magic always rests on the idea of symbolism and of language.
>
> The description of a wish is, *eo ipso*, the description of its fulfilment.
>
> And magic does give representation to a wish; it expresses a wish.

Thus far, the argument works as a dualism of the instrumental and the expressive, and I think that in the "Remarks," Wittgenstein does indeed incline toward just such a dualism. However, when exemplifying and explicating what he means by the expressive, he plainly and importantly transcends the dualism (1971: 33):

> The magic in *Alice in Wonderland*, trying to dry out by reading the driest thing there is.
>
> In magical healing one *indicates* to an illness that it should leave the patient. After the description of any such magical cure we'd like to add: If the illness doesn't understand *that*, then I don't know *how* one ought to say it.
>
> … [N]o phenomenon is particularly mysterious in itself, but any of them can become so to us, and it is precisely the characteristic feature of the awakening human spirit that a phenomenon has meaning for it. We could almost say, man is a ceremonious animal. This is partly false, partly nonsensical, but there is also something in it.
>
> In other words, one might begin a book on anthropology in this way: When we watch the life and behaviour of men all over the earth we see that apart from what we might call animal activities, taking food etc., etc., men also carry out actions that bear a peculiar character and might be called ritualistic.

In these passages, Wittgenstein seems to be suggesting that what he sees as the ceremonious or ritualistic actions carried out by human beings is not simply expressive but in some sense true to the world as we find it. Hence, he concludes that when an illness is told to go away, if it fails to take heed, then he "doesn't know how one ought to say it"—as if such magical practices really do conform to nature. Or again, he finds that in arriving at his (misguided) conclusions about magic as misguided science, Frazer might just as well have believed "that when a savage dies he is in error" (ibid.: 34). In other words, the magical observances in question are, like death (and taxes), in some sense, necessary, certain, and natural. The sense in which this is so is, as Wittgenstein says, "partly false, partly nonsensical, but there is also something in it." What he means exactly by this reserved affirmation bears sharply on the notion of the a priori and can be plumbed by looking more closely at his account of ceremonious conduct.[4]

According to Wittgenstein, the reason why Frazer sees the magical and religious notions of humans as mistakes is because he pictured them, rationalistically, as attempts to explain the world, that is, as theoretical endeavors. By doing so, Frazer put himself in a position to offer an explanation of magical practices, for he was then able to see the practices as the forlorn products of the mistaken notions. As an upshot, or so Wittgenstein (1971: 29) concludes (providing in the process a concise description of what Evans-Pritchard called the "if I were a horse" fallacy): "All that Frazer does is to make [these practices] plausible to people who think as he does."

But Wittgenstein points out that where a theory is not put forward, there can be no mistake, since ordinarily we use 'mistake' to characterize an incorrect explanation of things. If, then, the magical and religious notions at point are not intended as theories, they cannot be mistaken. "Was Augustine mistaken … when he called on God on every page of the *Confessions*?" Wittgenstein asks, rhetorically (1971: 29). Moreover, Wittgenstein finds it utterly implausible (as did Durkheim) that people construct and continue to deploy all these notions and practices "out of sheer stupidity" (ibid.).

If these notions are not attempts at explaining the world, then what are they? We have already seen that Wittgenstein was prone to regard them as expressive, but his descriptions are far richer than that. The notions are, to gather together his allusive and aphoristic remarks, strongly affective ("The crush of thoughts that do not get out because they all try to push forward and are wedged in the door"; 1971: 30); spiritual ("What narrowness of spiritual life we find in Frazer!" ibid.: 31); ceremonious or ritualistic ("The ceremonial [hot or cold] as opposed to the haphazard [lukewarm]"; ibid.: 32); highly relevant to our everyday lives and what makes an impression on us ("That a man's shadow, which looks like a man, or that his mirror image, or that rain, thunderstorms, the phases of the moon, the change of seasons, the likenesses and differences of animals to one another and to human beings, the phenomena of death, of birth and of sexual life, in short everything a man perceives year in, year out around him, should play a part in his thinking [his philosophy] and his practices, is obvious, or in other words it is what we really know and find interesting"; ibid.: 33); mythological ("A whole mythology is deposited in our language"; ibid.: 35); gesticulatory ("We have in the ancient rites the use of a very highly developed gesture-language"; ibid.: 36); and, finally, universalistic ("[T]here is something in us too that speaks in support of those observances by the savages"; ibid.: 34).

From this emphasis on affect, existential relevance, and gesticulation or bodily language, it is tempting to conclude that all Wittgenstein is doing is juxtaposing practice to theory. He is certainly doing this, but it is not all he is doing. It is crucial to see, especially in view of the evidently dichotomous way in which he divides the expressive from the instrumental, that the juxtaposition does not constitute a dualism. For when one adds up the content of all these remarks, one sees that what Wittgenstein is opposing to theory (and opinion and explanation and belief) is no simple counterweight, no opposing but equal principle. On the contrary, what he has in mind enjoys a certain fundamental primacy with respect to theory. As pre-eminently affective and bodily, spiritual and mythological, existentially relevant and universalistic, such magical and religious notions bespeak the bedrock dynamic on which theory, opinions, explanations, and beliefs necessarily rest.

If this is so, then these notions cannot themselves be matters of opinion: "The characteristic feature of primitive man ... is that he does not act from *opinions*" (Wittgenstein 1971: 37). Nor can they be open ultimately to explanation: "Even the idea of trying to explain [such practices] ... seems to me wrong-headed" (ibid.: 29). Rather, the sole form of accounting they are open to is description: "We can only describe and say, human life is like that" (ibid.: 30). In effect, they constitute existential certainties or, to use the technical philosophical term, the synthetic a priori.

Precisely because this kind of a priori is neither theoretical nor empirical, it obtains in a logical and ontological nowhere, between necessity and contingency. For this reason, it confounds explanation, the representational demands of which leave no room to maneuver in the face of ambiguity that is basic. When confronted with ambiguity of this kind, all one can do is show it. That is to say, by definition that which is basically ambiguous cannot be logically determined. Since it is neither this nor that, with respect to saying what it is, one can only say (as the Hebrew scriptures say about the godhead), saying everything and nothing at once, that it is what it is. This is why I think that instead of saying "We could say, man is a ceremonious animal," Wittgenstein says "We could almost say" this, and goes on to say that it is in any case a partly false and nonsensical proposition. Because man's "ceremonious" faculty, his capacity to make meaning, is precisely neither theoretical nor empirical, it is basically inexplicable. Any explanation of this faculty—that is, any attempt to rigidly designate it as either this or that—will in the very (creative and processive) endeavor of trying to do so necessarily go beyond itself and thus belie itself. As a result, although this faculty can be shown, or can show itself, it cannot be *said* as a truth-functional proposition, at least not without making a partial nonsense logically.

One provocative way of capturing such basic ambiguity is by reference to the so-called gestalt switch. About the famous ambiguous figure that can be seen as either a duck or a rabbit, Wittgenstein had this to say (in Monk 1990: 507–8): "Suppose I show it to a child. It says 'It's a duck' and then suddenly 'Oh, it's a rabbit.' So it recognises it as a rabbit.—This is an experience of recognition. So if you see me in the street and say 'Ah, Wittgenstein.' But you haven't an experience of recognition all the time.—The experience only comes at the moment of change from duck to rabbit and back. In between, the aspect is as it were dispositional." What is important here is Wittgenstein's claim that insofar as the ambiguity is basic, the experience of recognition is dispositional and depends on a change of aspect. The moment of change is immediate and therefore inexplicable. Moreover, it describes perception in terms of an irreducible relationship between the perceiver and what is perceived. That is to say, the question to ask is not what the figure really is or if its determination as anything at all is simply a function of something that goes on inside the head of the perceiver. Rather, the only useful or sensible question that can be asked is, what difference does the change of aspect make? The other questions do not admit of clear answers as long as the ambiguity, as between the figure and itself as well as between the perceiver and the perceived, proves basic. The attempt to see the gestalt switch in terms of such questions always leads down the futile path of having to decide between materialism and idealism, as if the thing had to be either object or idea. What Wittgenstein is trying to show by reference to such *gestalten* is that although idea and experience or thinking and seeing or, more comprehensively, the internal and the external are not the same thing, neither does it make sense to understand them as perfectly separate and distinct from each other.

The immediacy of the change of aspect implicates a creative process. That is to say, at some point in looking in to it, the synthetic a priori lacks an empirical genesis or even an origin through learning. Wittgenstein (1971: 36) alludes to this creative process in terms of what we ordinarily construe as the conduct of choice: "If a human being could choose to be born in a tree in a forest, then there would be some who would seek out the most beautiful or the highest tree for themselves, some who would choose the smallest and some who would choose an average or below-average tree, and I do not mean out of philistinism, but for just the reason, or kind of reason, for which the other man chose the highest. That the feeling we have for our life is comparable to that of a being who could choose his own standpoint in the world is, I believe, the basis of the myth—or belief—that we choose our body before birth." Here Wittgenstein is pointing out that humans are given to experience their "standpoint in the world" as somehow their own choice, and he seems to imply that this experience provides a basis on which humans come to believe that the mind is one thing and the body another ("the basis of the myth—or belief—that we choose our body before birth"). But he also suggests that in a (logically impossible) sense, one's "standpoint in the world" is in fact a matter of 'choice'. Hence, if one could choose to be born "in a tree in a forest," one might choose to identify oneself with the most "beautiful" or "highest" or "smallest" or "average" or "below-average" tree, and whatever the choice, it is taken for "just the reason, or kind of reason"—that is, I think, the 'reason' of self-fashioning—for which other persons choose the other trees to house their particular identities.

These choices, though, arising as they do somehow between thought and perception, cannot be altogether witting and free. Hence, Wittgenstein calls the proposition that our minds somehow obtain prior to our bodies—and, it must follow, as against Kant, the proposition that our conduct of choice can be perfectly autonomous—a "myth." It is for this reason—the reason that the conduct he is describing both does and does not amount to choice—that he qualifies by the conditional ("If one could choose") his picture of choice throughout. Nevertheless, this conduct is, I believe, a question of ethics for him (1971: 36): "We might say 'every view has its charm', but this would be wrong. What is true is that every view is significant for him who sees it so (but that does not mean 'sees it as something other than it is'). And in this sense every view is equally significant. It is important also that the contempt each person feels for me is something I must make my own, an essential and significant part of the world seen from the place where I am." Wittgenstein seems to be saying here that from the perspective of our faculty to make meaning of the world, no standpoint is more (or less) significant than any other. That is to say, synthetic a priori or foundations of human worlds, the standpoints of the highest tree and of the lowest, though different, are equal. If you live in the highest tree and your other in the lowest, that does not mean that the latter has got the world wrong—your other is not seeing it, as Frazer seems to think, "as something other than it is." And precisely in order to see this, Wittgenstein finds that it is "important" to make the other's "contempt" for us (a contempt issuing from the other's particular standpoint in the world), "an essential and significant part" of our own standpoint. By doing so, of course, by learning the other's language (another way, according to Wittgenstein [1971: 36, third footnote] to understand what it means to incorporate into our own view the other's outlook on us), we position ourselves to see the 'truth' in the other's standpoint as well as the relativity of our own.

Such an exercise, one that Wittgenstein practiced with incomparable rigor over the course of his life (indeed, in a sense it is this exercise that defines his philosophy), is by any other name ethics. For it is an exercise in self-liberation and self-creation by means of, paradoxically, the respectful acknowledgment of the other as other. As such, it also implies the understanding, which I believe Wittgenstein held, that the synthetic a priori, the certainties in terms of which we define ourselves and take our existential bearings, remain open to human judgment despite the fact that ordinarily nothing seems to speak against them. By the same token, it implies that although all such standpoints may be equally meaningful as ciphers of 'reality', and therefore immune to theoretical judgments of right and wrong, they are not necessarily off-limits to judgments of good and bad. That is, their nature as existential attitudes toward the world may render theoretical assessments of them misplaced, but it cannot save them from ethical evaluations. It is for this reason that I speak of these attitudes, these a priori, as primordial choices. However much they may be taken for granted and acted on in terms of certainty, they are also auto-constructed in terms of a good. Wittgenstein saw that such standpoints are subject to evaluations of use, but I cannot say whether he formally entertained the point I am making about ethical evaluations. The point, though, is certainly implicit in his argumentation and also, I should think, his conduct: he had a strong sense of the good and was not shy about judging others according to it (cf. Monk 1990: 278).

In view of this understanding of the synthetic a priori, it is no wonder that Wittgenstein concluded that Frazer's evolutionary account of the Beltane May Day or fire festival fails to furnish satisfaction. This festival, which took place in certain parts of Great Britain and Northern Europe up to the nineteenth century, centered on a cake, ritually prepared and divided into lots (one of which could serve as a selector), which were then distributed for purposes of determining a victim to be thrown symbolically into the fire. Impressed with the sinister aura of this festival, Frazer explained it in terms of the hypothesis that the festival found its ultimate origin in ancient rites of human sacrifice. But Wittgenstein points out that even if Frazer's evolutionary hypothesis proved wrong, we would still be impressed with the sinister character of the Beltane festival. In other words, although the genetic explanation may throw a certain light on the festival, it cannot account for our impression that there is something deep and sinister about it.

"I think it is clear," Wittgenstein says (1971: 38), "that what gives us a sinister impression is the inner nature of the practice as performed in recent times, and the facts of human sacrifice as we know them only indicate the direction in which we ought to see it." By "inner nature of the practice," he means (ibid.: 38), "all those circumstances in which it is carried out that are not included in the account of the festival, because they consist ... in what we might call the spirit of the festival: which would be described by, for example, describing the sort of people that take part, their way of behaviour at other times, i.e. their character, and the other kinds of games that they play. And we should then see that what is sinister lies in the character of these people themselves." Plainly, in this passage Wittgenstein is referring to 'cultural context', to the culturally certain foundations that distinguish and identify the people in question. The reason why we find something deep about this festival is, then, according to Wittgenstein, that the spirit of the festival, that is, its inner nature or existential meaning, smacks of the sinister. Put another way, the dark character in question is an aspect of who the rite's practitioners *are*, of their particular identity as cultural beings.

But Wittgenstein's key point looks beyond the cultural context of the people of the rite to embrace the observer's context. "What makes human sacrifice something deep and sinister anyway?" he asks. His answer is (1971: 40): "[T]his deep and sinister aspect is not obvious just from learning the history of the external action, but *we* impute it from an experience in ourselves." The impression is given not only because something deep and sinister rests with the inner spirit of the rite and with the character of the rite's practitioners, but also because "there is something in us too that speaks in support of those observances" (ibid.: 34). Here, with this turn to the beholder's share, Wittgenstein, despite his conspicuous and philosophically central discomfort with the idea of universals (he regarded as pathological the philosophical craving for generality), insinuates the universal—though not in the received sense of the notion. This movement is unmistakable in the sentence that brings his essay to a close (ibid.: 41): what we see in ceremonies and stories evocative of human sacrifice "is something they acquire, after all, from the evidence, including such evidence as does not seem directly connected with them—from the thought of man and his past, from the strangeness of what I see in myself and in others, what I have seen and have heard."

Thus, Wittgenstein argues that the context of meaning to which the impression at point must be referred includes the observer's experience and stock of knowledge. In effect, he sees the observer as participant of what she is observing, helping to define and construct it as it does her in return. This point reiterates Wittgenstein's rejection of both empiricism and intellectualism in favor of the understanding that although the perceiver and the perceived are relatively separate and distinct, there obtains between them a fundamental continuity. As partly a product of the character of the 'outside' observer, the impression of something deep and sinister directly ties the idea of the synthetic a priori to the idea of the universal. This is true despite the fact that by virtue of its syntheticism, this kind of a priori is essentially particularistic. The possibility of an a priori that is at once both particular and universal is a function of the fact that the implied universalism does not project a world of fixed things, but rather evokes a perceptual dynamic that continuously fires the possibility of a world in common. Although each and every synthetic a priori is culturally particular, insofar as it is a product of the human faculty for making meaning, it must be open to the active understanding of others. Thus, by not allowing our intellectualism to obstruct our vision, and by keeping a sharp eye out for the "connexions" and "intermediate links" (Wittgenstein 1971: 35) that make a gestalt, including especially the gestalt formed by the observer with the observed, we put ourselves in a position to see directly the deep nature of the festival and thus satisfy ourselves as to why it impresses us as sinister. The capacity to do this bespeaks a universalizing nature, but because this nature describes the observer as being in the picture he himself projects, it remains ever beyond the reach of logical determination. It is, however, distinctly manifest in human interaction and therefore in a sense can be shown.

I have argued that Wittgenstein's "Remarks on Frazer's 'Golden Bough'" offers an account of the synthetic a priori that radically revises the Kantian understanding. For unlike Kant, who held fast to the immaculate distinction between subject and object, inside and outside, and form and content, Wittgenstein (to leave aside his polemical argument about the expressive and the instrumental) relativizes these distinctions, making them definitively incomplete. As a consequence, while the distinctions do not disappear, their opposing principles enjoy a certain continuity with each other, meaning that they must be less than identical to themselves. This paralogical condition, a state of nondualism or basic ambiguity, yields an a priori that both is and is not certain, universal, and a matter of choice. The possibility of such an a priori stands with the picture of the human world as, in the first place, a dynamic of becoming, in which the said, for all its imposing power to fix and decide things, can never quite catch up with the saying. The said enters into the saying and may represent itself as the superior power, but it can never wholly supercede the primacy of its counterforce. For the human world proceeds in terms of meanings imprisoned in action, and although these meanings can be let out into the light of consciousness, if that light is to shine at all, there must always be further meanings that remain implicit and, in this sense, in the dark, behind the epistemic bars of practice—behind the limits of the self and self-consciousness.

I have read a good deal into the "Remarks," a brief text that has certainly not been regarded by the philosophical commentators as central in the corpus of Wittgenstein's work (cf., however, Zengotita 1989). Still, I believe that I can reinforce my interpretation by glancing quickly at another work by Wittgenstein, especially *On Certainty* (1972), in which he deals with the problem of the a priori rather directly.

Wittgenstein's friend and Cambridge colleague, G. E. Moore, in his attempt to refute philosophical skepticism, that is, the position that there is nothing about the world that can be known with certainty, offered as evidence to the contrary certain common-sense understandings. The most famous of these is his proof that his two hands exist, which he demonstrated by holding them up and saying "Here is one hand, and here is another." According to Wittgenstein, Moore's demonstration could hardly refute skepticism, since showing one's hands in this way cannot provide knowledge that one's hands exist. What it *can* do, said Wittgenstein, is make clear that it would be nonsensical to doubt the existence of one's hands. Moore, says Wittgenstein (1972: § 151), "does not *know* what he asserts he knows, but it stands fast for him."[5]

In other words, Wittgenstein drew a distinction between, on the one hand, the ordinary, everyday experience of not feeling any doubt and, on the other, the epistemological condition of having certain knowledge. Whereas the latter is a question of logic and rationality ("One says 'I know' when one is ready to give compelling grounds. 'I know' relates to a possibility of demonstrating the truth" [1972: § 243]), the former has to do simply with making sense or nonsense of anything at all. Were we to doubt the existence of our own two hands, as we hold them up for all to see, there would be nothing safe from doubt, including our being in the world and our senses: "Doesn't testing come to an end?" (ibid.: § 164). Wittgenstein was arguing neither that one's senses are perfectly reliable nor that different people cannot arrive at different existential certainties. Rather, he was pointing out that in order to make any sense at all, it is necessary that we take some propositions for granted, for these propositions (such as "here is my hand") belong to the frame of reference by virtue of which we can make meaning of the world in the least. If we did not conduct ourselves as if our hands exist or the earth abides beneath our feet, our world would lack any integrity whatsoever, and we could take no meaningful direction from it for purposes of getting on with life (ibid.: § 150): "How does someone judge which is his right and which his left hand?… If I don't trust *myself* here, why should I trust anyone else's judgment? Is there a why? Must I not begin to trust somewhere? That is to say: somewhere I must begin with not-doubting; and that is not, so to speak, hasty but excusable: it is part of judging."

Plainly, Wittgenstein is pointing to a synthetic a priori, which can be conceived of in terms of a taken-for-granted world or, as he calls it, a world picture (*Weltbild*). The sort of picture he has in mind is not a proper theoretical projection of things, but a practical, meaningful framework on the basis of which we can judge and determine, which is to say, come to terms with things. Regarding Moore-type assertions as "absolutely solid," says Wittgenstein (1972: § 151), "is part of our *method* of doubt and enquiry." By "method" here he does not intend a technical procedure but rather our everyday practice of making sense of things (ibid.: § 148): "Why do I not satisfy myself that I have two feet when I want to get up from a chair? There is no why. I simply don't. This is how I act." Hence, for all practical purposes, this taken-for-granted framework, this "substratum of all my enquiring and asserting" (ibid.: § 162) is groundless, without 'why': "The difficulty is to realize the groundlessness of our believing" (1972: § 166). Correlatively, Wittgenstein asserts (ibid.: § 152): "I do not explicitly learn the propositions that stand fast for me. I can discover them subsequently like the axis around which a body rotates. This axis is not fixed in the sense that anything holds it fast, but the movement around it determines its immobility."

The last quotation suggests why such indubitable propositions constitute a worldview. Wittgenstein holds that unlike theoretical premises, they do not stand alone, as matters of logic proper, but rather together: "It is not single axioms that strike me as obvious, it is a system in which consequences and premises give one another *mutual* support" (1972: § 142). "When we first begin to believe anything, what we believe is not a single proposition, it is a whole system of propositions. (Light dawns gradually over the whole)" (ibid.: § 141). Wittgenstein describes how this holistic learning takes place as follows (ibid.): "I am told, for example, that someone climbed this mountain many years ago. Do I always enquire into the reliability of the teller of this story, and whether the mountain did exist years ago? A child learns there are reliable and unreliable informants much later than it learns facts which are told it. It doesn't learn *at all* that that mountain has existed for a long time: that is, the question whether it is so doesn't arise at all. It swallows this consequence down, so to speak, together with *what* it learns."

The holism of synthetic a priori propositions helps us to understand how such groundless propositions can "stand fast." They are of course taken for granted, which means that normally they do not dwell in the light of consciousness and therefore are not open to question (as Wittgenstein says, some propositions are simply swallowed down together with what is learned). But there is more to this kind of pre-epistemological security. Because they are all tied together, these propositions are continually reinforced by all the other such propositions, in the sense that to question any is implicitly to question many, if not all. And since together they constitute one's world picture, that is, the picture according to which one goes about the activities of one's everyday, ordinary life (standing up, sitting down, going from one place to another, etc.), such questioning tends to pull the very ground from beneath one's feet. It is for this reason that Wittgenstein tells us that what holds these propositions fast is the movement around them (1972: § 114): "The child learns to believe a host of things. I.e., it learns to act according to these beliefs. Bit by bit there forms a system of what is believed, and in that system some things stand unshakably fast and some are more or less liable to shift. What stands fast does so, not because it is intrinsically obvious or convincing; it is rather held fast by what lies around it." Such propositions are groundless, then, because they themselves constitute the ground. And like any ground or horizon, they are fixed only relative to their correlative figure or theme, which in the present case amounts to one's everyday, precognitive practices.[6]

Gier (1981: chap. 8) finds that Wittgenstein distinguished two sorts of such synthetic a priori propositions, one having to do with grammatical rules and another that is a question of facts rather than rules. For example, "I cannot remember the future" runs contrary to certain fundamental Western understandings because it fails to adhere to the grammatical rules of usage. The proposition makes no sense since it defies the logic of grammatical convention rather than empirical fact: we simply do not use 'remember' in this way, to take as its object the future. But the proposition "I have only one body" is not a question of rules of usage; instead, it is bound up with empirical matters of fact.

Despite the difference between them, however, both kinds of proposition run irre-mediably between the analytic and the synthetic. Grammatical propositions constitute the logic of a language and the basis on which people act and make meaning. In this sense, they are a priori and enjoy an analytic nature. But plainly, as 'rules' of grammar, even if implicit ones, they are also subject to the material process of history and are thus synthetic. Hence, they obtain halfway between the formal and the factual or contingent. The other sort of a priori propositions have the form of ordinary empirical propositions but enjoy a special ontological status. "It is clear that our empirical propositions do not all have the same status," says Wittgenstein (1972: § 167), "since one can lay down such a proposition and turn it from an empirical proposition into a norm of description." By "norm of description," Wittgenstein intends a proposition that "gives our way of looking at things, and our researches, their form. Perhaps it was once disputed. But perhaps, for unthinkable ages, it has belonged to the *scaffolding* of our thoughts. (Every human being has parents.)" (ibid.: § 211). Such presuppositions are bound up, not with rules of usage, but with the way things are and what there is. They serve as pinions of reality, and, in this sense, may be thought of as analytic or even transcendental. But Wittgenstein's characterization of them as empirical propositions transformed into norms of description suggests that they too are synthetic in nature. Moreover, just as, like any rules, the rules of grammar are subject to change, so such hard propositions can lose their special status among empirical propositions. For example, whereas we have ordinarily always presupposed that every human being has two, and only two, parents, with the invention of the technology of surrogate motherhood, whereby the biological processes of ovulation and gestation are divided between two women, is it not the case that now some children may be said to have not two but three parents?[7]

Although on the surface of it, there do seem to be differences between grammatical and hard propositions, it is not clear to me that they are fundamentally different. Gier himself (1981: 175) suggests that the appearance of the distinction in Wittgenstein's work "reveals some possible confusion in Wittgenstein's thinking." I have brought Gier's discussion to bear here because it is exceedingly helpful in clarifying Wittgenstein's focus on the question of the a priori. For my purposes, what is important to see is that both grammatical and hard propositions constitute synthetic a priori. As such, neither is normally a question of truth or falsity; rather, both embody the conditions for determining what is true and what is false. In addition, both confound the distinctions between the analytic and the synthetic, or reason and fact, such that these distinctions are rendered essentially fuzzy and less than fast.

Merleau-Ponty

In his monumental work, *Phenomenology of Perception*, Maurice Merleau-Ponty takes Kant to task for failing to follow out his own program, "which was to define our cognitive powers in terms of our factual condition" (1962: 220–21). Had Kant done so, finds Merleau-Ponty, he would have arrived at "a new definition of the *a priori*" (ibid.: 220), in which the a priori is no longer cleanly distinguishable from the a posteriori: "From the moment that experience—that is, the opening on to our *de facto* world—is recognized as the beginning of knowledge, there is no longer any way of distinguishing a level of *a priori* truths and one of factual ones, what the world must necessarily be and what it actually is" (ibid.: 221). Put in a nutshell (ibid.: 394): "[E]very truth of fact is a truth of reason, and *vice versa.*" So much for Kant's continued adherence to a dualism of form and content, or of the analytic and the empirical.

In order to explain himself, Merleau-Ponty (1962: 394) appeals to a phenomenological notion of "founding" (*Fundierung*), by which he has in mind a dynamic two-way relationship, in which one sort of truth serves to found another, which in turn acts back on the first sort, making itself more than derivative and the founding truth less than primary. That is to say, in our practical engagement of the world, we manage, especially by means of language, to transform truths of fact into truths of reason. Although the latter truths can never break entirely free from their founding facts, they become sedimented into cultural forms (into, as Wittgenstein would say, the "scaffolding" of our thoughts) and therewith in-form the facts from which they derive, giving these facts, irremovably, a cultural character. In light of this dynamic picture of essential ambiguity, ultimately there is no distinguishing between the two kinds of truth, and wherever they *can* be distinguished, the distinction is relative. This I take it is what Merleau-Ponty has in mind when he maintains (ibid.: 393–94) that "there is not one of my actions ... which has not been directed toward a value or a truth ... Conversely, there is not one truth of reason which does not retain its coefficient of facticity."

In order to demonstrate that ideas or truths of reason are always tied to being-in-the-world, Merleau-Ponty takes up Descartes' example (in his Fifth Meditation, but harking back to Plato and forward to Kant) of the triangle as a pure idea, that is, as an idea in itself, cleanly detached from the empirical world. Merleau-Ponty's discussion is involved (1962: 383ff.; cf. Hall 1979), but the following highly anthropological observation by him—evocative of Wittgenstein's that "norms of description" can grow from hard to soft propositions—suffices here to indicate the spirit of his point (Merleau-Ponty 1962: 394): "[T]he alleged transparency of Euclidean geometry is one day revealed as operative for a certain period in the history of the human mind, and signifies simply that, for a time, men were able to take a homogeneous three-dimensional space as the 'ground' of their thoughts, and to assume unquestioningly what generalized science will come to consider as a contingent account of space."

What, then, of the other side of the two-way relationship he called "founding"? If, as against intellectualism, the truths of reason are always derivative, then must we, as dualism bids us, plump for empiricism? But the whole of Merleau-Ponty's great book is geared to show that neither empiricism nor intellectualism can do the ontological trick. For the founding facts in which Merleau-Ponty's "founding" begins are, like Wittgenstein's hard propositions, far from ordinary empirical facts. Instead, they are matters of basic ambiguity. Such ambiguity, which cannot be "resolved" but can be "understood as ultimate" (Merleau-Ponty 1962: 394), recalls Wittgenstein's thesis of truths that can be shown but, precisely because they are imprisoned in practice and do not stop for logical logic, cannot be said.

Merleau-Ponty, providing a loose and open-ended list of terms, does speak of the "founding term, or originator": "time, the unreflective, the fact, language, perception" (1962: 394). But he uses none of these terms here in an ordinary sense. Let me take up "perception" alone, as this concept forms the axis of his phenomenology and may serve to elucidate the other terms. "[T]he perceived world is the always presupposed foundation of all rationality, all value and all existence," he says (1964b: 13). Merleau-Ponty is interested in the presuppositions of our existence, the world as we live it before we reflect on it, which is what he means by "the perceived world." Hence, for Merleau-Ponty, the perceiving being cannot be in the first place a pure consciousness, as it is for, say, Descartes and Kant. Otherwise it would be, instead of pre-reflective, a disengaged self, like Descartes' *cogito* or Kant's transcendental ego. In order to transcend this dualistic conception of the perceiver as that which is wholly set over and against the world, Merleau-Ponty renders the perceiving being as a body-subject. Obviously, by making it out as no less bodily than mindful, Merleau-Ponty construes it, not as detached from but as participating in the world. In which case, unlike Descartes' 'I think', which extends in neither space nor time, it must be a matter of temporality and facticity.

Since the body-subject 'thinks', it must enjoy language, in the sense of expression. Language-as-expression reconfigures the world, making the world meaningful, and yet remains inseparable from being-in-the-world, which is to say, from bodily existence or experience. Language in this sense, as for Wittgenstein, is a matter of gesticulation and silence before speech. For Merleau-Ponty, it is the body that perceives and the body that speaks. And the body can do this because, in the first place, it is not the objective phenomenon that science projects. Purely objective phenomena, in Merleau-Ponty's as well as Wittgenstein's philosophy, are nothing but high abstractions, the production of which depends on the as-if existential detachment afforded by the intellectual or theoretical standpoint. Instead of an objective phenomenon, Merleau-Ponty's 'body' goes without organs.[8] A body without organs is integrally tied to the world and is therefore less than perfectly separate and discrete; but it is tied in a way so open and dynamic that its movements characteristically reconfigure its relationship to the world, thus always transcending itself in its act.

Even if the perceiving being remains tied to the world, though, perception seems still to presuppose a consciousness of sorts. Hence, Merleau-Ponty posited a *cogito* or 'I think', but, in critical contrast to Descartes', a tacit one. Such a *cogito* is the name Merleau-Ponty (1962: 371) gives to the self-consciousness that necessarily accompanies all perception, even if perception is essentially bodily, a movement toward the world in which the perceiving being transcends itself by reconfiguring itself in relation to the world: "All thought of something is at the same time self-consciousness, failing which it could have no object. At the root of all our experiences and all our reflections, we find, then, a being which immediately recognizes itself, because it is its knowledge both of itself and of all things, and which knows its own existence, not by observation and as a given fact, nor by inference from any idea of itself, but through direct contact with that existence." Plainly, as it proceeds in action, that is, "through direct contact with … existence," the *cogito* of which Merleau-Ponty speaks must be less than transparent to itself, which is why he calls it "tacit" (ibid.: 402).

But despite its pronounced nature as action rather than thought qua thought, the tacit *cogito* would not be a *cogito* at all, an '*I think*', if it eluded itself completely. For this reason, the idea of the tacit *cogito* might still evoke body-mind dualism, rather than the patent ambiguity of a body that is no less a subject than an object, and thus project perception as an act of consciousness. Seeing this and taking an even more radical ontological turn, one that dovetails with Wittgenstein's (1972: § 142) notion of a system of "mutual support," in *The Visible and the Invisible*, the book he was working on when he died, Merleau-Ponty (1968) reconceived "founding" in terms of "intertwining" or "reversibility." Instead of a movement in which one thing founds another that in turn reconfigures its source (as culture, our second nature, informs the human practice from which it springs), he conceives of a dynamic crossing arrangement (ibid.: 133):

> [B]etween my movements and what I touch, there must exist some relationship by principle, some kinship, according to which they are … the initiation to and the opening upon a tactile world. This can happen only if my hand while it is felt from within, is also accessible from without, itself tangible, for my other hand, for example, if it takes its place among the things it touches, is in a sense one of them, opens finally upon a tangible being of which it is also a part. Through this crisscrossing within it of the touching and the tangible, its own movements incorporate themselves into the universe they interrogate, are recorded on the same map as it.

Instead of citing the hands, then, as does Moore, in an exercise of ostension, to prove that we can have certain knowledge of the external world, Merleau-Ponty cites them in their dynamic relationship to each other, in order to describe how perception works and how it solicits faith in its act. That is, he brings our hands to bear, not as objects, but as modes of engaging or perceiving the world. The hand can touch because it too is palpable. It can make sense of (behave sensibly in) the world precisely because it is of the world, a part of the same "universe." There is a substantive identity between it and the world, such that its touch can be relied upon, not because it provides certain knowledge, but because, as Wittgenstein might say, what it touches resonates with it in practical harmony.

Precisely because there is such identity, however, because the hand's ability to touch depends on its status as itself tangible, its touch can never exhaust in perception what it touches. Its own palpability makes its touch self-referential and thus constitutionally limited ("a veritable touching of the touch, when my right hand touches my left hand while it is palpating the things, where the 'touching subject' passes over into the rank of the touched"; Merleau-Ponty 1968: 133–34). Only if the hand were itself untouchable, the veritable hand of God, would it be capable of transforming what it touches into an object pure and simple (and even then, judging from the Hebraic creation story, as in Michel-angelo's glorious Sistine depiction of it, such sheer objectification is dubious). In other words, the relationship Merleau-Ponty describes, the dynamic of perception, cannot be captured by subject-object dualism. The substantive identity between the body-subject and the object-world, the identity that makes perception possible, also precludes the possibility of grasping the perceived phenomenon totally, as a pure object. For its identity with its other ensures that the perceiving being must be less than identical to itself. And inasmuch as it is, it—and of course the perceptible other, which it also is—is by definition always already beyond itself.

This dynamic of identity within difference is for Merleau-Ponty the "ultimate truth" (1968: 155). That is to say, he describes the presuppositional foundation of human existence, not as a foundation in the positivistic sense of the term, a firm and unambiguous edifice, but as (perceptual) movement of the sensible body in the world. Of course, the shibboleth of identity-in-difference recalls Hegel's dialectic. But just as it is the nature of that dialectic to resolve itself, so it is the nature of Merleau-Ponty's never to reach final resolution, never to catch up with itself. For the identity that makes the movement of perception possible also ensures the difference that makes the movement ongoing. This dynamic, a bodily but sensible connectivity, is called by Merleau-Ponty (ibid.: 138 and chap. 4) "flesh," and, in view of the way in which it connects all things to one another in an open whole, a whole that is, paradoxically, less than a totality, he speaks of it as "the flesh of the world" (ibid.: 146).

Holism of this kind bears comparison to Wittgenstein's, wherein together with every proposition one learns, one also 'swallows down'—which is to say, learns unknowingly—a host of other propositions, for the latter are fundamentally linked to the former, as horizon to theme. Hence, with regard to such attendant propositions, Wittgenstein (1971: 34–35) bids us to "see the connexions," to show them "in a perspicuous way," a way that has nothing to do with genetic or explanatory relations but simply allows us to see all at once a meaningful configuration. Both holisms, Merleau-Ponty's and Wittgenstein's, are gestaltist in character, supposing that the meaningful forms of our existence are in a sense always already given, not exactly as ideas, but as lived and affective or 'bodily' predications—that is, as synthetic a priori. Although Wittgenstein does not use 'flesh' to describe what binds such propositions together, when one considers that the kind of horizon he has in mind is not properly propositional at all but a matter of concrete, everyday practice, Merleau-Ponty's term seems to fit the spirit of Wittgenstein's understanding well enough. Indeed, in light of the fact that Wittgenstein (1971: 41) critically includes in the horizonal context of any perception or understanding the beholder's share (to repeat the quote, with italics added: "the *strangeness* of what *I* see in myself and in others, what *I* have seen and have heard"), he approaches the very heart of Merleau-Ponty's holism: that the ultimate context and standpoint of every act of perception—the ineradicable, 'visually' enabling blind spot of the mind's eye—is the body-subject.

Of course, we ordinarily think of perception in terms of seeing rather than touching, and the other word Merleau-Ponty uses to speak of the intertwining—"chiasm"—is the physiological term for the crossing of the optic nerves that physically occasions vision. In starting with the example of the hands, Merleau-Ponty wants to show the basically bodily nature of perception, even when it is visual perception in question. As most any account of scientific methodology will exhibit, the dualistic picture of perception as an act of consciousness in relation to the external world is associated especially with our faculty of vision. The distance this faculty affords us from whatever happens to be under observation is so great relative to how our other senses work that it has encouraged us to conclude (mistakenly) that the break between the observer and the observed is clean. In sharp contrast, Merleau-Ponty (1968: 134) argues that we all see, like Lear's blinded Lord Gloucester, 'feelingly': "Between the massive sentiment I have of the sack in which I am enclosed, and the control from without that my hand exercises over my hand, there is as much difference as between the movements of my eyes and the changes they produce in the visible. And as, conversely, every experience of the visible has always been given to me within the context of the movements of the look, the visible spectacle belongs to the touch neither more nor less than do the 'tactile qualities.'" It must follow that visual perception too works as a crossing function (ibid.): "[S]ince vision is a palpation with the look, it must also be inscribed in the order of being that it discloses to us; he who looks must not himself be foreign to the world that he looks at."

If the seer is thus continuous with the seen, in looking at its other it is also seeing itself. In the visual domain, Merleau-Ponty describes perception along the lines of mirror-imaging, making self and other reverse—and therefore less than absolute—projections of each other. In his phenomenological account of the development of the child's perception of others, Merleau-Ponty (1964b: chap. 4) makes extensive use of the example of how children respond to their own image in the mirror. He finds (on the basis of psychological research) that whereas at first the child tends to see the visual image of its body in the mirror as enjoying a quasi-existence, it gradually learns to displace the image and grasp the mirror's crucial developmental lesson: "[H]e can ... be seen by an external witness *at the very place at which he feels himself to be*" (ibid.: 129). In the following passage, Merleau-Ponty (ibid.) attempts to lend support to the claim of an original and originary consciousness in which differentiation is less than complete:

> Many pathological facts bear witness to this kind of external perception of the self ... First, it is found in many dreams in which the subject figures as a quasi-visible character. There would also be phenomena of this kind in dying people, in certain hypnotic states, and in drowning people. What reappears in these pathological cases is comparable to the child's original consciousness of his own visible body in the mirror. "Primitive" people are capable of believing that the same person is in several places at the same time. The child knows well that he is there where his introceptive body is, and yet in the depth of the mirror he sees the same being present, in a bizarre way, in a visible appearance.

Granted, his comparison here of "primitive" people with children and pathological cases is anthropologically exceedingly crude and badly dated. But it makes a powerful difference to the anthropological import of the comparison that he aims to disclose by it, rather than (à la Frazer et al.) a mistaken perception of the world, a recognition that opens on the truth or a prioricity of nondualism, and therewith one that betrays the radical reduction carried out by intellectualization. Merleau-Ponty (1964b: 132) relates that Wallon, the psychologist on whose study he draws here, holds that once the child has learned to reduce the mirror image to an ideal space (that is, to intellectualize it), the image has become what it should be in an adult mind: "a simple reflection." But, says Merleau-Ponty (ibid.), "there are two ways in which we can consider the image—one, a reflective, analytic way according to which the image is nothing but an appearance in a visible world and has nothing to do with me; the other, a global and indirect one, of the kind which we use in immediate life when we do not reflect and which gives us the image as something which solicits our belief." In other words, he is suggesting that in fact the child's relatively undifferentiated perception has something fundamentally right about it (ibid.): "[T]he image in the mirror, even for the adult, when considered in direct unreflective experience, is not simply a physical phenomenon: it is mysteriously inhabited by me; it is something of myself." As Wittgenstein would say, it is not a mistake.

If Merleau-Ponty is correct, then the lesson to be learned when the child comes to better differentiate his mirror image from himself, such that he learns to take that image as an external perspective on himself and thence to see himself in terms of how he may appear to the other, is that, far from being perfectly separate and distinct from his other, in some concrete (but, crucially, always imperfect) way he *is* his other. Merleau-Ponty (1964b: 135ff.) goes on to cite Lacan's famous psychoanalytic study of the role of the "mirror stage" in the development of the self, to the effect that the child's eventual assumption of the viewpoint taken on by him, as this viewpoint is given in the mirror image, is what makes the self possible. For it is only by assuming an 'outside' perspective, that is, the perspective of the other, that a self can appear at all to what is otherwise a mere "lived *me*" (ibid.: 136). "To use Dr. Lacan's terms," writes Merleau-Ponty (ibid.), "I am 'captured, caught up' by my spatial image ... The specular image is the 'symbolic matrix ... where the *I* springs up in primordial form before objectifying itself in the dialectic of identification with the other.'" Put differently, the immediate me is drawn away from itself and *subjecte*d. But Merleau-Ponty (ibid.: 138; 140) is keen to stress that this development is made possible only because the lived me, the pre-eminently (but still not absolutely) undifferentiated childhood me, "is never radically liquidated": "[W]e must consider the relation with others *not only as one of the contents of our experience but as an actual structure in its own right.* We can admit that what we call 'intelligence' is only another name designating an original type of relation with others (the relation of 'reciprocity') and that, from the start to the finish of the development, the living relation with others is the support, the vehicle, or the stimulus for what we abstractly call the 'intelligence.'" For Merleau-Ponty, then, the intertwining constitutes a bodily a priori, one that, in view of its sensible or experiential nature, is no less synthetic than given.

Reversibility or the intertwining appears to make the self-other relationship symmetrical, but this appearance of symmetry, although provocatively instructive, is misleading. It is instructive because it points to novel realizations, perhaps the most jarring (and, when one considers the considerable ubiquity of 'the evil eye', ethnographically gravid) of which is that the seen as well as the seer must have the capacity of sight. Of course, when the seen is another person, there is nothing outlandish about this condition. But as soon as 'other' is used to include all that is not self, then it must be the case that visible 'things' as well as persons can return the seer's look. Merleau-Ponty takes this claim quite seriously, as in the following example of painters (1964b: 167): "Inevitably the roles between [the painter] and the visible are reversed. That is why so many painters have said that things look at them. As André Marchand says, after Klee: 'In a forest, I have felt many times over that it was not I who looked at the forest. Some days I felt that the trees were looking at me, were speaking to me ... I was there, listening ... I think that the painter must be penetrated by the universe and not want to penetrate it.'" I take it that Merleau-Ponty intends, against all logic, that the trees are actually looking at the painter as he is looking at them (*pace* Dillon 1988: 169). Under our received ontology (on which logic proper rests), this claim must be regarded as perfectly outlandish: trees as such do not possess organs of vision. But under Merleau-Ponty's (1964b: 163) revised ontology, in which the animate body is without organs, that is, does not amount to "the assemblage or juxtaposition of its parts," except in the abstract, the body is at once separate from and participant of the seen. In which case, reasons Merleau-Ponty (ibid.: 164): "It is more accurate to say that I see according to [the seen], or with it, than that I *see it.*"

Once one takes up the ontological perspective of nondualism, then even if the trees are not seeing in the strict sense, it is sensible to say in earnest that the trees regard the painter. The strict sense is highly abstract, a very useful but readily misleading meaning constructed by setting aside the lived world, the world in which I and the trees participate in each other, such that the trees can see as a function of me and "[t]hings have an internal equivalent in me; they arouse in me a carnal formula of their presence" (Merleau-Ponty 1964b: 164). In effect, the trees serve as a kind of mirror, and the mirror appears because "my body is made of the same flesh as the world (it is a perceived), and moreover ... this flesh of my body is shared by the world, the world *reflects* it, encroaches upon it and it encroaches upon the world ... they are in a relation of transgression or of overlapping" (Merleau-Ponty 1968: 248).

Nevertheless, the relation between the seer and the perceived, self and other, is definitely not symmetrical. The fact that there is only one flesh hardly means that significant difference is precluded. To the contrary, while reversibility entails commonality, it rests no less inescapably on difference. Hence, Merleau-Ponty tells us that all flesh is not the same (1968: 250): "The flesh of the world is not *self-sensing* (*se sentir*) as is my flesh—It is sensible and not sentient—I call it flesh, nonetheless ... in order to say that it is a *pregnancy* of possibles ... that it is therefore absolutely not an ob-ject, that the *blosse Sache* [brute fact] mode of being is but a partial and second expression of it ... The flesh of the world is of the Being-seen, i.e. is a Being that is *eminently percipi*, and it is by it that we can understand the *percipere* ... *there is* Being, not Being in itself, identical to itself, in the night, but the Being that also contains its negation, its *percipi.*" If the flesh of the world is not sensible in the same way as is my flesh (which is sentient), must we then conclude that Merleau-Ponty does not mean what he says when he describes the trees as returning the painter's look? As long as we bear in mind that self-sensing flesh remains flesh, that it is the issue of the flesh of the world (which equals a "pregnancy of possibles"), then the answer must be no. The flesh of the world really does see, but it sees potentially, a potentiality that is realized in the painter's capacity to see herself according to or with the trees. From this understanding of imminent vision, it is tempting to slip back into thinking that Merleau-Ponty's description of the trees as sighted is merely a figure of speech. But as long we see the painter, ontologically, as continuous with the trees, we must take Merleau-Ponty to mean just what he says.

Nevertheless, it would appear that the difference between the sensible and the sentient does constitute an asymmetry. The painter and the trees both do and do not see in the same way. It is important to recognize that the asymmetry runs deep—much deeper than may seem to be the case at first sight. Despite the fact that the difference provided for in the flesh of the world is a matter of degree, it is also, paradoxically, a question of kind. Since the being constituted by the flesh of the world is, as Merleau-Ponty says, not identical to itself but inclusive of its own negation, it cannot but present an infinite difference. And difference of this kind, unfathomable and irredeemable, cannot help manifesting itself in terms of values, that is, in terms of a difference between good and bad. It cannot because it bears with it the negative, which, when construed as an act rather than a concept, "slackens the intentional threads which attach us to the world" (Merleau-Ponty 1962: xiii). And to the degree that these "intentional threads" are slackened, that is, to the extent that we enjoy a relative 'distance' or distinction from the world, we are free to determine our own ends. In which case, the world, even as it ever remains our ground, is also, in imperfect but consequential measure, ours to refuse and thus to transcend.

There is value only relative to evaluation, and there is evaluation wherever there is a transcendent end, which is to say, an end that is no less willed than determined in the nature of things. Such an end—a primordial choice, if you like—involving as it does, implicitly or not, evaluation between one thing and another, amounts to a good and therewith implicates the not-good or, at least, the not-so-good.

In view of this argument about the critical role of negation and valuation in the flesh of the world, the asymmetry between the two ways of seeing, the painter's and the tree's, is not simply logical but also, by implication, axiological. The possibility of evaluation rests on the relationship of negation as between sensibility (the way trees see) and sentience (the way we see). With the development of radically sentient beings, beings in whom reflexivity (which Merleau-Ponty identifies as the elemental dynamic of corporeality) has become acute to the point of conspicuous reversal, the will becomes manifest. In effect, where there's the way (of all flesh), there's a will; and where there's a will, there's a transcendent end, which is to say, a synthetic good. Hence, the ontological fact of reversibility becomes also a uniquely human or ethical modality.

By their very nature, such goods are particular and contextual rather than universal. As synthetic, they are products of history, singular courses of events significantly determined by willful acts under conditions of fundamental uncertainty. These acts are performed by reflective but embodied beings and are therefore, like all material processes, subject to contingency. Nevertheless, there is one end that all the others presuppose, for which reason it may be said to enjoy a certain universality. I have in mind the end of having ends. No matter how hard we try, we cannot help but engage the world with a view toward some particular end. In other words, we always take a stand and thus define a good, even when we aim to refrain from doing so. Merleau-Ponty put it this way (1962: xix): "Because we are in the world, we are *condemned to meaning*, and we cannot do or say anything without its acquiring a name in history." While the relaxation of our ties to the world allows us to give meaning—that is, assign value—to our particular situation, the fact that those ties are slackened but never broken ensures that we cannot do otherwise. We remain bound—as Merleau-Ponty would say, 'embodied'—as the condition of our own freedom. As a result, the end of having ends enjoys a singular status.[9]

Like all other ends that are taken for granted, the end of having ends is both given and constructed—a synthetic a priori or primordial choice. But unlike our other ends, this end is given not only pre-reflectively but also ineluctably. Whatever humans do, wherever and whenever they exist, the end of having ends is necessarily implicit—which cannot be said of any of our other ends. Nor is this end a construct in quite the same way as the others. For unlike the latter, when this end is brought to the light of consciousness, it is not open to revision. We can do away with it to be sure, but only by ceasing to exist. Which is why, as I argue in this book, acts that run directly contrary to the end of having ends, although they are logically self-inconsistent and continue to entertain that end in all their contrariness, are essentially lethal. Nevertheless, the end of having ends remains synthetic, in that it is not a question of natural law but of human existence. It is made to appear only in virtue of beings whose defining nature it is to transcend or fashion themselves—not to *be* but to *become*.

Therefore, the end of having ends may be construed as, rather than a mere good, a hypergood. It is a synthetic a priori, but its syntheticity is more strictly limited and its a prioricity more categorically closed than is the case with the other goods. In the sense that the other goods always presuppose it, the end of having ends may be thought of as a kind of human universal. Its universality, though, has little to do with our received acceptation of this notion, which connotes a positively fixed certitude, a natural law. In contrast, the end of having ends remains an offer, but, to invoke the language of the cinema Wiseguy, "an offer that can't be refused." That is to say, like all offers it may indeed be refused, but its terms of refusal carry with them the threat of death.

As a hypergood, the end of having ends presents what might be called, oxymoronically, a natural good. What makes this end no less decidedly synthetic than given is that by determining the *producing* of synthetic ends or goods, it transcends itself. That is to say, it is determining, but what it determines is its own partial negation as a determinant. Uniquely defined by this hypergood, human existence, insofar as it takes itself as its own end, necessarily presents a natural (a priori) but axiological (synthetic) bias toward the end of having ends.

It must follow from the fact of this bias that the asymmetry defined by the difference between the sensible and the sentient, the seen and the seer, is a matter of value. It is not merely a question of qualitatively different ways of touching and seeing, but of relative worth. Just as in each and every one of our acts we are condemned to meaning, so we are predestined to differential value. But, one might well ask, which side of the difference—between the sensible and the seen on the one hand, and the sentient and the seer on the other—makes the greater good?

Merleau-Ponty's ontology leaves no room for doubt here. The goodness in question rests with the power not simply to discover or recognize one's own end but to generate the possibility of making and having ends. It would appear, then, that the end of having ends is identifiable with the dynamic of transcendence, the intertwining itself, and not with either of the two sides defined by this dynamic. It is true that if the two sides are taken in themselves, as if they obtained apart from their crossing, then there is no differentiating the one from the other by reference to relative worth. But as soon as they are defined as functions of their crossing, one side appears to enjoy a certain, general primacy over the other. Although both are eminently tied to the intertwining, the one is more so than the other. Indeed, even as they generate and inform each other, one of them—the seer and the sentient—always stands belated relative to the other. This is because, as *self*-conscious acts, seeing and sentience are logically inclined to exclude—as the outside or the other—the seen and the sensible, whereas the latter, as was noted earlier, include vision and touch as immanent parts or potentialities of their nature.

This differential of generative power is what Merleau-Ponty (1964b: chap. 2) is getting at when he speaks of the "primacy of perception" and pictures perception as most basically a bodily faculty. He is saying that the seen and the sensible, so long as they are understood dynamically by reference to reversibility, constitute the very core of our identity, and that that identity—what we are—must be the starting point of all our perspectives, reflections, and practices, however variable and diverse they may be. It is true that Merleau-Ponty does not speak of the asymmetry between the sensible and the sentient, the seen and the seer, as axiological. His later philosophy made it even less likely that he would do so. In *The Visible and the Invisible*, he attempts to move beyond any *cogito* whatsoever, even a tacit, experiential one, in order to put behind him once and for all the metaphysics of subject-object dualism. An ontology preoccupied with attenuating the notion of the self or a being equipped to decide merit is not likely to project what there is as innately a matter of value.

If, however, the asymmetry of seer and seen, of sentient and sensible, is aligned with that of self and other, then it at once becomes apparent that human existence is an exercise in value judgment. Deciding on which enjoys primacy of place—self or other—is paradigmatically an ethical question. And since the seer and the sentient always betray selfhood, even if only as a tacit phenomenon, the pertinence of the self-other duality in their case is patent. Merleau-Ponty did indeed come to abandon the tacit *cogito*, which notion he had originally entertained to capture the self-consciousness implicit in any act of bodily perception. But even his distinction of the visible and the invisible, forged in his effort to do away with any sense of the pure subject, continues to evoke the self-like (Merleau-Ponty 1968: 215): "Meaning is *invisible*, but the invisible is not the contradictory of the visible: the visible itself has an invisible inner framework (*membrure*), and the in-visible is the secret counterpart of the visible, it appears only within it, it is the *Nichturpräsentierbar* [originary not-present] which is presented to me as such within the world—one cannot *see it there* and every effort to see it there makes it disappear, but it is *in the line* of the visible, it is its virtual focus, it is inscribed within it (in filigree)."

Judging from this quotation, the distinction between the visible and the invisible greatly complicates Merleau-Ponty's earlier organizing distinctions, undercutting their residual dualism. On the one hand, the visible would seem to correspond to the seen and the sensible, but on the other, the invisible paints a much deeper picture than do the sentient and seer. For instead of simply naming an emergent development of the visible (such as vision and touch), the invisible points to the "inner framework" or "secret counterpart" of the visible. In other words, it points directly to the visible's supporting or sustaining framework, that which "renders [the visible] visible, its own and *interior possibility*" (Merleau-Ponty 1968: 151; my italics).

Thus, the invisible is an aspect of the visible, but, paradoxically, an aspect upon which one can never lay eyes. Merleau-Ponty calls this aspect "meaning," but one can sense the intonement of spirituality—a philosophical caution against empiricist idolatry—in his usage of the invisible. The point I am making here is that although the invisible is precisely other than the pure subject, it is not intended to do away with subjectivity but rather to conceive of it in irreducibly nondualist terms. The nondualism is focused in the consideration that the irreparable blind spot of the mind's eye, the hole of perceptional invisibility without which perception could not happen, is the body. The body is the unseen standpoint of every perception. But the key thing is that while the notion of the invisible rules out any sense of a pure subject, it nonetheless smacks of inwardness, of "interior possibility."

Thus, "the invisible" makes a stunning, productive paradox: it identifies self-transcendence or creation with the other rather than the self qua self. The invisible locates "interior possibility" or selfhood primarily in, instead of the seer and the sentient, what is participant of but invisible or other to the seen and the sensible as well as to the seer and the sentient. As a result, the self-other relation is undone as a dualism but not at all erased; it perdures as a primordial and ultimately unfathomable dynamic. If it is the case that the self-other relation obtains thus primordially, what there is is inconceivable, save as a question of differential value. It is a truth to which every religion seems to attest: even when self-consciousness is originarily attributed to the other rather than to the self, it renders the world in terms of the synthetic a priori, and the synthetic a priori is nothing if not value somehow given.

To come to the principal point, under these ontological conditions, by which the capacity to create or evaluate is associated in the first place with the other rather than the self, it is the other that enjoys the axiological primacy of the hypergood, not the sentient or even the sensible. In other words, it follows from Merleau-Ponty's ontology, that the universalistic bias toward the end of having ends, the at once (incomprehensibly) natural and ethical direction of our being, is toward the other.

The Synthetic a Priori and Ethics, Mysticism, and Magic

Merleau-Ponty does not couch his ontology of ambiguity and reversibility in the distinctly axiological terms I have used here. Indeed, although he wrote about the nature of human freedom and was politically concerned, he did not develop a systematic account of ethics. And although Wittgenstein essayed a lecture on ethics, he held that, in line with his dichotomy of showing and saying, philosophical ethics is an attempt to say what can only be shown. But I am anxious to show that Merleau-Ponty's as well as Wittgenstein's recasting of the synthetic a priori in uncompromisingly and irrevocably nondualist terms leads directly to the conclusion that, notwithstanding the driving objectivist pretension of science, at bottom we cannot perceive the world save in the language of non-indifference (cf. Evens 1995: 195ff.). A nondualist ontology entails the understanding that discretion is as generally necessary as it is necessarily particular in the world as we find it.

Merleau-Ponty's observation that we are condemned to meaning and Wittgenstein's that we are ceremonious animals implicate this picture of what I think of as the primacy of the ethical in human affairs. Both of these arguments bear on the diagnostic centrality of convention in human nature, and, as it is definitively void of instinct, conventional conduct proceeds according to its own evaluative ends. The interpretation of Wittgenstein and Merleau-Ponty as essentially, if inexplicably, concerned with the ethical nature of human existence is given support in the secondary literature, in the case of Wittgenstein substantially so (see especially Edwards 1982; with reference to Merleau-Ponty, see Yeo 1992).

I have drawn a number of suggestive parallels here between Wittgenstein and Merleau-Ponty. It has not been my intention, however, to make a rigorous, detailed comparison of their work; rather, I have tried to bring out a profound commonality of focus between them. That focus is their comprehensive concern to rethink the notion of the synthetic a priori in unrelentingly nondualist terms. As a result of this shared ontological problem, both thinkers, despite the fact that they are not normally mentioned in the same philosophical breath, and however outstanding the differences between them, developed remarkably comparable understandings of human conduct. These understandings picture that conduct as proceeding on the basis of, to highlight the paradox, foundations that are not foundations. In other words, the foundations are immanent and transcendent at the same time, both given and facultative. I have argued that this radically paralogical picture of human conduct necessarily committed both scholars to a counter-ontology, one that grasps what there is in terms of basic ambiguity and therewith processually as discretionary becoming or ethics, as I use the latter term here. I confess that the ethical implications of this ontology did not become transparent to me until I became familiar with Emmanuel Levinas's philosophy of otherness. Hence, when I dwell on ethics in the present work, more often than not I am drawing directly on Levinas for inspiration. At any rate, before leaving off this discussion of Wittgenstein and Merleau-Ponty, I want to point once more to the ethical force and heavy anthropological bearing of their work by citing their deep appreciation of what in Western thought tends to get dismissed as mere mysticism and magic.

Wittgenstein deleted (as "bad," i.e., "S" for *schlecht*) the following lines from his original manuscript of his remarks on Frazer's *The Golden Bough* (cited in Klagge and Nordmann 1993: 116–17):

> I now believe that it would be right to begin my book with remarks about metaphysics as a kind of magic.
>
> But in doing this I must not make a case for magic nor may I make fun of it.
>
> The depth of magic should be preserved.—
>
> Indeed, here the elimination of magic has itself the character of magic.
>
> For, back then, when I began talking about the 'world' (and not about this tree or table), what else did I want but to keep something higher spellbound in my words?

Wittgenstein is suggesting here that, like magic, metaphysical questions tend to evoke in us a sense of something deep and mysterious, something fundamental but also unfathomable. Hence, like magic, metaphysical philosophy—take, for example, the proposition that everything serves a purpose or that the universe is a vast mechanism or that what really exists are not trees or tables but monads—can be consequentially misleading, but not for that reason frivolous. On the one hand, since it makes logical nonsense, he does not wish to speak in favor of such 'magical' thought; on the other, since its depth needs to be preserved, neither does he wish to make fun of it. In effect, although he is far from uncritical of it, he takes magic very seriously.

The following quotation, which serves to link magic with ethics and religion, makes plain the respect in which Wittgenstein (in Monk 1990: 277) held such thought:

> My whole tendency and I believe the tendency of all men who ever tried to write or talk on Ethics or Religion was to run against the boundaries of language. This running against the walls of our cage is perfectly, absolutely hopeless. Ethics so far as it springs from the desire to say something about the meaning of life, the absolute good, the absolute valuable, can be no science. What it says does not add to our knowledge in any sense. But it is a document of a tendency in the human mind which I personally cannot help respecting deeply and I would not for my life ridicule it.

Merleau-Ponty too takes magical thought seriously (1968: 24):

> It was ... evident to the man brought up in the objective cognition of the West that magic or myth has no intrinsic truth, that magical effects and the mythical and ritual life are to be explained by "objective" causes and what is left over ascribed to the illusions of Subjectivity ... [T]he ethnologist in the face of societies called archaic cannot presuppose that, for example, those societies have a lived experience of time like ours [i.e., the experience of time as simply linear] ... and [he] must describe a mythical time where certain events "in the beginning" maintain a continued efficacity ... To be sure, we have repressed the magical into the subjectivity, but there is no guarantee that the relationship between men does not inevitably involve magical and oneiric components.

In point of fact, Merleau-Ponty is quite certain that "the relationship between men" does inevitably involve such components (1962: 365):

> It will perhaps be maintained that a philosophy cannot be centred round a contradiction, and that all our descriptions, since they ultimately defy thought, are quite meaningless. The objection would be valid if we were content to lay bare, under the term phenomenon or phenomenal field, a layer of prelogical or magical experiences. For in that case we should have to choose between believing the descriptions and abandoning thought, or knowing what we are talking about and abandoning our descriptions. These descriptions must become an opportunity for defining a variety of comprehension and reflection altogether more radical than objective thought ... We must return to the *cogito*, in search of a more fundamental *Logos* than that of objective thought, one which endows the latter with its relative validity, and at the same time assigns to it its place.

The philosophy "centred round a contradiction" is of course his own, keyed as it is to the body-subject or subject-object regarded not as a relationship between two autonomous principles but as opposing principles, each of which integrally defines the other—that is, as a fundamental ambiguity. The distinction between 'thought' and 'description', in which the latter concept denotes what ultimately 'defies' the former, seems identical in essence to Wittgenstein's between what can be said (i.e., thought) and what can only be shown (because when we try to say it, we cannot really know "what we are talking about"). And like Wittgenstein, Merleau-Ponty rejects the dualism, choosing instead to privilege the descriptional pole as more fundamental, not because it replaces logical thought, but because it founds it (endows it "with its relative validity" and "assigns to it its place"). In this connection, recall that for Wittgenstein, ultimately practice can be described but not explained, and far from refuting thought, it serves as its scaffolding. Practice is the "substratum of all my enquiring and asserting," says Wittgenstein (1972: § 162). "The difficulty is to realize the groundlessness" of this substratum (ibid.: § 166). Or as Merleau-Ponty puts it (1962: 365), once we discover this paradoxical layer of bodily or pre-logical reflection, "we shall understand that beyond [it] there is nothing to understand."

This groundless ground, which is altogether more radical than objective thought and beyond which there is nothing to understand, forms of course the land of the synthetic a priori, and both scholars, as we have just seen, use the word 'magic' to describe it. When they do, as is also plain from the quotations, they have in mind a kind of thinking that is usually associated with so-called primitive peoples. In anthropological literature, perhaps the key diagnostic of such thought has been apparent indifference to logical contradiction. It is especially in view of the logical law of non-contradiction that Wittgenstein and Merleau-Ponty find the word 'magic' appropriate to the sort of ground to which they are laboring to (re)turn the mind's eye. As this ground is also groundless, a foundation that is not a foundation, it basically flouts the law of non-contradiction and cannot be logically determined. Merleau-Ponty, again evoking the anthropological concern with thought that runs contrary to logical logic, speaks of this ground—on which objective reflection is said by him to rest—as "brute" or "wild" being (1968: 110).[10]

Wild being and the synthetic a priori implicate nondualism, and nondualism—since it can be shown but not said, that is, since it ultimately defies thought—is magical. Using an example from Wittgenstein, perhaps I can point more transparently to what these two thinkers are driving at when they speak of magic. With his inimitable genius for lighting up an issue at a stroke, Wittgenstein (1972: § 621) poses the following question: "[W]hat is left over if I subtract the fact that my arm goes up from the fact that I raise my arm?" In effect, he is posing the body-mind problem in an effort to clear up misleading expressions concerning willful or voluntary movement. To take an example of my own, if I were to ask a student to please close the classroom door (as I have done on occasion to make the present point), and she obliged, there would appear to be no mystery about what happened: the student took the meaning of my request, and, imparting physical energy to the door, closed it. But when I ask myself to raise my arm, and my arm goes up, a mystery immediately emerges. It seems that we know what caused the door to close; but what 'caused' my arm to go up? With this mystery, we can see that even the interpretation of the act of closing the classroom door is woefully inadequate. We so take for granted the possibility of intelligible communication between one another that we are inclined to see the student's behavior simply in terms of the physical energy she delivers to the door. But when the request is given internally—by oneself to oneself—the translation of request into physical movement poses an enigma for explanatory purposes. My request to her moved the student to move the door. To pose the question that escapes notice, though, how did the student move herself?

Ordinarily, we disregard the fact that the physical movement originated in something that we imagine to be irreducible to the physical, "to be without any mass" (Wittgenstein 1972: § 618)—call it, if you like, will or volition. Still, it is absolutely crucial to avoid the subject-object dualism that communicating with oneself, inside the cavity of one's own head, makes so inviting here, and to realize that what is mysterious is not volition in itself. For volition never really does appear *in itself*, that is, it never appears save as a component of physical action. What is ultimately mysterious and unfathomable is the action itself, which is as physical as can be but has as its defining end something pro-posed rather than given in the 'nature' of the case. The willing of the action *is* the action ("I raise my arm"), and yet its purposefulness contrasts with the fact of the action ("my arm goes up"). Logic proper has zero tolerance for such fundamental ambiguity. As a result, the action is ultimately inexplicable, in the critical sense that it cannot be clarified by reason as such. In Western thought, clarity is typically determined by the canonical laws of rationality, and each of these is predicated on the eschewal of ambiguity and contradiction in favor of mutual exclusion or absolute boundaries between one thing and another (cf. Evens 1983).

In the ethnographical literature, the condition of fundamental ambiguity has clas-sically been construed as a mistaken picture of the world, wherein ideal relations are taken for real ones, and it is this picture that was held by anthropologists to reveal magical thought (e.g., Evans-Pritchard 1956: 141–42). By striking contrast to classical anthropologists, who were inclined to see such thought simply as wrong, and for that matter to most modern anthropologists, who have tended to see it as merely sym-bolic, both Merleau-Ponty and Wittgenstein are suggesting that this magical picture of the world, although nonsensical for logical reasons and purposes, is not only pro-foundly meaningful but also in some existential sense penetrating, and that accordingly it deserves the greatest respect. The answer, then, to Wittgenstein's cutting question is that because it is enchanted, we cannot really say what is left over when we subtract the one form of arm-raising from the other, but we can (and do) show it. Here, in trying to say it with the imagery of a transcendental opening in the fullness of biological life, Merleau-Ponty deftly points to the remainder in question (1962: 189):

> The use a man is to make of his body is transcendent in relation to that body as a mere bio-logical entity. It is not more natural, and no less conventional, to shout in anger or to kiss in love than to call a table 'a table'. Feelings and passional conduct are invented like words. Even those which, like paternity, seem to be part and parcel of the human make-up are in reality institutions [here Merleau-Ponty footnotes Malinowski on the Trobrianders]. It is impos-sible to superimpose on man a lower layer of behaviour which one chooses to call 'natural', followed by a manufactured cultural or spiritual world. Everything is both manufactured and natural in man, as it were, in the sense that there is not a word, not a form of behaviour, which does not owe something to purely biological being—and which at the same time does not elude the simplicity of animal life, and cause forms of vital behaviour to deviate from their pre-ordained direction, through a sort of *leakage* and through a genius for ambiguity which might serve to define man.

Chapter 2

Blind Faith and the Binding of Isaac—the Akedah

[F]aith is a privative concept: it is destroyed as faith if it does not continually display its contradistinction to, or conformity with, knowledge ... The paradoxical nature of faith ultimately degenerates into a swindle, and becomes the myth of the twentieth century; and its irrationality turns it into an instrument of rational administration by the wholly enlightened as they steer society toward barbarism.

— Max Horkheimer and Theodor W. Adorno, *Dialectic of the Enlightenment*

Then Abram bound the youth with belts and straps ... / And stretched forth the knife to slay his son. / When lo! An Angel called him out of heaven, / Saying, Lay not thy hand upon the lad, / Neither do anything to him, thy son. / Behold! Caught in a thicket by its horns, / A Ram. Offer the Ram of Pride instead. / But the Old Man would not so, but slew his son. / And half the seed of Europe, one by one.

— Wilfred Owen, "The Parable of the Old Man and the Young"

All at once he feels weary of ganefs and prophets, guns and sacrifices and the infinite gangster weight of God. He's tired of hearing about the promised land and the inevitable bloodshed required for its redemption. "I don't care what is written. I don't care what supposedly got promised to some sandal-wearing idiot whose claim to fame is that he was ready to cut his own son's throat for the sake of a hare-brained idea. I don't care about red heifers and patriarchs and locusts. A bunch of old bones in the sand. My homeland is in my hat."

— Michael Chabon, *The Yiddish Policemen's Union*

In this chapter I examine certain a priori or primordial features of Western thought, in effect, aspects of the reality that this thought takes for granted. I do so by scrutinizing closely a story at the center of the Judeo-Christian tradition. This story, the Akedah or binding of Isaac (chapter 22 of the book of Genesis), has the theme of sacrifice. I intend to show that while it is instructive and positive in vital respects, this story bears at heart a terrible and consequential malevolence, what I have come to think of as a profound stupidity. Despite all the various thinkers, Jewish, Christian, and Muslim alike, who have managed, often with subtle and exceptional intelligence, to save for the good the figures of both Abraham and God in the story, the divine command to kill Isaac and Abraham's obedient response strike me as unacceptable, even by other-worldly standards.

In the case of a narrative like the Akedah, Gerhard von Rad asserts that "one must from the first renounce any attempt to discover one basic idea as *the* meaning of the whole. There are many levels of meaning, and whoever thinks he has discovered virgin soil must discover at once that there are many more layers below that" (1972a: 243). My interpretation directs itself to this multi-layered character, holding that there is no "one basic idea as *the* meaning of the whole" and accentuating the ambiguous nature of the story.

I read the story as an admonitory attempt to deal with the problem of how one can truly sacrifice oneself without at the same time defeating the existential purpose of the act of sacrifice, namely, to ensure life. The story's solution of a perfect gift (the gift of death), on which a lesson in faith is thought to hang, is the most pronounced but not, I think, the only solution that the story has to offer. This solution entails by logical contrast the idea of a perfectly imperfect gift, which is to say, a purely economical act or counter-sacrifice, where the other alone is 'given'. But both perfect and perfectly imperfect sacrifice, as the two principles of a dualism, lead, at least logically, to the same end—death. For this reason, following the tribulation of Abraham and Isaac, the story's final ('humanistic') substitution of beast for man presents another less harrowing and dramatic solution, an economy of sacrifice, but one that is itself economized or attenuated: the self is given, surrogatively and only in part to be sure, but nonetheless truly, thus ensuring the continuity of humankind.

There can be no doubt that continuity of life is an emphatic burden of the story.[1] But beyond the substitution of beast for man, the story implies an even more ingenious and saving solution to this problem, a substitution of spirit for matter—i.e., bloodless sacrifice. Here, I maintain, is the crux of the solution of perfect sacrifice, the demand apparently imposed on Abraham of total obedience or blind faith. The progressive shift away from bloody to spiritual sacrifice disposes a redefinition of 'faith' from a social and behavioral phenomenon to an interior idea. But by the same token, here too the story's approach to the problem seems to come to grief, since the willing total abdication of one's will to the other has, paradoxically, the dialectical force of self-aggrandizement. As is developed transparently in the sacrifice story of Jesus, a perfect gift implies the capacity of perfect election and therewith of perfect (i.e., godly) selfhood. The god-given command to man for a perfect gift actually sets him up for a fall, into the dire imperfection of self-aggrandizement. This imperfection is 'dire' because it disregards the vital significance of man's finitude, to wit, the significance of continuing or *imperfect* sacrifice as the very dynamic that is human existence. In which case, should we not question the figure of God in this story, as well as Abraham's utterly compliant response to this figure's lethal command? Accordingly, I argue that this story's figure of God has been (unduly) informed with an all too human desideratum of perfection, and that, in light of this chiastic reversal, whereby the flow of identity from God to man backs up, Abraham's blind compliance with God's terrible command amounts to an act of self-aggrandizement; it is an unwitting pretence by virtue of which Abraham appears to others and to himself as a reverential servant of God while his conduct describes nothing less contrary than godlike presumption. Thus, we may describe Abraham's murderous behavior toward his son as a kind of idolatry, perhaps the worst kind, whereby he is worshipping himself—that is, his *self*.

The story affords a deep mythic insight on the basis of which human existence may be construed as a sacrificial dynamic, a special point I develop in the next chapter (using Derrida's brilliant commentary on Kierkegaard's profound reading of the Akedah). Thus, the 'choice' in every primordial choice becomes an ethico-existential question of what is owing to the self and what to the other.

Blind Faith or Sacrificial Economy?

Perhaps the most famous intellectual interpretation of the Akedah is Søren Kierkegaard's *Fear and Trembling* (1985). In it, the great Danish thinker directs himself to the deep religious sense behind both God's murderous command and Abraham's devout conformance. By ordering Abraham to sacrifice his beloved son Isaac, God means to test Abraham's faith, and Abraham, suspending all the creaturely laws by which men ordinarily set store, aces the test, proving himself to be a veritable knight of faith. No matter how unspeakable the content and unintelligible the purpose of God's immediate command, it must be just and therefore cannot but obligate the one to whom it is addressed.

In light of Kierkegaard's profound interpretation, together with the comparison to the Akedah implied in the name for the Nazis' colossal murder, the Holocaust (whole burnt offering, in the Greek), J.-F. Lyotard asks (1988: 107), rhetorically but with stunning provocation, what, then, is the difference between the command to Abraham to destroy his son and the order to the Nazis to exterminate the Jews? That is, is there a difference that makes a difference between the divine command through which the Jews began their life as a people and Hitler's order to extinguish those same people forever? Both constitute prescriptions for unthinkable violence. And, by their very nature as matters of faith rather than reason or even ethics, neither means to leave room for refusal of any kind: if one is to count as a member of the faithful, one is obliged simply to comply, in fear and trembling, and in the darkness of basic rational and ethical impenetrability. Of course, in the case of Hitler, it is tempting simply to dismiss the leap-of-faith argument on the grounds that he was a raving lunatic. But how do we know that Abraham (whether a historical figure or simply a theological construct), likewise, was not a certifiable paranoid schizophrenic or, say, a sociopath?

Lyotard does find significant differences between the two cases. For present purposes, the key difference bears on the relationship (which for me, as will be seen, is a question of identity) between the slayer and the victim. Lyotard (1988: 109) asks, "[D]id the SS love the Jew as a father does his son? If not, how could the crime have value of a sacrifice in the eyes of its victim? And in those of its executioner? And in those of its beneficiary?" Lyotard is at pains here to show that the tendency to construe 'Auschwitz death' as 'beautiful death', along the lines of the story of Isaac, in which death has been associated with a knightly intrepidity and made to signify life and resurrection, is a regrettable misapprehension. As Lawrence Langer (1991, 1995) has made plain, this tendency toward palliation is deeply rooted in the Western imagination and betrays a psychological disposition to avoid coming to grips with the utterly nihilistic reality of the Holocaust.

Of course, the differences between the story of the Akedah and what took place in the Nazi death camps are profound. But they can be allowed to prescind the possibility of any continuities whatsoever only at cost of our self-understanding. The trouble with Lyotard's position is that his use of the differences to show that one of the two cases does not qualify under the Kierkegaardian religious picture leaves the leap-of-faith argument intact. In so doing, Lyotard continues to endorse the possible soundness of acts of unintelligible orderings and blind followings and therefore, notwithstanding his disqualification of the case of the Nazis, manages to make room for Hitlers yet to come.[2]

From the ethical perspective I take here, the argument leading to a leap of faith ought not to be trusted, at least not in respect of the biblical paradigm concerning what transpired in the land of Moriah. Kierkegaard was right to reject as decisive the Enlightenment promise of objective thought and Hegel's rationalistic universalism, whether in philosophy or religion. But he was wrong to think that the only alternative is to take a dauntless leap into immaculate subjectivism and blind faith. To be sure, we always find ourselves beholden to something we take for granted, on 'faith'; to adapt to my purposes Lyotard's Freudian idiom of repression, there is something always already forgotten (1990: 26–28). This finding, pertaining to an existential sense of faith other than Kierkegaard's, alerts us to the way in which our selves are fundamentally uncertain and limited, the sense in which they are abidingly other to themselves. But while our considered thoughts ever rest on other thoughts, unconsidered and in this sense built on faith, and may well inspire having faith and even a faith, this scarcely constitutes an argument for leaping into it—not in the unthinking way in which Abraham leapt to extinguish the life of his own child. At the end of the day, every faith-bound foundation amounts to a particular certainty, an a priori that is synthetic, which fact constitutes a pretty good argument not to leap but instead to step gingerly, with all the circumspection one can muster. Every particular certainty is necessarily a conditional certainty, and therefore ultimately an uncertain one subject to critical deconstruction.

As becomes clear in the course of the analysis to follow, my argument is not an attack on faith when this term is used in connection with openness to what is new, different, and other. Rather, I mean to question the common doctrinal conception of faith, as when the term is used, dualistically, in absolute contrast to 'reason'. This is the case when we speak, for example, of a 'faith-based' initiative and of the determinable religions as faiths. It is also the case when Kierkegaard interprets the Akedah, regardless of his express emphasis on act as opposed to belief and on the ineffable otherness of the figure of God. It is the dualistic opposition of faith to reason that makes possible a faith so complete as to be 'blind', a faith the perfection of which constitutes the measure of the damage it can do no less than of the devotion it demands.[3] But this notion of faith goes well beyond the existential sense set out in the preceding paragraph. Indeed, considered in terms of our constituting limitedness, simply as a condition of human existence, faith defines self-hood as ever open and uncertain. It thus betokens a patently creative state of being, and so gives reason to welcome the otherness of difference and what is yet to come.

But blind faith seems scarcely welcoming in this way; on the contrary, it privileges closure. By juxtaposing Abraham's choice to rational decision-making, Kierkegaard, eminently an existential thinker, manages to paint the choice as exquisitely free. But in so doing he covers over the truth of a choice taken in response to a command that is no less determinable than it is utterly inexplicable, and he averts the gaze away from the telling fact that Abraham's zealous choice has served for centuries, in three different monotheisms, as the very model of dogmatic faith. With all due respect to Kierkegaard's genius, it seems to me that while Abraham's choice must count as horribly trying, it was not truly authentic: it did not exactly issue from 'inside' himself and 'outside' any rule. Rather, whether or not through a deep and ulterior motive of his own, his choice was in critical part born of a veritable rule of rules, an instituting power that could not be more sovereign and the patriarchal closure of which is as exemplary as can be.

Even if Kierkegaard's religious lesson betokens a sound interpretation of the biblical story, I must refuse the lesson as it stands. There is, though, a way to read the point of the story without having to take on faith this lesson about faith. This reading holds that, broadly in line with Shalom Spiegel's (1993) finding concerning an epochal shift from human to animal sacrifice, the story is most pointedly about the linkage between sacrifice and surrogation. In other words, it is basically concerned to bring into relief prescriptively the vital human significance of sacrificial economy. If this reading is sound, then the sacrificial 'imperfection' of surrogation is, rather than a basic design flaw, the very thing that makes sacrifice effective and good.

Identity and Substitution

Beast for Man

In view of the divine promise of Abraham's continuity as embodied in his son, the identity between Abraham and Isaac is even fuller than that between Abraham and himself. In other words, given the story's central emphasis on Abraham's mortal immortality in the generations to issue from his son, the meaning of identity in the story is defined by a relationship before it is defined by reference to either the one or the other of the two individual parties to that relationship. In effect, identity or selfhood in this story is defined primarily by difference or multiplicity rather than sameness or unicity—the logical scandal on which postmodern thought might be said to turn.[4] In this light, from the standpoint of Abraham's worldly existence (in the main, the only kind of human existence Judaism has to offer), if God had allowed Abraham to proceed as originally instructed, then the act would surely have been in vain. Only in a religion that projects resurrection or 'human' life after death could such a sacrifice have proved life-giving. Indeed, the Akedah or the binding of Isaac is the biblical act of which the sacrifice and resurrection of Jesus are surely meant to count as a recursive perfecting.[5]

But in the case of the Akedah, by providing a beast in the place of Isaac, God at once makes the act of sacrifice as humanly vital as it is destructive and issues the warrant for surrogation. In doing so, God designedly identifies Isaac with the surrogate victim. On the one hand, because the victim is in fact a proxy, and thus truly victimized, there is reason for further sacrifice: guilt and indebtedness remain. On the other hand, the sacrifice works *as* sacrifice precisely because the victim is authoritatively identifiable with Isaac, and therefore with Abraham. In overall effect, the victimizing substitution of other for self is thematically incomplete. As a result, although murder takes place, abnegation remains the name of the rite. The story seems basically about how, in spite of the surrogation, the self is truly given.

Obviously, though, this sacrifice remains imperfect in that in the end what is given is not the self in the form of the son, but the son in the form of a beast. As a result, while it ensures the continuity of Abraham's seed and human life, it fails to put an end to guilt and the need for further sacrifice. By making the Son of God the Son of Man, and thus the Lamb of God, the sacrifice on Mount Golgotha seeks to redress this very imperfection.

The Son for the Father

There is yet another apparent imperfection in the logic of this paradigmatic scene of sacrifice from the Hebrew Bible, an imperfection that is, I think, no less deep and even more troubling—that in order to warrant the end of human sacrifice, God finds it necessary to command Abraham to take the life of another human being, his very own son no less, and that Abraham, although doubtless infinitely vexed by the contemplation of this horrible deed, sets out with unwavering determination to execute it. I speak here of imperfection because it is as hard to imagine any father *in his right mind* paying heed to such a filially violable order[6] as it is to imagine a god, who is defined in terms of perfection, having recourse to it. Put another way, in ordering Abraham to sacrifice Isaac, God is demanding from Abraham—who, as the creature rather than the creator, is definitively imperfect—the gift of perfection.[7] One might wish to take care here with the idea of perfection, and say that, in light of Isaac's part as the figure of Abraham's immortality, he is only the best Abraham has to give. But as such, from Abraham's perspective, a perspective that God's commandment to Abraham implicitly assumes, the gift of Isaac's death is indeed absolute, and in this sense the gift of perfection.

One evident explanation for this disturbing imperfection is that the warrant for surrogation presupposes the identification of Isaac as victim. This identification constitutes an indispensable condition for the establishment of sacrificial identity between the boy and the ram, such that the latter can take Isaac's place on the altar. And this identification cannot be made save for God's order to Abraham to kill his precious son and Abraham's active willingness to carry out the order, thus consecrating the boy. Indeed, in view of what Isaac undergoes in the story—bound stepwise to the altar, only to have his father's raised arm, knife blade in hand, stayed by the Lord at the moment of truth—it is no exaggeration to say that in a terribly meaningful sense the boy's life is taken and given at the same time.

This interpretation is generally consistent with Shalom Spiegel's classic Judaica study, in which the principal purpose of the Akedah narrative is seen as in all likelihood the establishment and justification of a great change in the character of ritual sacrifice, from a 'pagan' norm, according to which the victim is human, to a humanistic norm, in which a beast is substituted for a human (Spiegel 1993: 64). If this interpretation is correct, one might reasonably conclude (with Rad 1972a: 239; and Rabbi Leiner of Izbica, in Gellman 1994: 24ff.) that although Abraham and Isaac were made to suffer a terrible ordeal, God's order was a necessary deception (or, in Rabbi Leiner's usage, an "appearance"), and he never intended to allow Abraham to follow it to its final end. Of course, while this interpretation can thus clarify God's doings in the story, it leaves the motivation of Abraham's seemingly unconscionable conduct still to be comprehended.

Knightly Faith or Unholy Desire?

Like all stories, the Akedah has at least two sides, each of which serves the other as a deconstructive mirror-image, that is, one that reflects so acutely as to occasion critical self-reflection, the sort of prying reflection that opens oneself to question. In the present case, what is an imperfection from the creational side of the story—namely, surrogate or incomplete sacrifice—proves a perfectly vital force from the creatural side. The lesson seems to be something to the effect that humanity as such depends for its livelihood on a constitutive incapacity to complete itself or do things in the absolute, and that insofar as humanity seeks to transcend altogether this condition of conditionality, as is its wont, it courts destruction. A familiar story. Indeed, this tale of an infanticidal father whose devoutly murderous conduct is transmuted into the life of the generations by a salvific act of God may be seen to recall the life-disseminating properties of a great tree whose fruit remains immortalizing only so long as it stays beyond the reach of mortals. The fruit, of course, is the originary power over life and death, the fruit of the Edenic tree of life, and, as the story goes, at the end of the day it simply is not ours for the taking.

This reading follows from construing the highlight of the Akedah to be the substitution of an animal for a human in sacrifice. It is this substitution that realizes the story's theme as a turning movement from death to life. In light of reading the story from its endpoint of surrogation, the story's principal burden of instruction is to make the substitution of beast for human, and thus life for death, sensible in terms of the logic of sacrifice. The story performs this task by establishing vicarious identity between Isaac and the ram of God. The command by God to offer up Isaac, and Abraham's dutiful conduct in doing so, may be explained, then, simply as functions of the story's narrative task: the establishment of identity between Isaac and the sacrificial ram depends on the establishment of Isaac's identity as victim.

However, while God's command and Abraham's response may be readily understood in this way, when these two figures are seen as subjectivities or persons rather than simply as agents of the narrative, their actions inevitably raise questions of motivation. These are the questions that Kierkegaard addressed. And if I am right about the story's principal purpose as a demonstration of the vital significance of surrogation in sacrifice, these questions of subjectivity must have vexed the story's redactors too.

In point of fact, as one might expect if the story's main thrust lies elsewhere, the narrative provides precious little to go on in answering these questions. When God issues his command, he provides no reason for it, and Abraham appears to be as much in the dark about his own conduct as he is about the order from above. Indeed, Abraham's response to the command is so immediate that it seems very much like one's response to an 'order' issued practically by oneself to oneself: While carving the Thanksgiving turkey, I 'tell' myself to raise my arm, knife in hand, and my arm goes up. Although we take for granted self-movement of this kind, in fact it exhibits all the mystery surrounding the connection between mind and body, or, more appropriately in the present context, between spirit and matter. For in truth, as I argued (on Wittgenstein's philosophical authority) in chapter 1, the connection is neither exactly immediate nor mediate.

The sort of response Abraham gives to God's order, not instinctual but nonetheless more bodily than mindful, is what one might expect of a time and place in which the existence of God (or of gods) is not quite yet a matter of belief but constitutes the implicit certainty on the basis of which any belief whatsoever takes flight. In other words, insofar as 'faith' implies 'belief' in the sense of facultative acceptance (as it plainly does in Kierkegaard's Pauline usage), Abraham's behavior seems to be both more and less than a matter of faith. Put another way, his behavior may be thought of in terms of a sense of faith other than the one in question here, a pre-predicative and fundamentally social sense. Indeed, his movement is so automatic it might almost be described as motivationless.[8]

Nevertheless, the story does not want for certain contents that betray a subjectivist perspective. The stunning horror of what Abraham is asked to do could not but introduce the wrench of self-consciousness into the automated works of the divine structure of command. Doubtless, like Kierkegaard, the story's redactors, in their capacity as readers, felt the need to arrive at some understanding of what God and Abraham could have been thinking. Hence, when Isaac, a pious son but no fool, seeing the sacrificial appurtenances asks his father as to the whereabouts of "the lamb for a burnt offering," Abraham answers "God will provide." This answer is truthful, prophetically so. And yet it is also exquisitely ironic, concealing the awful truth from Isaac. From this one may infer that Abraham was hardly acting in all innocence, but was only too conscious of the horrifying nature of what he was about to do. (Harking back to Lyotard's jarring comparison between God and Hitler, Abraham's answer could be seen to find a parallel in the well-documented attempt of the Nazis to conceal [e.g., Lang 1990: 41ff.], from both the victims and the world at large, what they were doing in the death camps.)[9] Much the same may be said of Abraham's words to his two young helpers, when he instructs them to wait while he and Isaac go off to "worship." Notwithstanding its plain truth, the statement does more to conceal than reveal what is about to happen. And when he appends to this instruction (my emphasis) "*we* will come back to you," he is telling the servants (what had to appear to him) an outright lie, but which in fact proves to be yet another prophetic truth. Finally, in connection to the question of Abraham's and God's intentionality, the words of "the angel of the Lord" seem to leave no room for doubt. The angel informs Abraham (twice, no less) that he has been let off the hook because he did not withhold his son, "thine only son, from Me." These remarks certainly give truth to the interpretation that in this story God is out to try Abraham's faith, and Abraham means to prove that his faith is more than equal to the trial.

Still, there is something off-center about this strand of the story. The theme that what is on trial is Abraham's faith is somehow not quite in keeping with the more immediate theme of the story—that of the trial of Isaac's life. From the perspective of human law, as Kierkegaard stressed, Abraham's conduct must be judged repugnant. But, strikingly, Abraham's great and blind faith may be seen to constitute a threat even from the perspective of his maker. Given the nature of God's final intervention, it is logically implicit in the story's upshot that in a substantial sense Abraham's behavior was dreadfully wrong. The sort of gift Abraham set out to give is simply not for humankind to offer. The gift of perfection or death, as is the theme of Golgotha, is God's prerogative, not man's. Hence, at the end of this story, God has to step in to make things right. All this follows from taking the story principally as, rather than a rationalization of blind faith, a warrant to economize when sacrificing.

A Perfect Sacrifice

Because it is our habit to think of substantive identity in terms of singular individuals, it has been usual to see Abraham's action as simply homicidal, the attempted murder of an-other, albeit his own son. But if I am right about the way in which identity is defined in the story, as a matter of the *relationship* between Abraham and his son before it is a matter of the (non-)relationship between Abraham and himself ("non-relationship" only because we mistakenly tend to conceive of the self in entitative rather than relational terms), then Abraham's act should be understood in terms of self-sacrifice. In which case, we are talking about a selfless act of attempted suicide.

As a rule, selflessness is a good thing. But, and this is the point that I want to develop here, the act seems so perfectly selfless that it registers as the ultimate suicide. In binding Isaac to the altar, Abraham sets out to do himself in, but so completely as to prescind even the possibility of living on in the supreme manner in which, according to the biblical imagination, it is given to humankind to do so: through the generations that issue from Abraham's seed. Moreover, in light of the fact that these are the generations of God's promise, a promise of great and mighty nationhood (Genesis: chaps. 17 and 21), it might be said that Abraham intends to give himself a death so round as to be matchlessly complete. To attempt such global perfection is to presume the exercise of total control in matters of life and death, and thereby to arrogate to oneself godlike powers. If we choose to say (with Wittgenstein 1971: 35) that "nothing is so dead as death," then Abraham appears to be casting himself as the very substance and pure figure of death. In light of this picture, in acting as he did, Abraham exhibited not knightly faith but unholy desire.

One might be tempted to conclude, therefore, as against all received wisdom, that insofar as the command from God was a test, Abraham failed it alarmingly. As a god-fearing person, that is, one respectful of the infinite difference between humans and the Other, Abraham should have refused to comply with the command to offer his son as a holocaust, a perfect gift.[10] Of course, the fact that at the story's end the angel of the Lord states plainly that Abraham is to be rewarded for his compliant behavior seems to rule out any such interpretation. But perhaps the words of the angel, which so credit God's command as gospel, themselves reflect a redactional loss of perspective or the failure to represent truly what is otherwise than representable.

Whether or not one thinks that the stories of Genesis are somehow god-given, there can be no reasonable doubt that they have been propagated by human hands, and that, in any event, they naturally and inextricably include a human point of view. As a result, in some substantial sense, the creational as well as the creatural principals in these scriptural tales cannot but present an earth-bound perspective, a view from somewhere rather than nowhere. I suggest that in the Akedah, God-Elohim, that high and mighty patriarchal figure, in ordering Abraham to make of his beloved and only son (by Sarah) a perfect gift, displays a disposition that is only too human. I have in mind the disposition to make everything come out even, which is to say, to bring everything to a final end or to seek perfection. I do not necessarily mean to imply that representing God in terms of perfection makes of him a human figure (although it may, notwithstanding Descartes'

proof of the existence of God—that if inherently imperfect beings can conceive of perfection, then God must exist). I mean instead that inasmuch as God's movements are
pictured as having perfection as a desideratum, as if this quality had gone missing and
needs to be restored, the figure of God has been assimilated to a human sensibility and
aspiration. It was Rousseau (1992: 25–26) who spoke of self-perfectibility as the human
faculty that "develops all the others," and who, doubtless taking his cue from a biblical
theme, was inclined to see it as "the source of all man's misfortunes."

This interpretation suggests that in this story the figure of God, as profoundly
informed by otherness as it may be, might also share in the identity of Abraham. I have
already shown that as Isaac is identifiable with the ram of God, so Abraham is identifiable
with Isaac. As a matter of fact, the basis on which these identities are fixed leads one to see
that the same sort of identity-in-difference obtains between God and Abraham.

Anthropomorphism: From Abraham's Psyche to God's Mouth

The defining identity between Abraham and Isaac is both the same as and different
from the identity between Isaac and the ram. Isaac, after all, is tied to Abraham by
virtue of biological continuity, making the identity between them the only sort that,
at least for certain purposes, moderns are likely to take as seriously as that between
an individual and him- or herself. But it is crucial to recall that even in this biological
aspect, the identity between Abraham and his son is given by God in a miraculous
manner. When Sarah is 90 and Abraham 100 years old, God promises Abraham that
"Sarah your wife shall bear you a son, and you shall call his name Isaac" (Genesis: chap.
17). In effect, then, in the case not only of the ram but also of Isaac, it was indeed the
Lord who provided, consecrating identity between, on the one hand, Isaac and the ram
and, on the other, Abraham and Isaac, and therewith among the three of them.

By the same token, Abraham is identified with God. Isaac is the issue of Abraham's
loins, but those geriatric sinews are miraculously invigorated by God's initiative. It may
be seen, then, that in the child of their union—an unequal union, to be sure, of spirit
and matter—Abraham and God are in a sense made one 'flesh'; together they constitute
a marvelous identity in and of fatherhood. The fact of the story is that as a creational
elision between the figures of God and Abraham, Isaac's father is both one and two at
the same time—that is to say (a theme given added and more other-worldly emphasis
in the figure of Jesus), Isaac is both the son of man and the son of God.

None of this is to say that these three dyadic identities—Isaac and the ram, Abraham
and Isaac, and God and Abraham—are not also relationships of critical difference. That
between Isaac and the ram holds the difference of economy in sacrifice, a difference so
vital as to make a virtual world of difference between the cessation and the continuation
of a people called Israel. And that between Abraham and Isaac, as between God and
Abraham, holds the difference of belatedness, according to which one of the two parties
to each pair enjoys over the other the tremendous authority owing to generative others
and claimed by creator-patriarchs.

But these differences do not so much spring from or conceal identities as foster them.
I do not think that this story can be understood unless the god-figure's infinite and originary difference *from* man is placed alongside that figure's substantial identity *with* man,
for its meaning lies precisely in this paradox. The story pictures Abraham as a creaturely

extension of God's person, but, paradoxically, an extension with a mind of his own.[11] Hence, while Abraham responds to God's authoritarian command bodily, just as if he were a hand of God, his response is seen also to constitute an autonomous decision.

The story itself thus authorizes the identity between God and Abraham as flowing directly from God's creative initiative to his creatures. What I want to suggest here, though, is the possibility that identity also flows the other way—it backs up, so to speak, informing the figure of God with the figure of man. This is hardly a bold or novel thesis, in view of the well-known consideration that anthropomorphism is a characteristic feature of the Hebrew bible's depiction of the godhead (e.g., Johnson 1961, 1964). In the story in question, it seems to me that God's command to offer up Isaac registers just such a reflux of identity. By calling in all debts, that command expresses a diagnostically human want of perfection: it prescribes a sacrifice that would put an end to all sacrifice and therewith to life itself. In effect, although it issues from God's mouth, it smacks of an ever-present temptation on the part of humanity to overreach itself.

The interpretation of the Akedah as primarily a trial of Abraham's faith is predicated on the presumptive, utter righteousness of the order to take Isaac's life in sacrifice. If, though, it is correct that logically perfect sacrifice on the part of man must constitute a threat not only to the law of man but also to the primacy of the Other, then the interpretation to faith should not go unquestioned. It would seem that the justice of both God's command to Abraham, a mere mortal, to kill his own son and of God's subsequent approval of Abraham's zealous response is open to serious question from a perspective that is more than humanistic and runs deeper than the patriarchal warrant recorded in the story.[12] If it is to be identified with the creational force registered at the end of the story (by the promise of life), then the figure of God appearing at the beginning would seem to be disturbingly compromised. For whereas the creational force is a vital force, the command to cut Isaac's throat on the altar is so perfectly lethal, so globally destructive, that it is out of keeping with even the undeniable sense in which death may be construed as a chronic condition of life.

Between Perfect and Perfectly Imperfect Sacrifice

Total Economy and the Anti-sacrifice

If, then, the story's apparent lesson about faith is neither as plain nor patent as has been thought, can we dismiss it? I do not think so. For taken together with the lesson about surrogation in sacrifice, it yields an interpretation of the story that serves to enlighten beyond both lessons.

Generations of readers have noted that in this story the terms for the deity alternate between Elohim or God and Yahweh or the Lord, the former appearing five times in the first half of the story, the latter appearing in the second half, also five times (Spiegel 1993: 121–22). Accordingly, the story has been controverted as at least two-sided, one side centering on God's (Elohim's) test and command to bind Isaac (his 'power') and the other on the Lord's (Yahweh's) saving intervention and promise of life (his 'mercy'). Indeed, it has been argued by experts that the story is not simply two-sided but in fact is made up of at least two distinct prime documents (Spiegel 1993: 122ff.). For my purposes, though, what counts is that the two sides appear together as one story, and whether or not they are narratologically reconcilable, their pairing yields a discerning portrait of the human condition.

As I have shown, the highly suspect nature of the command to bind Isaac is brought to light by seeing the command as reflected in the mirror of the Lord's countermand to substitute a beast for the boy. In other words, in contrast to the vital economy provided by surrogate or imperfect sacrifice, perfect sacrifice looks stupidly lethal and therefore cannot emerge as a demand in any sacrificial logic determined by an overarching reproductive imperative. By the same token, when it is seen in the mirror of God's distinctly non-viable call for a holocaust, a pure gift, the economic relief brought by the Lord's provision of a surrogate victim also looms suspect. By insinuating the possibility of a *total* economy, one that is logically no less absolute than a perfect sacrifice, the offering of a proxy undermines the very ideas of gift and sacrifice. The economizing capacity of surrogation projects an image of a no-cost existence, wherein salvation is realized as self-savings—the 'I' banks itself with a miserly and ultimately self-destructive completeness.

In point of fact, every act of substitution in sacrifice is intrinsically open to interpretation as hypocrisy. No doubt there is cause to celebrate the Akedah narrative's evident implication that human sacrifice is a pagan abomination in the eyes of the Lord (Spiegel 1993). But what about the ram, whose innocent life is expended in place of the life that is owing? Instead of reading the story as a warrant to end human sacrifice, it can just as well be seen, from the ram's point of view, as an artful blind to draw attention away from the fact of the matter.[13] And the fact of the matter is that when in sacrifice the life of another is substituted for the life of the self, the self has chosen to deceive—often enough itself and always the other. Indeed, if surrogation is carried to its logical conclusion, then in principle the self remains undiminished while the other alone is eradicated.

Such a turn of events does more than make nonsense of the ideas of surrogation, gift, and sacrifice—it defines their negation. An immaculately economic act of sacrificial slaughter constitutes an anti-sacrifice, and as such is, like its exact antonym (perfect sacrifice), as lethal as can be. Despite its strong impulsion to misrecognize itself as a totality rather than a basic ambiguity, the self is, after all, nothing more than a powerful manifestation of self-other relations. What singularity it enjoys rests precisely with this its fundamental multiplicity, its constitutional dynamism, its becoming-other. In which case, of course, any attempt on the part of the self to obliterate the other, in an effort to complete itself by excluding the otherness on which it depends for its being, must lead to the extinction of itself as well as the other.

A Magical Movement

In effect, then, as reflected in the mirror of each other, both of the story's lessons at point here—blind faith and surrogation—look seriously flawed. But as a result of this narrative chiasm, the story holds out—perhaps beyond the redactors' intentions—yet another lesson, an even more profound and complicated one. I have in mind the lesson that as human beings we are caught irremissibly between the needful self and the obligatory other. What the Akedah shows is that Isaac is in fact doubly bound, to the Other who gave him life as well as to the life of the self thus promised him, and through him to generations of others to come. To take the allegorical meaning, we are damned if we fail to give ourselves on behalf of the other, and we are damned if we do not fail. Which means, of course, that salvation rests in managing to do both—an impossibility or a magic act if ever there was one.

As I have shown, both perfect and perfectly imperfect sacrifice come to precisely the same end: the end of time. This is because the double bind can be put off but not resolved. Human existence may be construed in terms of the process of putting off the dead end described by the double bind. This process amounts to a taking hold of both horns of the dilemma. In so doing, the dead end is postponed, making time. Of course, it is impossible to take both horns at one time—were it possible, the dilemma would not be dilemmatic. But one can manage to move between the horns in such a way as to realize them both for the time (of) being. This amounts to a kind of high-wire act, in which one moves, ever precariously, first this way and then that, between the two ends of the wire. The object of the exercise is to keep the two ends extant, not by reaching them but by reaching for them. Once reached, they spell death. In other words, whereas the ends themselves signify the end of time (a falling off the wire, into the abyss), the back-and-forth movement between them, a paradoxical movement of suspension or untimely time, constitutes time.

The story of Isaac's binding may be read to offer instruction in how to perform this magical movement. Isaac is pictured as bound by or condemned to the wire, suspended over a terrible and unfathomable abyss. He is caught between the altar rock of what is owing to the absolute other, from which the self issues, and the hard place of that self's impelling initiative, that is, the derivative but demanding power of the self to empower itself. Although fundamentally opposing, these two demands define each other. Indeed, they meet representatively in the singular figure of Isaac: on the one hand, he is God's gift, and therefore he is owing to and even (at least implicitly) participant in God; on the other hand, as other to the absolute otherness of God, he makes and is owing to himself, which is to say, to humanity or all the others. In the story, Isaac does not so much mark the spot where these two demands intersect, as if he were separate and distinct from them; rather, he *is* their crossing, a dramatic and personified dynamic of reversal. How is this so?

With Isaac's victimization, the story moves first toward death, in the direction of redeeming Isaac's (and Abraham's) debt to the Other. But with the provision of the surrogate animal, the story reverses course, moving toward the preservation of the self and humanity, and thus paradoxically redefining the original direction—God's directive—as life rather than death. From a logical point of view, the upshot is scandalous: a sacrifice that is not a sacrifice, a *holo*-caust that is not whole in the required sense (in the end, it is not Isaac qua Isaac that is immolated). The paradox is facilitated by two critical conditions. One is Isaac's ordeal, which, because Abraham acts in earnest, is palpable and far more than symbolic. By trying Isaac's life, this condition consecrates his identity as victim and therewith establishes identity between him and the ram of God. The other condition is of course the intervention by God, which provides and licenses the ram in substitution. As a result of these two conditions, in Isaac death is transfigured into life.

But like all tricks, even the most ingenious, this one is subject to exposure. And once exposed, its magical effect goes up in smoke. By projecting it in the sober illumination of its logical conclusion rather than in the bedazzling light of a divine stay, the act of surrogation too is betrayed as having death as an end. The slaying of the ram is the murder of an-other and therefore cannot foreclose the possible murder of all the others in the economizing interest of the self's saving of itself. Thus, the transfiguration of death into life, Isaac's resurrection, is exposed for what it is—a kind of trick. But it is the trick of a lifetime. It constitutes a vital rather than perfect economy. It negotiates the double bind, such that life can go on. It is an immensely creative enterprise.

A Magical Time or the Time of the Other

From an existential rather than logical point of view, the paradox at issue marks time— it marks the time it takes to convert a death sentence into a life sentence, a putting-off time, the time of one's (and one nation's) life. In the story, such time is registered as threefold. First of all, there is the time it takes to carry out the sacrifice. This time is pictured as an actual journey into a foreign land and then up one of its heights, both called Moriah, and then back again to the place known as Beersheba. The journey also describes a progression of sacrificial stages, moving from the call to sacrifice, to the consecration of the victim (Isaac being made to bear, like Abraham's beast of burden, the wood for the burnt offering), to the altar and immolation. Second, there is the time mentioned at the end of the story, a promised time pertaining to the proliferation and greatness of Abraham's posterity. Finally, there is the time marked in the powerful moment of truth, when Abraham takes the knife to his child, only to have his hand stayed instantaneously by the angel of the Lord. This kind of time, in which what happens happens all at once, is the time of creation—in effect, it is the no-time of eternity in which something is made from nothing, life from death.

All three kinds of time mark the time of the Other. Hence, the sacrificial journey goes up to and down from the place thenceforth called Adonai Yireh, or the mount on which the Lord sees (and is 'seen'). The time of Abraham's posterity signifies the time of futurity. Although God's promise appears to reduce this time to the certainty of the self and the present, the essential uncertainty and otherness of this time are given in the fact that the promise is decidedly the prerogative of the absolute other. Finally, the time of instantaneity is the time of creation, of the emergence of the singular and novel, of 'effects' irreducible to causes. This is the time marked by the point of crossing, that is, Isaac, in whose figure is projected the life-time of a people.

For purposes of the story, the most telling time is the third kind, the instantaneous time of creation. It is this kind of time to which the magic of the trick is keyed. Taken in its everyday sense, creation time is described by decision or choice. As it *is* the medium of determination, by definition a true choice cannot be told beforehand. A true choice is a quintessentially creative act. Even if in hindsight conditions for it can be isolated and identified, in critical part it constitutes its own condition and remains therefore, in a crucial sense, unconditioned. It makes difference.

The Choice to Choose: Spirit for Matter

The story of the Akedah plainly turns on a pair of choices. God issues to Abraham two commands: respectively, to kill and then not to kill Isaac. In regard to each, Abraham decides to obey rather than disobey. But the choice confronting Abraham exceeds, by a quantum leap, the question of compliance. Given its dire content, its instruction to cut off Abraham's line and thus (from the story's chauvinist perspective) the future of humankind, the first command obliges Abraham to make a choice between what is owing to God and what is owing to himself. Owing to God is not merely allegiance, though; more fundamentally, according to the command, it is life itself. And as a matter of God's promise, owing to Abraham is also life, but life in the unique sense of selfhood. At stake is not simply animate but, more profoundly, reflexive existence. Put another way, at stake is self-consciousness or human life. Put still another way, Abraham is due precisely the power to choose for himself, that is, to choose on behalf of his self.

Every choice of whether or not to obey a directive implicates the choice between having and not having choice. This is because for most practical purposes the choice to obey deprives one of any way to show that one has in fact taken a choice, whereas in the nature of the case the choice to disobey presents one as having chosen for oneself. When one chooses to obey a command, one's self-definition as a chooser, a self, becomes a matter of faith, since there is nothing to be seen in the manifestation of the choice that can serve to distinguish one as anything other than a mere function of the command. But choosing to do other than the other's bidding necessarily describes one indeed as the other's other and therewith as oneself.[14]

In this connection, what I wish to bring to light is that in the Akedah, the choice to choose, instead of being left implicit, is given added, even exceptional, emphasis. In view of the infanticidal content of the first command, Abraham is being asked to make a choice so hard that it cannot fail to highlight the question of choice itself. He is obliged to choose between being and not being. The question put to him, then, is Hamlet's. And as in the case of Shakespeare's prince, the question asks either that he deny himself, his own being, and suffer the Other's choice ("The slings and arrows of outrageous fortune") or that he assert himself by choosing to choose for himself ("For who would bear the whips and scorns of time, / … / When *he himself* [my italics] might his quietus make / With a bare bodkin [blade]?"). Whereas for Hamlet the 'good' choice is against "conscience" or the Other and for himself, for Abraham the reverse is the case. (In Kierkegaard's terms, Hamlet chooses what is for him the higher ethical value in his given situation, whereas Abraham trades ethics for the infinite, thus making him a knight of faith rather than a tragic hero.) But in both cases, at stake is the capital power to be a chooser, that is, to be empowered to create one's own world.

It is only because Abraham enjoys this creational power that the story can present itself in the thematic terms of a test of faith. How must Abraham prove himself? By forgoing this god-given power and trusting in God to call the shots, even though—and this is the critical point—he, Abraham, could have done otherwise. In effect, in resolving to slay his own son as ordered to do so by God, Abraham makes a sacrifice and is duly rewarded. But what exactly has he offered up? At the end of the day, for all that his beloved son has suffered materially, it is precisely not Abraham's self in any bodily form (including his son's body) that gets sacrificed but rather the self that is belonging to Abraham in spirit. He has agreed, at God's bidding, to return what God had given him in the first place: the power to choose to do other than God's bidding. This is precisely the power not of embodiment but of inspiration—this is the power given man when God breathed life into him, not when he formed him of dust from the ground. The substitution of a beast for a human being is warranted, as the story goes, because Abraham has indeed already sacrificed himself in a profound way—in spirit (cf. Sarnum 1966: 162–63).

The kind of being at stake in this story, then, is described by the power of choice, the magical or spiritual power to create worlds and make time. The story makes the point that if man is to benefit from this power to render being from nothingness, life from death, he must substantially acknowledge that he enjoys it only at God's behest, and therefore always within limits. Hence, while the story turns on an exercise of the power of choice by Abraham, the happy ending depends not on this choice exactly but on the ensuant one taken by God. It is God's intervention—God's choice, the choice of God—that creates the magical transfiguration of life from death. The story means to reaffirm, then, that the deity is the master chooser, the creator of worlds, a claim that has been in question at least ever since Adam and Eve got away, in a critical sense, with stealing the forbidden fruit. The narrative of Abraham and Isaac reminds us, in disturbing terms, that although the tree of the knowledge of good and evil may have fallen into the hands of man, the tree of life remains forever beyond his reach.

The 'Stupidity' of Blind Faith

Blind Faith vs. Pre-reflective Understanding: The Akedah and the Nuer Rite of Gar

The story then constitutes a specific, instructional answer to the question of why there is something rather than nothing. The answer is that life is a gift from God, and that the continuing enjoyment of this gift depends on abnegational sacrifice as a matter of blind faith, that is, as a matter of conscious but uncomprehending choice. It strikes me that this answer, while deep and salutary, also bears a grave danger. On the one hand, in a very powerful way it serves to remind us that choice is limited and never wholly witting, individual, and free (a scriptural shibboleth reiterated with a difference by postmodernism); on the other, by promoting the choice of *blind* faith, the answer can serve to foster Hitlerian aspirations.

In order to elucidate this judgmental conclusion further, I want to compare and contrast the Akedah to another answer to the question of human existence. Given that each and every culture may be regarded as a particular approach to putting off the dead end of being doubly bound, to living a dilemma and making time, there are indeed many other answers or myriad forms of human life. But there is a feature of the Akedah that serves to distinguish it categorically in the present connection. I can bring this feature into high relief by viewing it in light of a phenomenologically 'more primitive' treatment of the existential problem of the double bind.

The Nuer of East Africa also perform surrogate sacrifice, to the same life-sustaining purpose as expressed in the Akedah.[15] The ideal victim for the Nuer is an ox, and the key to this practice among them is their perception of identity with their cattle. This identity is established in an initiation rite called *gar* or 'the cutting', whereby all pubescent boys are made to undergo a severe scarification: several lines are incised, to the bone, in the boys' foreheads, starting from the center of the brow and extending to each ear. In effect, the horns of cattle are carved indelibly into the boys' heads. This bloody initiation into manhood empowers the initiates to perform, among other things, ritual sacrifice to Kwoth (Spirit or God). The cutting, then, appears to be a master rite, the root sacrifice that licenses all the others.

For general purposes, the formal and functional parallel between this Nuer ritual and the binding of Isaac is obvious. (At risk of putting too fine a point on it, it is worth recalling here that the Akedah's ram was, as preparatory to the fulfilling of its sacrificial role, caught in a thicket "by it horns.") In the present connection, though, there is a crucial difference. Whereas Isaac's trial is a matter of choice, and dramatically so, the ordeal of the Nuer youths is simply taken for granted as a part of the natural course of things. However it appears at first blush, this difference, as registered in the Akedah's theme of blind faith, is momentous.

While the Nuer do indeed 'trust' in Kwoth, they do not have 'faith' in him, if that usage is meant to convey that they have deliberated a decision to believe in him. By contrast and for all the automatism of his response, there can be no doubt that the Akedah pictures Abraham as having to prove himself by making just such a decision. In view of the shocking and seemingly insane and perfidious imperative to murder Isaac, the credibility of the God of Abraham must have looked open to question to Abraham's redactional authors, at least to some degree. Accordingly, Abraham is pictured as having to decide whether he should take the imperative—and hence the mouth from which it issued—as true. For the Nuer, though, Kwoth's designs are not open to human prerogative at all. Instead, Kwoth and the order imposed by him are entertained as matters of perception alone: Nuer see and experience the world in terms of them. In other words, whereas in the Akedah God is presented, in part but critically, as a function of Abraham's faith or belief, for the Nuer, Kwoth, like the earth, wind, and water, simply *is*.

The phenomenological ramifications of this ontological state of affairs, wherein God is an indubitable presence, run deep. For one thing, logically speaking, the situation in which humans would need to prove their acceptance of God as true or existing cannot arise. And for another, although there is a need to establish especial identity between the self and the surrogate victim, there is no need to warrant the reality of this identity by rationalizing it. In the case of both the Nuer and the Akedah, this identity is made by causing the intended victim to suffer a terrible ordeal, thus linking him to the sacrificial beast. But whereas for the Nuer the resulting identity, surely conceived of as Kwoth's design, is really real, for us it presents itself as, although serious, a kind of fiction. For this reason the Akedah finds it necessary to back up the identificatory warrant for the substitution with the implicit thesis that what in reality has been sacrificed is Abraham's spiritual power. It is as if because the identity between Isaac and the ram must in the end be deemed merely symbolic, and therefore a kind of cheat, the act of surrogation is in need of rationalization by reference to a more genuine sacrifice. Thus, notwithstanding the overt attention of the narrative, the most innovative critical sacrificial substitution in the Akedah is not beast for man, but spirit for matter.

Blind Faith: A Dualistic Development

By comparison to ritual sacrifice among a people like the Nuer, then, the Akedah's theme of faith betokens nothing less significant than a different world, a different sense of reality. It might be said that Nuer reality is keyed more to perception and actuality than to commitment and choice. The fact that Kwoth is readily perceived by the Nuer as, although separate and distinct from man, also close to man and participant in his world suggests that for them the distinction between spirit and matter is as fuzzy as can be. In light of this comparison, the Akedah's theme of faith becomes conspicuous by virtue of the incipient way it treats matter as one thing and spirit as quite another. In effect, the difference in question projects the difference between a dualistic and a nondualistic ontology.

A critical caution is in order here, for as it obtains specifically between these two examples, this difference can easily be overdrawn. The forgoing analysis plainly suggests that there is a great deal in the Akedah narrative to indicate that, in relation to the way in which the reality of God was experienced in Abraham's world, that world had much in common with the Nuer's.[16] We should not forget that the biblical story also blurs the boundary between spirit and matter, as in the identity it establishes between the finite figure of Abraham and the infinite figure of God. Nevertheless, the exegetically celebrated theme of faith in the biblical story, with its diacritical accent on the difference between spirit and matter, marks unmistakably a dualistic development. This development is further advanced and refined in the story of the sacrifice of Jesus, where the whole point becomes how spirit, in the figure of the creator, can save matter, cast as the creature, by offering itself up on the latter's behalf. In effect, then, the Akedah is on the road to dualism, a thesis crucial to my interpretation of the story and my willingness to credit Kierkegaard's Pauline reading in terms of blind faith.

Blind faith, in the sense of belief that is resolute but based solely on trust, is a servile attitude made possible by dualism. The Akedah's account of Abraham as self-sacrifice in spirit alone clearly implicates the dualism of spirit and matter as it revalorizes the very idea of obedience, away from obeisance or even reverence and toward sheer servility. This kind of sacrifice, wherein spiritual is substituted for material being, is recorded in the story as a supererogatory decision on the part of Abraham to obey God's abhorrent command. The surpassing nature of Abraham's decision rests with the nature of the risk: Abraham risks 'his' life, and all the promised life that his life includes, for God's sake. But the risk is brought to its critical edge by the fact that Abraham's decision is taken blindly, without knowing for what he is taking the risk. He knows only too well what he is risking, but he can have no idea of whether the risk is worth it or not. In effect, then, it goes wholly unmitigated, even by such knowledge as is standard in cases of risk-taking—the knowledge of whether the possible benefit warrants the risk.

Blind faith in this sense can emerge only where 'sighted' commitment is an option. In relation to faith, sightedness means having access to a reason for commitment. Abraham has no such access—he must commit in total intellectual darkness, on the basis of revelatory authority and obligation alone. God does not offer Abraham a ground for the command; he just issues it. The point is, though, that blind faith is blind, not because reason is not part of the picture, but because access to reason is denied under circumstances in which it *is* part of the picture. In point of fact, faith of this kind entails the idea of reason, which is to say, it supposes the clear differentiation of the intellect from the senses. For this reason, a Nuer cannot act in blind faith, at least in respect of Kwoth. True, he acts in the absence of any ground other than the perception of Kwoth, Kwoth being the certain ground on which everything stands and from which everything derives. For this very reason, however—that Kwoth for him is a matter of perception and not belief—the situation cannot arise in which the Nuer can conceive of a ground on which he can put the truth of Kwoth or his order to question. For under these epistemological conditions, any such ground would have to have as *its* ground the perception of Kwoth and his designs.

Put another way, for the Nuer, reason and the intellect, like spirit itself, are not clearly differentiated from the senses. As there can be, then, no reason qua reason that one can forgo in commitment, in such a world blind faith, the kind of faith Abraham's act is seen by Kierkegaard to epitomize, is simply not possible.

Total Risk

To return now to my value judgment, it seems to me that blind faith courts 'stupidity'. By this supposition I do not intend that such faith is in error, but rather that as a mode of thought, it too readily entertains malevolence.[17] On the explicit basis of revelatory experience and authority that goes not simply unquestioned but unquestionable, Abraham risks everything—not just his son's life, or even his own, but life itself. This global risk is occasioned by unalloyed faith, the presumption of which stands behind the command to Abraham to prove himself by sacrificing Isaac. As the story goes, the risk proved worth it, since it produced an extraordinary benefit— redemption so very substantial that humans were thenceforth effectively permitted to sacrifice themselves basically in spirit rather than in substance. This benefit amounts to a progressive movement—a veritable leap—in the direction of selfhood. The resultant differentiation of spiritual from material sacrifice and the story's thematic acknowledgment of Abraham's self, made implicitly but powerfully in the voluntary act of abnegation, indicate that what is gained is the superadded re-creation of the life of the self. It is paradoxically but precisely the spiritual power to choose and determine one's own world that gets expressed and redoubled in Abraham's decision to abdicate this power in the face of the Lord.

If Abraham had known beforehand that he had a world to gain as well as to lose, his faith would have been not blind but instrumental—a gambler's faith—and the risk, although still great, calculated. But the story treats the possibility of global risk as a function of perfect faith. That is to say, such incalculable risk is brought into play only because God seeks to test Abraham's faith. The roundness of the risk repeats and depends on the perfection of the faith.

Since a Nuer takes God's presence for granted, faith cannot be an issue for him. And since he cannot act in blind faith, unlimited risk is not about to define his situation. A Nuer does not sacrifice in order to show his faith, but rather to ensure the continuity of life. And even in this connection the sacrifice is not exactly a means to an end since, as a function of Kwoth's design, sacrifice constitutes its own satisfaction. Whether or not the sacrifice effects the immediate purpose (say, healing), it is only incompletely differentiated from everyday (profane) life and therefore enjoys the practical status of simply the living of that life. In other words, for the Nuer, sacrifice is practiced in much the same way as eating, sleeping, and interrelating. To be sure, in view of the fact that a Nuer offers up what he truly perceives as a part or extension of himself, there is risk. But the risk is limited, never total. For this reason, among the Nuer a sacrifice like Abraham's, one so rarefied that it can alter the need and nature of sacrifice itself, is unthinkable. Each and every sacrifice not only gives life, but, precisely because it is definitively measured, because it always falls short of payment in full, also ensures that the practice of sacrifice will have to continue in its current form. While some Nuer sacrifices are deemed more important than others, none can serve as a sacrifice so total that it can effect a redemption powerful enough to reduce the need, by a giant Abrahamic step, for further sacrifice.

Self-Perfection and the Inversion of the Hierarchy of Spirit and Matter

"No risk, no gain," to be sure. If Abraham's inordinately hazardous action yielded the considerable return of a marked intensification of human selfhood, then Nuer ritual practice must correspond to a relatively undeveloped or naive sense of self. That is to say, the act of sacrifice does not advance the Nuer along the road of self-development and, tautologically, toward the reduction of the need for substantive sacrifice. But the implicit value judgment here is pointedly complicated by the consideration that the Abrahamic leap of faith, which is also a leap of self-consciousness, not only carries grave risk but also encourages the turning of that risk into reality.

It is not hard to see that the self-development registered in the story of Abraham and Isaac reveals the operation of the principle of perfection. Indeed, inasmuch as that development ensures the perpetuity of Abraham's self as a leader of nations, of a premier worldly world ("In his seed all the nations of the earth shall be blessed" [Genesis: chap. 22]), it bespeaks Abraham's likeness to God—the first creator of worlds. But as it does, it holds out an image not simply of self-development but of self-completion. That is, it informs man with, above and beyond a strong sense of self, a sense of self the logical destiny of which is sheer self-containment and self-transparency. More precisely, the development in question defines man, teleologically and for himself, as that creature whose fundamental end in life is self-perfection. This holds true despite the fact that the story's narrative, with its stunning emphasis on the need for Abraham to submit his will to God's, gives a powerful, if unarticulated, lesson about the idolatrous deception of such an image. Indeed, it is the implicit operation of this perfectibilist self-definition that explains why the lesson has to be given at all.

How does the Akedah portray this image of self-completion? To stay with the story's theme of blind faith, the relationship between God and man is depicted as a matter of choice. God *chooses* to issue a certain command to Abraham, who in turn, on no other basis than faith, *chooses* to obey. Inasmuch as it is wholly intentional and creative—that is, agential and unconstrained by force, guile, or reason—the conduct of both epitomizes what it means to choose. The relationship is thus pictured as mediate rather than immediate, a tie between two selves each of which has the power to direct its own conduct toward the other and therefore stands to the other as other. The relationship is in this sense open: the tie has a significant degree of play in it. The play amounts to the power of choice and thus constitutes a spiritual rather than material freedom. As such, obviously, it is predicated on a prominent distinction between mind and body. It is this distinction, of course, which admits of the most novel change recorded in the story, namely, the substitution of material by spiritual being in sacrifice. In effect, by deferring his volitional power to God, Abraham performs not a bloody but a spiritual transfusion; he injects God or the Other with the life that is His, thus renewing that patriarchal figure and defining it all the more so as a matter of spirit.

Hence, the theme of blind faith entails a prominent distinction between matter and spirit. The character of the difference between man and God implicates the sharpness of this distinction. What is narratively featured is not the material but the politico-spiritual character of the difference. Insofar as man enjoys the power of choice, he is one of a kind with God and is thus implicitly equipped to displace the latter (or at least appears so to himself). The story furnishes an account of how God goes about containing this difference, ensuring against the threat of it.[18] But right from the beginning, the story secures the primacy of God's place by signaling that there really can be no contest, and that notwithstanding man's power of choice in the least, the relationship between him and God is ineradicably hierarchical rather than equalitarian, a relationship of authority rather than power. God's command is, although presumptively not Abraham's wish, certainly Abraham's witting but unquestioning commitment.

The hierarchical nature of the relationship is ultimately founded on generational priority: it is understood that man could not have created himself in the first place and is therefore owing to his Other. This fundamental asymmetry of creator and creature is inevitably glossed in terms of the ontological polarity of spirit and matter. Man's limited generative power or pro-creativity marks him as, although not exclusively, representatively material, while God's absolute generative power, creativity in itself, identifies him absolutely with the spiritual pole. Therefore, in respect of this polarity, man's power of choice, a godly attribute, presents a transcendence and makes of him a walking contradiction—a representatively material being that is nonetheless inspirited.

Herein rests the nub of the problem. Although the spiritual pole is in principle deemed superior, when it is prepossessingly introduced into man, that is, into the 'creature', it risks subjection to definition by its material counterpart. As a result of this unholy-holy admixture, the creature is ever tempted to define himself in terms of the limitlessness or perfection of the maker, and to conduct himself in such a way as to make that self-definition come true. Insofar as the main intended lesson of the story is about the vital need to acknowledge performatively God's supremacy, the threat of this antinomian turn of events may be seen to furnish the story's very raison d'être.

Hierarchical Inversion and Immaculate Boundaries

Referring to the idea of boundaries can flesh the point out. Plainly, because they extend in space, material things lend themselves to precise delineation. Spirit, however, characterized by zero dimensions, does not—its boundaries are definitively ethereal. Therefore, insofar as material boundaries are spiritually informed, one might expect them to present themselves as fuzzy and fluid rather than fast. But the same condition of ontological ambiguity offers the alternative possibility: where they are found together in the concrete individual, that is, nearer to the material end of the polarity, that end is enabled and even given to impose its inherent perspective on the spiritual pole. The boundaries of the individual thus look not merely but perfectly precise. Which is to say, for purposes of self-definition, they become absolutely exclusive or closed, dualistically defining the individual as against everything else.

As soon as the material perspective presents itself as the starting point of perception, the kind of boundary it disposes advances a definition of perfection in terms of fixity and closure. This definition stands in sharp contrast to any non-idolatrous apprehension of the Perfect, in which is featured precisely the unrepresentability of amorphous openness. And when the material notion of boundary is applied to the distinction between matter and spirit, it defines dualism. Considered as a dualism, this distinction is no longer simply sharp and prominent, but differentiates its polar principles immaculately. Consequently, matter comes to be seen as one thing and spirit entirely another.

More importantly here, though, is that such mutual exclusion allows material boundaries to appear as if they go unqualified by the basic ambiguity characterizing all 'things' we are inclined to speak of in spiritual terms. In effect, it is forgotten that such boundaries not only separate but also connect.[19] What is more, by virtue of the phenomenological emergence of boundaries of this immaculate kind, the world of spirit too comes to be apprehended as a closed whole, a kind of totality or individual. That world then gets defined by virtue of the boundary differentiating it from the material world, an exclusionary boundary. To detect the cognitive movement in this direction, we need only cite the dramatic example of the figure of Christ, in whom, apparently for the first time, spirit as such and in full comes to be contained phenomenologically within the confines of a material singularity, an individual human being. Surely, this is one crucial meaning of the 'incarnation' of Christ.[20] This meaning was not lost on the Canaque of New Caledonia, who take the spirituality of the world for granted. When their Christian missionary-anthropologist, Maurice Leenhardt, asseverated that he had introduced Spirit to them, they objected, saying that, on the contrary, what he had brought was the Body (Leenhardt 1979: 164).

The Displacement of the Other by the Self

The terrific irony is that Abraham's plain and powerful movement toward spirituality leads, not ineluctably but nonetheless forcefully, to the logical extinction of the very idea of spirit. Although it would seem to treat its two constitutive principles equally, in fact the dualism of matter and spirit always privileges the former. This is because the defining essence of dualism, mutual exclusivity, supposes a world in which things do not participate in but are instead exterior to one another. Notwithstanding the rationalism of Descartes' *cogito*, such a world is at bottom primarily material. Hence, in the dualistic contest between spirit and matter, spirit cannot really win. The contest implies that each of the two principles is essentially purposed to reduce the other to itself. But whereas logically the material principle can succeed in eliminating the spiritual one, by defining the world in quantifiable terms, in order for the spiritual principle to triumph, it has to reduce itself to the measure of the material. In the dualistic terms of the contest, it can win only by excluding or by wholly incorporating the material world, thus denying its own defining essence as basic ambiguity. Thus, with the advent of dualism, spirituality is insidiously denatured and denied.

The point can be made more concretely. One upshot of the Akedah is that spirit is put decidedly at the disposal of humanity and history. As the just reward for his act of self-sacrifice, Abraham, through his descendants, is re-spirated, or hooked up in perpetuity to a divine respirator. Once the life, nationhood, and supremacy of Abraham's posterity seem guaranteed, though, he is positioned to forget the experience of his own heteronomy. A presumption of perpetuity so imposing as to be received as in the order of things (as is promised at the close of the story) invites one to take oneself as self-contained, as one's own starting point. What does it mean to forget that one ever originates in otherness, if not that one has displaced in one's own mind the other with the self? And what is the self in this dualistic context but, at least at first, the sense that one has of oneself as a substantive denizen of the world of procreation. Hence, the starting point of perception looks to be, instead of a blind spot, or something always already forgotten, or what is otherwise than being, an empirically well-defined and highly visible phenomenon.

The narrative of the Akedah is finely attuned to just such a turn toward *self*-centeredness. The narrative tells a horror story, a story expressly meant to serve as a reminder that, for all the promise of their continuing existence as self-contained entities, men are in fact vitally and irredeemably dependent on what is other to them. The reminder is necessary because one of the forceful consequences of the development of self-consciousness is the loss of memory of the other as truly other. With each advance in the development of self-consciousness, man is given to feel more secure in the promise of his empirical being; correspondingly, he becomes less cognizant of the experience of his own otherness. The inevitability of this state of affairs is lodged in the reminder itself. I mean nothing so uncomplicated as that the reminder would not be necessary but for man's inclination to self-perfection. Rather, I mean the following eventful paradox: that the reminder cannot recall to man his essential heteronomy without at the same time reminding him of his autonomy. It works, even when it is meant to strike the fear of God into the hearts of men, by appealing to them in view of their power of choice, their power to do otherwise. For this reason, in their capacity as a phenomenology of mind, the biblical stories speak here of 'temptation' instead of, for example, 'determination' or 'dialectic'. With abiding insight, the stories grasp man's essential situation of consciousness as no less a matter of conscience and hence in terms of what is called here ethics rather than reason.

The Reduction of the Infinite

All this is inscribed in orthodox religion's password, 'blind faith'. As we have seen, this usage denotes that Abraham decides on the basis of faith alone, without benefit of reason or understanding. In effect, he makes his decision in view of what is invisible to him, of that to which he is perfectly blind. The reminder of his heteronomy is a reminder of precisely this: that the truth of God is no less certain for being objectively unknowable and unrepresentable. According to Midrashic commentary, at the moment his father raised his hand to take his life in sacrifice, Isaac was blinded (Shulman 1993: 4). With this interpretive insight the Midrash is surely indicating that, as a correlate of Abraham's pious decision, the blind spot that is the truth of God, the fount of all perception, is phenomenologically brought into relief. What Isaac was forbidden to see at that life-threatening instant was the very source of himself, that which gives life and takes it away.

The inherent but perilous temptation to self-perfection on the part of man makes it easy to see why it might be critical to institute a set of understandings, whatever their specific contents, that serve constantly to remind men of their fundamental belatedness, of the primacy of the Other. To forget this condition, whether in relation to other human beings, other kinds of animals, inanimate things, or, more abstractly, otherness as such, is a profoundly risky business. This kind of forgetfulness amounts to the attitudinal exclusion of that on which life ultimately rests—an exclusion the consequences of which are logically predictable.

But it is one thing to remain alert to one's fundamental finitude and quite another to take instruction from it as if the invisible ground imposing it issued commands on the model of a human order. To take instruction in this way makes not only a category mistake but also a consequential contradiction. For it implicitly renders the invisible ground present and even accounted for, as if it were man's to access in the way men facultatively access one another. True, in Abraham's case the ground remains for him out of sight, but it is presented plainly as within his earshot. God's fundamental invisibility certainly highlights his otherness, the way in which he differs from any determinate object in this world. However, although vision and hearing inflect absolute otherness differently, the voice Abraham hears speaks words that are clear and distinct, in the manner of human talk, talk that bespeaks, as vision betokens, not indefinitude, but the present-at-hand.[21]

I am again arguing, then, that Abraham's willingness to take God's instruction in this story actually constitutes not the knightly success celebrated by Kierkegaard's commentary but an egregious failure by Abraham to stay alert to his own fundamental limitedness. It is futile to question that in the general case there is always something to which we cannot but remain blind. Since any question cannot explain its own possibility without effecting an infinite logical regression of further questions, the question at point ultimately betrays the operation of the very blind spot it seeks to dispel. But if there is one thing that we have learned from the horrific events of the twentieth century, it is never to allow a specific command to remain unquestionable. Unlike an existential condition, each and every specific command is finite or contingent and therefore accessible in principle as to its rationale.

By trusting implicitly the justice of God's command, far from demonstrating trust in the invisible otherness that goes in the story by the name of God, Abraham actually violates that trust. The essential black hole of human understanding can be brought to the attention of human consciousness by the figure of God, but it cannot be brought to light. In claiming to know God's specific command, Abraham does not remember but forgets that there is always already something forgotten. He conducts himself as if he can—not cannot—know, for certain and concretely, without any doubt whatsoever, what the always already forgotten amounts to. He forgets that it is the intrinsic openness, not the determinacy, of the absolute other that needs to be kept in trust. It is because this memory fails him that he can be certain that the command he hears, all too humanly exact and patriarchal, issues from the mouth of God himself and, accordingly, be willing—quite insanely—to risk all of life, absolutely everything.

Abraham and Dire Madness

"When people are convinced they speak in the name of God," writes John Caputo (1993: 145), "then it is time for the rest of us to head for the doors." Who is it Abraham hears speaking? He can be sure of the invisible other, but can he be sure that that other has spoken a command to him to kill his own son? That kind of certainty implies that the command he hears issues from not an invisible other but another other, one whose voice is audible and articulate in this world. Such an other betrays a self, a positive creature that can see and direct itself in relation to others and to the invisible other. But unlike the voice of another such other, the voice Abraham hears does not resound for all to hear—it is for his ears only. Whose voice can it be, then, but his own? And who, then, is speaking in God's name, but Abraham—to himself?

Today, of course, Abraham's conduct would lead us to think him mad—schizophrenic, to be exact.[22] He experiences the voice he hears as coming from outside himself rather than as his own. But this experience constitutes and betrays a distortion of his relationship to the invisible other. That relationship is essentially bipolar: man is at once both part of and contraposed to that otherness. In his contraposition, he differentiates himself, ultimately as an individual; but in his participation, he remains always other to himself, including his own individuality. By projecting God as the said rather than the saying, in terms of words the denotative meaning of which can be fixed and deciphered, Abraham distorts this bipolarity into a kind of a monopoly. For inasmuch as he comprehends the otherwise than being in such mundane terms, he reduces it to determinate being, his very own. In his presentation of self, then, he has lost sight of himself as a singularly double-bounded creature whose part in the order of things is to contrapose it-self to that very order without ever ceasing to belong to it. In effect, he has defined himself in terms of one pole of his being only, the contrapositional one, allowing it to do double duty, as both itself and as his (voiced-over) patriarchal other.

By specifying God's order and acting on it, Abraham resolves in his own mind his opposition to that order. He thus presents himself as indistinguishable from it. He does so not by increasing his participation in it to the point of losing himself, as one might lose oneself (one's mind) in, say, a rampaging crowd. Rather, he collapses it into his own determinate being. To be sure, he truly experiences the voice as belonging to another. Nevertheless, his experience is solipsistic: he alone hears God's order.[23] Having managed to obscure the concrete way in which he continuously belongs to what is other to his self, he forgets that his mind is not simply conveyed by his body but is itself bodily. According to the story, he hears with his mind's ear (in the sense that one might see with the mind's eye), and he obeys. In other words, as in all dualistic epistemological contexts, he presents himself first as mind, then as body. *Pace* Kierkegaard, what Abraham discerns is not the subjective truth of God, but rather the precarious truth of his own subjectivity. In the event of this dualistic self-definition, the loss of mind Abraham suffers is—although articulated contrarily as an intensification of mind—not less for his having convinced himself that he has internalized God's infinite compass instead of having mindlessly allowed himself to be fully incorporated by it. Of course, these two outcomes are equally deadly. Indeed, Abraham becomes, if you like, a mad crowd of one, deranged and malevolent as regards his own child and even life at large.

Madness and the Eclipse of the Common World

By presenting himself so critically in terms of subjectivity, Abraham eclipses from view the one world common to us all. I do not mean the objective world according to science and rationality. Rather, I have in mind the world as we find it when we see it in relation to ourselves looking at it at the same time. Unlike the scientific picture of it, this world comprises the visible and the invisible, the material and the immaterial. By including in our 'view' the sense of ourselves looking at the world, we bring into account our own particular perspectives. And because these perspectives are particular rather than universal, they imply an infinite regression of enabling perspectives. They are therefore definitively limited, excluding from immediate seeing the ground that is the condition of their possibility. In which case, the objective world cannot be the world according to science. Instead, it is the world in which we participate and in so doing help produce by coming to terms with the particular standpoints of one another (and of the Other). The terms we come to are, in the first place, practical rather than ratiocinative. They reflect a dynamic bodily perception through which the fundamentally limited views offered by particular perspectives are articulated with one another to constitute a working world.

The objective world I have in mind, then, is a correlate of the mindful body before it emerges as a preponderantly theoretical proposition. The universality that admits of a shared world emerges with, rather than a view from nowhere, the dynamic, temporal articulation of motile human beings, who watch their step in relation to one another's movements.[24] As a result of this bodily complicity, we are enabled to fill in gaps of our own particular perspective, expressing in our very movements vis-à-vis others and otherness a working sense of the whole. This is the sense that prevails, say, when we navigate in vehicular or pedestrian traffic—the sense in which each of us grasps from our own particular position the same visible formation as well as our own relationship to it.[25] This working sense of the whole furnishes a basis on which well-defined cultural worlds (including the *sensus communis*) and properly theoretical ones may arise, and may in turn inform the particular perspectives regulating and enabling our perception of the world. And because it remains always infinite and open, this sense of the whole also implicates the possibility of divinity and occasions conceptualizations thereof.

In the Akedah, Abraham's solipsism—a dualistic turn of his self-consciousness away from bodily to hermetic, soulful perception—cuts off his access, in a crucial respect, to the common world just described. Hence, although the form of his actions can be understood (he sets out to make a burnt offering), their content, by reason of its unthinkable character, appears utterly incomprehensible (he intends to slaughter his own child). In effect, without appeal to an actually common world, he is no longer able to meet others and communicate with them as co-participants. This lived and mindful state of profound isolation, impregnable to deliberated self-repair, defines madness. Abraham cannot explain himself—not even to himself (insofar as that self remains still a question of, by contrast to an acutely subjective 'inner' construction, sensible articulation with others). Thus, apart from prophetic lies, he has nothing to tell his two servants and his inquiring son about his actions.

Faith and the Common World

Throughout the ages, concerned interpreters have striven to make sense of Abraham's conduct. In fact, if we take it as exegesis in its own right, the story itself tries to do the same. It accounts for Abraham's action as a proof of his faith in God. But this is far from explication by reference to the one world we all have in common. Instead, as Kierkegaard brought out in such depth, 'faith' denies any sort of objective world in favor of a profoundly subjective one. According to the argument from faith, the only thing we really have in common with one another is the fact of our solipsism. In which case, the argument in question can have force in one community only: the community of the faithful, or at least of those who take for granted belief as a natural attitude among men.[26] The argument derives its force not from demonstrating that Abraham's actions are other than malevolent, but from presuming, on the basis that Abraham is carrying out the orders of one who is not only almighty but also all-just, that the actions cannot but be benevolent.

But even among the community of the faithful, the argument is unlikely to obviate feelings of suspicion. On the contrary, because it is predicated on solipsism, the kind of faith at issue always stands on the edge of madness. Hence, Abraham is asked to prove his faith precisely by undertaking an apparently deranged act, one which can hardly make sense in terms of human decency. In connection with this act, for Abraham, evidently, it was enough to trust in God. But for all those trying to penetrate and justify Abraham's behavior, it is necessary to trust not only in God but also in Abraham's trust that he has indeed heard the word of God. In view of the heinous act he intends to perform and his inability to make the commission of the act comprehensible in human terms, why should we?[27]

We cannot help but have faith, but we need not be stupid about it. Earlier I indicated that by 'stupidity' I intend a structure of thought that fosters unnecessary violence. Here, though, I can add that the particular structure of thought in point does its disturbing work by obscuring the fact that our life depends not only on our separation from but also on our connection to the chronically inchoate world that we all have in common. The story of the binding of Isaac frames the abhorrent but perfect ethical enormity of Abraham's act as a measure of his faith. But it is just plain stupid to give credence to a man who is about to slaughter any child, let alone his own, on the grounds that the unrepresentable other is making him do it.

Abraham too is being stupid, although his stupidity is allied with madness. As I see it, in keeping with my 'theory' of sacrifice, the madness stems from anxiety of displacement, a fear that is fed by the critical focus on Isaac as the promise of Abraham's immortality. That immortality is fundamentally compromised, since it proceeds most concretely by Isaac's displacement of Abraham. When it is considered that Abraham is no ordinary father but the father of us all, a singularly potent patriarch, it becomes comprehensible in human terms why he might be moved to embark on the sacrifice of his son. He wants to displace the otherness of Isaac, his other and future self, before that otherness can displace him in his immediate and exceptional concreteness. An anxiety the object of which is so perfectly full and vital is enough to drive anybody mad.

That Abraham should exhibit this terrible anxiety is hardly surprising in view of the fact that the story pictures God himself as similarly stricken. The existential force of this anxiety mimetically pervades the story. God's menacing command to Abraham, no less than Abraham's sacrificial assault on Isaac, constitutes a shocking reminder of belatedness to the son, of the son's vital dependence on the father. Both the Father and the father of us all—God and Abraham—display a grave concern for their own continuation as a function of the filial piety of their offspring. This concern is not unrealistic. For inasmuch as the father's continuing existence is a matter of the son's continuing acknowledgement of the father's priority, it is the son who creates the father. But once the son exists on his own account, what is there to guarantee that he will continue to pay his filial dues in this way?

Abraham is driven mad by this anxiety. He is moved to divorce himself from the world of limits and compromise, thus creating his world as self-certain. The nature and logic of the command to kill his own son is an enabling expression of such madness. For one thing, the command is utterly uncompromising in what it prescribes. Abraham is asked to offer up his son, neither surrogatively nor synecdochally, but whole, as a holocaust. The command leaves no room for compromise, placing Abraham out of the human world and into an absolute one. For another thing, given its purpose as a test, the command asks Abraham to choose, as against life and choice, to obey. In so choosing, however, Abraham cannot help but revitalize, aggrandize even, his power of choice. For the fact that the choice confronting him is absolute—a matter of life and death—redefines that power in turn as absolute, implicitly representing him as godlike.

Abraham fails to conclude that the horrifying words he hears as coming from outside himself, but which, inaudible to others, resound in his head alone, must be his own. Can this failure define him as other than a madman? His actions stem from the fact that he has cut himself off from the world as it allows us to come to viable terms with one another as well as with otherness in itself. Notwithstanding the story's own obvious intentionality and the gist of so much exegesis, it is not really the temporal world (Kierkegaard's objective world) from which he withdraws, the world as it blinds us to our own basic limitedness. On the contrary, inasmuch as he forgets that he is participant in a primary world, the common ground of which makes it possible for each of us to meet and compromise and communicate with others, Abraham in fact succumbs to the temptation to regard himself one-sidedly in terms of his own worldly autonomy and subjectivity. And insofar as we choose to countenance his determined, lethal violence against Isaac, his beloved but most threatening other, we are displaying a lack of sensibility so egregious as to be nothing short of stupid.

Faith vs. Life

The argument from faith addresses only those whose subjectivity is sufficiently advanced along the road to dualism to make intelligible the idea of inner commitment. But the argument does not appeal to the world as we find it in our capacity as self-conscious bodily beings always already materially committed to—that is, constituent of and compromised by—one another in a dynamic and open whole. On this world all norms ultimately rest, since it amounts to the inherently indeterminate foundation by virtue of which norm-ing itself, in an endless repetition of difference, takes place.

In connection with this world, the argument from faith can occlude but not dispel the conclusion to the malevolence of Abraham's actions. For this world is quintessentially vital. It expresses itself above all as life, and presents life as good, in a singularly ambiguous sense. Life is good both because it constitutes its own *end* and because it *constitutes* its own end. Put another way, the world in question presents itself primarily as bent toward life—it has life as its good. At the same time, however, it presents life as peculiarly capacitated to determine its own good. In practice this ambiguity amounts to ethical existence, a uniquely tensile form of life wherein any overarching good leaves other goods fundamentally open to creative choice. The tension results, then, not simply from the power of choice, whereby the good is always subject to question, but from the paradoxical fact that this power is limited by life, that it necessarily has life as its prepossessing good. In other words, the good of life is no ordinary norm, but that by which all norms are constructed and judged. For this reason, although under the conditions of ethical existence death can be determined as a good, when death is granted dominion not as a function of life but in its own right, it is bound to sponsor malevolence.

That is why, despite the proven metaphysical attraction of the argument from faith, we remain uncomfortable in the face of Abraham's actions. Indeed, even Kierkegaard,

in one of four possible projections of Abraham's afterthoughts, considers that the patriarch might have entertained the conclusion of malevolence (1985: 47): "It was a tran-
quil evening when Abraham rode out alone, and he rode to the mountain in Moriah;
he threw himself on his face, he begged God to forgive his sin at having been willing
to sacrifice Isaac, at the father's having forgotten his duty to his son ... He could not
comprehend that it was a sin to have been willing to sacrifice to God the best he owned;
that for which he would many a time have gladly laid down his own life; and if it was a
sin, if he had not so loved Isaac, then he could not understand that it could be forgiven;
for what sin was more terrible?" The killing of one's own offspring, the arresting of
biological continuity, insofar as it cannot be justified by reference to human vitality,
qualifies representatively as a senseless act of death. Abraham is in no position to justify
his conduct as life-giving—his faith depends on precisely his inability to do this. If his
faith is to be proven, it has to be blind.

To be sure, the story justifies this justification of Abraham's conduct (justification by
faith) by rewarding him in fact with life. But there is something fishy about the logic of
this reward. Perhaps the story implies that although Abraham can know God's order
only as death-dealing, because it issues from God he can trust that the order is issued
actually on behalf of life. But even in this interpretation, the fundamental good of life
is given short shrift. It is subordinated to the interest in God, but a god depicted as
concerned primarily with the preservation of his position as God and only secondarily
with the principle of vitality. In this narrative figure, God speaks in the language of men
and is concerned to test their faith. The anthropocentric reductionism here is registered
in the story's treatment of the principle of vitality, which, in the cause of securing faith,
is patently instrumentalized.

Notice that the trouble is not that God is pictured in the dual terms of both life and
death. Such a picture only stands to reason. Rather, the trouble is that owing to the story's
elevation of faith over life as the 'first principle', the relationship between these two sides
of the same coin of the realm of animate existence is mediated so substantially as to give
death dominion in its own right. By tying it to the axiomatic supersession of the good of
life by patriarchy, death is no longer perceived as a condition of life but as an independent
phenomenon. It is so introduced in God's command at the beginning of the story: without so much as a how-do-you-do to the poor man—never mind an explanation in terms
of life—God, keen to prove Abraham, calls to him and simply instructs him to put his
beloved son to death. In virtue of this opening command, this test, that which primarily
conditions life in the story is not death but heedfulness of patriarchal authority. If this
observation is correct, then the promise of life to Abraham as a reward for his conduct
is, rather than what one might expect, an unqualified non sequitur. The very nature
of this reward implicitly and irrefutably defines his faithful but murderous conduct as
malevolent: where life is the essence of the good, and death is other than a condition of
life, there death must be what makes the bad bad. My point is, then, that by virtue of the
normative tenor of the primary world, the world in which we come to terms not only
with one another but also with otherness as such, Abraham's actions as well as the command that prescribes them cannot help but convey malevolence.[28]

Chapter 3

EXCURSUS I
Sacrifice as Human Existence

What makes human sacrifice something deep and sinister anyway? Is it only the suffering of the victim that impresses us in this way? All manner of diseases bring just as much suffering and do *not* make this impression. No, this deep and sinister aspect is not obvious just from learning the history of the external action, but *we* impute it from an experience in ourselves.

— Ludwig Wittgenstein, "Remarks on Frazer's *Golden Bough*"

Derrida's Kierkegaard

I have sought to address the profoundly vexing questions raised by God's murderous command to Abraham and Abraham's astonishing response. In my view, although it projects a malevolently mistaken, even stupid, picture of the prescriptive importance of absolute faith for human life (which is not to say that we can do without faith), the story features, fruitfully and with penetrating balance, the vital importance of an economy of sacrifice for human beings. But even should one find this reading productive, one might still wonder why the story couches these lessons in terms of sacrifice. That is to say, the questions of the command to Abraham and Abraham's response to it are one thing, while the question of why Abraham's terrible trial must proceed by sacrifice is quite another. Why does this religious story about the critical conditions of human life present itself in the terms of sacrifice?

In his foreword to Hubert and Mauss's (1964) classic study, Evans-Pritchard (ibid.: viii) remarks that the "literature on sacrifice is enormous," and in their introduction

Hubert and Mauss (ibid.: 1) observe that "[t]heories of sacrifice are as old as religions." I have no need here to try to review this literature and these theories. For my purposes, it suffices to suggest that for the most part, however varied it is, the literature displays the following as a usual feature: it takes as the object of study, and tries to explain, sacrifice considered as a rite. The guiding presupposition is, to quote Evans-Pritchard's expression of agreement with Robertson Smith (in Hubert and Mauss 1964: vii): "'[S]*acrificium*' is the basic rite in ancient (and primitive) religion." No matter, then, whether the theories are evolutionary, functionalist, structuralist, or something else; they tend to treat sacrifice as a constituent element of religion as such.[1]

In the present study, by contrast, sacrifice is grasped as in the first place—before it appears as a ritual practice and component of institutional religion—a structure of human social existence. By seeing sacrifice in this way, its ubiquity as a religious rite is made easier to comprehend. If religion, well differentiated as such or not, is understood as a prescriptive practice bearing on the spiritual aspect of being human, then it is not surprising that sacrifice enjoys so prominent a place in religions. For, speaking very broadly, the spiritual aspect of human existence has always to do with the question of what is owing to otherness considered as that which is ultimately irreducible to the self, and thus makes of religion a sacrificial practice of one kind or another.[2] I do not aim here to give a minimum definition of religion, but merely to suggest that inasmuch as all religions are keyed to a sense of self as vitally bound to a higher power, all logically entail sacrificial conduct, which is, ideally, self-abnegation of some sort. Exactly how this concern for otherness manifests itself in any particular ritual sacrifice is a matter for empirical research and interpretive analysis. For instance, in the previous chapter I tried to show, among other things, that displacement and indebtedness stand at the bottom of the Akedah, and in the next chapter I offer an interpretation of the Holocaust in terms of sacrifice similarly considered.

This conception of sacrifice as the dynamic structure of human existence suggests that neither sacrifice nor violence can be eradicated. Nevertheless, it also implies that sacrifice can take forms more irenic than utterly violent or powerful, and other than bloody or holocaustic. For all its murderous message, the Akedah provides an instruction on how to quit homicide as such, and, by implication, ultimately, bloody sacrifice altogether. Indeed, 'modern' religion is marked by its formal refusal of sacrifice of this kind, although all too obviously such sacrifice remains thematic in characteristic domains of modern life, including most conspicuously warfare.[3]

My answer, then, to the question of why Abraham's trial is framed as a matter of sacrifice is that the story is about the terms of human existence, and that it implicitly understands the structure of this existence as sacrifice. That is to say, it implies that ultimately there is no distinction to be made between sacrifice and any action that is peculiarly human—all human action has the form of sacrifice.

We can get our bearings here by examining Jacques Derrida's (1995) interpretation of the Akedah. More exactly, Derrida's is a tendentious reading of Kierkegaard's interpretation. The good Frenchman is primarily concerned to rethink the nature of the great Dane's axial distinction between what Abraham owes to his fellow humans and what he owes to God. According to Kierkegaard, the distinction tells the difference between ethical and religious obligation, and the latter sort of obligation necessarily takes precedence over the former, because it alone may be construed as absolute.

By reconceiving the god-figure in the story—generalizing (or, as Derrida would say, "disseminating") it away from the particularity of at least the revelatory religions—as purely and simply what is wholly other, Derrida mitigates the distinction. Propounding the dictum *tout autre est tout autre* ("every other is wholly other" or, as translated in the book, "every other (one) is every (bit) other"), Derrida argues that inasmuch as all others, including non-human animals, do in fact display what is wholly other, our obligation to them is also absolute. It is, he says (1995: 83), a question of recognizing in the "infinite alterity of the wholly other, every other, in other words each, each one, for example each man and woman." Kierkegaard conceives of the (religious) obligation to God in terms of singularity, as utterly unexampled, while he depicts the (ethical) obligation to all the others in (Hegelian) terms of generality. Derrida's point is that each of the other others is also a singularity, a unique being, and therewith wholly other and deserving of the attendant obligatory respect.

As Derrida sees it, this universalizing (but not 'universalist') reinterpretation does not so much refute Kierkegaard as supplement his point. It displaces Kierkegaard's emphasis on the absolute uniqueness of God, such that the extraordinary is disseminated, adding force to Kierkegaard's text—the force, I suppose, of being apprised that at each instant each of us is existentially tied to death-by-sacrifice, that is, to (as in the title of Derrida's book) the gift of death. This, Derrida (1995: 79) seems to hold, is the great force of the story of Abraham and Isaac, what makes (re)interpretation of the story so abidingly attractive. If we take Derrida's point, then, however intellectually perplexed we find ourselves as to the story's nature, at the level of existence we cannot but identify with Abraham and his dilemma.

The Akedah as the Human Condition

Derrida's reinterpretation has more than one notable consequence, to be sure. But for purposes at hand, the most outstanding is that it describes all self-other relations, that is, all human relations, as relations of sacrifice. In the Akedah, Abraham, feeling pre-emptively bound by God's order, finds it necessary to disregard—to sacrifice—what is owed to all lesser others, including to his own son (and, of course, to Sarah). Derrida's point is that this sacrificial turn of events is not extraordinary but in fact our quotidian condition. For insofar as we fulfill our obligation to any particular other, we are necessarily failing to do so to all the other others. In effect, we exist by virtue of sacrificing others. Such is the very structure of our conduct. Whatever we do in our agential capacity as responsible beings, that is, as humans, we necessarily manage to displace ourselves and/or others. Derrida's illustrations of this existential condition are impressive (1995: 69):

> By preferring my work, simply by giving it my time and attention, by preferring my activity as a citizen or as a professorial and professional philosopher, writing … in a public language, French in my case, I am perhaps fulfilling my duty. But I am sacrificing and betraying at every moment all my other obligations; my obligations to the other others whom I know or don't know, the billions of my fellows (without mentioning the animals that are even more other others than my fellows), my fellows who are dying of starvation or sickness. I betray my fidelity or my obligations to other citizens, to those who don't speak my language and to whom I neither speak nor respond, to each of those who listen or read, and to whom I

neither respond nor address myself in the proper manner, that is, in a singular manner (this for the so-called public space to which I sacrifice my so-called private space), thus also to those I love in private, my own, my family, my son, each of whom is the only son I sacrifice to the other, every one being sacrificed to every one else in this land of Moriah that is our habitat every second of every day.

Here Derrida manages to describe how sacrifice characterizes the entirety of our lives. He shows the ineluctable sacrificial nexus between his personal preferences and his obligations to his nation ("citizens"), the international community ("those who don't speak my language"), the creaturely world in general ("the animals that are even more other others than my fellows"), and, indeed, to his own "private" life, his family and each of its members in all of their singularity. A little later he goes on, as follows, to suggest that although it hardly would occur to us to think that the criminally murderous event described by the Akedah is any more than a scriptural account with a theological wallop, in fact not only does it happen in today's world, but we ourselves, simply by virtue of the "smooth functioning" of the social order in which we live, with its pronounced rule of law and moral discourse, organize it on a routine and massive scale (ibid.: 85–86):

> The sacrifice of Isaac is an abomination in the eyes of all, and it should continue to be seen for what it is—atrocious, criminal, unforgivable; Kierkegaard insists on that. The ethical point of view must remain valid: Abraham is a murderer. However, is it not true that the spectacle of this murder ... is at the same time the most common event in the world? Is it not inscribed in the structure of our existence to the extent of no longer constituting an event? It will be said that it would be most improbable for the sacrifice of Isaac to be repeated in our day; and it certainly seems that way ... Things are such that this man [Abraham] would surely be condemned by any civilized society. On the other hand, the smooth functioning of such a society, the monotonous complacency of its discourses on morality, politics, and the law, and the exercise of its rights (whether public, private, national or international), are in no way impaired by the fact that, because of the structure of the laws of the market that society has instituted and controls, because of the mechanisms of external debt and other similar inequities, that same "society" *puts to* death or (but failing to help someone in distress accounts for only a minor difference) *allows* to die of hunger and disease tens of millions of children (those neighbors or fellow humans that ethics or the discourse of the rights of man refer to) without any moral or legal tribunal ever being considered competent to judge such a sacrifice, the sacrifice of others to avoid being sacrificed oneself. Not only is it true that such a society participates in this incalculable sacrifice, it actually organizes it. The smooth functioning of its economic, political, and legal affairs, the smooth functioning of its moral discourse and good conscience presupposes the permanent operation of this sacrifice.[4]

Derrida is most critically concerned in these passages to show that our moral and ethical decisions are never finally justifiable, that at the end of the day we have no way to truly account for our various 'choices', all of which somehow involve the sacrifice of others, whoever or whatever they may be, on the altar of still other others. This is the case, as Derrida sees it, whether these choices are well considered or simply lived. In the penultimate chapter of this book, I will return to the vital question of ethical justification. For present purposes, though, what is important about these passages is their effective description of sacrifice as, in Derrida's words, "inscribed in the structure of our existence." Again, Derrida's stunning assertion that society operates necessarily according to, one might say, a hypocritical oath, whereby "the smooth functioning" of any social order's "moral discourse and good conscience" depends on permanent "incalculable sacrifice [of others]," is for the moment beside the point. The point I wish to make is, rather, this: being human, that is, conducting oneself in a manner that identifies one as human, takes the form of sacrifice. By no means does this mean that all forms of sacrifice (human, animal, vegetable, self, other, etc.) are ethically of equal weight or character; it just means that being human may be described as a sacrificial dynamic.

It is important to be clear that this picture of human existence in terms of sacrifice constitutes a description, not a theory, of that existence. It explains nothing. Instead, it is a way of looking at being human, a way distinguished, in my view (which may or may not be Derrida's), by its overriding prejudice for ethics. That is to say, it is a picture of human existence as, above all, ethics—a discretionary dynamic keyed to the good and bearing principally on the displacement of self and other. Hence, Derrida finds that whatever our preferences, in executing them, we betray all the obligations that they necessarily pre-empt: in preferring our professional duties, we fail to discharge non-professional ones; in preferring our public commitments, we fail to discharge private ones; in preferring our native tongue, we fail to give way to other languages; in preferring our cultural habits, we fail to make room for other cultures. These sacrificed obligations constitute 'Isaacs', as it were—sons and daughters all.

Self-Sacrifice and the Question of Responsibility

What is curious about Derrida's discourse here, however, is that it is couched largely in terms of the other, of how the discharge of our duties to the Other and to others displaces or sacrifices our duties to still other others. The 'self' is scarcely mentioned by him. Even so, the idea of the self is presupposed throughout his argument; indeed, it seems to serve therein as the blind spot of the eye of one's moral perception. The obligations of which he speaks, whether fulfilled or forgone, are meaningful as obligations only in virtue of self-responsible beings. His point seems to be that, as against the understanding of the usual moralisms, responsibility is fundamentally paradoxical. In Derrida's picture of things, it is impossible for the self to discharge its responsibilities to the other without at the same time being significantly irresponsible. Still, by failing to speak openly in terms of the self, he sidesteps a crucial question in relation to responsibility, namely, the question of self-sacrifice.

Derrida does, though, acknowledge the possibility of self-sacrifice. At one point in his text (1995: 69), after speaking of the sacrificial offering in the Akedah as *both* Isaac and Abraham, he feels obliged to remark parenthetically, "and it is the sacrifice of both of them, it is the gift of death one makes to the other in putting *oneself* to death, mortifying oneself in order to make a gift of this death as a sacrificial offering to God." Yet as we have seen, he basically debates the question of sacrifice in terms of the displacing of others, not of the self. Given that from the perspective of others one's self is also an other (it is so even to oneself, as when one turns one's gaze on oneself), perhaps Derrida means to include the possibility of self-sacrifice under the rubric of the sacrifice of others. In any event, self-sacrifice, while giving life to the other, would entail the irresponsibility of taking life from the other that is the self.

But even if this is the case, Derrida still manages to avoid addressing directly the question of self-sacrifice. It is reasonable to construe the self that is at stake in self-sacrifice as an 'other'. But it can never be just another other, for this sort of other is characterized by a uniquely incarnate co-incidence with the sacrificing self, such that it must bear peculiarly (but not exclusively) the responsibility for the act of sacrifice. In other words, the identity between the victim and sacrificer is, although irredeemably and significantly imperfect, so substantive and imposing that the victim is responsible for the sacrifice in a distinctive way.

In Genesis 22, Abraham is twice called by God and once by Isaac. Each time Abraham responds "Here am I." This phrase (Heb. *heneni*) amounts to an announcement of individual responsibility. In effect, in answering thus to his son and to God, Abraham declares that he, Abraham, inasmuch as he *himself is*, is owing to each. It is as if he said, "Here I am—me, myself, and I—on the proverbial spot!" Derrida too understands the phrase in just such terms of individual responsibility (1995: 71): "God ... addresses Abraham who has just said: 'Here I am.' 'Here I am': the first and only possible response to the call by the other, the originary moment of responsibility such as it exposes me to the singular other, the one who appeals to me. 'Here I am' is the only self-presentation presumed by every form of responsibility: I am ready to respond, I reply that I am ready to respond."[5] The point is that having responded "Here am I" to the address by the other, the other that is the self becomes the *self*-responsible other, which is to say, the self. Therefore, even if one wishes to identify as a kind of other the self that is at stake in an act of sacrifice, there remains a critical difference between sacrifice of this sort of other and of the sort we are inclined to think of as surrogatory. This is the difference between, in ordinary parlance, self-sacrifice and the sacrifice of others.

It is crucial to take care not to fall into the dualist trap of thinking of this difference as complete. If the self is always other to itself, then, obviously, the difference at point must be relative rather than absolute. In which case, responsibility too must be essentially relative. The relative character of responsibility is what Derrida is driving at when he maintains that for every responsibility discharged another necessarily goes begging. But in relation to the difference between self- and other-sacrifice, this relativity has yet another aspect: it means that responsibility can never be attributed unequivocally to a self. If the self is always in some measure other to itself, then plainly it cannot be wholly responsible for 'its' acts. The implications of this observation are shatteringly powerful. To the extent that one is other to oneself, the other must share in the responsibility for one's acts. Conversely, as the other of other selves, one is always also responsible for what the other does. In effect, as selves, that is, as uniquely discretionary beings, we are responsible not only *to* but also *for* the other. Put another way, just as one can never be held totally accountable, so, insofar as one enjoys a self, one can never be without some responsibility for what happens.

The fact that the difference between self- and other-sacrifice is relative, though, scarcely means that it is a difference that makes no difference. On the contrary, as is my main emphasis here, this difference is an element of the logic of existence as sacrifice. Because the fundamentally ethical character of that logic turns on it, this difference could not be more critical. On it rests the possibility of assessing responsibility at all: in the absence of any such difference, in which the self is identified as a self, as a reflexive and therefore agential being, 'responsibility' would be not simply relative but utterly meaningless. In which case, of course, there could be no moral universe, no world in which it makes sense to speak of even a relative difference between good and bad. But the fact of the matter is that the difference between self- and other-sacrifice (as between good and bad), fundamentally relative though it may be, will not go away. It seems undeniable that despite the intrinsically fuzzy boundary between self and other, axiologically it more or less amounts to one thing to offer up oneself on behalf of another, and something else to sacrifice the other on behalf of oneself. To think otherwise would be to deny that whether Abraham kills himself directly or does so (more profoundly) by making Isaac his proxy is significant. But it could not be more obvious that the Akedah would not have the same axiological force if Abraham had chosen directly to bind himself instead of Isaac—the story virtually turns on the son as the designated offering. Or, in anticipation of the chapter to follow, to take an example wherein the lack of ambiguity is even more conspicuous, to deny the difference between self- and other-sacrifice would be to deny that it would have made any significant difference if Hitler had chosen to kill himself instead of the Jews.

Chapter 4

COUNTER-SACRIFICE AND INSTRUMENTAL
REASON—THE HOLOCAUST

I thought about the victims. Plucked clean, people entered the circus with numbers around their necks ... They were forced to jump, perform, and listen to the sound of a whip. What sort of martyrs could they be! They didn't want to accept suffering, but it never occurred to them to struggle for a martyr's crown ... They ... would have burned the ark of the covenant if it had been available. They would walk on their heads if they were ordered to, and they would change their faith three times a week. They only wanted to live ... But they had been selected to be sacrificed, to die for something, for a cause that wasn't their cause.

— Jiří Weil, *Life with a Star*

I had to hold fast till the end, and die of living.

— Charlotte Delbo, *Auschwitz and After*

Because culture abhors an ethical vacuum, instrumentalism as value cannot hold. A return to value-as-such—value that, while not exclusive of instrumentality, is sui generis and irreducible to instrumentalism—is therefore inevitable. This consideration, though, should give the proponents of an ethical approach no cause for complacency. The self-destructive movement of unbridled instrumental reason may be logically inevitable, but this condition dictates nothing about the tenure of instrumental reason's predominance or the magnitude of the dreadful moral and material consequences of its course of self-destruction.

I aim to show here, for one thing, the 'suicidal' telos of unqualified instrumental reason, committed as it is to destroying itself by concretely taking the lives, in one way or another—including outright murder—of those who fall in with or in the way of its presumption. For all its proven and substantial promise of benefit, instrumental rationality is always peculiarly sociocidal. But it is not always apparently so. To see plainly the alarming possibility of human suffering implicit in instrumentalism's self-destructive advance, it is important to look at an example in which instrumental reason was allowed to have its way largely unobstructed by other relevant principles or values, which lent themselves, by virtue of their own character, too readily to instrumentalist reduction. When combined with dualism, the decided predisposition of these particular values fostered about as pervasively penetrating an instrumentalism as one can imagine in the context of human social existence. Dualism logically demands not a tensile and continuing dialectical reversal of the order of opposing principles (in this instance, value and utility), but rather the exclusion (or eradication) of one of the two principles altogether (in this instance, value), thus collapsing the dialectic and, in a fatefully meaningful sense, stopping time. The example I have in mind is the Holocaust.[1] In adducing this example, my purpose is both to bring into relief the terrible material, human significance of instrumental reason's predisposition to undermine itself and to offer understanding of the genocide perpetrated by the Nazis

Because the facts of the Holocaust are well known, there is no need here to make a case about the stunning human toll taken by the Nazi endeavor to annihilate the Jews and other groups of people regarded by the Nazis as undesirable. A look at, for instance, Raul Hilberg's (1985) classic history is enough to set the record, if not straight (for there is much for historians to debate), at least commandingly attested.[2] What is at point here is the radical question of how to understand what happened, how to comprehend it. What happened so violated the modern idea of humanity that it made nonsense of the taken-for-granted social-evolutionary conception to which that idea serves as the normative core—namely, civilization. Despite the supreme difficulty of interpreting the Holocaust, the attempt to do so must be made, and there exists a range of arresting, insightful, and ethically profound accounts.

The interpretation to follow makes especial use of two kinds of these accounts. One centers on, as just broached, the contribution of unqualified instrumental reason. The other takes up a condition under which such reason was given free rein to move to its own logical conclusion—in the "geometric madness"[3] of the death camps. The condition I have in mind is religious intentionality. While rationality and technology might have enabled an unprecedented realization of a certain religious impulse to perverse power, the terrible, implicit promise of that very mythic power imbued the instrument of reason with a mighty existential force.

What I have to say here is consistent with the thesis that the Holocaust is (or has become) emblematic, even as it also remains, as does every atrocity, a "*unicum.*"[4] I picture what happened not as an aberration but as one conceivable phenomenological conclusion of Western thought and practice. To be sure, if the Holocaust is somehow continuous with Western understanding, it has to be open to an imposition of meaning in terms of that understanding. This must be the case despite the radically nihilistic way in which such events rend the moral fabric by virtue of which civilization has sought to make itself meaningful. I agree here with Giorgio Agamben (2000: 41) when he opines that it is hypocritical to ask how people could have done such atrocious things (as if acts of this kind do not come naturally enough to humans), and that the only really fruitful question asks under what conditions people do come to do these things. Although my argument features in this connection instrumental rationality, National Socialism hardly lacked a proliferous framework of values. But this framework lent itself peculiarly to instrumentalism and, paradoxically, to the eradication of value-as-such.[5]

Most critically, the explanation given here locates the meaning of the Holocaust, at least in large part, in the Judeo-Christian mythical paradigm of sacrifice. More specifically, the death camps realized an identitarian possibility profoundly implicit in that paradigm and perpetually experienced, by those routinely informed by that paradigm, including the religious and non-religious alike, as temptation. The temptation of which I speak is to a self-identification whose defining axis is predicated directly on absolute power over life and death and, correlatively, on the ultimate instrumentalization of human existence.

The interpretation offered here helps, I think, to make intelligible the "useless cruelty" suffered by the victims of the Nazis, but, most emphatically, not by extending to it any redeeming value.[6] On the contrary, the temptation built into the Judeo-Christian paradigm of sacrifice, as a negative 'value', is precisely to an order of things in which value-as-such does not exist, and which amounts, thereby, to a universe in which death alone has dominion. In the absence of genuine value—that is, of an end irreducible to sheer means—the only end that can confer meaning is death itself. Death becomes not merely the inevitable endpoint of organic human existence but, stupidly, the end to which that existence willfully aspires in order to realize itself as meaningful being.[7] Put another way, in the interpretation given here, one deep meaning of the Holocaust issues directly from the nihilistic order obtaining inherently as enticement—the temptation of temptation—in the Judeo-Christian ethos and definitive of meaninglessness in this ethic's mythico-semantic universe.[8]

There is an underlying 'logic' to the Nazi project of extermination, but it is a lived rather than logical logic. Doubtless, many of those who participated in these horrific acts were motivated out of fear or bureaucratic ambition or military sense of duty or peer pressure or anti-Semitism, etc. At bottom, though, atrocious acts on this scale and of this magnitude are not so much questions of motivation as of utmost self-identity, that identity whereby primordial choices are immediately revealed and without which one would have no idea of who one is or where one stands in the world. Instead of one thing moving another, acts of this kind describe self-movement, a near-natural conduct presenting a second nature. In effect, they virtually constitute their own end. In the case at hand, the acts in question exhibit a perverse logic of sacrifice. Because it is informed—dualistically—by a sense of self-perfectibility, this logic inverts the vital purpose of sacrifice, making it purely homicidal. Conceived of on the basis of perfectibilism, sacrifice projects only two logical conclusions: either unqualified self-immolation or total other-liquidation. Both of these conclusions are murderous without concession to a reverence for life, a reverence that is profoundly complicated by the consideration that human life as such is meaningful only insofar as it transcends bare biological existence. Because the logic in question is embodied before it is discursively articulated, it clarifies how something so patently abstract as rationality can manifest itself in act before word, as practice. Once it is assimilated to a primordial choice, such an abstraction becomes, rather than an instrument of one's thoughts, part of the scaffolding of one's self-identity and thus immediately actionable.

There is one more feature of my interpretation that is important to mention at the outset: although it aims to make the Holocaust intelligible, at the same time it indulges no determinism, whether causal or interpretative. If the meaning of the Holocaust rests with nihilism powerfully implicit in the sacrificial paradigm that defines, in the Western tradition, what it means to be a human being, then that meaning functions explanatively by reference to the idea of choice, not cause. For, as was detailed in the last two chapters, the Judeo-Christian paradigm of sacrifice describes human existence as a conduct of choice. It is for this reason that the nihilism lodged as an existential possibility in this paradigm can be viewed as temptation rather than inevitability. It is crucial to understand this character of the interpretation, for it means that although it may make the project of the death camps comprehensible, in no way does it displace the question of responsibility. On the contrary, it does its work by directly confronting this question.

The argument proceeds in four basic steps, the first three of which bear squarely on the question of rationality. First, drawing on a reconsideration of Kant's moral thought, by Berel Lang and in line with postmodern criticism of the Enlightenment, I propose not that universalist reason was the sole or even pre-eminent cause of the Holocaust, but that—although not a sufficient one—it was a necessary condition of the *possibility* of the Holocaust. Second, bringing instrumentalist reason into account, I argue, following Louis Dumont's iconoclastic analysis, that the Nazi ideology exhibits, rather than a genuine social holism, a grave individualism. Third, I link Kant's ethical universalism to individualism by reference to dualistic thinking and the concomitant conception of boundaries as immaculate rather than fluid.

The fourth—and most essential—step turns to the issue of sacrifice. Appropriating and thus transforming to phenomenology and ethics Richard Rubenstein's deep psychoanalytical treatment of the death camps, I bring out the existential bearings of theoretical concepts so roundly abstract as universal reason, individualism, and dualism. That is, I point to the mechanism by which they can become synthetic a priori, such that their realization is guaranteed by the thoughtless, routine performance of everyday life. I do so by offering an 'ontology' of human existence as a structural dynamic of self-identifying in relation to the other. This dynamic necessarily takes the form of sacrifice: whatever self-identity the dynamic realizes can exist only at the expense of either self or other. Selfhood can occur only by displacing its own and/or an-other self, describing a process of give-and-take. This last step of the argument is the most pivotal for my overall enterprise. It carries forward the axial ontological step taken in the last chapter, in which I redefine human existence, inclusively, as the conduct of sacrifice. By picturing human existence and the conduct of sacrifice as one and the same, I position myself to show the way in which dualism, and the rationality it disposes, can be embodied in human acts of mass death. By way of the Judeo-Christian mythic tradition of sacrificial and discretionary existence, the living of which issues in, in fundamental part, Western man's self-identity as Man, and the logic of which entails perfection as a delusory and fatal but immensely alluring, even gravitative, end, unqualified instrumental reason can come to be incorporated seamlessly in the fabric of our selfhood so as to manifest itself immediately as practice.[9]

Universal and Instrumental Reason

The Claims of Particularism

According to the present account, Nazism was in critical part a product of modern reason, more especially, of 'enlightened' reason. The argument has been focused and articulated with care by Berel Lang (1990: chap. 7). He asserts that Nazism's genocidal ends are critically linked to the Enlightenment's diagnostic goal of freeing humans from institutional and historical authority, and for intellectual and moral autonomy. This goal is predicated on the faculty of self-responsible reason, considered as a universal human capacity. As is crucial to Lang's argument, in Enlightenment thought the capacity of self-responsible reason comes to define the very identity of 'human being'.

Using Kant as a central figure of the Enlightenment, Lang observes that in Kant's writings, what makes something reasonable, including ethical judgments, is universalizability. Accordingly, for Kant, a course of action is moral only inasmuch as it can be applied universally, without contradiction, and an agent is moral only inasmuch as his or her conduct exhibits the faculty of universal reason. These two conditions of morality are plain to see in two of Kant's formulations of his famous notion of the categorical imperative: (1) a reason is moral, which is to say, a genuine reason, only if it is a logically consistent reason for all agents in a relevantly similar situation (that is, only if it is universalizable); and (2) only every rational being, that is, only every being capable of universal reason, should be treated as an end in him- or herself (that is, as an agent).

In view of the significant internal diversity of Enlightenment philosophy, it is important to be clear that Lang is not arguing that Kant is *the* representative thinker of the Enlightenment. He is merely contending that the two themes central for Kant's thought identify Kant "with central themes of the Enlightenment more generally" (1990: 180). The two themes are described by Lang as "[1] the impulse for universalization in the account of human nature and as a principle of both moral and theoretical 'conduct,' and [2] the autonomous, nonhistorical … self" (ibid.).

As I read him, Lang maintains that under this principle of universalizability, any claim for particularism is in principle not only contrary to rationality but also presumptively inferior and open to arbitrary evaluation. In part, therefore, trouble comes in relation to the question of what to do about claims for particularism. They are by definition 'violations' of the moral law. But because they obtain outside the universe of rational judgment, their value is subject to arbitrary decision.

In relation to arbitrariness, though, Lang seems to make an additional, even stronger point. If I understand him correctly, he argues not only that the principle of universalizability is helpless when it comes to evaluating claims for particularism, but also that that principle cannot decide when an agent's self is in fact consistent with self-responsible reason. Since the principle of universalizability is purely formal, it cannot appeal to empirical evidence in order to arrive at a judgment.[10] Therefore, the principle can furnish no sure way to tell whether an agent has acted out of self-responsible reason rather than something else. Without knowing what exactly the initiator of an act had in mind, however reasonable the act may appear by objective standards, how can one know whether or not that person has acted out of reason? Of course, often one can ask an agent to account for her actions. But since any agent is always situated in particular circumstances and therefore can never clearly qualify as a disinterested observer, her testimony will always be suspect. ("In actual fact it is absolutely impossible," writes Kant [1964: 74–75], "for experience to establish with complete certainty a single case in which the maxim of an action in other respects right has rested solely on moral grounds and on the thought of one's duty ... We are pleased to flatter ourselves with the false claim to a nobler motive, but in fact we can never, even by the most strenuous self-examination, get to the bottom of our secret impulsions.")

In light of this argument, and of certain historical particulars of the Holocaust, the Nazi genocide takes on, although not inevitability, a kind of likelihood. National Socialism was nothing if not consumed with the principle of universalizability: "It was not only that the Nazis repeatedly emphasized that they were thinking always of their own place vis-à-vis everyone else but that the principle of universalization was applied wherever they had power; they had, in effect, incorporated that principle into nationalism. In doing this, the Nazis were in effect urging the replacement of history by a version of reason" (Lang 1990: 192).

The Jews, on the other hand, with their insistence on identifying themselves on the basis of historical particularism, were easily made to represent the claim for particularistic evaluation as against the Nazi's universalistic ambitions. Moreover, in light of the radically imposing nature of self-identity staked by the Nazis to the principle of universalizability, the particularism of Jewish identity came to define the Jews as the less-than-human counterpart to the comprehensive humanity of the Nazis.[11] Given the presumptive inferiority of the particular in 'Enlightened' thought, and the huge space left for arbitrary judgment by the principled incapacity of the rule of universalizability to decide on particularities and determine intentionality, the Jews were not only a 'natural' target of the Nazi's drive to universalize Nazism—they were also a people denied in principle any way to redeem themselves. Indeed, there were no principled limits on the Nazis in how they chose to treat the violation presented by Jewish particularism. Here is a pivotal moment in Lang's argument to this effect (1990: 187–88):

> The [Enlightenment] conceptions thus outlined mark out an analogy between the elements embodied in the "principle" of genocide ... and the structural form exemplified in the conceptions of the universal self and of the ahistorical, universalizing judgment which have been proposed here as basic themes of Enlightenment thought. In the conceptual framework presupposed in the phenomenon of genocide, a crucial distinction is asserted between members of a group to whom certain rights are ascribed by virtue of that membership and individuals who are not members of that group, whose humanity is thus brought into question and whose "rights" then become contestable. Furthermore, if the rights at issue ... are fundamental—for example, as such a definition might distinguish between humans and subhumans—exclusion from the first group means that virtually no controls remain for the determination of the status (or rights) of those who are excluded. This does not by itself ensure that the consequences of such exclusion will be severe, but it does mean that there are no limits *in principle* to what those consequences may bring. The fact of difference becomes in effect a prima-facie justification for whatever response is made.

Lang is not arguing that the Nazi genocide was an inevitable result of Kantian thought.[12] Rather, his point is that the genocide made manifest a certain latent conceptual content of that thought. The fact, then, that Nazism stood self-consciously opposed to the humanism and liberalism of Enlightenment ideals makes no significant difference to Lang's position, for he is proposing that an affiliation of thought took place on the plane of "the internal structure of ideas" (ibid.: 194), not that the Nazi ideology extolled an Enlightenment program.

One might be tempted to think, on the basis of Lang's argument, that had Kant admitted claims for particularism into his moral philosophy, the Nazi genocide would not have occurred or at least would have been made a less likely turn of events. Lang (1990: 199) does indeed point, by contrast, to a Western "anti-utopian" tradition opposed to "notions of human perfectibility and a universalist standard of human nature and society on which such notions are based." In this tradition, which received perhaps its "single most important formulation" by Aristotle, "the pluralist view dominates" (ibid.). The issue, though, is not whether particularistic claims are admitted, but whether they are admissible. Of course, the Nazis could not have failed to bring such claims into consideration. But because the claims had to be regarded as fundamentally inadmissible, they were subject to arbitrary elimination along with their claimants.

As opposed to Lang's position, it is both sensible and more intuitive to argue that in their bid to utterly except whole bodies of people from the human world, it is the Nazis who best represent particularism, and that, given their foundational role in the rise of Western civilization, it is the Jews who exemplify universalism. According to Bauman (1988: 50), the Jewish tradition is the one and only "particularity" that "gave credence to the program of universalization." But the truth of this inverse perspective notwithstanding, it is crucial to stay focused here on the force of Lang's point about the linkage between Kantian universalism and Hitlerism: that the National Socialist ideology of universal and timeless sovereignty assumed for Nazism the mantle of absolute reason, and therewith the charge of ridding the world of any self-identity that could be construed as anathematic to such presumption. Given this point of view, the Jews, who, in the face of the powerful advance of Western universalism—which is to say, against all reason—managed to maintain their identity as 'the chosen people', presented an archetype of such odious particularism.

Modern Individualism and Hitlerian Racism

Lang's philosophical argument receives novel support from Louis Dumont's bold anthropological investigation of German ideology and Hitlerian totalitarianism. In his critical study of the rise and nature of economic ideology, Dumont (1977) suggests that Nazism has to be understood in terms of modern ideology. Although the Nazi ideology invoked holism, the holism in question presupposed a radical individualism and therefore was substantially different from the 'authentic' social holism often associated with past social orders.[13] Dumont argues that the Nazi totalitarianism resulted from the attempt to subordinate a deeply rooted and predominant individualism to the primacy of society as a whole. Such a titanic contradiction, he finds, is bound to manifest itself as violence (ibid.: 10ff.). What Dumont seems to have in mind is (apropos of Lang's position) this: since it operates in a context of well-developed individualism, such pseudo-holism cannot but be suppressive. What it suppresses, of course, is the individual or particular, which, although now prominent, has been ruled out of order.

In order to demonstrate this thesis, Dumont undertook an intensive study of German ideology and Hitler's thought (1986: chaps. 4–6). Basically consistent with Lang's account, Dumont finds that on behalf of their claim to paradigmatic social holism, the Nazis depicted the Jews as the representatives of selfish individualism, in stark contrast to themselves as an 'Aryan' people always prepared to make supreme sacrifice in the interest of the social whole.[14] The opposition between themselves and the Jews, then, amounted to a transformation of that between the social whole and the individual. In the case of the Jews, the violent and absolute nature of this opposition was fixed by biological reference, in a perversely Darwinian appeal to racial difference and instrumental competition over sheer physical existence. Thus, instead of a social world in which the hierarchical primacy of the whole over the part is implicit and conditional on value-as-such, National Socialism constructed a world in which the pre-eminence of the whole depended on the forcible exclusion of 'the individual' and its (alleged) societal representatives.

As Dumont saw it, then, the Nazi construction really presented an inversion of an authentic social whole. The Nazi hierarchy of whole and part was Hobbesian rather than 'true', constituted by an artful and atomistic relationship of *Führerprinzip* (Dumont 1986: 169): "the great Nazi parade in which each human atom marches past in goose step and where the Führer, the sole object of each one's faithfulness, vociferates from above as in a trance where each one's anxiety is transmuted into numberless force." The resulting hierarchy was, as Hobbes would have had it, but an artificial man. For Dumont, the most critical point to understand about Hitlerism is the fundamental way in which it was based on "modern individualism," on the equalitarian idea of the individual as wholly autonomous. Indeed, with an insight that runs well beyond his structuralist persuasion, Dumont goes so far as to submit (ibid.: 168), "Hitler projected onto the Jews the individualist tendency he felt within himself as threatening his 'Aryan' devotion to the community."

Lang (1990: 195) cites Dumont's study in relation to the consideration that Nazi particularism—the movement's intense nationalism and rabid emphasis on distinguishing Aryans from others—was ideologically bound up with a ruthless (Kantian) universalism. Herein rests a deep consistency between Lang's argument about Kant and Dumont's contention that Nazism is essentially an ideology of individualism, for Kant's "universal reason," let us not forget, constitutes a principle of radical individualism (cf. Taylor 1989: 363ff.).[15] In Lang's argument, the kind of universalism in question can allow no distinctions outside of that of the Aryan nation itself. For Dumont, the universalism of the Nazi social whole stems from and finds its nemesis in that of the modern individual, which it therefore must eradicate. Thus, in essence, Lang's and Dumont's respective positions are much the same. Judging from the logic of their positions, it would appear that both thinkers draw their overall idea in common from a single philosophical source: Hegel's argument (1977: 355–63)—doubtless on the example of the French Revolution—concerning the reign of "terror" under conditions of "absolute freedom." In his *Phenomenology of Spirit*, Hegel reasons that absolute freedom—which is to say, freedom utterly unencumbered by otherness—expresses itself in national oneness. In doing so, it entails the violent exclusion of all distinctions with any content of their own, including of course the distinction of the individual ("The sole work and deed of universal freedom is therefore *death*, a death too which has no inner significance ... It is thus the coldest and meanest of all deaths, with no more significance than cutting off a head of cabbage or swallowing a mouthful of water" [ibid.: 360]). For Hegel, Kant's idea of the autonomous individual shares in the aspiration to absolute or universal freedom. And like Lang's argument, Hegel's constitutes a critique of Kant in this particular regard, since for Hegel the notion of the individual as wholly self-contained leaves no room for true otherness and therefore ignores the dialectic. In respect of Dumont, Hegel's argument aims to rethink the whole along the lines of Rousseau's 'general will', whereof the whole and the part, although truly one, also continue to enjoy a relative autonomy from each other. Without doubt, the political superiority of a structure of this kind—dialectical and nondualist—is implicit in Dumont's analysis of Nazi holism as false.

Dumont's argument is especially cogent and provocative in relation to the question of racism. In taking up that question, Lang (1990: 195ff.) remarks not only that the Nazi version of Social Darwinism is compatible with the relevant Enlightenment themes, but also that it received positive promotion from the ideal of history as progressive, an ideal issuing from the perfectibilism implicit in the Enlightenment theme of universal reason. Dumont, however, concentrates on the correlation of racism with radical individualism.

In his classic study of the Indian caste system, Dumont (1970) propounded, in connection with racism in the United States, that the modern ideology of individualism renders illegitimate the significant difference of social identity, promoting the conception that all persistent difference is substantive rather than facultative. Inasmuch as the ideology of egalitarian identity applies to the moral character of human beings—as it does in Kant's principle of self-responsible reason—it defines away the possibility of significant spiritual difference. It thus makes distinction a question of the body rather than the soul—"as if," in Dumont's words (ibid.: 255), "once equality and identity bear on the individual souls, distinction could only be effected with regard to the bodies."

Dumont drives this provocative argument home in relation to Nazi racism. There he draws on Hitler's devout attachment to the Social Darwinian proposition that all men are created equal, but only in the sense that each is pitted against the other in a struggle to the death of all against all. "The idea of struggle is as old as life itself," orated Hitler (cited in Dumont 1986: 170), "for life is only preserved because other living things perish through struggle ... In this struggle, the stronger, the more able, win, while the less able, the weak, lose. Struggle is the father of all things ... It is not by the principles of humanity that man lives or is able to preserve himself above the animal world, but solely by means of the most brutal struggle."[16] As Dumont reads this proposition, underlying Hitler's worldview is an intensely individualistic and biologistic ontology. In this ontology, relation is done away with in favor of substance, and, correlatively, difference is denied by force, the only form of selection conceivable under such a brutally materialistic ontology, in favor of natural unity. Dumont concludes: "The only residue that [Hitler's] grim ... individualism could tolerate under the heading of community was the 'race': people think the same and ... live together because they are physically, materially identical" (ibid.: 175).

In other words, to give Lang's argument a Dumontian turn, by ontologically legislating against difference, the ethical principle of universal reason left it open to, and even moved, Hitler at once to grasp persistent social distinction as principally a matter of biology and to endeavor to eradicate it. The moral universalism of Kant's principle of reason and the incapacity of this principle to decide claims for particularism, then, promotes, by way of a dialectical transformation, a ruthless, ontological individualism.[17]

Dualism and the Dialectical Identity of the Universal with the Instrumental

Starting with Lang's argument, I have traced a dialectical movement of ideas, in which the principle of universal reason gradually undoes itself. Logically triggered by this principle's implicit absolutism, a shift takes place from idealism to materialism, and from value to power. More broadly put, when value is taken as absolute, as perfectly exclusive of power, it promotes its own collapse into sheer instrumentality. In the present case, the Enlightenment conception of humanity as totally free in its relations with the world tends toward a social order based on unfreedom—in a word, totalitarianism. For Lang, this reversal is constrained by the judgmental incapacity of the principle of universalizability in the face of the inevitable claims of history. For Dumont, it issues from the contradiction between the universalistic and equalitarian conception of the individual and the fact of the fundamental structural difference between the whole and the part, which difference marks the ultimate irreducibility of the former to the latter. But whether one emphasizes Kantian idealism or Kantian individualism as the engine of the reversal, what seems to be the trouble is the principle of universality: as a political ideology, the intrinsic totalism of universalization translates into totalitarianism.

Strictly speaking, my thematic focus in this segment of the argument is not the degeneration of the principle of universalism but rather that of the principle of instrumental reason. But if the argument about a dialectical movement from value to power is correct, then the principle of universal reason, for all its ethical purport, must carry within itself the seeds of instrumental reason. In effect, the self-destruction of the principle of universal reason and the self-destruction of instrumental reason come to the same thing.

There is nothing mysterious about this particular idea of the identity of opposites. Horkheimer and Adorno have already argued this thesis, with stunning force and acuity, in their monumental *Dialectic of Enlightenment* (1998). There they set out to show that the universalistic (or "democratic") "disenchantment of the world," "the dissolution of myths and the substitution of knowledge for fancy," has as its essence "technology," and is at bottom "instrumental." They could not be more blunt, as in these words summing up Francis Bacon's reasons for enlightened enterprise (ibid.: 3–4): "What men want to learn from nature is how to use it in order wholly to dominate it and other men. That is the only aim. Ruthlessly, in despite of itself, the Enlightenment has extinguished any trace of its own self-consciousness. The only kind of thinking that is sufficiently hard to shatter myths is ultimately self-destructive." They conclude (ibid.: 6): "For the Enlightenment, whatever does not conform to the rule of computation and utility is suspect," and "Enlightenment is totalitarian."[18] Similarly, my argument has been that given the inevitability of historical particulars, the principle of universal reason is moved to invert itself into instrumental reason, and that the latter principle shares in the overall movement of self-de(con)struction. Universal and instrumental reason are of a piece, and both display a certain proclivity to expose, in practice and at great human cost, their own fundamental limitations.

Although their positions are substantially interconsistent, Lang and Dumont respectively identify different forces behind the movement of self-de(con)struction. For Lang, the difficulty rests with Kantian idealism, whereas Dumont cites individualism and materialism as sources of the trouble. But if the movement of self-de(con)struction is common to the principle of universal and of instrumental reason alike, then the constraining force must be broader and more comprehensive than either idealism or materialism. Logical dualism presents just such a subsuming force.

Both universalism and individualism are products of dualist thought. The totalistic idea of identity conveyed by both of these principles presupposes the conception of 'immaculate' boundaries. Immaculate boundaries are conceivable only through a logic of dualism—a logic that rules out or logically 'excludes' the possibility of a 'middle', that is, of an ambiguous boundary that both separates and connects. As individualism is definitively exclusionist, so universalism is expansionist. But a boundary that both separates and connects cannot issue in the terrible expansionism and exclusionism that define the Holocaust; only the idea of boundaries that are immaculate can produce aspirations so godly grandiose.

The Holocaust, then, presupposes a Cartesian universe, one in which the boundary between one thing and another is immaculate. In such a universe, the difference between self and other is total, making conceivable a self that is perfectly identical to itself. In holding out the possibility of a perfect self, a self that makes a universe unto itself, dualism encourages the self to exclude all that is other to itself. Whether such exclusion takes the form of incorporation or elimination, it constitutes a kind of expansion. Indeed, if incorporation is construed in biological terms (the picture implicit in Nazi racism), then it is but a stage in the process of 'elimination' (cf. Rubenstein's [1966: chap. 1] psychoanalytical conjectures).

Put another way, dualism promotes the conversion of the other into an instrument of the self. But here 'instrumentalism' takes a quantum jump beyond the material notion of utility. It refers to a process of identity construction, wherein one makes oneself into a cosmic figure at the expense of the other, whether the other is used practically, as an instrument of utility, or, more profoundly, hermeneutically, as an instrument of self-definition. This sort of instrumentalism, as I will show shortly, features the structure of sacrifice.

Ironically, the Kantian idea of the human being as an end in himself lends itself to such instrumentalist ambition. Considering oneself as an end in oneself, one is given impelling reason to treat others not as ends but as means. All that stands between this objectivistic outcome and the ethical state indubitably prescribed by Kant's categorical imperative is the hypothesis of pure, self-responsible reason as the human condition. If that hypothesis fails substantially to take the measure of humankind—if, as Lang claims, the human condition comes to both more and less than such reason—then the idea of oneself as an end in oneself can lead to the unqualified objectification (and, correspondingly, de-subjectification) of the other and indeed even of the self. Here, then, is an ambiguity that facilitates the conversion of universal reason into instrumental reason—the ambiguity of, as Dumont might say about the Kantian individual, the particular as the universal.

This ambiguity is inherent in Descartes' *cogito*. To be sure, Kant's 'I think' differs from Descartes' in crucial ways, since it is patently formal (a unity of consciousness or transcendental apperception), not substantive (Descartes' 'thinking stuff'). But it nonetheless shares in the Cartesian idea of the ego as fundamentally exclusive. Descartes' radical distinction between mind and body differentiates the individual self in absolute terms (as does Kant's between sensibility and reason). By doing so, Descartes establishes a timeless, universal human identity, an identity that cuts across all social difference—ethnicity, tribe, culture, class, gender, etc.—to constitute a common humanity. Modern democracy, with its precepts of 'equality before the law' and 'one man, one vote', and the like, is ultimately predicated on an identity of this kind: each person is basically equal to, or the same as, the next in that he or she is capacitated as an autonomous creature of reason. By the same token (i.e., the transparent identity of the subject to itself), logically speaking and paradoxically, however, every human being is given to see everything that he or she is not (including, of course, 'others') in purely instrumental terms—as if everything other has as its sole purpose the satisfaction of one's own needs. If anything, in view of the perfect epistemological closure of the Cartesian ego, this particular logical predisposition is even more impelling than that directed to the idea of a commonality of all humankind. Under the *cogito*, one is given no irrefutable reason to regard anybody, save oneself, in terms of genuine subjectivity. I submit that this paradox, whereby the same dualist logic that defines a universal humanity also brings about a global instrumentalism among men, is crucial for understanding how the civilized world can be so representatively uncivilized. In fact, despite this world's characteristic representation of itself as the apotheosis of moral consciousness, such conduct is a deep-seated and elemental expectation of the very idea of civilization.

Of course, in practice a wholly self-identical self is an impossible dream (one that tends more toward a nightmare). There can be no self without the other. Both Lang's attention to the historicist fact of particulars that stand unavoidably in the way of universalism and Dumont's focus on the structuralist consideration of the whole as irreducible to the individual constitute acknowledgments of otherness as a prerequisite of selfhood. Accordingly, both structure and history are partly identifiable with the Other, and neither can be disregarded without dire risk to the survival of the self.

From the fundamental belatedness of the self relative to the other, it follows that any attempt on the part of the self to eliminate the other is self-defeating. Indeed, ultimately an attempt of this kind describes a form of self-consumption, a suicidal act of cannibalism. If this observation is correct, then in exterminating Jews and other bodies of people, the Nazis were also killing themselves. In order to see better the suicidal and cannibalistic character of instrumental reason's trajectory of self-de(con)struction, it is necessary to turn from a philosophical to a more existential point of view. The vantage point I have in mind comprehends the Holocaust in terms of sacrifice. By referring the question of the role of rationality in the Nazi project to the conduct of sacrifice, I can clarify how instrumental rationality—paradigmatically abstract and a proper means if ever there was one—can manifest itself as a lived end, a conclusively inhuman and lifeless form/end of existence.

Terminal Sacrifice and the Cannibalism of the Self

In his powerful psychoanalytical (and theological) interpretation of the Holocaust, Richard Rubenstein projects, unmistakably, the picture of the death camps as altar sites of ritual murder (1966: chap. 1). He approaches the Holocaust in terms of Freud's well-known primal scene, wherein, in an original horde comprising a father and his wives and sons, the sons murder their father, literally devouring him, in order to take sexual possession of their 'mothers.' The general object of the killing is the freedom to gratify any and all instinctual desires. But the guilt occasioned by the horrendous deed is so great that the sons establish instead the rule of law (taboo), making the father into the Father, a far more powerful figure dead than alive. In effect, the sons establish civilization (as it is known in the West).

According to Rubenstein, the Nazis re-enacted this primal scene, only to the inverse effect: instead of civilization, they created a demonic and barbaric order. Essentially, they sought to realize the primal sons' original aim of complete freedom. The impediment to achieving complete freedom among them was not the original father figure of Freud's story, however, but a version of, given a psychoanalytical perspective, a derivative father figure—the god of Judeo-Christianity. As a Christian nation, Germany was subject to the restraint of this god. It might be said, then, in order to make a world where all things were permitted to them, the Nazis found it necessary to kill God.

Put another way, the Nazis were committed to making themselves wholly identical to themselves by eliminating otherness. This otherness found one of its implicit paradigmatic representations in Christianity. However, given the substantial degree to which German identity was bound up with Christianity, such a goal naturally posed extraordinary political and psychological difficulties.[19] Ironically, in coping with these difficulties, the Nazis were assisted by Christianity itself.

As Christ was a Jew, Judaism is plainly identifiable with the origin of Christianity—with, so to speak, the Father of the Father or, if you like, the Son's Father. After all, Christianity is, "however Hellenized," a Jewish religion (Passmore 1970: 76). Hence, in the Nazi deicidal designs, the substitution of Judaism for Christianity was an easy first step for the perpetrators to take, so easy in fact that it was scarcely noticeable. What is more, the step was greatly quickened by the mythic structure of Christianity, which profoundly depicted the Jews as deicides themselves. In effect, the Jews had already been targeted as fit to kill in a ritual drama staked to nothing less powerful than the promise of eternal life.

It is apparent that in light of Rubenstein's understanding, such killing takes a form of sacrifice.[20] Indeed, the Holocaust prominently displays certain features and a logic that are, in one theory or another, diagnostic of sacrificial undertakings.[21] The logic I have in mind is that of communion, an act of identification with God or the absolute other. Given a sense of distance between self and other—which, of course, distinguishes the self as it distinguishes the other—this act of identification requires both a medium and a mode. The mode is consumption: what better way to construct an identity between self and other than through the incorporation of a common stuff or, what amounts to the same thing, of each other. The medium, then, must be some kind of victim, a theanthropic and theriomorphic holocaust. For vital reasons, such victimage requires surrogation to some degree. If the sacrifice is selfless in every conceivable way, that is, if it is total (a *holo*-caust), then it is not identity but dis-identity that is established: the self is exterminated rather than reinvigorated. As a distinctive feature of the process of substitution, the surrogate victim is consecrated as a victim and is thus dedicated to its mediatory purpose. In this way, it is marked or differentiated as fit to sacrifice.

Despite the considered reluctance to discuss the Nazi death camps in terms of sacrifice, it seems to me apparent that the Holocaust describes conduct of this kind. That is to say, the genocidal activity of the Nazis evokes, disturbingly, what we ordinarily call the conduct of sacrifice. Using Jews and other categories of people as surrogate victims, as 'holocausts', the Nazis sought to identify themselves with—or more precisely, as—absolute or godlike power. The death camps were nothing if not a formal presentation of power over life and death. This power was so massive and efficient that the very existence of these camps must surely have been experienced, by perpetrators and victims alike, as a summons to otherness of divine proportions, a voiceless but all too concrete invocation of an (un)holy otherness. "With heart and soul they [the Nazis]," writes Jean Améry in his survival account (1980: 36), "went about their business, and the name of it was power, dominion over spirit and flesh, orgy of unchecked self-expansion. I also have not forgotten that there were moments when I felt a kind of wretched admiration for the agonizing sovereignty they exercised over me. For is not the one who can reduce a person so entirely to a body and a whimpering prey of death a god or, at least, a demigod?"

It edifies to recall here that in chapter 3 of the biblical story of Genesis, it is just this power over life and death, represented by the Tree of Life, that God scrambles to deny humankind, making it impossible to access by relocating Adam and Eve. Once they have succeeded in appropriating to themselves the other godly power prohibited to them, the knowledge of good and evil, God evicts the first couple from the Garden of Eden.

Here then, in essence, were two characteristic movements of ritual sacrifice: presentation and invocation. To these two were added two more: consecration and slaughter. The consecration took the form of killing before the slaughter, a preparatory murder. In Primo Levi's remarkable account of life in Auschwitz, perhaps there is no theme more felt and pronounced than that the camps were designed to kill men as Man, as human beings, before dispensing with them materially. He calls on us to consider if "what man's presumption made of man in Auschwitz,"—"killed in our spirit long before our anonymous death"—"is a man" (1961: 8, 49).[22] The first killing, depriving men of their moral definition, and therefore of their definition as humans, transforms them into "beasts" (ibid.: 38, 39), consecrating them as fit to slaughter.

Admittedly, it is deeply disturbing to construe the Nazi genocide as sacrificial in nature. It is disturbing, I think, because sacrifice is ordinarily associated with a received good rather than a monumental evil. It is not hard to point to what it is about this particular instance of what we would normally deem religious activity that makes it utterly perverse: its complete perfectionism.

The Nazis sought to perform a sacrifice that would put an end to sacrifice once and for all—a sacrifice that would take away all the sins and guilt of the world, making further acts of redemption unnecessary. Obviously, in attempting to perform so complete an act of sacrifice, they had squarely before them, long and thoroughly bound up with German culture, the powerful model of Christ. But for reasons, I surmise, having to do with the kind of perfection held out by reason itself—the mathematical, Cartesian perfection of self-containment—the Nazis deviated, consequentially, to say the least, from the model.

In Christianity, humanity remains ever indebted to its Other, to God the Father. For in the principle of the thing, God sacrifices his Self, in the form of his Son, for the benefit of humanity or His other. The perfection is God's doing, the logic being, surely, that God alone can offer himself up whole and still live. In this way, in principle, man's debt may be redeemed, wiped out forever. But as is positively crucial to see, the debt is recovered only by re-establishing it on an even deeper, more universal—i.e., more perfect—plane. Thus, the perfectionism of Christ, although patent, includes as an integral facet the imperfection of a final or perfect indebtedness to the Other.

Grasping implicitly the holism of this logic of sacrifice, the Nazis too set out to perform a perfect sacrifice, to redeem humanity wholly and thereby identify themselves as—and make themselves into—gods.[23] There is no doubt that the Nazis understood that others would perceive their actions as radically evil. Yet their project of extermination expressly pictured itself in terms of redemption. (If we fail to take this consideration into account, I do not see how we can even begin to comprehend the fact that so many people proved willing, and if not willing at least more or less ready, to carry out the hideous tasks entailed by that project.[24]) But in undertaking such an act of sacrifice, blinded by reason's promise of self-containment through total enlightenment, they failed to see that that same logic of sacrifice can work only so long as the act can be construed as primarily benefiting the other rather than the self. Ultimately, it is precisely in its respectful attention to the other that the self receives its definition as self, as an autonomous agent.

By definition, the figure of selfhood is demonstrable only insofar as it stands out against its ground. If the self fails to contest that ground, to actively stand against it, it has no way of showing to others or to itself that it is in any worldly way distinguishable in it-*self.* The ground of the self can vary. It is pertinent here to take the familiar range of variation given in the Hebrew Bible, from patriarchal order to the order of desire. Implicitly, the Nazis saw the ground as the former—*the* patriarch or God. But in making their opposition to that archfigure of Judeo-Christianity total, they at once constructed and disclosed the operative ground as sheer desire. To contest absolute power absolutely is to define the stakes of the struggle in terms of omnipotence, and omnipotence is nothing so much as desire perfected, the desire of desire. They thus failed to grasp that through the logic of sacrifice, the establishment of selfhood entails not only opposition and self-distinction but also, and even more fundamentally, concrete abnegation and credible other-regard. If selfhood entails active opposition, it is even more rooted in passivity, the passivity of belatedness, of having been created from what precedes it, that is, from otherness. As a result of this failure, the Nazis served to identify themselves not as gods but as human beings vainly trying to become such. Indeed, their acts identified the Nazis as all too human, to evoke here not only Nietzsche's psychology of human fallibility and the will to power, but also Arendt's ethically crucial insight into the banality of evil. Although it constitutes a unicum, the Holocaust was far from an aberration. Perpetrated largely by ordinary human beings, it did not have to happen.[25]

In this same connection, it should not be forgotten that in making this soteriological 'blunder', which caused untold "useless suffering,"[26] horribly wasted the lives of millions, and left the Western world in an ethical abyss, the Nazis were assisted, however bitter the ironies of this observation, by the evident way in which the Christian attempt at perfect sacrifice also failed. I have in mind that right from the beginning, the blame for the Crucifixion escaped the tremendous gravity of Christ's vicarage, to be placed again on man, and on certain men in particular. Indeed, insofar as Christ is held to be both man and God, a divine incarnation issuing from Mary's unsullied womb and demanded by the salvationist logic of Christ's sacrifice, could the blame for his death not have fallen also on men? And given that as a new-born Jewish religion Christianity is distinctly meaningful only in virtue of the displacement of its fatherly predecessor, could these men have been other than Jews? Indeed, are not the Jews in a conspicuous sense identifiable with the very god who gave his son for sacrifice, and does it not follow, then, that we are looking here also at another consequential sacrifice, one overshadowed by the brilliant luminosity of the Son's by the Father, namely, that of the father by the son? And although it does not make sense here to say, with Freud, that the object of the son's act was to take sexual possession of his mother, his father's wives, can it be doubted that the object was to take the father's place?

Indeed, is it not the case that there is, paradoxically, a patricidal logic profoundly implicit in the story of the Son's filicide—that ultimately the life of the son as the Son, that is, in his majority, as God, depends on the displacement of the Father? This logic is diffused by the story's theological narrative of the Father's resurrection of the Son, whose life He gave in sacrifice. The redemptive point of the story rests distinctly on the consideration that the Son's life is indeed sacrificed by the Father, who manages to save, by dint of the Resurrection, his own divine goodness from the opprobrium that normally would follow from an act of filicide (just as the staying of Abraham's hand preserved both God and Abraham for the good). Yet the Son's life was not only given but also taken. And here the story apparently diverges from the strictly theological narrative by laying the responsibility at the feet of the Jews, identifying them as deicides and, therewith, targets of ritual murder themselves. Remarkably, though, the contradiction resolves itself, since the Jews, as the generative source of Jesus (Y'hoshua [Joshua] in Hebrew), are irrecusably identifiable with the Father, the very Father that gave the Son in sacrifice. In effect, then, the patriarchal figure of God is preserved, but only at the cost of targeting it for elimination. Put another way, at its inception the story of the sacrificial slaying of the Son by the Father contains within itself a potent instigation to the murder of the Jews and, correlatively, of God the Father.[27]

Thus, the gloriously beneficient plan of this perfect sacrifice was logically flawed, such that men still felt the need to redeem themselves by continuing to 'sacrifice' other men—not just any men, but those others who by virtue of the originary Christological plan cannot but be regarded as representatively other, namely, the Jews. This flaw, an imperfection given not in principle but all the same by design, has plagued Christianity from its inception, and it served in part to furnish the Nazis with a supreme victim for their utterly perverse sacrificial endeavor.

I want now to bring home this central point about the Holocaust and a perverse logic of sacrifice by looking more closely at the issue of surrogation in relation to the Nazi genocide. What is striking about the use of the Jews as the victims is the Nazi projection of them as wholly other. The Nazis did their best to dis-identify themselves from their victims, making the surrogation out as complete and thereby as something really other than surrogation. Intuitively, though, what makes an act of sacrifice sacrificial is an identity—a 'communion'—between the sacrificer and the victim. Thus, in the example of Christianity, if God's Son were not also the Son of Man, and so identifiable with men, then he would not be a natural donor for man's needful redemption. In which case, the selfless act of giving would be unintelligible as a gift. If the victimage is to count as vicarage, as gift, then an acknowledged identity must exist between the donor and the victim—between God and his Son on the one hand, and between man and God's Son on the other. Plainly, this case is complicated by the fact that the gift from God to man must count at one and the same time as a gift from man to God.

In the Nazi example, however, the surrogative shift from self to other is meant as uncompromising; the identity between sacrificer and victim is emphatically denied, a denial grounded in the certainty of biological discreteness. As a result, to come to my main point, the meaningful character of sacrifice is not so much obviated as inverted. Where there appears to be no such identity whatsoever, the act of killing can occasion no feelings of indebtedness, for what is understood in such perfectly radical difference is precisely that nothing can be owing to the victim. Moreover, where this is understood, neither can the killing occasion guilt. Guilt can arise only if the victim is thought to have been wronged. But a victim that is perfectly objectified can have no rights to violate.[28] Outside of the killing itself, that is, the final canceling of the debt, there is perhaps no activity more ruthlessly systematic in the history of the Nazi persecution of the Jews than the stepwise deprivation of their rights (Hilberg 1985: esp. chaps. 2, 3; Remmling 1987).

Finally, in the absence of an identity between the sacrificer and the victim, the act of killing can hardly be regarded as a gift—under these circumstances, life is only taken, not given. If the victim is thought to have nothing at all in common with the sacrificer, neither party can be regarded as giving of himself. On the contrary, in relation to the act of killing, the agent can be identified only as an exterminator, and the victim as some kind of pest. The sole form of abnegation open to such an agent is the heroic prosecution of the killing itself, a monstrous sense of selflessness to which the Nazis were only too ready to lay claim (Bonhoeffer n.d.: 18; Hilberg 1985: 136–37). And since the victim is defined as of another nature entirely, a nature that runs contrary to acts of personhood, she or he cannot intelligibly be construed in the role of donor: the Jews were victims, not martyrs.[29]

Notwithstanding the apparent paganism of the movement, Rubenstein lays great weight on the thesis that Nazism can be comprehended only as "a negative reaction to the Judeo-Christian world"—it is, he says, "an inverted and demonic transformation of Jewish and Christian values, combined with a Romantic hankering after a paganism it never understood" (1966: 18, 19). Partly in line with this thesis, I have argued here that the form of sacrifice constituted by the death camps amounts really to an inversion of the received nature of sacrifice: the Holocaust was, I should say, an anti- or counter-sacrifice.

Most commonly, 'sacrifice', precisely in virtue of the loss thus entailed, connotes a life-giving or life-constituting act. The Nazi death camps, however, were solely death-dealing. Why, then, speak of the Holocaust in terms of sacrifice? In effect, I have already addressed this question in the preceding chapters. But the question is so acute, it pays to digress a moment, to recapitulate the argument in brief. Does it not make sense to see these acts simply as murder (even if ritualistic), thus reserving the formal notion of sacrifice for its usually positive acceptation? To be sure, I have documented for the Holocaust an impressive array of features that typically mark ritual sacrifice as we normally understand it. I have also shown that the Holocaust largely enjoys the form but not the meaning of sacrifice, at least not the expected meaning. Given the considerable consensus today in Holocaust studies to refrain from describing in terms of sacrifice the mass killing that took place, why, then, insist on doing so? Because from a phenomenological and existential point of view—the view I have taken here—the acts were truly sacrificial.

Plainly, the killings inverted the received meaning of sacrifice, most conspicuously as regards the relationship between sacrificer and sacrificed. The Nazis (stupidly) saw no identity between themselves and their victims, only difference. They thus removed the element of self from the loss and effectively reformed the 'sacrificial' act into a matter of killing alone. In the terms of the institution of sacrifice, if the self fails unconditionally to identify with the victim, then, whatever the express purport of the act, it must be defined in terms of its lethal intentionality alone and stand bereft of any life-constituting end. But this very move—to the slaughter of the other as wholly other—continues to convey something essential in at least the Western tradition of sacrifice, namely, its implicit perfectibilism. In result, what the Nazis perpetrated con-stitutes a limit case of this tradition; it is what transpires when the sacrificial impulse is carried to one of two logical conclusions. In the one conclusion, which I call here perfect sacrifice, the self is given as a whole, without surrogation, with the intended consequence of either the complete cessation or the resurrection of life.[30] In the other conclusion, only the other is destroyed, but with the total redemption of the self or, in other words, absolute selfhood as the end in mind. In this instance, the end is identical to that of almost all ritual sacrifice, namely, renewed vitality. But here too, as in perfect sacrifice, there is no surrogating, or, more exactly if also self-contradictorily, surroga-tion is total. Therefore, I regard it in paradoxical terms as a counter-sacrificial form of sacrifice and speak of it, correspondingly, as perfectly imperfect sacrifice. Both of these limit cases ensue from the perfectibilist principle, and both, regardless of their express objective, insofar as they are humanly rendered, come to the same effect: death as its own end. In the one case, there is no economy of sacrifice, whereas in the other, there is nothing but economizing. As a result, both are non-viable, for in the one noth-ing is saved and in the other nothing is given, and where life is neither saved nor given, there simply is no life to speak of.

If one adheres fast to the formal concept of sacrifice, as it is understood iconically in organized religion, then one is less likely to discern the perfectibilism at point. This remains true even if, from a logical point of view, this principle is hard to miss in a development as notable as that of the representation of events in the Akedah on the one hand and the Crucifixion on the other. Whereas in the Akedah, Abraham's perfectibilist disposition is rationalized and thus hidden by God's commandment to sacrifice Isaac and then to refrain from making so perfect an offering, in the Crucifixion perfectibil-ism is, as a human faculty, effectively overshadowed by the attribution of its realization to the deity. Indeed, it is implicit in both stories that, considered as a human quality, self-perfectibility amounts to the ambition to displace God or become godlike and is therefore condemnable. This is evident in the Akedah's axial emphasis on the vital significance of blind allegiance to God, and even in the Crucifixion story's assignment of blame to some men, which, since the men so charged were represented as the anti-Christ, serves only to alienate from ordinary humanity the inclination to perfectibility. By contriving to repress perfectibilism as a human faculty, these stories seek to sup-press it among men. The upshot is, though, that the stories, precisely in virtue of these counter-measures, harbor this principle subliminally, as a terrible temptation, one that implicates the antinomian force of unbridled desire.

It is by looking beyond the bounds of the ritual concept to its existential basis that one can begin to think of sacrifice in these terms.[31] Inasmuch as we experience ourselves as agents of our own behavior, we cannot but conceive of ourselves as self-responsible. We thus find ourselves—as a condition of our existence as selves—owing at once to ourselves and to our others. On the one hand, as selves we are by definition in our own care, a self-interested state of being, colloquially regarded as 'human nature'. On the other hand, because selfhood is inconceivable apart from otherness, we are also obliged to watch over our others. Put another way, since the self is inherently always other to itself (to quote Emily Dickenson, "I wonder what myself will say"), it is also responsible for its other. The trouble is that we cannot discharge this double human commission at one and the same time, since, given the ontological primacy of self-and-other over either of its polar principles, self-serving behavior entails displacement of the other, while other-regarding behavior amounts to self-denial. In effect, we experience ourselves as caught fast between what we owe to ourselves and what we owe to our others. We exist, thus, as a sacrificial dynamic. In this light, it is hardly surprising that the temptation to resolve this dilemmatical existence once and for all, in a perfectibilist call to make ourselves totally selfless or, alternatively, wholly autonomous, never ceases to present itself. As Rousseau observed (1992: 25), self-perfectibility is a faculty of the human condition, residing "among us as much in the species as in the individual."

To return now to Rubenstein (1966: 38ff.), in his psychoanalytical approach, the "camps' principal industry" was to 'eliminate' people—to make shit out of them—in order to affirm a world of "anal freedom," one keyed to the infantile desire to do whatever one pleases, in effect, to be God. On the evidence, even if one is not particularly disposed to psychoanalytical interpretation, Rubenstein's presentation might appear immensely compelling. As forceful as it is, however, by referring the Holocaust to a naturalistic explanatory scheme, Rubenstein's account risks defining away the crucial moral component of the Nazis' project (cf. Lang 1990: 158–59). Lang too, like Rubenstein, makes the point that the death camps are not comprehensible as a utilitarian endeavor. But he makes it in such a way as to studiously avoid obviating the issue of the moral accountability of the agent. His exposition of the point allows me to return to the themes of universalism, dualism, and instrumentalism.

Reviewing the argument for regarding the Final Solution as, from the Nazi point of view, a prudential undertaking (the argument accepting that the Nazis simply believed the ideological rationale that they were ensuring the state of public health by exterminating a pestilential population), Lang concludes as follows (1990: 19):

A bitter irony appears here in the form of an inverted conception of moral agency: the agent of genocide does not treat his victims as a means; he attacks them as ends in themselves and on grounds of principle rather than inclination. There is no use that the agent wishes to make of his victim, nothing he requires or wants of the latter except to deprive him of all claims of selfhood. In the act of physical destruction on the basis of group identity, all claims of the individual are denied: the agent is here entitled, even obligated, to act toward his victims in a way that demonstrates that they have no claims as persons. To act otherwise—to take account of the individual as a person or even to allow this as possible—would in these terms be a fault, a moral parody in the sense that anthropomorphism always is. The principle applied here asserts that certain persons may—more strongly, ought—to be treated not as ends in themselves, but as the negation of ends in themselves.

In other words, because the victims are defined not as means to but rather as the antithesis of ends, the killing constitutes its own end: it is valuable in itself. It is undertaken not for reasons of interest, inclination, or gain, but as a representatively 'moral' endeavor—that of the de-termination of ends. As the "negation of ends in themselves," the victims are by definition absolutely excluded from any human world, while the perpetrators are enabled to define themselves unequivocally as ends in themselves.

The sacrificial logic of the death camps is thus patently dualist and universalist. As it entails absolute exclusion, so it implies exhaustive expansion. The death camps exhibit this sacrificial logic, but in the living of it. The camps *are* this logic. In speaking of 'logic' here, then, I am being anything but intellectualistic, for I have in mind not logical logic but logic imprisoned in action, or lived logic.[32] Using the description of human existence as a structural dynamic of self-and-other, we can see that the death camps constituted a form of life that took industrial murder as the very point of its being. The camps presented a sacrificial logic whereby the self seeks to secure itself by annihilating whatever it finds irreducible to itself, which is to say, recalcitrant otherness. Existentially speaking, however, this logic is disastrously 'stupid', by which I mean that it fails to see that in consuming the other, the self necessarily sets upon and digests itself. This sort of archstupidity is not an error or mistake in any ordinary sense. It is not basically a matter of a false notion or representation. It is rather a primordial choice, and as such a structure of thought and form of life in which the will crushes the understanding. In result, the self alienates itself from its own ground to the point of encyclopedic malevolence—the calculated infliction of useless cruelty and suffering on all otherness, and the consequent demise of any self at all, including of course that of the instigators. Whatever else he was, Hitler was an infinitely 'stupid' man in that he was utterly insensible to the universally malevolent and destructive nature of the logic of his own self-fashioning. The sacrificial logic of which I speak was not a motive per se. The magnitude and horror of the acts at issue seem to imply not motivation but a peculiar kind of devotion, the kind that one is given over to by dint of one's most basic self-identity—the identity without which one would have absolutely no idea of who one is or where one stands in the world. The desire to become gods did not so much move the Nazis, as if it was separate and distinct from who they were, but rather constituted their very being, their (in)humanity. In effect, their species identity was keyed to the self-identity of a madman, whose madness, in a constitutional alliance with stupidity and malevolence, expressed itself as a "specifically human form of bestiality,"[33] an absolute destructiveness conduced by the desire to make oneself (one's Self) omnipotent.

To say that this logic constitutes its own end, though, is not to say that it is not also instrumental. But it is so in an anomalous sense that runs underneath utilitarianism proper. Above I exposited this sense in terms of cosmic identity construction, whereby one's other is made the hermeneutic instrument of one's self-identification as an omnipotent totality. Because it aims to proceed to the point of perfection, the resulting objectification of the other logically enjoys the primacy of a first principle, an essence or foundation on the basis of which instrumental reason as such can actually emerge as an intelligible proposition. That is to say, the perfect desubjectification of the other transforms the other into not simply an instrument but the essence of instrumentality, thus inaugurating an instrumental rationality as such. But the critical point here is that because it seeks to invert the other's status as an end in itself, the moral load of 'death camp' logic is the negation of morality itself. Without the other as an integral of the self, the self stands bereft of an object of moral responsibility.

It is implicit in this interpretation of the death camps that, as Lang (1990: chap. 1) critically argues, the Nazis knew what they were doing. If it is the case that despite the ideological justifications in terms of racist utility, at bottom the genocide was performed for its own sake, then it follows that the Nazis understood well enough the moral implications of their actions. On some variable plane of consciousness, they grasped what they were willing, as well as what they were bringing, into existence—a monumental and representative evil. There is abundant evidence that the regime as a whole organized—and many of the perpetrators invited—denial and repression concerning the moral monstrosity it had built (Hilberg 1985: 274ff.). Perhaps the most imposing fact in this connection is, as Lang's (1990: 25ff.) analysis stresses, the extraordinary pains that the Nazis took to conceal their genocidal activities. Correlatively, it could have been no less apparent to the Nazis than it is to any student of their brutal regime that precisely a profound identification with the victims was logically presupposed by the camps' terribly demanding work of dehumanization. At this juncture, though, what I want to bring out is that the genocidal victimization by the Nazis did not stop short of themselves.

When push came to shove, it is a fact that the Nazis privileged as a matter of policy their commitment to exterminate especially the Jews over the concern to prosecute the war effort (Lang 1990: 16, 17; Rubenstein 1966: 1, 2). It is only if one sees the Nazi intentionality as acutely 'religious' in nature that one can understand the Nazis' willingness to accept military defeat, so long as their success in the enterprise of exterminating the Jews was ensured. In effect, they seemed hell-bent on destroying themselves on behalf of their burning intention to sacrifice, once and for all, the Jews. Rubenstein concludes that once reality no longer gave way to his will, Hitler "had no choice but to eliminate reality by eliminating himself" (1966: 43), which he did, having taken the trouble to write just hours before his death the following admonition: "[A]bove all I charge the leaders of the nation and those under them to scrupulous observance of the laws of race and to merciless opposition to the universal poisoner of all peoples, international Jewry" (quoted in Lang 1990: 19n16).

The willingness of the Nazis to take their own lives expresses the same sort of radical victimage to which they subjected the Jews and other victims. Because it is an organon of perfection, 'death camp' logic is insatiable and therefore self-destructive. When it became militarily impossible to continue to assert itself in terms of the 'master race' by exclusion of and expansion over the Semites, Hitlerism was bound to turn against itself with the same rigorous perfectionism it had applied to the Jews. Accordingly, its sights shifted antithetically from total victory to total defeat (cf. Burke 1969: 408). Rubenstein asserts (1966: 37):

> There is a psychological cannibalistic element in regarding eliminating the other as the only possible mode of dealing with him. This was the characteristic mode of behavior of the Nazis in dealing with their opponents in the East both in and out of the camps. It finally became their characteristic mode of dealing with themselves. When it became impossible to envisage total victory, the real Nazis could envisage only total destruction as the other alternative. Some, like Goebbels, actually gloried in the thought of the total destruction of their country and welcomed the Allied bombers as bringing a necessary catharsis which would ruin the old and create the eventual conditions of a purified, truly Nazi Germany.

At no point did it occur to the most strongly convinced Nazis that there might be a way in which their country, if not their inner circle, could live in a world which was in any way resistant to their claims. This was the most archaic incorporative mode of dealing with limit and frustration—one seeks to do away with that which impedes.

Even if they had prevailed militarily, the Nazis would eventually have come to stand in their own way. Victory would surely have turned their uncompromising gaze onto themselves and the irrepressible way in which they themselves represented the otherness that serves to thwart self-completion. In projecting the possibility of immaculate limits or self-containment, the underlying dualism of that gaze rejects effective limits. Effective limits are themselves relative, as regards the boundaries they draw, and for this very reason viable. Such limits delineate a self whose boundaries are necessarily circumscribed—one that is, paradoxically, both autonomous and heteronomous. In contrast, a perfect limit is a limit unbounded and thus the equivalent of no limit at all. Such a limit holds out the possibility of the self as a totality. Under this condition, the self may be construed as a death camp of one (a picture of the self uncomfortably close to Foucault's celebrated critical view of the modern self). Rubenstein, making effective use of his psychoanalytic bag of tools, puts this in terms of the reality principle (1966: 41):

> Instead of facing facts, the Germans became increasingly unable to accept reality. The goal of German life under the Nazis was to reconstitute the world in such a way that it could conform to primitive German wish and fancy. This was done through propaganda, military enterprise, and above all the death camps. The wish to structure things after their deepest and most archaic wishes would have driven the Germans, had they won, to make the death camp into the authentic prototype of the future Nazi state ... In the long run, reality will always have the final say, if only in the grave ... Ultimately the terminal expression of this rejection of reality must be deliberate self-destruction. The killer's final victim must necessarily be himself.

During the roundup of the Jews in Poland, Poles themselves began to suspect that they were next (Hilberg 1985: 214–15). They were only intuiting the logic of the German enterprise. If the Nazi identity always demands for its self-assertion the consumption of a totally opposing other, then the Nazis could not have stopped the mass murders at the sacrifice of the Jews, the European Gypsies, the mentally ill, the homosexuals, or even the Poles. Logically, they would eventually have had to fall upon and devour themselves. Indeed, if one starts with the premise that the Nazis were basically identifiable with their victims—as one must—then in carrying out the Final Solution, the Nazis had all along been searching 'within' for their victims.[34]

In his book *Heidegger and "the jews,"* Lyotard (1990: 3) writes (using the lower case, the plural, and quotation marks) "the jews" as the name of all those souls, who, like "real Jews," are "the object of a dismissal." Real Jews, "in particular," have been afflicted with such a dismissal. In the Occident, the Jews have been a people of choice—a veritable chosen people—whenever a currency is demanded to satisfy a deeply felt need to put 'paid' to a certain obligation, an obligation that is, however, essentially unredeemable. The obligation Lyotard has in mind is the standing obligation of the self to the other, to whom the self always owes its existence and remains hostage. As it is always presupposed, the other can never be fully retrieved or represented. Lyotard speaks of it, in

Freudian terms, as the primally repressed; hence, it is that "which must be remembered as something which never ceases to be forgotten" (ibid.). In effect, the invisible other immovably stands to remind us of our own belatedness and indebtedness. In Western thought, the Jews in particular have assumed the role of mnemonist in respect of this fundamental debt.[35] As a consequence, whenever someone—be it Nazis, Christians, monarchs, republics, etc. (ibid.)—in a fit of unbounded ambition, tries to cancel the debt, to forget that there is something that never ceases to be forgotten, the Jews have been typecast in the role of vicar. Of course, in result only the messenger is diminished or wiped out—the debt remains.

Plainly, Lyotard's penetrating reflections on the primally repressed resonate sharply with Rubenstein's religious notion of a fundamental human limit and Lang's philosophical thesis of the inevitability of claims for the particular. But I draw here on Lyotard for the pointed way in which his simple but profound neologism, "the jews," brings home the stunning irony of Nazism.

To cite from the back cover of Lyotard's (1990) book, "the jews" represents "the outsiders, the nonconformists: the artists, anarchists, blacks, homeless, Arabs, etc." What is most critical about Lyotard's notion, though, is that the corresponding list is in principle interminable. As one may gather from Lang's deconstruction of Kant's Enlightenment principle of universal reason, as well as from Rubenstein's discussion of the Judeo-Christian idea of deicide, the drama of striving to become perfectly transparent to oneself is, in one version or another, deeply written into Western thought. In this drama, at any given time, depending on circumstances, any people can become the victims or "the jews." Although the Holocaust may have become the exemplar of genocidal activity, the role of "jew" and, for that matter, obviously, the role of "nazi" remain subtly but largely inviting in—and are enacted only too routinely on—every stage of our social existence. The Judeo-Christian mythic paradigm of sacrifice and identity presents a primordial choice, a synthetic a priori of Western thought, in which the temptation to (specifically human) inhuman activity is a constitutive feature. As a result, although each fall to this temptation is singular and particular, dependent on its own peculiar confluence of choice and historical circumstance, the inhumanity of which I speak may be found, in various forms and intensities, in different socio-political settings.

By trying to forget that there is something that never ceases to be forgotten, then, the Nazis forgot their own "jewishness." They forgot that by excluding the point of view of the other, one necessarily acts to seal off the possibility of one's own future. They forgot that in the pursuit of the perfect sacrifice, one eventually would have to get around to oneself. And with this ironic turn, the spell of uncompromising rationality breaks, at least for the time being, illuminating the horror of it all and bringing back the primally repressed as the unforgettable forgotten.

Here, then, is a comprehensive and profoundly 'reflexive' lesson of the Holocaust, one which, by all signs, remains still to be taken. It rests with a certain telos implicit in the Western self-identity of 'human'. This identity conveys a primordial choice that is keyed to the attribution of enlightened, moral consciousness, to be sure, but also uncritically linked to the dualist principle of perfectibilism. The lesson is, surely, that we need to rethink our very idea of what it means to be human, such that we include the possibility of inhumanity—paradoxically, a specifically human, malevolent kind of bestiality—as, rather than simply the annulment of this meaning, a manifest condition of it. By doing so, by rethinking moral consciousness as innately open to its own deathly negation, we serve to remind ourselves that in truth our powerful capacity to make ourselves depends not on perfection but, in the sense of finitude, on imperfection. In this way we can effect a leap in consciousness beyond that so richly recounted in the biblical story of Adam and Eve's expulsion into a moral universe of their own. We can remake our-selves again, this time in the image not of an almighty god, with unlimited access to the Tree of Life, but of an imposingly creative being. The self-becoming of this new being rests not only on a wondrous autonomy but also, paradoxically, on a critical and exactingly discretionary understanding of its own fundamental heteronomy.

Chapter 5

Bourdieu's Anti-dualism and "Generalized Materialism"

Sticking a gun in his ribs, a thief addresses Jack Benny, the famous American comedian who portrayed himself as a notorious cheapskate and who told this joke:

Thief: Your money or your life.
Benny: [He says and does nothing.]
Thief: Are you crazy? I said, "Your money or your life."
Benny: I'm thinking it over!

Preliminaries

My concept of primordial choice virtually entails the idea of practice. Indeed, as it designates a process of selection that is less than perfectly witting, individual, and free, primordial choosing really is just another name for practice. In recent decades, no social scientist has done more to develop a theory of practice than Pierre Bourdieu. Like his, my concept is intended as a master wrench in the inordinately difficult task of dislodging the bedrock dualism that afflicts anthropological and social theory. But while I have learned from Bourdieu's penetrating and influential theory,[1] my concept deviates from his significantly, for, consistent with its nominal emphasis on a notion of choice, my concept sees practice in terms of ethics rather than power. This difference is absolutely critical to the task of undoing dualism. One very productive way of distinguishing my own theory, then, is by critically explicating Bourdieu's against the implicit backdrop of this difference.

Bourdieu's sociology approaches that of Durkheim in influence, scope, and ambition. Indeed, in keeping with a prevailing movement of social theory, Bourdieu's theory of practice strongly revises the normativist sociology of his fatherly precursor into one keyed to power. Bourdieu's is a grand theory—immensely powerful, penetrating, comprehensive, and sophisticated. I argue here that for all its prodigious accomplishment, it is also flawed at its core. When one looks for the configuration of meaning that makes Bourdieu's theory consistent, what one finds is a conceptual framework that falls discordantly short of its own ontological promise. To be sure, Bourdieu's organizing concept of practice squares off decisively with the besetting ontological problem of sociological and anthropological theory: the problem of subject-object dualism. But, as I aim to show, Bourdieu remains consequentially caught in that dualism. For this reason—that Bourdieu's theory continues to harbor the principal problem it is designed to meet—I maintain that the theory is basically deficient.

I believe that Bourdieu fails to overcome this root problem because instead of attacking it directly on grounds of ontology (the evident ontological tone of his conceptual tools notwithstanding), he tends to approach it as a matter of epistemology. That is to say, Bourdieu seems even more concerned to secure a better scientific perspective than to rethink directly the reality on the basis of which any such perspective makes sense.

Broadly speaking, as an authoritatively positive purchase on the truth, a scientific perspective evokes, in some form or another, Cartesian dualism. It is just such dualism—wherein things utterly mutually exclude each other and thus define absolute boundaries—that makes it possible to conceive of an object (or subject) in itself. Because it is predicated on objectification, a scientific perspective is bound to evoke this dualism as long as it goes unqualified by a directly theoretical revision of Descartes' ontology. It is plain that Bourdieu's scientific sociology is meant to undo Descartes' ontology. But driven especially by his powerful critique of intellectualism, Bourdieu's sociology holds up a practical and piecemeal rather than directly theoretical perspective. As a result, for all the considerable force of his efforts to avoid dualism, in the end he fails to do so.

This failure is registered most comprehensively in his avowed materialism, the dualist (and reductionist) position that tugs most tenaciously at his theory of practice. In this connection, Bourdieu never does manage to put himself in a position to give the reality of the immaterial its singular ontological due. It is true that by appealing to the socio-cultural operation whereby power and production are masked symbolically in moral terms, he richly seconds these basically material processes with the effective or virtual reality of the immaterial. But as might be expected from his wholesale characterization of moral terms as "masks," he never does see that before it is a matter of power and production, human practice is a question of value qua value, which is to say, a question of ethics.

These criticisms are likely to seem ill conceived or worse to the knowledgeable, sympathetic reader of Bourdieu. For not only is Bourdieu's sociology plainly novel in its ontological designs and ethical in its aspirations, but it has also been brilliantly defended by its author against the thrust of criticisms, like mine, that see it as reductionistic. Most particularly, in an expansive analytic interview, Bourdieu has produced what may be thought of as a metalogical commentary on his own ideas.[2] The questions of the interview were thoughtfully constructed and articulated by his colleague and one-time student, Loïc J. D. Wacquant, "both to disentangle the central conceptual and theoretical nodes of Bourdieu's sociology and to address the recurrent objections and criticisms that the latter has met from its foreign readers" (Bourdieu and Wacquant 1992: xii). Bourdieu's responses to these questions and Wacquant's expert interpretative commentary are notable aids in deciphering Bourdieu's work. The responses are also deeply insightful about the ontological nature of social reality and exhibit, as in all of Bourdieu's work, a surpassing clairvoyance into the exceeding complexity of social dynamics.

Given this state of affairs, I confess that I have sometimes found myself caught up short in following my critical observations through to their conclusions. For every fault one finds in Bourdieu's theory, there appears already to exist a compelling reply by him to the effect that one must have misread. And for every revision one ventures in respect of these so-found faults, it seems possible to identify an equivalent position already well formulated by Bourdieu as a vested component of his sociology.

But circumspection is not resignation, and for all the apparent force of Bourdieu's replies to his critics, I have not been able to dispel my objections. In relation to the criticisms that have been leveled at his theory, his defensive comments often strike me as more convinced than convincing. Although I would not characterize them in terms of "evasion," "sophistry," and "an easy turning of questions"—the common pitfalls of analytic interviews Wacquant took pains to guard against (Bourdieu and Wacquant 1992: x)—I am inclined to think that they do exhibit, unhappily, the sort of inherent fudging to which, as has been brought into high relief by Bourdieu himself, practice as such is definitively given. In view of the fact that Bourdieu is, for obvious reasons, very keen to present his theory as more a function of practical enterprise than theoretical design (ibid.: 34f., 158ff.), perhaps the appearance of "reinforced dogma" in his responses to critics is not surprising. The notion of reinforced dogma is due to Karl Popper, and Bourdieu's avowedly practical practice of theory lends itself too readily to the sort of ad hocing that, according to Popper (1965: 37, 244), makes refutation impossible. As a result, when the theory is considered in the round, what its conceptual contents imply and entail on the one hand tends to be secured by idealistic self-representation against critical attack on the other. If this observation is right, then the theory must be two-faced, comprising both an operational framework and a meta-commentary that helps to secure that framework by misrepresenting it. The effect verges on dogmatization, a downright anathema from the perspective of the liberating purpose to which Bourdieu expressly puts his sociology.

To guard against the practical dogmatization of his theory, Bourdieu would, I think, have to reconsider his "fear" of the "oversimplifications" that "are the inescapable counterpart of 'theoretical talk'" (Bourdieu and Wacquant 1992: 140). Reflecting his certain, almost native grasp of the fallacy of intellectualism as well as his acute awareness of the complexity of social life, this fear has surely served to motivate his sociology of practice. But ironically, it also bears a profound threat to practice, for, like intellectualism, it too can betray a utopian desire to resolve the tension of theory and practice once and for all. Correlatively, it may reveal a failure to see the dialectical importance of the "oversimplifications" of "theoretical talk" for the realization of reflexive sociology, and for the relative liberation of human consciousness from unnecessary determinacy and for elective choice.[3]

Bourdieu concedes that his writings "may contain arguments and expressions that render plausible the systematic misreadings that they have suffered." But he finds that "in many cases" the criticisms of his work are, in addition to being "misreadings," "strikingly superficial" (Bourdieu and Wacquant 1992: 79). Doubtless, in view of the exceeding difficulty, iconoclasm, and sophistication of his thought, "in many cases" he is right. But he seems blind to the distinct possibility that under the influence of his own argument about practice, which rightly makes practice out to be diagnostically resistant rather than open to refutation, he has misread his own work in ways that serve to close it to insightful criticism.

In this chapter, I examine Bourdieu's theory by reference to the ontological question. I do so by scrutinizing how the theory effectively treats the dualism of subject and object in three topical areas of strategic importance to his thought as well as to the question of dualism, namely, human agency, otherness, and the gift.[4] In his reflections on his own work and on his detractors' objections, Bourdieu plainly (but not decisively) anticipates some of the criticisms to follow here, and I will cite him to this effect as I proceed.

As Bourdieu and Wacquant record (Bourdieu 1990b; Bourdieu and Wacquant 1992; Wacquant 1989), critical commentary on Bourdieu does not lack for charges of materialism and inadequate treatment of human agency. My exercise in this book, though, is driven principally by a goal other than merely critical, a positive and more ambitious goal: to show that practice is more fundamentally a matter of ethics than of power. This goal represents an outstanding conceptual difference with Bourdieu, and I believe it lends to my critique the distinction of, so to speak, an attempted paradigm shift. In effect, I am not so much trying to contribute to practice theory as to disclose ethics as the most inclusive basis of human social life.

Underlying my difference with Bourdieu is my guiding precept that the only way truly to unlock the inordinately powerful epistemological shackles of dualism is simply but critically to assume a fresh ontology, one that projects reality as basically ambiguous as between the material and the immaterial. It would be a mistake to think, then, that since I am criticizing Bourdieu for starting from his ontological point of view rather than mine, my critique is simply a matter of theoretical preference and has no hard sociological bite. My point is precisely that the principal problem on which Bourdieu's sociology so rightly rests cannot be satisfactorily addressed if such a shift of starting points is not made. To think of my difference with Bourdieu as merely one of philosophical attitudes misses the point: it is precisely a difference of this kind on which the radical sociological advance projected by Bourdieu depends.

I also contend that in the human realm the basic ontological ambiguity of which I speak manifests itself as ethics. Put another way, the nondualism Bourdieu's sociology professes to stand in search of *is* ethics. Hence, running right through the following critiques of Bourdieu's approach to human agency, otherness, and the gift is a measured but persistent and thoughtful projection of 'ethics' as capable of doing what 'power' cannot: effectively eliminate the dualism Bourdieu so insightfully determines as the universal wrench in the works of the social and human sciences.

I should add, as a cautionary remark, that under the rubric 'value' I include 'antivalue', by which I mean power. Therefore, no one should conclude that by embracing ethics as 'human nature' in its diagnostic mode, I have fallen into the dualistic trap of excluding power and material motives as critical features of social life. Rather, in the paralogical perspective offered here, they are opposed to ethics but only as modalities thereof. Put another way, whatever the extent of their role in social life, they are always already ethically informed and determined.

I proceed first by resuming Bourdieu's theory in broad but key respects; second, by critically assessing his crucial concept of the habitus, as regards its conception of the body and in relation to the idea of human agency; third, by examining his theory in connection to its treatment of the anthropologically defining problem of otherness; and, fourth, by questioning at its conceptual core his signature analysis of the gift.

Practice

In book 1 of his *The Logic of Practice* (1990a; henceforth cited as *Logic*), largely a reworking of his landmarking *Outline of a Theory of Practice* (1977; henceforth cited as *Outline*), Bourdieu has done his readers the great service of setting out his theoretical approach in a systematic and economical form. The book lends itself peculiarly, then, to a close reading of certain of Bourdieu's key theoretical understandings, especially as they pertain to anthropological thought.[5]

Bourdieu begins by pointing to what he regards as the arresting predicament of social science: the opposition between subjectivism and objectivism, or, in his words, "the spurious alternatives of social physics and social phenomenology" (1990a: 140). His principal task, then, is to supersede this misguided theoretical dualism. In solution, he proposes a dialectical theory, according to which "organizing consciousness" and "automatic behaviours," or intellectual structures and objective actions, are involved rather than simply contraposed. The ontological synthesis of this dialectic is practice, a structured structuring process that proceeds not according to rules as such but to the needs of the moment. It follows that practice can never really be normatively bound or synoptically captured by a timeless theoretical model; indeed, as its problems are practical, as they cannot be plumbed beforehand, practice necessarily excludes the question of its own theoretical rule. Practice, then, describes a circular causality in which social life is produced and reproduced by objective, material conditions as they are apprehended by agents through structures of perception, while the structures of perception are themselves informed by, in one manner or another, the objective conditions.

Exactly how, though, does this circular causality or dialectic work? How through practice are the structures of consciousness transmuted into behavior and the material conditions into intellectual representations? These are, of course, questions of body-mind dualism. In response, Bourdieu offers an ingenious concept based on the idea of bodily incorporation of ideas: the famous habitus. This concept describes systems of durable dispositions that serve to generate and organize practices as well as representations. And because they are embodied, that is, because they are dispositions rather than ideas as such, the habitus function "without presupposing a conscious aiming at ends or an express mastery of the operations necessary in order to attain them" (1990a: 53). By conceiving of the body in this way, as practically informed by ideas, Bourdieu gives a brilliantly novel answer to the question that has plagued all Durkheimian sociologies, structural-functionalism and structuralism alike: just how does society make you do it? Put less colloquially (but more trendily), the concept of the habitus provides a fresh solution to the problem of how society reproduces itself.

Such a concept presupposes that the body, in its dynamic fullness, can be mindful—that it enjoys, in Bourdieu's words, "the capacity for incorporation" (1990a: 57). What does a capacity of this kind look like? Conceived of as a "living memory-pad" (ibid.:

68), the body raises some of the same sort of questions as the mind itself in relation to attunement with the world. Is the body an empty slate, or does it constrain certain meanings by its very nature? The thrust of Bourdieu's theory makes it plain that for him the body's capacity for incorporation is predisposed by practice. That is to say, as I read his usage, the root meaning or categorical end that opens the body to development as habitus is, in a word, survival in the sense of material production and reproduction.

Not surprisingly, therefore, Bourdieu construes his theory as a materialism, although a "generalized" one, in that it gives consciousness and even subjectivity a certain due (1990a: 17). In this theory, human life is pictured as a struggle for existence under conditions of essential uncertainty. The struggle describes a competition over the means of production and reproduction. Under capitalism, the competition is acknowledged for what it is—a practice of economic interest and calculation. But in pre-capitalist societies, where self-interest and egoistic calculation do not receive thematic recognition and remain undifferentiated, capital as such cannot obtain. Instead, it appears as "symbolic capital," that is, as capital masked and denied. Hence, a ritualistic gift, from seller to buyer, rounding off a transaction, helps to create profit by disguising it in terms of non-economic exchange. It is important to understand, however, that symbolic capital is genuinely ambiguous as between its two natures, for its operation as capital virtually depends on its "misrecognition" as something other than capital, that is, as something symbolic. In this sense, according to the theory, consciousness and the subject remain irreducible and enjoy a real autonomy (ibid.: 41).

The upshot of the struggle over the means of production and reproduction is the establishment of relations of domination. Where literacy and formal education are found, economic wealth can function precisely as capital, furnishing a basis on which to institutionalize relations of inequality or political authority. Both literacy and formal education serve to objectify resources, to detach them from particular contexts, allowing thus for their rationalized accumulation. The monopolization of the instruments of accumulation sets the scene for the institutionalization of the relations of dependence that issue from such monopolization, explicitly identifying these relations as pre-eminently political and economic.[6]

Where, however, the means of objectification and accumulation of resources are lacking, the resources can be preserved only as habitus, that is, only as they are incorporated or embodied in practice. Under these conditions of relative undifferentiation, relations of inequality cannot differentiate themselves as such in institutional terms of polity and economy. Instead, they can proceed only in disguise, under a veil of personal and moral relations. In this way, basically arbitrary relations and distinctions are transformed into legitimate ones, as in a "good faith" economy in which interested transactions are always couched in terms of honor and gift rather than contract and calculation (1990a: 114–15).

Although Bourdieu describes an evolutionary shift from pre-capitalist to capitalist societies, it is critical to his argument that these are precisely not mutually exclusive kinds of social arrangement. Just as capital, although incognito, operates in pre-capitalist settings, so symbolic capital and the habitus are important features of capitalist orders. Indeed, Bourdieu's project of objectifying objectification—to expose the social determinants and historical interests of theoretical scholarship—is directed against the kind of habitus and symbolic capital characterizing modern societies (1990a: 25ff.).

There is much to learn from Bourdieu's intellectually masterful and intricate constructions on practice. The importance of the focus of his notion of practice, on a bodily logic that is not "logical logic" and is keyed to a principle of uncertainty, is capital and can hardly be overestimated. But it is no less important to see that his notion is predicated exclusively, and therewith reductively, on a concept of power: capital, of course.

In prominent places, Bourdieu's vocabulary fairly smacks of reductionism. "Game," "strategy," "interest," "generative model," and "capital" are terms closely associated with materialism of one kind or another. In reply to those who have charged him with reductionism (e.g., Elster 1983: 43, 69–71; Ferry and Renaut 1990: chap. 5), Bourdieu has argued that the criticism is itself based on a reductionist reading of his work. According to Bourdieu, the reader can arrive at such a charge only because he or she fails to set aside the various antinomies that the concept of habitus aims to transcend (Bourdieu 1990b: chap. 7; see also Bourdieu and Wacquant 1992: 24–26). Thus, for example, if the dualism of mechanical compliance and strategic choice is obviated, then "strategy" must take on a meaning other than the reductionist one attaching to it in rational choice theory, that is, other than that of "the product of a genuine strategic intention" (Bourdieu 1990a: 62; see also Bourdieu and Wacquant 1992: 128f.). Bourdieu's point is well taken, but of course its effectiveness depends on how well the concept of habitus succeeds in accomplishing its task of synthesis. It seems to me that for all its synthetic force and intention, 'habitus' falls notably short of the mark.

The Habitus and Human Agency

In order to show this, let me start with the concept of habitus itself in relation to its specific predication of the body. Most essentially, the habitus presents embodiment or incorporation as constraint. Indeed, the concept paints a picture of Durkheim's "mechanical solidarity," but in terms of a dialectical materialism that adds much to the plausibility of the Durkheimian category. Overridingly, the concept of the habitus is devised to account for, and does profoundly illuminate, social "reproduction." Bourdieu (1990a: 60–61) states that "the *habitus* tends to ensure its own constancy and its defense against change through the selection it makes within new information by rejecting information capable of calling into question its accumulated information, if exposed to it accidentally or by force, and especially by avoiding exposure to such information." He continues (ibid.: 64): "The *habitus* is the principle of a selective perception of the indices tending to conform and reinforce it rather than transform it, a matrix generating responses adapted in advance to all objective conditions identical to or homologous with the (past) conditions of its production; it adjusts itself to a probable future which it anticipates and helps to bring about because it reads it directly in the present of the presumed world, the only one it can ever know."

To be sure, the habitus is characterized as "inventive": it is given to "regulated improvisation" because it is underlain by a "practical sense" (Bourdieu 1990a: 57). The concept does address itself, then, to the question of change. But it does so in terms of constraint still, not agency. In connection with the question of change and invention, Bourdieu's theory looks for understanding to the dialectic of the habitus (embodied history), institutions (objectified history), and "the situation." What it is usual to call in dialectical theories 'contradiction' seems to have everything to do with an outcome of social transformation: there may be "cases in which dispositions [habitus] function out of phase and practices are objectively ill-adapted to the present conditions because they are objectively adjusted to conditions that no longer obtain" (ibid.: 62).[7] In a situation of this kind (what Bourdieu calls, if I read him right, a "new situation"), the strategies of the habitus "can invent new ways of fulfilling the old functions" (ibid.: 291), and "be the source of misadaptation as well as adaptation, revolt as well as resignation" (ibid.: 62).

The point is that transformation is wrought somehow within the dialectical relationship, apparently without benefit of agency. As Bourdieu says (1990a: 53), the whole process is "arbitrary" (in the Saussurean sense of heterogeneous connection) and, correlatively, "conductorless." Structure governs the habitus, which in turn structures the structures, while the overall process is driven practically, as an exercise in survival (ibid.: 55). As near as I can tell, this dialectical theory presents a kind of evolutionary explanation in that it proceeds by positing (a) an objective but uncertain world of necessity, (b) a conventional world, comprising both institutions and the habitus, and (c) a problem-solving, competitive practice of survival that powers the articulation of convention and necessity. The objective and conventional worlds govern or select each other, as they are mediated by "a claim to existence" that manifests itself as competitive and practical ingenuity (ibid.: 53). Something of the sort, I take it, is intended by the following (ibid.: 55–56):

> The genesis of a system of works or practices generated by the same *habitus* ... cannot be described either as the autonomous development of a unique and always self-identical essence, or as a continuous creation of novelty, because it arises from the necessary yet unpredictable confrontation between the *habitus* and an event that can exercise a pertinent incitement on the *habitus* only if the latter snatches [selects?] it from the contingency of the accidental and constitutes it as a problem by applying to it the very principles of its solution; and also because the *habitus*, like every 'art of inventing', is what makes it possible to produce an infinite number of practices that are relatively unpredictable ... but also limited in their diversity. In short, being the product of a particular class of objective regularities, the *habitus* tends to generate all the 'reasonable', 'common-sense', behaviours (and only these) which are possible within the limits of these regularities, and which are likely to be positively sanctioned because they are objectively adjusted to the logic characteristic of a particular field, whose objective future they anticipate. At the same time ... it tends to exclude ... all the behaviours that would be negatively sanctioned because they are incompatible with the objective conditions.

Whether or not I have got Bourdieu's dialectic right in picturing it as a piece of evolutionary logic, it would seem that, like evolutionary movement, at bottom the dialectic lacks any meaningful moment of human agency, a moment that entails self-conduction and thereby attribution of responsibility to a person or persons. The habitus function as "principles which generate and organize practices and representations that can be objectively adapted to their outcomes" in the absence of explicit intentionality and operational expertise (Bourdieu 1990a: 53). The practices and representations "can be collectively orchestrated without being the product of the organizing action of a conductor" (ibid.). It should be borne in mind here that by eliminating "conscious aiming" and "express mastery" as necessary features of practice, Bourdieu does not mean to imply the operation of unconscious agency. Taking it as "a kind of *Deus ex machina* which is also a God in the machine," he rejects the thesis of unconscious agency along with the finalism, materialism, idealism, and naturalism of Lévi-Strauss's anthropology (ibid.: 40–41). But of course if one grants, as I do (following Wittgenstein and Merleau-Ponty), that the "principles" that "the *habitus* function as" betray primordial choices, choices that at one time did involve conductor elements but have become, through the socialization of consciousness, matters of preconception and habit, then there is as regards "practices and representations" a meaningful sense in which we might speak of unconscious agency and, for this reason, at least limited accountability. Surely we can hold accountable Adolf Eichmann—who served to 'conduct' freight-car deportations of veritable hosts of human beings in what was exemplarily a practice of mass extermination—for permitting himself to be rendered thoughtless and his certain grasp of the ethical implications of his conduct to be smothered by devotion to duty and career (see, in this volume, chap. 4, note 12).

If, as Bourdieu says (1990a: 62), the "*habitus* contains the solution to the paradoxes of objective meaning without subjective intention," then the key to the solution is the body. It is the body that is capacitated both to incorporate and animate history as systems of "durable, transposable dispositions," rather than rules and intentions. But in this theory, the body serves as a body, as *res extensa*, not as an agent. Still showing signs of his early persuasion to structuralism, Bourdieu is at pains to eliminate intentionality as a critical feature of practice. Accordingly, insofar as the body plays an active role in relation to the habitus, whether we have in mind the activity of incorporation or of structuring, it does so as an orientation to practical problems, that is, in Bourdieu's dialectic, as a material drive to persist entitatively in a contingent universe.

By 'human agency' I mean that use of the term where we talk about agency in terms of moral responsibility. I have in mind, then, precisely non-arbitrary and conducted, but not necessarily individualistic, moral force. In the absence of such force, it is hard to see how the habitus can accomplish its sociologically appointed task of dialectical synthesis. The lack of purposeful and self-reflexive agency seems to leave the field of social practice to mechanism.

Of course, at this point I am vulnerable to Bourdieu's charge of continuing to (mis)read his theory reductionistically. I can only respond that while I credit—indeed embrace—the logic of his reply to those critics who have charged him with reductionism, I find that "*habitus*," despite the synthetic task allotted to it and the remedial claims made for it by its creator, does not transcend the dualism of subject and object. For all of his powerful, unequivocal rejections of objectivism and mechanism, and despite his open talk to the contrary,[8] Bourdieu's theory fails to make the possibility of human agency as such a condition of practice. As a result, in the end, it reiterates rather than ablates the dualism. If it is not to reduce to monism, nondualism requires that moral force, as well as mechanical process, be given its due. As Bourdieu's theory stands now, moral force, although often invoked, is only simulated (as symbolic capital), while mechanical process, although repudiated in principle, is proffered in fact. By foreclosing the ontological possibility of an element of creative agency that can produce a hiccup in the habitus, a discontinuity in the smooth reproduction of its practices, Bourdieu's scientific realism appears also to foreclose the possibility of the raising or liberating of consciousness.

Bourdieu's mechanism is highly sophisticated and for that reason elusive. Above I found it helpful to depict the logic of Bourdieu's theory as evolutionary. Here it helps to point out that his theory has much in common with the powerful mechanism one finds in cybernetic theory. Bourdieu posits a system of practice that operates largely through the self-correcting device (feedback loop) of the habitus. As self-correction simulates self-reflection, so the system simulates purposive behavior without real purpose. It is true that the system is governed by an overall purpose, namely, survival (negentropy). But this purpose resides in the whole of the system, not in any part having a purpose—there is no agent. Even if there is no agent in the system, could there perhaps be agency? The answer to this question depends on, inter alia, whether or not we wish to count negentropy as an authentic purpose. While it is the case that negentropy differs anti-thetically from entropy, which, as an intrinsic end, counts really as a non-purpose, it also differs fundamentally from purposes such as justice or love, which are set before one, by oneself or others, as the "pro-posed whereto" of one's action (Jonas 1966: 115).[9]

All this raises the question of whether Bourdieu really has gotten away from the structuralist's reductive picture of "agents as automata or inert bodies moved by obscure mechanisms towards ends of which they are unaware" (1990a: 98). Or perhaps he has simply introduced mechanisms so sophisticated that, like the mechanisms in cybernet-ics, they are hard to recognize as such—even by himself.

To be sure, Bourdieu makes a forthright case for the "reality" of subjectivity: "[T]he existence of symbolic capital, that is, of 'material' capital misrecognized and thus rec-ognized, although it does not invalidate the analogy between capital and energy, does remind us that social science is not a social physics; that the acts of cognition that are implied in misrecognition and recognition are part of social reality and that the socially constituted subjectivity that produces them belongs to objective reality" (1990a: 122). But if the operation of symbolic capital as capital supposes the "objective reality" of subjectivity, then I am led to wonder: Why is "capital," rather than "the symbolic," the first force of the designation? Why does not the existence of symbolic capital "invali-date the analogy between capital and energy" in some fundamental way? Why is not practice principally motivated by symbol rather than capital? If it were, then would not practice have the overall purpose of transcending itself as power driven? Are we not to understand that this purpose, rather than that of accumulating symbolic capital, stands behind Bourdieu's imposing attempt to objectify social scientific objectification?[10]

Similar questions may be raised about Bourdieu's use of "invention" or "improvisation" and "time." Given the absence of creative agency, what sense can these concepts make? Can there be invention if there is no moment of the "unpredictable novelty" diagnostic of genuine agency ("the conditioned and conditional freedom it [the habitus] provides is as remote from creation of unpredictable novelty as it is from simple mechanical reproduc-tion of the original conditioning" [1990a: 55])? Has time really been reintroduced into social theory if the principle of uncertainty finds an "objective basis" in the "probabilistic logic of social laws" (ibid.: 99). Probability does not rule out determinism. Moreover, given the plausibility of a closed system with chance elements, even indeterminism is not enough to admit of a truly open system, one in which, as Bourdieu says, things could always have been "otherwise" (ibid.; cf. Popper 1974: 1074). If invention, improvisation, and even time are to make sense in human terms, what is needed is the ontological pos-sibility of 'give' in the systemic flow of things, a limited but consequential vacuum by virtue of which radical novelty—the kind of unfamiliar and unprecedented creativity that characterizes imaginative endeavor—is given room or even called forth.

The body, however, may be conceived of as critically more than a non-conscious vessel of social regularity and reproduction. For me, the embodiment of culture is, above all, a creative process in which the body not only turns convention into habit, facilitating constraint, but also creates. Is not moral selection, that is, selection that obtains between the subjectlessness of natural selection and the self-transparent agency of perfectly witting choice, no less bodily than it is reflective? The idea of the less-than-conscious character of selection of this kind takes one of its cues from the notion of, so to speak, the 'body creative'. For better or for worse, the conception of the body as an agent of choice remains true to the essence of Merleau-Ponty's ideas—from which Bourdieu drew inspiration (cf. Bourdieu and Wacquant 1992: 20, 138n92; Wacquant 1993: 245)—as the habitus does not. Those ideas convey an ontology of ambiguity in which the body is a mere vehicle of neither structure nor structuring, but is understood, paradoxically, to perceive in its own right, as a 'body'.

Let me elaborate the contrast. "The practices of the members of the same group," writes Bourdieu (1990a: 59), "... are always more and better harmonized than the agents know or wish, because, as Leibniz ... says, 'following only (his) own laws', each 'nonetheless agrees with the other'. The *habitus* is precisely this immanent law, *lex insita*, inscribed in bodies by identical histories, which is the precondition not only for the co-ordination of practices but also for practices of co-ordination." Compare this description of the "immanent law" (which the habitus "is precisely") to Merleau-Ponty's characterization of the "unknown law" of speech as bodily rather than intellectual (1962: 183; emphasis added):

> Thought is no "internal" thing, and does not exist independently of the world and of words. What misleads us in this connection, and causes us to believe in a thought which exists for itself prior to expression, is thought already constituted and expressed, which we can silently recall to ourselves, and through which we acquire the illusion of an inner life. But in reality this supposed silence is alive with words, this inner life is an inner language. "Pure" thought reduces itself to a certain void of consciousness, to a momentary desire. The new sense-giving intention knows itself only by donning already available meanings, the outcome of previous acts of expression. The available meanings suddenly link up in accordance with *an unknown law*, and once and for all a fresh cultural entity has taken on an existence. Thought and expression, then, are simultaneously constituted, when our cultural store is put at the service of this unknown law, as our body suddenly lends itself to some new gesture in the formation of habit. The spoken word is a genuine gesture, and it contains its meaning in the same way as the gesture contains its.

Whereas the emphasis of Bourdieu's "immanent law" is on the inscription in the body of identical histories, that of his compatriot's "unknown law" is on the gestural creativity of the body, or, as Merleau-Ponty says (ibid.: 181), on the body as "a power of natural expression." For Merleau-Ponty, the body exhibits a primordial signifying intentionality, conceived of here by him as a "void of consciousness," which constitutes a creative openness. In Merleau-Ponty's scheme of things, it is this openness, rather than the uniformity of habit, that makes possible communication or tacit orchestration (ibid.: 193–94):

> In order that I may understand the words of another person, it is clear that his vocabulary and syntax must be 'already known' to me. But that does not mean that words do their work by arousing in me 'representations' associated with them, and which in aggregate eventually

reproduce in me the original 'representation' of the speaker. What I communicate with primarily is not 'representations' or thought, but a speaking subject, with a certain style of being and with the 'world' at which he directs his aim. Just as the sense-giving intention which has set in motion the other person's speech is not an explicit thought, but a certain lack which is asking to be made good, so my taking up of this intention is not a process of thinking on my part, but a synchronizing change of my own existence, a transformation of my being.

I have discussed Merleau-Ponty's work intensively in chapter 1. Here I merely wish to indicate that although both Bourdieu and Merleau-Ponty look directly to 'the body' for assistance in surmounting Western dualism, for the latter the body does not merely facilitate constraint, leaving invention to the mother of practical necessity, but above all functions as a creative agent. Whereas Merleau-Ponty has abandoned the Cartesian body in favor of one that does not reduce to 'the bodily', Bourdieu seems still to cling to it as a machine that defines reality in its own image.[11]

The principal issue here is not the comparison between the two thinkers, of course, but the question of whether Bourdieu's evident allergy to the idea of genuine agency hinders his anthropological efforts. It seems to me that it does. Let me try to prove the point by showing that, when push comes to shove, Bourdieu fails to acknowledge the anthropological other's otherness.

Otherness

In treating the anthropological question of "magical or religious actions," Bourdieu (1990a: 95), invoking Weber on behalf of an account in terms of the logic of practice, asserts that such actions should be construed as "this-worldly." As they are "entirely dominated by the concern to ensure the success of production and reproduction, in a word, survival," he says, "they are oriented towards the most dramatically practical, vital and urgent ends" (ibid.). The argument is a reaction to the various attempts to account for such actions in terms of objective meanings, such as, for example, Durkheim's functionalist predication of moral integration or Lévi-Strauss's structuralist thesis of logical integration. These accounts, he argues, constitute forms of reductionism and essentialism: they cut off practices "from their real conditions of existence, in order to credit them with alien intentions, [dispossessing] them of everything that constitutes their reason and their *raison-d'être*, and [locking] them in the eternal essence of a 'mentality'" (ibid.: 96)

Apparently, Bourdieu intends to comprehend magical and religious actions as symbolic but wholly practical. They are, he writes (1990a: 95), like "wishes or supplications," emerging in situations of extreme distress (such as "death or misfortune"), and having "no other purpose than to say or do something rather than nothing." In a word, they are performative, done for their own sake, "without any signifying intention." Their apparent foolishness stems from the fact that, as a function of the habitus, they "apply strategies" to the "natural" world that are suited, however, to the "social" world. As applied to nature, strategies of, say, authority and reciprocity—which is to say, strategies that work solely on other human beings—have a certain hopeless or "forlorn" quality about them (ibid.).

Bourdieu's argument strikes me as critically remedial. Yet it seems to go a step too far, constituting a reductionism in its own right and making it impossible to entertain the possibility of "alien intentions"—that is, the possibility of irreducible otherness.

The concept of otherness is hardly new to anthropology, which discipline has been defined as the study of *other* cultures. In recent years, however, under a well-meaning reflexivity of post-colonialist anthropology, there has been a decided tendency to reject—as 'othering'—the very idea of otherness. Behind this tendency rests the supposition that the attribution of otherness amounts only to a move in an imperialist game of political domination. In the view taken here, however, the trouble is not otherness per se but the easy and power-laden presumption that what is other is also singularly inferior. Given this point, ironically, any attempts to eradicate the idea of otherness, however well-intentioned, may do more to perpetuate than to combat the violent conceit of colonialism. By denying otherness, these efforts too manage to belittle the distinction and authenticity of the other.

Here, in diametric contrast to colonialist (and even post-colonialist) presumption, otherness—that is, precisely what cannot be wholly assimilated to the self—is afforded a certain axiological primacy. In this I take my cue from the thematically ethical philosophy of Emmanuel Levinas (1991).[12] According to Levinas, otherness defines the self's end. Although this usage may be unusual to social science, there is nothing especially mystifying about thinking of death as a final imposition of otherness on selfhood. Because otherness is thus de-finitive, Levinas grants it the respect owing to that in relation to which everything else must count as belated—ethical respect. Since relative others are, from another perspective, just other selves, they are of course no more nor less than human. Nevertheless, as others they also represent otherness in the deep sense just described, and insofar as they do, they warrant the kind of respect owing to, now in Levinas's religio-philosophical terms, the Other.[13]

In the case of the ethnographic other, this axiological warrant is peculiarly dramatic. Since at least the time of the nineteenth-century anthropological evolutionists, magico-religious thought has been a notorious and problematic site of the ethnographic other's otherness. In view of its implicit attribution of axiological primacy to otherness, such thought stands as uniquely representative of otherness as such and, correlatively, as jarringly other from the perspective of Western rationality, which is rooted in the Greek idea of the philosophical pursuit of the truth (see here Voegelin 1957 and, in this volume, chap. 13). And the truth, in this powerful tradition, is determinable (with the assistance of *logos*, to be sure) only by means of an act of radical disengagement from the world as we find it. As a result of this act, the one, as the truth, is distinguished from the many, which presents the world of sense perception and appearance rather than reality. This distinction finds its philosophical conclusion in Descartes' Platonic dualism of mind-subject and body-object. In effect, the perspective of rationality qua rationality is the perspective of the *cogito* or the unitary self, and as such it excludes otherness as irrational.

Bourdieu's argument about magico-religious actions—that they are simply matters of practice—sharply recalls Wittgenstein's in this regard. Wittgenstein also tells us that "magic does give representation to a wish; it expresses a wish" (1979: 4e). Compare here how Wittgenstein interprets the act of kissing the picture of a loved one (ibid.): "This is obviously *not* based on a belief that it will have a definite effect on the object which the picture represents. It aims at some satisfaction and it achieves it. Or rather, it does not *aim* at anything; we act in this way and then feel satisfied."

But the analogy to magical and religious acts among so-called primitive peoples is, although deeply enlightening, significantly inexact. For, as Bourdieu himself points out

(1990a: 95), ritual practices appear to confound the "social" with the "natural." In so doing, they convey a meaningful picture of the world other than the received picture in Western thought. Whereas the received picture is predicated on pronounced dualism, in virtue of which moral rules and natural laws signify mutually exclusive worlds, the former picture supposes an ontology of fundamental ambiguity. In such an ontology, an act can never be either social or natural, but always both and neither. By the same token, nature cannot be wholly indifferent to strategies of authority, since such strategies constitute not only culture or not-nature but also second nature. In which case, in this ontological picture of things, it is mistaken to construe ritual practices as simply performative, as if they did not also purport to accomplish something instrumentally.

Bourdieu's thesis about the magical act's confusion of the natural world with the social, even though the confusion is not intellectual, reminds one of Wittgenstein's conception of philosophical confusion: a lack of clarity resulting from failure to see that the same word can change in meaning from one context to another (cf., e.g., Malcolm 1994: 78–79). Just as this conception led Wittgenstein to think of the philosophical endeavor of clarification as a kind of liberating therapy, so, as I will cite later, Bourdieu is given to conceive of his project to objectify scientific objectifying, thereby freeing it from the fetters of everyday practice, as a kind of sociological therapy. But here, in relation to the magical and religious acts of which Bourdieu speaks—the sort of ritual practices typically reported in professional ethnographies—I am suggesting that his thesis about confusion may well beg the question. By deciding in advance that the natural and social worlds are indeed discrete, he precludes from consideration the possibility that such magical thought is not only practical but also in some significant, if limited, sense right.

Ritual practices are, too, characterized by an 'aim' or 'signifying intentionality', even if only utterly ambiguously. And this intentionality is, due to its failure to draw an immaculate boundary between what is social and what is natural, precisely 'alien' to the predominant intentionality of the modern worldview. The intentionality of ritual practice seems to remain opaque and impenetrable to the idea of identity so central to the logic of Western thought.[14]

To be sure, to return to Wittgenstein's provocative example, the picture of ontological ambiguity is implicit also in the modern's act of kissing a photograph; the 'bodily' intentionality of this act too runs deeper than wishful expression. But in this case, that picture is implicitly denied by virtue of the received ontology, which is patently dualistic as between the instrumental and the expressive. For reasons of this denial, the act tends to represent itself and be construed as simply emotive, as if it lacked any engagement of the 'real' world. Therefore, as its representation of itself informs in part what it is, it is best regarded as an act of ritualism, not ritual.

In their attempt to define magical and religious actions as exclusive of 'aim' or 'signifying intention', both Bourdieu and Wittgenstein draw an immaculate boundary between intentional purpose and practice. As a consequence, neither thinker is in a position to detect the signifying intentionality of the acts in question. Hence, in spite of their own remedial intentions, both thinkers end up by reducing such actions to the simply performative.[15]

By appealing to the notion of practice, Bourdieu finds that he has addressed the so-called problem of primitive mentality. Like Lévi-Strauss before him, Bourdieu seems to think that he has not so much answered as done away with the question of meaningful worlds that appear "alien." Through the solvent of "practice" rather than "structure," otherness is supposedly dissolved by him into ritualistic behavior. In this way, he makes otherness intelligible in terms familiar to Western thought, converting apparent difference into identity. If my criticism is right, though, this trick is performed at the cost of concealing the element of real difference. The nondualism whereby such magical and religious actions constitute their own end and yet—however nonsensically from a strictly logical point of view—display a certain instrumental intentionality gets lost in the epistemological shuffle.

In effect, in his rush to show that the actions in question are matters of praxis rather than *logos*, Bourdieu reduces the meaningful side of these actions. The otherness that is eclipsed by his analysis is not instrumentalism per se—which of course can scarcely be regarded as other from the point of view of Western thought. Rather, the otherness is instrumentalism that does not admit of rigorous definition in terms of means rather than ends. Such instrumentalism is less than instrumental in the received sense of the term, since it is assessed not simply by its objective effect, as a means to an end, but above all by its own 'moral' character, as an integral of the end. As instrumentalism of this kind cannot be meaningfully detached from the inherently discretionary constitution of the actions, its otherness rests with its implicit predication of a nondualistic world in which the operation of discretion has no need of explanation but is taken for granted as first and fundamental.

Thus, despite its emphatic attention to the symbolic, Bourdieu's notion of practice conceals the meaningful or moral side of social life and human practice, reducing it to a question of material survival (magical or religious actions are, as Bourdieu says (1990a: 95), "entirely dominated by the concern to ensure the success of production and reproduction, in a word, survival"). It then conceals the act of concealment by picturing the symbolic as having acquired, in the service of capital, a certain autonomy in its own right. But, to reiterate, if the symbolic enjoys a reality of its own, why is it always in the service of capital? Why do the tables never turn?

Bourdieu's failure truly to give meaning its due stands with his remarkable interpretation of Weber as an implicit materialist and his rejection of the phenomenological idea of lived experience. Although Bourdieu's reading of Weber (as carrying "the materialist mode of thought into areas which Marxist materialism effectively abandons to spiritualism") is both ingenious and useful (1990a: 17), it is frankly absurd in its willful blindness to Weber's obvious sociological preoccupation with the idea of meaning as such, a preoccupation that profoundly informed his analytical work.[16]

As regards phenomenology, Bourdieu's (1990a: 25–26) point that the idea of "lived meaning" is fundamentally limited is of course well taken. As he says, lived meaning or taken-for-granted knowledge cannot comprehend its own possibility, since this possibility always entails conditions that necessarily escape capture by the taken-for-granted. For example, the meanings of deference and insolence, as they are lived, are unreflexive or a priori. But their occurrence is nonetheless conditional on a socio-cultural context of hierarchical relations that can be determined only through objective analysis, such as statistics. Or so Bourdieu would have it. A more self-evident example is that lived meaning cannot comprehend the movement of practical transcendence involved in bringing into cognitive relief meanings that are lived before they are cognized. The practice of theorizing or objectifying cannot be grasped in terms of the taken-for-granted without making a logical nonsense of the reflexive movement that the practice constitutes.[17]

But a question arises here as to the nature of just what it is about practice that always escapes description through the idea of lived experience. For Bourdieu, as far as I can make out, this phenomenologically indescribable nature finally betrays (reduces to?) material production and reproduction. The trouble is that such a view implicitly objectifies the indescribable, ontologically limiting it in advance and therewith, contrary to Bourdieu's own express theory, denying the diagnostic feature of practice—temporality as open-endedness or abiding unforeseeableness.

Doubtless much of what is lost to the concept of lived meaning is open to the sort of objectification Bourdieu extols. But not all. Even hierarchical relations, so ready a target for materialist analysis, possess a nature that is downright inimical to analysis of this kind, as Louis Dumont (1970) has propounded and elaborated in his momentous study of the Indian caste system. Indeed, I would contend that at bottom this nature defies description not only by praxeo-logic and phenomeno-logic, but also even by Dumont's own quasi-structuralist logic of value. In my view, it is a nature that is indescribable in principle. As value qua value, the value that finally organizes any hierarchical order always supposes basic ambiguity and therefore a relative suspension of the deterministic ties that otherwise bind. It is this ultimate open-endedness, by definition indescribable, that allows for, calls forth even, the creative choice that makes value-as-such—and without value there can be no hierarchy (Evens 1995: 213–15). This truth applies even in the case of hierarchical relations expressly based on wealth and power. Although in a plain sense wealth and power sum up anti-value, they are themselves products of moral selection, and thus they too presuppose the possibility of value-as-such.

The only way to describe the indescribable without at once simply belying one's description is, as Levinas (1969: 27–28; see also S. Smith 1986) has shown, to focus on the way in which the indescribable interrupts phenomenology. In Levinasian terms, the experience of that which cannot be experienced discloses the fact of radical otherness. To be sure, in its fundamental contingency, so does the material side of existence. Production and reproduction place on display otherness of this kind, but they do so only as markers of what cannot be wholly grasped in terms of entitative, visible reality.

I am inclined to think that the magical and religious actions Bourdieu describes—to remedial but still shortsighted effect—as this-worldly and performative are in fact predicated on the apprehension of such radical otherness. It is this apprehension that informs thought and action that take for granted the ultimate efficacy of addressing commands to 'nature'. For what gives rise to the apprehension of such radical otherness is precisely the experience of what cannot be comprehended by experience, that is, of what somehow obtains between matter and spirit. As neither this nor that, as precisely otherwise than anything at all, radical otherness must always elude specification by a signifier. In which case, like a naturally lawful nature that responds to authoritative commands, it is the impossible. But it is an impossibility betrayed by the existence of every human being, of every biological creature given to reflexivity so profound as to notably reconstitute that biology on command. The biology is reconstituted to the point where it becomes impossible to distinguish between where biology ends and reflexive instruction begins, that is, to the point of bodily demeanor, carriage, gesticulation, embellishment, interaction, etc.—in a word, habitus.

Founded in an otherness that is at once both materially limiting and spiritually liberating, human beings are caught fast between material existence and agential deliberation. Forced thus to be free, to mediate their own material existence by way of self-making, intersubjective 'choices', human beings everywhere are necessarily, before production and reproduction proper, a question of ethics. For in virtue of the relative autonomy they enjoy from their own material constitution, such creatures are in a singular position to forgo, on behalf of their other—which is to say, on behalf of a self that is constructed in indebtedness to its other—not simply their own creaturely comforts but, much more pointedly, their very survival as creaturely beings. Thus, one must take great care not to be misled when considering production, reproduction, and survival in relation to human practice. Whereas these notions ordinarily serve as substantives of a kind, what is principally at stake in human practice is not substantive identity but self-identity, a primarily moral or transcendental rather than material end.

Conceived of as an order issued to or a request made upon the natural world, when the latter world is defined solely by opposition to the social world, a rain-making ceremony, for example, is indeed "forlorn" (Bourdieu 1990a: 95). From the perspective of modern technology, which measures success naturalistically, in terms of instrumental effect alone such an order or request appears outlandish. But from the perspective of human practice considered in the round, as ethics, a ritual of this kind expresses a profound truth—that discretion obtains no less 'naturally' in the world than does determinacy, and, correlatively, that in refashioning themselves, as is their lot, humans also manage to remake their world.

The rainmaker's mistake is not that he confuses the natural with the social world—that is what he has got right! His mistake is that, precognitively focused on the continuity between the two relatively distinct worlds, he is in no position to take optimal instrumental advantage of the marked degree to which the one works in isolation from the other. The modern's mistake, though, is no less "forlorn" and perhaps far more consequential. It is that, critically blinded by short-term interest and the commanding efficacy of instrumental success, he has forgotten that the boundary between society and nature is itself limited, and that in the long run, respect for the way—however remote and gradual (cf. Evens 1983)—in which the natural world registers the commands of the social world pays crucial dividends. Of course the rainmaker notices, as Wittgenstein quipped (1979: 2e), that "it does rain sooner or later anyway." But the rainmaker's action also acknowledges that the way in which he conducts himself is somehow tied to the way things are, to the blowing of the wind and the falling of the rain—even if (since it falls between lawful regularity and conformity to a rule) it is not possible to describe and comprehend just how. Whatever else radioactive winds and acid rains demonstrate, ordinary causality included, surely they demonstrate this ultimately inscrutable but deeply consequential connection, whereby human purpose informs natural process.

The conspicuous otherness of magical and religious thought springs from the fact that they are themselves predicated on the presumption of radical otherness. Such thought and action presume a universe in which the existence of discretion has no need of explanation but is taken for granted, making futurity genuine rather than a present yet to come or a knowable quantity not yet known. By reducing such thought and action to practices of material survival, even if these practices be performative rather than simply instrumental, Bourdieu manages to deny their otherness as well as the essential manner in which they are keyed to time and uncertainty.

The Gift

That Bourdieu's theory of practice implicitly stops time and excludes ethics is, ironically, perhaps nowhere more evident than in the example he deploys as the signature of his theory of practice as essentially temporal: the gift. Indeed, more generally, to hark back to the preceding two critical sections of this chapter, his analysis of the gift implicates his failure to give otherness its due and to grasp the inventiveness of habitus in terms of creative, bodily agency.

In breaking with structuralism, Bourdieu (1977: 4ff.) begins his *Outline* with a critique of Lévi-Strauss's reformation of Mauss's "phenomenological" approach to gift exchange. According to Lévi-Strauss, by focusing on the native experience and native theory of gift exchange, Mauss was in no position to explanatorily penetrate to the objective truth of such exchange, namely, the unconscious model of reciprocity. Bourdieu (ibid.: 5), however, points out that the "full truth" of the gift rests between Mauss' phenomenological (subjectivist) truth, on the one hand, and Lévi-Strauss's structural (objectivist) truth on the other. These are, respectively, the opposing truths of irreversibility and reversibility in exchange. In Bourdieu's words (ibid.), "any really objective analysis of the exchange of gifts, words, challenges, or even women must allow for the fact that each of these inaugural acts may misfire, and that it receives its meaning, in any case, from the response it triggers off, even if the response is a failure to reply that retrospectively removes its intended meaning." In short, the truth that structural objectivism excludes—the "full truth"—is the temporal "structure" of gift exchange. It is this structure, argues Bourdieu, that allows a pattern of exchange ever open to definition as reversible to be experienced and presented as irreversible, that is, as a gift.

There is no denying the penetrating shrewdness of Bourdieu's insight here. But what I wish to emphasize is the evaluative thrust of his insight (1977: 6)—that gift exchange is a "fake circulation of fake coin," a matter of "manipulation," "strategy," "misrecognition," "self-deception," and so on, apparently to the point of excluding the possibility of bona fide irreversibility. In other words, although Bourdieu acknowledges the perception of the possibility of a gift, he omits the possibility itself from consideration. Judging from his account, there is no such creature. Put another way, for Bourdieu. all giving is Indian giving, the kind by reference to which the North American Indians were given, perversely, a bad name.

But it seems obvious that time permits not only bargaining and strategic interacting disguised as giving, but also genuine giving and receiving without expectation of payment. Time does this even if giving cannot be experienced as such, or even if there is not any giving qua giving. Time constitutes a function that chronically ruptures totality or 'reciprocity' and makes history liable to ethical transcendence. In the first place, time is neither money nor power but openness, and this openness gives the social world to choice, and therewith to creation and gift(edness), no less than to the closure of exchange.

In his profound study of the gift, *Given Time*, Jacques Derrida (1992) points out that neither Mauss nor, to his knowledge, any other anthropologist has truly addressed the question of the gift. "[T]he gift is annulled in the economic odyssey of the circle as soon as it appears as *gift* or as soon as it signifies *itself as* gift," so that "a consistent discourse on the gift becomes impossible: It misses its object and always speaks, finally, of something else. One could go so far as to say that a work as monumental as Marcel Mauss's *The Gift* speaks of everything but the gift: ... economy, exchange, contract" (ibid.: 24, 26).

Obviously, despite his differences with both Mauss and Lévi-Strauss on the question of the gift, Bourdieu is no exception to Derrida's observation about anthropologists. Indeed, Bourdieu's argument that the gift is always counterfeit is based on the insight, which he shares with Derrida, that once the gift appears as gift, its logic becomes that of exchange and calculation. But whereas Bourdieu concludes from this penetrating insight, with a terrible material consistency, that the gift is delusory (a "fake circulation of fake coin"), Derrida (whose study of the gift is sprinkled throughout with the conditional "if there is any") draws from it a profoundly different lesson—that the gift remains always an open question. Of course, since, by his own understanding, he cannot mention the gift without at once annulling it, in arriving at his conclusion, Derrida offers up a maddeningly inconsistent discourse. He does so with all deliberation, though, aiming to make sure that he does not miss his object and speaks always, finally, of nothing else—of that which, by definition, cannot be known.[18]

Despite the fact that it does not present itself as such, Bourdieu's discourse too is, in the final analysis, consequentially less than consistent here. For as there can be no symbolic capital without the possibility of capital in the strict sense, so, obviously, there can be no counterfeit gift without the possibility of the real thing. Except here the real thing—gift—is precisely that which breaks the circular flow of the operations of the material world, the world of capital and exchange.

In effect, with his thesis of the gift as counterfeit coin, Bourdieu manages at last to turn the tables: by virtue of the logic of this thesis, unwittingly but ineluctably, he pictures the world of exchange as standing fundamentally in the service of—indeed, as owing its meaningful existence to—a self-starting world, one that does not lend itself to consistent representation in the material terms of capital. What is more, with this turning, the opposition between gift and capital is, paralogically, settled without being abolished. Since, precisely unlike capital, gift always remains its own end, considered in their chiastic and paradoxical role as 'foundations' to each other, gift necessarily enjoys a certain primacy over capital, the ultimately unfathomable primacy of a first principle. Accordingly, instead of symbolics thought of as a kind of epiphenomenal capital, what we have here is capital thought of as a lesser (because materially limited) version of an infinitely more productive principle.

Bourdieu (1990a: 41) is right: "gift" always presents a "misrecognition" enabled by time. But by taking this finding to entail that gift is indeed impossible (rather than a cipher of *the* impossible), that the question raised by the idea of the gift is closed, Bourdieu ends up by reducing the social world to exchange and power. This is the case notwithstanding his seductively resonant concept of symbolic capital, the theoretic deception of which helps allow for Bourdieu's materialism to be (mis)recognized as something other than reductionism, other than a "social physics" once removed but not discarded.

The folly of Bourdieu's reductionism is ironically evident in his brilliant and profoundly critical efforts to objectify the objectifying subject (1988), attempting thus to liberate sociology from its epistemological illusions and account for the production of himself as a sociologist disposed to do just that. In one of the few interview questions that seems truly to have puzzled Bourdieu's thoughtful but patently sympathetic interlocutor,

Wacquant puts his finger on a major fault line running through the theoretical mass of Bourdieu's project (Bourdieu and Wacquant 1992: 194):

> If I understand you correctly, then, science is still the best tool we have for the critique of domination. You fall squarely in line with the modernist project of the Aufklärung (and in sharp disagreement with the postmodernists) in that you argue that sociology, when it is scientific, constitutes an inherently politically progressive force. But isn't there a paradox in the fact that, on the one hand, you enlarge the possibility of a space of freedom, of a liberating awakening of self-consciousness that brings within rational reach historical possibilities hitherto excluded by symbolic domination and by the misrecognition implied in the doxic understanding of the social world, while, on the other hand, you simultaneously effect a radical disenchanting that makes this social world in which we must continue to struggle almost unlivable? There is a strong tension, perhaps a contradiction, between this will to provide instruments for increasing consciousness and freedom and the demobilization that an overly acute awareness of the pervasiveness of social determinisms threatens to produce.

Wacquant seems duly discomforted here. How is a person bent on sociological liberation supposed to live with herself once she has been liberated and has seen the social world for what it is—a power-driven, deterministic universe enabled by the routine self-deception of its constituents? Is not such a would-be liberator wittingly living a lie? If the social world is as fundamentally determined as Bourdieu asserts, then is not the consciousness-raising enterprise of liberation he extols an exercise in futility? Indeed, is not the exercise itself just another form of the misrecognition that serves to ensure the maintenance of the status quo? Wacquant does in fact lay stress on the consideration that since it occasions "disenchantment," Bourdieu's proposed exercise is bound to promote a "passively conservative attitude" (Bourdieu and Wacquant 1992: 195). But I wish to explore another implication of the "contradiction" between Bourdieu's sociological determinism and his liberationist designs—that it opens him to a charge of inauthenticity and supposes an epistemological objectivity so round as to be Cartesian or dualist in effect.

If Bourdieu's theory of practice is correct, then it must be the case that, whatever his express intentions, his efforts to free social science from its practice of power are really self-interested efforts to accumulate capital of one kind or another. Considered as a self-understanding—and Bourdieu is keen to impress that its capacity to comprehend its creator is one of its prominent distinctions—his theory of practice can only describe his (as everybody's) explicitly normative designs as witting or unwitting deceptions. Thus described, his designs function not only to mask but also, even more perniciously, to construct the very world they are expressly meant to transcend.

In his bold and important study of the world of the French university, Bourdieu (1988: chap. 1) attempts to invalidate in advance the interpretation of his work as a play in a practical game of power rather than a contribution to scholarly knowledge and scientific sociology. He does so by suggesting that the reader who wishes to objectify without being objectified—that is, the reader who has yet to be emancipated *from* ordinary social practice and *for* enlightened sociological theory—is disposed to make such an interpretation. The trouble with this discursive gambit is that it places the reader in a double bind. If the reader charges Bourdieu with academic capitalism, then he must be wrong; but if he omits to make this charge, allowing Bourdieu's theory of practice to go uninterpreted as itself a mode of practice in a field of competition over power, then he cannot be right. There is something oppressive about this attempt to pre-empt the reader's interpretation, so much so that it tends to make Bourdieu's practice of theory doubly suspect, as both artful and wrong.

If Bourdieu's claim to be charged with saving sociology for epistemological transcendence and theoretical control is to be credible, then his theory has to allow for a kind of 'capital' that is more than material yet less than symbolic—for a genuine surplus value. Put another way, he must grant that every economy and exchangist enterprise presupposes an inaugurating value, one that is finally irreducible to capital. Given such a value—an incommensurable 'capital', a not-capital, or, to wit, a gift—then any socio-economic order is, as Durkheim and Mauss surmised, a whole by value, an intersubjective reality, before it is a ring of exchange among monadic subjects or supremely pragmatic objects.[19] But holism of this sort, struck by an inaugurating value (what I am calling here, presuming [*pace* Kant] a heteronomous rather than autonomous subjectivity, a "primordial choice"), projects the whole as, rather than absolute, basically ambiguous. Such an essentially open whole intimates—with the gift—infinity and paradox. As a result, it cannot be wholly objectified and, correlatively, does not lend itself to self-transparency, to the final resolution of the gap between subject and object. Its ambiguity is basic, always displaying the observer's participation in what is observed and thus the insuperable limits of objectification.

One can only applaud Bourdieu's efforts to objectify objectifying, his offer of a sociological therapeutic, a veritable—as he proposes, after Freud and Wittgenstein—socioanalysis (1988: 5). But given his theory, how can we accept him at his word when he describes his offer as uncompromised by routine practice, that is, as a gift? Does he not propose here to offer up his subjectivity, his self, whole? And is the result not open to the same critique as applies to father Abraham in the Akedah, that of dialectical reversal? Insofar as Bourdieu's efforts project a picture of flawless objectification, a final resolution of the gap between subject and object, they are based on a reductionism logically akin to the dualist arguments his own theory of practice does so much to discredit.[20] Indeed, ironically, his apparent presentation of himself as an objectifier uncontaminated by dispositions less than suitable to scientific motives, a surpassing *lumière*, ultimately evokes the bodiless view-from-nowhere afforded by the Cartesian *cogito* (cf. Dreyfus and Rabinow 1993), a godlike expanse. This is the case, for all his thematic repudiation of the philosophy of consciousness and his definitively Marxian aspiration to turn on its head the epistemological hierarchy composed by philosophy on the one hand and social science on the other, placing the latter on top. Logically speaking, is it not open to us to describe the product of so sanitary an act of self-objectification—a virtual resolution of the subject-object tension—as pure consciousness, the dimensionless stuff that sheer, godly grandiose selves are made of? It is difficult to overestimate the salubrity of self-objectification, but all too easy to underestimate the harm it can do. Bourdieu seems less than alert to the consideration that acute reflexivity is critically double-edged. By giving one to stand back from one's 'ground', such reflexivity conduces objectivity; but in doing so it also prompts one to think of oneself as wholly detached, that is, as a self-possessed or Cartesian subjectivity. Reflexive action threatens to do other than therapeutic good if it forgets to attend resolutely to its own limitedness, to its 'foundation' in fundamental ontological ambiguity.[21]

The tension between subject and object, the tension in which "the spurious alternatives of social physics and social phenomenology" (Bourdieu 1990a: 140) find their source, is here regarded as essential. It can be resolved, as Bourdieu maintains, neither by material-ism ("social physics") nor by idealism ("social phenomenology"). With all due respect to his powerful critical theory, though, nor can a "generalized materialism" do the trick; the tension, inasmuch as it is essential, can only be mediated. The process of mediation is a matter of survival to be sure, but survival as meaningful existence, above and beyond—although not sublimely detached from—material production and reproduction.[22]

The subject-object tension may be construed as a distinctly human space and time. Since it is tensile or dynamic, such space describes work—it is a workspace. But not work simply, or even basically, in the physical sense of expenditure of energy, for the tension is a matter of responsibility wherein the self is charged or bound by the other to construct the purpose to which the effort is put. In other words, the work is the trans-forming of space into place or, in Cartesian terms, into purposeful extension. In effect, the space amounts to a dynamic openness that condemns humanity not so much to toil for a living (a condition hardly confined to humans) but, what is infinitely more trying, to do so by creating or giving purpose. The task of determining one's own end, that is, of situ-ating or de-fining oneself, renders even toiling for a living an option, albeit a mortal one. It constitutes a moral rather than economic mode of production, and of the two is by far the more demanding. The exquisite severity of this 'trial by labor' can be evoked by construing it in terms of a vital struggle, but not for survival in the usual sense of the word. Rather, it is a struggle for self-definition, and therefore with one's very ground. This profoundly disjunctive image—of a creature whose nature it is to determine its very own nature—projects all at once what it means to have to work for a living and yet to have the choice to do otherwise. Humanity may be said to be 'con-demned' to this eccentric, tensile space of existence because, considered as a dynamic of self-mediation, humanity is indistinguishable from the tension itself.[23]

The temporal nature of this dynamic is not really a question of its occurring *in* time, but rather of its character *as* time. Openness of purpose describes time as uncertain, unknowable, and incalculable. In other words, it describes an essential futurity, one that at bottom is irreducible to time-present. For no matter how well and truly one fills the future with conventional purpose, thus dissipating the uncertainty and constituting the time of now, in doing so one cannot help but re-create the context of irreducible futurity in which one is condemned to continue to do so. Thus, such time ever escapes the odyssey of the economic circle, in which case, of course, it can only be described as—as in the title of Derrida's book—given.

To be sure, as Bourdieu (1977: 5) says, the gift receives its meaning from the "response it triggers off." But paradoxically, the response, by definition an economic decision, receives its possibility from the originary value without which no economy can launch its circle of exchange. As it cannot be caught by that circle, the value consti-tutes an indebtedness that can never be redeemed. Put differently, as it is irreducible to the self-sameness of the circle, it is representatively other. For this reason, the conduct it inaugurates, even that of exchange and power, logically remains a matter of ethics before economics. Before it can be counted as conduct in the everyday terms of the material world, it must be informed by otherness.

Put yet another way, in terms of sacrifice, all human conduct takes place in the face of the other or otherness. This human dynamic of self-and-other is plainly gifted in that it is peculiarly discretional. Since the self could not have created it-self in the first place, the gift necessarily comes from the other. Moreover, because it is discretional, it constitutes a gift of life, but life in a sense that will not reduce to material survival, a sense described, rather, by purposefulness above and beyond such survival (for instance, Abraham's patriarchal immortality as a great and mighty nation). And because the vital capacity of this gift as discretion amounts to moral consciousness, the resultant self always finds itself—insofar as it finds it-self at all, and notwithstanding any accompanying resentment on its part—beholden to the other. But since the self is definitively self-responsible, it is also in a sense owing to itself. As one result of this peculiarly human condition, wherein one exists tensionally, divided morally and vitally between self and other, all human behavior describes the conduct of sacrifice—something always has to give. This living tension marks all human choices, even those the self makes between others (if one gives to X, thereby giving short shrift to Y, one's sacrifice of Y always remains subject to evaluation by reference to the axiological polarity of selfishness and selflessness). As another result, all human conduct constitutes an answer to the identitarian question of, not in the first place, who or what am I? but rather, what justifies me? The ethical question trumps the directly ontological question, thus making a non-ontological ontology.[24] Obviously, given that this tension between self and other is the human condition and therefore admits of no final resolution, the only viable way to proceed, as Bourdieu could not make plainer, is economically. But just as obviously, every such economy presupposes an aneconomic horizon, without which the economizing can make no sense. There must be something—an originary gift or value or sacrifice—to economize. Perhaps because this horizon is the very figure of the impossible, that is, always horizonal but never extant, Bourdieu fails to capture the ontological truth of its originary role in relation to human social reality, and in doing so, reduces that reality overmuch, to the final detriment of his sociology.

It is the case that, to cite Wallace Stevens's onto-culturological poetics (in H. Bloom 1976: 203), "we make of what we see … / a place dependent on ourselves"; but it is also the case "that we live in a place / That is not our own and, much more, not ourselves." It is tempting to conclude, with both Stevens and Bourdieu, that this trying state of affairs makes culture a supreme fiction. But, as seems to be understood by the poet but not the sociologist, this conclusion follows necessarily only if by 'fiction' one intends something that is indeed exquisitely symbolic and imaginative yet no less commandingly real than empirical reality itself. Whereas for Bourdieu the confected quality of human social purpose corresponds at bottom to a faculty of deception and self-deception, Stevens speaks here not of *illusio* but of "a world of poetry indistinguishable from the world in which we live,… [since the poet] creates the world to which we turn incessantly and without knowing it and … gives to life the supreme fictions without which we are unable to conceive of it."[25] To spin it my way, if reality is irremediably ambiguous as between choice and circumstance, then human practice is above all, before it is either material truth or *illusio*, either economics or symbolics, a self-responsible endeavor in the face of otherness and the other—in a word, an ethics.

As practice, ethics, like power, does not entail agency in the sense of a purely internal, mental substance, conscious or unconscious. I cannot fault Bourdieu's salubrious Wittgensteinian stance that the notion of a mental self, a wholly subjective phenomenon that makes thinking possible, is needless, a kind of, in Wittgenstein's derogatory usage, myth (Malcolm 1994: 54–55). Nevertheless, the practice that is specifically human is no less agential than it is powerful, no less ethical than pragmatic. For it does proceed, in part but fundamentally, by creative agency. The agency involved is primarily intersubjective, holding first of all between self and other—the material and the immaterial, the visible and the invisible—before it obtains as individual consciousness. In this utterly profound sense, as Bourdieu's Durkheimian sociologism registers, such agency is indeed social.

But the point to see here, in connection with Bourdieu's logic of practice, is that agency of this kind necessarily transcends materialism, not actually explaining purposefulness or intentionality, conscious or less-than-conscious, yet making it understandable that what we speak of in such terms takes place in this world. The ontological ambiguity that conditions human agency and marks human practice cannot be eradicated by self-objectification, for the ambiguity is the condition of human life. As such, despite appearances, it does not really allow for that life to take the form of an unbroken circle. There is no mechanism of production and reproduction, not even a pragmatic one affirming contingency as a basis for action, that can fill the gap of the ambiguity. Put another way, also keeping in mind Wittgenstein, there is no key to the grammar of human practice, for the grammar is a question of self-fashioning in the face of otherness and therefore entails creative or gifted as well as pragmatic choice.

The possibility of giving, then, is ineradicably implicated by the fact of material existence. As production and reproduction, no more than lived experience, can finally plumb the conditions of their own possibility, they betoken a nature that is somehow, at bottom, morally charged and irredeemably challenged by alterity, a nature that transcends or exceeds—that is other to—itself. It is this ultimately inexplicable nature, this unknown, always already forgotten law that makes sense of the admonishment to seek to liberate ourselves from the play of power and gives us insight into how it is possible to conceive of an intention to understand understanding. The sort of transcendence involved is ethical: it betrays a bodily consciousness that, in a logically impossible act of excess and re-creation, folds back on itself to yield consciousness as conscience and choice. To recall the earlier two critical sections of this chapter, it betrays 'bodily' invention as intention, rather than as conductorless, 'practical' ingenuity, and it implicates an irreducible otherness, a bodily being that is always other to itself—a veritable intersubject. In result, practice as production and reproduction becomes, diagnostically and simultaneously, mediation by moral or creative agency. Given this picture of human practice, materialism, even when it is generalized, is not enough.

Chapter 6

HABERMAS'S ANTI-DUALISM AND "COMMUNICATIVE RATIONALITY"

A whole mythology is deposited in our language.

— Ludwig Wittgenstein, "Remarks on Frazer's *Golden Bough*"

Jürgen Habermas's magisterial sociology takes 'rationality' beyond considerations of instrumental action and power, straight on the road to ethics. Also a grand exercise in practical reason, it nonetheless differs roundly from Bourdieu's sociology of practice. Whereas Bourdieu finds the answer to rationality proper and subject-object dualism in a bodily, historical, and political process (the habitus), and stresses the remedial force of scientific sociology, Habermas engages essentially the same problem by appeal to what he regards as the pragmatic universal conditions of linguistic communication, and argues for a rationality keyed to ethical consensus instead of power.[1] Put grossly, with no attempt to do justice to the exceptional depth and complexity of the ideas of either thinker, it is the difference between a kind of materialism on the one hand, and a kind of idealism on the other.

Just as for reasons of my reliance on a notion of practice I found it necessary to take up Bourdieu's imposing sociology of practice, so for reasons of my concern to develop a rationality centering on value rather than instrumentality I need to consider Habermas's prodigious attempt to save rationality for social theory and human interaction. Here my point of contention begins with Habermas's treatment of mythic thought. Habermas's (1984: 43ff.) evolutionary notion of "communicative rationality" renders this kind of thought as utterly, if not fundamentally, irrational and certainly backward. This consideration suggests to me that in spite of his richly reasoned rejection of instrumentalism as the sole basis of rationality, his theory somehow fails still to transcend the kind of rationality in which instrumentalism finds its logical inspiration.

Habermas's treatment of the question of mythic thought affords a revealing perspective from which to arrive at critical insight into the nature of his theory. More importantly here, though, insofar as his theory fails to escape the gravity of rationality proper, it betrays the logic from which the commanding authority of Western rationality derives, namely, dualist or binary logic. This logic, by prohibiting contradiction absolutely and demanding conclusive answers (which is to say, final solutions), prods Habermas to undermine his own posits of ethical order and fundamental intersubjectivity. As in my discussion of Bourdieu, it seems to me that the inconsistency in Habermas's argument arises for reasons of failure to rethink radically enough Western ontology. Whereas Habermas hopes to save humankind for rationality by appeal to the pragmatics of language, he begs—no doubt intentionally but, I believe, to the detriment of what he wants to accomplish—the ontological question of language itself. His failure to look beyond language in terms of the pragmatic conditions of the truthful exchange of information to language as communicability, that is, as the very possibility of speaking to and understanding one another at all, is tied to his failure to discern well enough the difference between rationality in terms of logic qua logic and reason qua ethics.

Mythic Thought as Closed

Although he points unreservedly to the excessive narrowness of a criterial focus that is restricted to cognitive-instrumental success alone, Habermas, well primed by the Enlightenment's opposing of *logos* to *mythos*, readily falls in with the early views of Robin Horton's (1967) anthropology. Horton's thesis centers on the well-known distinction, inspired by Karl Popper's (1962) powerful critique of dogmatism in Western social thought, between "open" and "closed" systems of thought.[2]

Horton acknowledges that mythic thought is indeed characterized by a certain rational aspect. From his neo-Tylorian perspective, such thought is a kind of pre-scientific groping, which differs from science proper in especially two ways. First, it is posed in the idiom of persons rather than things. Second, it remains mired in a closed world, a world in which critical thought is prescinded by dogma and taboo. Such a world is diametrically opposed to the open world of critical (in Popperian terms, rational) thought.

I am not partial to Horton's designation "idiom" for the thematic emphasis that archaic peoples place on "person" as opposed to "entity." As I see it, that difference is more substantive than "idiomatic" allows, for it betrays a divergent grasp of reality. It can be glossed as simply another idiom only at risk of a significant misunderstanding—as if personification and reification were merely different ways of expressing the same thing.

As to the second difference Horton highlights between science and traditional religious thought, that is, the difference of open or critical versus closed or uncritical thinking, my position deviates radically from his. The attribution of epistemological closure and openness to, respectively, mythic and scientific thinking throws real light on the nature of the difference between the two modes of thought. Unfortunately, the rationalistic brilliance of the light also serves to obscure an aspect of the nature of that difference that is equally—if not more—edifying: the crucial sense in which it is the mythic world that is open and the scientific one that is closed.

By distinguishing between instrumental rationality and what he calls communicative rationality, Habermas intends to capture the possibility of a moral world as such. 'Person' versus 'thing' is not for him simply an idiomatic distinction. The concept of communicative rationality is a question of, no less than formal consistency between means and ends, a dialogue unconstrained by forces other than those of reason, or, in his oft-cited phrase, an "ideal speech situation." The ideal speech situation is that situation at which any discursive argument worthy of its name ought to aim (cf. McCarthy 1978: 434n4). In effect, communicative rationality is a question of ethics. Habermas argues that in a communicative universe, interlocutors necessarily presuppose the possibility of distinguishing not only between truth and falsity but also between normative correctness and incorrectness, sincerity and insincerity. Thus, they lay claim to truth in three "worlds"—the objective, the normative, and the subjective—and presume the possibility of arriving at consensus in such terms. These three kinds of "validity claim" are, he argues, pragmatic conditions of any human communication aimed at mutual understanding, and therefore constitute universals.

Habermas is thus keenly alert to the vital fact that rationality is a matter of not only propositional logic but also the conditions of social interaction. Nevertheless, his position leads him to conclude one-sidedly, with Horton, that mythical thought is simply closed relative to modern thought. In other words, mythical thinking aims at anything but the ideal speech situation. Taking a cue from Horton's reservation (cited in Habermas 1984: 65) that the absolutism of scientific thought has tended to drive out the "poetic quality" of everyday life, Habermas does observe emphatically that from mythical thought we can learn about the danger of hypostatizing instrumental rationality. He thus positions himself to give a certain credit to the arguments of scholars, like Winch, who oppose evaluating mythical thought simply by reference to rationality in the strict sense of the term. But Habermas does not allow this insight to qualify the one-way directionality of his evolutionary picture of mythical thought as closed in relation to the modern understanding of the world. For him, by bearing on the worlds of normative rightness and subjective truthfulness in addition to the world of objective truth, the closed quality of mythical thought just becomes more comprehensive.

In view of the fact that mythical thought differentiates subject from object only "deficiently" (Habermas 1984: 49), this thought is in no position to adjudicate well between (or as Habermas puts it, to say yes or no to) validity claims and remains unreflexive as to its own status as a system of representations. Obviously, if subject and object are not sharply distinguished from each other, the subject is hindered from standing back and assessing the validity of its own claims, whether these are about the objective, social, or subjective reality. Following Piaget, Habermas speaks of the cognitive uncoupling of the object world from the subject as "the decentration of an egocentric understanding of the world" (ibid.: 69). In these terms, he concludes (ibid.: 70):

The more the worldview that furnishes the cultural stock of knowledge is decentered, the less the need for understanding is covered in advance by an interpreted lifeworld immune from critique, and the more this need has to be met by the interpretive accomplishments of the participants themselves … Thus … we can characterize the rationalization of the lifeworld in the dimension "normatively ascribed agreement" versus "communicatively achieved understanding." The more cultural traditions predecide which validity claims, when, where, for what, from whom must be accepted, the less the participants themselves have the possibility of making explicit and examining the potential grounds on which their yes/no positions are based.

Plainly, Habermas gauges the openness of a way of thought according to a single standard: the greater the degree to which thinking is immune from critique, the less open it is. By "immunity from critique" here, Habermas is apparently referring to preclusion of the possibility of responding yes or no to a validity claim. Obviously, where differentiation remains only relative, it is not possible to answer in such conclusive terms, and this is the case if we are considering not only the validity claims of the objective world but also those of the normative and subjective worlds.

Two Kinds of Openness

In effect, despite the emphatic, remedial attention Habermas gives to the normative and expressive aspects of communicative interaction, for him the standard of openness is univocal. But if we are to do justice to its ethical nature, we need to grasp openness in terms of two dynamically intertwined meanings: for the one, openness refers to the scope of choice, the degree to which the world is open to the subject's discretion as considered in terms of his ability to respond to the world in decisive terms; for the other, it refers to the measure to which the subject himself is open to the other. The second kind of openness does not reduce to self-criticism, when such criticism is taken to mean the capacity to respond yes or no to the self's claim. On the contrary, the second kind of openness entails the self's fundamental uncertainty in the face of the other.[3]

Habermas's pragmatic understanding of openness largely corresponds only to the first sense. Immaculate differentiation constructs the world in terms of, to be sure, choice. It projects the world as a place of alternatives so discrete that they offer themselves to unequivocal affirmation or denial by a discretionary subject. Plainly, this sense of openness is tied to binary logic, a logic that wields the power of clean division. Even when the set of things among which one is choosing does not reduce to two, as long as the available choices are perfectly separate and distinct from one another, one is enabled to proceed in binary fashion, by saying, unambiguously, yes or no to each.

But the second sense of openness—openness as receptivity to the other—constitutes the more profound condition of the capacity of choice and ultimately belies immaculate differentiation. It is only in view of the other that selfhood makes any sense at all. Before the world can be rendered radically open to choice through telling difference in decisive terms, there must obtain the capacity for discretion. This capacity ultimately amounts to the ability to stand against one's own ground: it is by virtue of such an act of resistance and distanciation that one can discover, and thus develop, one's discretionary force or selfhood. But at the same time, it is crucial to see that the capacity to stand out as against one's ground can issue only from that ground, for were the capacity otherwise derivable, then, accordingly, one's ground would also be otherwise. What else but one's ground can give one to be, can sub-ject one? In Judeo-Christian thought, this creative dynamic of discretion is paradigmatically conceived of in the chiastic terms of a creature fashioned in the image of its creator. In other words, selfhood is in the first place not a matter of one's choice but of pro-jection by one's ground, which is to say, in this tradition, by the Other. And since, in this case, what is thus created is selfhood, that is, the capacity to choose for oneself, the pro-jecting is indistinguishable from a subject-ing.

The two kinds of openness may also be described with reference to the idea of arbitrary choice. When the line dividing one thing from another is imperfect, as is the case with regard to self and other, it is logically impossible to give an unambiguous yes or no to the one over the other. Since the differentiation between them is relative and incomplete, saying yes to the one thing cannot but mean saying yes, in some measure, to the other and no to both. Moreover, under these conditions and by the same token, whatever one's choice, it must always be subject to a value other than one's own. That is to say, one cannot plump for x without at the same time giving way, in degree, to y. In any event, one's choice, although highly personal, must always proceed in part according to a value external to one's own preference, and in this sense can never be merely arbitrary. As soon, however, as things are pictured as perfectly separate and distinct from one another, then one's choices lend themselves to arbitrariness in that they appear, to oneself and others, to be constrained by one's will alone. The effort is to perfect openness as it is described by arbitrary selection, at the expense of openness to one's other, the kind of openness from which discretionary powers derive in the first place. In result, to use a convenient terminology, value is reduced to preference.

To expand on an example in the introduction, take the issue of abortion in the United States. Both sides of this acutely divisive debate are inclined to reduce choice in just this fashion. According to the "pro-life" side, the champions of a woman's right to choose have torn away the vital gravity of abortion by regarding it as a matter of prefer-ence or arbitrary choice. To the extent that they see the question of abortion as utterly predetermined, though, the "pro-life" proponents fail to comprehend the very idea of choice, the idea of selection the autonomous agency of which is levied by the essential ambiguity of the options. The sense of choice open to them is the reductive one keyed to preference rather than value and definitive of acts of consumption. On the other hand, inasmuch as the "pro-choice" side fails to see that "a woman's right to choose" comes to more than mere personal and political preference, to bear the diacritically human value of non-arbitrary selection in which external value is not simply oppressive but also enabling, this side too projects a reductive sense of choice and, what is more, helps to promote abortion as a discretionary behavior more suitable to the shopping mall than to what is potentially a human life defined in all its singularity.[4]

Despite the myopic propensities of the two sides, their respective choices and valid-ity claims—on the one hand, to carry the fetus to term and, on the other, to miscarry it—ultimately convey 'choice' as this word is used to denote non-arbitrary selection. Both options implicate the selfsame idea of life as it is peculiarly distinguished by just this deep sense of choice: in the one case, the life of a human fetus, which is indeed 'soulfully' capacitated, and in the other, the life of the maternal bearer, discretionary and therefore no less soulful than the fetal life so borne. The opposing positions of the debate are hardly mutually exclusive. Together, in the basic ambiguity of their opposi-tion, they pose a choice not between good and evil but between options both of which are life-threatening, in the fundamentally dual sense of 'life' we tend to take for granted when we speak of human life in particular—creaturely life and life as factitious or self-chosen. In effect, then, the debate defines, rather than a contest between mutually exclusive causes, a true and vital dilemma that calls for unremitting choosing in precisely the sense of the term at point: the dynamic, ethical sense—the sense distinctive of life as it is peculiarly human.

On the logic of this discussion, it would appear that, ironically, there is actually something dehumanizing or, to be more exact, desubjectifying about Habermas's standard of openness. Given the complexity of his position, it may seem startling to associate him with brute decisionism. But as is implicit in, for example, Augustinian moralism—whereby good and evil are perfectly distinct from each other, making it possible for Augustine to picture evil as the product solely of man's divided will—validity claims perfectly differentiated from each other offer themselves whole cloth to resolution by the will of the chooser alone. Such claims differentiate self from other (in Augustine's argument, 'Other') in the same immaculate way they are themselves differentiated. The irony is that although it presents a veritable picture of the enlightened (liberated) self, subjectivity so complete, so utterly composed, signifies determinism rather than choice. The self may be constitutionally opposed to the other, but in the end the capacity of the self to choose still depends on making a choice for the sake of the other, that is, on admitting external value.

Seeing itself as wholly autonomous, the self threatens to cut itself off from the very moorings of selfhood by denying them. The resulting subjectivity is as bogus as it is conspicuous, for the self's defining capacity, its ability to create itself and its world, is not thus enhanced but undercut. The abortion debate, in which, in their typical representations, the options could not be more starkly differentiated from each other, constitutes a forcefully blunt illustration of the point. The total closure of each side to the call of the other, although logically stupid, not only prescinds any creative construction of an in between, but also (in a stunning irony the truth of which is plain to see in the homicidal behavior of both sides of the debate) undermines the very value finally at stake—that of life in its peculiarly soulful or human presence.[5] In the absence of ambiguity, what is there to 'choose' but the Same, the pre-existing order of identity and difference, whether this order is construed as a matter of divinity or rationality or common sense or tradition or something else? Of course, a choice taken on the basis of, say, religious or rational truth may present itself as based on anything but arbitrary or subjective preference. But once the chooser incorporates them as primordial choices, such truths come to define her self-identity. They no longer function as external values but, to the contrary, work to cut the chooser off from such values. These truths then effectively become the will (even if a divided one) of the chooser, and as such constitute choices for her own sake rather than for the sake of the other. This is why a Father Abraham or a Mother Teresa remains susceptible to criticism as self-interested.

What is fundamental to the meaning of heeding the call of the other is not making the call one's own, but remaining ever open to it—enough to make a choice for the sake of the other. If I make a choice solely on the basis of what I take to be my true, inner, or self-certain self, then I represent myself as fixed and unchanging and thus foreclose on my creative capacity, defining my choice more in terms of constraint than freedom.[6] For a self to express its autonomy, it must remain alert to its own fundamental uncertainty in the face of the other.

Seeing something of the sort, Michel Foucault found that, far from the celestial abode of freedom it is supposed to shine forth, the modern self, tied as it is to the idea of heroic self-control, constitutes the most comprehensive form of incarceration hitherto known to humankind. As I see it (a thesis I develop in chapter 11), Foucault's charge is that if by selfdom one means creative agency, then the modern self is scarcely a self at all.

Relative Differentiation

If, in the interest of openness, the modern self seeks to substitute for creative agency a necessitarian calculus of certainty, then it can do no better than to rely on propositional logic to ensure its goal. The binary nature of this logic guarantees outcomes that are certain. It is by definition identitarian logic. By excluding the middle, the inbetween, this logic contrives to remove all brokenness and uncertainty; in effect, it dismisses otherness or any difference that cannot be reduced to the same. Correlatively, it cannot tolerate contradiction. Authentic choice, wherein the uncertainty as to which option to take is in principle fundamental, is thus made logically impossible. If this picture is sound, then even if the sort of decisive differentiation Habermas takes as the measure of openness contributes somehow to choice, it cannot do so primordially. Authentic choice supposes what Habermas calls "deficient," but I prefer to call relative, differentiation.

No one should doubt that Habermas's concept of communicative rationality does implicate the kind of ethical openness I have in mind. The recommendation that ideally the speech situation ought not to proceed on the basis of power and constraint is emphatically a celebration of the primacy of the other. It proposes that one ought to be open to one's other, not because one is so forced, but because such openness is good—it reaches toward mutual understanding. But because Habermas ties validity claims comprehensively to either-or logic, he undermines the very recommendation that does most to distinguish communicative rationality from cognitive-instrumental rationality.[7] The insistence that the validity claims of all three worlds—the objective, the normative, and the subjective—answer to yes/no resolution assimilates ethical to logical openness, thus tending to reduce goodness to *episteme* and *logos*, and communicative or pragmatic rationality to theoretical rationality.

I suspect that the difficulty rests with the fact that Habermas weights each of the three worlds as equal to one another. By doing so, he omits in his approach to allow for the superiority of the ethical over the rational, a superiority that the approach highlights in the very notion of the ideal speech situation—a quintessentially normative notion. If moral value rather than coercion is to define the speech situation, allowing reason, considered as reasonableness by contrast to theoretical rationality, to prevail, then the approach must give overall precedence to relative over absolute differentiation. To do this, the questions of sincerity, normative rectitude, and even of fact, although resolvable for the time being, must be seen as always open—that is, they must all be seen as ultimately normative, when this term is taken in its ethical rather than political sense, to mean a matter of discretionary rather than criterially correct determination.

If the questions of sincerity, normative rectitude, and fact are subordinated finally to logical and evidential conclusion, they will serve to foreclose on further questioning, thus undermining the fundamentally ethical nature of the situation and making

Habermas's concept of communicative rationality dogmatic. While legislating against contradiction may economize getting on with things, insofar as it rules ambiguity out of court, it mandates not for theory as an aid to practice, but for rationality as against life. Put another way, such 'lawmaking' tends to pit efficiency against choice qua choice in a way in which an overriding preference for efficiency is effectively secured by one of the 'powers that be' in Western civilization, namely, the great force of abstract logic.

The Question of Non-contradiction

It is illuminating here to restate this critique by referring it to a matter that will play a central role in part 2 of this volume, the question of non-contradiction. In an exercise of exemplary clarification, Martin Jay (1992) has essayed, in relation to Habermas's work, the debate over performative contradiction. Habermas's organizing idea of communicative rationality is keyed to the combating of, instead of propositional or ontological inconsistency per se, the incongruity that holds "when whatever is being claimed is at odds with the act of claiming it" (Jay 1992: 265)—to wit, a performative contradiction. As a concept, performative contradiction falls directly between the Aristotelian notion of contradiction as a purely logical phenomenon and the Hegelian-Marxian notion of contradiction as an ontological reality. Hence, the concept is important to Habermas's linguistic turn away from, on the one hand, rationality in the strict sense and, on the other, social ontology proper. For Habermas, intersubjectivity is best understood by reference to neither idealism nor materialism, but rather the pragmatics of language. What is for Habermas a performative contradiction, though, is for postmodern thinkers a permanent and irreducible condition of human existence. Using Foucault, Gasché/Derrida, and De Man/Nietzsche as foils, Jay makes plain the opposition between postmodernism and Habermas's critical concern with performative contradiction.

Because it too seems to implicate a subject-object dualism, I cannot embrace in its entirety Nietzsche's iconoclasm that the logical canon of non-contradiction is simply "a subjective empirical law, not the expression of any 'necessity' but only of an inability" (quoted in De Man 1979: 119). Still, I have great sympathy for the postmodernist position that what goes by the name of performative contradiction is positively fundamental for human existence. Indeed, in part 2 I shall argue that from the perspective of practice, the act of affirming and denying one and the same thing is not exactly a contradiction, a fault to be eradicated, but instead may constitute an act of resistance. The assertion that something both is and is not what it is flies in the face of entitative ontology, since this ontology is keyed to the logic of identity. As a result, such an assertion tends to blur the distinction between matter (a thing) and non-matter (no-thing). And when it is performative rather than purely logical, such an assertion directly manifests ontological ambiguity, thus denying mind-body or spirit-matter dualism. In so doing, it also presents the situation of choice, an aporetic situation that marks an opening or ambiguity in the order of things, such that room exists for creational movement, for the self (in its otherness) to fashion itself. Herein, in fundamental ontological ambiguity, rests peculiarly the human situation. Obviously, despite its preoccupation with 'choice', a bugbear for postmodern thought, this argument has something very substantial in common with those postmodernists who would "deny the possibility of any noncontradictory consistency" (Jay 1992: 274), that is, who regard performative inconsistency as a human condition.[8]

On the other hand, I would also argue (see chaps. 11 and 12, this volume), with Habermas, that there is much to be gained, both epistemically and ethically, by attending with critical concern to contradictions, performative and otherwise. Ought we not expect people to make the effort to conduct themselves according to their word, and to conduct their theoretical arguments according to reason? For the sake of argument, take, hypothetically, a thinker whose postmodernism is vulgar enough to maintain the wholesale rejection of Enlightenment reason and the modern self. Can he mount this argument intelligibly save on the basis of that very reason and sense of self? Is not such a performative contradiction cause for critical concern?

I wish, then, to embrace both the position of Habermas and that of his critics. How can I bring this off without contradicting myself? The appearance of inconsistency in my position depends on the presence of a profound inconsistency in Habermas's argument. The postmodernist theses of subjectlessness, heterology (*différance*), and fundamental existential tension and the Habermasian ideal of unconstrained communication center alike on the ultimate openness of human existence. This is true despite the fact that postmodernists, seeing the glass half-empty and emphasizing the picture of limitedness made by this openness when it is cast against the background of Enlightenment aspirations, are inclined to understand this condition in terms of power, whereas Habermas, seeing the glass half-full and concerned to fulfill the liberating promise of the Enlightenment project, grasps the condition in terms of ethics (cf. Honneth 1991).

The trouble is, however, that Habermas's ideal of unconstrained linguistic communication is not in keeping with his assertion of the pragmatic truth of the law of non-contradiction, as this assertion is set forth in his argument. The law of non-contradiction does its work by constraining a resolution, a yes or no response, rather than by creating openness to further questions, to otherness. For this reason, hoisting Habermas on his own petard, Foucault (1984: 42) responded to Habermas's criticism by calling it Enlightenment "blackmail" (see also R. Bernstein 1992: chap. 5). Habermas's point was that Foucault exhibited "arbitrary *partisanship* of a criticism that cannot account for its normative foundations," that is, a performative contradiction. Foucault's response was that in the name of freedom, Habermas means to force Foucault into an Enlightenment position whereby whoever is against normative foundations cannot be for normative ideals. In effect, putting aside for the moment the apparent futility of this critical exchange, Foucault turns the charge of performative contradiction back onto Habermas.

If the concern for performative contradiction is to adhere to the call for the ideal speech situation, a situation basically defined by its openness to redefinition by the other, then the concern must fall short of demanding conclusiveness. The only way I can see to conform to a law of non-contradiction while at the same time making it less than conclusive is to relativize it. (For obvious reasons, eradicating it, as postmodernism might lead one to deem desirable, will not do the trick.) In the present work, I propose to relativize the canon of non-contradiction by attributing to the ethical demand for openness hierarchical primacy whereof that demand comprehends the logical canon. As a result, the two principles are reconciled even as they stand opposed to each other.

Because it serves to exclude the middle, the primacy apparently afforded by Habermas to the validity claims of the objective world over those of the normative and subjective worlds checks any such hierarchical or asymmetrical order. And in the absence of such a (disorderly) order, the principles of non-contradiction and unconstrained communication can obtain solely as contradictories, as I believe they do in Habermas's theory. Where they do, needless to say, it appears unreasonable to hold at one and the same time the postmodernist thesis of fundamental inconsistency or *différance* and the Habermasian commitment to validity claims. The contradiction between the principles of non-contradiction and unconstrained communication may be read in the very idea of communication in Habermas's discourse. For Habermas, paradigmatic communication takes place between equals. Obviously, this notion of communication aligns with the ideal of unconstrained linguistic interaction. However, when the self and the other in communicative exchange are regarded as equals, the other appears as just another self. Among equals, there can be no genuine otherness—unlike 'separate but equal', which epitomizes the social ideal of modernity, 'other but equal' is nonsense.[9] The notion of equality supposes not difference but the identity that derives from membership in the Same.

Hierarchy, Equality, and the Relativity of Binary Logic

I suggest, then, despite Habermas's express contrary intentions and appeal to communication as the medium and mark of the generative priority of the 'intersubjective', that his idea of communication implicitly describes as basic the self and the individual, not the other and society. The conception of society brought into relief by the idea of equality already presumes a third-person perspective, a non-participant, detached perspective wherefrom society appears as, instead of an intersubjective dynamic, a totality in terms of its objective constituents. The constituents are viewed from the 'outside', as if from nowhere in particular, and as societal by virtue of, in the first place, their common, objective identity as rationally capacitated individuals rather than their nature as essentially interpersonal. In other words, they are seen as bound together by external relations only, as if they were all nothing but third persons to one another. In this way, they are enabled to apprehend one another universally, as identical fungible units—that is, as equals.

In the absence of third persons, one would never have the option of seeing the other objectively. One could only meet the other face to face as what is participant with but always beyond and irreducible to oneself. Such immediacy describes communication as a becoming other to oneself. But when society is considered primarily from its third-person aspect, communication becomes a matter of reciprocation between identical selves rather than participation between self and other. Under these conditions, relations between one another can only be indirect: it is as if one's experience of the other is never direct and immediate but rather always modeled on one's experience of someone one does not know but knows *of*. As a result of this detachment, what goes on in the way of communication is bound to fix rather than transform the self: when it threatens self-certitude, communication, conceptually secured from the immediacy between concrete interlocutors, seems especially constrained to break down. In this event, the self appears as essence rather than dynamic, as a modality of determinacy instead of freedom.[10]

To once again deploy in illustration the example of the abortion debate, the fact that the debate evolved as a sheer power struggle implies that the two sides stand to each other, formally, as equals. This does not mean that one side may not be (or become) more powerful than the other, but that even were this the case, unless the dominant power were converted into authority of some kind, the two sides would still be identical to each other as units of structural contraposition. Were either side to acknowledge the legitimacy of the other's argument, there would then obtain between them a relationship of authority—in this case, an ethically based asymmetry or hierarchy—and the debate could be settled on grounds other than power as such. As they stand, however, the sides are virtually impervious to each other's call. Each is constrained more fundamentally by its idea of itself as perfectly self-contained than by the content of its ideas about abortion. This hermetic self-identification defines, with the same absolute edge, the limits of the ideas on abortion, cutting each side off from the arguments of the other. Correlatively, the alternative choices confronting the sides are defined binarily, leaving no ground on which either side can open itself to the other. Given the closed nature of the sides, the choices become questions of sheer preference and, in this sense, arbitrary. Put differently, the debate's rhetoric of religious and moral values is deceptive, inasmuch as it tends to conceal the fact that the boundaries defining the two sides are so fixed and impermeable that they cannot admit of value that does not issue from the conceit of the Same.

In effect, looking through a tenacious and facile dualism, each side sees the other as, if not radically evil, at least dead wrong and accordingly as deserving of nothing save total defeat. Neither side is epistemologically free to entertain the force of the other side's argument. The relevant validity claims are framed so as to permit a response in terms of yes or no, but can either side say anything but no to the claims of the other, and yes to its own? The self-certitude of the sides and the dualism it expresses present a picture of the Enlightenment turned against itself. Leaving the issue between them preponderantly to power, the sides sorely constrict the play of otherness or difference.[11] Otherwise, they would see their way to reaffirm the value of fetal life and of the life of the child-bearer at the same time, since, as peculiarly discretionary or (to use the biblical descriptor) inspired, it is the same 'life' at stake in both cases.[12]

In a well-known article, the philosopher Judith Jarvis Thomson (1971: 48ff.) asks that we imagine waking up to find ourselves attached by dialysis to a famous musician who is dying of kidney disease. We have been kidnapped, or so the hypothetical goes, to serve for a period of nine months as a life-support system, at the end of which time the musician will be able to survive on his own. The question posed by Thomson is this: given that the musician will indeed expire if detached, does he have a right not to be detached and is it "morally incumbent" on us to accede to the situation. She expects that we would find an affirmative answer to these questions "outrageous" (ibid.: 49), which in turn suggests to her that there is something fishy about the presumption of the argument against legalized abortion—that the right to life simply trumps the right of the bearer of the child to control her own body in this connection. Putting aside the question of rights, for my purposes what is striking about Thomson's imaginary case is this: although at first blush it is (in line with Thomson's purpose) a perfectly outlandish set of circumstances, the case models not simply certain situations of unwanted pregnancy but, profoundly, the human situation in general.

If one considers that each of us is fully capacitated at any given time to harm our neighbor, if not to rise up and kill him, then in this eminently concrete sense, each of us is indeed responsible for our neighbor's life. Typically, in the event of such vio-lence, we are inclined to ask how it could have happened. Perhaps, though, the more profound question is, why does this not happen all the time? In view of our general capacity to do grave damage to others, the very existence of our neighbor constitutes an imposition on us not to harm him, and thus invests us morally, realizing our endowment as ethical beings—in a word, as selves. In effect, speaking ethically rather than physiologically (which is not to say solely immaterially), we are all already vitally attached to one another, and, like Thomson's medical hostage, always having to decide whether or not to pull the plug.

In point of fact, we do pull the plug in countless ways and measures, from warfare to murder, rape, torture, hate crimes, anger, revenge, abuse, willful neglect, complacency, etc. What is more, considering that our 'neighbor' is ultimately Everyman, our respon-sibility necessarily exceeds our moral resources, meaning that we cannot help doing violence to others. Here I have in mind Derrida's (see chap. 3, this volume) critically arresting argument—that our obligations can be discharged only in the particular, such that to fulfill one such obligation is to sacrifice others. In attending to the well-being of one of our neighbors, the welfare of others must be allowed to go begging. Of course, this practical limitation cannot excuse failure to seek, in any particular context, the 'fairest' possible way to discharge our obligations, that is, to make every effort to do justice. Nevertheless, since triage is a necessary condition of moral choice, there is a substantive sense in which the answer to the question of why we do not do violence to our neighbor all the time is: "But we do." Of course, violence of this kind, resulting from the limited good, logically entails that (as we all already know and largely expect anyway) ordinarily we do indeed refrain from doing harm to others.

What I am anxious to highlight in this discussion of Thomson's hypothetical example are not specific answers to these questions about violence, however, but the idea that whatever the answers are, they cannot help but presuppose the fundamentally ethical nature of selfhood and the human condition. What the example (like the reality it is meant to model—that of the relation between a woman and the fetal life she car-ries inside her) brings into relief is this: in respect of one's selfhood, the existence of the other constitutes both threat of displacement and vital condition. We are caught, as an irremediable foundation of our being, between the threat to our Selves, posed by the very existence of the other, and the other's entreaty not to suffer harm, a plea so passive that even a fetus can make it and without which our selfhood would go unrealized.

If this predicament describes the human condition, then it follows that when in fear of the chronic threat of the other we grant onto-epistemological dualism absolute supremacy, we are in effect aspiring to fully autonomous selfhood. And when we are, we promote the perception that the bidding to forbear our neighbor is nothing but a constraint on our freedom, and thus construct our relationship with her exclusively as a matter of power. As a result, we act to cut ourselves off from the condition of our humanity, that is, our selfhood. If, then, the principle of dualism, upon which rational determination as such is grounded, is as a rule allowed to define ethics, then it does not foster but rather denies freedom. It seems to me that, understood principally as the ability to give a yea or nay response to validity claims, 'openness' conveys just this state of affairs and (re)constitutes the self as essentially closed. But when openness means primarily the ability to acknowledge the other in his or her full singularity, that is, as value, then it serves to interrupt the self in its very self-absorption. In result, the self licenses itself to become other to itself, which is to say, to continue to (re)make itself. In light of this dynamic, the self appears only in the making. If it is understood that when one says "I," one is not in the first place referring to a thing but rather to an agential process that is relative and uncertain, but singular nonetheless, then one defines oneself as open to begin with and not simply as a fungible unit or third person.

When society is construed as different from or more than a genus-like phenomenon uniting similar individuals, then the relations constituting it obtain between participants who are both like and unlike each other. They are dyadic, face-to-face relations, in which one's participation is ill described by the clean detachment that springs from the perspective of the third. Rather, one's self in these relations is substantively generated by and finally subordinated to the relation itself, such that the relative other always transcends the self. The other, representing the enveloping relation in which the self finds itself, exists on a plane different from the plane of the self. In effect, then, the self veritably emerges as invested by and beholden to the other. Under these conditions, before it can be an exchange of information and ideas, communication amounts to participation or communion. Such communication makes the self constitutionally open to question and responsible to and for the other. Accordingly, the ideal speech situation is keyed in the first place not by politics and logical consistency, but by ethics and ontological ambiguity.[13]

If the ideal speech situation is construed in terms of ontological ambiguity, then, obviously, it bears out the postmodernist thesis of openness as difference. But it also speaks the truth of Habermas's thesis of the universality of communicative openness between human beings. Defined ultimately by reference to the hierarchical primacy rather than the equality of the other, the ideal speech situation denies not the pragmatic need to provide yes or no answers to the validity claims of truth, sincerity, and normative propriety, but the need to provide these answers as final and as utterly mutually exclusive of each other. It is the economizing finality or absolute status of rationality and canonical logic, not their situational validity, that is called into question. Binary responses may then be seen as fruitful for certain times and purposes and not for others, bearing in mind that 'fruitful' here refers ultimately to ethical rather than instrumental advantage, to the advantage of having and creating ends. Indeed, the time we refer to as evolutionary may be seen to select for binary logic, as Habermas contends, but only so long as it is understood that such logic and time remain ethically circumscribed and informed by choice, however else they are constituted.

Jay (1992: 273–74) reads Habermas in a way that makes this powerful thinker's position perfectly consistent with the picture of binary logic as relative and of the ideal speech situation as based on difference rather than sameness: "Habermas, in fact, has been very careful to emphasize that intersubjective communication is necessary when the parties involved are not identical. Consensus or consistency means not perfect unity but merely an always provisional willingness to agree on the basis of a process of validity testing that can be revised later." But while Habermas's writings leave no doubt that this picture is the one he intends to project, it is nevertheless incongruent with his particular notion of communication and his standard of non-contradiction. Jay's own critique suggests as much. He points out (1992: 275–76) that language has non-pragmatic aspects that are socially consequential and may not lend themselves to logical resolution; that if Habermas's non-subjectivist charge of performative contradiction against postmodern thinkers is to stick, he will have to forge a notion of agency that admits of responsibility as it denies subjective sovereignty; and that some social conflict may result from interests that are in fact irreconcilable by "discursive adjudication." These criticisms may be taken to imply that Habermas has failed fully to relativize or situationalize the demand for non-contradictory consistency. Were Habermas's demand really consistent with the proportional picture of the ideal speech situation and of binary logic espoused here, he would scarcely have concluded that the evolutionary line of ethical development leading from myth to modernity is straight and unambiguous. He would instead have been in a position to see that despite the strong impediment it puts in the way of yes/no responses, what I have called here mythic rationality takes for granted discretion in a way so profound that the defining openness of the ideal speech situation is featured there paradigmatically, in embryonic form.

I suspect that the contradiction in Habermas's thought—between the demand for non-contradiction and the call for ethics—rests finally with his notion of language, a notion critically informed by the horror of metaphysics. To get away from social ontology on the one hand and sheer rationality and the philosophy of consciousness on the other, he appeals to language-as-speech as the medium of intersubjectivity. For all his concern to feature intersubjectivity as a reality of its own kind, though, there remains a residual positivism about Habermas's linguistic turn. Although his discussions of language exhibit an immense scholarship (e.g., Habermas 1984: 94ff.); although he distinguishes, in the certain terms of both Humboldt and Mead, second-person from third-person language (e.g., Habermas 1992: 162f., 172f.), expressly grounding his theory in the former; and although, correlatively, he attributes priority to *parole* over *langue*, performance over structure, his usage seems still to cling somehow to language as a third-person phenomenon, as if language obtained only objectively. For Habermas, as he has masterfully set out (1987a: 43ff.), instead of the Durkheimian 'social', the reality behind intersubjectivity, or what Durkheim called moral solidarity, is language. But notwithstanding his universalistic pragmatics and concept of communicative action, in the end Habermas seems, just like Durkheim, hard put to know how to construe the underlying reality as anything but entitative, as a positive fact that gives the non-metaphysical truth to intersubjectivity.

My suspicions here are grounded especially in the fact that although Habermas emphatically attributes generative primacy to the other (e.g., 1992: chap. 7), he omits to conclude that the self and the other, the speaker and the hearer, of the speech situation must therefore be asymmetrical. He continues to regard them as equals, thus failing to see that the interlocutor, as the representative of the situation of locution, enjoys peculiarly the hierarchical privilege inherent in the speech situation's comprehension of the speaker. In the absence of this insight, even second-person language retains the appearance of a positivity, a medium of exchange between discrete entities.

Once it is conceded, however, that the generative priority of the other is tantamount to the hierarchical primacy of encompassment, language may be seen as something more than a medium of exchange—it may then be grasped as proximity or participation as such, that is, as connection that is 'real', but no less negative than positive for all that.[14] Since hierarchical encompassment entails ontological ambiguity—that is, the ambiguity of a thing the boundaries of which are less than entitative and fast—it necessarily admits of separation in connection.

Lest the attribution of hierarchical primacy to the other be thought of as utterly inimical to Habermas's project, I hasten to add that he himself makes this connection, although, again, without seeing it. In an essay—a veritable tour de force—on the subject of individuation and socialization, Habermas (1992: chap. 7) engages the paradox Durkheim featured in *The Division of Labor in Society*, the paradox of the individual as a social phenomenon. In short, taking G. H. Mead's ideas in hand, Habermas argues that while the self is ever dependent for its realization on the perspective of the other, it can nonetheless individuate itself by projecting the other on which it depends.

In other words, by seeing itself from the perspective of an other that does not yet exist, that is, a future other, the self remains fully social even while it transcends convention. However, the conception of the other as futurity—in a word, as time and uncertainty—depicts the other as not equal but transcendent; it depicts the other as that which solicits the participation of the self but always remains above, beyond, and ahead of it. What is more, considered in this way, the post-conventional other remains continuous with the other it has displaced, the other of the here and now. To be sure, the future normative order captures the uncertainty of otherness in a way that the current one does not. But the latter, as Durkheim taught so steadfastly and well, enjoys no less critically the commanding and comprehensive position of otherness. Indeed, as I have argued here with respect to mythic rationality, the traditional normative order displays in a pronounced and representative fashion the discretionary force accompanying the principle of uncertainty in human affairs. It follows that despite the opposition of futurity and convention on which Habermas (so insightfully) dwells as the key to understanding authentic individuation, his three worlds are not of equal weight. The normative world, considered in terms of the norming rather than the norm (that is, not the standard but the process of creating the standard), must enjoy the primacy of generation over the objective and subjective worlds, for of the three worlds, it is the one tied most definitively to discretion and uncertainty.

Because I have been concerned in this chapter to scrutinize Habermas's notion of rationality, I have not sought to take up directly his conception of moral consciousness. But there can be no doubt that that conception follows from his primary concern to save the social world for reason as such. To lend support to my argument about Habermas's failure to escape the gravitational pull of rationality proper, let me make a quick conjecture about his evolutionary picture of moral consciousness. To extrapolate from his deployment of Kohlberg's (and Selman's) ontogenetic account of moral development, Habermas (1990: 126; see esp. 116 ff.) views the crucial shift as a "passing from the conventional to the postconventional level of moral judgment. The social world of legitimately regulated interpersonal relations, a world to which one was naively habituated and which was unproblematically accepted, is abruptly deprived of its quasi-natural validity." The contents of this evolutionary shift are rich and complicated, but he conceives of it especially as the development of morality itself (ibid.: 208): "Morality thrives only in an environment in which postconventional ideas about law and morality have already been institutionalized to a certain extent." What is of interest here is that although conventional society is nothing if not normatively based, it is in essence bereft of morality in Habermas's scheme of things. Given the critical role of differentiation in Habermas's evolutionary theory, there is of course a sense in which he is quite correct—in which morality cannot be said to obtain until it has been distinguished as such. But that sense depends on the kind of boundaries that only dualism can produce, the kind so hermetic and impervious to light that they are impossible to see through. Habermas apparently fails to see what is representatively ethical about conventional or traditional society. This failure dramatizes his inclination to grasp evolution as plainly and simply progressive and to give pride of place to rationality and selfhood proper over ethics and the other. I expect that this is the case notwithstanding his express commitment to discourse ethics, which he defines emphatically as intersubjectivist.

Habermas on the Inhumanity of the Holocaust

Habermas's project—to save Enlightenment rationality for the good—apparently originated in a realization he had as a teenager, while listening to a broadcast of the Nuremberg trials (quoted in R. Bernstein 1992: 202): "At the age of 15 or 16, I sat before the radio and experienced what was being discussed before the Nuremberg tribunal, when others, instead of being struck by the ghastliness, began to dispute the justice of the trial, procedural questions, and questions of jurisdiction, there was that first rupture, which still gapes. Certainly, it is only because I was still sensitive and easily offended that I did not close myself to the fact of a collectively realized inhumanity in the same measure as the majority of my elders." Bernstein (ibid.) surmises that with this realization Habermas began to formulate the question that was to drive his social theoretical thinking: how could such a ghastly inhumanity have interrupted the course of Enlightened civilization, "the cultural tradition of Kant, Hegel and Marx in which the ideals of reason, freedom and justice had been so prominent"? As a university student, Habermas became familiar with Horkheimer and Adorno's (1998) response to this question. In their brilliant *Dialectic of Enlightenment*, these two extraordinary Frankfurt School thinkers argued that although Enlightenment reason presents itself as the means to liberate men from the authoritarian mind-lock of the uncritical normative order of mythic tradition, in point of fact the liberation, which in practice amounts to the development of the subject, leads back, with dialectical intensity, to mythic domination. The domination inherent in Enlightened thought is realized in, instead of magico-religious enchantment, the instrumentalization of the whole, as described by the rationalist opposition of subject to object. Given the perfectionism or totalism implicit in the very idea of rationality, this opposition takes the form of fascism—of man over man, and man over nature, including his own nature (the insight Foucault was to develop so prodigiously).

Although deeply influenced by this argument, Habermas took issue with its own brand of totalism, that is, the global way in which it closes off any possibility of speaking truth to power. He undoubtedly agreed with Horkheimer and Adorno's picture of Nazism (and other inhumanities) as an expression of mythic thinking. But for him, the Nazi death camps represented a reversion to such thought rather than a dialectical inevitability of the Enlightenment. Doubtless, he saw this reversion, in keeping with Horkheimer and Adorno's position, as a function of instrumental reason. But it nevertheless remained for him a "rupture," not simply in the goodness of his understanding of the order of things, but in the course of civilization itself.

Habermas's task, then, was to show that Horkheimer and Adorno's argument about the futility of Enlightenment thinking is mistaken. With this task in mind, he eventually drew his key distinction between two kinds of Enlightenment rationality, instrumental and communicative, arguing that the former presupposes the latter. In effect, he proposed to understand the Enlightenment in terms of an instrumental rationality that is basically dependent on a rationality intended to undermine all power save that of the force of the better or more valid argument.

The trouble is, as I have maintained throughout, that because it is assessed as claims that can be decided by autonomous yes/no responses (someone either is or is not sincere, and is normatively and factually correct), validity for Habermas presupposes an immaculate objectivity and therewith a clean distinction between subject and object. As a result, far from clarifying the primacy of communicative over instrumental rationality, he manages to define the former in terms of the latter, for it is precisely its logical binarism that gives to cognitive-instrumental rationality its commanding efficiency.[15] By definition, conclusive decisiveness (not excluding the settlement of claims to validity) bespeaks instrumental power. Every totalizing commitment to a judgment constitutes a move to ignore the fundamental ambiguity of any social situation, and therefore necessarily does violence, in some degree, to one side or another.

Still, as Habermas asserts, what he calls communicative rationality remains a critical standard, an ideal to which to aspire. Although immaculate differentiation of the subject must, by virtue of its concomitant development of objectivity, make conceivable the idea of validity, in itself dualism is not a fundamental precondition for the emergence of such a rationality. All that is necessary is substantial but relative differentiation—differentiation that is imperfect but still sufficient to admit of the idea of validity by contradistinction to power. Considered as an ideal as well as an idea, validity allows one to define one's self by reference to truthfulness (Am I sincere, moral, and factual?), and thus to center one's selfhood in terms of responsibility to and for the relatively objective nature of the issue. That nature depends on optimal, but not unqualified, distanciation from instrumentality—one is positioned to consider one's own material interests and choose to try to subordinate these to the question of truth. To be sure, by the same token (the ideal's capacity to represent the self to itself as responsible for truthfulness), this ideal also makes possible the witting misrepresentation of one's self, even to oneself, as, say, 'an honorable man'. In other words, the ideal necessarily allows to appear together with itself such psycho-social phenomena as the liar, the confidence man, and the self-delusional self.

More important for present purposes, though, is that as soon as the ideal nature of validity qua validity is mistaken for actuality, misplacing it as concrete and absolute (instead of situationally relative), all claims to validity are opened—beforehand and automatically—to the charge of misrepresentation. They then effectively appear, right from the start (and, on some plane of consciousness, even to the claimant), as plays of power masquerading as ethics.[16] What makes the postmodern picture of modernity's Everyman (a picture of a dupe by virtue of a comprehensive confidence trick perpetrated by systemic, socio-cultural power) an intellectual commonplace is validity's presentation of itself as absolute. Were differentiation regarded basically as relative and incremental instead of absolute, then claims to validity could not be faulted out of hand, but rather would always be subject to appraisal as to their soundness or, in effect, their validity. This is the procedure that most scholars, for instance, take for granted, including those committed to the radical deconstruction of reason.

Pace Habermas, then, immaculate differentiation is not a key to communicative rationality. And while substantial but relative differentiation is, even it stands in the service of a more fundamental condition—I have in mind openness to the other. Communicative rationality is a value-rationality, and in relation to any such organon, objectivity is desirable—not in the first place because it yields truth and closure, but because it can produce openness to the other. However, when regarded as an end in itself, as tends to be the case under the conceptual order of immaculate differentiation, objectivity effects closure rather than openness. It then defines a perfectly objective universe: instrumentalizing the other as well as, in the end, the self; raising into question the plausibility of value-rationality; and giving rise to a terrible ontological closure in its own right—the uncritical closure (a profound dogmatism) of rational certitude. Such closure describes both self and other as objective, and consequently as uniform and perfectly quantifiable.

In the absence of any qualifying condition, conceived of in this way (that is, as numbers or things), people become simply objects of manipulation instead of, in any binding form and meaningful measure, ends in themselves. But if it is never wholly detached from the axiom of openness to the other (which is to say, if it is not dualistically delineated), objectification becomes, as Habermas claims for it, a crucial step in the advance of value-rationality. Openness to the other amounts at heart to deferral to the other, and thus indexes an essential ethical asymmetry between the absolute, unquantifiable singularity of oneself and of the other. By virtue of its immediate relations, every other implicates other others with whom one does not stand face to face, but to whom one is, by virtue of value-rationality, nonetheless also responsible. No dyad obtains alone, for on the horizon of every immediate relationship loom third parties—that is, other others. It follows that one is owing to all the others, each taken in its nature as an end in itself. In which case, one must be responsible to a totality of others—a totality, however, that is non-totalizable or diacritically defined by internal difference.[17]

It is not possible, then, to defer to all the others. Under such conditions, deferring to one entails giving short shrift to others in an interminable political economizing of self-other relations. Opening oneself to one's other in, say, an intimate relationship by definition excludes all the other others. The categorical reduction of the other is thus imposed by the structural implication of other others in one's immediate relation to any other. It is here, in the structure of the self-other relation, that reason enters as an authentic value. By constraining disinterest, reason acts to universalize self-other relations. In the event of this objectifying reduction of all the others, reason defers to them on an equal and impartial basis, thus, paradoxically, preserving each in its irreducible (Kantian) singularity. Put another way, reason constitutes justice as a considered, equitable distribution of unavoidable injustice. In this (economistic) fashion, it serves, on balance and as the concept of communicative rationality supposes, the fundamental ethical interest of openness. As soon, however, as reason is taken as an end in itself—as it is under the epistemological rule of dualism—it undermines the very openness that makes it 'reasonable'. For it then reifies truth, picturing what is true for the present as immutably true and therewith occasioning a mythic order of domination, eclipsing the fact that truth, for all its demonstrable objectivity, is ultimately produced by people in their capacity as supremely facultative. That is, instead of reducing others in order to ensure their freedom, reason qua reason makes the reduction its own end. In doing so, as Horkheimer and Adorno seized on, it reconstitutes both self and other as tyrants over themselves (their own natures) and one another, and fosters the kind of geometric madness that so characterizes the modern era, from World War I to the Holocaust and beyond.

Habermas has been criticized, to opposing agendas but for much the same reason, by both the right and the left as regards his position on the Nazi occurrence in German history. His grasp of this barbaric episode as a historical singularity, in which Western Enlightenment was put on hold by a Hitlerian 'conventionalist' mentality, is no less out of keeping with those Marxian thinkers who see the emergence of the death camps as integrally tied to the advance of capitalism and to Enlightened thought than it is with the neo-conservative and anti-communist thinkers who portray the criminal acts of the Nazis as unoriginal versions of crimes already innovated by Bolshevism (see S. Cohen 1993: chap. 3; Friedlander 1992: 13–14; Habermas 1989; Pecora 1992). Inasmuch as the right-wing critics in Germany are keen to dismiss, in the interest of normalizing their national identity, the factuality of their history, one can credit their position only by keeping the door open to more of the horrific kind of history they aim to bend to their own nationalistic designs. The arguments of the left-wing critics, however, although unduly limited in their scope, enjoy real force.

Habermas's absolution of Enlightenment reason is shortsighted. While he sees that the dualism characteristic of rationality can empower validity, he fails to discern fully enough, as the criticism from the left maintains, that that same totalizing logic stands on all fours with instrumental domination. With Horkheimer and Adorno, he grasps the way in which mythic traditionalism closes the mind by stunting the growth of reason, but he fails to perceive that that same enchantment of the world radically expresses the openness to the other which marks the human condition as self-determining in the face of the other—that is, as—in my (Levinasian) usage—ethics. Horkheimer and Adorno well understand that mythic traditionalism is already Enlightenment, since it inaugurates the liberation of the self. But they, too, fail to see that the liberating impulse is given precisely in the dominating primacy of the other, a primacy acutely definitive of enchanted worlds. For all its immense power to hide the possibility of reason from the mind's eye, that primacy is not predominantly 'power' in the received (instrumentalistic) sense of the term, but rather in its diagnostic nature as openness to the other—power's embryonic foil.

By refusing to allow the ghastly twentieth-century acts of mass murder by civilized men to move him to abandon the goals of the Enlightenment, Habermas does humankind an inestimable service. But in his endeavor to take up the mantle of Enlightenment thought, his headway is seriously limited by his failure to see clearly enough the distinction between rationality as logic, powered by dualism, and reason as ethics, fostered by openness to the other. The latter sort of reason does not exclude the former but rather puts and keeps it in perspective, thus relativizing it and the certainties in which it issues, whether these bear on probity, normative correspondence, or factual truth. Even when their objectivity is unimpeachable and substantial, these 'certainties' are always a matter of practicality, never of truth qua truth.

PART II

THE ETHNOGRAPHIC OTHER
The Ethical Openness of Archaic Understanding

In part 2, I turn to a primary and abiding anthropological site of otherness, namely, the question of mythological or 'atheoretical' thought. Like many other scholarly disciplines, anthropology has been characterized by a felt need to systematically exclude *mythos* in favor of *logos*. This character is of course patently evident in respect of the anthropologists known as the nineteenth-century evolutionists. But it remained in effect, differently but no less predicatively, in the most prominent anthropology of the twentieth century. In their concern to refute their predecessors, these twentieth-century anthropologists were keen to save traditional thought from the charge of irrationality. By and large, they did this by advancing a 'symbolic anthropology' of one form or another. This anthropology portrayed mythic and magico-religious thought as basically figurative, so construing its intentionality as having nothing to do with logic as such, and therefore as in no way deprecating the rational capacity of peoples particularly given to such thinking. Thus, this anthropology preserved the epistemological primacy of rationality. But by the same token, it also continued to obscure what might be thought of as the 'realist' force of mythic thought, the significant respect in which this thought is not tropic but earnest. In light of my argument about dualism and rationality, I want to reassess mythic thinking and show that in a fundamental way it takes for granted what I am construing here as the ethical character of human existence.

The Chapters

In order to develop a nondualist rationality attuned to the idea of ethics as existence, in part 2, I turn directly to an abiding anthropological issue, namely, the question of enchanted worlds or mythological thought—the ethnographic other. The discussion focuses on the condition of indifference to contradiction, perhaps the main condition cited in opposition to the logic of such thought. The very idea of a rationality that is indifferent to contradiction gives rise to serious objections. In the first two chapters of part 2, I confront a pair of these objections. The first is that instrumental rationality is plainly superior by reference to technological control. The second is that mythic rationality's apparent indifference to the law of non-contradiction immunizes it to the principles of truth and reality. In addressing in chapter 7 the first objection, which is often ignored by anthropological relativists, I contend that the judgment as to instrumental rationality's superiority is in an important sense well-founded, but is itself enabled by mythic rationality. In addition, I propose that technological superiority does not necessarily entail a superior picture of how things are, a proposition that obliges me to offer an adumbration of why in fact science works so imposingly. In taking up in chapter 8 the second objection to mythic rationality, I set out the ontological thesis most critical to my project, which is also the most anthropologically novel point I have to make: that mythic rationality's apparent indifference to the law of non-contradiction is indeed evident (if also relative), but that, at the same time, it presents a naive gloss on and expression of the condition of ambiguity and choice, and therewith of the inevasible primacy of the ethical in human existence. I underwrite this claim by construing mythic rationality as a mode of selection. In contrast to natural selection, where no agent as such exists, as well as to rational choice, where the agent is in principle unambiguous, the mode of selection constrained by ethical practice exhibits a basically ambiguous and pre-eminently creative faculty—in short, moral agency.

My monographic interpretation of an Israeli kibbutz (Evens 1995) constitutes an ethnographic demonstration of my thesis about ethics, contradiction, and choice. But in order to show that the point is well taken in relation to non-Western and so-called primitive peoples, in the next two chapters of part 2, I undertake separate, close readings of two East African peoples, the Dinka and the Azande. In chapter 9, I demonstrate that the Dinka's relative but characteristic indifference to contradiction is critically linked for them to the matter of choice and sacrifice, and, by comparing and contrasting a Dinka origin myth with the biblical story of Genesis, I am led to differentiate between a naive and a more acutely self-conscious sense of choice. Still concerned with indifference to contradiction, but now focusing directly on moral accounting, in chapter 10 I compare and contrast the proceedings of the poison oracle among the Azande to scientific explanation and then, more intensively, to a hyperbolically representative case of modern psychotherapy. The analysis features the way in which Zande oracular practice, by contrast to much modern psychotherapeutic interaction, gives primacy of place to otherness over selfhood, and thus exhibits—notwithstanding its violent obsession with witchcraft accusations—a fundamental ethical openness.

Chapter 7

TECHNOLOGICAL EFFICACY, MYTHIC RATIONALITY, AND NON-CONTRADICTION

If ... present-day science in its perplexity points to technical achievements to "prove" that we deal with an "authentic order" given in nature, it seems it has fallen into a vicious circle ... scientists formulate their hypotheses to arrange their experiments and then use these experiments to verify their hypotheses; during this whole enterprise, they obviously deal with a hypothetical nature.

[T]he world of the experiment seems always capable of becoming a man-made reality, and this, while it may increase man's power of making and acting, even of creating a world ... unfortunately puts man back once more—and now even more forcefully—into the prison of his own mind, into the limitations of patterns he himself created ... What is new here is not that things exist of which we cannot form an image ... but that the material things we see and represent and against which we had measured immaterial things for which we can form no images should likewise be "unimaginable." With the disappearance of the sensually given world, the transcendent world disappears as well, and with it the possibility of transcending the material world in concept and thought.

— Hannah Arendt, *The Human Condition*

Mythic Rationality

My principal focus now is a likely objection to a certain distinction. The distinction is a kind of rationality, which I call mythic, and which stands in logical contrast to the instrumental kind. The objection pertains to the evident indifference of mythic rationality to the law of non-contradiction. I regard mythic rationality as a form of normative rationality; it is, to use Weber's familiar term, a value-rationality (*Wertrationalität*).

As such it concerns itself primarily with deciding ends rather than means. Ultimately, I aim to show that mythic rationality's relative indifference to the logical law of non-contradiction is, when seen from the perspective of practice rather than theory, the very dynamic of choice.

Although it cannot be defined in terms of the consistency between means and ends, mythic rationality is intelligible, penetrating, and non-arbitrary as an organon of comprehension and human practice. Moreover, not only does it exhibit a certain coherence of meaning, but also it enjoys an imposing and fundamental hierarchical primacy over instrumental rationality. The primacy I have in mind is that of encompassment: while it runs logically contrary to instrumental rationality, mythic rationality also includes its instrumental counterpart as a secondary and relatively undifferentiated operation.[1]

The hierarchical privilege of mythic rationality rests with nondualism. Just as the proven technological force of instrumental rationality depends on that rationality's definitive dualism, so mythic rationality's capacity to generate instrumental action has its source in a failure to differentiate in certain terms one thing from another—which is to say, to differentiate things dualistically.

I confess that as a central designation of my argument, the term 'mythic rationality' makes me uneasy.[2] It risks essentializing mythological thought as something that in an important sense it is not—namely, a kind of *logos*. I am using 'mythic rationality' to bring into relief the limitations of the idea of rationality as a measure of a modality of human existence, a modality the rationality of which is diagnostically given to presentation of itself in terms of its own basic limits. In the long run, the object is to reconstruct or relativize rationality qua rationality by referring it to a kind of thinking that, although undeniably marked by a significant form of closure, is constitutionally keyed to its own deconstruction. This key is cut in mythic rationality's basic and diagnostic deference to the Other. In effect, mythic rationality is never expressly itself. As ever thematically other to itself, mythic rationality has little autonomy as rationality in the strict sense, the sense of *logos*. In this particular respect, then, it does not obtain as a mode of thought. It is, therefore, doubly mythic: it is not only, as Lévi-Strauss exposited, a 'wild' kind of thought, but as such, it is also (Lévi-Strauss's structuralism notwithstanding), as I elaborate below, not, strictly speaking, thought at all.

The thesis that such thought, owing to its capacity to entertain discretionary force at large, constitutes a rationality in its own right, one that enjoys a certain significant superiority over its instrumental counterpart, is bound to raise at least the following two serious objections. First, instrumental rationality possesses a demonstrable efficacy and plain advantage in relation to technological control. In the face of such undeniable and imposing technological power, is it not idle to speak of the superiority of any value-rationality? Second, and correlatively, is it not the case that the nondualism of value-rationality is so crippling logically as to make it impossible to discriminate truth from falsity and, therefore, to distinguish between consistency and inconsistency of means to ends? Under such an epistemological regime, how, then, is it possible to lead a truly effective material existence? In other words, can my position account for the demonstrable efficacy of scientific knowledge and discount the apparent truth that what I am calling mythic rationality exemplifies precisely what is commonly meant by irrationality? I take up the first objection in this chapter, leaving the second for the next.

Hierarchical Superiorities

Charles Taylor and the Commanding Superiority of Scientific Rationality

In an essay that takes the issue of the rationality of pre-scientific culture well beyond the mire of much of the anthropological and philosophical debate, Charles Taylor (1985b: chap. 5) makes a powerful case for the need to take into account the conspicuous existential clout of science. His argument hinges on two main points. The first is that incommensurability between the scientific and the pre-scientific modes of thought and action does not obviate the need for assessing the one as against the other; rather, it conveys rivalry, thus actually demanding such assessment. The second is that since advanced technological control must reflect a greater understanding of the world, at least of the physical world, in this respect modern science must be judged (and invariably is, even by members of cultures in which science is not the prevailing mode of practice) distinctly superior to pre-scientific culture. This argument enables Taylor to have the cake of relativism and eat it too. While the acknowledgement of incommensurability preserves the relativist position, the contest between the incommensurable orientations produces an existential standard—one that is not laid out in advance—by which to judge the two modes of thought and action.

I find Taylor's argument both provocative and enlightening. I too wish to show that the concept of rationality is richer than the acceptation of it in terms of logical consistency allows, and that the additional content can come out when comparing cultural ways that are apparently incommensurable. Yet, in contrast to Taylor, I am concerned to emphasize the way in which this enriched concept of rationality gives a kind of superiority to the mythic rather than the empiricist perspective. It is edifying to explore this difference between Taylor's and my position.

Perspective and Hierarchy

In *Two Kinds of Rationality* (Evens 1995), I argue that the normative and the instrumental definitions of the situation of the Israeli collective I studied, Kibbutz Timem, are both commensurable and incommensurable. This argument holds common cause with Taylor's point about incommensurability. What he speaks of as a rivalry that demands judgment between incommensurables is something like what I have in mind when speaking of incommensurables as also commensurable. The key to the difference rests with my claim that between the mythic and instrumental perspectives there exists a phenomenologically ineliminable hierarchical relationship.

Taylor's assertion that the two perspectives compete somehow for the same space implies that both are essentially incorporated into a greater whole. This must be so even if the specific nature of this whole is always impossible to determine in advance, or, more exactly, is ever under construction. It is my contention that by reference to its genial capacity in relation to instrumental thought and practice, the mythic perspective enjoys a privileged relationship, an especial identity, with just this fundamentally indeterminate whole.

This hierarchical privilege places the contest between the two perspectives in a broader light than Taylor's argument strictly allows. In this light, the superiority claimed for the instrumental perspective seems odd, if not contradictory. Whereas the degree of technological control afforded by modern science may be, as Taylor asserts, so spectacular as to demand comparative judgment, what permits such paralogical judgment is the mythic perspective. In other words, the perspective that is judged inferior when the technological prowess of science prompts commensurability is in relation to the act of commensuration itself the enabling perspective. It is this perspective's definitive nondualism, its predisposition to regard all boundaries as fluid by virtue of encompassment, which makes possible the patently creative practice of commensuration (between incommensurate discourses or perspectives on the world), attention to which, as Taylor observes, can so enrich the concept of rationality.

In order to make sense of this apparent inconsistency, it is necessary to recall that the hierarchy logically distinguishes two planes of relationship: one of encompassing relations and one of exclusionary relations, or the superordinate plane and subordinate plane, respectively. The superiority of the instrumental perspective belongs to the latter hierarchical plane and should be understood accordingly.

The Short Memory of Instrumental Reason

When it is understood as a feature of the subordinate plane of the hierarchical order, the instrumental perspective is obviously secondary. Its secondary rank may also be told in terms of the following consideration, concerning the logic of arriving at such a judgment. Only by the willful occlusion of the full nature of the mythic perspective can the superiority of instrumentalism be established. The judgment in favor of instrumentalism entails a prior judgment as to ends: it can be made if, and only if, the end of instrumentalism is adopted as the standard of measurement. This end is implicitly dualist; as a matter of principle it excludes the idea of intrinsic good in favor of defining good in terms of utility alone. But the mythic perspective trades in ends as such, by which I mean here ends that deny an immaculate distinction between ends and means, and therefore that entail 'means without end', a quintessentially nondualist dynamic.[3] For this reason, although one might wish to argue that judgment in favor of mythic rationality also entails a prior judgment as to ends, the latter judgment cannot logically exclude instrumentality.

Judgment to the superiority of instrumentalism constitutes a compromise of the hierarchy, about which, however, although the compromise is not without effect, there is something false. By virtue of the judgment, the kingdom of ends is transfigured into a universe of means. But the transfiguration is accomplished due to an egregious memory slip, wherein the enabling role of the mythic perspective as an opening onto a universe of authentic, nondualist ends is not really eliminated but merely repressed, and hence neglected.

Perhaps the self-inconsistent nature of the judgment to instrumentalism's superiority over the normativism of myth can be most neatly focused by reference to the relational principles differentiated by the hierarchy. The judgment favors the plane of the hierarchy where exclusionary rather than encompassing relations are the rule. As a consequence, since exclusionary relations commission incommensurability, over and against commensurability, the judgment makes itself—makes its own determination—incomprehensible. Thus, the superiority of, for example, science over magic supposes that science can be perfectly demarcated from magic, making the judgment to superiority, although empirically demonstrable, nonsense. The point is that the superiority of the instrumentalist over the mythic perspective is derivative and cannot help but presuppose the latter perspective as presenting a primary superiority.

The Relative Superiority of Technological Control

Instrumental Success, Atheoretical and Historical Judgment

What, then, of the weight of the justifications Taylor (1985b) adduces for the judgment he essays? He relies on two in particular, which he finds are intricately tied together. One is the fact that the "spectacular degree of technological control" afforded by modern science simply "commands attention and demands explanation" (ibid.: 149). "[T]heoretical cultures score successes which command the attention of atheoretical ones," he says, "and in fact invariably have done so when they met" (ibid.: 150). The other justification amounts to the presumptive explanation of such instrumental success: "[M]odern science represents a superior understanding of the universe, or if you like, the physical universe" (ibid.: 148). Although these two justifications have considerable warrant, they should not go without qualification. It would appear that wherever it has become available, modern science enjoys a stunning measure of technological clout. Instrumental success is impressive. And of course it may be regarded in terms of superior rationality, but only when the concept of rationality is accepted, as usual, to mean logical and empirical consistency. Taylor, however, wants to move beyond this sense of rationality to a richer notion. In relation to this richer notion, one informed by the capacity to surmount incommensurability, modern science not only does not measure up but also runs contrary.

Just how contrary may be detected in a paradox that goes unrecognized in Taylor's account. Taylor (1985b) distinguishes the scientific and pre-scientific perspectives as theoretical and atheoretical (disengaged and engaged inquiry), respectively. But he finds that the judgment of the superiority of modern science is commanded as "a facet of our activity" (ibid.: 149). This means, I take it, that the judgment arises as a matter of practice in contrast to thought qua thought. But this, in turn, must mean that the superiority (as distinct from the instrumental success) of the theoretical orientation is established as a function of atheoretical engagement.

This circumstance not only points unmistakably to the limits of the superiority of modern science, but also insinuates the historical character of the judgment involved. The fact that, for reasons of its technological power, modern science everywhere has won acclaim does not preclude reappraisal in the future. Is not the contradiction inherent in the judgment of instrumentalism's superior rationality likely to advert attention to the shortcomings of this form of rationality? As people become aware of a sense of rationality richer than the utilitarian one, are not the limits of the way in which instrumentalism is superior bound to make themselves felt? In turn, will they not—no less than has this perspective's outstanding technological capacity—draw acknowledgement? And as they do, may one not expect the judgment of the superiority of modern science to undergo qualification?

In point of fact, however, empirically the state of evaluation has never been as plain as Taylor's account might suggest. It seems true that the technological control deriving from science has nowhere failed to impress or, as Taylor notes, to command attention. But it is also the case that the judgment of the significance and worth of this conspicuous success has for the most part been perplexed and equivocal. Put another way, although instrumental success always solicits desire, it is not always deemed desirable.[4] A glance at the ethnographic literature shows that the imposition or adoption of modes of thought and of techniques forged by science leads not necessarily to the abandonment of traditional ways but tends to produce their disorder, modification, and even revitalization (see, e.g., Burridge 1969; Darrouzet 1990). Furthermore, an anxious critical concern over the axiological vacuum that science creates—which serves as a fitting environment for the uninhibited pursuit of technological perfection—is a conspicuous feature even of the modern reflective life (cf., e.g., Horkheimer and Adorno 1998). Taylor's very choice of words to describe the manner in which science gains control over people suggests just such a form of alienation. Science does not solicit recognition or beg consideration; rather, it "commands" attention.

Why Science Works: the Efficacy of Perspectival Myopia

Taylor's (1985b) second justification for the determination of instrumentalism's superiority is the heavier claim by far. The assertion that "[t]here is an inner connection between understanding the world and achieving technological control" (ibid.: 147), such that control of this kind bespeaks a superior knowledge or picture of the world, would strike, were it simply correct, a decisive blow for modern science's defining superiority in the contest with pre-scientific thought. That epistemological truth is the explanation for superior technological control is not, however, self-evident.[5]

In principle, it is possible that science works for reasons other than those it articulates in explanation of itself. A great deal of extraordinary work in the philosophy of science has shown that science does not proceed in practice as it represents itself in theory. To cite two celebrated examples, it has been forcefully argued that the principles according to which science operates are not, as science itself has maintained, positive method and foundation, but "anything-goes" or "all's fair in the conduct of inquiry" (Feyerabend 1978) and "paradigmatic" or precognitive commitments (Kuhn 1970).[6] It seems only reasonable to grant, though—Humean skepticism notwithstanding—that such consistent and powerful technological success suggests that there is something basically sound about the scientific picture of the world. I propose that that picture, an essentially mechanistic picture, is, so to speak, half-right (in which case, of course, speaking logically, it must be doubly wrong). This understanding of the truth of science may be assimilated to the picture of the competing perspectives as hierarchically interrelated. Half-truth is about what one would expect from a perspective obtaining on the subordinate plane of the hierarchy. As the view from the part, such a perspective sees precisely one-half of the state of the world. By losing sight of the holistic aspect of things, this perspective might be said to suffer from loss of perspective.

But this kind of myopia may serve as an important condition of science's technological effectiveness. A loss in ability to estimate the relative importance of things, which is to say, their value or pro-portion (by which I mean, their relation to the whole), appears to result in a gain in ability to control them and to predict instrumental outcomes, at least for the short run. This momentous exchange of powers is, although not easily explained, in keeping with the logic of hierarchy. Since the view from the whole is inherently unclear and horizonal, it gives one a sense of fundamental uncertainty. By eliminating awareness of any need to take this 'uncertainty principle' and its like into account, orthodox science allows itself to proceed as if the world operated according to mechanical forces alone, without significant impact from contingency.

Streamlining Trial and Error According to Logical Conclusiveness and the Principle of Certainty

Another way of characterizing a world of mechanism is in terms of the relations between its inhabitants. The occlusion of the holistic perspective produces a picture of a world of things that have no essential connection with one another. In other words, in the world as it thus appears, boundaries are not relative but absolute. Such boundaries are fundamentally associated with a reality that begins with entities as such, that is, with what is usually termed 'physical reality'. Thus, when laying claim for modern science to "a superior understanding of the universe," Taylor (1985b: 148) quickly adds, "or if you like, the physical universe." Science, he says, "achieves greater understanding at least of physical nature" (ibid.: 149).

It is curious that Taylor's qualification—"the physical universe"—is made almost as an afterthought and is then left largely unremarked. The idea of physical nature logically involves a conceptual dichotomy no less consequential than that of the physical and the metaphysical, and highlights the remarkable dualism of the world of modern science. Indeed, immaculate boundaries, entities, and dualism are all of a piece. Immaculate boundaries reify, thus distinguishing things dualistically, as mutually exclusive.

The logic of a world lacking holistic perspective is, then, dualist. It excludes the possibility of a middle ground, a betwixt and between. Instead, it holds that a thing is what it is and not something else. Therefore, should it discern otherwise, that is, should it identify contradictions, it insists that they demand for their resolution absolute decision. In this connection, the mission of this logic is to search and destroy. It is nothing, then, if not conclusive (Evens 1983).

Logical conclusiveness promotes prediction and control. To detect how, it helps, following Karl Popper's (1972) evolutionist view of scientific method, to construe in terms of trial and error the process by which humans confront problems.[7] Combined with dualist logic, this process exhibits a terrific efficiency. In principle, dualist logic will not abide ambiguity, which gets abandoned by it as dogma, myth, irrationality, and the like. By moving one to decide error unambiguously, and thence to eliminate it, it leaves one with what has worked (but not necessarily with what alone will work), and with a pretty good idea of what is likely to work for prudential purposes. In effect, by streamlining the process of trial and error according to a principle of selective, instrumental certainty, dualist logic leads to prediction and control.

The point is that the superior technological control associated with scientific practice is consistent not only with the thesis that scientific practice provides a superior picture of the way things are, but also with the thesis that scientific practice necessarily betrays a radically limited understanding of the world. In other words, or so I suggest, what gives to scientific intelligence the practical superiority of which Taylor speaks is precisely its critical blind spot—a usefully ignorant principle of certainty.

Epistemic Gain as Value-Rationality's Loss: A Risky Business

To be sure, the technological success of modern science suggests that, as Taylor proposes, the world does operate as science says it does—in terms of things subsisting outside of one another, which is to say, physicalistically—to a degree stunning enough to command our attention. It must, then, be the case that modern science constitutes an advance in knowledge, an epistemic gain.

But technology's gain can nonetheless constitute a loss for humanity as such. By obscuring the uncertainty that conditions the representative situation of choice, neglect of the view from the whole—which is to say, neglect of the sense of limitation which that view provokes—can seriously undermine choice. What is more, such neglect not only undercuts humanity's ethical capacity; it also places human existence at exceptional material risk. The reason for thinking that modern science's view of the world is as narrow (and to that extent illusory) as it is accurate and superior should not be dismissed as *merely* ethical, as the dualism of principle and effective practice might tempt one to do. It is important to see that the thesis of orthodox science's myopia comprehends practical matters in a way more far-reaching than expediential. I have in mind here considerations no less concrete than toxification of the global environment and nuclear holocaust. The possibility of such events coming to pass is only too real, and obviously their imminence has much to do with what I am calling here the myopic technological power of modern science.

It could be argued, and often is, that an even more powerful science could eliminate such threats. But this is 'fox in the henhouse' reasoning. It fails to grasp that these threats of global suicide are fundamentally conditioned by indeterminacy, that is, by the fact that, no matter how good our science, it is fundamentally impossible to be absolutely sure of what the future holds. Science, however, succeeds precisely by shunting aside the principle of indeterminacy to tap into the world as it lends itself to definition in terms of exact boundaries and positive determinations. Put in terms of an earlier distinction, science in the strict sense is for the short term, achieving its remarkable effectiveness by way of the constitutional omission of the long term and consideration of essentially unknowable futurity from its account. The combination of immense technological efficacy and constitutional shortsightedness makes modern science a monumentally risky business.

It is important to note that Taylor, too, makes it plain that the superiority of the scientific understanding of the world is significantly limited. He sagely cautions the reader that in arriving at his judgment of scientific superiority he does not intend "global superiority" (1985b: 149), which is to say, I take it, superiority in all things. He also raises the possibility, if I read him correctly, that, all told, modern science has done more harm than good. He remarks that, given a predominant goal of locating our proper place in and coming to terms with the order of things, "[a]rguably [modern science] has been disastrous" (ibid.) This goal, which he speaks of "as coming into attunement" with the universe and characterizes as largely diagnostic of an earlier stage of our civilization (ibid.: 142), obviously resonates with what I have been calling mythic rationality. With this goal in mind, he writes: "[I]t may be that considerations which we in theoretical cultures can no longer appreciate so overweigh the balance in favour of the pre-theoretical ones as to make them offer the overall superior form of life" (ibid.: 150).

Nevertheless, Taylor makes no systematic case for a judgment of this comprehensive kind. Rather, he is concerned to exact commensuration on the plane of instrumental efficacy alone. The hierarchical framework I am proposing pictures a double judgment, however, such that the superiority on which Taylor dwells is subject to a superiority of a higher plane. The latter is privileged by the originary primacy of the process of commensuration itself. Moreover, as I have argued, the one judgment is no more existentially insistent than the other. Although short-term needs and goals may come to shield the long term from the mind's eye, in point of fact we live both terms simultaneously, the one no less needfully than the other.

In practice, the double judgment describes a historical and phenomenological (but by no means predetermined) dialectic whereby the shift from the relatively undifferentiated world of myth to the highly differentiated world of science logically and existentially anticipates a further shift—a de-differentiating one, in which the scientific picture of the world gets redefined by reference to its fundamental limitedness. This redefinition preserves science for the instrumental leverage and partial truth it affords, but, by reason of authoritative ethical containment, it preserves it as an enlightened shadow of its former self. In other words, instead of allowing the alienated condition of a science that determines the evaluative mode of humankind, the redefinition would ensure the reverse: that humans determine the value of science by thoughtful reference to what is peculiarly human, namely, the ongoing creating and re-creating of ends, in a becoming that defines humanity as ethical process. It is important to emphasize, though, that the redefinition does not really eliminate the conflict between instrumentalism and normativism. Rather, it serves, precisely by appeal to the higher superiority of the normative perspective, the perspective that opens out on our creative capacity to make and remake value-as-such, to heighten our sense of responsibility for the unremitting choice that these two perspectives present.

Chapter 8

EPISTEMIC EFFICACY, MYTHIC RATIONALITY, AND NON-CONTRADICTION

Contradiction. Why just this *one* bogy? That is surely very suspicious.

Why should not a calculation made for a practical purpose, with a contradictory result, tell me: "Do as you please, I, the calculation, do not decide the matter"?

The contradiction might be conceived as a hint from the gods that I am to act and *not* consider.

— Ludwig Wittgenstein, *The Wittgenstein Reader*

I wish only to point out that the accusation of contradiction is not decisive, *if the acknowledged contradiction appears as the very condition of consciousness.*

— M. Merleau-Ponty, *The Primacy of Perception*

I turn here to the second tough objection that my argument about the superiority of normative rationality is bound to provoke, namely, the paralogical nature of such rationality. My response falls into three main parts. First, I argue that in its operation, mythic rationality does not exactly exclude the law of non-contradiction; instead, by way of nondualism and hierarchical encompassment, mythic rationality relativizes that law. Second, I contend that mythic rationality is principally a 'logic' of life rather than thought as such, and therefore must be understood above all in terms of what I call practice. And third, I seek to establish that from the perspective of practice, the apparent willingness to entertain contradictions bespeaks a dynamic of choice and, therefore, the human condition. By 'the human condition' I have in mind what I call, by contrast to natural selection as well as to rational choice, moral selection.

Relativity and Contradiction

Judging Mythic Rationality

It is not easy to avoid the conclusion that the mythic perspective is representatively irrational. The celebrated efforts of modern anthropology to do just that serve as testimony to the taxing challenge of the task. By cultivating tolerance of contradiction, the nondualism of the mythic perspective appears to make this perspective perfectly nugatory as a basis for technically effective thought and action. In extolling the virtues of the logic of theory as such—which is to say, binary logic (Evens 1983)—this objection to the mythic perspective ties in with the imposing, commonplace thesis that scientific thought enjoys, overwhelmingly, superior technological efficacy. But to hark back to the preceding chapter, the association of the objection from logic proper with the thesis about the material force of science should put us on guard. It suggests that the objection makes its way by evaluating mythic rationality in the terms of its instrumental counterpart. As a consequence, the objection fatefully omits to grasp the peculiar logical force of mythic rationality and register this rationality's enabling role in relation to the instrumental variety.

It is transparent that the judgment here against the mythic perspective is predicated on the logical standards of the competing perspective. The mythic perspective is irrational if, and only if, it is defined in terms of the logical criteria we employ in settling scientific questions. These criteria compose what logicians call the 'laws of thought'—the laws of identity, of the excluded middle, and of non-contradiction. But to proceed in this way is not, of course, to bring reasoned selection to bear on the judgment between the two perspectives. Instead, it is simply to presume the overriding validity of just those criteria that the nondualism of the mythic perspective throws into question.

In view of the consideration of what I see as the mediative primacy of the mythic perspective, such presumption looks highly suspect. Evaluating mythic rationality by reference to rational rationality and its law of non-contradiction is something like measuring the quality of passion by reference to the logic of calculation (bearing in mind here Rousseau's observation (1992: 26) that "it is impossible to conceive why someone who had neither desires nor fears would go to the bother of reasoning"). Obviously, there is something amiss about this procedure. How can nondualism be the object of properly logical appraisal, if appraisal of this kind is a definitive power of a singularly dualist outlook?

More exactly, logic as such construes the mythic perspective, with its capacity to abide contradiction, as erroneous. But unlike theory proper, the mythic perspective does not present a strict representation of the world that can be decisively adjudged true or false. A perspective that fails to draw a manifest distinction between one thing and another cannot admit of the absolute difference between map and territory necessary to make conceivable the idea of representation qua representation. In turn, obviously, where no representation as such is projected, that is, where a theory is not put forward, there can be no mistake. Therefore, the mythic perspective cannot be simply erroneous.[1]

Relative Access to Objective Truth

If, then, there is something absurd about attempting to assay the value of mythic rationality in terms of logical rigor and technological control, in what terms should this value be fixed? It needs to be determined predominantly relative to the question of ends. Therefore, mythic rationality must be measured by appeal to the relative merits of the form of life it describes. In effect, its standard of comparison is a matter of ethics before it is a matter of utility or logical proof. It is a question of what *to be* before it is a question of what *will do* (cf. Tugendhat 1986). It is a question of reason, as reason stands fundamentally alloyed to moral choice.

By the same token, though, mythic rationality must be concerned at some level with practical effect. In point of fact, the nondualism of mythic rationality does not simply stand opposed to instrumentalism—by definition it embraces it as a relatively undifferentiated function. As Charles Taylor (1985b: 140ff.) observes, to describe the difference between the two perspectives in terms of sheer opposition would be unintelligible from the standpoint of the mythic perspective, and therefore ethnocentric. It is worth quoting his balanced and plainspoken presentation of this crucial insight, in which he simply sidesteps our powerful disposition to think dualistically (ibid.: 143–44; in this volume, see also chap. 4, note 12): "It certainly would not help to say ... that ritual practices in some primitive society were to be understood simply as symbolic, that is, as being exclusively directed at attunement and not at all at practical control; or that the body of religious beliefs was merely expressive of certain attitudes to the contingencies of life, and not also concerned with giving an account of how things are."

Mythic rationality is nothing if not concerned with effective action. It is just that it does not define 'effective' in terms of instrumental success alone. It includes, as an integral of the definition, an appraisal of the end to be effected. As a consequence of ever keeping in view the character of the end, the means are assessed not simply for their instrumental outcome but also for their intrinsic connection to the ends. That is to say, they are assessed for their power not to yield the ends as products but to embody them in practice as works.[2]

If, however, the mythic perspective does pertain to practical control, then, as Taylor says, it must also have an interest in representing the way things are in their empirical aspect. In this case, it must follow that regardless of its failure to adhere faithfully to the law of non-contradiction, this perspective cannot fully want for a capacity to discriminate between success and failure, and therefore between truth and falsity.

The difficulty with the position that condemns the mythic perspective as logically absurd and empirically useless is its absolutism. The picture of that perspective as radically impotent for instrumental purposes is seriously and self-servingly distorting. If one's reflections on the mythic perspective begin with logic proper, then, to be sure, the alliance with contradiction must appear, so to speak, unholy.[3] If contradictions are thought not to matter at all (instead of taking them as sites for further contemplation or, as Wittgenstein proposes in the epigraph to this chapter, a hint to act and not consider), then inconsistency between an idea and a description of the facts can serve to refute neither the idea nor the empirical description. In such a case, one can never be in a position to decide one's practical options on the basis of instrumental success.

But seen from its own perspective, mythic rationality does not appear in the absolute terms of logic proper—at least, not in the first place. In the first place, consistent with its definitive disinclination to draw boundaries that cut unambiguously, this rationality is manifested as no less lived than reflected. In other words, it does not accord with the picture of itself as either life or logic. Rather, from its own perspective, mythic rationality appears to be both logic and life, or, what comes to the same thing, neither.

In short, the mythic perspective exhibits an ontology of ambiguity. If 'ontology' is taken in the strict sense, though, as that department of metaphysics concerned with being in the abstract, then an ontology of ambiguity is disturbingly aberrant. By virtue of its picture of the world, such an ontology cannot unequivocally tell the physical from the metaphysical, and as a result, it projects a lived logic, a rationality ever in-the-making (cf. Evens 1983).

Put still another way, the nondualism of mythic rationality does not reduce to monism. From the decisive point of view of logic proper, an outlook that fails to distinguish unequivocally between life and logic must be deemed monist. In fact, monism is an intelligible proposition solely on the basis of the dualism of logic as such. Monism is nothing if not a kind of totalism, and totalism and logical dualism go hand in hand. This is concisely expressed in the law of identity, according to which a thing is what it is and not something else.[4]

The nondualism of the mythic rationality amounts instead to a kind of relativism—the relative kind. Whereas most relativisms, failing to come free from the grip of dualistic thinking, are presented in absolute terms,[5] the relativism of mythic rationality is decidedly equivocal. Accordingly, it lends itself to assertions of truth even as it affirms comprehensive ambiguity. Failure to distinguish absolutely between one thing and another does not mean failure to distinguish between them at all. On the contrary, it is the idea of absolute distinction that opens the world to definition in terms of the eradication of difference. Absolute distinction projects perfect exclusivity, thus making identity without difference conceivable. But an ontology of ambiguity implies a total lack of difference no more than it does an absolute whole. Rather, it trades in the idea of unremitting but relative differentiation. In such an essentially equivocal picture of reality, while a thesis cannot produce an antithesis as such—which is to say, it cannot produce a contradiction in the strict sense—it can issue in an assertion that is relatively antithetical. By the same token, it can conclude in an assertion of relative truth. That is, it can propose the truth of one thing as against another relative to some purposes, even while relative to others, it identifies the two things with each other.

To adduce a characteristic ethnographic instance, Godfrey Lienhardt (1961: 147) tells us that the Dinka, who take for granted that divine powers are living agents affecting their everyday lives, "can discuss the prospects for the harvest without necessarily introducing the free-divinity Abuk, to whom good harvests are attributed, and one can discuss thunder, lightning, and rain up to a point as purely 'natural' phenomena, without talking of Deng or Divinity. To take a slighter example, a Dinka may complain of a cold or a headache without reference to Powers as the grounds of these minor discomforts. Should the cold turn to high fever, or the headache become persistent and agonizing, his thoughts will turn to the possible activity of Powers." As I read this telling piece of ethnography, past a certain point of inquiry—the point of excess, extremity, or anomaly—the Dinka are prepared to tolerate what appear to us as contradictions. Evidently, a Dinka is unconcerned about asserting at the same time both 'x', that agricultural production, lightning, thunder, rain, or headaches are natural, and 'not-x', that they are 'supernatural', which is to say, not-natural. Thus, a Dinka will distinguish between the truth of 'x' and 'not-x' for certain purposes and fail to do so for others.

Yet despite this illogicism, as is the crux of Lienhardt's argument here, a Dinka is perfectly able "up to a point" to negotiate his reality in instrumental or "natural" terms.

The fact that the Dinka's taken-for-granted world is populated no less by divine powers than by natural forces, and that it therefore—as against all the prejudices of formal logic—fails to make a fast distinction between what moderns regard as the material and the immaterial or the visible and the invisible, does not abolish but rather only relativizes the truth of instrumental advantage.

Thus, such an epistemological regime plainly displays a certain tolerance for contradiction. Moreover, because it does not entertain the idea of absolute difference, it is constitutionally inhibited from transmitting truth conclusively. Nevertheless, or so it seems, mythic rationality is not unprepared to tell what is relatively true from what is relatively false. Neither, therefore, is it wholly prevented from availing itself of instrumental advantage. "The same savage who, apparently in order to kill his enemy, sticks his knife through a picture of him, really does build his hut of wood and cuts his arrow with skill and not in effigy," Wittgenstein observed (1979: 4e). It was, of course, especially Malinowski who brought home to anthropology that despite their outstanding magico-religious presentations, primitives (so-called) are exceedingly practical.

Hierarchical Structure and Perspectival Alternation

The key to mythic rationality's access to the logic of instrumental rationality is hierarchical encompassment. By failing to differentiate cleanly between fact and value, mythic rationality does not exactly exclude facts. Rather, it grasps them no less in terms of value than of fact—but there remains for mythic rationality a fact of the matter. Therefore, unlike rationality proper, which defines myth as meaningless, or worse, and value as metaphysical, mythic rationality actually includes its counterpart.

This difference between the two kinds of rationalities corresponds to the twofold consideration that, first, by definition mythic rationality cannot sanction a hard and fast boundary, and, second, where such a boundary is epistemologically unavailable, there can be no thoroughgoing exclusion. As a result, mythic rationality is constitutionally inclusive. It is therefore always poised to construct and deploy an at least implicit or relatively undifferentiated variety of instrumental rationality.

In effect, the hierarchical ordering of the two rationalities presents, as a structural dynamic, an easy alternation of perspectives on the truth. On the one hand, there is the perspective of truth proper, on the other, the perspective of relative truth. Whereas from the former, truth values are assigned decisively by means of formal logic and to the end of technical success, from the latter, truth is transmitted relatively, according to 'choice' of ends, as an ethical matter. The alternation is brought about by the hierarchical encompassment of the logical perspective by the ethical one. The structure of encompassment makes the boundary between the two perspectives fluid rather than fast, defining each in terms of the other, and both together as two and one at the same time. As a result, movement between them becomes perfectly natural, like the movement of perception in a gestalt switch, whereby, for example, a figure you are seeing as a duck suddenly comes into view as a rabbit—an intrinsic perceptual dynamic.

This set of alternatives may appear to be available also to instrumental rationality. In this rationality, too, a shift of perspectives from the truth of fact to that of value and back again can and does occur. But in the case of this sort of rationality, far from taking a natural course, such a movement must look wholly contrived, logically impossible, or even miraculous (as in, say, the material truth of biological reproduction and the theological truth of virgin birth). Because the logic of instrumental rationality—logic in the strict sense—is predicated on a perfect distinction between fact and value, under the rule of this logic, the only way to get from its kind of truth to the other is by a suspension of good sense, of mental competence, or of the real world. For this reason, instrumental rationality cannot tolerate its counterpart; or, rather, when this rationality is in the epistemological ascendant, it tolerates the co-existence of values as alternative ideational systems only by making value qua value the equivalent to nonsense. Accordingly, it is inclined to reduce value to its instrumental co-efficient (Dumont 1986: chap. 9).

It is this view—from the rationality of instrumental advancement—that portrays mythic rationality as logically absurd and absolutely cut off from effective practice. As is textbook knowledge, anthropologically the nineteenth-century evolutionists— Tylor, Frazer, etc.—surveyed 'primitive mentality' from this view. But even the currently privileged interpretation of magico-religious discourse as a matter of figurative language—an interpretation associated with duly celebrated anthropologists such as Evans-Pritchard, Lévi-Strauss, Victor Turner, and Clifford Geertz—continues to presuppose the view from instrumental rationality. Appearances notwithstanding, the interpretation does not really question that view. Rather, by insisting that such discourse is intended not logically but tropologically, the interpretation tries to save 'primitive man' for formal logic and from the charge of fallacious reasoning. Obviously, the charge of fallacious reasoning follows from presupposing formal logic as a parameter when judging magico-religious thought and action.

It is not really the case, then, that the structural alternation in question is available to instrumental rationality. Because of its master predication of immaculate boundaries, this rationality posits the opposition between the truth of fact and the truth of value as complete. Accordingly, to assert both truths at the same time, as does the alternation of perspectives, is, in this rationality, to run afoul of the law of non-contradiction. In other words, by crucial contrast to mythic rationality, which by virtue of encompassment enjoys relative access to the truth of its counterpart, instrumental rationality holds the two kinds of truth as, by logical decree, perfectly out of reach of each other.

Instrumental impotence and willingness to accept contradictions thus appear unambiguously as features of mythic rationality only from the point of view of an autonomous instrumental rationality, one liberated by forgetfulness from its mythic counterpart. From the vantage of mythic rationality, however, the contradiction between the two kinds of truth, as well as the inattention to instrumental success, is relative. The 'law' of the exclusion of contradictions operates here, too, but only as one pole of a containing structure of alternation—a mythic rationality.

Because it is contained, this law is binding only situationally, making the question of contradiction relative rather than decisive. A situational shift of perspective to the encompassing order—a shift made possible by a dynamic hierarchical structure—puts the relationship between the two kinds of truth in a new light. In this light, the one kind of truth is not only opposed to but also consistent with the other. The relationship of encompassment constitutes a boundary that connects as it separates: insofar as it describes a duality of truths, it divides; but insofar as it pictures one term of this duality as encompassing, it contains and connects. By virtue of assuming the encompassing perspective, then, in a sense both kinds of truth obtain at the same time, and the contradiction between them—as well as the law of non-contradiction itself—is relativized.

Mythic Rationality as a Form of Practice

But talk about kinds of truth—as if primarily at stake are what is called in technical logic 'truth values'—makes it seem as if the alternation is a matter of different epistemologies plain and simple. It is crucial to see that 'to assume the encompassing perspective' is not exactly to make an epistemological move, as if that perspective were simply a question of the relationship between knower and known. Were we to think this, it would be implicit that mythic rationality is after all primarily a theoretical endeavor, a tool for securing objective knowledge. If this were so, there would be no reason to avoid assessing it solely in terms of the critical organon of theorizing, namely, technical logic. In the event, the very idea of encompassment would have to be judged as incoherent, as a piece of intellectual sleight of hand in the interest of putting up with contradictions and bringing about "the breakdown of science, and of criticism, i.e. of rationality" (Popper 1965: 322).

In point of fact, however, the view from the encompassing perspective calls into question the presumption that all thought and action can be satisfactorily evaluated in terms of epistemology. Precisely because it cannot sanction immaculate division, the encompassment relationship does not admit of an observer sufficiently detached from the world observed to make the epistemological predication of knower and known acceptable as a blanket description of the way things are. Viewed from the encompassing perspective, the observer always participates in the world under observation. For this reason, the thrust, whether explicit or simply presumed, to make the humanities and even the human sciences into science in its classical acceptation is building on a model of scientific practice that has been thoroughly rebuked by developments in the twentieth century (going back at least to 1927, the year in which Heisenberg's famous 'uncertainty' paper appeared in print).

For reasons of such ontologically unavoidable observer participation, the encompassing perspective is from its own point of view as much a matter of practice as of theory. Participation entails existential engagement, thus condemning the observer to action and limiting the degree to which it is possible to stand back and simply watch what happens. In describing reason and truth, then, the encompassing perspective shifts away from the image of a neutral subject mapping an external territory and toward a conception of existential practice by human agents who are both in and of the world. To move from the instrumental to the encompassing perspective is not really to make an epistemological sea change. Rather, it is to relocate one's understanding from a situation defined sheerly in terms of the epistemological relationship of knower and known to one where existential practice is not only the order of the day (as it is everywhere) but also taken for granted (as it is not, under the rule of instrumentalism).

By 'practice' I intend action that is essentially informed by ideas, that is, intrinsically meaningful action. Defined thus, action is not entirely differentiable from thought. Put from the other side, under this notion of practice, ideas are always 'imprisoned in action.[6] Contrary to both commonsensical and certain reflective usages, then, practice can never be simply the implementation of theory. As it includes thought as an intrinsic moment of its unfolding, practice is always more than action defined by contrast to thought. Put another way, practice obtains prior to the wholesale distinction that makes conceivable the very idea of theory, the distinction between action and thought or between presentation and representation. Indeed, under this notion of practice, theory presents nothing if not a kind of practice—the kind dedicated to liberating ideas from action in the interest of making practice more efficient. Correlatively, practice defined as the implementation of theory is simply practice that has as one of its informing ideas a dualistic distinction between theory and practice.[7]

Practice as Moral Selection

If practice is neither wholly blind mechanism nor all-seeing theory-in-practice, then it must be, in some critical measure, self-governing. If it is not simply deterministic, then it must proceed by its own lights. But if its vision is fundamentally limited, then it must go forward creatively. In order to bring this singularly mediatory process into relief, it helps to construe practice as a mode of selection. As such, it falls somewhere between natural selection and rational choice. The word 'selection' in 'natural selection' amounts to a figure of speech, whereas in 'rational selection', the word denotes choice grounded in positive knowledge. The kind of selection I have in mind, a process neither natural nor, strictly speaking, rational, is genuinely agential but essentially uncertain. I call it moral selection.[8]

The principal advantage of grasping practice in such terms is that it focuses attention on the way in which practice amounts to a process of choice that is, first, authentic or creative, second, social, and third, less than fully conscious. When we are confronted with a practical rather than theoretical question, the decision is above all a matter of becoming rather than truth in the strict, logical sense. Put another way, such a question demands not that we select the true over the false answer but that, given the socially possible options, we choose what it is we want to be, or, more precisely, the direction of our becoming. Put still another way, the question is not about a technically driven calculus of means to an end, but—again given a heterogeneous social structure marked by a multiplicity of possibilities, not all of which are necessarily compatible with one another—about the selecting of the ends themselves.

Choosing one's own ends is necessarily a creative process, for one's ends de-fine or de-limit who one is. Insofar as one selects one's own ends, one originates oneself. Such an act of self-fashioning—a primordial choosing, if you like—is not wholly derivable from what preceded it, since it alters the conditions of action, constructing a logic of action that would not apply had the act not itself 'acted' (cf. Burke 1969: 64ff.). In a certain sense, then, inasmuch as the act constitutes its own motivation, practice must be without 'why' (cf. Caputo 1987: 262). That is to say, it is essentially open as to its course, not only in that it is underdetermined, but also in that it is constituted by choice. In other words, practice is creative.

Practice is also fundamentally social. Openness to the future is nothing if not receptivity to otherness. If one remains essentially underdetermined, then one must ever be open to redefinition according to one's encounter with one's other—including one's social other. For this reason, practice is not basically a matter of perfectly autono-mous individual subjects making choices. On the contrary, it presents the kind of selection that depends on irreducible 'intersubjectivity'. Therefore, the social process of selection I have in mind cannot be satisfactorily understood through, for example, the received idea of democratic decision-making. This idea pictures social choice as the sum of autonomous individual choices, whether they are rational or not. What I have in mind by practice, though, is selection that is generated pre-eminently between one individual and another.

Obviously, since choice of this kind is irreducible to the individual, it cannot be a matter of subjectivity plain and simple. With reference to the individual, the kind of choice in question is preponderantly less than conscious. It proceeds largely at the back of the minds of the individual choosers, which is to say between them, for where an individual's mind is substantially less than self-aware, it is also to the same extent there undifferentiable from the mind of the other. Although moderns tend to take for granted that the unconscious resides somehow strictly within the confines of the individual, this picture of hermetic closure was not always the case in Western thought.[9] To choose a familiar ancient example, the identity between less than self-conscious 'minds' is not only what the serpent, with a force both subtle and visceral, enfigures in the biblical story of Genesis; it is also what this wily creature had in 'mind' when advising Adam and Eve of their likeness to God.

An intersubjective choice is ultimately keyed not to knowledge as such but to *tacit* knowledge (cf. Polanyi 1967). It is important to be clear that 'tacit knowledge' is an oxymoron: we are talking about knowledge that is not strictly known.[10] For example, in my study of an Israeli kibbutz's obsessive propensity to define, without final regard to empirical adequacy, its most difficult internal social problems in terms of conflict between the generations, I argue that the members of the kibbutz move to this defini-tion of their situation in much the same way that one moves to leave a room through the door rather than through the wall (Evens 1995)—that is, automatically, without need for reflection. Like the self-identity of 'material individual' for modern man, the self-identity of 'peculiarly moral creature' in the kibbutz is so inseparable from who the members of Kibbutz Timem really are that the manner in which it moves them is indis-tinguishable from self-movement. And that self-identity is, as I show in my study (ibid.: esp. chaps. 6 and 7), an intrinsic feature of the Hebrew biblical usage of the notion of 'the generations' as a definition of the situation.

To sketch an analogy that highlights the moral as well as the 'natural' character of such selection, the movement is akin to the way in which humans assume upright posture. Just as in the case of this extraordinary carriage, by virtue of which human beings define themselves by taking a stand against their own ground (Straus 1966), the self-identity conferred by the Judaic idea of generation defines human relational space as moral. The patriarchal creator's instruction to his son to take on his (the patriarch's) own image—that is, to be a creator (a chooser) in his own right—obliges the son to take a stand. As a result, the space-time of the generations is defined as peculiarly moral, giving to the occupants their critical bearings in the world.

The biblical figure of the serpent in the Genesis account of the generations is, yet again, edifying here. The manner in which this figure is drawn presents an illumination of moral selection. In its assumption of the prone position, the serpent plainly evokes upright posture as a key to the relational space of the generations as being representatively moral space. To see this, one need only call to mind that the serpent's lowly bearing was altogether a matter of choice: it both chose this bearing, by virtue of its volitional act of temptation (of Eve), and was chosen to it, by dint of the discretionary punishment meted out by God.

Paradox and Transcendence

Now that I have described what I have in mind by moral selection, I can return to the question of indifference to contradictions. To do this, it is important to see that choice that is essentially creative, social, and tacit is also fundamentally paradoxical. This paradoxical nature may be read directly from moral selection's integral association with practical questions.

In the case of theoretical questions, one is confronted with the need to affirm or deny the existence of a certain state of affairs. Here the truth is presumptively unequivocal and depends on, and only on, whether or not that state of affairs is in fact the case. In principle, such truth is independent of one's decision to affirm or deny it. With practical questions, by contrast, the truth depends also on the response to the question. Here the truth is tied to the need to constitute ends and determine what will be. In effect, such truth is conditioned by choice and is relative to the chooser's intentionality, including the moods, emotions, and immediate or ready-to-hand concerns that condition choices and attach to synthetic a priori, even if the chooser's intentions are not exactly known to him or her. Thus, as I have elsewhere shown (Evens 1995), in Kibbutz Timem, 'conflict between the generations' constituted at once an empirically deficient but hermeneutically correct definition of the situation. Its truth depended on the 'decision' of Timem's members to identify themselves repeatedly and existentially in such terms. In so doing, the members constructed the self-identity and conventional world without which the course of empirical events in Timem could not be genuinely meaningful, for the same reasons that, outside of a particular cultural context, a wink and a nod would be nothing more than physiological motions.

How does practice produce truth of this kind? As an act of choice, practice transforms what there is. More exactly, by virtue of this act—which marks the site of our elaboration of what is by means of our elaboration of it—what there is transcends itself. In so doing, it interrupts itself, paradoxically standing against itself, describing the transcendence that is human existence.[11] By definition, what there is always correlates decidedly with positive reality: the facts of the matter, the status quo, the reality that one feels as pressing, the situation into which one has been thrown. From this ontological consideration—that what there is and positive reality stand together—it follows that self-transcendence presents a phenomenological shift of emphasis from positive toward negative reality. To make the point in more familiar terms, the movement in question, a movement of opposition or resistance, constitutes an experiential swing from matter toward mind or spirit, that is, from what there is toward what is otherwise than what there is. By contrast to 'positive' and 'negative', though, 'matter' and 'spirit' (at least in Western discourse) tend to convey a dualism I want to avoid, namely, that of body and mind, or of the physical and the metaphysical. For the fact of the matter is that positive reality (or what there is) is always already irredeemably informed by the metaphysical, which is to say, convention (or what is otherwise than what there is). To capture this nondualistic usage, whereby 'positive reality' does not lack a metaphysical co-efficient, one might say, following a linguistic distinction due to Levinas (1991: 45f.), that what there is conforms to the said rather than the saying.

The slack needed to satisfy moral selection's demand for open possibilities is given only through opposition to what I am calling here positive reality.[12] But the shift of ontological emphasis, from positive to negative, is always limited. The act of contraposition can never be complete. Because the act itself serves as an ineliminable link between the transformation it has wrought and what there was, the opposing movement cannot reach its logical climax. Put another way, although its ground may shift with the course of its movement, practice as moral selection always remains grounded—it never manifests itself as what is wholly perfectly otherwise than positive reality. As a result, although the shift from positive toward negative is a difference that makes a difference, it does not eliminate the positive. The movement in question may be pictured as spiral, such that the resulting negative reality becomes a fresh positive one, promoting, endlessly, further transcendental re-creation, including even vast metaphorical structures.

Contradiction as Resistance and Choice

Thus, practice or moral selection presents a profound paradox. The contraposition of positive and negative described by moral selection constitutes a relationship of connection in separation. If we examine this paradox in terms of the two kinds of truth, we come up against a manifest contradiction. Insofar as practice separates a negative posture from a positive reality, it differentiates the subjective or relative truth associated with sheer conventionalism from the objective truth predicated by empiricism and formal logic. But insofar as in the very act of separation it cannot fail to link together what it sets apart, practice defines these two kinds of truth in terms of each other. In effect, both absolute and subjective truth are relativized, yielding a hierarchy of truth in which the relativized variety is constitutionally encompassing.

But the consideration I wish to feature here is that moral selection displays a logically painful contradiction: objective and subjective truth are distinguished as contradictories that inform each other. This contradiction points straight to the venerable anthropological problem of rationality, ethnographically brought into focus by peoples who apparently have trouble telling the real (the objective) from the ideal (the subjective). Thus, the Dinka assert that a cold or a headache is at the same time natural and not-natural—that is, that objective truth is also not-objective.

At this juncture, however, I aim to clarify that what, from a logical point of view, presents an unwarranted willingness to tolerate contradictions is, from the standpoint of practice, the very dynamic of choice. The two sorts of truth correlate with what may be called the ontological poles of human identity or being. Plainly, transcendence supposes an opposed behavioral predisposition that can be overcome. It is fruitful here to apprehend this predisposition in terms of one standard (and typically dualistic) representation of positive reality, namely, instinct. The instinctual pole may be defined in terms of such animal practices as taking food, excreting wastes, sexually reproducing, etc. Accordingly, the transcendental pole may be defined in terms of the transcending or remaking of its instinctual counterpart—the provoking and socializing of it, or even the capitulating to it.

From a logical point of view, the tensional structure of these two poles presents a paradox and entails the contradiction of opposing kinds of truth that somehow share their identity. Whereas the instinctual pole corresponds to objective truth, the transcendental pole points directly to the kind of truth (often regarded as disreputable) associated with subjective deliberation. Logically, however, the tensional structure itself identifies the two kinds of truth as one. One quick way of making this outcome perspicuous is to articulate an interrogative consideration that is irritatingly implicit here: how can the transcendental pole be regarded as less instinctual than the instinctual pole proper, the logically opposing pole? Is it any less 'natural'? Is not the instinctual pole always already conventional? Are human acts of eating, excreting, sex, and the like not as cultural as they are natural?

Strikingly, however, should we take a different perspective, switching from that of logic proper to that of practice, the apparent contradiction is transformed into a dynamic of choice. From the perspective of practice, the relationship between the two poles is not simply a logical structure of contraposition—it is a movement of resistance. It describes a standing against, an experiential and consequential, but ever limited, transmuting reality from a representatively instinctual toward a transcendental pole.

To take up the Dinka example once more, the contradiction of an affliction that is at the same time both natural and supernatural describes, when seen from the standpoint of practice, the conduct of choice. By apprehending the natural as also supernatural, the Dinka projects reality in terms of encompassment by the divine. In so doing, he ascribes his affliction ultimately to discretionary agency, thus leaving open to himself the possibility of removing the affliction by choice. By appealing to the divine, the Dinka is in a position to redefine himself as unafflicted—that is, to dispose his own end(s). In effect, he can press back against the pressure of reality, so defining himself as, in part, self-transcending. He thus displays himself as a creature in which the ideal and the real are definitively and inextricably confounded. He *is* the back-and-forth movement through which the differentiation of the real and the ideal is made possible.

It may be objected that, depending on the nature of the affliction, he cannot in fact define the affliction away. But of course, it is precisely the nature of the affliction that is in question here. Whereas modern thought is inclined to identify this nature along the lines of body-mind dualism, the Dinka determines it nondualistically. The ethnography shows that while the Dinka draws a distinction between afflictions as material or as spiritual, he finds that all afflictions are, if not especially, at least finally spiritual. In effect, the distinction is imperfect. The Dinka is taking for granted that at bottom his cold or headache—and, indeed, all that there is in the world—no matter how palpable it be, must be chalked up to Divinity, an encompassing, experiential reality in which the Dinka himself, in his own peculiar but incomplete way, participates. The Dinka's contradictory definition of the situation discloses that he never forgets that he, in his creative capacity, although roundly and surely limited, participates in situating himself. In so apprehending his situation, he not only represents himself *as* but virtually also makes himself *into* an agent.

Hence, before it is a question of figurative or logical thought, the Dinka's conduct is a matter of practice as moral selection. This consideration is not altered by the technical results of his act. Of course, as modern medicine seems increasingly hard put to deny, it is by no means empirically certain that even the most biologically based afflictions are perfectly resistant to wishful remediation.[13] But even if the Dinka's affliction fails to yield to such discretionary measures, he will have succeeded in making himself into a creature that makes himself by standing against his own positive condition, that side of himself represented by the instinctual pole.

What better way to describe an ontological shift away from instinct qua instinct than in terms of choice? If the transcending of instinct is not an action of and toward choosing, then what is? Even if it is less than perfectly self-conscious, resisting one's specific inherent or taken-for-granted propensities amounts somehow to the withholding of assent, therewith implicating the possibility of giving it.

But since this action is still a far cry from choice in the strict sense, that is, choice keyed by acutely self-conscious agency, as it remains so closely tied to the strings of the instinctual pole, it enjoys a primordial character. The kind of action in question continues to exhibit determinacy in such pronounced measure that the facultative component of the action, although it is imposing, cannot be made clear and distinct. Therefore, the question of agency remains fundamentally perplexed. This consideration correlates directly with the understanding that practice is always less than fully conscious and is representatively intersubjective. Among the Dinka, these conditions are enfigured in Divinity, a representation of external but encompassing discretionary power. The chief consideration here, though, is that choosing of this primordial kind conditions the possibility of choice as such. Every highly autonomous choice presupposes this first 'choosing' between choosing or not, that is, between transcendence and instinct. In other words, what I am calling here moral selection may be regarded as the root of all choice.

Obviously, then, from the perspective of practice, the entertaining of the contradiction between the two kinds of truth amounts to conducting oneself in terms of choice. The shift from the one pole toward the other both distinguishes and conjoins the two kinds of truth, implicitly asserting a blatant contradiction. We are now in a position to see, however, that what on the plane of logic proper signifies an irrational willingness to tolerate contradiction, on the plane of practice is nothing but the behavior of choosing. Conceived of as lived, the contradiction between the two kinds of truth betrays the very dynamic of choice.

The considerations that, first, mythic rationality is especially representative of the logic of practice and, second, practice is a kind of selection, what I call the moral kind, oblige us to reappraise mythic rationality's willingness to tolerate contradiction. To be sure, mythic rationality does appear to assert contradictories at one and the same time. But whereas to do so in theory is, by definition, always unwarranted, to do so in practice is to display the conduct of primordial choice.

Of course, this finding raises the crucial question of the relative value of mythic rationality. Even if this rationality does not intend a theoretical posture per se, are we not better off assuming one? The present exercise, given its preponderantly theoretical force and nature, obliges me to answer in the affirmative—but only insofar as taking such a posture undergirds, rather than undermines, the possibility of moral selection. I will seek to develop this answer in the remainder of this study. For now it must suffice to point out that although in itself mythic rationality is not existentially unavoidable, the conduct of primordial choosing is. Put another way, there is no doing without some kind of value-rationality.

For all its theoretical posturing, not only is modern science, too, as a host of strong critics (including M. Polanyi, Kuhn, and Feyerabend) have shown, not free from the problem of rationality, but it exhibits it fundamentally. In light of (to favor Kuhn's famous notion) paradigmatic commitment, science, like mythic rationality, confounds the real with the ideal. Although I do not take this finding to mean that there is no significant difference between scientific and mythic rationality, I do infer from it that both rationalities display the primacy of moral selection in human existence. The fact is that, ultimately, it is simply not possible to tell the real from the ideal. The movement from the instinctual or the real toward the transcendental or the ideal is the human condition, and that movement obtains prior to the two poles themselves.

The finding that mythic rationality is peculiarly representative of moral selection makes it appropriate to reappraise—but not to overlook—this rationality's willingness to tolerate contradictions. If the structure of choice involves inescapably the contradiction between the two kinds of truth, then since every distinctively human act is an act of choice, every such act as an act must run afoul of the law of non-contradiction. However scrupulous one's logic, one cannot avoid enacting contradiction: to be existentially entrammeled in contradiction is what it means to be human. Surely, it must follow that mythic rationality, whatever its shortcomings, has got something fundamentally right.

Here I have set out my position about choice and contradiction largely in the abstract. In the next chapter, in light of this position, I examine comparatively the story of Genesis and, following up the ethnographic example adduced in this chapter, the East African people known as the Dinka. Needless to say, in connection with the Dinka and preliterate or traditional social orders in general, the question of tolerating contradictions has a notorious anthropological saliency.

Chapter 9

CONTRADICTION AND CHOICE AMONG
THE DINKA AND IN GENESIS

You see, it is the ancient legend of paradise . . . That legend referred to us of today, did it not?. . . There were two in paradise and the choice was offered to them: happiness without freedom, or freedom without happiness . . . They, fools that they were, chose freedom. Naturally, for centuries afterward they longed for fetters, for the fetters of yore . . . And only we found a way to regain happiness . . . [W]e helped god to defeat the devil definitely and finally . . . Paradise again! We returned to the simple-mindedness and innocence of Adam and Eve. No more meddling with good and evil and all that . . . The Well-doer, the Machine, the Cube, the giant Gas Bell, the Guardians—all these are good . . . For all this preserves our non-freedom, that is, our happiness.

— Eugene Zamiatin, *We*

In response to the anthropological problem of rationality, I have argued that what, from the point of view of theory, can be construed as indifference to the law of non-contradiction amounts to an act of resistance and a dynamic of choice, when seen from the standpoint of practice. That is to say, what classical anthropology was inclined to perceive as backward and irrational discloses instead the essentially ethical nature of human existence. In light of this contention, the finding of logical indifference is thus shown to be less a figment of the anthropological imagination than a profoundly shortsighted conclusion. In other words, notwithstanding the most distinguished recent anthropology, including structuralism, hermeneutics, and the (Bourdieuian) theory of practice, the anthropological problem of rationality addresses a real difference, one of imposing empirical force. But the difference is profoundly relative, reflecting the epistemological ascension of theory qua theory, and is therefore best understood by reference to the complexly nondualistic relation between theory and practice.

In the present chapter, my argument comprises five parts. I open by introducing in brief the issue of choice in relation to the story of Genesis. I argue that Adam's choice reveals a profound contradiction between determinacy and self-fashioning. In the second part, I set out to document for the Dinka an implicit ontology of ambiguity, according to which self and other, and the natural and the supernatural, are at once identical and distinct. I contend that this logically absurd state of affairs makes sense when it is understood that for the Dinka the other and the supernatural enjoy the hierarchical privilege of encompassment. I also maintain that this hierarchical privilege is primarily performative rather than contemplative in nature. In light of these arguments, the contradictions of a self that is other and of an unnatural nature take on the appearance of active resistance rather than abstract logic. In essence, the contradiction betrays a dynamic of choice. In the third part, I proceed to treat Dinka temporality with reference to such an ontology of ambiguity and, more briefly, to relate this ontology to the fact that the Dinka take practice not primarily as a means to an end but as its own objective. In the fourth part, I show that the Dinka themselves project the picture of contradiction as an existential condition of choice. That the Dinka grasp themselves in terms of choice seems a critical finding in light of the unreserved suspicion under which the rhetoric of choice has fallen in postmodern intellectual discourse.[1] Finally, in the fifth part, I compare my findings on choice among the Dinka to the question of choice in Genesis. Here I suggest that while the parallels between the two are striking, by thematizing choice itself, Genesis ups the ante.

The Paradigm of Genesis

Adam's Choice

It seems to me that every human act is rooted in the contradiction of a choice that is not a choice, one that is at once a matter of choice and of determination. Adam's act of disobedience in Genesis 2 and 3 constitutes a paradigmatic representation of what it means to make such a choice. Plainly, the act of disobedience was predisposed. Indeed, in the story, had God not set Adam up to take a fall, the act could not have been meaningful in terms of disobedience. If God had not cut Adam on the bias and had left him solely to his own devices, as if he were entirely his own authority, then the claim for the absolute, creative authority of God would have to go unwarranted. In which case, how could Adam's conduct be defined as deviant? Yet in some irrepressible sense, the choice was Adam's: although he was substantially predisposed to take a fall, he was also constructed in such a way that he could have done otherwise.

Thus, Adam's agency conjoins contradictory kinds of truth: it joins together the truth of determinacy or fact and the no less essential truth of choice or convention. In other words, Adam was created both as a determinate product of existence and as a function of moral selection: he was created both by his other and by himself; he both did and did not fashion himself. The spirit of this contradiction is rhetorically embodied in the figure of the serpent as well as in the act of disobedience. The act of disobedience, recall, is conspicuously appetitive yet critically transcendent, while the figure of the serpent is supremely tellurian yet deeply reflective.

The truth of determinacy is registered by Adam's belatedness. But how exactly does the story register the truth of choice? Of course, choice is given fundamentally in the Creator's creativity. But as a component of Adam's make-up, choice is defined in the story as the difference made in God's Creation by a creature re-creating itself in practice. This difference amounts to resistance, a positive torsion of negation, a creative act. The pressing back against the pressure of reality constitutes choosing. This is the case even if reality is pictured, as in Genesis, as already conventionally informed by God.

Thus, the story presents a theoretical contradiction—a choice that is not a choice— as an act of resistance. In effect, the story's assertion that Adam both did and did not create himself is not primarily a theoretical proposition; it betokens, instead, a choice-constituting movement of defiance. In actively resisting reality as it was defined by God's imperative, Adam at once differentiated and conjoined two kinds of truth: objective determinacy, or God's creation, on the one hand, and subjective self-fashioning, on the other. In so doing, a point to which I will later return, he also objectified the option of choice—the option between being chosen and choosing for the sake of oneself.

An Implicit Ontology of Ambiguity

Experience and Participatory Selfhood

It is edifying to compare the example of Genesis to that of the Dinka, whose tolerance of seeming contradictions is ethnographically well recorded. According to Lienhardt (1961: 147), the Dinka have no problem discussing such phenomena as poor agricultural harvests, bad weather conditions, colds, and headaches "as purely 'natural' phenomena." But they do so only "up to a point." Beyond that point, when these phenomena and their like persist and become particularly worrisome, the Dinka's "thoughts will turn to the possible activity of Powers." Evidently, the Dinka are unconcerned about asserting, at one and the same time or by turns, that something is natural and that it is not-natural (supernatural). It would appear, thus, that the Dinka are prepared to tolerate patent contradictions. As I see it, in order to make intelligible the Dinka's apparent indifference to canonical logic, it is necessary to grasp their assertion not primarily as a theoretical proposition but most particularly as an artifact of practice. In what follows here, I attempt to give interpretive force to this characterization of the Dinka assertion.

With acute phenomenological insight, Durkheim observed that the sentiment of a natural order existing in itself depends on a social determination of reality, a determination on the basis of which what moderns typically regard as religious perceptions and understandings can no longer truly be taken for granted (see note 5 in this chapter). Following Durkheim's insight to its logical conclusion, Lienhardt argues that Dinka religion must be understood not as a set of beliefs and principles, but as, to use his words, natural and social experience: "[T]o attempt to produce an account ... of a kind of Dinka 'creed' ... would be to start by concealing what ... is the clue to our understanding of the facts—that is, that Dinka religion begins with *natural* and social experience of particular kinds" (1961: 96; see also 32, 158, 159).

I take it that the notion of experience propounded by Lienhardt and the notion of practice understood here are critically linked by a focus on a world that is lived before it is rationalized. Although the Dinka may "up to a point" offer an account of lightning and headaches as "purely 'natural' phenomena," the ethnography documents that at no point does he see himself as wholly detached from such phenomena. That is to say, the Dinka never regards himself as purely an observer of lightning and headaches, but always finds himself to some substantial degree existentially engaged in and by them. Put differently, his self-awareness is sharply curtailed by his experience of participation in his other—which is to say, his experience of his own otherness.

But this does not imply that the Dinka lacks a developed sense of self. Rather, 'participation' describes a sense of self that remains firmly tied to the basic ambiguity of self and other.[2,3] The reflexive component of this self is keyed to a certain moment of the ambiguity—the moment of resistance to the other. The ethnography is unequivocal about the saliency of such existential resistance. Lienhardt documents frequent conflict between Dinka fathers and their sons, and, citing a "Divinity/man : father/child analogy" among these people, he highlights the Dinka cultural "theme of *opposition* to Divinity" (1961: 42–43; cf. Deng 1972: 71, 73). The fact of this opposition suggests that for the Dinka, fatherhood and Divinity represent the weighty and ultimately intractable authority of what there is or, better, of what stands behind what there is.

Resistance of this kind registers in the Dinka's cultural universe a certain difference between, on the one hand, the Dinka as a volitional creature with his own ends and, on the other, a pressing reality whose forces may run contrary to those ends. The resistance may be regarded, then, as the enactment of a 'contradiction' between a nature defined in terms of what there is and a supernature defined in terms of a moral faculty for self-fashioning. Construed thus, however, the contradiction appears to be nothing but the conduct of choice. The kind of opposition in question, the kind that distinguishes self-propulsion from motion by force of 'nature', is the expressive activity we speak of as choosing.

A Non-natural Nature

Should we consider things from the other side of the equation, the possibility of choice is tantamount to the performative contradiction of a 'non-natural nature'. Such a nature systematically and actively transcends itself—in effect, for all its irrefragable naturalness, it is also supernatural. Through one of its elements (humankind), nature transparently exceeds itself to become second nature. It is true that for the Dinka it is usual to attribute the values of 'natural' and 'supernatural' to both man and Divinity, and that it is Divinity, not man, who is especially associated with supernatural power or originary moral force (Lienhardt 1961: 28). But this consideration does not vitiate the argument about the Dinka's capacity for refusal as a phenomenological key to the emergence of his consciousness of his own agency.

His capacity to oppose the 'powers that be' does indeed bring the Dinka to an awareness of choice, enabling him to distinguish his self for himself. It thus alienates him from his ground and positions him to view reality in terms of its behavior apart from moral selection—in terms, that is, of what Westerners call natural causes or objective reality. But for reasons of his preponderantly participatory purchase on things, the Dinka's ground is never far beneath him, serving to restrict his naturalistic view to but a glimpse. He never really does see nature in the round, as if he himself were cleanly severed from it. Accordingly, the capacity for choice implicit in his opposition to the given is experienced by him as belonging not simply to himself but at the same time, and more fundamentally, to the order of which he finds himself to be a part, the order of things at large. As a result, as paralogical as it may seem, this order remains for him as subjective as it is objective.

Thus, although it is evident that the Dinka experiences a distinction between what we call nature and the supernatural, it is no less plain that for him nature is both natural and supernatural. For reasons of this logically scandalous and diacritically ambiguous construction, Lienhardt (1961: 28) finds that the distinction in question ill describes Dinka religion: "I have not found it useful to adopt the distinction between 'natural' and 'supernatural' beings or events in order to describe the difference between men and Powers, for this distinction implies a conception of the course or laws of Nature quite foreign to Dinka thought." But whether or not one chooses to describe Dinka religion in these terms (in the end, Lienhardt seems unable to avoid their use, although he encloses them in marks to indicate a special sense),[4] the important point is to understand that where the line between the 'natural' and the 'supernatural' is but fuzzily drawn, the former must be morally constituted and the latter given in nature. Lienhardt (ibid.: 54) makes the point this way: "To the Dinka, the moral order ... is given ... in much the same way as for practical purposes we regard the physical order to be given." In effect, the relevant Dinka distinction is acutely and irrepressibly ambiguous, making nature more than natural and—for moderns, stranger still—the domain of the supernatural less than unnatural.[5] It follows, impossible though it is to make logically plain, that the Dinka distinction recognizes neither nature nor supernature as such.

Basic Ambiguity and Lived Contradiction

Lienhardt's phenomenological interpretation of Dinka religion centers on the insight that their religion is virtually keyed to the experience of essential ambiguity. The thesis that the spiritual beings of Dinka religion amount to images of the Dinka's prepossessing experience of his own ambiguous constitution forms the core of Lienhardt's argument about the reality behind—the 'rationality' of—Dinka religion. The ambiguous constitution in ethnographic question is that of a self-endowed creature whose self is nonetheless commandingly circumscribed by his other. Lienhardt tells us that Dinka refer primarily to Divinity when they "have to adjust themselves to situations in which they involuntarily find themselves, and where clear oppositions and ambiguities of thought and experience occur." Correlatively, he speaks of the "evocation of the notion of Divinity by paradoxes and contrarieties of experience" (Lienhardt 1961: 55). Dinka myths depict the human condition as "one of *conjoined opposition* between men and Divinity," he observes, "a relationship in which, at once together and apart, they are held in a tension which it is part of the function of religious rites to regulate and maintain" (ibid.: 37). The Dinka understand their existential situation in the dilemmatical terms of being caught constitutionally between creaturely subjection and their capacity to manage themselves: "Men now are—as the first man and woman ... became—active, self-assertive, inquiring, acquisitive. Yet they are also subject to suffering and death, ineffective, ignorant, and poor" (ibid.: 53).

It should not be too hard to see that the experience of ambiguity driving Dinka religious practice implicates the issues of both contradiction and choice. To take the question of contradiction first, if one assumes the point of view of formal logic, the Dinka ambiguity of self and other may be understood to assert the contradiction that phenomena such as lightning and headaches are at one and the same time both natural and not-natural. Insofar as the Dinka experiences his self as such, as its own agent, these phenomena appear to him as part of an exterior, objective world. But insofar as—in accordance with the ambiguity saturating his existential identity—he experiences his self as participant of his other, then the selfsame phenomena appear to him as events of a world morally empowered in its own right—what moderns call a supernatural or enchanted world.

Starting from the position of formal logic, the contradictory accounts of lightning and headaches are suspended in the abstract as commensurate and symmetrical propositions about the world. Therefore, inasmuch as each is the antithesis of the other, rationally they cannot be entertained as continuous with each other. But the Dinka *does* appear to entertain them so. When he shifts from the naturalist to the supernaturalist account, far from replacing the one with the other, the Dinka is invoking the contradictory account on top of or behind the naturalist one.

However, the perspective from formal logic seriously impairs one's vision in relation to the Dinka ambiguity, for while the ambiguity has an implicit theoretical moment, its quintessential character is, by diametrical contrast to theory proper, its livedness. Before it is articulated as thought, it is felt—"experienced," Lienhardt would say—in practice. As a consequence, the logical canon of non-contradiction has only an indirect relevance for it. Because the ambiguity issues from practice, the so-called contradiction must be in the first place enacted. That is to say, before he sits back and takes stock of things, the Dinka's conduct itself projects at a stroke contradictory pictures of lightning, headaches, and the like. It cannot be otherwise, since his conduct is unidentifiable as Dinka outside of the ambiguity of self and other that critically informs it, providing the key to its meaningfulness.

If, then, the two logically opposed projections of the world correspond respectively to the autonomous and heteronomous sides of the Dinka's self, and if the distinction he draws between the one side and the other is essentially porous, then his behavior cannot help but exhibit both projections at once. Remarkably, then, as he approaches the phenomena of the world with a view toward their natural origins, by the same token he approaches them as if they follow from or present supernatural causes.

Hierarchical Containment and Epistemological Alternation

To see just how the Dinka are enabled to enact at the same time contradictory behaviors, it is important to understand that from the point of view of practice, the two sides of the Dinka's self are neither commensurate nor symmetrical. Given that the heteronomous side cannot admit of a clean break between the Dinka and his world, it must enjoy the hierarchical privilege and primacy of encompassment. For this reason, the heteronomous side merely supposes its autonomous counterpart. The autonomous side, however, in a sense also inescapably implicit in the fact of encompassment, actually presupposes heteronomy. Put another way, whereas the heteronomous side (like a native land without an autochthon) would go unfulfilled without its counterpart, the autonomous side (like a part without a whole) would be inconceivable without its overarching foil.

The asymmetrical structure of the relationship between the two sides of the Dinka's self is another way of talking about the porosity of the boundary between them. The asymmetry allows the Dinka to shift epistemologically from one account of the world to a contradictory account without giving it a second thought. When lightning, headaches, and the like are perceived to become increasingly life-threatening ("Should the cold turn to high fever, or the headache become persistent and agonizing"), the Dinka's thoughts turn from "purely 'natural' phenomena" to "the possible activity of Powers" (Lienhardt 1961: 147). By virtue of the hierarchical containment of the one account by the other, there is no effective obstacle to such epistemological alternation. Hierarchical containment is in a plain sense logically naive. For practice that remains thus uninformed by logic qua logic, a contradiction in the strict sense is the merest of formalities.

Practice and Conjoined Opposition

Hierarchical containment is effected in and by practice. The consideration that practice can never be quite contained by its practitioners, but in the end may be counted on to bring the latter up short, bespeaks its hierarchical superiority. Practice ties together the practitioners' active subjectivity with their passive subjection to their other. Whereas their subjectivity describes the alienation from the world that is necessary to make conceivable the very idea of natural causes, the subjection points to the supernatural power that lies above and beyond nature. Practice is itself, then, the relation between the two sides of the Dinka's self and, correlatively, between the contradictory accounts of the world.

The Dinka can turn his thoughts, without logical embarrassment, from naturalism to supernaturalism because he begins his 'thinking' from the perspective of practice rather than that of logic. From this perspective, the two accounts are not abstracted from but remain somehow imprisoned in action. As such, they are performative before they are representational; they predispose reality before they propose it. Put differently, they are not so much a question of the canons of formal logic as of the ethics of human practice; in the first place, they entail choice, not logic. These accounts project the order of things not as something subject to our decided and exact control, as in logic, but as something to which, because we are of it, our choices can make a difference, although that difference itself is ever subject to a mastery not our own.

The perspective of practice does not eradicate the difference between the naturalist and the enchanted account. The difference is, however, critically mediated—not in logic but in practice. By virtue of practice, the two accounts are inseparably conjoined in a moral, Siamese twinship. The alternation of the two accounts is a play on the paradoxicality of the relationship between them, a relationship in which the one account contains its contradictory. The interconnection of conjoined opposition allows the Dinka to flow 'logically' from the one account to the other, without, however, dedifferentiating them.

Time and the Dinka

Two-Timing Time

It is illuminating to make the point about fundamental ambiguity also in relation to the question of temporality. As far as formal logic is concerned, the two Dinka accounts obtain in homogeneous time, the units of which are internally univocal and qualitatively indistinguishable. Practice admits of this sort of time, in which both past and future are merely modified presents. Homogeneous time begins with the certainty of the present; the temporal flow of practice is punctuated by reference to a definite 'now'. This circumstance produces exclusive occurrences, fixing practice categorically in terms, then, of well-defined events and the sameness of the subject who is the index of the now. I refer to this sort of time as the short term.

Such time is homogeneous, each moment being 'just another moment' and internally unambiguous. Under the rule of this sort of temporality, if two accounts of things are mutually contradictory, it would be irrational to hold both at the same time. But practice also marks another kind of time, one that serves to distinguish practice from pure theory and is neither homogeneous nor exactly eventful. This sort of time is defined by reference to the essential ambiguity of practice.

As a process of moral selection, practice describes 'behavior' as ontologically ambiguous as between behavior and meaning. In Cartesian terms, such behavior obtains directly between stuff that takes up space (*res extensa*) and stuff that enjoys the physical dimensions of an idea (*res cogitans*)—to wit, zero dimensions. The ambiguity is dynamic, presenting—before each of the stuffs appears in its own right—a movement of circumscribed opposition between the two. This movement entails that the resistant stuff, by virtue of actively standing against the other, delineates itself as subjective agency, but also as, by virtue of its irrevocable belatedness, subject to the other. Thus, practice describes human behavior in the spatial terms of being in between—a tensional or negative space, an absence or openness that not only makes room for but virtually commands or constitutes choice.

The human agent experiences this condition of circumscription as an ultimate limit and ground. Lienhardt's ethnography makes it abundantly clear that for the Dinka, although death and suffering are not impregnable to the designs of human agency, they are at bottom a matter of what happens regardless of those designs. ("Yet they are also subject to suffering and death," lament the Dinka, about themselves, in relation to their capacity to control the order of things.) Our ground is finally beyond our volitional reach; in the end, we do not happen to it—it happens to us. Although one may experience one's own dying, one can never experience one's own death (Levinas 1969: 232ff.).

Put in terms of temporality, our ground—the characteristic paradigm of Western thought notwithstanding—is irreducible to time-present, to a temporality keyed to the here and now of our own subjective universe. Instead, it amounts to what I call the long term: an essential futurity, an indeterminate and indeterminable 'not yet', an-other time, or, better still, the time of the Other—in Dinka terms, the time of Divinity.

The fact of circumscription, then, marks a time different in kind from the homogeneous temporal mode. This time is not subject to the closure of the present; rather, it bespeaks an ineradicable openness, corresponding to the essential uncertainty of practice, to the way in which practice constitutionally evades every attempt to fix it categorically, the way in which it always eludes the designs of its practitioners. If such time cannot be punctuated by reference to a definite 'now', then it cannot be broken down into well-defined, fungible units. Nor, therefore, can it define events as such; it corresponds, instead, to events-in-the-making.

The relationship between these two kinds of time is like that between the two sides of the Dinka's self—asymmetrical. Because the time of the Other serves to put a cap on human agency, it enjoys a certain authority over its counterpart. The authority I have in mind has the quality of the authority enjoyed by an author to create ends. Obviously, authority of this kind is predicated on a principle of uncertainty.

In relation to essential uncertainty, time-present is really a mode of deferral, a putting off of an ultimate end. Whether it is measured in the fungible units of geometry or (as among the Dinka) in the existential ones of lived experience, deferring is (to recall the capital punishment handed down by God to Adam in the story of Genesis) time done as a life sentence. For present purposes, the chief point is that so long as it is not obscured from consciousness (as it is not among the Dinka), the time of the Other describes as singularly ambiguous any conception of the now. Time as deferral marks time-present all right, but it marks it as time contained by another temporality, one irreducible to the certainty of the now. In effect, it marks it as two-timing time.

No Time for Contradictions

Such ambiguous temporality casts yet another fresh light on the Dinka's apparent willingness to tolerate contradictions. Put straightforwardly, although the Dinka asserts at the same time both that lightning, headaches, and the like are natural and that they are not-natural (supernatural)—since for him 'the same time' includes different temporal planes, that is, opposing but hierarchically conjoined modalities of time—strictly speaking, his assertion is not classifiable as a contradiction. The assertions of naturalism and of supernaturalism are made on different temporal planes, one of which also contains the other as a counterweight. Thus, they are made *at* the same time but *in* different times.

In accounting for phenomena such as lightning and headaches in naturalistic terms, the Dinka is not excluding but rather including the opposing account in terms of supernatural powers. The one account is posited in the certain temporal mode of the Dinka's here and now, while the other is posited in the irrecusably uncertain time of Divinity, a past and future always beyond the purview of the Dinka's present. Since the time of Divinity encompasses the Dinka's time-present, both accounts are posited *at the same time,* and the Dinka is 'logically' free to shift discursively and epistemically from one account to the other.

The consideration that the time of Divinity is comprehensive reveals that such time correlates peculiarly with practice. Practice also representatively displays the way in which the 'whole', as encompassing, remains ever beyond the possessive reach of the 'part'. We arrive again at the critical point: the Dinka assertion is made in practice and not as a statement of theory proper. In effect, the Dinka's conduct toward lightning, headaches, and the like counts at once as both naturalistic and supernaturalistic, because it always occurs on opposed but conjoint temporal planes. Given that the Dinka assumes his phenomenological stance in the world at the hierarchical point of crossing of the two temporal modes, whatever the Dinka does, the conduct in question exhibits at one and the same time both naturalistic and supernaturalistic meaning.

Time and Reproduction

In pointing out, in a famous dictum, that it is not possible to prepare for peace by preparing for war, Einstein was wrong (notwithstanding his good intentions). Ironically, he was wrong for the very same reason that those moderns who champion the cause of such (logically ridiculous) preparations are wrong: there can be no success in such an endeavor so long as conduct is restricted phenomenologically to a temporality reducible to time-present. Restriction of this kind tends to be the case under conditions of modernity. Where time is registered as essentially ambiguous, as between such temporality and the long term, however, a course of action as logically absurd as the one Einstein disparages is well within reason.

The Dinka ethnography provides a neat and ready illustration of the point. Their view of reproduction shows just what it means, in connection with such logical nonsense, to stand phenomenologically at the point where the one temporal mode transverses the other (Lienhardt 1961: 41–42; emphases added; cf. Deng 1972: 30, 127):

In Dinka there are important interconnexions between notions of creation and of fatherhood, though the verb 'to create' is never interchangeable with the verb 'to beget'. Divinity created (*cak*) men in the beginning, and the men he created begot or bore (*dhieth*) children. Divinity did not 'beget' or 'bear' men, and it would be a linguistic mistake in Dinka either to use this expression for the creation of men by Divinity, or to say that father and mother 'created' their child. Yet *the notions are linked. Dhieth* means both 'to beget' and 'to give birth to', so that verbally the activities of men and women in procreation are not distinguished from each other. When a man was asked to explain what happened in coitus, he described the physical act, and added 'And that is called begetting (*dhieth*), and Divinity will then slowly create (*cak*) the child in the woman's belly.' *Divinity thus has a creative function in the formation of every human being*, and when human beings are barren their barrenness is explained by reference to it; when a woman fails to bear a child despite intercourse with a man known to be able to beget children, it is commonly said that Divinity has 'refused' her a child, and at sacrifices masters of the fishing-spear or prophets commonly ask that Divinity may allow women to bear children. Men, therefore, beget children in association with the creative operation of Divinity, which is thus the real and ultimate "Husband (man) of the cattle, Husband of the women ..." as it is expressed in a Dinka hymn. *The ideas of 'creator' and 'father' are fused with each other* when Divinity is thought of as the active source of life for his 'children', men.

In other words, although the Dinka distinguish between creating as supernatural and procreating as natural, they also grasp the two processes as fundamentally linked or fused or associated. Such that, for this people, the generative force of procreating is founded, ultimately and in every case, in a creative, or what we moderns might call a supernatural, act.[6]

This patently ambiguous picture of reproduction has its source in the overriding degree to which it is projected from the standpoint of practice rather than theory as such. From this standpoint, a participant vantage, encompassment is experienced as absolutely prior. That is to say, what the Dinka takes most for granted, what he finds 'real' above all, is the relative holism or imperfect differentiation of the supernatural and the long term. This purchase on reality translates into an absolute predisposition, a pre-reflective (bodily) inclination even, to assimilate, in every case and for the nonce, the natural to the domain of the supernatural. This is so even though the difference between the two domains remains intact throughout. In the event, the Dinka perceives the natural pole of reality for 'the time being', and the un- or supernatural pole for 'the time of "not yet"'; all the while, however, he does not fail to see the natural pole as a modification of the domain of the supernatural and the present as a function of the time of Divinity.[7]

An End in Itself and Divine Time

A correlative way to show that designating the Dinka assertion as a contradiction fails to satisfactorily comprehend the nature of the assertion is to recall that the normative process I am calling here practice is not primarily instrumental—it is, rather, its own end. The priority attributed by the Dinka to practice, the priority of authorship and circumscription, means precisely that practice takes place on its own behalf. It means that practice cannot be referred beyond itself, that it is self-founding. Because practice is thus the bottom line of the Dinka's reality, because it presents a reality deeper and more comprehensive than substantival reality, it is not for him an attribute. It is, instead, the very essence of the order of things.

The Dinka's approach to such phenomena as lightning and headaches constitutes an answer, not to the theoretical question of what these phenomena are, but to the practical question of what the Dinka wants to be in respect of them. It is an expression of how he desires to fit into the order of things. Put another way, his answer intends primarily to define, not to explain, his phenomenal situation. As the Dinka sees it, the answer is predominantly given *for* him, by order of Divinity, rather than *by* him. But whether one sees oneself or one's other as the chief defining agency, the main point here is that, as a definition of the situation, the Dinka's answer cannot be fairly judged by reference to the law of non-contradiction. In relation to expressions of how things ought to be, the relevant standards are not formally logical but quintessentially ethical.

In addressing the venerable anthropological question of contradiction in relation to Dinka religion, Lienhardt pursues just this line of argument. Speaking about sacrifice, the key rite in Dinka religious practice, Lienhardt asks (1961: 291): "[I]f sacrifice is made for the recovery of a sick man, for example, and he dies, why is sacrifice not regarded as ineffective, in the same way as a technical act which fails to produce its desired result?" Lienhardt's thoughtful answer should be consulted in full, but it may be summed up by his pithy observation that "the objective of a sacrifice is achieved in the act itself" (ibid.: 291ff.). Which is to say, I surmise, that although, in its aim of forestalling a bad end, sacrifice marks the time of events, in its more fundamental end of discharging responsibility to the other, sacrifice keeps the encompassing, aleatory time of Divinity.

Contradiction as Choice

Experience of Choice: The Scylla of Other and the Charybdis of Self-Absorption

I have argued that the experience of ambiguity at the center of Dinka religion implicates what scholarly observers have tended to misconstrue as contradiction in the strict sense, and that the apparent contradiction is really the situation of choice. The notion of contradiction predicates mutually exclusive propositions. Between contradictory propositions there can be no truck, no room to maneuver epistemologically. Either the one or the other, but not both, must be the case. But as we have seen, the ambiguity at the center of Dinka religion defines, rather than epistemological closure, an existential clearing, a fluid movement between the two sides of the Dinka's self; correlatively, it describes a play between the corresponding, apparently contradictory views of the order of things.

This play amounts to a space and time of choosing. The polarity of naturalism and supernaturalism presupposes the performative duality of the Dinka's self. While his self remains primarily participatory, and thus (in being itself) endemically of its other, it also exhibits an alienatory capacity that makes it possible for the Dinka to grasp the world in naturalistic terms, as relatively 'outside' or objective. The alienation signifies the resisting, the standing against that is choosing; it marks a time of deferring and discloses a space of moral or creative selecting.

In light of the ethnography, to come now to my final point, there can be no doubt that the Dinka, too, grasp their experience of ambiguity in terms of choice. For the Dinka, one of the most salient features of the predominant side of his self, the side of otherness or Divinity, is its facultative nature—it exhibits the essential uncertainty that is associated with discretionary power. In their creation stories, Man is said to have offended Divinity by a particular act, moving Divinity to withdraw in degree from Man. In commenting on these stories, the Dinka are inclined to emphasize the "smallness of the fault" for which Divinity leaves Man in the lurch (Lienhardt 1961: 53): "Divinity's withdrawal from Man as the result of a comparatively trifling offence, by human standards, presents the contrast between equitable human judgements and the action of the Powers which are held ultimately to control what happens in Dinka life." In other words, man's other is characterized by a singular and consequential arbitrariness, the kind of unpredictability that is associated with absolute discretion.

Likewise, man's offensive/resistant role in Divinity's decision to withdraw is depicted in terms of choice. For example, in the creation myth, which Lienhardt reports is common to all Dinka whom he knew (1961: 35; 1973; cf. Deng 1972: 126), Divinity and men were originally contiguous, being connected by a rope stretched horizontally such that Man might hoist himself up as he pleased. Under this asymmetrical but side-by-side regime, death was unknown, although Divinity restricted the vitality of men by rationing the amount of grain they could have. The first woman, however, driven by greed, proceeded to plant more than the allotted amount of grain. In the course of doing so, she struck Divinity with her hoe, causing him to sever the rope and withdraw. As a result, men suffer hunger, sickness, and of course death. This story and the other creation tales Lienhardt records make clear that what moved Divinity to choose to withdraw was Man's self-regarding choice to exceed the limits Divinity set for him—that "Man in a sense chose death" is, Lienhardt (ibid.: 36) concludes, implied by these stories.

Clearly, the distance established by the withdrawal of Divinity from Man is a construction of the difference between nature and supernature. By pulling Himself away, Divinity places man in a situation of subjectivity, allowing man (up to a point) to understand the world objectively, in terms of natural causes. But far from representing the difference as a contradiction, the Dinka story presents it as a choice: as a result of Man's defiant gesture, Divinity chooses to withdraw from Man, thus creating a moral space in which Man is utterly condemned to dispose, in certain part, his own fate.

Here the difference between nature and supernature has little to do with declarations that admit of truth in the strict sense. Instead, it serves as a condition of proclamatory truth, truth that is occasioned by moral selection. The difference places Man in a situation where he must fashion his own identity by choosing, time and again, between the alternatives presented by the difference: whether to continue to offer resistance to

Divinity's rule, treating the world as the instrument of men, or to conform to the path laid down by Divinity, dutifully participating in the world according to supernal force.

Man must choose time and again because he has no choice in regard to the matter of choice. The alternatives do not confront him in theory but in practice, veritably defining the kind of creature he is. That is to say, together they fix his most fundamental identity—in effect, he is the tension they present. Therefore, the alternatives condition his every undertaking, and since they are opposing options, he is caught between them for all practical purposes. When he chooses to follow Divinity's designs, in a sense he is being less than his divinely given self; but when he attempts to defy Divinity, he then jeopardizes the ongoing existence of that very same self. His human condition, then, is precisely that of choice: he must steer, by his own lights, a tight course between the Scylla of self-annihilation by virtue of total emersion in his Other and the Charybdis of self-destruction by way of the folly of excessive self-absorption.

Ritual Practice and Dispositive Choice

Lienhardt (1961: 37) interprets this condition as "a tension [between Divinity and men] which it is part of the function of religious rites to regulate and maintain." Ritual practice, then, is the Dinka's principal response to his existential dilemma. Such practice addresses the Dinka's dilemma, not by trying to resolve it, but by putting time between him and it, deferring the double-bind and allowing him to get on with the business of living.

It is by now a classic argument in anthropology, as forged especially by the Manchester School, that ritual has the power to temporarily reconcile social principles that are fundamentally at odds. Indeed, ritual is a mediatory form in the deepest possible sense, a 'magical' sense: in and by its performance, it transacts essential difference. Like practice, it is action in which the ideas representing it are *essentially* imprisoned. In ritual, doing is always privileged over understanding. It is not, then, a *theory* of practice, but rather a *practice* of practice, albeit a formal one. If theory is practice that aims to make practice a more efficient instrument, then ritual is practice that aims to secure the very possibility of practice. In effect, ritual practice constitutes its own end. Although it does *represent* what it accomplishes (as has been the organizing emphasis of the great bulk of the many recent anthropological discussions of ritual),[8] it also *presents* it (as has not been well enough understood by anthropologists).

The critical point here is that the meaningful character of ritual is keyed to practice rather than theory. Like the creation myths that go hand in hand with it, ritual is a response not to theoretical but to practical questions, questions focused on the creative determination of ends rather than means. Dinka rites and myths may function, as Gluckman et al. surmised, to preserve a certain social world. More fundamentally, though, they constitute generative expressions of that world. They address the correlative questions what is the 'nature' of things? and who or what am I? not by asserting truth values, but by declaring and enacting—publicly, dramatically, and, above all, dispositively—choices for *this* state of being rather than *that*. In effect, they answer by engaging and committing to the reality they proclaim the person who performs and recites them.

Answers of this kind cannot be sensibly evaluated in terms of truth and falsity; rather, they require moral acceptance or rejection. Therefore, when an act of sacrifice among the Dinka fails "to produce the required result which is the proximate occasion of sacrifice" (healing a wound, say), the Dinka do not conclude, by way of appeal to the law of non-contradiction, that the premises of the institution of sacrifice have been refuted (Lienhardt 1961: 291). Instead, in accord with the thematic, moral nature of their act, they conclude that "Divinity has refused" (ibid.). If the forgoing account of contradiction and choice among the Dinka is correct, then that conclusion is as it should be.

A Choice Comparison: The Dinka and Genesis

Ritual vs. Radical Choice

The parallels between the picture of choice presented by the Dinka material and that projected by the Hebrew genesis story are remarkable. Both focus on a performative contradiction, delineating perspicuously a representative situation of choice by dint of which humans come to realize their moral capacity. Indeed, the Dinka creation myth sketched above and Genesis 2–3 have their narrative plot substantially in common: (1) at first, man and God/Divinity are immediately present to each other; (2) God/Divinity proscribes man's self-development; (3) in an appetitive act, the woman violates God's/Divinity's proscription; (4) as a result, a caesura is formed between God/Divinity and man; (5) as a further result, man suffers pain and death.

However, there is a consequential, even epochal, difference between the situation of choice expressed by Genesis and that projected by Dinka culture. Although choice is thematized as deviancy and responsibility in both cases, in Genesis it is thematized also as such, as choice qua choice. That is to say, Genesis depicts choice directly in terms of the options not only between compliance and transgression but also between choice and not-choice. It does this by lacing the forbidden fruit with the epistemic arsenic of the knowledge of good and evil. So fortified, the fruit becomes food for thought. But 'thought' here must be understood very specifically as reflection on the possibility of deciding one's own 'good'. In other words, it is a question of deciding what it is 'good to be' and thus of begetting one's own world.

In effect, whereas the Dinka cast choice in terms of a narrow line running between fixed options, that is, as ritually circumscribed, Genesis amplifies choice exponentially. In Genesis, the act of disobedience confronts humans not only with choices, but also, and especially, with the very *idea* of choice.

By contrast to the Dinka account, in which the transgressive act creates a significant but controlled tension between man and Divinity, the full projection of the idea of choice appears to stretch the distance between man and the God of Genesis past the breaking point. The power to choose to choose implies sheer choice, a total absence of restraint, and therewith the possibility of the death of God. If one may choose not only between the specific options of 'a' and 'b'—say, an apple and a pomegranate—but also between leaving things as they are and making of everything an option, then one must be one's own god. That is to say, if 'a' and 'b' stand explicitly for 'non-choice' and 'choice' respectively, then it appears possible to determine one's own choices. Under these conditions, if one chooses the alternative of non-choice, then one effectively opts to leave things as they are, acceding to the available choices as they present themselves. Even in this case, though, there is the implication that one could have fashioned one's own choices, for in effect, the option to leave things as they are supposes the condition of self-restraint. In turn, this condition holds out the possibility of self-determination, which is to say, of determining one's own choices. The effective appearance of this truly radical possibility—which has informed the development of selfhood in the West so profoundly—does much to explain the cautionary affect and content of the biblical message in general.

The option of determining one's own choices is precisely what the choice to choose insinuates. If I can viably deny the choices presented to me, I will not only have refused to play the game of selection according to the Other's rules, but also have already altered the manifold of choice. Following such denial to logical perfection, I will have managed to include in the manifold of choice not only the choices forgone by my taking one from those offered, but also all the choices excluded in the very manifold put before me (by the Other) in the first place. In so doing, it must follow that I will have appropriated to myself absolute choice or, what amounts to the same thing, freedom from the risk of uncertainty. Thus, by successfully withholding assent, I will have brought about a novel choice, namely, the choice for my Self as a Chooser or Creator of worlds. In effect, I will have begun to re-create the world according to my own designs—in my own image.

By contrast to the concrete choice between an apple and a pomegranate, the choice between choice and non-choice projects matters onto the plane of generality. This ontological conversion, from the particular to the general, is precisely what Genesis accomplishes by casting good and evil as gastronomic and epistemic at the same time. As food for thought, the distinction between good and evil anticipates all logical distinctions proper, that is, all distinctions that brook no middle. Indeed, I suggest that transformation of food into thought is, even if remotely, inceptive of Descartes' ontological syllogism leading to sheer mind as the only certainty, as well as, it must follow, to dualism. As a result of this transformation, the choice to choose becomes construable as the dualist choice between choicelessness and unlimited choice. In effect, the choice to choose holds up an 'evil' vision of itself as absolute, tempting humans to think of themselves as entirely their own masters. There is thus a palpable sense in which the ambiguous relationship between God and men has been resolved in favor of a clean break or, more exactly, the complete dissolution of otherness.

With the epistemological availability of the projection of himself as completely free, man seemingly affords himself the perspective of total subjectivity. Correlatively, from so sheer a perspective of interiority, the world appears to be wholly exterior, an objective Nature. As a concomitant result, whatever resists naturalistic reduction—that is, whatever stubbornly presents itself as beyond Nature—must be unnatural. In this way, the category of the supernatural comes to connote the ridiculous rather than the sublime. In turn, absurdly, this circumstance exerts considerable pressure to objectify even the experience of interiority, the experience by virtue of which objectification itself becomes meaningful.

In effect, although the story must be regarded as only embryonic in this regard, Genesis takes a sharp turn toward the possibility of the perfect dualism from which both science and history spring. I say 'history' because the conception of man—indeed, of "the whole of reality," as Lukacs put it (1971: 145)—as a temporal product of human action presupposes the dualistic figuration of men as perfectly autonomous choosers. I include 'science' because the conception of the world as open to examination in terms of lawful regularities finally presupposes the dualistic exclusion of any supra-mundane agency from interference with the natural course of events.

To be sure, Genesis hastens to add that the assumption of sheer choice on the part of men is a delusion of grandeur. Adam may have discovered that he possesses a creative will in his own right, but it is God who expels him from the Garden into history, not failing, in an act of beneficent care, to provide him with a suit of clothes for the worldly journey. Man's newly found sense of autonomy notwithstanding, God neither dies nor fades away. Instead, gradually, over the course of Western history, He recedes behind the scenes, as the invisible and providential force that makes the visible world possible.

In other words, the biblical story depicts the appearance of choice qua choice on the part of humans as but an appearance. Indeed, the idea of appearance arises along with that of choice, for once man constructs himself in terms of an exclusive interior self, it becomes possible for him to present himself as other than what he regards himself to be, in this sense, differentiating his appearance from his reality. The dualities of appearance and reality and of choice and non-choice are, in fact, coeval.

Nevertheless, the appearance of choice qua choice is a consequential watershed. By sharply projecting a picture of sheer self-determinacy, even if this picture amounts to a false impression, a kind of self-deception (it is hard to disagree with the story's kerygmatic caution here), the appearance sets in motion the transformations of the human world that eventuate in modernity. As the postmodernists have mightily belabored, the diagnostic traits of modernity, including positivism, rationalism, historicism, economism, politicism, etc., are all predicated on man's dualistic definition of himself as an immaculate subject.

Epilogue: On the Nature and Efficacy of Ritual

The forgoing discussion comparing ritual practice and radical choice intimates an onto-phenomenological perspective on the notion of ritual. It suggests that, strictly speaking (and assuming possible other features that anthropologists have brought forward to define it), ritual appears only where participation remains relatively unaffected by the thematic development of instrumentalism and subject-object or mind-body dualism. By 'participation' I have in mind, as must be evident at this juncture, not simply symbolic but also actual connectivity. In contrast to Lévy-Bruhl, though, I do not see this connectivity as a function of a 'law' of participation (a notion that, given its theoretical resonance, tends to conceal the ingenuous nature of what is in question). Instead, I see it as an inherent truth of experiential holism, the 'logic' of which can best be captured in terms of such roundly paradoxical concepts as, for instance, Dumont's "hierarchy" and Hegel's "dialectic" (Dumont's concept being, of course, distinctly Hegelian).

Ritual practice is a peculiar exercise in hierarchical encompassment, the axial structuring structure of any participatory order. Practice that is formally given over to mediation, in the deep, magical sense intended here, is inconceivable under conditions other than participatory ones. In performatively subsuming or referring to itself, ritual presents a chiastic dynamic in which ineradicable difference (as between the ideal and the real) is transformed for the time being into its mirror image, namely, identity. The transformation is effective but ephemeral. Let me comment first on the effectiveness or efficacy of ritual, leaving the question of the ephemeral character of ritual's end product to follow.

The transformation wrought by ritual is effective because it buys time, so to speak, temporizing a form of life. The ritual dynamic appears to model auto-affection, whereby, according to Kant (quoted in Agamben 1999: 109), we "must behave toward ourselves as passive," thus marking time as the tensile difference between the passive self and the selfsame self standing against itself. This standing-against entails the experience of oneself as momentum, that is, as the transcending motion described by resisting oneself, one's ground. On this understanding, time amounts to one's sense of oneself as the interval of transformation of the passive self into the active self, an ongoing process. Time, then, is the experiencing of dynamic difference—the back-and-forth change—between passive and active selfhood.

It must follow that time and selfhood come to the same thing, for paradoxically, the difference constituted by a passive, self-transcending self must also be experienced as a coincidence of the passive and the active. It is the same passive self being, in its becoming, both passive and active. Plainly, then, such coincidence constitutes the self. More exactly, it describes the self as self-constituting, a dynamic rather than a thing.

In Kant's argument, all this takes place as inner sense. If time were nothing but inner sense, however, if it were reducible to the self, then what would prevent the self from constituting itself as complete? If there were nothing that stands outside the self, beyond the self's control, why could the self not simply secure itself *in itself*, thus stopping time, in the interest of eternity? To be sure, such a self—one that is perfectly identical to itself—is, notoriously, a Western ideal. The fact, though, that the self always amounts to time as well as coincidence, to difference as well as identity, suggests not only that such self-completion is chimerical but also that in the absence of an outside, the Kantian inner sense makes no sense. Put differently, the temporal nature of the self entails that the self is always already other to itself, that in itself it describes a self-other relationship, that because there is always something that cannot be internalized, unambiguous selfhood is a contradiction in terms.

Heidegger, who famously equated being and time, saw this inconsistency in Kant's understanding. Kant, he says, "takes the subject—the 'in me'—as the starting-point for this problematic" (Heidegger 1978: 248). By contrast, Heidegger argues (ibid.: 47–48; emphasis added): "To have a determinate temporal character presupposes something … which is permanent [and] cannot be 'in us', 'for only through what is thus permanent can my Dasein *in time* be determined.'" Or, as he puts it more directly (ibid.: 248): "Kant presupposes both the distinction between the 'in me' and the 'outside of me', *and also the connection* between these." But we can appeal here as well to Durkheim, for the temporal world into which Heidegger tells us we are thrown—the "outside of me" and the "permanent"—is, for Durkheim, the social world. Durkheim acknowledges, with Kant, that our experience of the shift from one state of consciousness to another makes possible the conception of time. But he emphasizes, as against Kant, that this experience "is far from being enough to constitute the notion or category of time," since "my time" remains always predicated on an "abstract and impersonal frame" that surrounds us (Durkheim 1915: 10). For Heidegger, that frame is the world into which we are thrown; for Durkheim, it is society. The category of time, says Durkheim (ibid.: 439, 440) (like the other "pre-eminent concepts" that have "a preponderating part in our knowledge") has the function of "relating the variable to the permanent, the individual to the social."

I am now in a position to offer an explication of the efficacy of ritual. I have argued, first, that time and selfhood are the same thing, and, second, that time is the betweenness of self-and-other, of inside-and-outside. If the second point is the case—that inside and outside are differentiated from each other only incompletely—then, although at first blush it might seem otherwise, the inner sense cannot be the originary model for ritual process. Rather, it is the other way around: the individual self issues from the self-other dynamic, in relation to which the figure of the other or outside enjoys a certain priority, namely, the priority of encompassment. Unlike the figure of the self, that of otherness lends itself to exclusionary boundaries only when it is defined in terms of the self rather than in its own right (see chap. 11, this volume). Given that time is being (as is asserted in the first point above), the reality of the self is not primarily a matter of self-reflection; instead, it depends ultimately on otherness, including the otherness intrinsic to social practice. In this connection, ritual, as a particular kind of social practice, lends itself to phenomenological understanding.

The peculiarity of ritual is that it is a practice of practice. This means that it distinguishes itself by its material and purposeful intensity of focus on the reconstruction of reality. This intensity of focus is performative but at the same time far more than theatre, for what it performs is the ordinary construction of reality, without however presenting itself as mere fiction, as performance qua performance. Theatre explicitly defines itself as the unreal, thereby profoundly (though not totally) undercutting the possibility of the participants (performers and spectators alike) becoming, through self-constituting, the characters in play. Ritual, on the other hand, presents itself as somehow inherently even more real than quotidian reality, thus acutely promoting the constructing and reconstructing of this reality, including especially the subjectivities at stake in it. In effect, the ritual process *is* the very process of self-constituting, but with a magico-religious edge that is ordinarily either demoted, or for all practical purposes, missing in everyday life.

Herein rests the efficacy of ritual. By making the most of the zone of indistinction between the process of everyday life and the dramatic performance of that process as keyed to the good (whatever the culturally specific take on 'the good' might be), ritual exponentiates the creative capacity of the everyday process to constitute both self and world. The amplified zone of indistinction is realizable because human existence is from the start, to recall Wittgenstein (see chap. 1, this volume), "ceremonious" or "ritualistic," a peculiarly human characteristic that in effect betrays "the fact that," to invoke Heidegger now (1978: 32), man is an entity that "in its very Being, that Being is an issue for it." Thus, ritual appropriates to concentrated effect the very manner in which humans construct themselves and their worldhood. In other words, ritual is nothing but an amplified form of the existential way in which we ordinarily constitute, in body and soul, who we are. For this reason, granting the ontological truth of body-mind nondualism, ritual can in fact heal the sick as well as injure, even fatally, the fit and the whole.

The ritualistic characteristic that, according to Wittgenstein, humans bear in their everyday existence—the characteristic of self-constituting, of treating their own nature as an issue for itself—describes an ongoing dialectic of deconstruction and construction. One makes oneself by, at the entreaty or behest of the other, standing against oneself, all the while filling with content the vacuum thus created. In other words, presenting the dialectic of the passive self as activating itself, the self, in virtue of the other, undoes itself, thus making room for its transformative re-creation. In effect, as I have propounded earlier (chap. 3, this volume), human existence is sacrificial in nature. It is no wonder, then, that the dramatization of this existence, which I am treating as ritual in the strict sense, always takes a form of sacrifice. Anthropology

has routinely treated sacrifice as a ritual per se. In fact, however, it is existence-as-sac-
rifice—the human condition (the condition of mortal beings who nonetheless enjoy
a certain immortalizing say over their transience)—that provides the basis on which
all ritual qua ritual models itself.

I have distinguished between ritual and theatre by reference to the self-understanding of each. I maintain that theatre sees itself as performance, whereas ritual, although
certainly performative, presents itself (to itself and thence to others) as the very reality
it is representing. The anthropological problematic of ritual may itself be referred to this
distinction or its like. To judge from the disciplinary record, while the ethnographic
observer generally discerns that the participants of the ritual apprehend it as much more
than performance, she herself, no matter how seriously she credits the intelligence of
those whom she is studying, has difficulty seeing it as anything but performance. For
this phenomenological reason, the efficacy of ritual—ritual's evident existential hold on
those engaged in its practice—typically remains (if the observer is not able to explain it
away, as does nineteenth-century evolutionist and twentieth-century tropist anthropology) utterly alien in her considered awareness.[9] But precisely because the anthropologist
is professionally inclined to address ritual from a non-participatory perspective, this
problem of ritual becomes one that in the first place demands a theoretical explanation.
How are we to account for the continuing practice of such rituals as truly observant rite
if in fact they are merely performance? It seems to me that before the observer can usefully turn to a theoretical explanation, she must cast a reflexive eye on the question of her
own disbelief, which finds its source in the aporia of performance (representation) and
participation (presentation). Like that of theory and practice, which it does indeed implicate, this aporia is, in the West, typically seen in dualist terms, and is thus made absolutely impervious to mediation. In result, the anthropological reflexivity that is required
is impossibly complicated, since it entails theoretically dismantling one's perspective,
which, however, is, by trade, precisely the perspective of theory as opposed to practice.

My point is that the anthropologist's analytical picture of ritual must in the end
incorporate herself, but not simply as a spectator, even should she take account of her
interests, political or otherwise, in the abstract. Rather, the picture must include herself
as a thinking being, when 'thinking' is conceived of, not by contrast to practice, but *as*
practice, a bodily, affective, and purposeful engagement in and of the world. Long ago,
Rousseau (1966: 49), writing about "the Orientals," luminously captured this radical
sense of ethnographic reflexivity:

> For a proper appreciation of their actions, men must be considered in all their relationships:
> which we simply are not capable of doing. When we put ourselves in the position of others,
> we do not become what they must be, but remain ourselves, modified. And, when we think
> we are judging them rationally, we merely compare their prejudices to ours. Thus, if one
> who read a little Arabic and enjoyed leafing through the Koran were to hear Mohammed
> personally proclaim in that eloquent, rhythmic tongue, with that sonorous and persuasive
> voice, seducing first the ears, then the heart, every sentence alive with enthusiasm, he would
> prostrate himself, crying: Great prophet, messenger of God, lead us to glory, to martyrdom.
> We will conquer or die for you. Fanaticism always seems ridiculous to us, because there is
> no voice among us to make it understood. Our own fanatics are not authentic fanatics. They
> are merely rogues or fools. Instead of inspirational inflections, our tongues allow only for
> cries of diabolic possession.

Whatever Rousseau means when he says that we "simply are not capable of" considering men "in all their relationships," inasmuch as the difference between the perspectives of theory on the one hand and practice on the other is, while fundamentally relative, ineliminable, we cannot hope to theorize practice essentially. What the anthropologist *can* do, however, is to record in her theory the change she (her-self) has undergone as a result of being there, that is, being in and of the world conveyed by the ritual event under observation. She can for the moment put aside her theoretical prejudice and allow her own voice—as it made her 'fanaticism' bodily understood to herself—to speak descriptively, in her theory, of just that sacrificial experience.[10] But precisely because her special task is theorization, she cannot simply take for granted the nondualism of theory and practice. By contrast to the ritualist, her principal aim is precisely to explain, for which purpose she must do her best to set aside her participatory self.

This difference is not peculiar to the situation of ethnography; rather, it is a particular manifestation of a universal condition. One can never make a picture that represents perfectly the image of the observer and that of the observed, if only because there will always be one participatory perspective that must remain invisible, namely, the last exercise in self-transparency, the perspective that makes continuing reflexivity possible. To see the infinite regression here, one need only imagine oneself observing the observed, and then observing oneself observing the observed, and so on.[11]

Because it takes for granted performance as veritably constituting and reconstituting the reality thus performed, ritual is nothing but a dramatistically concentrated mode of the ordinary process of self-constituting. Put another way, ritual distills and sublimates the description of being as time, that is, as becoming—a sacrificial dynamic in which the self becomes other to itself, and thus, by dint of the other, abnegates in order to make itself anew.

Having thus addressed the question of ritual efficacy, I turn to the other question I posed above, that of the ephemeral character of ritual's transforming effect. Obviously, insofar as this effect is temporal, it must be transitory. It is so for the same reason that it is efficacious: as peculiarly a matter of practice (a practice of practice), it must perforce reaffirm for the long term the difference (between the ideal and the real) it sublates for the time being. Put another way, it cannot finally undo this difference, for it is this very hierarchical difference—wherein the Selfhood implicit in the said and the set is encompassed by the uncertainty or otherness unspoken in the saying and doing—that enables ritual's creative effectuation. As the chiastic dynamic on which it turns implies (a dynamic of crossing as between the real and the ideal), although the transformation wrought by ritual is vitally more than an illusion, it is done with mirrors. But instead of feeling obliged by our rationalistic prejudices to demonstrate that therefore the transformation is but smoke, we need to come to terms with the obvious: that, to the contrary, ritual efficacy is the very proof of body-mind nondualism. Of course, insofar as it is instrumental, the ritual is subject to failure—the rite may not succeed, for example, in healing the sick or setting right a wrong. But because ritual is primarily its own end (in the sense that it is means without end or, in a word, practice), it is instrumental only relatively and in lesser part. For this reason, instrumental failure only goes to show the ultimate primacy of the other, the uncertainty that critically distinguishes all practice. With this acknowledgment of the determining role of the other, such instrumental failure, in effect, also bespeaks the truth of nondualism.

The anthropological difficulty in seeing the efficacy of ritual stems from the dualism that, for certain purposes of inquiry, necessarily defines the discipline. In a 'magical' move that denies the reality of magic, thus making disappear the phenomenon of the ethnographic observer's embodied participation in the observed, dualism too, ironically, demonstrates mind-body nondualism. To see the ontic continuity between observer and observed, it is necessary for the former to look at herself looking at the latter, where 'looking', however, is a view from somewhere rather than nowhere, but a somewhere that entails (as in, for instance, the notion of the 'evil eye') the beholder's substantive integrity with what is being seen. Failing to entertain that the problematic of ritual efficacy is a matter of ontology, anthropology has been constitutionally poorly positioned to see that this efficacy becomes comprehensible wherever reality is grasped in terms of basic ambiguity. Given dualism, a reality without firm definition can qualify only as an outlandish idea. But it is nonetheless real.

Chapter 10

CONTRADICTION IN AZANDE ORACULAR PRACTICE AND IN PSYCHOTHERAPEUTIC INTERACTION

This scientific and philosophical revolution ... can be described roughly as bringing forth the destruction of the Cosmos, that is, the disappearance, from philosophically and scientifically valid concepts, of the conception of the world as a finite, closed, and hierarchically ordered whole (a whole in which the hierarchy of value determined the hierarchy and structure of being ...), and its replacement by an indefinite and even infinite universe which is bound together by the identity of its fundamental components and laws, and in which all these components are placed on the same level of being. This, in turn, implies the discarding by scientific thought of all considerations based upon value-concepts, such as perfection, harmony, meaning and aim, and finally the utter devalorization of being, the divorce of the world of value and the world of facts.

— Alexandre Koyre, *From the Closed World to the Infinite Universe*

In this chapter, taking up the case of yet another East African people, the Azande, I continue the demonstration of my thesis about the integral connection between the conditions of authentic choice and what is, in logic, contradiction. Whereas in the preceding chapter I focused largely on choice in itself, here I stress the question of choice in relation to moral accounting. As I did with the Dinka, I examine the Azande comparatively, setting their oracular procedures off against a modern, Western pseudo-psychotherapeutic interaction. My concern remains to relativize the law of non-contradiction by referring it to a notion of practice defined axially in terms of self-other relations, when these are conceived of as above all ethical in nature. Although the Azande oracle is in principle mystical (and therefore on all fours with a worldview in which patently mythical forces such as witchcraft and sorcery are thought to occur naturally), and psychotherapy rational, both forms of inquiry display a definite indifference to contradiction. The reason for this indifference rests, I contend, with the consideration that both focus on practical rather than theoretical questions.

Nevertheless, in the pseudo-psychotherapeutic interaction (and, I would argue, in psychotherapeutic interaction proper), the presumption of theory qua theory is a difference that makes a difference. That presumption, a representative diagnostic of much modern practice, comports a principle of epistemological certainty, removing the ground from moral accounting while privileging naturalistic explanation. In this light, I will propose an anthropological gestalt switch according to which it is the selfcraft of much psychotherapy rather than the witchcraft of the Azande that must count as 'closed'. A substantial difference between witchcraft, a cultural corollary of the Azande oracle, and selfcraft, a diacritical practice of modernity, rests with the fundamental openness of the former, an openness whereof discretion is taken for granted as a modality of, by contradistinction to convention, what there is. For this reason, strange as this may seem, the Zande practice of witchcraft holds out the possibility of moral choice in a fundamental way that selfcraft tends to obscure. Although their witchcraft bears, thematically, relations of hostility and fails to acknowledge choice in the sense associated with modernity and radical individualism, there is something fundamental to learn from the Azande about moral accounting.

The Anthropological Rationality Debate

In these times, when the only worthy intellectual position is deemed one that has already succeeded itself (a post-whatever), the 'anthropological rationality debate' may seem old-fashioned. The debate's standard edited collection, Bryan Wilson's *Rationality* (1970) was succeeded by Hollis and Lukes's *Rationality and Relativism* (1982). But if Tambiah's (1990) Louis Henry Morgan Lectures are any indication, and a 'straight from the horse's mouth' monograph like Akiga's (1939) is not to be ignored, then the problem stands. Akiga's account of the Tiv, his own people, although not unmediated by Christian training and Western education, exhibits an otherness that seems in the end to resist reduction to figurative language. Although it is not a 'straight from the horse's mouth' monograph, Maurice Leenhardt's *Do Kamo* (1979) also documents such irreducible otherness.[1]

In his richly argued critique of the notion of mentalities, the classicist G. E. R. Lloyd (1990) has profitably questioned the wholesale use of the metaphorical-literal dichotomy to describe socio-cultural orders in which the dichotomy is epistemically unavailable. Although he argues that the emergence of this dichotomy cannot help but change perception, he does not seem to hold with the possibility of a reality in which the categories of metaphor and letter are not simply unavailable but in a sense ontologically mistaken. On the contrary, for all his acute attention to the historical character of Western categories, and to the condition of different contexts and styles of thought, Lloyd (ibid.: 5) seems still to presume standard Western ontology—as when he declares: "Collectivities do not think, only individuals do."[2]

Sperber (1985) too rejects the 'symbolist' approach that reduces to figurative language the apparently irrational statements often reported in ethnographies. Taking a well-considered rationalist perspective keyed to cognitive psychology, he argues that all peoples necessarily entertain some representations as representations rather than as facts per se and that correspond to ideas understood only incompletely. On Sperber's approach, then, if I understand him correctly, when the ethnographer is earnestly told by his informants to go, say, dragon hunting, he should take 'dragon' neither as a statement of fact nor as a figure of speech, but rather as a perfectly ordinary representation that happens to be vague and one or more times removed from the cognitive plane of brute factuality. However, since even when it is entertained as indistinct and only factually involved (rather than factual per se) the idea of a dragon continues to challenge the received suppositions of Western reality, the problem remains. The difference between Sperber's position and what I set forth here is radical, and may be summed up by comparing his notion of "semi-proposition" (ibid.: 49ff.) with my notion of "half-logic" (Evens 1983). Both posit fuzzy boundaries, but whereas "semi-proposition" is epistemological, distinguishing cognitions that are vague and unspecific, "half-logic" is para-ontological, conflating the cognitive with the bodily, the ideal with the real.

It is my impression that there exists today a forceful, if limited, disciplinary tendency to conduct one's ethnographic and anthropological researches as if there is no problem of rationality. I suggest that especially for reasons of the prevailing influence exercised by the approach from figurative language, making a tropological anthropology, and by the intellectual deconstruction of Western reason, it is sometimes thought or even taken for granted that the problem of rationality was simply a figment of the anthropologist's romantic or colonial imagination. Somewhat ironically, in view of his rationalism—and although one can hardly speak of him as post-structuralist—Lévi-Strauss's (1963a) powerful deconstruction of totemism heralded the tropological dissolution of the problem of rationality. For that matter, so did Evans-Pritchard's *Nuer Religion*, in which the analysis from figurative and poetic language displays a subtlety and depth perhaps unparalleled by anything since, including Geertz's hermeneutics (notwithstanding the direction of his critique of Evans-Pritchard; see this chap., note 3).

Maurice Bloch's *Prey into Hunter* (1992) provides a skillful example of a recent work in which it appears simply to be taken for granted that there is no problem of rationality. His symbolic interpretations of rituals, myth, etc., strike me as always rich and often brilliant. But the problem of rationality presented by the ethnographical observations Bloch analyzes, the problem of what sense it makes in the first place to entertain what appear to us as patently nonsensical representations, goes largely unaddressed by him—as if to say that once we have described the particular cultural symbology of representations that equate birds with spirits, or men and women with cattle, we have exhausted the anthropological problem presented therein. Bloch's book, no more than many other recent works, seems to accept that the problem of rationality has been completely done away with by symbolic anthropology and the culturological thesis of troping the light fantastic.

Obeyesekere's *The Apotheosis of Captain Cook* (1992), on the other hand, espying a residual Frazerian aspect to structuralism, still finds it necessary to demonstrate that there is no problem of rationality. Mounting a virtual diatribe against Sahlins's (1985) thesis regarding the deicidal/regicidal killing of Captain Cook in the South Seas (and in the process giving a fresh, multi-faceted professional substance to this sort of ritual killing), Obeyesekere argues that the very idea that the Hawaiians could have mistaken a human being for a god is a product of a Western, colonialist mythological conceit. His critique is keyed to a Weberian (and, I venture, Malinowskian) notion of 'practical reason' as a kind of universal biological and cognitive capacity. But his argument from the concept of pragmatic reason, despite his explicit avoidance of utilitarian reductionism, seems to make it impossible for any people, anywhere or anytime, to entertain notions in which 'the real' and 'the ideal' somehow include each other. Ironically, then, it would seem that while seeking to destroy European colonialist myth-making, he manages also to promote, uncritically, one of the key principles from which this myth-making has drawn epistemological sustenance—rationality in the sense of *logos*. As Sahlins, in his book-length refutation (1995: 8–9), puts it, Obeyesekere manages to endow the South Seas natives in question with the "highest" Western "bourgeois" values. In this regard, as I see it, although Obeyesekere stresses practical rather than intellectual reason, he remains close to Lévi-Strauss. His concept of practical reason, no less than Lévi-Strauss's of intellectual structure, deploys—if in a more particularistic and context-sensitive way—a thesis of figurative usage in order to save 'native peoples' from the charge of pre-logical mentality.

The critical intellectual pounding taken by the idea of rationality, and by the consequential authority that this idea has fostered, has been profoundly remedial. But the crucial consideration that a line demarcating reason from magic, or science from metaphysics, cannot be fixed in absolute terms, hardly means that no line may be drawn at all. Were we to think this, the spirit of absolutism (or, to use the cant postmodernist term, totalism) intrinsic to the received idea of rationality will not have collapsed but rather prevailed. Lines of demarcation come in many kinds, including the kind I draw here: the basic but fuzzy kind, the kind that both separates and connects. As I see it, the failure of much recent anthropology to acknowledge fundamental, authentic otherness signals, for obvious reasons, what Wittgenstein would have called a loss of problem.

The Problem

When I was a graduate student, my doctoral supervisor, Max Gluckman, telephoned me to put off an appointment, saying that his dentures had broken. Always the anthropologist, he responded to my expression of sympathy by asking, rhetorically, why the misfortune had befallen him just when it did, and then, following this question with another, why he would choose to answer by invoking chance rather than witchcraft. Somewhat late on the uptake, here I explore these questions in connection with the problem of contradiction and choice.

Like most if not all of his colleagues, Gluckman had been profoundly influenced by Evans-Pritchard's (1937) study of witchcraft and oracles among the Azande (singular, Zande). Although that study is well-trodden ground for anthropologists and philosophers alike (e.g., see Wilson 1970), it still provides a rich ethnographic and analytic resource in relation to the problems Gluckman posed.[3] Indeed, it is a good bet that when Gluckman's dentures broke that morning, the contingency of the event brought Evans-Pritchard's monograph to his mind, leading him to reflect aloud on the questions at point.

Evans-Pritchard employed the first of Gluckman's questions—Why me, why now?— to suggest that an account of contingent misfortune in terms of witchcraft or the like is really far from silly. After all, so far science has had very little to offer in the way of a direct answer to the question of contingency. As to Gluckman's second question, that is, why some people account for such contingent misfortune by reference to an enchanted world rather than 'the' natural universe, Evans-Pritchard could answer only by pointing to the 'mystical' premises of Azande thought. His answer is unsatisfactory, not because it is mistaken, but because he was inclined to think of mystical notions, by contrast to scientific ones, as mistaken. Mystical notions, he wrote, are "patterns of thought that attribute to phenomena supra-sensible qualities ... *which they do not possess*" (1937: 12; emphasis added).

I want to project a different, more positive picture of what Evans-Pritchard called mystical notions by pointing to the ontological and epistemological conditions for offering and maintaining such notions. In so doing, I hope to throw light in the direction of Gluckman's questions. More particularly, I want to address the question of moral accounting in relation to contingent suffering. I take it that by juxtaposing the explanatory concepts of chance and witchcraft, what Gluckman basically wanted to know is why he was culturally disposed to understand his misfortune in terms of natural causation rather than moral agency (cf. Gluckman 1965: 218). Whereas 'chance' (as Gluckman used it that morning) connotes an indifferent probability, 'witchcraft' conjures up agential doings on the part of someone or other.

My argument throughout turns on a notion of practice. I make the argument by comparing and contrasting the Zande oracular procedures to certain pseudo-psychotherapeutic ones from a modern setting. The instance of pseudo-psychotherapy is taken from Peter McHugh's (1968) rigorous ethnomethodological study of the organization of meaning in social interaction, based on a 'laboratory experiment' in which college student volunteers were told deceptively that they were undergoing a new, simplified form of psychotherapy.[4]

Although I am primarily interested here in the question of moral accounting, I start my discussion in terms of the anthropological problem of rationality, the problem to which Evans-Pritchard's great monograph on the Azande most directly addresses itself. Of course, an abundance of excellent ethnographic work has appeared since the publication of Evans-Pritchard's study in 1937, but barring mindless presentism, it still makes good sense to employ that study in an attempt to think again through a fundamental problem. When it comes to rethinking ontological and epistemological aspects of the problem in mind, the restudy of this classic work offers the student the strategic advantage of case material that, for reasons of its intimate association with the disciplinary emergence of the problem, lends itself uniquely to the possibility of an interpretive gestalt switch. The switch of interpretation that I intend here proposes two discernments: first, that a practice like Zande witchcraft is, in a limited but profound sense, open rather than closed, and, second, that therefore, in studying a people like the Azande, we can learn not only about them but also from them. What we learn is, I think, that moral accounting is predicated most fundamentally on a perception of discretion as a primordial feature of the world, and not in the first place as a reasoned product of Kantian individuals.[5]

Although in its crucial turn to a notion of practice my argument is in keeping with a good deal of current anthropology, in its openly ontological intentions and unembarrassed projection of 'otherness' per se the argument departs sharply from regnant disciplinary emphases of tropology and broadside relativism. In order to deal with the apparent difference between peoples whom anthropology has traditionally studied and the people of anthropology, the present argument takes another direction. Under the liberal anthropological watchword 'different tropes for different folks', relativism and tropology move decidedly to avoid the presumptive attribution of inferiority to the other. For all that, however, inasmuch as the very idea of figurative language is, like that of rationality proper, peculiarly Western, by reducing cultural difference to a question of such language, relativism and tropology manage to collapse the other into the Occidental self. In so doing, ironically and despite appearances, they drive even deeper that self's arrogation of epistemic rank.[6]

By contrast, under the philosophical influence of Emmanuel Levinas (1969, 1991), I embrace here the difference between self and other as no less irreducible than relative, such that it can be meaningfully engaged but not finally resolved. Moreover, far from presupposing the superiority of the Occidental self, my approach attributes to the other, on the basis of ethics rather than exotics, a certain axiological primacy. It thus flatly refuses the association of otherness with inferiority, the stupid but impelling association of the present time. And by privileging the other in a fundamental way, it does so without collapsing the difference of the other into a relativistic symmetry, the fearfulness of which rests with its necessary description of all value judgment as essentially arbitrary, a matter of power rather than principle.

Put more simply, I argue here that there is something profoundly compelling, if not true, about the world as the Azande find it, that is, an oracular world inhabited by witches. This truth (bearing on the existential nature of discretion) is worth knowing, but because it really is other or unfathomable in our own received Occidental terms, it cannot be assimilated by us save at a certain ontological cost—the cost of the world as we know it, which is to say, not the enrichment, as one may be used to hearing, but rather the veritable transformation of our-selves.

Witchcraft, Poison Oracles, and Rationality

The ethnography of Azande oracles is well known. The Azande make all important determinations and decisions by consulting their oracle, which operates through the administration of a strychnine-like substance to fowls. Thus, having suffered a misfortune and so regarding himself as bewitched, a Zande will consult the oracle in order to discover the identity of the culprit. Keeping to questions that can be answered only by yes or no, effecting thus a crude digital machine, he feeds the oracular substance to a chicken, instructing the substance to kill the chicken if he has identified the witch correctly and to save it if he has not (or vice versa).

From the perspective of empirical science, the question that arises about such a system of inquiry is how it can last, for it seems riddled with contradictions. In response, Evans-Pritchard took two main lines of argument. First, he observed: "Contradictions between their beliefs are not noticed by Azande because the beliefs are not all present at the same time but function in different situations" (1937: 475). This observation is a corollary of his argument that the Zande "actualizes [his] beliefs rather than intellectualizes them ... [T]heir ideas are imprisoned in action and cannot be cited to explain and justify action" (ibid.: 82–83). In other words, Evans-Pritchard argued that, in a specifiable sense, a contradiction among the Azande might not be a contradiction because their beliefs are not primarily matters of theory but of practice. Obviously, this argument anticipates Bourdieu by more than three decades. Second, Evans-Pritchard pointed out that once its initial premises are granted, the oracular practice of the Azande proceeds in tolerably rational fashion, even though it is finally organized to reinforce itself.

Here is an example of how contradictories may be separated situationally, keeping the contradiction from being seen as such. The Azande do understand that the substance they employ for oracular purposes is what we would call a natural poison. As a result, they also know that if it is administered in sufficiently large doses, it necessarily kills. Yet this knowledge has no bearing on their conviction that when the substance is given to a fowl in the oracular situation, the fowl's fate is owing to oracular rather than natural causes. As Evans-Pritchard put it, the two sorts of knowledge "are functions of different situations and are uncoordinated" (1937: 319). Plainly, as it is hard for modern thought to see why the naturalistic knowledge is irrelevant to the oracular situation, Evans-Pritchard's argument depends here on the very idea of situation. Suffice it to say that if his argument is to work, 'situation' must be defined overridingly by reference to immediate practical aims and consequences, making theoretical knowledge as such—that is, knowledge that transcends particular situations—definitively irrelevant and phenomenologically indistinct.

What about contradictions that occur within the oracular situation itself, the kind we might expect in the course of, say, a scientific experiment? For example, what do the Azande do when the oracle contradicts itself irrecusably? Here they respond in a manner that tends to secure their system of thought from the threat of such contradictions but that is nonetheless significantly rational in the received sense of the term. After receiving the oracle's answer on important issues, the Zande will repeat the question, this time, however, reversing the order of the answers in relation to the chicken's reactions. That is to say, if in the first run, yes was linked to the outcome of death, in the second, no will be so linked. In other words, the Azande check the reliability and consistency of the oracle by, as we would put it, repeating the experiment. Or the Zande might test the oracle's power of discrimination by seeing if it gives different answers to different questions.

When the Azande are confronted with an oracle that contradicts itself or with one that is non-discriminating (one that gives the same response no matter what the question), evidently they feel compelled to account for the oracle's failure. Thus, they behave much as would be expected under the rule of logic as such, exhibiting an awareness that if the oracle's failure goes utterly unaccountable, then conviction in the oracular system cannot stand firm. To account for the failure, the Azande appeal to initial conditions of the case at hand. For example, they might suggest that a taboo had been violated or that the oracular substance had been extracted from the wrong sort of creeper. It is crucial to see, though, that they do not select in explanation just any initial conditions; they select ones that, given reality as the Azande find it, logically entail the consequence in question. Once it is admitted that there are two kinds of creeper, one of which produces an overpotent oracular substance, it becomes logically appropriate to argue that in the case of a poison that kills fowls indiscriminately, the wrong kind of creeper is to blame.

The Azande restrict their explanatory selection of initial conditions in yet another, perfectly logical way. They tend to look to conditions that admit of independent testing. Plainly, were they to test their conjecture about an excessively strong oracular substance by citing the fact that it kills the fowls indiscriminately, their argument would be stupidly circular. Instead, they are likely to shelve the substance for several months, waiting for it to "cool" (Evans-Pritchard 1937: 331). Should it still prove defective after this 'test', Azande will be inclined to abandon the explanation of 'excessive potency' as wrong and seek another.

Furthermore, in their accounting procedures, the Azande not only appeal to initial conditions but also implicate what, given their reality, we would regard as universal laws or regularities. The explanations that the Azande offer for oracular failure would be perfectly illogical if this people did not take for granted certain lawful relations, such as the operation of the poison oracle through the medium of fowls and the connection between the observance of taboos and the success of the oracle. Obviously, if for the Azande the world were such that fowls thrive on the oracular substance or that the violation of taboos has no impact on the effective operation of that substance, then their explanations could have no logical force.

I have just described five features of the operation of the Zande oracle that are correct by reference to the strict sense of rationality: (1) Azande test their oracle for reliability; (2) they do not ignore contradictions resulting from these tests but rather seek to account for them; (3) in explaining them, they appeal to specific initial conditions that can deductively generate the explicandum; (4) these initial conditions do admit of independent testing; and (5) in arriving at their explanations, Azande appeal not only to initial conditions but also to universal laws or regularities. These five ways of approaching a practice constitute ingredients of scientific thinking. Yet Evans-Pritchard found the Azande explanations of the oracle's failure wanting, calling them, in a felicitous but pejorative phrase, "secondary elaborations of belief." As he saw it, the explanations serve not to explain the contradictions but rather to explain them away, thus exposing the oracle, to the outside observer, as dogma. Indeed, so effective did Evans-Pritchard (1937: 319) find the defense mechanisms of the Zande structure of belief, that he opined: "Let the reader consider any argument that would utterly demolish all Zande claims for the power of the oracle. If it were translated into Zande modes of thought it would serve to support their entire structure of belief." How, then, do the Azande manage such epistemological closure?

There are at least two critical ways in which Azande reasoning falls short here of logical rigor. First, for all of the apparent testing of the oracle's reliability, the questions asked of the oracle are, generally speaking, too imprecise to determine whether or not the answers are successful. Thus, instead of asking, will I kill a bushbuck if I go hunting tomorrow? the Zande is likely to ask whether or not he will have a good hunting season if he hunts in one part of the bush rather than another. Obviously, whereas the precise content of the former question would allow the answer to be easily tested against the empirical outcome, the content of the latter—with its vague notions of 'a good hunting season' and 'parts of the bush'—makes the nature of the connection between the answer and the empirical outcome far less determinate. Moreover, the vague character of the binary answers also leaves a great deal of space for ad hoc interpretation. Thus, in the case of a man who was informed by the oracle that he would die if he made a certain journey but who proceeded to make the journey without mishap, only to make it again and then die, it was said that the oracle had not been wrong but had looked ahead (Evans-Pritchard 1937: 348). Clearly, given the broad content of the questions asked of the oracle and the vague character of the answers, there is always enough interpretive room to save the oracle from refutation. As Evans-Pritchard put it, "The answers either cannot be tested, or if proven by subsequent events to be erroneous permit an explanation of the error" (ibid.: 340).

The second critical way in which Zande accounting procedures fail to meet the demands of logical inquiry bears directly on the issue of testability. As a crucial measure of scientific rationality, the explicans should be testable independently of what it is introduced to explain. I have already indicated that in explaining their oracle's failures, Azande do cite conditions that yield to independent testing. But such testability is a matter of degree, and in the final analysis it is especially in connection with this parameter that Zande accounting procedures come up short when they are evaluated by reference to rationality as such.

Take the case of an oracular substance that kills fowls indiscriminately. As stated above, Azande are likely to attribute this unsatisfactory result to an excessively potent oracular substance, one extracted from the wrong sort of creeper, and to store the substance, allowing time for it to 'cool'. Evans-Pritchard records that if, after it has been allowed to 'cool', the substance still fails to perform satisfactorily, Azande "either throw it away or seek to discover whether witchcraft or some other cause is now responsible for its failure to give correct judgements" (1937: 331). On the one hand, should they throw it away, we may safely infer that whether their explanation of the substance's faultiness is right or wrong is not for the Azande a question worth pursuing. So much for their spirit of scientific inquiry. On the other hand, should they seek to determine whether witchcraft or something else is the cause of the problem, they fare no better on the canons of explanation proper. Evans-Pritchard does not identify the causes other than witchcraft that the Azande might adduce to account for the oracle's poor showing. But it is fair to assume that whatever these causes might be, should they too fail to convince, the Azande would then turn to witchcraft as the cause. That is to say, eventually the Azande will arrive at witchcraft to explain the fault. And we already know what the test for witchcraft is—the poison oracle. In the end, thus, the Zande accounting procedures describe a circle.

Here, then, we see why Evans-Pritchard found the Zande's system of thought to be notably closed. Construed as a system of rational inquiry, the Zande poison oracle involves too much imprecision of language and too little possibility of testing explanations independently of the effects that need explaining. The imprecision of the explanatory predicates invites ad hoc hypotheses or 'explaining away', and the sharp curtailment of continuing explanatory referral to logically higher-level statements—that is, the tautological closure of the system—makes deep refutation unthinkable (cf. Popper 1968: chap. 6). In a word, considered as a system of thought, the Zande oracle cannot be falsified.

Exhibiting an umbilical attachment to anthropological views he did so much to refute, views that picture primitive peoples as mentally incompetent, Evans-Pritchard was inclined to attribute the unfalsifiable nature of this system to the fact that the system is epistemologically founded in mysticism. "Azande see as well as we," he wrote, "that the failure of their oracle to prophesy truly calls for explanation, but so entangled are they in mystical notions that they must make use of them to account for the failure" (1937: 339).

Today, however, we know that unfalsifiability is hardly confined to mystical systems of thought. In the wake of the work of such scholars as Burtt, Hanson, Popper, Kuhn, Lakatos, Feyerabend, and others, it is plain that science itself is given, perhaps fundamentally, to securing itself against refutation. As a technical concept, 'falsifiability' is due to Karl Popper, whose powerful (if also well-criticized) model of scientific rationality I have been employing all along here as a standard against which to measure the strengths and weaknesses of the Zande oracular system construed in terms of rational inquiry.[7] Popper (1965) forged his model as a descriptive and normative critique of the received theory of modern science as an inductive endeavor. He finds that the inductivist's affinity to highly probable hypotheses is counter-intuitive to good science (ibid.: 287). Since that affinity advantages hypotheses that stay close to the known facts, it promotes ad hoc or stop-gap thinking and disadvantages hypotheses that can be tested independently of the facts to be explained. Popper speaks here of "reinforced dogma," by which he means theoretical representations that are so constructed as to be more or less immune to critical attack (ibid.: 327, 334). When one considers that their respective subject matters were once taken to define a line of demarcation between magic and science, the degree to which Evans-Pritchard's analysis of Azande oracles and Popper's critique of the received theory of modern science share a common critical understanding is quite remarkable. In point of fact, I take it that Popper's concept of "reinforced dogma" and Evans-Pritchard's notion of "secondary elaboration of belief" are impressively synonymous.

Selfcraft and Foul Therapy

However, it better suits my purpose here to leave off the example of modern science and cite instead a different sort of parallel discourse to Zande oracular practice, but one no less peculiarly modern. In a work in which he investigates the problem of how meaning is constructed in social situations—the so-called problem of the 'definition of the situation'—the sociologist Peter McHugh (1968) describes an experiment he conducted on college students. Having been told that a new form of psychotherapy, the novelty of which rests with its simplicity, was being tested, the students were instructed as follows: first, to relate to the therapist a personal problem; second, to ask the therapist questions about the problem that can be answered by only yes or no, and then to comment on what they take to be the meaning of the answers; and, third, to summarize what they believe they have learned from the therapeutic exchange. Unbeknown to the student, the 'therapist', delivering his 'answer' from another room over an intercom, determined his response by reference to a list of random numbers. In other words, his answers had been predetermined and would have been the same regardless of the question. The following is an abridged version of one of the resulting pseudo-psychotherapeutic interactions, although one in which the therapist's answers, instead of being determined simply randomly, were structured to test the strength of the student's faith in the given definition of the situation (ibid.: 93–98).

[Student's account of his problem] I've been attending the University of Miami, until I came up here this year. Last year I met a girl down there and fell in love with her. I want to marry her. However, my brother's met her and he thinks she's too bossy and it'd be a mistake if I married her. My father seems to like her, but my mother hasn't met her yet. I know she's right for me, but how can I convince my brother she is? My mother will make her decision when she meets her, but in the meantime my brother might say something that will influence her before then. My father doesn't talk to my mother, so he won't be any help. I really know she's right for me regardless of what anyone says, but I'll need the go-ahead of my family if everything's to go right.

[Question] My brother met the girl I love several months ago, but he doesn't think I should marry her. Should I try to show him she's changed, and will be all right to marry now?

[Answer] No.

[Comment] You mean I shouldn't try to convince him she's changed, once somebody makes up their mind about something like this there's no changing them. Especially my brother. It's no use even trying. People just hold on to what they believe no matter what, so I'm better off going ahead with another plan. But I still want to change my brother's mind. While it isn't easy to do this by just talking about it, maybe if he sees her he'll realize she's changed and isn't so bossy any more. I hope so.

[Question] Could I go about this, instead of telling him, by letting him see her and see that she's changed for himself?

[Answer] No.

[Comment] You mean that she will be the same to him even if he sees for himself. No matter whether I tell him or he sees it for himself he won't want me to marry her, she'll be just as bossy as ever regardless of how she acts in front of him. Too bad I have a brother like that ... The question is, will he change ever, or is there nothing I can do?

[Question] Will he ever change his feelings about her?

[Answer] No.

[Comment] Hmm. Really? This isn't easy to take, even though I can see what you mean. You told me that it doesn't matter whether he is told, or even if he sees her, he'll stick to his guns and always be against it. This means I can't go on worrying about what he thinks or changing his mind, but concentrate on seeing that he doesn't interfere. Of course, maybe he won't ever change, won't ever like her and [will] always think she's bossy, but still he might realize it doesn't matter to me and I'm going to marry her whatever he says or thinks ...

[Question] Even if he never likes her, will he decide it's no use doing all this objecting and drop it?

[Answer] No.

[Comment] He won't drop his objections ... [M]y father seemed to like her, he doesn't have the same opinion my brother does. And my mother hasn't met her yet, maybe she wouldn't mind either ...

[Question] Even though my brother disagrees, would the rest of the family go along with the marriage?

[Answer] No.

[Comment] They won't consent to the marriage. Well, there's nothing left but to break off with the family. That'll be hard on everyone, but after all, I love her and that's the most important thing. You don't go through life with your brother, or your mother and father either ... Maybe if I get a job paying good money and could support her, they'd come around later.

[Question] If I got a good job with a good steady income, will they agree I made the right choice?

[Answer] No.

[Comment] Christ, you keep saying no all the time ... Maybe I can't influence you either. I mean you keep saying everything I don't want to hear. I mean can this be psychotherapy?...

[Question] Do you want me to influence you in this conversation?

[Answer] No.

[Comment] [15-second silence] Well, maybe it's not put right. I can't make him understand, know about my family that makes them different. These answers, though, I don't know, psychologists must be pretty good to do this. There aren't many who could.

[Question] You must be pretty good, aren't you as good as most psychologists?

[Answer] No.

[Comment] No. No. Wow, he doesn't think he's as good as most psychologists. Wow. So what kind of advice is he giving? Bad advice. This can't be psychotherapy, I mean what kind of help is that? Do you think you're any good, and he answers no. In fact, it's been no to everything I've said. Hasn't it?... Maybe it's no regardless.

[Question] Do you say no regardless?

[Answer] No.

[Comment] Well, that's good. I mean, what would that mean, saying no regardless?... What is the purpose of this? Supposedly a simple method of giving advice. But maybe it's supposed to be so simple even an incompetent psychologist can use it ... You can learn something about yourself just by talking about it. Maybe that is their reason here, to teach the person about himself ...

[Question] Do you think I should marry the girl?

[Answer] No.

[Comment] That must be it. They are trying to find a way of advising that teaches you more about yourself ... Even if I get bad advice, I will be better off because I will know myself better after I'm finished ... Like I know now for sure I'll marry the girl regardless of what my family says ... Before I came in here, though, I didn't know that ... So there's something to [this kind of therapy] ...

[Student's summary of the exchange] For a while I was worried that this was a bad situation. I didn't know how to take your advice when you said you weren't a very good psychiatrist, but then I realized it could still teach you something about yourself ... I was especially helped when I realized that I should go right ahead with my plans ... Very interesting. Even a poor psychiatrist can be helpful if you just talk about yourself.

It would be hard to find from a modern setting a more stunning, and for that matter entertaining, parallel to the Zande oracle.[8] Like the Zande interrogating his chicken, the student put his questions to the alleged therapist in the hope of determining an auspicious course of action and/or remedying an unhappy situation. From the perspective of rational inquiry, the no's uttered by the 'therapist' were tied to the student's questions in the identical (heterogeneous) fashion that the binary responses of the poison oracle are to the Zande's queries. Although the student had ample logical opportunity to refute decisively the definition of his situation, in fact he clung to that definition, always managing to turn contradiction into confirmation: he was told outright by the 'therapist' that the therapy was not much good; the 'therapist's' declaration that the answers were not in fact responsive to the questions was enough to give the student pause but not to move him to abandon the definition of the situation; the fact that all the responses were the same regardless of the question would have put off, as we know, even an Azande; the illuminated paradox of the 'therapist's' reply of no to the question "Do you say no regardless?" did not even break the student's epistemic stride. In the end, the student was able to reinforce the therapeutic definition of the situation by telling himself—an ad hoc gambit or secondary elaboration of belief if ever there was one—that he had learned his own mind and that the foul therapy to which he had been subjected was meant to facilitate just such an onanistic enlightenment.

Here, then, is a mode of inquiry intimately associated with a pre-eminently modern practice—let us call it 'selfcraft'—that seems no less unfalsifiable than Zande oracular thought. Yet in principle, the pseudo-psychotherapeutic proceedings, although they had a hidden purpose, were no more founded in mystical notions proper than is bona fide psychotherapy founded in such notions. The considered principles at the core of psychotherapeutic interaction are meant to attribute to phenomena nothing that cannot be derived from empirical observation or logically inferred from it.

Practice and Rationality

If the profound resistance to falsification exhibited by such systems of inquiry is not attributable to mystical notions as such, how can we account for it? We can do so, I think, by expanding on Evans-Pritchard's situationalist reply to the riddle of when a contradiction is *not* a contradiction.

Obviously, a system secure from inductive refutation is one in which the particular case in itself can never be adequate to discredit the general case—the case of how things stand in general. Such a logically scandalous condition describes an epistemological state in which, regardless of the particular case, the general case remains always thoroughly presumptive. Since in this state of reflection it is taken for granted that the particular case must serve as an instance of the general case, the former can never be understood to run truly contrary to the latter—apparent contrariness will be explained away or disregarded. Put another way, where the general case is utterly taken for granted, where it constitutes the pre-reflective ground of all reflection, the particular case cannot achieve a degree of differentiation from the general case sufficient to make conceivable employing it to test the validity of its ground. In the event, even apparent contradictions can serve only to confirm the general case.[9]

Such blind presumption of the general case obtains under, and only under, conditions where the primary purpose is not truth but 'livability'. In a word, it obtains where the situation is directly defined by practice rather than theory. Where this condition prevails, what counts in the first place is not whether one's representation of things is a good likeness, but whether one's actions work.

But what does it mean to say in the present connection that something works? As Hume showed (making a nonsense of commonsense empiricism in the process, arch-empiricist though he was), a practical effect is never really closed (see Popper 1972: 4). A practical effect cannot provide a properly rational basis for concluding that what has just happened will continue to happen. From the fact that every time a coin has slipped from one's fingers it has always fallen to the ground, one cannot conclude, on the basis of logical logic, that the next time it might not rise. Hence, in order to assess the significance of a practical effect, one must ever look forward to the effects yet to come. More precisely, it is simply not possible for the inductivist to take into account all of the relevant instances. Accordingly, as Bourdieu (1990: 81, 82) says, "practice is inseparable from temporality" such that it identifies itself "with the imminent future of the world, postulating the continuity of time." Put differently, practice presumes the general case considered not as the aggregate whole but as the essentially uncertain or ambiguous whole. The presumption of continuity or generality is not due to a psychological mechanism of association, as Hume thought (see Popper 1972: 6), but presents the very nature of human practice. In light of this understanding, to say that something works is to say simply that it is livable in the general case, in other words, that it allows one to get on with the business of human existence. I take it that this is the import of Evans-Pritchard's finding when, during his fieldwork among the Azande, he decided to regulate his affairs in accordance with the oracle's decisions and was led to remark (1937: 270): "I found it as satisfactory a way of running my home and affairs as any other I know of."

Just as the Zande consulting his oracle is preoccupied with practical rather than theoretical problems, so the student consulting his 'therapist' was concerned to make a decision not simply representing but actually effecting who he is and where he stands in the world. Since a decision of this kind is essentially uncertain and creative, the process of its determination cannot yield to the precise terms of formal logic and the conclusive tests of scientific rationality. Although that process does not wholly lack a theoretical coefficient, the 'theory' attaching to it is consistently enveloped in practice.

It is only when practical problems are differentiated as such, liberating theory to represent itself as above and beyond practice, that it becomes possible to construct a rational system as such. With this onto-epistemological revolution, thought is positioned to stipulate beforehand what will count as evidence for refutation and, more importantly, that something should so count. Once accounting procedures can present themselves as non-participant in what they aim to illuminate, they appear free of the contingencies of practice. In the event, they can project the world as timeless and complete, and therefore as open to a rule of precision and certain truth, of limpid representation and independent testability. At bottom, then, what serves to demarcate the Zande oracle from scientific inquiry is nothing so substantial as the imprecision and circularity of the former, qualities not foreign to the practice of science, but rather the fact that the Azande are not given to the conception of such an epistemological rule. That it is possible to decide beforehand, in theory and out of time, a rule of evidence for falsifying unequivocally the general case can scarcely be dreamt of in their universe.

Thus, the imposing degree to which the structures of thought at issue here are unfalsifiable may be explained by reference to their primarily practical nature. This account returns us to Evans-Pritchard's (1937: 82–83) precocious solution to the anthropologically pregnant riddle of when a contradiction is *not* a contradiction—to wit, when it remains "imprisoned in action." Taken as an epistemological starting point, practice, although it never lacks for an element of theory, does not admit of the clean dualistic break between theory and practice that makes contradiction conceivable and practically relevant as a canonical instrument of thought. The reflective release of theory from practice, while occasioning only a limited freedom, enables theory to represent itself as sui generis, thus projecting the world as concordant to rules of evidence that are fixed and decisive.

Moral Accounting

At this juncture, I can turn to the question of moral accounting. Perhaps it will have been noticed that although the proceedings of both the Zande oracle and of McHugh's kind of psychotherapy are indeed practically driven, it is not the case that McHugh's poor dupe lacked access to the canons of rationality proper. Given the modern content and setting of McHugh's experiment, the participating student not only *could* have appealed to the logical law of non-contradiction but, notwithstanding the practical aim of the interaction, in a certain sense *should* have.[10] Of course, it is easy to picture even the most savvy of rocket scientists falling for McHugh's obnoxious but ingenious sociological con game.

The epistemological power of practice aside, however, what I want to emphasize now is that in the modern setting, practice is informed by theory as such, that is, theory that (mis)represents itself as essentially free of practice. As a consequence, although it continues to display a mighty resistance to falsification, practice is indeed transformed. The transformation that counts here is that practice tends to lose its moral definition. Perhaps the most visible difference between the Zande oracle and McHugh's therapy is that between witchcraft and selfcraft as modes of forging practical decisions. Although, in light of the philosophy of someone like Kant, at first blush it may seem to us exactly otherwise, the move from witchcraft to selfcraft exemplifies also a decided shift away from moral toward natural accounting. It marks an ontological shift from a world that runs most essentially according to moral agency to one the dynamics of which are principally matters of mechanical determination. In the former, existence is primarily a question of creative, discretionary selection, as conduced by an existential and ultimately irresolvable ambiguity of selfhood and otherness, and is only secondarily 'natural'. In the latter, existence is primarily entitative, a function of natural determinations in which ambiguity is systematically eradicated in favor of self-identity, making moral agency distinctly epiphenomenal.[11]

As forms of practice, both witchcraft and selfcraft presume the general case or the whole. But whereas witchcraft points to the essential ambiguity or uncertainty of the whole, selfcraft, by affording the whole the firm boundaries of the individual qua individual, tends to fix or totalize it. Ambiguity stands as a critical condition of the operation of moral force, however, which is nothing if not a creative force for signification under conditions of essential uncertainty. That is to say, on the one hand, moral force creates and re-creates meaning out of ambiguity; on the other, basic ambiguity calls up, over and over again, the creative force of moral agency. In this light, given its ontological presumption of basic uncertainty, witchcraft may be construed as a mystical practice on the experience of moral force at large in an uncertain world. Although the experience of the world as primordially subject to discretion cannot of itself commit one to a world populated by witches, it certainly provides a genuine basis for the phenomenological emergence of such a world.

If, however, uncertainty is obscured or belittled, selection as a creative and therefore specifically moral enterprise makes little sense. By picturing the world in terms of the apparent concrete integrity of the individual, the conceptual confinement of selective force inside the bounds of the individual makes the world appear, accordingly, ever more thingified and certain. As a result, selection itself is projected as a positive rather than intrinsically creative dynamic. Thus, whether we have in mind mechanical computation or instrumental choice, selection is rendered as natural rather than moral.

No wonder the Enlightenment idea of the moral agent has fallen on hard times. Insofar as it is predicated on the self-contained or natural rather than existential individual, it is ultimately self-defeating. The essential ambiguity that is occluded by naturalistic individualism, the ambiguity of the individual that exists outside of and as other to itself, intimates genuine otherness—otherness that is irreducible to the unambiguous. If reduction of moral agency to the self-identical individual undermines the authenticity of otherness, then what sense can there be in making it categorically imperative that one should always treat other people as ends in themselves?[12]

The upshot is that when logic qua logic and selfcraft are added to oracular proceedings, the proceedings are transfigured into therapeutic ones, and the situation loses its moral definition in favor of naturalism of one kind or another. Much of modern psychotherapy is predicated on the idea that one can lay oneself open in order to assess and identify one's natural self, as if one possessed a self in the same way that one possesses a heart and lungs. Indeed, McHugh's student, impelled by the aberrant circumstances to carry the therapeutic situation to its solipsistic conclusion, understood himself to have arrived at his decision as if it had been predetermined as a component of his true, innermost self. There is no idea of genuine choice or creative movement in such a decision.[13]

One might be tempted to think much the same of the Zande, albeit for reasons of reduced rather than unqualified autonomy. Given oracular decision-making, the Zande does not grasp the decision as his and, therefore, strictly speaking, as choice. But he does grasp the answers of the oracle as genuinely responsive, as pronouncements of the other considered not as a therapeutic or rational interlocutor, but as a genuine moral agent. For the Zande, the oracle speaks with the authority of an other that is irreducible to the self and identity.[14] By contrast, for McHugh's student, the dialogue was reduced to a monologue, a self-certain process of selection in which there is no room for the other qua other and therefore for genuine moral agency.

My response to Gluckman's question, then, of why he was predisposed to attribute the instance of his dentures breaking to chance rather than to malign moral agency, is that the phenomenological release of theory from practice, and of the individual from its social context, such that these distinctions are defined dualistically, tends to undermine moral accounting of contingent suffering. For while these grand turns to dualism make scientific inquiry possible, in the end they tend to take the very life out of the idea of moral force.

However, as has become thematic in today's intellectual environment, naturalistic explanation is itself a form of practice and moral discourse. Even as it effectively conceals from itself its role in this regard, it takes a stand in and constructs a virtual world. Indeed, although I stand by my forgoing argument, there is even a crucial sense in which modernity and selfcraft may be seen to advance rather than undercut moral agency—an exceedingly difficult sense that I address in part 3.[15] I mention it now in order to facilitate a concluding observation about the anthropological authority whose questions began this chapter. Deep down, in spite of his anthropologizing about the difference between his and the Azande view of contingent misfortune, Gluckman knew that moral accounting still counts. When I pressed him that morning long ago, he confessed (a confession he was wont to make whenever something untoward happened to him) that he had been bewitched after all. Only he had no need of a magic oracle to identify the evildoer—the name was a matter of the anthropological record.[16]

PART III

FROM MYTHIC TO VALUE-RATIONALITY
Toward Ethical Gain

In part 2, I argued that there is something fundamentally amiss about evaluating mythic rationality in terms of the law of non-contradiction. I have also maintained that what appears in this rationality to be outright willingness to tolerate contradictions is in fact the very situation of choice. In view of the comparative aim of this discussion, am I then obliged (ironically by reason) to conclude that we ought to abandon rationality qua rationality in favor of a return to myth per se? If, by insisting on a lawful scheme of things, rationality proper essentially subverts the process of moral selection, while myth, by taking value for granted in the order of things, facilitates that process, then surely it is time to reject formal logic and scientific thought. Should we not adopt instead a more primitive mentality, for all its ghosts and goblins? Depending on what exactly one intends by 'primitive', there is something of value in this admonishment. But a romantic and absolute call to mythic reason is scarcely the lesson of my exercise. Rather, I wish to urge that both rational and mythic reason have advantages as well as disadvantages, and, more critically, relativizing relativism, that the human promise of modern reason, a promise that is registered in the metalogical emphasis on choice in Genesis, remains still to be kept.

The Chapters

The thesis that atheoretical thought is in a certain paradigmatic way ethically privileged over modern rationality raises the specter of primitivism. In part 3, I clarify that primitivism is not what I intend, and I propose that, despite all the violence and destruction they have conditioned, the reason and selfhood of modernity continue to promise ethical advance. In chapter 11, then, the first chapter of part 3, I argue (complicating the distinction, set out in chapter 8, between two kinds of choice) that while mythic rationality is closed to alternatives but open to otherness and therewith value, scientific rationality creates alternatives but shuts down 'authentic' choice. I follow up this argument with a critical discussion of the modern self. In light of Foucault's socio-political critique and the criticism it has attracted, I propound that it is not the modern self as such that is problematical, but the dualism with which it has emerged. Chapter 12 essays the ethical promise of the modern self. In it, I propose that by overcoming dualism (by which I mean keeping it in check), the modern self makes itself critically aware of its own vital limits. The result is not, however, a new mythic rationality, but—embracing Enlightenment liberationism by discarding Enlightenment perfectibilism—a value-rationality in which the fundamental openness of mythic rationality gets amplified. Put another way, acknowledging that every a priori is ultimately synthetic, the modern self opens itself freely to its own underlying otherness. This dialectical transformation, a re-enchanting of the human world, implicitly identifies the human condition as a double bind, in which our very existence is constituted as an essential tension of self-and-other and correlatively as a conduct of creative or responsible choice.

The book's argument about ethical advance raises unmistakably, as with the well-known social theories of a shift from tradition to modernity, the questions of progress and ethical justification. In view of the murderous and genocidal events of the twentieth and twenty-first centuries, these questions have been cast under the deepest suspicion. Focusing on the question of ethical justification, chapter 13, the second excursus, revisits Derrida's interpretation of the Akedah (recounted earlier in chapter 3) to engage his argument against ethics. Following the philosophy of Emmanuel Levinas, I maintain that the self-other relation always presupposes the ethical primacy of the other over the self. But since the other is by definition ultimately impossible to circumscribe and to fix categorically, and because in a paralogical but profound way it includes the self, the ethical ground that the other constitutes is essentially ambiguous. For this reason, the goodness of one's decisions remains ever open to question and relative to responsibilities left unaddressed or even denied. But although an essentially ambiguous ethical ground leaves us necessarily to our own devices and uncertain, it does not leave us directionless. In this crucial connection, I maintain that the ethically hierarchical primacy of the other, whose basic ambiguity is the key to any existence that is peculiarly ethical (to wit, human existence), serves as a master precept, the substantive force of which amounts to a caution, on pain of the non-viability of humanity as such, against decisions that suppose absolutism.

In chapter 14, I explore implications of my argument for the practice of anthropology. I clarify that while the thesis of ethical advancement is critical to my position, in no way does it entail the evolutionary inevitability of such a course of events. Correlatively, consistent with the concept of the synthetic a priori, and citing in illustration a substantive example of such a paralogical principle, I relativize but do not eliminate the idea of the universal. The discussion leads me to compare and contrast the Greek or philosophical to the Hebrew or ethical worldviews. Their mutual interpretive intrication notwithstanding, I argue that the thematically ethical one can facilitate the anthropologist's quest to site him- or herself 'outside' so as best to approach otherness. In effect, drawing out an implication of the book's overall argument about nondualism and the peculiar character of humankind, the chapter proclaims the radical idea that anthropology is, at the end of the day, ethics.

Chapter 11

EPISTEMIC AND ETHICAL GAIN

Descartes' syllogism revised: "I think, therefore I am ... Descartes."

— Marshall Sahlins, professional conference, Ascona 2003

The first idea was not our own. Adam
In Eden was the father of Descartes
And Eve made air the mirror of herself ...

— Wallace Stevens, *Notes Toward a Supreme Fiction*

Prologue: The Paradox of Self-Consciousness and Foucault's *Las Meninas*

In the duly celebrated first chapter of *The Order of Things*, Foucault (1970) offers a penetrating interpretation of Velasquez's baroque masterpiece, *Las Meninas*. The interpretation meticulously describes and plumbs Velasquez's graphic portrayal of himself portraying himself. Instead of trying to summarize Foucault's round and close reading, I cite here a felicitous passage from a brief essay on Borges (and H. G. Wells), in which the author, Robert Philmus (1974: 2–3), relates Borges's fascination with paradox to *Las Meninas*. The passage well and briefly describes the contents of the painting and also evokes the focus of Foucault's interpretation:

> The self-consciousness involved in portraying oneself as the creature of one's creation is baroque, the sort of self-consciousness Velasquez graphically epitomizes in his masterpiece *Las Meninas* (1656). The scene is the artist's studio. In the foreground the maids of honor [the

meninas] assume various attitudes. On the rear wall hangs what at first looks like, but is too luminous to be, another of the many paintings adorning the room: it is a mirror reflecting two figures who do not otherwise appear in the "fictive" space of *Las Meninas*; they belong to the "reality" outside the spatial limits of the canvas. All the same, the presence of their mirror images has the intellectual effect of confounding any nice discrimination of art from life, a confusion Velasquez deliberately intensifies by placing the mirror symmetrically in balance with a door opening on interior space also outside the confines of the space depicted (the symmetry calls attention to this baroque analogy between mirror and door). Initially, the maids of honor detract from the viewer's perception of the artist who stands self-deprecatingly to one side, in partial obscurity, poised with brush and palette before a canvas whose dimensions, it can be inferred, are similar to those of *Las Meninas* itself. This artist, of course, is Velasquez, who has portrayed himself in the act of painting *Las Meninas* from a different angle.

   Las Meninas is a compendium of baroque predilections and conceits: the fondness for paradox (which the mirror of art and life typifies); the metaphysical tricks of perspective and point of view (illustrated by the divergent angle of vision of the Velasquez who depicts himself vis-à-vis the self-portrait within *Las Meninas*); the tendency towards infinite regress (consciousness of being self-conscious ... *ad infinitum* ...).

Like Borges, Foucault was concerned with the paradox of representation and infinite regress. Indeed, Foucault opens the preface to his book with Borges's epistemologically jarring fable of a "certain Chinese encyclopedia" in which the taxonomic order of animals is so absurd as to be "unthinkable." That is, whereas the taxonomic categories can be set out in language, the connection between them cannot be thought in relation to any spatial ('real') reality. Take, for example, the category of "all the animals included in the present classification": how can we represent the reality of a category that includes all the categories of which it is merely one? This is the kind of logical absurdity, a paradox of self-reference, on the basis of which Russell and Whitehead constructed their famous theory of logical types, which holds that a class cannot be a member of itself. Foucault finds in *Las Meninas* a critique of the very idea that this reality can be finally captured in a representation.

   It is curious that the painting takes its name from the maids of honor, for, as Foucault brings out, *Las Meninas* is visually organized around the figure of the Infanta (the princess), whose image is dead center. But as Foucault is keen to reveal, there is a second center, this one belonging to the other space that the painting 'depicts', the space of the 'reality' standing outside of the spatial limits of the painting. This space is conjured up by the mirror on the rear wall in the scene, which, reflecting two onlooking figures, obscures not only the line between art and life, but also between inside and outside. It is precisely the perspective of these two onlookers, who happen to be the king and queen, which, although peripheral or horizonal to the scene, constitutes the other center of *Las Meninas*. The royal couple is presumably what Velasquez is painting on the canvas facing him in *Las Meninas*.

   For Foucault, the crucial point is that whereas the first center is visible, the second remains essentially invisible. True, the king and the queen are made to appear, but only in reverse of themselves, as a distant mirror image—"the frailest duplication of representation" (Foucault 1970: 308). While that image cuts across art and life, inside and outside, it does not destroy these distinctions. As onlookers of the scene directly depicted in *Las Meninas*, the royal couple's perspective is fundamentally the same as whoever is viewing this masterpiece. It is primarily the perspective of one who is standing outside looking on and in. It thus 'reveals' reflexively not only the king and queen but also us, as viewers of the painting, and especially Velasquez, as the painter in the act of painting himself painting. In effect, then, Velasquez paints himself into the picture, but only by simultaneously re-creating himself outside of it, in objective reality so to speak—and as visually unavailable.

Because *Las Meninas* thus registers the invisible as an ineradicable condition of the visible, Foucault sees it as furnishing an early critique of the prevailing Western notion of representation during the seventeenth and eighteenth centuries, Foucault's classical age. He distinguishes this period from the Renaissance and also from modernity, which, roughly, begins with the nineteenth century. In the Renaissance, representation was based on a principle of similitude, such that between the representation and the represented there was held to be some sort of substantive resemblance. In the modern age, given the dualism of the Kantian distinction between analytic and synthetic knowledge, representation remains but becomes essentially problematic. The classical notion of representation, the one at issue in *Las Meninas*, is, like that in modernity, dualistic, but in an uncomplicated and idealist way. It is predicated on the understanding that one need look for the truth no further than the representation itself, since, as the independent product of reason (in the sense of Descartes' *mathesis*), representation is its own guarantee of truth.

In the character of its critique, in which the visible is shown to be fundamentally linked to the invisible, the painting in fact anticipates by three hundred years or so an idea developed by Foucault's teacher, Merleau-Ponty—the ontological and paradoxical idea of the 'chiasm'.[1] This idea, discussed above in chapter 1, refers to an encompassing dynamic that embraces both of the parties to the order of reversal betrayed in a mirror image. Between his movements and what he touches, Merleau-Ponty maintains, there must exist a substantive kinship. He describes this kinship in terms of the movement of his hands touching each other, such that each hand is felt from within but also feels itself as something that is touchable from without. Thus, the line between the inside and outside is naturally blurred, marking "crisscrossing … movements [that] incorporate themselves into the universe they interrogate" (Merleau-Ponty 1972: 133).

Framing his description in the realm of the tactile rather than the observable, Merleau-Ponty does away with the need to postulate a *cogito* (not even a tacit one). As a result, he manages to incorporate the unseeable into bodily reality, such that the body always already displays a dynamic coefficient of mindfulness or invisibility—here the 'reflection' of *Las Meninas* crosses with 'reflexion', when this word refers to a relation that exists between an entity and itself. In this way, Merleau-Ponty can describe directly how the movements of the two partakers of the 'chiasm' constitute or, perhaps better, exhibit the chiasmic order—or *universe*—encompassing them. Indeed, in this connection, the mirror reflection in Velasquez's painting can be read from its literal side, in terms of a gestalt switch rather than a mere reflection or representation of reality. I have in mind here not only Wittgenstein's point that the two perceptions composing a gestalt switch are ontologically equal, but also Merleau-Ponty's example after Paul Klee, in which the painter feels that things he is portraying are looking at him rather than the other way around. There can be no doubt that the mirror image in *Las Meninas* is about reciprocal looking. Not only is Velasquez outside the picture, looking in at himself at work, but he is also looking at himself *from within* the picture, as he stands before the canvas. In the event, he likely felt himself being looked at by the painting, a sensation he recorded on the canvas by painting his own figure at his painterly work—*looking*. In effect, he has given the painting a pair of eyes with which to see—his own. The expression 'a creature of one's creation' seems to register the ambiguity here. Velasquez's 'creation' is *Las Meninas*, and, whether he was aware of this or not, in this great work he is telling us, on the one hand, that he has created it and, on the other, that it has created (perceived, distinguished) him.[2]

In unearthing the critique he finds in *Las Meninas*, Foucault confines his illuminations to the deep structure of the painting itself; he is, doubtless by design, unconcerned with the intentions of the painter. In fact, however, in respect of this intellectually absorbing masterpiece, the painter's sense of what he is doing or has done may well throw an essential light on the paradoxical structure under discussion. Needless to say, the fact that *Las Meninas* lends itself prolifically to assessment as a critique of a theory of representation does not allow us to conclude that Velasquez so intended or saw it. To my mind, Velasquez must have felt that he had succeeded not merely in representing reality but in creating it. It is highly evocative to consider that by placing himself in the painting as outside of it, and by representing this reflexive position in the image of the royal couple, he manages not only to identify himself with the latter but also, in his creational role as artist, to usurp their encompassing centricity of, in this Catholic monarchy, divine power. He is his own model. Thus, in the painting's allusive or peripheral space of unrepresented reality, he effects, as befits a mirror image, a reversal, whereby his self-deprecating position in the space directly represented in the painting, a position of eccentricity (to the side of the Infanta), is transformed into a position of centricity. Indeed, it becomes the supreme center, since it is his position, and not the center of the physical composition, that implicitly conveys reality in all its creative and creational force and compass—the reality of the painter, of the 'creator', at his work. In effect, Velasquez creates not only the royal couple, their daughter, and her maids of honor, but also, like God, his very own self. He portrays himself as, to quote Philmus (1974: 2), the "creature of his own creation." Although on the surface the painting presents itself as otherwise, it is essentially a self-portrait, one perhaps unlike any other, because in it the artist's face is made to 'appear' most stunningly offstage and as distilled into its creative perspective.

If this interpretation makes sense, then it adds to Foucault's analysis a fundamental feature of the lived dynamic that goes together with the logic of the paradox—the dynamic of self-consciousness. This dynamic describes an infinite regression, whereby in considering itself, the self cannot help but manifest itself as other to itself. The vital feature I have in mind is that by its very nature, this dynamic state of being is an ethical one, for, in accordance with the paradox, it virtually determines its host as an optative dialectic of self and other. In other words, self-consciousness proceeds as a responsive back-and-forth movement between the self-as-other and the other-as-self. And inasmuch as it is a matter of both responsiveness *and* selfhood, it implicates self-responsibility.

But this self-responsible movement is informed by an inherent propensity of the self to blind itself cognitively to its own ineradicable otherness. This is because by its very nature every act of self-observation necessarily eclipses the observing self, producing a temporary blindness of the self to its own irreparable otherness or impossibility. It therewith occasions the temptation of the self with the possibility of self-completion. Yet this enticement to perfection sorely misleads, for, as Foucault's *Las Meninas* shows, the self-portraitist can never really fix himself in the act of painting. No matter how many times he steps back to do it, there is one more instance of himself at work that cannot be made visible: himself picturing himself painting, then picturing picturing himself painting—to infinity. If self-consciousness tends to close itself off to itself in its function as other to itself, then presumably the stronger the state of subjectification, the greater the temptation to regard oneself as perfectly self-transparent—as the creature of one's own creation, as a virtual immortal. Indeed, the paradox of self-consciousness is also the story of Genesis: having been created in the image of his maker (a chiastic paradigm if ever there was one), man is ever liable to capitalize on the creative ability thus given him, to the endpoint of displacing his creator, that is, his other.

One way to live through this perfectibilist temptation is to remind ourselves of the fact that ultimately we remain invisible to ourselves, that we are founded on invisibility. In intimating this admonition to grasp that we are ultimately invisible to ourselves, an invisibility that abets and becomes Foucault's explicit call for the elimination of the modern concept of man, one can only doubt that this French thinker had the biblical tale in mind—even though the latter narrates in one and the same breath the inaugura- tion of human life *and* its mortal coil (the original Western diktat of Foucault's notion of the death of man). Much more likely, given his predilection for reflexive anthropol- ogy, it must have struck Foucault, as it struck Wittgenstein, that "it never occurs to a man what the foundation is on which his [auto-]investigation really rests—unless perhaps *this* has occurred to him" (Wittgenstein 1979: 6n).[3]

Thus, *Las Meninas* may be interpreted not only as depicting but also as constituting a 'chiasm' or gestalt switch. It depicts the center (the visible or the theme) as the periph- ery and the periphery (the invisible or the horizon) as the center. In addition, it con- stitutes on the one hand a luminous critique of a dualist notion of representation and on the other an early but profound example of the dualistic and presumptuous sort of selfhood that goes together with such sophisticated epistemological certitude. That is, while the painting seems to betray the artist's ambition to arrogate to himself the power of the whole, it also shows the logical absurdity of just such unbridled ambition.

As regards Foucault's differentiation of the three chronological periods or 'epistemes', it would appear that with the shift from the Renaissance to the Cartesian dualism of the classical age, there occurred a certain disenchantment of the world, whereby connectiv- ity in the order of things could no longer be taken for granted. But with the advent of the modern age, when the concept of man seized the place left vacant by a notion of rep- resentation that could not, as Foucault's interpretation of *Las Meninas* shows, represent itself, there occurs a certain re-enchantment—or so Foucault's (1970: esp. chaps. 9–10) well-known critique of the modern notion of man as an illusion (or, perhaps more accu- rately, as delusional) and his beaming forecast of "the death of man" might suggest.

Scientific Closure

With his powerful critique of dogmatism in Western social thought, Karl Popper (1962) inspired a well-known distinction between 'open' and 'closed' systems of thought. In light of this distinction, it has been commonplace to attribute epistemological closure to mythic thinking, ascribing to rationality proper the openness we associate with critical thought. There is substance to this bifurcate attribution. Nevertheless, it is too easy, since, as was shown in part 2 of this volume, it serves to obscure a crucial sense in which it is the mythic world that is open and the scientific one closed.

The closed nature of a universe explicitly defined by mythic thinking is a function of dogmatic or, more accurately, in contrast to Foucault's classical age, innocent presumption. Under such an epistemological regime, it is simply taken for granted that the world is as it is traditionally represented, in which case the representations are construed as no less real than representational. If the correspondence between reality and what moderns see as representation is a matter of presumption rather than theory or belief, then the distinction between reality and representation can scarcely constitute a difference. As a result of so utterly naive a certainty, such an epistemological universe does not so much quash as make inconceivable other ways of picturing the world. It closely circumscribes the capacity of humans to create worlds and effectively precludes criticism.

By the same token, however—that is, by virtue of such pre-reflective closure—value, in the sense of moral worth, is conserved. Closure of this kind pertains no less to the world than to minds. As it is pre-reflective, the terminal boundaries laid down by this closure are not differentiated simply as matters of the mind, and they therefore close the world as they close the mind. But a closed world is definitively (although not necessarily unambiguously) whole; it is a world that is one before it is many—even as it is always both. Obviously, such an encompassing world cannot admit of perfect separation between itself and the creatures inhabiting it. It therefore denies to the humans who project it thoroughgoing self-consciousness, the kind of self-consciousness toward which Velasquez advanced. If their sense of self were radical and acute, they, rather than their world, would be regarded as whole. While subjective consciousness cannot define itself as complete and comprehensive, neither can it project the world as perfectly objective. In the absence of an immaculate division between subject and object, nothing can ever present itself as objective per se. Thus, the world must remain, to some degree, and from the beginning and forever, morally conjured—enchanted from the outset. In such a world, the presence of value (agnation, cognation, salvation, freedom, life) needs neither justification nor explanation—it simply *is* (cf. Koyre 1957).

By contrast, scientific rationality disposes toward the reduction of all value and moral order to mere convention. At the same time, it formally admonishes its practitioners to exercise rather than avoid self-criticism, and in this sense it encourages open minds. But the fact that such critical openness is rooted in a view of the world as cleanly divided between subject and object should give us pause. This immaculate division frees us to grasp the world as possibly other than our picture of it, and therefore to see our picture of it as open to revision. But because a universe in which the line dividing the subject from the object is taken as total leads to the reduction of all value to the pole of subjectivity, it renders any value a matter of caprice and utility. Correlatively, the world itself suffers radical devalorization. In any event, obviously, self-criticism, the prescriptive icon of scientific openness, cannot be construed in terms of value-as-such, and appears instead to have the admonitory force of a utilitarian principle or naturalistic constraint.

Surely there is something amiss about this state of affairs. Although in an emphatic sense scientific thought is diagnostically open by contrast to mythic thought, in another sense the reverse is the case. Science promotes self-doubt at the same time that it defines away moral force. For all its commanding material efficacy, the openness of science can badly mislead: in the absence of moral capacitation, how can self-criticism indicate genuine openness? If openness means anything at all here, surely it means receptivity not to one's self, but to one's other, such that the self is open to redefinition by the other—that is, by otherness as such. But in a universe where value is reduced to utility, the other is deprived of any real defining or creative force. Instead, the other is grasped implicitly as an instrument of reason and therewith is reduced to a variation of the self in question, the rational or scientific self.

Thus, in the final analysis, the substantial openness occasioned by the scientific principle of self-criticism is incoherent. At the same time that it conveys a certain receptivity to criticism, it also marks a decided closure, a staunch resistance to anything but the same. To be sure, in this instance 'the same' invites and includes criticism not simply from one's self in the strict sense, but also from one's others. But insofar as moral capacity has been epistemologically confined by Descartes' *cogito*, an airtight egoity reduced to reason, how can one's others be truly other? Does not criticism coming from these others also represent 'the same'—subjectivity as delimited by reason? In which case, how can the world ever appear other than as objective, the complete subject's absolute complement and instrument?

The point is that the openness of scientific thought is, although materially consequential, appreciably lame or even inauthentic. The identical turn of consciousness that makes the idea of self-criticism thinkable—the turn toward theoretical reality and representational truth—tends also to conceal, and so to erode, the moral capability that makes this idea meaningful. While it occasions the appearance of self-criticism, the dualistic differentiation of subject and object attacks moral being at its heart. By cleanly detaching the subject from the object, it makes the world one's oyster, so to speak, opening the range of immediate optionality in spectacular degree and, in this sense, facilitating 'choice'. Yet by the same token—the rendering of the world as a function of the object of one's choice—it makes nonsense of the idea of receptivity to genuine otherness, that is, to otherness that is irreducible to the subject or the same. In short, scientific openness creates options as it denies the paradigmatic situation of choice. Where ambiguity is wanting, there can be no choice in the deepest sense of this term.

In what is to follow, I will return to this paradox of scientific openness in an effort to probe its nature more deeply. The main point here, though, is that in a certain fundamental sense, it is scientific rather than mythic rationality that effects epistemological blinkers, perversely concealing and thereby closing itself off from its own enchanted foundations. For instance, scientific cosmology can and does ask how the universe got its beginning. But in doing so, it displaces the question of why there exists anything at all, of why there is something rather than nothing. In effect, the 'ontological' wonder of the universe and, correlatively, value qua value are therewith removed from view. They no longer have anything to do with otherness as such, but rather are relegated to matters of instrumental worth and mechanical complexity. Scientists may well subjectively register this wonder, but this will be deemed irrelevant to the operation of their science. The wonder is devalorized in that it is treated as merely subjective.

If at first blush this finding about the closure of science seems strange, we need only remind ourselves of Thomas Kuhn's famous book, *The Structure of Scientific Revolutions* (1970). In it, Kuhn describes 'normal' science as in a palpable sense deeply dogmatic, and the shift from one scientific 'paradigm' to another as, by contrast to purely rational choice (and as I grasp the implications of his argument), akin to religious conversion. Indeed, Popper himself, who never doubts that science can be satisfactorily demarcated from religion, builds his position of "critical rationalism" in light of his revolutionary insight that at bottom the adoption of the rationalist attitude is a question of faith, an "irrational *faith in reason*" (Popper 1962: 2:230–231).

The Closure of Scientific Anthropology

Inasmuch as scientific rationality is naturally inclined to close itself off from its own foundations in 'irrationality', such rationality makes it impossible to comprehend as different but also intelligent the enchanted worlds of other cultures. For this reason, the existence of the discipline of scientific anthropology bears ironic witness to the closedness of rationality as such. Coupled with the rationalist reservation that one's own picture of the world may be a mere representation, so that one is ever obliged by reason to remain open to other such pictures, the encounter with ones that are other as well as apparently unintelligible provides, of course, the very raison d'être of anthropology. Anthropology is moved by reason—more specifically, by the open-mindedness reason champions—to seek out other worlds, ideally, worlds where no Western person has gone before. By token of the selfsame notion of reason, however, anthropology's access to a world intelligible in any other way but that of rationality is closed. In effect, scientific anthropology is predicated on an epistemological openness the practice of which exposes itself as a Promethean exercise in closure. Accordingly, the discipline is resiliently hindered from finding a world to be both different and intelligible. If anthropology succeeds in making an-'other' world intelligible, then it is highly suspect that that world will therewith have been assimilated ('colonized', to use the term of the day) to the world as rationalism finds it.

From the nineteenth-century evolutionists to the twentieth-century tropists, anthropologists have been predisposed by the rationality underlying their precept of open-mindedness to reduce the other to the self they take for granted. Tropological interpretation of other configurations of thought may constitute a horse of a different color, but it still trots out what, in his critique of the evolutionary interpretations, Evans-Pritchard (1965: 24; emphasis added) labeled, with both wit and acumen, the "if *I* were a horse" fallacy. Whereas in asking themselves, how would I think were I primitive man? the nineteenth-century anthropologists transported themselves as rationalists, their twentieth-century successors, before they put themselves in the place of primitive man, failed to bracket the taken-for-granted conception of the figural as diametrically opposed to the literal. It is only very recently that anthropologists have begun to grasp firmly that in order to make otherness intelligible without reducing it to the same, they themselves must be open to redefinition in terms of the other. To take an equine eye view, they have to leave their 'I' behind.

Foucault's Critique

The Closure of the Modern Identity

The profound way in which science is a closed system of thought is hardly confined to science as such. Rather, it is a pervasive feature of modern identity. In recent years no one has demonstrated this point more formidably than Foucault. Harking back to my treatment of the Holocaust, and in accord with common interpretation, I read

Foucault's work as, speaking broadly, a reaction against the unintended totalitarianism of Kant's ethics. But at the same time I am inclined to agree with those students who find that Foucault might well have thrown out (also unintentionally) the baby with the bathwater (see esp. Norris 1993). By contrast to the way in which I take up the work of Bourdieu and Habermas in part 1, I do not in the main intend here a critique of Foucault. Rather, without aiming to do justice to the richness and scope of his analyses, I find it convenient to cite his powerful critique of Western epistemology in order, first, to confirm my thesis that this epistemology bespeaks a profound closure and, second, playing on if not a self-inconsistency at least an ambiguity in his argument, to move from this thesis to another—namely, that the way in which this epistemology is open rather than closed offers a fundamental good.

Foucault "lays bare a modern system of power," writes Charles Taylor (1985b: 152), "which is both more all-penetrating and much more insidious than previous forms. Its strength lies partly in the fact that it is not seen as power, but as science, or fulfillment, even 'liberation.'" Indeed, without a doubt Foucault's work has as one of its key themes the thesis that the prevailing concept of the self in Western thought is, in stunning contrast to its patent presentation of itself as the epitome of autonomous agency, a superlative form of power and domination.[4]

For Foucault, the self in question is especially a manifestation of the totalism —and hence totalitarianism—inherent in a historically particular technology of control or form of power, which, because it originates with Christianity, he calls "pastoral power" (1983: 213–15). But it is a most insidious and egregious manifestation, since it amounts to totalism internalized, a veritable colonization of the self by the self. His picture of the modern self resembles nothing so much as the anti-utopian nightmares of Huxley, Orwell, Zamiatin, and others, in which totality, in the form of the state, alights on the self's internalization of control as the most efficient means to exercise its absolute rule. Except, of course, in Foucault's work the account is no cautionary tale or dystopic illumination, but an anti-utopian, historical description of the modern reality (see Foucault 1979). In this reality, according to Foucault, totality, considered principally as an anonymous socio-cultural power, has its way by socializing individuals to accept discipline by disciplining themselves. If constraint and closure logically inhere in perfect, which is to say dualistic, subjectivity, then the modern self presents these properties brought to a diabolically logical conclusion: far from evoking Kant's exalted 'moral law within', as it pretends to do, the modern self employs this ideology of an autonomous self to mask and create the 'master-slave relationship within'.

Foucault's One-Sidedness

In his critical appreciation of Foucault's work, Taylor (1985b) argues with surgical precision that Foucault's position is in at least two crucial ways self-inconsistent. First, he points out that by failing to make 'power' intelligible in relation to conscious action (which does not necessarily mean reducing it to conscious purpose), Foucault renders the notion incoherent. If it is not finally connected with purposeful human action, power seems indistinguishable from the idea of an impersonal and universal force, such as a cosmic will. Indeed, the concept seems to conjure an ether-like medium through which all social forces, both negative and positive, get transmitted.

Second, Taylor reasons that Foucault's critique of 'truth' and 'liberation' as instruments of a modern stratagem of control, whereby persons are socialized to subject themselves to domination, presupposes both truth and liberation. If people have somehow been duped into collaborating in their own subjugation, then it is hard to avoid concluding that through the exposure of their delusion, truth will out and liberation prevail. If there is no 'true' self to liberate, then who or what exactly is the subject of deception and control? As one critic puts it (using a phraseology that gets around the provocative Foucauldian thesis of 'truth' itself as a power regime and the problematical usage 'true self'), "[I]f the concept of power is to have any critical political import, there must be *some* principle, force or entity which power 'crushes' or 'subdues'" (Dews 1987: 162ff.)

Before he develops these two lines of critique, Taylor (1985b: 164) mentions yet a third. There is, he says, something "terribly one-sided" about Foucault's analyses of the modern self. He supports this charge by appeal to what amounts to a two-pronged argument. First, he declares that while Foucault's interpretation of the modern self as a technique of domination is deeply insightful, it completely overlooks that the rise of this self's humanity also brought undeniable goods: "a concern for the preservation of life, for the fulfilling of human need, and above all for the relief of suffering" (ibid.: 155). Second, he points out that as part and parcel of the modern identity, these ethical concerns give to this identity another side, making its concomitant forms of discipline conspicuously ambivalent: "[C]ollective disciplines can function in both ways, as structures of domination, and as bases for equal collective action" (ibid.: 165). That is to say, the same new forms of discipline that have served to enable domination have also conditioned the establishment of egalitarian and participatory institutions and practices.

Although Taylor chooses not to pursue this line of critique fully, I am inclined to think that it sets out what he finds most disturbing about Foucault's work. Indeed, Taylor (1985b: 166) is sufficiently galled by the French iconoclast's tendentious neglect in this connection as to call him a *"terrible simplificateur."* To see why Taylor feels so strongly on the matter, it helps to cite another piece of scholarship, one by the sociologists Berger, Berger, and Kellner (1973). In their thin but useful and balanced discussion of the evolutionary displacement of 'honor' by 'dignity" as an ideological axis of social order, they manage to suggest, in even stronger terms than Taylor (and just as if they had Foucault in mind), the hard-to-deny ethical goodness that attaches to the modern identity (ibid.: 95–96):[5]

[T]he unqualified denunciation of the contemporary constellation of institutions and identities fails to perceive the vast moral achievements made possible by just this constellation—the discovery of the autonomous individual, with a dignity deriving from his very being, over and above all and any social identifications. Anyone denouncing the modern world *tout court* should pause and question whether he wishes to include in that denunciation the specifically modern discoveries of human dignity and human rights. The conviction that even the weakest members of society have an inherent right to protection and dignity; the proscription of slavery in all its forms, of racial and ethnic oppression; the staggering discovery of the dignity and rights of the child; the new sensitivity to cruelty, from the abhorrence of torture to the codification of the crime of genocide—a sensitivity that has become politically significant in the outrage against the cruelties of the war in Vietnam; the new recognition of individual responsibility for all actions, even those assigned to the individual with specific institutional roles, a recognition that attained the force of law at Nuremberg—all these, and others, are moral achievements that would be unthinkable without the peculiar constellations of the modern world. To reject them is unthinkable ethically. By the same token, it is not possible to simply trace them to a false anthropology.

Returning now to Taylor, it is important to be clear that he is not denying that the ethical ideals of modernity condition self-delusion of colossal proportions and, correlatively, operate decidedly as instruments of power. Rather, he is proposing, as I understand the force of his argument (as well as that of Berger, Berger, and Kellner), that the rise of those ideals also affords human consciousness an ethically critical perspective, the relative goodness of which can be questioned absolutely only by abandoning a strong purchase on ethics. If these ideals are not genuine goods, then what is? In addition, Taylor is asserting that the ideals have helped to shape social institutions and practices, promoting egalitarian and participatory social orders in contradistinction to ones based on authoritarian principles as such.[6]

The Self as Ambivalent

Taking a cue from what he sees as Foucault's one-sidedness, Taylor (1985b) argues that the modern identity is distinctly two-sided. As a consequence, modern society "slides" between one side and the other, between the directions of domination and of free and participatory agency, "both for and against despotic control" (ibid.: 166). Taylor's emphasis on the ambivalence of the modern self (leaving aside for the moment the difficulties that this emphasis presents in its own right) is powerful. As it allows for Foucault's deconstruction of that self as a 'false anthropology', so it admits of a genuine liberated subjectivity or true openness of mind attaching to the modern self's humanitarianism. The idea of an ambivalent self stands to put right the flaws Taylor identifies in Foucault's position. In light of a *relatively* bifurcated self, there is no need to posit such incoherencies as power and self-delusion that lack a subject; the idea of a two-sided self, the faces of which, although essentially bound together, are capacitated to stand off against each other, can make clear just how the self can enslave and delude itself.[7]

But I want to emphasize here the capacity of Taylor's argument to comprehend the modern identity as a difference that makes a difference between, to employ Popper's distinction, open and closed societies. This difference holds despite the firm finding that so-called open societies have a marked and pernicious propensity to practice what they preach against. Taylor's position suggests an appreciation of the authenticity of the openness of the modern identity and its conceptual trappings, including, of course, scientific rationality.

To highlight the critical importance of allowing for such an authenticity, it helps to point to yet another way (one that Taylor omits to mention) in which seeing the modern identity as ambivalent can repair Foucault's argument (as Taylor represents it). I have in mind that in the absence of an authentic side to the modern self, it becomes difficult, if not impossible, to account for the possibility of a Foucauldian critique. If the modern identity makes no place for truth in some genuine or aboveboard sense, where can a Foucault find a platform from which to mount his intellectual attack?[8]

Foucault's Positive Self

In view of the richly subtle character of Foucault's arguments (which, as in the case of Bourdieu's arguments, makes them highly resistant to criticisms directed at their crux), Taylor's account may not be entirely fair to Foucault. Although I find Taylor's critical insights trenchant, in fact, Foucault expresses positions that are in certain respects—with very different emphases of course—consistent with Taylor's remediations. In one of his interviews, taking up the question of ethics and acknowledging the current problem thereof as one of lost foundations, Foucault (1984b: 343) states that his "point is not that everything is bad, but that everything is dangerous." From this he concludes: "If everything is dangerous, then we always have something to do. So my position leads not to apathy but to a hyper- and pessimistic activism." For him, then, "the ethico-political choice we have to make everyday is to determine the main danger." Judging from this salutary position statement, the main difference between him and Taylor may be one of emphasis. Whereas Foucault advocates—in essence, his ethics—a "hyper- and pessimistic activism," Taylor, in his critique *to* ethics, seems concerned to save us from pessimism and dispose us toward the good, not simply as the practice of confronting the bad, but rather toward the good as such.[9] Still, if the key aim of Foucault's ethics presupposes isolating and identifying "the main danger," the criterial problem remains: what are the grounds for this determination, and does not this ethical practice (dare I say, *discipline*) presuppose both truth and liberation, as well as a selfhood pertaining to which the danger is dangerous?

Perhaps, then, it is not so surprising that Foucault, even if only by default, points to a side of the modern self that is implicitly positive. If his critique is to enjoy the force of critical reflection, then it must eliminate its vulnerability to the charge that it is ethically anchorless. If he is not to sound "as though he believed that, as an historian, he could stand nowhere, identifying with none of the *epistemai* or structures of power whose coming and going he impartially surveys" (Taylor 1985b: 182),[10] then he cannot avoid embracing some conception of the good life, and acknowledging an anchor for such a conception in the modern self he so roundly excoriates.[11]

As Taylor points out (1985b: 182–84), in his last works Foucault did adumbrate a concept of a positive self as rooted in the tradition of Western thought. Indeed, at least three such concepts may be found in Foucault's thought. First, he held up as a good a form of subjectivity based on the ancient Greek idea of 'self-mastery', according to which the self is something to be made rather than renounced and deciphered. Far from a profound nature that needs to be plumbed, this subjectivity operates as an aesthetic endeavor whereby one makes from one's own life a work of art.

Foucault's effort to point to a superior subjectivity reminds us that the picture of the modern identity as ambivalent, while it avoids the incoherence Taylor finds in Foucault's critique, raises a pressing, critical question in its own right. If the modern identity has a good side, then what is it? To be sure, as Taylor and Berger, Berger, and Kellner proclaim, the development of such ideas as human dignity and human rights seems to testify to such a side. But what exactly is the nature of the subjectivity that conditions these goods? If the oppressive side is intimately associated with the radical individualism and intensive self-consciousness of the modern self, then what in the way of subjectivity is left to the good?

As a response to this question, Foucault's appeal to aestheticism and self-fashioning corresponds to his theoretical need to avoid any posit of a deep, underlying or fixed and centered self. Obviously, a self that continuously makes itself also makes unnecessary the idea of a true or foundational self. In addition, having put the blame for the oppressive character of modern subjectivity on Christianity and its Augustinian precept of self-confession, Foucault seemingly had reason to turn away from the Judeo-Christian and toward the Greek component of the Western tradition of thought, to search for clues to an acceptable subjectivity.[12]

The second idea of a positive self, intimated by Foucault, is this. Again in a late essay, Foucault (1983: 216) speaks of the need "to promote new forms of subjectivity through the refusal of [the] kind of individuality which has been imposed on us for several centuries." The kind of individuality he has in mind is the kind linked to the totalizing power structure of the state. But what I want to feature here is Foucault's advocacy of a subjectivity defined by a capacity for refusal (ibid.: 216): "Maybe the target nowadays is not to discover what we are, but to refuse what we are." Here Foucault champions subjectivity constituted by a capacity for resistance. Indeed, not surprisingly in view of his dark picture of power unleashed and ubiquitous, Foucault's work is fairly shot through with an idea of resistance, an idea that has exercised, despite its lack of theoretical elaboration (Dews 1987: 164), a significant influence on today's intellectual life.

To come to the third concept of a positive self, Foucault's early work foreshadowed a notion of 'authentic' self. This is evident in his thesis, in *Madness and Civilization* (1965), that by excluding mad people we cut ourselves off from any experience of the transcendent, thus constituting ourselves illusorily or, to use my words, falsely (cf. Dews 1987: 162). If we allow that madness and criminality are for Foucault a cipher of otherness, as they evidently are ("through studying madness and psychiatry, crime and punishment, I have tried to show how we have indirectly constituted ourselves through the exclusion of some others: criminals, mad people, and so on" [Foucault 1988: 146]), then he is implying something to the effect that the truth of the self is its intrinsic openness to its other.

Anti-dualism: The Phenomenology of Mind and Body

The Openness of the Modern Identity

Given their vagueness, it is difficult to say exactly what Foucault had in mind by these three allusions to a positive subjectivity and how he understood them vis-à-vis one another. But at this juncture, his designs make no difference to my argument. Whatever he intended by them, I wish to deploy the three sketches of positive subjectivity as signposts to the way in which the modern identity comports openness as such.

Self-fashioning and resistance play a crucial conceptual role in my interpretation of the social life of an Israeli kibbutz (Evens 1995). I argue there that Kibbutz Timem's routine fluency with the idea of generational conflict betrays a primordial choice. As I have earlier described, a primordial choice is a choice that takes itself as its own purpose, in effect, fashioning itself. What is more, in the case of Timem, the choice at point not only is itself self-fashioning but also is a choice *for* self-fashioning. Put differently, it is a choice of a self-identity defined in terms of the activity of self-identifying; this is the self-identity moderns are wont to call 'moral being'. Paradigmatically, this self-identity, issuing from a Hebrew patriarchal biblical tradition, is advanced as such through generational conflict in an act of filial resistance: by expressly refusing their fathers' demands, the sons constitute themselves as moral beings. Put differently, paradoxically, the sons constitute themselves as their fathers' creatures or, what comes to the same thing, in the image of their fathers, for, above all, that is the image the fathers intended and struck by means of their revolutionary social endeavor.

By measured contrast to Foucault's historiographical emphasis on epochal discontinuity, here self-fashioning serves as a diacritical mark of a very modern identity. To be sure, kibbutz self-fashioning and the Greek notion of an art of life can hardly be equated. Whereas the latter is peculiarly aesthetic in character, the former is expressly moral. Nevertheless, the two ideas have in common a fundamental understanding— that the self constitutes itself not in view of an instrumental or conceptual purpose, but in practice, as its own purpose.

Moreover, in the identity in question, self-fashioning and resistance do not serve as bases for separate and distinct subjectivities, as Foucault's notional explorations might suggest, but rather as integrals of each other. The self that makes itself does so not by itself, which would only resurrect the specious specter of an essential self, a self one possesses in the same way that one possesses a heart and lungs. Instead, it makes itself as at once against and beholden to its other. It is evident that a subjectivity defined in such terms is impressively open. As is central to my argument about Kibbutz Timem (as well as the Nazis), the act of resisting one's decreed or ascribed or given identity elaborates one's identity as self-fashioning. It does so by ostensibly marking one's articulation with the world as, in significant part, a relationship of optionality. Given this self-identity, human existence is informed with the value of choice so strikingly that the world can take on the appearance of the human being's prerogative. In effect, the world and oneself are in fact opened significantly to re-creation in terms of one's choices.

Radical Subjectivity and the Practice of Science

This state of consciousness, in which the world appears as something from which profit can be extracted, is a key condition of the practice of science as such. The appearance of science qua science presupposes the subject's apprehension of him- or herself as thoroughly detached from the world. By realizing emphatically a boundary between subject and object, self-fashioning as resistance projects the possibility of just such detachment. The grand metaphysical predications of science proper—whether we are talking about the proposition that the world is such as to yield certain truths (positivism); or the understanding of impressions as bearers of truth guaranteed by immediate confrontation with the world (what Nietzsche called the "dogma of immaculate perception"— empiricism); or the identification of the realm of truth with logical system and order (rationalism, Descartes' *mathesis*); or something else—are all keyed to the idea of a clean break between the observer and the world observed, that is, to subject-object dualism.

The main product of science, by its own accord, is knowledge. In fact, when all is said and done, scientific knowledge enjoys an exceptional instrumental efficacy. Although this efficacy is typically exaggerated and deeply abused through totalization, simply to deny it on the basis of relativism is plainly absurd for at least two reasons.

First, such denial tends to be self-inconsistent; second, the extraordinary efficacy of scientific knowledge seems undeniable. I must agree with thinkers who argue that in science there is a legitimate sense in which we can say "we know more than we did before" (Popper 1970: 57), that "epistemic gain" is a fact (Taylor 1985b: 147ff.). As I argued earlier, by virtue of its predication of absolute truth, science proceeds as if the contingent nature of the world—in more metaphysical and social terms, the discretion of the Other—were neutralized. As a result, it raises human consciousness or frees it to explore the world in terms of conscious choice. This state of affairs makes the exploratory process, a process of trial-and-error elimination, exceedingly efficient. Insofar as the world does indeed operate as if it were perfectly regular (which, to judge from the imposing instrumental successes of science, it does to a wonderful degree),[13] such exploration can yield progressive knowledge.

By 'progressive knowledge' I have in mind, say, the finding that witchcraft does not work according to the description of the physical world implicit in its practice. To be sure, most anthropologists would be willing to acknowledge the efficacy of witchcraft where witchcraft is taken for granted. But few, I wager, would want to attribute that efficacy to witches.[14] Even more pointedly, I also have in mind the conclusion that the autonomous self, the self considered as a fixed and immutable essence, does not exist, and that the apparent efficacy of such selfcraft, like the efficacy of witchcraft, is achieved by way of profound self-delusion. (It is hard to imagine even the most convictive of anti-foundationalists denying the latter claim to progressive knowledge.) By contrast, the marvelous efficacy of, for example, antibiotics or vaccination against smallpox is indeed achieved by design (cf. Tambiah 1990: 132f.).

This state of consciousness, whereby the world is significantly opened to exploration by intentional choice, is not confined to scientific endeavor. It is evident also in the moral realm. The thematically well-developed concerns for human dignity and human rights also display a spectacular openness. These values admonish precisely openness to or respect for the other, and hence provide the axiomatical foundation of egalitarian and participatory democracy. Although we may not wish to conclude that values of any kind should count as progressive knowledge, it seems more than difficult to repudiate, as Taylor and Berger, Berger, and Kellner have urged, the principled goodness of these values. This goodness is assayed on, so to speak, an openness standard.

Openness as Closure: Dualism and Immaculate Boundaries

If the modern identity is thus a picture of openness, how can it also be as pernicious as Foucault makes out? Or, to use Taylor's image, how can the society corresponding to this identity 'slide' so precipitously in the direction of oppressive closure? The answer rests with the paradoxical character of resistance. I have argued throughout this study that the act of resistance (deviation, disobedience, erring, dissent, etc.) inscribes a perspicuous boundary on the plane of human existence. By markedly differentiating an agency of resistance from a counterpart conceived of as an imposition, this boundary serves to constitute humans as such, as subjects defined by relative autonomy. Accordingly, humans become self-fashioning creatures that, paradoxically, choose (for) themselves. And in so choosing, they at once create their world. As the physician entails disease and the policeman disorder, so every self-identity necessarily comports with a corresponding world. In the case of the self-identity in question—that of self-maker or autonomous subject—the corresponding world is one open to humanity's designs, an object world.

In so opening the world, however, subjectivization also effects a consequential closure. The same boundary that delineates the subject serves to seal the subject against what it is not, against what becomes its outside. In effect, the same development that opens the world to humanity's designs at once closes humanity off from the world insofar as the world transcends those designs. And, of course, the world never does fail to present a face of truly enigmatic or transcendent otherness. Accordingly (to accentuate the paradox), as man opens himself to his other through self-construction, the other as such vanishes from the picture man is able sensibly to project. In other words, under conditions of sovereign selfcraft, openness to the other tends to destroy itself in its own advance.

For purposes of showing how this paradox works, it is important to identify the make-up of the boundary that, by opening him *to* his other, alienates man *from* his other. This boundary amounts to a form of consciousness, namely, reflexivity or self-consciousness. The genial act of resistance produces man as an acutely reflexive creature. Obviously, by showing him to himself, reflexivity opens man to what was in a sense other to him. By the same token, however, it closes him off to a fundamental aspect of himself—the aspect, of course, that remains impenetrable to the eye of reflection, Foucault's "unthought" (1970: 325ff.). Wholly defined in terms of reflexivity, a self is bound to exclude from itself the essentially less-than-conscious or other.[15]

Functioning as a boundary, then, acute self-consciousness is naturally inclined to present itself as immaculate. As I have reiterated a number of times, every boundary necessarily both separates and connects. But because it so naturally prescinds as alien the less-than-conscious, self-consciousness renders its own necessary connective charge perfectly inconceivable and therefore deeply problematic. In effect, the development of the autonomous self is disposed to conclude logically in unadulterated separation, in (to chant the philosopher's drone) metaphysical dualism.

The philosophical showcase of Western dualism is, famously, Descartes' distinction between 'thinking substance' and 'extended substance'. The distinction is associated with the notorious Cartesian *cogito*. Such an account of the self as the 'I think' is a logical conclusion of the generation of the self through and by reference to consciousness. With an arresting irony, however, the resulting self puts a premium on physical boundaries. The dualism to which self-consciousness is predisposed finds its most compelling representation in the material world. Once that world is differentiated dualistically, such that it appears solely in opposition to a mental world, it lends itself to description in terms of absolute entities. Without a 'stuff' that obtains naturally and integrally betwixt and between, the physical world presents itself as comprising mutually exclusive bodies, the boundaries of which may be defined in the exact terms of mathematics.

Thus, although the perfect closure of the self to the other is in fact a function of consciousness, with a terrific cunning, consciousness manages to throw (project?) its totalizing effect onto the material world. In so doing, it makes it seem as if such closure is an aspect of natural law, an immutable character of what there is. Put differently, consciousness tends to foster a picture of self-development in terms of nothing less apparently natural than incarnation in the specific sense of individuation. In this connection, it is edifying to recall that in *Do Kamo*, Leenhardt (1979: 164), who set out to bring Christ to the Canaque of New Caledonia, reports that this people found, much to their missionary-ethnographer's revelation, that it was not the spirit but the body that he imported.

All this bespeaks the terrific epistemic power of dualism. The power derives from the deceptive way dualism engages taken-for-grantedness. On the one hand, dualism deploys a raised or enlightened consciousness, in the form of radical self-consciousness, to vanquish taken-for-grantedness. A consciousness that thinks for itself, and thinks of itself as self-transparent, is let loose on the closed-mindedness of archaic or 'primitive' thought. On the other hand, however, by erecting an epistemic boundary between the conscious and the less-than-conscious, a boundary that in the nature of the case attributes to itself the firmness of a physical boundary, dualism enlists in its onto-epistemological struggle the support of taken-for-grantedness. With a surgical but wholesale excision, the boundary excludes what is counted as outside, allowing the inside (consciousness) to take itself for granted totally, without institutionalized fear of external disturbance. In effect, dualism exposes taken-for-grantedness only the better to conceal it. By presenting it as thoroughly exposed, dualism affords taken-for-grantedness the exquisite subterfuge of doing what it is cut out to do while presenting itself as undone. As a result, taken-for-grantedness is hidden both by its nature and by its exposure. Thus doubly hidden, it becomes twice as powerful. The result is an extraordinary epistemic tenacity, a mind-lock that, for reasons of its deviousness and comprehensiveness, is perhaps unequaled in the history of consciousness.

Dualism and the Failure of Human Rights: Exclusion or Recognition of the Other

This epistemological state of things casts light on the strikingly schizoid character of modern social life, the character addressed directly by Taylor's (1985b: 166) thesis of a "slide" between the 'bad' and the 'good' ("both for and against despotic control"), and touched on remotely by Foucault's astute and universalistic assertion that there is no good that does not also bear danger. Take, for example, the values of freedom and human rights, axiological insignia of modernity. Given the openness of reason, these values must be relative to other possible values (for instance, slavery and autocratic control), and therewith in principle open to question. Yet they appear to be held as absolutes, so much so that appeal to them (by, say, a nation-state) can elicit supremely sacrificial behavior.

Linking it to the question of refugees and statelessness, Agamben (2000: 20) argues that the notion of human rights is naive, and that its "real function" is to inscribe in the modern state sheer or naked life (*zoë* or life as it is common to all living creatures), in contradistinction to life the distinguishing form of which is concern for its own living (*bios* or politico-ethical life), as the true basis of state sovereignty. It is naive because precisely where it ought to count exemplarily—the case of refugees and citizens—it proves worthless. The "solemn evocations of inalienable rights of human beings notwithstanding," countless organizations (the League of Nations, the United Nations, etc.) and even individual states that have sought to address the problem of refugees have not been able to do so satisfactorily, with regard to the question of ensuring human rights (ibid.: 18–19). What is more, as was demonstrated terrifyingly (but not only) by Nazi Germany, even citizenship cannot guarantee these rights. What the notion of human rights *does* do, however, given its implicit naturalism and discursive role as an a priori, is to expose sheer biological existence—the power over life and death—as the central point of the meaning of state sovereignty in the West.

Raymond Geuss (2001: 144) tells us: "A 'human right' is an inherently vacuous conception, and to speak of 'human rights' is a kind of puffery or white magic." He goes on (ibid.):

> The point about magic is that the particular nature of the formulae used and the names of the spirits invoked ("rights", "the will of God", nature) matter less than that those on the receiving end *believe* in the reliable efficacy of whatever is invoked. To say that all humans have a natural or human right to self-determination, although the Indonesian government effectively prevents various groups in the archipelago from determining for themselves how they wish to live, means that we think the Indonesians *ought* to allow some groups to determine their own political life and we *wish* there were a mechanism which could be invoked to ensure this outcome. But, of course, there is not, and the powers-that-be in Indonesia know that there is not—that is the assumption of the whole train of thought.

Geuss's basic point is that in the absence of an effective mechanism of enforcement, talk of human rights is, strictly speaking, meaningless, but that given its powerful moral weight, the discourse of these rights can function to stabilize a governmental system. It does this by allowing people to think, illusorily, that the system is founded in a body of goods afforded by nature or God and that, real conditions of powerlessness and oppression notwithstanding, they enjoy "a sphere of unrestricted and certain competence" (ibid.: 151–52).

If the modern values of freedom and human rights are in fact conventional, from whence does their certain nature derive, if not from Cartesian and Kantian reason? They follow from Descartes' and Kant's proofs of, respectively, the ontological and de-ontological primacy of the rationally endowed individual, such that they have taken on the appearance of natural goods. One can be certain only that oneself, in its manifestation as thinking stuff, exists, according to Descartes; and by Kant's reckoning, given their capacity to calculate (even if by means of practical rather than pure reason) universal, moral judgments, each and every human individual is deserving of respect in her- or himself. The certainty is, then, of the logical kind. But since it is taken to be *the* logic, that is, the veritable key to the universe, including the human universe, the organon at point (classical Aristotelian-Boolean binary logic) is received as natural, not at all conventional. Thus, in complete contrast to the kind of values found in 'atheoretical' social settings, these values are taken for granted not because they are preconceived understandings, but, incongruously, because they have stood the test of reason—they are logically, and in this sense demonstrably, correct. Put another way, the relevant kind of certainty is sophisticated rather than ingenuous and reflects the rise of the dualism of theory and practice. The values are taken for granted, not in the fashion that, for instance, the sun and the moon are, but in the way of propositional truth. And precisely because this kind of certainty presents itself as enlightened rather than naive, as having expelled benightedness, its might is singular. As it is based on the canons of logic, which are definitively dualist, this certainty divides itself from the untruth with an absolute cutting edge and thus arouses fierce devotion from those who identify themselves in terms of this truth. In effect, the chosen values exclude their opposition

to the tune of perfection. Seeing itself as having defeated the naive certainty of igno-
rance, the profound manner in which it itself is based on faith is almost totally eclipsed.
Thus, by dint of the incongruous innocence born of certain knowledge, it makes its
own certitude virtually prepotent. Far from setting us free, the truth, as it is sanctified
by *logos,* and as Foucault tirelessly argued especially in relation to science, constitutes a
phenomenally cunning form of captivity: its refined and knowing presentation of itself
as the very foil of *mythos,* and as formally and unambiguously demonstrable, makes it
overpoweringly self-legitimating.

What is also remarkable about the way in which these values are entertained is that
it promotes, in a tacit but nonetheless systematic fashion, the very conduct proscribed
by the values. This occurs for at least two reasons, a practical one and a phenomenological one. First, where values are not predicative or differentiated as such, that is, where
they are not categorically distinguished from reality, they tend to secure compliance by
definition. Under such conditions, it is largely presumptive that conduct is somehow
consistent with the regnant values, even when, as measured 'empirically', the conduct
runs manifestly contrary. Put another way, the ambiguity diagnostic of this kind of
socio-cultural order, in which fact and value are not perfectly separate and distinct,
measures conformity in kind: it too lends itself to ambiguous determination. But where
values are distinguished unambiguously as principles, conduct apparently out of keeping with them lends itself to unequivocal judgment in terms of right or wrong. The
clean divide between principle and practice defines conformity as essentially a matter
of rational determination, as if action were nothing but an exact replica of principle that
is rendered in the concrete. In effect, the principle serves as a prescriptive sociological
blueprint from which the edifice of social action is meant to issue and to correspond,
detail for detail. In the event, the amount of room for seeing action as only ambiguously
consistent with principle is severely limited—the action either is or is not consistent.[16]
Where the question of conformity is defined in this logically rigorous way on the model
of representation—which is to say, where theory and practice are regarded dualistically,
and where practice is supposed to unfold geometrically as true to plan—deviancy is
bound to emerge as a routine or practical expectation. As is news to no one, the rationalized demand of conformity notwithstanding, it may be taken for granted that practice always exceeds and is other than the principled principle from which it is assumed
to flow; in which case, deviancy can be counted on.

The second reason that under this epistemological dualism deviancy is a likely
conclusion is phenomenological. Because the values are assigned to the realm of things
logical, that is, the realm of *res cogitans* or 'thinking stuff', their status as value is effectively devalorized. Reduced to reason, values as value—which is to say, insofar as they
are ends in themselves—lose their signifying bite. They become constructs of reason
and thus means rather than ends. As a result, nominal ends though they are, given
that it is understood that such values are instruments nonetheless, they are in principle
subject to the most penetrating cynicism. It becomes not simply easy but even impelling to slide from seeing them as principled goods to seeing them as covers for ethically
execrable or dubious behavior, and, indeed, to using them so. If it is correct that values
of the kind in question promote deviant behavior in these two ways, both practically
and phenomenologically, then it stands to reason that their adherents will be virtually
predisposed to practice what they preach against.

Take, for example, the principle of equality before the law, which is closely tied to the precept of freedom and, in democratic regimes, is itself a fundamental right. Needless to say, since the application of the law is a matter of interpretation of fact, circumstance, and the law itself, in practice in any particular case—even should we make the eminently questionable assumption that, speaking generally, fair-mindedness prevails in this endeavor—actual adherence to the formal principle of equal treatment can hardly be counted on. To take a specific and controversial issue from the US, that of 'affirmative action' in the context of access to higher education, we can see how mechanical it is to deploy the letter of 'equality' against the spirit of 'liberty'.[17] Opponents of affirmative action argue that by establishing an actionable preference for admission of African American students to institutions of higher education, this law constitutes reverse racism and is therefore an infraction of the principle of equality. Obviously, though, this argument ignores an in-place, long-standing racial inequality. What perhaps is not so plain is that this pre-existing inequality violates, in a comprehensive and pernicious manner, the principle of freedom. For, insofar as black students are not proportionally represented in institutions of higher education, we are bound to conclude that African Americans are being deprived of their right to self-fulfillment[18]—the very right that, according to the most esteemed writers on this matter (Dahrendorf 1968: 184–85), sums up all the rights that together best define the meaning of freedom. In effect, the opponents of affirmative action are deploying, perversely, the principle of equality as an instrument of injustice and unfreedom. In result, their position gives the truth to Marx's charge that under capitalism these values are merely formal and encourages the cynicism that is bound to grow under so fictive a state of things.

In connection with this point about dualism and the predisposition to do other than one says, the predication of universality in the value of human rights is concentrically edifying. The intrinsic universalism of the notion of human rights may be traced, in important part, to Descartes' *cogito*. By defining the human being in terms of self-containment on the basis of reason, the argument 'I think, therefore I am' renders humanity primarily in terms of the autonomous individual. That is, what makes us human is not our group or societal affiliation but rather our individuality as defined by—and, in principle, only by—the capacity for reason. Plainly, then, Descartes' 'proof' differentiates a universal humanity, one that cuts across all social and cultural boundaries, whether race, creed, class, ethnicity, nationality, or the like. Wherever an individual capable of reason is found, there stands a human being. Building on Descartes and tying moral consciousness integrally to reason, Kant identified the human individual as the proper beginning and object of all moral conduct. For Kant, the other person too—by virtue of the fact that, given her capacity for reason (and hence universalizing judgment), she is a possible source of moral law—is an end in herself and deserving of respect. Thus, Kant's position implies a universal moral order and underwrites the idea that every human being should have certain fundamental rights.

There is, though, stemming from the originary Cartesian dualism, a critical hitch in this universalizing of rights. If, as Descartes maintained, the mind constitutes an interiority the confines of which are in practice delimited by the material individual, but at the same time the mind is exclusive of the body, then how is it possible for the mind to know anything at all about what is exterior to it, including of course other individuals? That is to say, returning now to Kant's ethical universalism, how is it possible to discern that the other person is, indeed and without a doubt, a person and 'possible source of moral law'? To the contrary, if the personhood of the 'I of reason' is the only reality about which one can be certain, then whatever is not-I, which is to say, everything outside the I, stands by definition at the I's disposal. Here, then, the universalism is not ethical but definitively instrumental, a decidedly Hobbesian universe.

Thus, the Cartesian dualism registers a stunning ambiguity: at the same time that it allows for the projection of a common humanity with universal rights, it also constructs a sweeping instrumentalism. It is crucial to see, though, that, unlike basic ambiguity as between fact and value, wherein the dividing line is fuzzy rather than fast, this ambiguity manifests itself as a binarism. For this reason, the slide from moral to instrumental universalism is decisively sharp—less a 'slide', perhaps, than an inverse transposition, a switch. What is more, although in principle the ambiguity enjoins the universalism of human rights, in practice it privileges instrumentalism. Just as the ambiguity rests wholly on the capacity of reason as the sole measure of the human individual, so it is reason that constitutes the implicit measure of the force of each side of the ambiguity relative to the other. Accordingly, the impossibility of the Cartesian self knowing the other enjoys a distinct leverage over the predication of a common humanity, for it is logically prior: before you can discern another mind or moral consciousness, you have to be able to recognize a human being outside of yourself. In other words, the exclusion of the object by the subject trumps the recognition of the personhood of the other by the self.

This asymmetry, wherein the implicit instrumentalism of the logic of the Western notion of human rights deductively outweighs the moral import of the notion, translates into a powerful phenomenological impetus. Precisely because it is the implicit rather than explicit principle of the ambiguity, instrumentalism is digested, along with the gestalt of human rights, simply as an element of one's identity as a human being. As a result, whereas action according to the conscientious admonishment of the value on human rights demands deliberative commitment, the implicitness of instrumentalism moves people as a matter of course, without need of reflection. Moreover, because it enjoys logical supremacy in an epistemic gestalt the defining essence of which is reason, it moves them, ironically, with a special intensity (an irony compounded by instrumentalism's habit of belittling and even dehumanizing others—including, representatively, women, children, and so-called primitives—who appear, instead of rationally calculating, especially emotional and value-bound). In the view set out here, then, notwithstanding the pernicious shibboleth of 'free market' ideology, that self-interest is, so to speak, the bottom line of human nature, the prevalence of instrumentalism in the West is a phenomenological function of onto-epistemological dualism.

If this phenomenological inquiry into the Western notions of value and universalism is sound, then, owing to their patent dualism, what these notions teach in effect is treatment of all humans *in principle* as persons or ends in themselves and *in practice* as means to one's own ends. That is to say, the model they offer for what it means to be a human being includes a tacitly fundamental and therefore impelling drive to practice what they preach *against*. In which case, in order to account for the slide to instrumentalism, we need to add to the explanatory factors of naiveté, state power, ideological dupery, and compensatory psychological belief the phenomenological condition of the dualistic ambiguity comported by the Western precepts of freedom and human rights.

Indeed, I submit that the radical reduction—seen by Agamben to reside in the very idea of human rights—of the human individual to naked life, to the exclusion of the ethico-political singularity of this life, is made possible by onto-epistemological dualism.

Dualism at Fault

We have now arrived at the overall critical point: it is not the modern self as such that produces the pernicious technology of control against which Foucault mounts his powerful critique, but the ultimately contingent dualism to which that self is given. It is dualism that effects a perfect barrier between self and other, epistemologically sealing off the one from the other and defining each as a totality. Such perfect closure makes genuine openness, the space of moral play, inconceivable, leaving the epistemological field to the objectification of both self and other. In effect, it colonizes the self as it colonizes the other. Moreover, because reflexivity moves the self to present itself as a subject, even as it treats itself like an object, it enables the self to facilitate its own subjugation by disguising or misrecognizing it as self-determination.

It is important to recognize that for Foucault, the exemplary thinker behind the kind of representation that he took *Las Meninas* to annul was indeed Descartes.[19] Because the classical 'episteme' was keyed to Cartesian dualism, it was taken for granted that representation, being purely a function of the intellect, was exclusive of the represented. Whereas in the Renaissance likeness and resemblance were grasped as mediating between the representation and the represented, classical representation regarded itself as perfectly separate and distinct from what it represented. But this autonomous representation of itself was of course profoundly nearsighted: by giving short shrift to the represented, classical representation was really in no position to see its own beginnings in lived reality. In effect, the subject was obscured twice over, for even its ultimate invisibility was rendered invisible—that is, put out of mind. To be sure, with the inception of modernity, the vacant place of the artist-Creator was filled in with the figure of 'man'. But this construction also issues from Descartes' dualism and its *cogito*, and thus serves even more effectively to eclipse the fundamental ambiguity of the visible and the invisible.

I expect that Foucault's analytically piercing genealogy of the modern self and his examination of techniques of subjectivation also reveal, at least implicitly, his negative view of Cartesian dualism. In any case, though, my point is that the self that disciplines itself by subjecting itself to the terrorism of the modern confessional, attempting to search and destroy by assimilation or denial all that it finds within itself that reflexivity cannot call its own, does not exhaust the modern identity. Although Foucault's emphasis on distinct epistemological structures is analytically gravid, a gradually developing dualism serves as a connective thread in Western discourse, starting at least with the biblical Hebrews, and tying together the classical with the modern age. It is developed dualism, not the modern identity in its entirety, that makes possible the kind of grand self-illusion that preoccupies Foucault's critique. And it is dualism that makes analytically intelligible Taylor's remedial description of a slide to social closure. The dualism of the modern identity constantly threatens to eclipse the progressive openness of that identity, and all too often succeeds in carrying out its threat. Because dualism projects immaculate boundaries, the eclipse tends to be total, blocking off the openness at stake from sensible viewing.

Dualism is deeply embedded in the modern identity. It is impelling in the development of the self as an autonomous agent. The more acute that self-consciousness becomes, the more that it interiorizes itself, and the more that the other takes on the appearance of mere exteriority, a finite stuff that takes up space but is otherwise quite meaningless. In effect, as conscious choice is amplified, the universe is made to appear as a place in which moral force as such—that is, other-regard—is conceivable only as a superstructure, an instrumental delusion or 'myth'. Ironically, then, self-consciousness removes the basis for its own claim to moral authority, thus objectifying—which is to say, subjecting—itself.

Dualism's Vulnerability

Although the process of dualism is impelling, it is not inevitable. As the weight of its own lived contradictions becomes too much to bear, dualism is inclined to collapse, to the benefit of the genuine openness it implicitly comports. This collapse is especially well elaborated in the work of 'critical theory', a tradition of thought that, in certain fundamental respects, Foucault extends (cf. Dews 1987: 150ff.; Feenberg 1986: 267n48; Taylor 1985b: 159f.). Earlier (chap. 4, this volume), in a demonstration related to critical theory, I represented the Holocaust as a concrete watershed of the collapse of Western reason. For the sake of looking to a school of thought very different from critical theory, let me briefly mention here an account of this collapse, which, for reasons of its focus on what is commonly understood as a disease, brings home in yet another (although not catastrophic, certainly devastating) way what it might mean to say that a contradiction of the kind in question is 'lived'. I have in mind Gregory Bateson's (1972: 309–337) provocative discussion of alcoholism. Although Bateson's cybernetics may seem a far cry from Foucault's discourse analysis, the parallel between the two thinkers as epistemological critics is arresting.[20]

According to Bateson, before it is a disease in itself, alcoholism is a symptom of a disease. It is part of the everyday cultural configuration of alcoholic addiction in the West to associate alcoholism with a failure of will power. The idea that the alcoholic is peculiarly lacking in self-control is a feature of the popular understanding. Indeed, that idea tends to be applied to all manner of addictions in Western social thought, as witness Nancy Reagan's notorious campaign against drug addiction in the United States, in which addicts and would-be users were exhorted to "Just say no."

As Bateson sees it, however, it is precisely the expectation of such mighty self-discipline that constitutes the disease, for pitting the self against the other in absolute terms, an opposition that makes nonsense of the self's 'ecological' attachment in the world, is self-defeating, even suicidal. Hence, in Bateson's view, in a sense alcoholism is less a disease than a cure for the Western dis-ease of radical selfhood.[21] But, of course, as a cure, alcoholism displays the dualistic self not only, as Foucault might have said, rebelling against its own discipline, but also virtually coming apart under the weight of its self-contradictions.

In chapter 4, I analyzed the Nazi death camps—an exclusionary practice so thorough that it could only end by cannibalizing itself—as the most stunningly emblematic example of the propensity to self-destruction lodged in the modern idea of the absolutely self-contained self. In this chapter, though, I have cited two other examples of how dualism produces fundamental contradiction: the modern self, as pictured by Foucault, and, speaking generally, the other as pictured by scientific anthropology. To reiterate, as Foucault sees it, the modern self is a contradiction in practice, in that its autonomization amounts to a punishing form of control. As regards scientific anthropology, the very rationalism that moves it to discover the other ensures that what it discovers can be only a backward or, at best, equivalent form of itself.

Even more revealing, perhaps, is that both Foucault and modern anthropology continue to show the effects of the contradictions that stoke their critical fires.[22] Foucault's repudiation of the modern sense of self so completely undermines the very idea of the self that it tends to make incoherent his claim that that self is self-deceived. And his repudiation of the 'episteme' in which that sense of self is situated is so round that it makes it impossible to understand how, ethically, a Foucault could have arisen in the first place. Likewise, in renouncing its scientific forbears so completely, some post-structuralist anthropology makes the emergence of its own critique incomprehensible. And by extirpating its foundations so radically, modern anthropology removes the possibility of investigating the other at all: in the absence of some valid sense of an inquiring, ethical self, how can the anthropological idea of the other be genuinely meaningful? It is not so surprising, then, that in much recent anthropology, otherness is eclipsed by an intense critical focus on the anthropologist's self, and access to the otherness of the human other has become, instead of cause for searching perplexity, an ideological matter of odium.

Chapter 12

TRANSCENDING DUALISM AND AMPLIFYING CHOICE

"Didn't I tell you so?" said Flask; "yes you'll soon see this right whale's head hoisted up opposite that parmacetti's."
    In good time, Flask's saying proved true. As before, the Pequod steeply leaned over towards the sperm whale's head, now, by the counterpoise of both heads, she regained her even keel; though sorely strained, you may well believe. So when on one side you hoist in Locke's head, you go over that way; but now, on the other side, hoist in Kant's and you come back again; but in very poor plight. Thus, some minds for ever keep trimming boat. Oh, ye foolish! throw all these thunder-heads overboard, and then you will float light and right.

— Herman Melville, *Moby Dick*

Nondualism and Openness

Logico-practical manifestations of contradiction such as genocide and alcoholic disease show that living the contradictions generated by dualism can be devastating. By excluding ambiguity, dualism constitutes the possibility of contradiction as such and correlatively of a world the truth of which corresponds to thought as such—that is, a rationalized world. In such a world, subject to the rule of thought considered as an organon in its own right with its own logic of necessity, non-contradiction is rendered lawful or nomic. Human existence taken as practice—as a tensile movement between thought and action, the creative but ordered movement I am calling choice—is depicted as impossible in principle. What is more, insofar as it is taken for granted that the world corresponds perfectly to reason, that is, insofar as rationalism prevails, human life is made unlivable in fact. The burden of having to practice not to practice but rather to complete and perfect and theorize becomes an unbearable and self-destructive deception.

Therefore, it seems only prudent to search for a nondualist understanding. To head off what, in my experience, is a routine turn of mind, it is crucial to establish right off that nondualism is not necessarily synonymous with monism. If dualism describes boundaries as immaculate, then, logically, nondualism may be seen as consistent with their description as non-existent or as real but fluid. Their description as non-existent necessarily yields monism but virtually presupposes dualism, for it is only by starting to think from the predication of immaculate boundaries that one is logically enabled to arrive at the preposterous idea of a seamless or absolute unity. The description of boundaries as fluid, however, basically parts company with dualism, producing an epistemological starting point of fundamental ambiguity. Under this description, a boundary may be held both to exist and not to exist.

The critical point, though, is that if boundaries are construed as immaculate, then the self is severed cleanly from the other. But if, instead, boundaries are construed as fluid, then even supposing self and other remain irreformably distinct, the difference between them becomes imperfect. The nondualism I have in mind, then, pictures the self as no less essentially open to than different from the other.

Openness is thus a critical feature of nondualism. At this point, it is worth recalling that in addition to aesthetic self-making and resistance, Foucault pointed implicitly to a third basis for a positive subjectivity, namely, openness to the other. Foucault aside, should we add to resistance this kind of openness as a requisite for a positive subjectivity, the result is a form of self-fashioning that guards against the terrible excesses of the modern identity yet preserves what is so undeniably valuable in it. In effect, openness brings perspective to the self-consciousness arising from resistance; it makes self-consciousness aware of the other as a condition of the self. For this reason, the creative character of the resulting form of self-fashioning is ethical even before it is aesthetic.[1]

Two Kinds of Openness

In order to say more about the bearing of resistance and openness on each other, and of both on self-fashioning, it is necessary to make clear that, as may have become apparent in the last chapter (see also chap. 6, this volume), 'openness' has been applied in two different ways here. I have used it to denote, on the one hand, freedom of choice and, on the other, receptivity to the other. Plainly, in the former sense, openness is associated with the modern self, the subject that unchains itself to explore and make its own world. Receptivity to the other, however, conveys the idea of a non-subjective (but not objective) moral force, and evokes (to hark back to part 2) the space-time of mythical thought, the kind of basically ambiguous and indeterminate universe that leaves room for creation. Construed in terms of self and other, the first kind of openness is keyed to identity or substantives; it refers to self and other as separate entities. The second kind, however, begins with difference (the imperfect difference between identity and difference or, say, Derrida's *différance*) and presents self-and-other as an irreducible relational space, the space of time and of moral play or creativity.

Plainly, the difference between these two kinds of openness is critical. From the point of view of the modern self, the difference may be glossed as the difference between choosing and being chosen. The openness diagnostic of the modern self cannot in itself overcome this self's inability to account for what it is not—the other. (As Merleau-Ponty

(1962: 249) drolly observed: "The existence of other people is a difficulty and an outrage for objective thought.") By critical contrast, selfhood built on the essential ambiguity of non-entitative openness naturally includes its counterpart—the modern self. Plainly, therefore, this kind of openness enjoys a generative primacy and in this sense a certain hierarchical privilege. In light of this hierarchical relation, if the difference between the two kinds of openness is the difference between choosing and being chosen, then it must be the case that we have been chosen to choose. To bring home the profound paradoxicality of all this, the hierarchical structure obtaining between the two kinds of openness is, as Levinas (1987: chap. 8; 1991: 99f.) insists, a form of anarchy, a hierarchy based otherwise than on a universal or first principle, an *arche*. How better to describe a governing relation the first order of which is choice?

The Modern Transcendence of Modernity

The paradox of *authori*tarian anarchy makes it easier to understand how it is that the openness associated with the modern identity can condition the operation of its primordially privileged counterpart. The fact is that freedom to choose, by which I now mean the subjective power enjoyed by the individual who apprehends himself in terms of autonomous choice (the Kantian individual), can materially affect and effect the openness on which such freedom is grounded. That this is so is demonstrated by the autonomous self's capacity to surmount the naive dogmatism of a mythic system of thought, such as that of the Dinka or, hyperbolically, of the paradisiacal Adam. The development of a strong sense of one's own autonomy frees one from the closure of tradition and opens the world to the probing of technical reason. It streamlines, as Popper (1965: 312ff.) has argued, the process of trial and error that produces technical advance and allows for the proficient development of efficient instrumentation, eliminating at the same time the instrumental misdirection of a world populated by ghosts, witches, and things that go bump in the night.

The force of the autonomous self vis-à-vis the encompassing other is demonstrated also by the radical closure effected by the advent of that self. While the autonomous self frees humans to develop instrumentally, it also cuts them off from the openness from which they draw their inspiration for autonomous endeavor. The modern self is inclined to throw out, along with the ghosts and the witches, the moral force that gives the truth to imaginary figures of mythic thought[2] and that also inspires humans to create a world of their own. Radical self-consciousness constrains a tendency to regard as meaningless or worse everything that does not accord with rational thought as such, thus rendering ethics as the grand superstition of our time and granting instrumentality unlimited rule.

But the power of the autonomous self vis-à-vis the other is demonstrated no less by its capacity to overcome this closure than by its capacity to produce it. For example, a critique like Foucault's is well construed in terms of the modern self caught in the act of transcendence—turning the openness of optionality, on the model of which the modern self fashions itself, to the ends of the openness of receptivity. Put another way, Foucault's critique finds its basis in the very self it denounces, displaying that self's genuine openness at work. By intimating the 'foundational' nature of otherness in a way that curtails the self, the change called for by Foucault's critique does indeed compromise autonomous subjectivity. It is critical to see, though, that the compromise, radical as it is, is nonetheless made in order to ensure selfhood by somehow setting it right—not in order to return to a more mythic self-identity (cf. Taylor 1985b: chap. 6).

The main point I want to make in this chapter is this: even though it stands logically opposed to the kind of relatively subjectless openness taken for granted in the mythic attitude, the modern identity serves also to validate that very openness.[3] Whether we cite the opening of the mythic attitude to rationality proper or the closing of the modern mind by virtue of rationality or indeed the reopening of that mind to genuine otherness, we witness the operation of consciousness on the primordial openness from which it issues and for which it stands. In effect, the process of negation continues to speak for the negated. This logically absurd operation is possible only because primordial openness is naturally delegating: one wants to say that it delegates *authority* to what it is not, thus realizing itself as openness in the very appearance and operation of its opposite. The Hebrew myth of Genesis may be seen to describe the idea. Although the events proceed according to the negation of an originating order (Yahveh's Paradise), producing worldly selfhood (the fallen Adam), the myth never fails to remind us that by delegating its authority to its creation, the originating order gives rise to its own negation while nonetheless remaining fundamentally undiminished.

How Transcendence Works: Bracketing and Anthropology Redeemed

The operation in question proceeds by what phenomenologists call 'bracketing'. Bracketing, says Husserl (1970: 135)—or as he also calls it (borrowing from the Greek for 'cessation' or 'disconnection') *epoche*—denotes "a withholding of natural, naïve validities and in general of validities already in effect." That is, consciousness takes leave of itself, putting itself and its world in fresh perspective. By setting aside or suspending what it takes for granted—its synthetic a priori—it creates epistemic distance between itself and the latter, thus allowing itself to see both the world and itself anew. As it does, of course, it necessarily presents itself to the world and to itself as autonomous subjectivity—a Self.

Although bracketing is definitively an operation of reflection, it is also, and fundamentally, an act of resistance. Whether we are talking about a thought experiment or about movement in the concrete, the act by which the status quo is put aside and consciousness raised is violently subversive; it is a tearing away, a resisting of how things appear to be, allowing them to appear otherwise, changing their face. What is more, since the appearance of things is neither simply a property of them nor merely an imposition on them by a viewing subject, but rather an intentional and participatory relationship between viewer and viewed (see chap. 1, this volume), bracketing subverts the self at the same time as it subverts the world. Such resistance may of course be willed. But given that it participates in what it stands against, it requires for its emergence a trace of otherness, an opening from which it can take momentary leave of, and a fresh fix on, the status quo. Although otherness is always on the horizon, waiting indifferently for an invitation to motivate being, its subversive operation can be sparked.

Religion, of course, however dogmatically it may conduct itself, takes its principled meaning from a devout concern for or appeal to otherness. But, as is of special interest here, so does anthropology. This 'scientific' discipline amounts to the secular pursuit of the spark of otherness. Its prohibition against ethnocentrism is nothing if not a call for openness to the other. But at this point, we can see that a *pro*scription on ethnocentrism is not enough. There must also be an express *pre*scription for ec-centrism, that is, for preparedness to redefine the self in terms of the other, to place oneself over against oneself on the side of the other.[4] Put in these terms, for all its routine, textbook collaboration in the institution of knowledge, anthropology may be said to have as a matter of principle a 'bad attitude'. It is, in theory at least, an epistemologically subversive activity, a kind of professional *résistance* in the politics of knowledge.

Resisting Resisting: Postmodernism and the Ethical Self

This somewhat wishful picture of anthropology makes it out to be an academic disciplinary manifestation of modern identity's promise of self-transcendence, a postmodernism in the making. At any rate, the modern romance of the other has certainly promoted a significant shift of content in the idea of self-identity. This shift goes by the name of 'postmodernism'—denominative hyperbole, to be sure, but nevertheless significant for that (cf. Calhoun 1991; Habermas 1987b; Harvey 1989; McGowan 1991). By contrast to the epistemological move from myth or order to history, what is truly remarkable about the postmodernist shift is that, in its staunch resistance to the status quo, it opens to question resistance itself. Whereas the rationalization accompanying the move to modernity constructed the absolute self by means of resistance to the arbitrary, discretionary force of the other, postmodernization is inclined to resist or bracket this very resistance insofar as the latter occasions a sense of an essential or absolute subjectivity.

Although its own positive emphasis on resistance, and on a subjectivity reinspired by relativity, makes of postmodernism a distinctly modern movement, it features in this way (and in spite of what it intends) modernity in the act of self-transcending. The postmodernist turn to practice and discourse as well as the turn of critical theory to communicative rationality are assaults on the totalizing that results from the modern self pitting itself against the other in uninhibited opposition. When it is interpreted as less than absolute, the modern consciousness turns out to be a form of practice or discourse or intersubjective reason. Starting to think about the self as an open-ended for(u)m, a form of life—whether we speak of practice, discourse, or communicative rationality—is, at least by intention, a way of undermining the ability of consciousness to delude itself by aggrandizing itself as complete unto itself.

A Self-Circumspect and Forward-Looking Self

Thus, through its own characteristic openness, the modern self can open itself to the other. The addition of openness to the other as an essential feature of the modern self develops this self by alerting it to its own limits. It gives to that self perspective on itself, perspective that, without resistance to the delusions of grandeur promoted by uncritical resistance, is sorely lacking. The resulting self continues to be self-fashioning, but not primarily in the pastoral sense of self-controlling, nor even in the aesthetic sense of self-creating. Rather, the overarching sense is the ethical one of self-responding in the face of the other, as Levinas would say (1991). Such a self makes itself by answering, in one way or another, to the needs and demands of the other. It is a self-circumspect self, one that makes choices in the knowledge that its ability to do so is fundamentally encumbered, that self-consciousness is fundamentally limited. It is a self that is aware of its own intrinsic otherness and that fashions itself accordingly, always in view of its heteronomous aspect, conscious of the knowledge that it is essentially indebted to its other precisely for the gift of creativity.

Although the shift of selfhood at point draws on and moves toward primordial openness, it does not reduce the self to mere participatory subjectivity, to a mythic consciousness, but continues to develop it as self-fashioning (cf. Levinas 1957). The shift takes a step back, to be sure, but only to go two steps forward. Put another way, by becoming aware of its own fundamental limitedness, self-consciousness does not return to a more naive state but rather amplifies its acuity by apprehending incomprehensible otherness as the foundation of the self.

Just as Adam and Eve's resistance to God's imperative developed their capacity for choice by thematizing that very capacity, so the modern self's resistance to the epistemological rule of self-certain choice develops this self's ability to choose by further objectifying it (cf. Bourdieu 1990: esp. chap. 1). By incorporating it as a repast of things both good and evil, the first couple rendered the world ambiguous and themselves agents of their own construction through choice of nourishment. As it unfolded in Western thought, the biblical difference of good and evil was taken, as a rule, to be absolute, thus defining boundaries as immaculate (see P. Brown 1988; Pagels 1988; Taylor 1989: chap. 7). Correlatively, it implicated the subject as simply over and against the object, that is, as a wholly autonomous agent. By reconceiving the difference between good and evil as, albeit fundamental, relative rather than absolute, the so-called postmodern self projects both itself and the world as modal. Under this apprehension, boundaries continue to be demarcating, but now they are understood as fluid too. A boundary of this kind does not fail to distinguish one thing from another, but it also marks each as ineradicably continuous with the other. It does not fail to distinguish subject from object, but it also situates the subject in the world.

Amplified Choice

Given this state of basic ambiguity, choice remains highlighted, since both optionality and agency are featured. At the same time, however, choice is no longer certain. It becomes intrinsically difficult to choose between options, not because of moral frailty or mental incompetence, but because good and evil or truth and falsity become less than apodictic, and (as I will elaborate momentarily) because the agent of choice becomes less than autonomous. An uncertain choice is one that presents itself unambiguously as a choice, but for which, as a matter of principle, the appropriate response cannot be decided beforehand—that is, the response cannot be deduced, logically or deontologically, from what holds prior to the choosing. Although it continues to thematize choice, a modal world brings into relief not mutual exclusion but ambiguity: one chooses between alternatives both of which are, in some variable but significant sense, right or good (or, indeed, wrong or bad). Furthermore, rationality as such cannot select the right or good alternative, since under conditions of basic ambiguity, it is the decision itself that determines in part the 'goodness' or 'correctness' of the options.

Obviously, far from muting the significance of choice, the postmodern proclamation of the limitations of choice actually heightens its significance. Choice becomes more authentic in at least two ways: first, it becomes true, in contrast to algorithmic, selection; second, it not only serves to select but also helps to create the value of the outcome.

If, then, choice of this kind is essentially indeterminate, what makes it more than mere caprice? It can indeed proceed arbitrarily, leading straight to, in Joseph Conrad's deeply arresting phrase, the heart of darkness. The charge of ethical vacuity has commonly been leveled against postmodernist thought (for a virulent example, see A. Bloom 1987; Hirsch 1991). Judging from the tendency in 'cutting-edge' social science to construe social inter-action solely in terms of power, the anti-foundationalism of postmodernism has indeed been influential in derogating the idea of moral authority. But however one reads post-modernists (I choose, with, e.g., R. Bernstein 1987; McGowan 1991: 29f., 89ff.; Norris 1987: 228ff., to read Derrida as an ethicist rather than a nihilist), while the ambiguity of choice is fundamental, it is not total; it does provide axiological direction of a sort.[5]

Choosing under conditions of the ambiguity produced by an incomplete boundary amounts to choosing between 'a as not-a' and 'not-a as a'. In other words, the alterna-tives distinguish themselves as a matter of emphasis. The point is that although in any given situation the choice between, say, good and bad may well be transparent for all practical purposes (as Holocaust and other genocides demonstrate), in essence the choice always remains an ethically charged matter of emphasis. To see why, it is neces-sary to explore at some length the question of agency.

Heteronomous Agency

With the transition to a self-circumspect self, the nature of the subject as a responsible agent also changes. A subject that is defined as simply over and against the world, that is, the monadic subject of modern times, is ultimately responsible only to and for itself. Hence, under the epistemological ascendancy of the monadic subject, other-regard is construed magically as altruism or selflessness and is impossible to justify except by reference to self-interest. In nation-states where monadic individualism constitutes the axial synthetic a priori, the invocation of 'sacrifice', on behalf, say, of waging war, is—although all too effective—typically a witting or unwitting cover, a thin piece of bureau-cratic rhetoric even, for self-interested enterprise. Underneath this moral discourse of humanism ('collateral damage', 'smart bombs', 'freedom', 'democracy', and so on) lurks the primary concern of material and political power. Although the powers that be (at least in democracies) may find it necessary to invoke ethical arguments for their mili-tary projects, affording moral causes a certain political leverage (cf. Walzer 2004), the driving force is ever rooted in the inherent self-interest of the Cartesian subject.

But when the subject is understood as innately situated in the world, its responsibil-ity to and for itself naturally includes its other. In a world where boundaries both con-nect and separate, not only choice but also agency is incompletely differentiated. The ambiguity of such a world extends to the agent, which appears as an essential tension between itself and its other. Just as the choice of 'a' presents itself also as 'not-a', so the agent of choice presents itself in part as its other. Insofar, then, as the agent is an agent, it is ambivalently responsible not only to and for itself but also to and for its other, for it is in a way itself-as-other.

What is more, since its responsibility is founded in its otherness, concern for the other enjoys the primacy of place that is warranted by generative priority. Throughout this work, I have argued that resistance keys self-consciousness and moral agency. But at this juncture, it needs to be brought out that the phenomenon of resistance is not an absolute first but already presupposes moral agency, in the form of a commanding object of resistance. Thus, Adam's consciousness-raising act of disobedience is inconceivable apart from a prior imposition on him of an order that implicitly comports the moral possibility of refusal.

Obviously, such primordial moral force cannot be understood by starting one's account from a monadic self. Since a monadic self can never be conceived to have created itself, it always betokens an-other. By contrast, however, the order of otherness thus implicated may be understood to account for the inception of the self. Whether we are considering the wholly other or just our neighbor, otherness is experienced as limiting. By definition, the limits associated with otherness are delimiting. In relation to human beings, what they delimit is subjectivity or facultative consciousness. According to Merleau-Ponty (1962: xix), we are condemned to meaning. In the present context, however, this judgment of existential phenomenology is best understood as a commandment to choose. Whether we choose to choose or not, we cannot help choosing, that is, making meaning. In this sense, appearances notwithstanding, fundamental indifference is never really an option.

In effect, then, the limits in question charge us with selfhood. And as a result of being chosen thus to choose, we are profoundly challenged, not simply to take responsibility for ourselves, but, given the heteronomous origin of that responsibility, even more critically, to take it for our other. We are 'naturally' accountable to and for our other, since the commandment to choose issues primordially and irrefragably from the other.

Thus, while resistance is a condition for the development of self-consciousness, the emergence of selfhood signifies a subjectivizing imposition on the part of the other. In other words, even before it is a matter of resistance or opposition as such, subjectivity is given in the essential ambiguity of otherness. Its irreducible difference from otherness notwithstanding, subjectivity is otherness involuted. I speak of involution rather than conversion, since the other as other stands contracted yet undiminished by the change.[6]

The primacy of otherness, though, is not that of determinacy or rank but of authorship or creative encompassment. As a result, the allegiance owed to the other is, although positively implicit in the human situation, optional. It can in a sense be repudiated. Indeed, otherness is privileged precisely because it founds the anarchy of authentic choice—an ethical state in which the commandments of the other may be opened to question.

Double Binds and Being Situated

The Double Bind of Authentic Choice

Such a paradoxical condition describes a double bind. By imposing choice, the condition places a premium of development on autonomization and self-fashioning and on the interrogation of one's other. But by making choice essentially dependent on other-regard, the identical condition makes it ethically imperative that the self attends to the other. Owing to the foundation of ethical possibility, and therefore of humanity, other-regard enjoys the privilege of ethical rank. Still, by denying instrumental realization any material purchase whatsoever, sheer abnegation presents a real threat to the survival of humanity. In other words, even if other-regard is ethically privileged in relation to self-interest, it has a definite interest in instrumental efficacy. By the same token, self-interest enjoys a certain ethical force. To hark back to the thesis of chapter 2 in this volume, perfect self-sacrifice and unmitigated self-interest are two sides of the same utopian coin: the former displays the totalism that has its source not in the ambiguity that privileges other-regard but in the dualism brought about by self-interest narrowly conceived.

In effect, humans are constitutionally obliged to choose at once the opposing options of autonomy and heteronomy. On pain of death, both moral and physical, their choices must be at once disinterested and self-interested. On the one hand, insofar as one chooses simply with an eye to one's very own self, by treating the genial other as non-existent—as dead, or as good as dead, which is to say, as death-camp stuff—one undermines one's capacity to choose. For what gives life to one's choices—that is, what makes them meaningful—is having to choose in the face of the infinite uncertainty that the other presents. Without consideration of the other, one's choices become inauthentic,[7] always decided beforehand, thus implicating the sort of totalitarian state of control and self-control that Foucault was so keen to expose. On the other hand, insofar as one chooses the path of total self-immolation, one arrests the material development of moral agency. In this way, one makes nonsense of the promise—a gift of moral vitality—of the one to whom the sacrifice is addressed, that is, the other.

Clearly, humans are caught directly between self-commitment and indebtedness to the other. This conflicted condition is binding, not for reasons of epistemology or even deontology, but because the survival of humans *as* humans—that is, as Other-made creatures who nonetheless fashion themselves—depends on their ability to fulfill both of these commitments at once. Although they run contrary to each other, neither commitment can be satisfied without also satisfying the other. In a nutshell, in order to pay one's ethical debt, conducting oneself according to the current moral order is not enough; one needs to advance one's moral capacity. However, should one advance this capacity to its logical (totalistic) conclusion in an effort to pay out the debt in full, one cannot help but renounce one's ethical foundation.

Given the truly vital nature of the need of human beings to pull off this basically impossible feat, to speak of them as caught in a double bind is misleading, for it suggests that the bind is somehow extraneous to their identity as humans. In fact, however, the bind constitutes the very humanity of humans: being human is the structure and the dynamic presentation of this bind.

The Double Bind as the Condition of Choice

The concept of double bind is due to Gregory Bateson (1972: part 3, esp. 201–270), who forged it as a tool for understanding the genesis of schizophrenia. As he saw it, in the context of the family, double-bind dynamics were liable to produce this cruel mental illness. It is important to understand, though, that Bateson did not suggest that double binds always lead to schizophrenia, but rather that they do so under certain conditions. These include, above all, an authoritative, parental injunction against the transcending of the bind. In the event that the double bind consists of contradictory injunctions, then there obtains yet a third injunction forbidding resolution.

It seems to me that Bateson's attempt here to differentiate what it is about double binds that causes mental illness fails. A third injunction, instructing against transcendence, is a common, if not general, feature of double binds. Thus, to cite the double bind of Genesis, God—the figure of parental authority par excellence—issues three crucial injunctions: (1) an explicit commandment not to eat a certain fruit; (2) by way of the pronouncement of this initial condition ("thou shalt not ..."), the understanding that it is indeed possible to partake of the fruit and therewith an implicit commandment to eat of it or, if you like, to choose for oneself; and (3) a death-threatening commandment ("in the day that you eat of it you shall die") against attempting to transcend the bind thus composed. While it has been argued, in the Augustinian tradition of Christianity, that this Judaic double bind produced a profoundly pathological condition (original sin), one requiring universal redemption, the pathology thus alleged bears of course on man's moral rather than his psychological health. It afflicts his soul, not, as in Bateson's paradigm, his psyche.[8]

I suspect that in seeking to identify the manner in which double binds foster schizophrenia, Bateson might have done better to feature, rather than the structure of the bind, the family as a structure. My surmise is that, assuming that Bateson is onto something here, what turns a double bind peculiarly into a condition for the genesis of mental illness is the imposing capacity of the modern family to constitute its own relatively closed social setting (cf. Taylor 1989: 289ff., 561n13). This circumstance limits one's authoritative others to the family circle, making it effectively impossible for one to 'get outside' or 'break' the bind—bearing in mind that, for all practical purposes, the family circle and the bind are synonymous. As a result, the great creative force of the bind is turned wholly inward, applying itself solely within the subject's self instead of between that self and others. Under these conditions, the double bind does not cease to stimulate world-creating, but the resulting world is strangely confined to an individual—the 'victim'.[9]

These conjectures aside, however, the important point here is that Bateson did not exactly characterize the double bind as unhealthy in itself. On the contrary (although perhaps he did not fully read himself in this way), he was inclined to understand it as a condition of creativity. Thus, there is no doubt that, paralleling his analysis of alcoholism (see chap. 11, this volume), Bateson saw schizophrenia as a creative, remedial response—that is, one with survival value—to a double-bind situation. By way of his later distinction between contradiction and paradox, and his grasp of the double bind as founded on the latter rather than the former, he came to the conclusion that the double bind and human communication walk hand in hand.[10]

It is my thesis that the double bind, as the human condition, is the representative situation of choice. The force that the double bind exerts to generate creativity is the force of choice. By constituting humans squarely between the alternatives of self-interest and other-regard, and by making each alternative somehow dependent on the other's satisfaction, the double bind ensures that humans cannot help but conduct themselves according to creative choice. Since the essential ambiguity of their directivity deprives them of acting wholly out of instinct, they have no choice but to choose. In the event, they are forced to be creative. They must choose in so ingenious a way that the alternative not taken is also given its due. In effect, they must make their own way between the alternatives; they must create a world of their own. Humans have no choice but to choose their way out, the idea of choice here being taken, not primarily in the strict sense, to mean individual and wholly conscious selection, but, in the strongest possible sense, to mean an activity that virtually creates its own subject and object.

Formulaic Modes of Transcendence

Given that the bind is fundamental and essentially irresolvable, 'the way out' can only be a temporizing of the problem. That is to say, whatever the mode of transcendence, it can put off, but not eliminate, the creaturely end defined by the double bind. In effect, it puts time between you and that end. In other words, the mode of transcendence makes time. The resulting time always exhibits a particular temporality and corresponds to a particular form of life. Being creative by fiat, every mode of transcendence is histori-cally unique, constituting such a temporality and form of life. When they are not only socially constituted (as all are) but also socially appropriated, temporalities and forms of life amount to what anthropologists call socio-cultural systems.

In their particularity, systems of this kind come in an infinite variety. But in relation to the human condition of being doubly bound, most, if not all, may be seen, at least up to now, as variations of one degree of complexity or another on two themes. Since every mode of transcendence is a way of deferring the lethal force of the double bind, every mode is limited by the parameters of that bind. These parameters, as we know, are essentially dual. Accordingly, if the object of the exercise is somehow to live all at once contradictory but equally vital injunctions, it is possible to identify two broad ways of doing this—two generic modes of deferral or temporality.

The first is this. By privileging the injunction of other-regard, humans position themselves primarily in the time of the Other, that is, sempiternal time. With this posi-tion, humans are enabled to define all their behavior as at bottom Other-directed, even should the self-interested character of their behavior be so outstanding as to command immediate acknowledgment. By virtue of its encompassing nature, sempiternal time is virtually double time, allowing the phenomenological conversion of historical time into the time of the Other (cf. chap. 9, this volume; Duerr 1985: esp. chap. 11).

This mode of transcendence, which might be called ritual or long term,[11] constitutes a powerful way—gauged in terms of survival value—of coping with the double bind. However, as much as it facilitates nomian conversion, so it curbs the development of man's capacity to develop himself. Correlatively, it retards the advance of instrumental success. With the liberation of self-interest from the axiological yoke of Other-regard, self-development and instrumentalism can come into their own: they can become so imposing and efficient as to virtually command attention. In view of this consideration, the first mode of transcendence makes a very substantial concession to the stultifying force of the double bind.

The second broad mode of deferral ultimately privileges the tacit injunction of self-interest. Here, the approach to the double bind is to postpone the satisfying of the con-tradictory injunction, until perhaps, as in, say, messianic Christianity, the end of time, or, reductively, to identify that injunction, in the manner of, say, rational choice theory, with that of self-interest. We might speak here, taking Weber's cue, of 'disenchanted' or short-term transcendence. This mode of transcendence has conferred on humankind an extraor-dinary instrumental advantage. However, by shortchanging the principle of Other-regard, it may well have brought the lethal logic of the double bind very close to its conclusion.

While these two modes of transcendence amount to mediatory 'strategies' for juggling opposing imperatives, and give a conspicuous tenor to the manner in which people go about their lives, neither can wholly relieve a person of the task of choice in any particular situation. Every human situation demands afresh the choice between self-interest and other-regard. A cultural formula to swing to one side of the bind rather than the other cannot erase the bind's presentation of itself in every human situation; it can only predispose the choice. But no matter how impelling the predisposition may be, even if it comes to describe a bodily impulsion or (in Bourdieu's terms) habitus, it cannot render altogether invisible the difference and optionality on which it is predicated.

Whether we have in mind a Nuer from East Africa, for whom Other-regard in the form of agnation is the dominant principle, or a modern rationalist, for whom self-interest is hegemonic, each and every situation implicitly confronts the individual with the choice between the two imperatives. And even if by cultural definition the principle of self-interest should be regarded as patently secondary, or that of Other-regard as epiphenomenal to self-interest, the two principles never fail to jointly define the situation. The cultural formulas can relativize but not abolish them, since humanity as such amounts to the very site of the existential tension these two principles represent.

Conversely, were there cultural formulas for fusing self-interest and Other-regard in a foolproof manner, there could be no human being. Such utopian formulas would amount to the perfect resolution of the double bind, the existential tension from which people derive their identity and vitality as humans. That is, in the absence of this tension, humans could not exist as moral creatures—beings whose life's work is making choices.

Situationalism and the Conversion of Moral Energy

The proposition that the double bind, regardless of man's best efforts to transcend it, always defines the human situation may be called situationalism. It holds that there is no final solution to the double bind, or that no matter how forceful man's cultural predisposition, it can always be dealt an arresting blow by the particular situation. Every particular situation brings man up short, in variable part, in relation to his own agency. The ineliminable contingent aspect of every particular situation defines the situation as open in such a way as to place man once again between the alternatives that define his existence. The openness of the situation amounts precisely to the fact that the opposition of the alternatives becomes problematical—doubly binding—all over again.

Take again my case study of an Israeli collective (Evens 1995). Despite their profound ideological and organizational commitment to collectivism, the members of Kibbutz Timem found themselves in the situation of having seriously to debate the possibility of making a compromise with the principle of self-interest. Ideologically, the choice had been predetermined, and yet, in the particular situation, they found themselves having to make it yet again (and again, and again). Owing to a state of highly reduced democratic participation, an anathema in this direct democracy, they were obliged by circumstance to entertain the possibility of changing the rule of voting from open or public ballot, a hallmark of their ardent collectivism, to secret or private ballot. Ideological commitment aside, though, even the powerful impulsion of embodied commitment, or the habitus, cannot obviate the force of situationalism. Thus, the same situation of Timem's democratic process posed a serious challenge to the members' transposable disposition to produce and reproduce generational relations and orientations. In this community, there is perhaps no cultural disposition more comprehensive and deeply embodied than that of the purchase on social life in terms of the thematically moral universe obtaining between father and son, that is, than that of generational relations. The problem of democratic participation and the antinomian proposal to institute the secret ballot were indeed debated and perceived largely in terms of generational conflict. But although the generational disposition was not dislodged by Timem's dilemmatic social situation, it certainly was threatened, for empirically the troubled state of affairs did not in fact coincide with the generational division. Therefore, had the members elected to define their situation—that is, themselves—strictly in terms of the empirical state of things—which, given their technical sophistication, they were perfectly capable of doing—rather than in terms of generational conflict, the moral self-identity attaching to each generation would have been impaired, if only with a piecemeal force and through neglect.

Situationalism means not simply that agency in human affairs does not belong wholly to humans; it means also that for its subsistence, human agency depends on just this sort of incompleteness. By imposing limits on the capacity of human agency, the task of mediation set by the double bind makes humans their own agent. In the absence of the double bind predicament—a 'situation'—humans have nothing against which to effectuate themselves, to become agential (cf. Taylor 1979: 157).

At this juncture we can see why the choice between alternatives that differ as a matter of emphasis is necessarily and primarily ethically charged. The double bind describes alternative options of just this kind—as I put it earlier, a choice between 'a as not-a' and 'not-a as a'. If the alternatives did not somehow share in each other, if each did not depend on the other's satisfaction for its own, the bind would not be doubly binding. It would then be possible to opt once and for all for one of the alternatives over the other, thus taking the life out of choice. But this bind makes such a solution impossible, paradoxically forcing humans to become their own agent.

Becoming one's own agent means making authentic choices, choices that ultimately can be referred only to oneself for the taking. There is no final algorithm for their resolution; there is nothing for it but to choose, in the strongest sense of the term. People may present the choice as referable to God or Reason or Nature or what have you, but there is no escaping the fact that, in some consequential measure, people themselves are the site or medium of the choice—not simply in the sense that choice must work through them, but, more strongly, in the sense that the choice depends in fundamental measure on their mediation or creative agency.

It is provocative to speak here—with the boldness of the theoretical (meta)physicist—of situationalism or the double bind as conditions of the production of moral energy. These conditions conduce the conversion of what there is into an energy (or, perhaps better, an anti-energy) that amounts to self-responsible force. But unlike the case between Einsteinian mass and energy, the conversion takes place, not formulaically, but by virtue of authentic choice. Instead of an extraordinarily large number, the speed of light squared, we have as our 'multiplier' moral selection. In view of the fact that the resulting moral energy makes possible an Albert Einstein, it represents an even more imposing and magical process than does the production of a tremendous amount of concentrated physical energy from the tiniest particle of matter.

Wisdom as an Imperative of Practice

The conversion under consideration is primarily an ethical matter. Indeed, it displays as correlatives the two distillate meanings that signify the ethical. I have in mind, first, that the process of conversion entails responsible choice or, what is the same thing, self-responsibility, and, second, that it demands a choice between self and other. The reason why these two meanings are correlative of each other is that, in a crucial sense, the first presupposes the second. That is to say, humans are not born self-responsible but become so only in the face of the other. It is the sense of otherness, a feeling of indebtedness and limitation, that awakens in humans the sense of self and therewith of agency. From Genesis to modernity and postmodernity, and from their primitive to their modern presentation of self, humans receive their humanity by virtue of the limits set by the other. This derivation is what it means to be situated and doubly bound; humans are, in the most vital of ways, bound to their other.

It must follow, however, that other-regard enjoys a certain primacy in the ethical process, indeed, the primacy of a 'foundation'. Clearly, without an ultimate foundation, choice would be not finally ethical but, by contrast, merely arbitrary. Still, the foundation at point here, namely, other-regard, is not fixed in the way of a *logos* or a natural nature. In the end, it cannot instruct you exactly how to choose, but only that you must. Other-regard advocates its own selection, but less as what is right than as what is relatively good—more exactly, as a good the absolute nature of which occasions choosing as a process of selection between relative goods. In other words, Other-regard advocates its own selection as a matter of choice. This makes it, so to speak, a foundation that is not a foundation.

When to choose in the direction of the self and when in the direction of the other is a question that cannot, in any final way (short of death or lobotomy), be utterly closed beforehand. Ethically, what is demanded, then, is what I want to call wisdom. Given that one is always caught between equally vital demands, by 'wisdom' I have in mind a sense of judicial balance. This acceptation is perhaps in keeping with received usage.[12] The need for balance arises against the backdrop of equally vital but conflicting demands; hence, the idea of balance seems to entail that of compromise. Yet it is useful to distinguish balance from compromise; indeed, compromise seems to imply a failure of balance. This confusion is easily dispelled. What is meant by balance is not that there can be no compromise, but that, in the interest of the maximum preservation of the possibility of choice, there must be a balance of compromise. Inasmuch as balance is not achieved, one of the conflicting demands has not received its due relative to the other. In this sense, then, balance itself may be compromised.

A sense of balance can be built up through experience (cf. Rad 1972b). Hence, ritual and rationality may be regarded, in certain of their social manifestations, as institutionalized stores of experiential wisdom. They present contrary approaches to turning out a balance between self and other, each approach having its own costs and benefits. Perhaps closer to the point here, though, are what we might call 'rules of thumb'. In contrast to formal or institutionalized rules, which, however ambiguous they may be, present themselves as jurally or even naturally binding, rules of thumb are self-defined in terms of their strategic value in everyday life (cf. Rawls 1955). They present themselves as sets of pragmatic, empirical generalizations for negotiating reality as it is defined by jural rules and ontological presuppositions.

Nevertheless, wisdom is no more reducible to strategies for everyday life than it is to institutions. Inasmuch as I am deploying the concept to designate the effecting of moral balance in the face of uncertainty, wisdom cannot be regarded simply in terms of pre-existing rules, even if they are only tactical. Given uncertainty, wisdom must be characterized by the capacity to improvise radically. By that I mean that the strategies must anticipate the possibility of their own redefinition. They must ultimately define themselves not as rules as such but as rules-in-the-making (cf. Bourdieu 1977: 22ff.; Giddens 1979: 65ff.). The experience of uncertainty demands that any collected wisdom remain fundamentally open to what it cannot know in advance. It must be prepared to effect balance in the face of genuine uncertainty. Put differently, it must be in a position to take each situation on its own merits, in its singularity.[13]

Still another way of putting this point is to think of wisdom not simply in terms of tradition or reason but also in terms of practice. Here wisdom amounts to approaching the world in accordance with the realization that the world is not ultimately securable in theoretical terms. Wisdom thus includes the understanding that, for all one's prior experience and knowledge, the determination of a solution to one's predicament cannot be reached outside of existential, practical engagement. And since such engagement is by definition intersubjective, less than wholly conscious, and determining of its own outcome, the understanding in question registers one's own limits.

Inasmuch as any body of wisdom fails to incorporate acknowledgment of its own limits, it is hampered in its task. Plainly, both traditional and rational epistemologies fall short in this way: both fail to take seriously enough the situational character of human existence. Whereas the traditional sort is keenly attuned to the situated condition of human existence, it is constitutionally predisposed to occlude the implications of that condition for the development of the human capacity for choice. On the other hand, the rationalist sort, in its zeal to ensure and advance just that capacity, tends to make light of the uncertainty implicit in being situated, thus prescinding from the openness that ultimately makes choice possible.

Chapter 13

EXCURSUS II
What Good, Ethics?

There is in effect something that humans are and have to be, but this something is not an essence nor properly a thing: *It is the simple fact of one's own existence as possibility or potentiality.* But precisely because of this things become complicated; precisely because of this ethics becomes effective.

— Giorgio Agamben, *The Coming Community*

Derrida and the Rejection of Ethics

This work is predicated on the paralogical thesis that the groundlessness of human nature founds that nature as ethics. That is to say, the groundlessness itself is the precondition of human or ethical existence. Paradoxically, then, since ethics can make no sense outside of a foundation, groundlessness may be said to constitute a foundation that is also not a foundation. Such a basically ambiguous foundation (ambiguity as foundational) raises the following acute perplexity, at least when it comes to ethics: how can a foundation that is not positively grounded guide decisions of value, that is, decisions that serve to create and determine the relative good? In response, I have argued that since its non-identity amounts to otherness or that which cannot be reduced to the self, such a foundation affords a certain primacy to the other, a primacy which, however, can determine no specific choice but the choice for choosing. Put another way, because the primacy of otherness can satisfy itself only by founding the self, it calls for the exercise of choice as wisdom or the transcendental endeavor to maintain both self and other at the same time. Success in this endeavor constitutes the time of humanity or human existence. The perplexity of how a foundation that enjoys no positive identity can offer any guidance whatsoever is so difficult and pressing that I wish to engage it once more, this time by revisiting Derrida's work on the Akedah and deploying critically his argument against ethics (if it is against ethics).

In his discussion of the Akedah, Derrida is principally concerned to show that responsibility is paradoxical. He takes as his point of departure Kierkegaard's argument that in order to fulfill his obligation to God, Abraham found it necessary to violate his obligation to his fellow human beings. Conceiving of God as the wholly other (rather than as the patriarchal figure drawn in the scriptures), Derrida (1995: 78) argues that every other enjoys the "singularity" of the wholly other and therefore is owed the attendant moral respect. In effect, Derrida blurs the distinction between the Other and all other others. As a result, disseminating[1] Kierkegaard's point, he arrives at the conclusion that it is possible to fulfill one's responsibilities to any other only by failing to discharge one's responsibilities to still other others. Put differently, attacking moralism—the construal of relevant alternatives in terms of an immaculate distinction between good and evil—as necessarily hypocritical, he concludes that one can be responsible only by being irresponsible.

We have here, then, an argument against ethics, or at least against 'ethics' in its received, moralistic sense, as the science of differentiating decisively what is moral from what is not. For it follows from this line of argument that it is not possible to justify one's ethical decisions ultimately. Since, as a singularity, every other is owed respect absolutely, by definition there is no way to absolve the decision to sacrifice any other to any other other (Derrida 1995: 70–71):

> I can respond only to the one (or to the One), that is, to the other, by sacrificing that one to the other. I am responsible to any one (that is to say to any other) only by failing in my responsibilities to all the others, to the ethical or political generality. And I can never justify this sacrifice, I must always hold my peace about it. Whether I want to or not, I can never justify the fact that I prefer or sacrifice any one (any other) to the other. I will always be secretive, held to secrecy in respect of this, for I have nothing to say about it. What binds me to singularities, to this one or that one, male or female, rather than that one or this one, remains finally unjustifiable (this is Abraham's hyper-ethical sacrifice), as unjustifiable as the infinite sacrifice I make at each moment. These singularities represent others, a wholly other form of alterity: one other or some other persons, but also places, animals, languages. How would you ever justify the fact that you sacrifice all the cats in the world to the cat that you feed at home every morning for years, whereas other cats die of hunger at every instant? Not to mention other people? How would you justify your presence here speaking one particular language, rather than there speaking to others in another language? And yet we also do our duty by behaving thus. There is no language, no reason, no generality or mediation to justify this ultimate responsibility which leads me to absolute sacrifice; absolute sacrifice that is not the sacrifice of irresponsibility on the altar of responsibility [i.e., moralism], but the sacrifice of the most imperative duty (that which binds me to the other as a singularity in general) in favor of another absolutely imperative duty binding me to every other.

So, according to Derrida, in respect of singularities, we always stand caught between competing obligations, all of which are absolute and for this reason equally binding.

This conclusion, that being doubly bound is being human, strikes me as positively critical. Indeed, I do not see how one can overestimate its importance. It captures precisely, as

I have argued throughout, the condition that makes ethics possible—the human condition. Because we always find ourselves suspended between equally binding obligations, we have no choice but to make choices. We are thus condemned to meaning. No matter whether we go about this wittingly or not, we cannot help but create values and therewith purpose or meaning. Doing so amounts to choosing one obligation over another (one other over another other). We thus resolve, not finally, but for the time being (the time *of* being), the impossible bind that defines the human condition.

Perhaps no one has brought home this condition with greater philosophical acuity and directness than Jacques Derrida. But his argument seems to take the life out of ethics at the same time as it describes ethics as the human condition, for while being caught between equally binding obligations constitutes the condition of choice, no allowance for a justifiable way to break the obligatory tie appears to make ethics impossible. For this reason, I surmise, Derrida speaks all along of sacrificial decisions as 'preferences', as if there were no significant difference, not even a relative one, between a preference and a value, between what is desired and what is deemed desirable.[2] If value (in the sense of moral precept) is not truly capable of final justification, then value turns out to be nothing but preference. Even if, as in the case of 'sacrifice', the specific value logically precludes preference, where good reasons cannot be adduced in conclusive justification of said value, it too turns out to look like no more than self-interested partiality. Hence, Derrida does not choose to think of the condition he describes, in which man is ever doubly bound, as ethics. On the contrary, since he cannot find any justifiable way to calculate one obligation against another, he sees, with Kierkegaard, the sort of choice Abraham made as "hyper-ethical," or what is above and beyond ethics (Derrida 1995: 71).

It is crucial to emphasize that the 'ethics' Derrida rejects is the received concept, according to which obligation is a lawful matter of determinate moral prescriptions and therefore of final justification. Indeed, what he does (and does so well in respect of one philosophical concept after another) is to demonstrate that the conventional Western notion of ethics is quite simply full of holes, that it is virtually impossible. Given the conspicuously ethical character of his discourse, though, it seems fair to say that hyper-ethics is for Derrida the truth of ethics—his ethics. As John Caputo (1993: 4) writes in his *Against Ethics*, plainly implicating Derrida as a stimulus and fellow iconoclast: "The deconstruction of ethics is ethics' own doing, ethics' own undoing, right before our eyes. It is something that happens to ethics and in ethics, something going on in ethics, with or without Jacques Derrida."

Nevertheless, in result of Derrida's failure to find any way to justify decisions between obligations, there remains something forlorn and even sordid—while also brilliantly insightful—about his picture of human social existence. Thus, Derrida (1995: 85–86) observes that "the smooth functioning" of any civilized society and its "discourses" on morality, law, and rights are in no way spoiled by the fact that this society, because of the nature of its politics and market economy, "*puts to* death or ... *allows* to die of hunger and disease tens of millions of children," the very neighboring "fellow humans" at whom the discourse of ethics and rights is also directed. Referring to the "sacrifice of others to avoid being sacrificed oneself," Derrida (ibid.: 86) continues that this society does not just participate in such "incalculable sacrifice," but "it actually organizes it," for the smooth functioning of the law, economy, polity, and credible conscience of this society "presupposes the permanent operation of this sacrifice." It is difficult to say whether Derrida means to suggest that human society in general is thus duplicitous. He confines his comment to 'civilized' society. But if there is no way to justify sacrificial choices between different others, then a society that does not constitutionally indulge hypocrisy seems a logical impossibility. I am reminded here of Bourdieu's similar thesis that without misrecognition and *illusio*, that is, without self-deception as to the basic arbitrariness of its purposes, no society could operate (Bourdieu 1984: 250; 1990: chap. 4).

Derrida's thesis about the impossibility of justifying choices between singularities seems to exclude the possibility of ethics, now not simply in the term's rigid, moralistic acceptation, but even when we take 'ethics' more broadly to imply that good reasons for such choices can be given. Yet in respect of this latter sense of the term, in which good ethical reasons may be distinguished from the moralistic and casuistic, Derrida himself plainly takes stands that are hard to regard as other than ethical. For example, following his reading of the Akedah, he (Derrida 1995: 95ff.) offers by way of comparison an interpretation of the Gospel according to Matthew. He finds that whereas Abraham's sacrificial gesture is utterly without calculation, economic or otherwise, Matthew portrays the sacrifice of Jesus as the founding of a heavenly economy. By virtue of that economy, as Derrida reads the Gospel, the essential aim of sacrifice becomes to rise above earthly economic reward, to be sure, but to do so precisely in order to benefit from a return (the heavenly return of eternal life). The contrast with the Akedah—in which Derrida finds it difficult to construe Abraham's sacrifice as anything but a pure gift, without expectation of return—is plain. Thus, he offers a powerful critique of Matthew, who chides the Jews as hypocrites and profiteers, while he himself promotes, in terms of nothing less prudential than a cost-benefit analysis, the ultimate in economies. In effect, Derrida seems to be rendering an ethical judgment, one about the profound irony and hypocrisy of Christianity's attitude toward Jews and Judaism, and about a stereotype that has contributed hugely to some of the most unspeakable acts of comprehensive, outright violence that human beings have suffered by their own hand. As it certainly bears on the treatment of the other by the self and seems also to implicate an idea of the good, it seems fair to deem this judgment ethical.

Indeed, Derrida's 'universalizing' shift away from the particularism of the three great revelatory religions (Judaism, Islam, and Christianity) toward the primacy of otherness *simpliciter* gives an unmistakable ethical tenor to his book about sacrifice. Although it is not easy to nail down exactly why, what I call Derrida's ethical evaluations seem somehow out of kilter with his insistence that as between competing obligations to absolute others, one must choose without benefit of the possibility of providing good reasons for one's choice. No doubt Derrida's judgments against murderous competition among the revelatory religions and Christological 'anti-Semitism' represent his own 'preferences'. But they are much more than matters of taste or caprice. Just as in the case of our expectations of a juridical decision for which there is neither precedent nor logical deducibility in the law (cf. Wisdom 1969: 249), the judgments issued here by Derrida, although they cannot be founded in formal certainty, are far from arbitrary. Rather, they appear to be reasoned and thereby open to justification. Even if he cannot offer ultimate justification for these judgments, that is, even if the justification can be neither final nor, as measured against the apodictic, 'good enough', Derrida can supply strong reasons for preferring tolerance and self-aware understanding to intolerance and hypocritical distortion of others and otherness.

Uncertainty as the Foundation of Ethics

Given the logical irrefutability of Derrida's argument—that in respect of obligations each of which is absolute, there is no way to justify choice between them—how can we save for justification such apparently ethical judgments as Derrida delivers? If we are to remain able to distinguish among our other-regarding decisions by reference to relative goodness, then we must. Do we really want (prefer) to forgo ethical judgment as such in respect of, say, the Nazi death camps? Do we want to allow the actualization of those camps to go unconsidered in terms of a distinction between good and evil—even if, as Derrida may be read to argue (with Foucault), there is nothing so good that it does not also do harm, and (a thesis conveyed by my critical depiction here of anti-sacrifice as itself a form of sacrifice) no evil so radical and demonic that it does not bear the stamp of everyday human endeavor? It is crucial to understand the overarching nihilism of the Holocaust in order, precisely, to promote the realization that in principle each of us—and not just the 'next guy'—is by nature capacitated to perform such acts, that acts of this kind do not arise from another but from our own all-too-human world. Such an understanding does in a substantial sense relativize Holocaustal events, opening them not only to interpretations that seek to find some redeeming or providential nature to them (cf. Langer 1995), but also to 'revisionist' and 'negationist' interpretations that tend to deny and belittle the representative evil manifest in these events. But that selfsame relativization makes plain that our capacity to choose between good and evil is at once a capacity to determine the good and the evil and, by reminding us that our choices always bear the risk of nihilism and self-destruction, helps to prevent us from forgetting our share of responsibility for 'the evil' we humans do.[3] This, surely, is Derrida's point too. Yet by leaving matters there, with a dazzling description of the existential condition of openness that constitutes us as ethical beings, the ethical lurch to which he consigns us remains aporetically unrelieved—that is, his hyper-ethical ethics gives us little or nothing in the way of reason that can assist us to carry on our ethics ethically.[4]

If we proceed absolutely according to the proposition that all other-regarding obligations are absolute and therefore equally binding, then truly there is no difference between one's preference to sacrifice all the other cats to the cat you feed every morning and the Nazi preference to kill all the Jews and Gypsies on the altar of racial purity. Yet, to recall an earlier quotation, Derrida himself, jabbing the reader with what presents itself rhetorically as an afterthought but surely is not, cannot help but acknowledge that difference (1995: 70–71; emphasis added): "How would you ever justify the fact that you sacrifice all the cats in the world to the cat that you feed at home every morning for years, whereas other cats die of hunger at every instant? *Not to mention other people?*"

I cannot fault the proposition that every other is wholly other. But I am inclined to think that there is something wrong with the lesson Derrida draws from it, or at least with the way he presents the lesson. The truth of the proposition—that we are ultimately suspended between competing obligations to others—helps us critically to understand why we are condemned to authentic choice, that is, to choices that result in the veritable creation of meaningful worlds. The issue is, though, how we go about making those choices. And I do not see that because we have no access to ultimate justification, we thus have to do without any recourse whatsoever to good ethical reasons, in the sense of reasons bearing on the good. On the contrary, precisely because we are bound by competing obligations between which there is no final solution, we are forced to make our own way. In so doing, no matter how we choose to inform our choices—whether aesthetically, prudentially, politically, indifferently, etc.—they always implicate at bottom an ideal of the good and bear on the self in relation to the other. In this light, even if there is no firm foundation on which to found an ethics qua ethics—or, rather, precisely because there is no such foundation—our choices cannot help but be fundamentally ethical. In other words, notwithstanding the original Greek sense of the term,[5] the crucial condition of ethical existence is not foundational certainty but the essential uncertainty that attends any form of life characterized by the possibility of responsibility and selfhood.

Because we are suspended between necessarily competing obligations for which there exists no certain standard by which to decide in favor of some as against the others, we are forced to establish our own certain standards, our own synthetic a priori. In effect, we are forced to make creative choices or, as Rousseau (1950: 18) had it, capturing the essential paradoxicality of the human condition (but with a meaning still different from mine[6]), we are "forced to be free." In this sense—that we have no choice but to make choices that create meaningful worlds—we are ethical beings.

Obligation as Existential and the Truth of Subjectivity

But we are ethical not only because we enjoy freedom of choice but also, and more fundamentally, because our choices bear on competing obligations. That is to say, choice is forced on us precisely because our condition of boundenness is a matter of responsibility. Why, then, is the double bind that constitutes the human condition primarily a question of obligation or indebtedness? That is, why are we always already obligated from the start? Why do we find ourselves ever indebted to the other—to others, to otherness?

My answer is, as I have argued throughout, that basically our selfhood is itself nothing if not such indebtedness: we cannot find our*selves* at all without at the same time finding ourselves owing. To the reader who wishes to dig deeply into the discursive intricacies of this answer, I recommend that she or he consult Emmanuel Levinas (esp. 1991), from whose profound work I have taken it. Following Levinas, I can say this much: conceived of in this fashion, the self is born not in self-consciousness but in responsibility. That is to say, the self emerges in the first place as an offspring of the other, not in identity to itself, but in relational difference from the other. Although this assertion runs deep, the evidence for it is remarkably plain: our belatedness (none of us could have given birth to ourselves), our mortality, and our creaturely vulnerability to pain and suffering. Each of these conditions signifies in certain terms our limitedness or our originary dependence on otherness, on that which does not reduce to the self. Put directly in ethical terms, these conditions show that from the start our lives are constitutionally forfeit to the other, whose place we have taken for the time (of) being. Put another way, whatever place I occupy, it might have been taken up by someone else—by an-other. The living of our lives, in these terms, then, virtually amounts to a continual paying out of this indebtedness. This is why the personal and cultural ways that we can live, while infinite in number, may each, including the least charitable, be construed as a form of sacrifice.

It might be said that since all creatures presuppose otherness and also suffer and die, these conditions hardly warrant discussion as a question of ethics. But the point is that only self-conscious creatures can experience these conditions as such. Hence, for example, although all creatures must die, only humans are obviously self-aware of their mortality. This consideration is dramatically rendered in the biblical story of Adam and Eve, whose death sentence turns out to be principally a matter of their learning that they are mortal and is thus a 'life sentence'. Such self-awareness or self-consciousness depends on selfhood as responsibility, as is also announced in this biblical story of the first couple, who, in the commandment to refrain from consuming certain fruits, are addressed by God as self-responsible creatures before they become self-conscious ones (that is, before they have eaten of the forbidden fruit). Even prior to the emergence of our reflexive selves, we obtain, as liable selves, selves whose selfhood is determined as a contraction of the other, such that we consist precisely in and through our contractive tie, our boundenness to and by the other. Given that in our case this boundenness is conspicuously chiastic—constituting us so substantially as reflections ('in the image') of the other that our creaturely capacity for creation is itself 'godlike' or wondrously reflexive—we cannot help experiencing our bounden nature, which is to say, our very selves, as ties of obligation, of indebtedness. Once the reflexive act takes place and one discerns one's self in its singularity, the responsibility is seen for what it is, as responsibility. And when that happens, the responsibility becomes a matter of choice as between responsibility and irresponsibility. This is not to say, along the lines of the kind of moralism Derrida debunks, that one can evade one's responsibility by choosing the path of irresponsibility, but rather that by so choosing one can discharge one's responsibility in a fashion that is more death-dealing than life-sustaining.

Self-consciousness, then, notwithstanding a good deal of structuralist, poststructuralist, and postmodern ratiocination, is not an illusion. It is, rather, the self's discovery of its own responsibility to and for the other. As a specific replacement for the other, one is constitutionally put on the spot, so to speak, uniquely answerable to and for the other for whom one is filling in. As such, ultimately no one else can fill in for the self in discharging that responsibility. If someone else could, if the responsibility could be delegated, then it would not be *you* that is on the spot. Put another way, no one can finally replace you in your replacing of the other; no one can occupy your place without your ceasing to be who you are in your singularity. Hence, although others may sacrifice themselves (or be sacrificed) on your behalf, no one else can actually suffer your suffering or die your death. When one sees oneself in relation to the other, that is, when one manages to objectify oneself, one does not simply, in the process of reflection, create a self. Rather, one discovers one's singularity as the assignation of the other. That is why when one considers one's self as an-other, in the third person, one never becomes just another other. Unlike all other others, the other at the end of the reflexive gaze, the mirror-image, is never quite distinguishable from the self defined in all its singularity as responsibility.

Thus, between being constituted as responsible selves and ever bound by competing obligations, each of which is absolute, we are essentially ethical. As inherently responsible beings caught in an obligatory double bind, we are forced to determine our own standards of good and bad, which is to say, we are forced to choose in the strongest possible sense of the term. It is this powerful sense of choice that Derrida is pointing to when he declares that every other is wholly other. With this declaration, he describes the human condition in terms of an obligatory double bind that makes it impossible to justify in final terms a choice between one such obligation and another. For if all our obligations are absolute, then they are equally binding. As a result, the choice one makes must be a creative choice, a choice that does not so much abide by the good as determine it for the time (of) being.

However, by the same token—our fundamental ethical groundlessness, by virtue of which we are thus constituted as choosers—we are given a kind of ground on the basis of which to make our choices. I say 'kind' of ground because it is not a ground in the received sense; it is not an essence or underlying reality. Rather, the state of groundlessness, as its own end, constitutes its own good. To be sure, one can say the same about any state of human affairs. For instance, Hitler's Germany also projected itself as its own good. In this respect, though, there is a critical difference between just any state of things and the condition of groundlessness: forcing us to be free, to make choices, the latter is not merely its own good but the condition for the emergence of any good at all. By not determining the good for us but by leaving us to decide it for ourselves, ethical groundlessness makes human existence as such possible. Unlike, say, Nazi Germany or, for that matter, most if not all nation-states and institutions, it does not ask us to make a moral choice between a predetermined good and bad. Rather it forces us to choose in the sense of determining the nature of the good and the bad; that is, it forces us to create our own worlds, making possible Nazi regimes as well as democracies yet to come. The point is that precisely because groundlessness, as its own good, does not present itself as a positivity, it constitutes a master good, a good that founds the ethical determining of goods. For this reason, any choice can be evaluated by reference to the manner in which it takes this 'ground' into account. While such measurement is inherently temporal and inexact, and is often very difficult to take with any real confidence, it is far from arbitrary.

Derrida's deconstructional penchant to leave his reader always in a state of ethical suspension, no matter what the issue, strikes me as nothing but an observant, philosophical acknowledgement of just this ground—groundlessness. But Derrida's characteristic emphasis on ethical suspension alone, although profoundly significant for the idea of choice, seems not to see that this ground can serve as a measure of the relative goodness of choices, that is, that it can offer broad but deep guidance in the determination of the good. He fails to see that while this (non-)ground may leave us hanging, it also offers us positive direction on how to go about touching down long enough to put off the bad end and 'hang in there', so to speak, thus allowing us to get on with the living of our lives, mortal though they be.

How can groundlessness do this? Groundlessness amounts to otherness, that is, to that which is irreducible to the self. More exactly, groundlessness is irreducible to the substantive principle of identity in terms of which any self, even a fragmented one, takes its cue.[7] Therefore, the very idea of groundlessness presupposes the difference of self and other. The possibility of axiological direction inherent in the situation of groundlessness turns on this difference.[8] The self-other relation is fundamentally paradoxical, presenting a peculiar and basically irresolvable tension: as the self is originarily and fundamentally dependent on, and therefore always owing to, the other, it can maintain itself only by denying itself, that is, only through abnegation. This is what is meant by the claim that the self is inherently responsible to and for the other. As a replacement of the other, the self *is* only insofar as it answers to and takes responsibility for the other. In other words, such responsibility virtually defines the self's being. However, since the self is also always other to itself—that is, since it constitutes a kind of other in itself—it must follow that the self also owes a certain responsibility to itself. Therefore, in discharging its obligation to the other, the self is also obliged to watch over itself. Plainly, then, the self is doubly bound, caught between two vital obligations—to its other and to itself. For this reason it can never discharge either obligation completely, but can only jockey back and forth between them.

The Essential Tension of Self-and-Other

I have thus arrived at a conclusion very similar to Derrida's about ethical suspension and the impossibility of satisfying one's obligations in full. As I pointed out in chapter 3, however, Derrida expresses his conclusion in terms of competing obligations exclusively to others, whereas mine focuses specifically on the obligatory bind presented by the self-other relationship. In point of this difference, it seems to me that the various conflicts of obligation that Derrida adduces—obligations to others—can all be parsed, and inevitably are, in terms of the binding tension between self and other. This is obviously the case in such examples as speaking one's own language and feeding one's own cat rather than, respectively, other languages and other cats. But even in the case of, say, attending to one's profession rather than one's family, where each of the competing obligations appears to be owing to the self rather than the other (to one's own profession and one's own family rather than others), the point seems to hold. Although in this sense in performing the tasks of one's profession one is addressing obligations similar in kind to those owing to one's family, insofar as such activity is perceived as detracting from one's obligations to one's family, it is open to interpretation (by oneself, one's family, and others) as self-ish and thus evocative of the conflict between self and other.

In this connection, the choice imposed on Abraham is highly instructive. At first, the choice between God's command and man's law appears to have nothing to do with self-interest. Intuitively speaking, is the social injunction against infanticide any less other-regarding than the religious imperative to have faith? Yet there can be little doubt that relative to God's command to Abraham to sacrifice Isaac, the injunction against infanticide enjoys a merely creaturely significance, inclining the story's redactors to assign to the choice of disobedience on Abraham's part the value of self-interest.[9]

The finding that all choices among conflicting obligations, even if the obligations may be overtly other-directed, always suppose the choice between self and other seems to me logically patent. In view of the line of argument implied by a number of powerful thinkers in recent decades—that selfhood is largely a mere convention of Western thought or, wherever it is found, a deceptive fiction—this conclusion is bound to look suspect. But if we are at all inclined to grant the possibility that we—that is, our selves—by virtue of creative decisions, even in the case of largely unwitting decisions, make a difference, then the finding seems unavoidable. For if in some significant measure we are answerable for what happens, if we are in effect not merely agents but responsible ones, then our selves, even if they are constructs and do not enjoy the same substantive reality of, say, our hearts and our lungs, constitute a difference that makes a difference.

Insofar as our selves are effective actualities, they are defined by choice. I have argued, following Levinas, that before it is anything else, the self is a matter of responsibility to and for the other. But with that responsibility comes the capacity of choice. As fundamentally liable to be called to account, the self has no choice but to conduct itself as a chooser. And if every choice presupposes a self, and the self is constituted as a replacement of the other, then every choice presents the obligatory bind between self and other. That is to say, every choice confronts the self with the paradox of having to make a choice that fulfills the self's obligation to the other and to itself at the same time. In effect, as dischargers of fundamental responsibility, we turn on the way in which we manage the choice between self and other.

To be sure, we cannot help but discharge this responsibility (even as we can never manage to relieve ourselves of it fully), no matter how prone or determined we are to make irresponsible choices. By 'irresponsibility' here I mean of course something different from the necessary irresponsibility determined by Derrida to accompany every responsible choice. Rather, I have in mind choices taken without due sense of responsibility. But the possibility of such choices only indicates that the way we go about discharging the responsibility attendant on our selfhood varies according to the manner in which we approach the self-other axis.

Because it presents a fundamental paradox, this axis can never be viably approached with final resolution in mind. That is to say, the question whether one has chosen more toward the pole of self-interest or of other-regard is basically always open. Hence, to stay with our biblical example, the character of Abraham's choice as more selfish or self-less remains instructively open to question. But this is not to say that in some cases—for example, the Holocaust—the question may not be crystalline for most practical and ethical purposes. Indeed, what is so glaring about the case of the Holocaust, as I suspect is duly reflected in Derrida's ethical suspensionism, is the radical way in which it was enacted according to moral certainty: the closure of Nazism as regards the definition of the good in virtue of the self-other relationship was absolute.

The Asymmetry of the Self-Other Relation

The paradoxical nature of the self-other relationship, the fact that it presents an essential tension, is well in line with Derrida's persistent emphasis on the human condition as one of ethical suspension. However, the self-other relationship qualifies that emphasis in a transformative way. Although the relationship is fundamentally paradoxical (the two poles to the relationship defining each other, making them not exactly separate but nonetheless distinct), it is also irredeemably uneven—indeed, it constitutes an axiological hierarchy. As I observed in chapter 3, Derrida leaves implicit the way in which the self-other relationship underlies every set of conflicting obligations, preferring instead to talk about the situation of such double boundenness in terms of other-directed obligations alone. Had he attended expressly to the critical role of the self-other relationship in the human condition, however, I think it would have been difficult for him to avoid having to acknowledge that ethical suspension itself, as based on the asymmetry of the self-other relation, provides a certain axiological direction.

Following Derrida, what sets up the double bind, by virtue of which there can be no final justification for choosing between obligations to others, is the crucial consideration that every other is wholly other, which is to say, that all such obligations are absolute and therefore equally binding. Nevertheless, there is one other to whom we are bound relatively rather than absolutely, namely, of course, the other that is oneself (one's self). Because the self is belated and presupposes the other, or because reflexivity entails self-alienation, the distance one needs from oneself to observe oneself, the self is always other to itself. But of course it can never become wholly other to itself without ceasing to be a self at all. Accordingly, inasmuch as it is owing to itself (and, as I have argued, it does bear a certain responsibility for its own welfare), the implied obligation must be less than absolute. The self is not owing to itself in the same infinite (but not uncontested) degree as it is owing to the other. Because it is the responsible one, the self is the one other to whom one's indebtedness can be economized without compromising the nature of the obligation. The self amounts to the indebted other, the other whose life is always already forfeit in the nature of the case.

Given the self's distinction as the one other to whom one's obligation is finite, the polarity it constitutes with the other as such can serve as a measure for the relative good-ness of one's choices. According to this axiological measure, the pole of otherness is essen-tially privileged over that of the self. Of course, to reiterate, as the self-other relationship is a paradox, this measure is intrinsically imperfect. Since the two poles of the relationship define each other, the self can privilege neither itself nor the other unambiguously. Hence, Abraham's choice to heed the word of God, a choice taken in all sincerity and so appar-ently selfless as to be stunning, is open to interpretation as radically self-aggrandizing. At work here is the idea that a choice of such enormous gravity as Abraham's contributes no less totally to his definition as a chooser—as a self—than it does to the possibility of the total destruction of the human world to which such selfhood corresponds.

But while ambiguity ensures vacillation between the poles of self and other and rules out the possibility of final logical certainty, it hardly precludes relative clarity of evalu-ation. In many cases, the question of whether one has chosen more to the benefit of oneself than to that of the other, or vice versa, is, although never decided, perspicuous. That is to say, the goodness of a choice as measured by its relative selflessness or selfish-ness may be manifest, even on the weight of reason and the evidence.

Again, take the example of the Holocaust. The fact of the horrific death-camp exter-mination of millions of 'others' leaves little room for seeing Nazism as anything but self-aggrandizing—indeed, as I have argued, self-deifying. It is of course true that the Nazis projected their program of extermination as a selfless act, a heroic effort to save the world from what they saw as racial and cultural degeneration. Why, then, is the Nazi projection of themselves any less valid than the picture I have just presented? On a purely relativist perspective (that is, one which sees foundationlessness in absolute rather than relative terms), the formal self-understanding of the Nazis must be con-sidered no less sound than any evaluation, which observation would of course lend support to the Holocaust revisionists and deniers.

The Intrinsic Connection between Self and Other

But even on intellectual grounds, we need not embrace such absolute relativism. Every-thing depends on how one perceives the self-other relation. If that relation is seen in terms of dualism, then the relativist position seems unavoidable, for dualism describes self and other as mutually exclusive values, making their opposition a matter of power alone. And if power is all that counts, then there really is no essential difference between one viewpoint and another: ethically speaking, one is as good as another, and they can be told apart only by virtue of which one of them succeeds in imposing (in today's academic cant, 'hegemonizing' by force, intimidation, deception, and so on) its definition of the order of things on the others.

But once the self-other axis is seen as a genuine tension, then self and other turn out to be no less bound to each other than they are opposed. As such, their opposition is always tempered by connection, as in turn is the influence of power to decide between them. For if they are intrinsically connected, then their opposition has always already been mediated. Insofar as it has, power is pre-empted by 'necessity', in the ethical and hence anomalous sense that, in any particular situation, however they stand with power, some viewpoints are intrinsically to be preferred to others.

The connectedness I have in mind is ethical, but it is substantive too. Despite the inordinate stress we moderns place on our biological entitativity, our physical well-boundedness, we are not perfectly self-contained. On the contrary, our skins are porous and our bodies palpably endowed with both conspicuous and minute orifices, through which substances get in as well as out, making the line between our inside and outside fluid. In breathing, for example, we inhale and exhale air from and to the outside, an outside that, notably, includes the other's inside.

The example of breathing is tendentious, as it also is forcefully relevant to the way in which our connection to one another transcends substantiality. The ordinary meanings of inspiration and expiration provocatively extend beyond the physical, bearing on the spiritual nature of human existence. To choose a paradigmatic literary and scriptural example, in Genesis the life that God breathes into the first human being is the life of the spirit as well as the body, a gift for which we, as Adam's beneficiaries, pay dearly by our 'expiration'—our mortality. For reasons of its fundamental paradoxicality, this continuity of meaning between the physical and the spiritual cannot be logically resolved or *said*. Still, it is *shown* each and every time a human being manages to say anything meaningful at all, for meaning betrays consciousness that is reflexive and creatively purposeful. The self, then, is bound over to others at once materially and, in its responsibility to the other, that is, its very selfhood, spiritually.

As opposition is always already mediated, it must count as belated. It is tempting to assert the contradictory also: that because it always mars connection, opposition too must count as belated. But this would be wrong, for whereas connectivity allows for, indeed includes, opposition as an integral part of its make-up, oppositionality excludes connection, by definition. Of the two principles, only the one that allows for rather than excludes the other can enjoy primacy between them. Between oppositionality, which entails mutual exclusivity, and connectivity, then, the latter necessarily enjoys the primacy of a first principle.

Connectivity and Ambiguity

It is absolutely crucial to see, though, that 'first principle' does not have here its usual acceptation as a primary element or determinate essence. To the contrary, it describes ambiguity that is basic. Although on the face of things it may seem otherwise, opposition takes its leading cue from the principle of identity. By projecting mutual exclusivity, opposition supposes perfect boundaries and therewith identity rather than difference. Put another way, dualism and monism are logically two sides of the same coin, functions of each other and the idea of self-containment or identity. It is only when opposition is also mitigated by connection that it allows for difference. Although it would appear to describe identity, connectivity always presupposes difference and boundaries that both separate and connect. To be sure, as connected to one another, things constitute a whole. But if this whole were absolute, it would suppose absolute boundaries and opposition rather than connection and fuzzy boundaries. As it is a matter of connectivity, the whole I have in mind, then, is always open and never circumscribable. That is to say, the holism of this whole is founded on difference rather than identity. Hence, the whole is describable only indefinitely, as 'that which is what it is' rather than as anything in particular or determinate.

When self and other are regarded simply in terms of opposition, as a dualism, they appear to stand to each other as equals, with nothing basic between them to mitigate their separate identities. But when they are regarded in terms of both opposition and connection, that is, as an ambiguity, the other-pole, regardless of the configuration of power, enjoys a certain superiority over the self-pole. Under this conception, whereby the relationship is understood as a tension, the pole of the other is not experienced as a determinate identity (as it is under dualism), but as peculiarly representative of fundamental ambiguity and originary difference. In effect, it is experienced in terms of the relationship between the two poles, rather than itself as a separate and distinct identity. The reason for the other's privileged position in this regard is that whereas the self (fragmented or not) is definitively keyed to the principle of identity, projecting itself as a thing in itself, logically the other can never be so circumscribed—when it is, it becomes self rather than other. To say, following the self-identification of the Wholly Other in the Hebrew bible, that the other 'is what it is' (*ehye asher ehyeh* or 'I am that I am') is to say exactly that the other cannot be identified using the 'is' of substantive identity, that it cannot be determined by a name, that it is irreducible to any be-ing or thing. The other is irreducible to self or anything that can be conceptually clarified or represented without fundamental contradiction. If it could be comprehended in this way, the way that exemplifies what we ordinarily mean by 'clarification', it would be not other but self.

Hence, the axiological priority of the other does not allow for ultimate justification of ethical decisions. If otherness cannot be unambiguously delineated, then neither can judgment based on the priority of otherness—that is, it cannot be justified once and for all. Its ambiguity means that precisely how one should choose is fundamentally unclear. Indeed, the basic ambiguity of otherness makes its nature as the good a matter of its dispensation of the capacity to determine the good. In other words, otherness is the good because it imposes on selves the need to determine their own good, that is, their own ends or their own nature. It thus imposes responsibility. The capacity to determine the good is given in the ambiguity of the other. The one ethical end we cannot do without, the one ethical end that is given us, is that of ultimate ambiguity or uncertainty as to our identity. In the absence of this end, there could be no humanity. Such ambiguity ensures that while human life entails constant judgment-making, final judgment remains ever suspended. Human life takes place within the space-time defined by this suspension.

The end of ambiguity constitutes the limits of our capacity to determine our own good. As such, of course, it is part and parcel of our mortality, for it is our mortality, and all that it entails (suffering, belatedness, fear, doubt, etc.), that makes our determinations meaningful to us. If our capacity to determine our own good were not limited, if all goods or ends were available to us without restriction, such that we had neither to suffer nor die, there would be no premium on choosing one good or end over any other. It would not matter which end one chose. If one could always also choose the choice forgone, no choice would in fact be surrendered, and choice would not be meaningful. Neither would time.[10]

Measuring the Good

Hence, at the same time ensuring that we must choose our own ends, basic ambiguity presents to us a good according to which we can measure the ethical value of our actions and decisions. But, again, if this good is essentially ambiguous, if it is a yardstick the dimensions of which are constitutionally inexact and therewith basically resistant to any calculus properly so-called, then how does it constitute a standard of judgment? To the extent that any decision seriously and comprehensively runs contrary to this good, we can be sure that that decision threatens human existence. But if this good is essentially indeterminate, how do we know that a decision has run up against it?

Clearly, I cannot with exactitude and in the particular determine the good, not without contradicting my thesis that the ultimate good is in fact basic ambiguity. But this limiting circumstance in itself signifies the way in which such a hypergood can provide ethical guidance, for it implies that any act or decision that smacks of the absolute is essentially life-threatening and therefore patently suspect. What follows from this is not, of course, that we must make all of our ethical decisions according to simply arbitrary standards. Were that the case, we would not have avoided absolutism but, to the contrary, embraced it in the form of an absolute relativism. Nor does it follow that we are being instructed always to take 'the middle of the road', when that old saw is understood in its everyday acceptation to mean (in terms of another old saw) 'moderation in all things'.[11] As defined by the hypergood of basic ambiguity, the 'middle' cuts an infinitely wide swath, to include, paradoxically, both ends and the middle. It is just that under such ontology of ambiguity, the ends can no longer make sense as cleanly detached and wholly opposed to each other, that is, as ends in themselves. Accordingly, what follows from taking basic ambiguity as the ultimate good is this: it is ethically sage to avoid as stupid (in the concrete sense bearing on violence unto death) any decision that smacks of absolutism in the sense entailed by the presumption of wholly fixed and certain goods.

In effect, the ultimate good of basic ambiguity serves as a kind of lodestar, a guide by which we can steer our ethical course. It is a guide that works, not by pointing directly at a fixed and final destination, but by indicating when we have deviated from the course in such a perilous way that the journey itself becomes critically jeopardized. The guide tells us when we are off course by sounding the alarm where and whenever our good ship (or ship of goods) veers toward an absolute end—an end that threatens to put an end to human existence, an end to journeying of this essentially ethical kind altogether. The basic good at stake, then, is the possibility of life, but life that in the living of it is no less a matter of self-determination than of biological continuity. That is to say, the good is the possibility of life that determines its own good.

I do not suppose that such a basically ambiguous guide, one that can offer no unconditional, sure, and determinate destination, can do much to address Derrida's feline dilemma: whether one ought to feed one's own cat or rather attend to the less fortunate cats in this world who lack a master to provide for them. This is not to say that this dilemma has no ethical bearing, but simply that the good of basic ambiguity has, as far as I can see, no cutting edge in its regard. It is worth pointing out, however, that by feeding his cat, Derrida is after all feeding *a* cat, an-other, even if that other is his own cat. He therefore not only has expressed a certain preference (for his cat over other cats) but also has performed a certain good, even if that good has, as Derrida makes plain, an ethical downside.

However, it is not difficult to find representative examples of the kind of broad but critical ethical instruction for which I argue here. Obviously, my interpretation of the evil presented by the Holocaust is keyed to the global absolutism of the Nazi project. Indeed, in my view, Nazism may be taken as a modern paradigm of politico-ethical absolutism, an absolutism that can be traced back to the utopian aspect and force of Enlightenment rationalism as well as to momentous epistemic turns, bearing on sacrifice, found in ancient Judeo-Christianity. In my reading of the Akedah, I located a dramatic mytho-logical image of such a turning, in which the stunning representation of sacrifice as absolutely selfless serves dialectically to encourage a phenomenological shift toward the hermetic closure of the self as well as to sanction the possibility of sacrifice that targets the other and is anything but sacrificial in the proper sense. However, in line with what it means to be on course ethically, I also found in that story a contrary representation. According to this representation, anathematic sacrifice and unimpeachable perfection in sacrifice, mirror images of each other, are both condemned in view of the nihilism they project. By implication, this representation may be taken to recommend imperfect but not absolute economy of sacrifice—my 'middle' or nondualist course.

But let me conclude here by showing that the sort of ethical foundation I have isolated and identified, a non-foundational one, can make sense even of the powerful ethical judgment, bearing on the Gospel according to Matthew, that Derrida himself insinuates in his argument against ethics in the received sense. This judgment goes well beyond the Gospel itself, of course, to implicate Christianity's constitutional depic-tion of the Jews. Derrida does not fail to provide an explication for his judgment that Matthew's characterization of the Jews as the representative economizers or destroyers of spirit makes a jarring irony. In the example of the Akedah, Abraham sets out to sacrifice his most precious possession, the life of his son Isaac or life itself, apparently without any expectation of return. In the face of this example, Matthew's perorations on sacrifice as an exchange of worldly for other-worldly goods overtly and reductively equates sacrifice or transcendence to economy and immanence. Matthew's hypocrisy is twofold: first, he accuses the 'others' of a debasement that he himself devises; second, he commits the debasement, all the while claiming for himself the representation of sacrifice as wholly untainted by economic measures.

Plainly, Derrida is presenting Matthew's hypocrisy as his reason for judgment here. But underlying this mighty hypocrisy, to make my point about the ethical yardstick of self-and-other in relation to absolutisms, lies a globally ambitious religious self-cer-tainty in virtue of which the other is positively excluded as absolute evil. In other words, Matthew's claim to certain truth in matters of the salvation of the self is built on the total exclusion of the other, the stupidity or lethal promise of which has been kept only too well down through the ages and especially in the twentieth century, humankind's century of atrocity. Derrida might be taken to allude to some such observation when, at the end of his book, he cites, as follows, Nietzsche's ferocious critique of Christianity and its founding (according to Nietzsche, economistic) theme of perfect sacrifice (Derrida 1995: 113–24): "The justice which began with the maxim, 'Everything can be paid off, everything must be paid off,' ends with connivance ... at the escape of those who cannot pay to escape—it ends, like every good thing on earth, by *destroying itself* ... The self-destruction of Justice ...! we know the pretty name it calls itself—*Grace* ...! it remains, as is obvious, the privilege ... of the strongest, better still, their super-law." Derrida (ibid.: 112–13) himself states: "The genealogy of responsibility that Nietzsche refers to in *The Genealogy of Morals* as 'the long history of the origin of responsibility ...' also describes the history of moral and religious conscience—a history of cruelty and sacrifice, of the holocaust even (these are Nietzsche's words), of fault as debt or obligation ... a history of the economy of 'the contractual relationship' between creditors ... and debtors ... These relations appear as soon as there exist subjects under law in general ... and they point back in turn 'to the primary forms of purchase, sale, barter, and trade.'"

These unrestrained condemnations ring all too true. History shows that under the admonishment of perfect redemption and sacrifice (the "everything" in Nietzsche's "everything must be paid off"), we can expect dire perversity: instead of justice, justice denied; instead of grace, might; instead of responsibility, other-sacrifice and non-answerability; and instead of politico-economic fair play and egalitarianism, calculating and extreme differential advantage. But despite their diametric lines and tone of hopelessness, I cite these condemnations in the interest of remediation. My ontological argument leads me to think that notions of responsibility, the good, and sacrifice are not only worthwhile but also unavoidable in human affairs. Although these principles (as Derrida shows) can never be perfectly secured for the good (in contradistinction to power), it is onto-epistemological dualism that calamitously weights things on the side of their perversion.

Derrida's pre-eminent deconstructive exercise is to demonstrate that by their very nature these notions are beset with aporias, and that as principles they cannot be faithfully discharged without at the same time being violated. My primary interest, though, is in rethinking these notions in order to put them on a better footing, one that takes into account the great force of demonstrations like Derrida's, but finds that the aporetic condition, while fundamental, is nonetheless subject to positive as well as negative mediation. Where dualism prevails as an organizing a priori—that is, where self and world are 'naturally' predicated on the basis of mutual exclusivity—the negative enjoys a definite primacy; for example, conceived of in terms of perfection, the concept of sin, to remain meaningful, is bound to produce perfect sinners. It is my supposition that were nondualism to prove so irresistibly convincing as to become an ontological pre-conception, a synthetic a priori, such that self and world would be constituted primarily as matters of relativity (Heidegger's Dasein or 'being-there'), notions such as ethics, responsibility, and sacrifice would be seen not solely as functions of power. In this case, although the suspension of judgment would abide, as therefore would the good's relativity to power, the good would not be reducible to power, and we would no longer be at a total loss as to the good. In effect, the good would be relative also to itself, in the form of life defined as determinative of its own good, and beyond that, as the Other and otherness that makes possible this ethical form of life. In the event of such an enabling good, it becomes possible in truth to speak truth to power, as power would be relative not only to itself but also to the good.

Allow me to illustrate what I mean, drawing on Derrida's (1995: 95ff.) critique of Matthew, and mine of the Akedah. Bouncing Matthew's biblical lesson of sacrifice off that of the Akedah, a story in which Derrida finds a representation of sacrificial giving that he cannot fault, the French philosopher is enabled to reveal in Matthew's Gospel a duplicitous economism and spiteful exclusionism. As regards the Akedah, I have argued—using Nuer sacrifice in counterpoint, and despite this biblical story's redactors and the majority of its interpreters—that it too may be read as a narrative of self-aggrandizement and murderous intent on the part of Abraham, who is charged by God with making the gift (of death) to the Other. Both critiques, Derrida's and mine, proceed according to reason, making their points logically and by means of careful comparative analysis. But at the back of the reasoned argumentation, both erect their censure on grounds of the positive presumption of openness to the other/Other. In both cases, this presumption of something beyond power and self-regard serves as a guiding good by virtue of which one can arrive at an ultimately uncertain but ethically compelling judgment. The judgment remains finally uncertain because the validity of this good cannot abolish the essential condition of judgmental suspension and the resultant relativism. This much is shown by the consideration that, by appealing to the same sense of the good and using the same discourse of reasoned analysis but different comparative cases, the two critiques arrive at exactly opposing interpretations of the ethical character of the Akedah.

What the good in question does do, however, is relativize relativism, thus opening it to the paradoxical possibility of a relative absolute. That is to say, this good—actually a hypergood, since it enables the construction of different goods—makes it possible to take, for the time (of) being, decisions the moral force of which differ from one another by degrees, according to their relative nearness to this good, a distance measured through reason. For instance, I have argued that Hitler's death-camp project tends to be so easy to judge as downright evil, not because it failed to entertain a good, but rather because, on the basis of rational reflection, the good it projected, an absolute absolute, cannot but be assessed as a complete negation of the one good that allows distinctively human existence: the hypergood of relative selflessness or openness to the other, not on behalf of the *Volk* as the nation-state (relative to other peoples, a consequentially selfish and exclusionary good), but of otherness as such. The good of ethics, then, is the making of man as that creature who makes himself by virtue of this good; it is the good of living as a self-constructed form of life, an existence above, but intimately tied to, the sort of life that all living beings enjoy.

One suspects, though, that it is no accident that in interpreting Matthew, Derrida appeals implicitly to the good of openness. In point of fact, his 'deconstruction' may be said virtually to entail this good. Behind Derrida's teaching to deconstruct received and taken-for-granted concepts and ideas is the implicit understanding that by doing so, we prescind from them, undercutting their capacity to foreclose our future. In so doing, we keep ourselves open to what is yet to come, namely, that which can be alluded to but not known.[12]

Chapter 14

ANTHROPOLOGY AND THE GENERATIVE PRIMACY OF MORAL ORDER

What else should our lives be but a continual series of beginnings, of painful settings out into the unknown, pushing off from the edges of consciousness into the mystery of what we have not yet become, except in dreams that blow in from out there bearing the fragrance of islands we have not yet sighted in our waking hours, as in voyaging sometimes the first blossoming branches of our next landfall come bumping against the keel, even in the dark, whole days before the real land rises to meet us.

— David Malouf, *An Imaginary Life*

The Rationality of Generation

The Case of the Kibbutz

In *Two Kinds of Rationality* (Evens 1995), I demonstrated that in Kibbutz Timem, the Israeli collective in which I did 20 months of field research, the idea of the generations constitutes a primordial choice. As such, this idea forms its own end and cannot be measured intelligibly in terms of rational choice. A primordial choice obtains exemplarily between cause and reason, and is thus irreducibly creative. Ultimately, therefore, it can be understood only in terms of itself. But the consideration that a primordial choice is finally inaccessible to the logic of instrumentalism should not be taken to mean that such a choice cannot be reasonably assessed as to its relative worth. Were that the case, the conscious choice between one form of life and another would be not merely in large degree a question of preference but absolutely arbitrary—in which case, of course, power would be granted a free hand.

As against this nihilist picture, a picture that seems to enjoy in today's intellectual world the same wide, almost magical currency as have the ideas of profit created from nothing and a self-transparent self, I argue for a form of rationality 'higher', in the sense of 'better', than the instrumental kind—a value-rationality. My argument is predicated not on any particular end, but on the end of having ends. Obviously, an end the point of which is the continuing creation of ends does not admit of an absolute distinction between means and ends—it amounts to, in Agamben's formulation, means without end. Put in a way to address more plainly the postmodern critique, my argument derives its principal force from a foundation, but one that is precisely not a foundation in the received (positivist) sense of the term. I am talking about ethics, an encompassing or hypercharged foundation that promotes the ongoing proliferation of foundations.

Taking my cue from Kibbutz Timem's ethnography, my discussion in *Two Kinds of Rationality* concentrated on mythic rationality as a representative form of value-rationality. Its unthinking openness to the Other makes of mythic rationality an organon bent primarily toward the ends limit of the means-ends continuum. However, precisely because its artlessness impairs without cause the possibility of the development of choice, mythic rationality ought not be the end of value-rationality. This is the case, even if value-rationality must ever begin in mythic thought.

The case study at the heart of *Two Kinds of Rationality* focuses on a proposal to change the rule of voting in Kibbutz Timem's General Assembly from open to secret ballot. The General Assembly is the institutional nerve center of the community's direct democracy. In this radically collective social order, the proposal evoked the morally charged distinction between the general or public and the particular or private will, and it split the community according to the difference between expedient action and ideological principle. It thus brought about a crisis of legitimacy and thematized the self-perception of a 'fall' away from the ideal state of things. The proposal to adopt the secret ballot grew out of an evident failure of attendance at the General Assembly, and as a solution to this problem of democratic participation, it struck many as running directly contrary to the basic principles of the collective. Although the state of fallenness was understood to result from advancing social differentiation, more particularly it was defined in terms of conflict between the generations, the youthful generation being held to account. Yet there can be no question that, from a strictly empirical point of view, whereas the former explanation was sound, the latter was tenable only insofar as it served to instantiate the growing social differentiation. In fact, the conflict divided only imperfectly along the lines of generational difference, and the growth of internal heterogeneity in the community reflected many differences other than that of generation, for example, labor branch, neighborhood, friendship network, ties outside the community, joining group, age-peer group, etc. (Evens 1995: esp. chap. 4).

The case study raises the question, then, of the rationality of the kibbutz members' choice of definitions of their situation. My answer to that question is that although an exacting empiricist account would have been more correct in that it would have corresponded more precisely to the facts of the matter, the explanation 'conflict between the generations' was truer in the sense that it better met the community's moral demands of the situation. Timem's members were caught in a crisis of legitimacy, brought on by the notable degree to which the collective had become internally heterogeneous. The amount of heterogeneity occasioned social conditions, such as the failure of democratic participation, which conspicuously belied the community's key ideological premise of resolving the contradiction between the individual and society. In effect, the perfectibilism of the community's approach to the self-other relationship, what I have called the human condition of double boundenness, had come, ironically, to exacerbate the stultifying effects of the bind.

The problem confronting the members was not simply how to increase democratic attendance, but how to do so without undermining their thematic self-identity as exceptionally moral beings, above and beyond what was regarded as the typical standard for human communities. In accordance with the ideological goal of synthesis, as is summed up in the kibbutz precept of 'voluntary collectivism' (a notion very like Rousseau's 'general will'), this self-identity was predicated as critically on other-regard as on autonomous individual choice. While acknowledgment of the increasing social differentiation of the membership did a sound job of describing the brute facts of Timem's development, it could not address the moral questions raised by that development. Or, rather, it sanctioned the tackling of these questions predominantly in a purely instrumental way—as if they had nothing to do with irresponsible acts on the part of members—and thus threatened to sap them of their moral definition. Therefore, the superior empiricist account of matters could not sustain the community's explicit definition of itself in terms of other-regard, that is, in terms that seemed irreducible to matters of expedience. The notion of conflict between the generations, on the other hand, irrefutably could, even as it captured synecdochically the more inclusive condition of social diversification.

In its chiastic image of a creature (son) fashioned after its creator (father), 'generation' defines an autonomous and creative self whose autonomy and creativity are conditioned fundamentally by dependence and creatureliness. It thus describes a world whose creatures are bound to choose or create, on behalf of the Other, for the sake of themselves. Such a doubly bound universe can obtain only by a deferment, a 'time' that is made by the conduct of having to run continually between two vital ends, now toward the self, now toward the other. Plainly, this universe, although it admits of the possibility of a well-developed self, not to mention an uninhibited instrumental consciousness, is, before it is anything else, a matter of other-regard and practice as ethics.

Thus, by defining their situation in terms of conflict between the generations, Timem's members were enabled to reaffirm, in the face of the community's growing social differentiation and at the risk of instrumental reductionism, the emphatically moral character of their self-identity: the creation of a 'new man', for whom the other must take pride of place. As a result, at a stroke, they both liberated themselves (their *selves*) and acknowledged the inevitability of the contingent march of events. Rather than collapsing self and other into each other in a triumph of the general will, the liberation worked by respecting the difference (asymmetry or heterogeneity) between self and other. Another way of seeing this result is as follows: by embracing 'generation' as a definition of the situation, the members replaced, at least in practice, their ideological commitment to surmount contradiction with the goal of coping, on an ethical basis, with the double boundenness of human existence.

Myth, History, and Ethical Rationality

Kibbutz Timem's resort to a mythic rationality therefore displays a sage, if transpersonal and not unalterable, reason. At this juncture, however, it may have become apparent that the idea of generation, although founded in myth, exceeds the measure of mythic rationality. Whereas mythic rationality proper gives short shrift to the individual subject as such, the biblical myth of Genesis is focused, diacritically, no less on the possibility of self-development than on the primacy of the Other. The generational relationship pictured by the myth stresses the son's emergence as a self by virtue of the father's otherness; the axiological primacy of the father is registered in the son's belatedness.

The direct way in which the myth of Genesis transcends its own mythic nature to comprehend non-mythical consciousness is perhaps most readily seen in relation to the treatment of time. Whereas the creation of humankind takes place in a kind of quasi-historical time, a sempiternal cosmic order in which innocence reigns and death has no dominion, the expulsion from the paradisiacal garden initiates a processing of the cosmic order, thus constructing a temporality in which creaturely choice takes hold and death becomes the rule. We may say, with Eric Voegelin (1956), that the myth 'documents' a shift of forms of consciousness, from "order" to "history," the latter form having been peculiarly (although perhaps not uniquely) a creation of Israel.[1] In this myth, both kinds of temporality are counted in terms of the generations (*toldoth*)—"the generations of the heavens and earth" and "the generations of Adam" (ibid.: 168ff.).

Voegelin demonstrates by means of linguistic evidence a striking consideration—that the notion of generation undergoes a change of meaning as it bears on the two kinds of temporality. In relation to the generations of the heavens and the earth, the term means creative activity, whereas in relation to the generations of Adam, it means procreation. Moreover, "the reader will not doubt that the *toldoth* of Adam continue the *toldoth* of heavens and earth. The authors intended the meanings of creation and procreation to merge in a co-operative process; the order of being is meant to arise from the creative initiative of God and the procreative response of the creation" (Voegelin 1956: 170).[2]

The point I want to make is that, as a myth, Genesis is itself an admonitory interpretation of the transformational shift from a mythic to a potentially instrumental or self-involved rationality. It is a deep account of what it feels like to be *self*-conscious. As such, it responds, with a phenomenological and aesthetic sensitivity perhaps unequaled in Western thought, to the question of how it is possible to get from a state of naiveté, in which self-consciousness is only rudimentarily developed, to a state in which consciousness becomes acutely aware of itself. However, although it undeniably pictures the resulting consciousness as raised, it plainly serves notice that the autonomous self is given by its nature to overextend itself, and that it remains ever subject to the heteronomy of the initial state.

In effect, Genesis may be read to recommend neither a mythic nor an instrumental rationality. Rather, it is given over to the promotion of a form of reason based on the need to choose responsibly—which is to say, to choose to be chosen. This interpretation is not exactly in keeping with the received interpretation, which, as over and against the idea of choice as a good, emphasizes the story's denouement as a fall. In the present reading, the kind of rationality at stake respects the double bind as a condition of human life, encouraging the rise of the self as above all conscious of its own final limitedness. In a word, we are talking about ethics or value-rationality.

Therefore, as a definition of Timem's situation, 'generation' is eminently reasonable. From the perspective of rigorous empiricism, so inexact a definition fails to do justice to the brute facts, mistaking in part the ideal for the real. But from the standpoint of a primordially chosen ethical universe, the definition in question transumes the facts, recognizing them as moral and thus reinforming them with moral force. In effect, 'generation' served to redefine the very facticity of the facts, showing them as selected no less by moral than by causal forces.

Nevertheless, although it drew attention away from the facts as positive and ineluctable, somewhat misleadingly throwing blame onto one particular category of members as against another, 'generation' did not exactly mask the contradiction underlying Timem's troubled state, namely, the contradiction of the comprehensive clash between the kibbutz principle of pragmatic social endeavor, on the one hand, and that of a union between the individual and society, on the other. Unlike, say, a definition such as 'witchcraft', that of 'generation' does not acknowledge moral force simply at the expense of empirical understanding. Rather, by featuring the development of the autonomous subject as a categorically moral being, it also features the self-critical subject presupposed by systematic empirical inquiry.

Therefore, arguably the definition 'generation' moved, if only tacitly and temporarily, to open to critical view the principled incongruity underlying the development of the kibbutz. Because in practice it replaced the ideological ambition of synthesis with a definition of the human condition as basically ambiguous, it brought the kibbutz closer to making that change in principle. This does not mean that it made the change inevitable, nor does it mean that had the members stuck fast with the more empirically valid definition of their situation, they would have absolutely precluded the moral one. But it does suggest that they would have eroded it, if only incrementally, by making it that much less relevant. Defining the situation in terms of conflict between the generations reiterated the relevance of moral definition; it served to remind the members that the self-development making so much difference in their social life depended, fundamentally, on the difference they themselves could make by way of responsible choice. Thus, the members' selection of a definition represented the consequential and omnipresent choice between choosing and not. It thematized the relentless need to choose and, correlatively, the fundamental priority of ethics.

Universality

The rich way in which the idea of generation, as it has been explicated here, is attuned to what I have called the human condition raises the issue of the universality of the story of Genesis. While I have indeed argued from, and on behalf of, a kind of universal, it is certainly not a universal in the received sense, the sense that grew out of dualistic thinking. Obviously, the thesis of the human condition as a double bind projects, in place of a positive foundation, basic ambiguity, an ethically gravid in between. The universal in question is, then, to borrow a usage (from Derrida), not so much a presence as an absence; it is, to raid still another turn of phrase (now from Levinas), otherwise than being. Although I do not accept that the story of Genesis constitutes a universal, it seems that the deep and subtle manner in which it expresses 'the universal' is exceptional.[3]

The comparative interpretation of Genesis and the Dinka myth of creation, undertaken in chapter 9, is suggestive here. Although the Dinka myth also pictures human being as a dynamic tension, and thematizes choice as deviancy and responsibility, it does not highlight choice *as such*—it does not feature the choice between choosing and not. By bringing into high relief the very idea of choice, Genesis puts an exquisite edge on the human condition, penetrating even more deeply its tensile nature. However, the remarkable hermeneutic power of the story in this regard should not be taken to mean that the story has transcended context and particularism, but that even contexts have contexts. By focusing so sharply, so penetratingly, on the manner in which humans present themselves in the double-bind dynamic, the story does not make a bottom line (an Atlas of a turtle, so to speak, to recall Geertz's famous Indonesian piece of deconstructionistic wisdom about foundations), but rather, in a context of imposing generality, points to the inscrutable bottom line.

The idea here of contexts within contexts suggests that something can be more or less foundational without, however, being absolutely so (cf. Rotman 1987). The idea recalls the notion, adumbrated earlier, of 'formal priority'. But whereas that notion is based on logical relations, what I have in mind now supposes an order of phenomenological priority. It includes the proposition that although what comes second is not reducible to what comes first, it must somehow express the latter. More comprehensively, though, it holds that any human creation, including logic (cf. Quine 1953), is conditioned, and that some conditions are more foundational, in the sense of being, rather than fixed and inalterable, more fundamental and constituting than others. This holds true even as regards the constitution of synthetic a priori and primordial choices, themselves endowed with great constituting force. For an example of such phenomenological primacy, I cite Merleau-Ponty's axial thesis that since embodiment is a necessary condition of perception, it must somehow inform all human creation. The body, then, conceived of, not as a thing (ironically, a conception based on the possibility of a disembodied perspective, a view from nowhere), but as the blind spot or aperture that enables perception to occur, enjoys a profound—although still not absolute—degree of foundational significance in respect of human activity.

The point about the relative foundational nature of Genesis can be given substantive force by reference to the way in which the particularism of the story is subject to deconstruction. This particularism is given in a number of ways, but perhaps none more conspicuous, at least in today's intellectual environment, as in the patriarchal relegation of the female principle to second fiddle. The story's picture of Eve as a concupiscent temptress has underwritten centuries of male chauvinism in Western society (Lerner 1986). Yet by referring the evident degradation of Eve to the story's own critical emphasis on the situated, and therefore limited, nature of all things human, the significance of the female principle in the story can be reversed.[4]

In its depiction of Eve as specially linked to the serpent and, correlatively, peculiarly responsible for the so-called fall, the story depends on the account of the serpent as enjoying godlike knowledge and of Eve as the principle of vitality rather than morbidity—she is the 'mother of all that lives'. Yet the story fails to address how so lowly a creature as the serpent can be omniscient and how so 'easy' a figure as Eve can be the universal mother. Clearly, these attributes of Eve and her cunningly twisted partner insinuate that there is between the figure of Eve and the figure of the story's first principle, the Creator, a representative identity. Thus, in its explicit thrust, the story appears to conceal or repress an implicit image of Eve as a first rather than second principle.

Of course, as Derrida has amply shown, any story can be deconstructed. The point here, though, is that Genesis does not simply yield to deconstruction but specifically teaches it.[5] What is astonishing is that the story provides, as its central lesson, its own rule of deconstruction—in political terms, a rule of ordered anarchy. The story is there to remind humans that although their endeavors (whether we are talking about world building or story telling) exhibit a godly creativity, they are always subject to revision by the Other. The richly formulated referral of full-blown self-fashioning to otherness, a prescription for ethical deconstruction, is what makes this story so extraordinary.

The Body of Eve and the Female Principle in the Kibbutz

In light of this discussion of Genesis, I return now to the kibbutz. If 'generation' evokes, and the feminine principle enjoys, an especially representative role in respect of the Other, then, notwithstanding the 'father-son' bias of their idiom, Kibbutz Timem's members were picturing themselves in terms of the feminine principle. In selecting 'generation' to define their situation, they were unwittingly projecting their revolutionary community as pre-eminently feminine in spirit.

The most conspicuous independent evidence for this conjecture is the persistent preoccupation of the kibbutz with the so-called *baayat hachavera* or 'problem of the female member'. This social problem has been the focus of a great deal of debate in the kibbutz, including kibbutz federation and inter-federation conferences. In brief, the problem is that whereas the kibbutz was ideologically predicated on a goal of gender equality, it is a prevailing perception in the community that the goal was not met. For instance, the facts that women have not shared equally in positions of authority and that the great majority of women work in the 'service' rather than 'productive' branches of the economy have been taken as evidence of this shortfall (cf. Bowes 1989; Spiro 1979; Tiger and Shepher 1975). Thus, women are implicitly designated as a major and stubborn impediment to the achievement of the ideology's design—in other words, like the sons, they have been perceived as a representative form of the Other.

Interestingly enough in this connection, so has the body. As a profoundly moral endeavor the success of which is predicated on physical labor, the kibbutz has always shown a certain intolerance for physical frailty. For example, I observed a number of instances of individuals who were ashamed of being sick, and I was told that women who cried out from pain while giving birth were found lacking in courage. Given moral perfectibilism, the body is bound to represent an intolerable drag on the spirit. Like self-interest and the separate will of the individual, the body is implicitly regarded as an obstacle whose contingent character needs to be overcome by moral exertion.

But, to come to the point, the feminine principle and embodiment enjoy a very special association in the phenomenology of the kibbutz. In addressing the issue of sex-role differentiation in this community, Yonina Talmon-Garber (1965) stressed the way in which child bearing interferes with the aim of equal work for women. Leaving aside for the moment the question of how biological difference affects the possibility of social equality, what is of interest is the perception, which the kibbutzniks undoubtedly share with Talmon, that the 'problem' resides in the gender-unique generative capacity of women. Women are being represented, then, especially in terms of their reproductive anatomy, which in turn is thought of as an obstacle to the realization of the ideological vision. Thus, as outstanding representations of the uncertainty of the Other, the body and the feminine are intimately linked to each other.

For all of this biologism, however, the depreciation of the feminine principle has the force of a phenomenological Trojan horse. The self-evidently ambiguous way in which the female anatomy embodies embodiment resists reduction to the terms of procreation. Rather, it inscribes a centerless center, a gravid negativity. Her anatomy bodies forth, in a way hard not to notice, a veritable (Merleauian) image of the body as the blind spot enabling all perception. Therefore, the feminine is bound to represent, at one level of consciousness or another, not only procreation but also creation: it embodies 'generation' in a way that spans, to recall Voegelin's (1956) phrase, the "creative initiative" of the other and the "procreative response of the creation."

It would seem, then, that in appealing to 'generation' as a definition of the situation, Timem's members were counting themselves, in their moral capacity, as pre-eminently female and as other. I venture that this remarkable image of the body social constitutes the deepest wellspring of the idea of the kibbutz—a revolutionary endeavor devoted to the ethical regeneration of not only Judaism but also humankind. In light of this conjecture, the notably patriarchal idiom of 'generation' in the kibbutz may be taken to betray a powerful anxiety over the felt dependency on women, a dependency of vitality and creativity. Similarly, the same anxiety probably stands behind the community's apparent tendency to hold the feminine principle, rather than ideology, responsible for the failure to live up to the goal of gender equality.

Anthropology as Ethics

'Greek/Jew Is Jew/Greek': Philosophy vs. Ethics

This discussion of Genesis has a strikingly provocative implication for the discipline of anthropology. The interpretation of the story pictures the meaning of 'generation' as keyed to the thesis of the generative primacy of otherness. It describes the human condition as above all a matter of ethics, and, correlatively, it commends appeal to the other as the most vital way to realize the capacity for choice.

Openness to the other is an axial motivation of anthropological research. However, for all the anthropological talk about ethnocentrism, just what it means to be thus open is a tough question—so tough, in fact, that the intellectual evolution of the discipline may be read in terms of answers to it. As long as there is no immediate need to do justice to the range of variation or analytical subtleties of the particulars of the scholarship in question, it is fair to say that the prevailing answers have been two: whereas initially openness meant trying to understand the other by assimilating it to the Occidental 'self' in its rationalist mode, today it means trying to do the same but by assimilating it to the Occidental 'self' in its romantic or symbological mode. In view of this shift— from rationalist to symbolic analysis as the privileged basis for comparative anthropology—the discipline first saw the other as intellectually inferior, and then, by denying any real difference (that is, by seeing such difference as simply a question of figurative language), as intellectually equal. Either way, though, and this is the main point, the other is absorbed into the self—the other's otherness is never truly acknowledged. The discipline may be inherently outward bound, but no matter what befalls it during its journey, it almost always manages to return home.

Underlying this grand intellectual self-deception is the paradigm that delivered the discipline into being and according to which the discipline continues to work. The paradigm is scientific, of course, having the goal of arriving systematically at the objective truth. More roundly, the paradigm is philosophical, for the language of science is philosophy. That is to say, the language is Greek, having been forged as an articulation of a certain epochal experience that took place in the early Aegean civilizations. I am referring here to the Hellenic revolution of being, from a mythic consciousness, in which humanity is only weakly differentiated from the cosmos, to a consciousness in which man is well-differentiated as an intellectual being.[6] Considered as the reflective expression of this leap of being, philosophy denotes the love (*philio*) of wisdom (*sophon*) and accordingly prescribes a search for the truth. The truth of something is that which the thing is in itself. It is not how the thing appears, since then there would be no truth but only the plurality of things as given to the senses. In other words, in this perspective, truth is the one, not the many, and it is wholly independent of the observer and the act of identifying it.

Plainly, philosophy is predicated on an act of disengagement from the world as we find it and on a rigid distinction between subject and object. Nevertheless, in this Greek tongue, the truth is ascertainable only through appeal to one's own self—more precisely, through a specific faculty of the Soul, the intellect (*Nous*). With the assistance of logic (*logos*), the intellect is enabled to determine the true nature of being. It should be clear that the determination of the truth is not a question of the influence of society on the soul, but rather of the soul's direct relationship with the One. Indeed, in this scheme of things, society, because it creates in humans desires and appetites that run contrary to wisdom and the right or just order of things, tends to be an unhealthy influence on the soul. Put another way, society as such presents the many, not the one. (As Plato redeems it in *The Republic*, revamping it according to the idea of the good, society is transformed into the relationship between the individual's soul and the divine intellect, and in this sense it is deprived of the genuinely social.) Hence, philosophy (by contrast to myth) has its beginning in the soul's resistance to the destructive force of society.

The overall point is this: the philosophical pursuit of the truth, when considered in light of the origin of this pursuit, reduces to the self's examination of itself. Although philosophy proposes to direct its investigations outside, its searchlight is originarily oriented inward. Not surprisingly, then, in principle all it can find is the same. Indeed, the very philosophical idea of arrival at the truth presupposes reduction to the personalized self or the same. Put from the other side, if the only genuine knowledge (*episteme*) is knowledge of the thing itself, that is, of identity, then the relationship we call knowing constitutes a violent suppression of the other. Inasmuch as the discipline of anthropology has its origin, as all science does, in this epistemological consciousness, it too is bound to find in its defining subject matter—that is, the other or the different—only the selfsame.

Of course, it is not the case that so reflective a pursuit as philosophy failed to feel the dogmatic constriction imposed by this problem. Kant in particular, in his three famous critiques, employs reason to examine its own limits, and thus, pointedly in the third critique (*Critique of Judgment*), manages to direct himself to the 'outside'—the other/Other rather than the self—that conditions the possibility of limited or relative selfhood. Carrying on Kant's involutionary movement, so-called postmodernist thought has definitively engaged this utterly axial and enormously consequential problem of the Western mind-set. Because postmodernism is itself peculiarly an outgrowth of the very way of thinking it aims to deconstruct, the struggle has about it a confounding air of heroism as well as futility, of tricksterism as well as great depth. In the present relevance, the work of two postmodernists in particular, Derrida and Levinas (neither of whom thinks much of the term), is especially instructive.

Both of these scholars have explicitly linked their respective assaults on philosophy to a remedial idea of the other, and both have discussed this idea in virtue of what Matthew Arnold (1925: chap. 4) spoke of as the opposing forces of Hellenism and Hebraism. The problem for both thinkers is how to locate a site from which it is possible to question radically philosophical discourse. Since, however, the only language properly available for the act of questioning is the language of philosophical discourse itself, the problem is intellectually punishing, with a severity that can only be described as Sisyphean. Indeed, as Derrida (Derrida and Kearny 1984) points out, the very search for an-other site from which to discourse deals a blow to the critical endeavor, since the substantive connotation of the notion of site or place (*topos*) is a determination of the ontology under assault. Preferring to rely on certain logically disturbing writings in the literary tradition instead, Derrida rejects as unsatisfactory both the Greek and the Jewish tradition as non-sites from which to mount his critique. Still, he regards it as "essential" to think through the issue posed by the relationship between these two traditions, and, more importantly, he "feels" that the other he steadfastly seeks at the limits of philosophy has as its model the Jew, "that is, the Jew-as-other" (ibid.: 107).

Levinas, on the other hand, has unequivocally concentrated a lifetime of critical effort on the task of recuperating the Hebrew tradition from the Greek. He has done so, however, not in order to avoid speaking Greek—to go home, as it were—but, on the contrary, to find a remedy to the 'allergy' of Greek language to the Other. Levinas's (1986) opposing of the story of Abraham to the myth of Odysseus neatly describes the point of his endeavor. Whereas Odysseus leaves his home of Ithaca only to come back in the end, Abraham departs from Ur for an unknown land, never to return. In other words, the respective itineraries of these two culture-heroes express the difference between arriving at the same and going always toward the Other.[7]

This difference could not be more meaningful. The image of departing only to return home conveys an attitude of round reductionism. The attitude projects the other as that which must be converted/colonized into the identity of the self—or, better, into the self as an identity. Plainly, there is in this attitude no sense of the self as truly open to the other; nor is there genuine acknowledgement of or respect for the other as other. By contrast, the image of a radical departure, a leaving home forever, takes otherness very seriously as the condition of the self. But in this image, the self is no longer conceivable as something self-enclosed, a thing in itself; rather it must be construed as a journey, always between places, never a place of its own. Such a self is intrinsically open to the Other. It is not a self secure in its own constructions, but one (un)founded in the fundamental uncertainty of the Other.

Levinas (e.g., 1991: chap. 5) speaks of this Abrahamic relationship between self and other as irreparably asymmetrical. By this he means that the relationship does not reduce to the self—which is to say, it cannot be totalized. He also means that there is a difference of level between self and other, in favor of the latter. Although inextricably linked, the two parties are not reciprocals of each other, since the self owes itself to the other in a way that is ultimately irreversible. Throughout the present work, I have used the notion of hierarchical encompassment to describe this kind of basically ambiguous relationship. I expect that Levinas would have found my usage objectionable on the grounds that an encompassment relationship implies identity. However, although such a relationship makes possible the self's construal of itself as an identity or totality, and therewith the idea of an absolute whole, in fact the collapse of difference implicit in the notion of encompassment can occur in one direction only—the direction of the Other. And precisely because the Other is all-encompassing, because it includes what it is not, it cannot be fruitfully conceived of in terms of positive limit boundaries. On the contrary, the whole it makes, far from being absolute, can only be considered as, to use Levinas's (ibid.) turn of phrase, otherwise than being (or than self or identity). At any rate, whether we employ 'asymmetry' or 'hierarchy', the meaning in question describes a relationship of creation in which the creature-self is endowed with the creator-other's capacity to create, but always to a degree limited by the creature-self's indelible belatedness.

As an upshot of this picture of self and other, Levinas and Derrida may be read to espouse a construction on reality as fundamentally open rather than closed, an order keyed primarily to difference rather than identity and to ethical rather than instrumental rationality. In socio-pragmatic terms, an order of this kind suggests a polity based on a principle of well-ordered anarchy—which is, I suggest, about as good a guess as any as to what Derrida has in mind when he prophesies a "democracy yet to come" (cited in McGowan 1991: 115). But the notion of ordered anarchy, a term familiar to anthropologists,[8] flows directly from Levinas's (1987: chap. 8) characterization of the subject as "responsible for its responsibility," and from this profound thinker's call for a revolutionary change of consciousness, from philosophy to ethics.

The Odyssey and the Exodus: The Practice of Anthropology

How, then, does this account of the difference between an odyssey and an exodus bear on the question of the implication of 'generation' for doing anthropology? Clearly, the journey of Abraham has a great deal in common with the biblical story that, on the face of things, has done more than any other to shape Western political thought and action, namely, the Exodus (Walzer 1985). Both stories tell of a leap of being into an essentially open or uncertain future and therefore of deliverance into freedom. But it is hard to think of a biblical departure more radical—both as regards the nature of the locational change and the representative character of the persons changing locations—than that of Adam and Eve from the Garden of Eden.

The first two humans move from the 'inside' of God's immediate providence to the 'outside' of a world in which death, but nothing else, not even death's 'when', is certain. The movement has all the vitality of a birthing, and it opens out onto a life of fearful insecurity. But at the same time as they move from an inside to an outside, Adam and Eve go in the opposite direction, from an outside to an inside: by becoming demonstrably self-conscious, they develop themselves as their own inside. As a result, having been put on the spot or set up by the Other to take a fall, they become acutely responsible for their own responsibility—they become actively moral creatures. They thus owe the intensity of their human distinction to the very exilic existence that ensures their insecurity. Although they have in a sense gone out from the other into themselves, their self-movement, a dramatic and uncertain journey of the generations, always remains mortgaged to the other. The attempt to repay this mortgage in full, as is terrifyingly expressed in the story of Isaac's binding, risks bringing Generation—that is, the passing of the generations—to a precipitous close.

As I see it, the discipline of anthropology, like the other social sciences, aims to study how people move. What distinguishes anthropology, however, is that it intends to do this by taking the perspective of the other. This distinction, as I argued earlier, gives anthropology an advantage in the field of critical thought. By definition, anthropology is engaged uniquely in the postmodern pursuit of an-other site, a place of otherness, from which to begin (re)thinking. The genial implication of 'generation'—in its sense as movement toward otherness—for the practice of anthropology is just this: the endeavor to learn *about* another culture needs to be founded, directly and knowingly, on the endeavor to learn *from* that culture.

This 'rule' or 'method' of research is far more consequential than it may seem. It is not a simple piece of advice about showing respect for the other. In counseling respect for the other, the rule takes 'respect', in a very deep and substantial way, to mean not mere politeness but a certain deference.[9] Deferring to the other means admitting to the other's otherness and necessarily entails a withdrawal of the self. In light of such self-contraction, it follows that anthropological research involves a fundamental measure of sacrifice on the part of the anthropologist, a generosity, a giving without expectation of return.

The religious language here should not be allowed to mislead: I am indeed talking about anthropological research. The relevant understanding of religion is not that of an institution in its own right, paralleling politics, economics, kinship, etc., but that of, say, Nuer or Dinka 'religion'—religion as existence. The notion of respect in question here is very like what the Nuer and Dinka call *thek*—a willful shrinking of the self in the face of the other (Beidelman 1981; Evans-Pritchard 1956: 177ff.; Lienhardt 1961: 124ff.). Considered as a rule for doing ethnographic research, respect of this kind for the other directly informs the quest for knowledge with the imperative of responsible choice.

Making the prime directive the goal of learning from, rather than about, the other, gives anthropology a new attitude: the other is no longer seen primarily as an object of study, but as a teacher in its own right. As a consequence, knowing is transformed from a suppressive into a responsive relationship, from an act of self-enclosure into a generous, other-respecting act of self-creation. By presuming the authenticity of the other's otherness, taking it as somehow otherwise than one's current self, the self is opened to otherness, and therewith to the possibility of self-transcendence.

Such anthropology appears to offer a solution to the logically impregnable problem of how to locate another site, outside one's own, from which to revise one's thinking. The solution is this: one is always already sited (sighted) in just this way—at a non-place, on the threshold (cf. Derrida and Kearny 1984: 11; Duerr 1985). It is the ambivalent sense of existential location, rather than that of the omnipresence which corresponds to omniscience, that the possibility of anthropology presupposes. Regarded dualistically, the distinction between an inside and an outside is pernicious nonsense. This judgment is recorded mythologically in the arresting ambiguity of the first couple's expulsion from Eden—as I mentioned above, in going from an inside to an outside, they went also from an outside to an inside. Therefore, in a logically scandalous but evident sense, at no point did Adam and Eve stand exactly inside or outside; rather, they stood always on the threshold of these alternative locations. To be sure, depending on the particular perspective one chooses to adopt (and one has always already so chosen), the first man and woman may be said to be located on either one side or the other of the threshold. Thus, after they have departed from the Garden, from the perspective of the self, they are inside looking out, whereas from the perspective of the other, they are outside looking in. An outside-inside distinction obtains—although significantly more indistinct, to be sure—even in the prelapsarian state. But the point of the story is precisely that one's perspective is a matter of choice: right from their Edenic beginnings, Adam and Eve are situated in such a way that they have to choose between the perspectives at hand.

The point of the present exercise is that by choosing the perspective of the other— that is, by adopting an attitude of respect toward the other as other—the anthropologist is positioned to take advantage of his or her existence on the threshold. Presuming that one can learn from, and not only about, the other raises one's consciousness, virtually giving relative access to the other's otherness and therefore to a site from which to rethink one's selfhood. To say that one's consciousness has been raised means that it has become alert to its own limitedness, to its own otherness. The solution, then, is in the epistemic preparedness to entertain the other as other.

Admittedly, under a discursive regime that puts this idea of the other out of episte-mological play, it is more than difficult to arrive at the intelligibility of such an attitude. Nevertheless, the fact that the perspective of the autonomous and rational individual tends to occlude from the mind's eye the other's otherness hardly means that the perspective of the other is unavailable. The latter perspective always remains at least implicit, at the margins of what is intelligible from the standpoint of the self-enclosed individual, whether we have in mind ethnographic or historical otherness, madness or magic, gender or genocide, parody or poetry, or something else.

Practically, we may think of the accessing of the other as a question of translation. In light of the ineluctable gap between self and other, it has been pointed out that eth-nographic translation is intrinsically incomplete; it must always fall short of its mark (Geertz 1973b: chap. 1). But under the rule of the primacy of the other, it is understood that good translation not only fails to get to the bottom of the other's terms, but also manages to alter the terms of translation. In other words, good translation is reciprocal; something is lost in it, but on both sides of the equation.

There is, though, a misleading aspect to the picture of translation in terms of loss of meaning or failure to rescue what is out there. The possibility of distortion in trans-lation rests on the idea that there is something to recuperate, a 'said' (Geertz 1973b: 19). And, indeed, there is. But like the said of the anthropologist, the said of the other betrays a 'saying', a process of arriving at a said—the very process that I am calling here, with regard to the anthropological enterprise, translation. The said thematizes the say-ing; however, as its processive guarantor, the latter always transcends the former. It must follow that, in a palpable sense, what one is trying to capture in translation is more an absence than a presence, more a becoming than a being. Even when it is considered as context rather than energy, culture 'is' one of those magical, twilight 'entities' about which it may be said 'now you see it, now you don't'. As context, culture always transcends what it is—its said-self. In this light, a point that interpretative anthropology continues to refine, the intrinsic incompleteness of ethnographic interpretation is less a question of distortion than of creative construction.

But the chief point I wish to bring out via this discussion pertains to the significance of the changes wrought by ethnographic translation to the terms of the anthropologist, not those of the other. By informing these terms with the perspective of the other, anthropological translation certainly serves to enlarge the universe of human discourse. It does so not simply by supplementing that universe but, more fundamentally, by supplanting it. Successful ethnographic translation unsays the anthropologist's said, thus opening the latter to the other. Unlike the socio-cultural settings it typically researches, anthropology is especially blessed with a deliberative capacity for continually unsaying the said. This description portrays anthropology as reflexive, to be sure, but, curiously enough, only insofar as anthropology retains the other's otherness as its principal concern. Under the rule of learning from the other, the discipline's reflexivity is not a matter of self-involvement or self-expansion, but of self-deconstruction on behalf of the other.[10]

If *alteration* of the anthropological self can serve as a measure of the success of ethnographic translation, then the authority of the ethnographic account, although necessarily contestable, must come to more than a matter of the ethnographer's differential hermeneutic advantage. Indeed, the authority derives from the other, not from the self. The deconstruction of the anthropologist's terms amounts to a withdrawal of self in the face of the other. This withdrawal bespeaks the other's authorization of the ethnographic account. In other words, the authority of the ethnographer derives from a mode of sacrifice. Plainly, authority of this kind is ethical before it is political—it truly is authority, not simply power.

Inasmuch as an ethnographic account is about the said rather than the saying, authority remains an issue of correspondence to the facts of the matter. However, since it can never fully escape from its interpretative dependence on saying, any said must itself remain open to interpretation. Ultimately, there is no fact of the matter, and in the face of this consideration, at some point of epistemological appraisal the orthodox authority of rational science virtually loses its authorization. When this happens, evaluation may become a free for all, abandoned to factors largely external to the quality of the ethnographic account, factors of prestige, position, influence, happenstance, etc.—in a word, power. Alternatively, evaluation may seek to rely on a very different sort of authority, the authority of the Other.

The authority of which I speak is dialogical: it issues from and in dialogue. But, an absolutely crucial caveat, this should not be taken to mean that authorization of the ethnographic account is referable in any simple way to the subject of the anthropologist's study. The anthropologist who, as a rule, abandons, on the basis of a principle of absolute relativism, her or his ability to judge others implicitly endorses power rather than ethics. The soundness of the ethnographic account does not depend on the express approbation of the subject of research. If it did, then it would amount to the authority of another self. But the ethnographic encounter does not take place simply within each of the participants, or even in some neutral unity or absolute totality of the two, but actually between them, in a dimension to which they alone have access at the time. The dialogue does not reduce to a monologue. The dimension of the between is the otherness for which the ethnographic other representatively stands, the threshold dimension of saying. The authorization derives, then, from the dialogue itself, not from the other's self. I am arguing that the alteration of the anthropological self, a mutation that is radically facilitated by an attitude of respect for the other, may serve as an index of that authorization.

Sacrifice may seem an inapposite source of authority in relation to writing ethnography. But when this notion of authority is applied to the evaluation of ethnographic accounts, all it means is that the most defensible accounts are the ones that do most to make the other's otherness, by contrast to the other's likeness to the anthropologist's self, intelligible. As a rule of thumb, the best accounts may be identified by virtue of their display of radical alterations to the anthropological self. The standard is, then, the degree to which the anthropologist has learned from the other.[11]

"It's All Greek to Me"

In a comparative exercise, Michael Herzfeld (1987) has richly argued that the peoples studied in modern Greek ethnography offer an especially bright mirror in which anthropology can see itself. His argument runs as follows. Pointing out that Greek ethnography and theoretical anthropology are connected both metonymically and metaphorically, he finds that Greek ethnography constitutes a unique reflexive basis on which to do ethnography of anthropology itself. The result pictures anthropology as focused on the construction of its own identity as an ethnographic authority. In this ethnography, the discipline is analogous to the Greek state, which is centrally engaged in the endeavor to control within its political boundaries the differences that threaten the Greek identity. The 'political boundaries' for anthropology amount to its epistemological domain and are very grand: they coincide with humankind, of course. Within this domain, anthropology, in order to justify its existence and satisfy its need for the object of its research, has had to exoticize peoples, thus constructing radical others. The radical other, in stark contrast to anthropology's understanding of itself as a discipline of the objective truth, is pictured as largely ruled by ideology and primitive or archaic practices. The disciplinary process of other-constructing stands out sharply in Mediterranean ethnography, in light of the fact that this area of the world is, far from an exotic horizon, anthropology's cultural backyard.

What is of particular interest here with regard to Herzfeld's intelligent study is, of course, its focus on the Greekness of anthropology. By bouncing theoretical anthropology off Greek ethnography, Herzfeld is led to see anthropology as largely an exercise in self-aggrandizement or the epistemological promotion of the Same. He studies both anthropology and the Greek state as discourses, focusing on the political rather than conceptual or philosophical content.[12] And he finds that, if I understand him, what leads both anthropology and the Greek state astray is the diagnostic dualism of their 'discursive constructs'. The focused concern to maintain the absolute or dualistic integrity of their respective identities is what motivates these two kinds of discourse.

The trouble is that Herzfeld appears to have boxed himself in. Although he expressly declares his faith in theoretical anthropology, a faith to which his study well testifies, in view of his findings, it is difficult to discern any reason for his devotion. Because they are partners in a single discourse, the comparison of theoretical anthropology with Greek ethnography facilitates a demonstration of the thesis that anthropology is prone to exoticize the other. However, for the very same reason, that is, the metonymical partnership of the two enterprises, the comparison also makes it rather easy, or at least not terribly difficult, to define the other's otherness away. Once it is demonstrated that the other is a construct of the anthropologist, what is left but the selfsame? Ironically, then, the very thing that recommends the comparison and facilitates the anthropological deconstruction of anthropology—namely, the closed circuit of things Greek—at once risks pulling the ground from beneath the discipline's feet altogether. For, in the absence of otherness, what is the point of anthropology?

As is apparent from Herzfeld's study, he does find purpose. Indeed, it is obvious that he respects difference; that he finds anthropology caught, as a radical condition of its enterprise, between self and other, theory and practice; and that he thinks it possible to get sufficient distance from the discipline as to be in a position to criticize it fairly. Still, given the findings of his comparative analysis, it remains difficult to comprehend the possibility of thus escaping the gravity of dualistic construction. What is the source of his optimism? Herzfeld (1987: 22) recommends an interpretative approach along the lines of Evans-Pritchard's ethno-historiography that is specifically inspired by Vico's "etymology" ("a means of dramatizing the socially and historically contingent character of institutions"), as well as by a dialectical picture of human existence. But although he tends to present this remedial approach as having grown out of his comparative ethnographic study, it seems likely that he brought the approach with him.

In fact, Herzfeld does point to a tradition of thought that has its source outside the circle of things Greek. He is inclined to think that the dualistic pursuit of identity, the pursuit that characterizes the Greek state and theoretical anthropology alike, is critically informed by the biblical figure of the fall. In its etiology of original sin, the idea of the fall expresses the difference between unity and diversity, perfection and corruption as, at least until the millennium, absolute. But 'the fall' is of course a Greco-Christian, not a Hebraic, concept. In the story of *Genesis*, there is in fact no direct mention of a fall; rather, the first couple are "sent forth" (*shillach*) and "driven out" (*gerash*) from the Garden. The idea of the fall, with its enormous cosmological power to excite thoughts of redemption through a resurrected perfection of identity, is, in relation to forms of cosmological consciousness and as epitomized in Augustine's great work, basically more philosophical than revelatory.

Herzfeld has learned a great deal from Greek ethnography. But the lesson is all Greek to him. As a consequence, while it can assist anthropology to reflect on itself as a political endeavor, it cannot very well instruct the discipline in another language. The reference to the Christological trope of the fall suggests that it may be desirable not merely to look at but to look through the mirror of Greek ethnography toward another discourse underlying theoretical anthropology and Western social thought—the Hebrew.[13]

It is easy to fall here into a picture of a Eurocentric contest over who is to rule the anthropological world—Greek or Jew.[14] Such a contest would be not only anthropologically odious but also useless. The point is how to employ the language of anthropology to site itself on its own margins, as directed toward the other. In relation to this goal, a contest between Greek and Hebrew is silly, because, for one thing, the two discourses are, like Judaism and Christianity, inextricably intertwined ("Jewgreek is greekjew," James Joyce said) and, for another, for all of their universalistic yearnings, each of them defines a particular cultural context. Nevertheless, it would appear that the Hebraic aspect of the language of anthropology, an aspect that goes largely unnoticed in the discipline, offers a bay window in the house of identity through which one can look to the other to make a difference to the self.[15] And this remains the case, even if Hebrew is no longer recuperable in some pure form from its expression in Greek (cf. Robbins 1991).

Anthropologically, the relationship described by the Hebrew notion of 'generation' pictures the self as a journey toward, rather than away from, the other. In this picture, otherness abides. Accordingly, the exoticization of the other is less a question of constructing its difference than of construing it as inferior to the self. In fact, the other ever retains a certain opacity in relation to the self. Therefore, coming to know the other presupposes an ineradicable, if also commutable, openness or incompleteness on the part of the self. The generational other cannot be terminated or incorporated by the self, because the self is always owing to the other. It must follow that knowing the other is not like knowing the self in its selfness. The self can 'know' the other in the sense of approaching it, but even then only insofar as the self is open to its own *alter*ation. Thus, in the generational picture, knowing the other constitutes a form of sacrifice, making this kind of knowing an ethical relation. Such knowing admits of political design, but only because it is predominantly ethical.

Ontologically, 'generation' describes the relationship between self and other in terms of a boundary that is both ineradicable and fluid. A boundary of this kind is nondualist but not monist; it delineates a fundamentally asymmetrical relationship in which the other encompasses the self as a contrary. As a consequence, the self is enabled to participate in the other, but not to reduce the other to itself. On the other hand, the self is reducible to the other, but only by becoming other than itself. In effect, then, the relationship describes a dynamic of becoming, in which the self, whether it likes and knows it or not, is always moving toward the other.

In this 'ontology', reality or the whole is fundamentally ambiguous. As such, it cannot be described adequately in ontological terms (as 'reality' or 'the whole'), in that it is precisely otherwise than anything at all. Therefore, it is a non-foundational foundation. Whereas a foundation in the received sense of the term always starts from and returns to the same, this one starts from and moves toward difference or otherness. As 'the whole', it is, then, dynamic rather than fixed and absolute. And as 'reality', it must admit of a plurality of realities or perspectives on reality, ensuring only that each of these is fundamentally moral in nature—which is to say that each operates by virtue of the situational break in necessity as defined by the ambiguity of reality. In this light, one might well say that the self has been given a break by the Other.

Thus, the Hebraic aspect of Western thought lends itself peculiarly to anthropology as a study of the other's otherness.[16] Since it affords the other the primacy of generation, this aspect defines the discipline as ethics rather than method or control, and it defines knowing as self-sacrifice rather than self-empowerment. I cannot say about Vico—who, as Herzfeld suggests (1987: 168), probably was, through Collingwood's influence, one of Evans-Pritchard's intellectual ancestors—but surely Evans-Pritchard himself and his most direct anthropological inspiration, Durkheim, were deeply moved by the Hebraic element in Western social thought. I take it that the strong commitment of both of these scholars to the idea that society is a moral order—an extraordinary idea to propound in the context of constructing a science—is biblical and revelatory at bottom. I have elsewhere argued (Evens 1982b, 1995) that this idea stands at the heart of Evans-Pritchard's turn to historiography, a turn essentially to ethical narrative in contradistinction to scientific analysis. As to Durkheim, one must recall that he was a direct descendant of a long line of rabbinical scholars and, before his decision to study philosophy, had prepared himself for the rabbinate (Alpert 1961: 15; Lukes 1973: chap. 1). I suggest that, whatever else it is, his sociology, with its driving but ontologically antipathic thesis of the moral nature of society, is also Judaism revised as positive science.[17]

The Productive Limits of Reflexivity

It is not the case that in order to mount a critique of anthropology as a discipline bent on aggrandizing the self by epistemologically subjecting the other, one need look into the mirror of Greek ethnography. A critique of this kind has been developed monographically and theoretically with some regularity in recent times. I regard such *explicitly* reflexive critiques as important.[18] But although they vary greatly in character and quality (Herzfeld's, for example, is distinguished especially by the specifics of its comparative dimension), speaking very generally a faint odor of the 'politically correct' hangs about them. When they proceed more or less chiefly on a basis of socio-political causes, these critiques are not just a question of theoretical contestation; they then also connote moral superiority. In light of this consideration, it behooves the discipline to reflect on their reflexivity by proposing some 'ethnography' of the ethnography of anthropology, for it seems that there is more to such critiques than simply trying to put right anthropology's social scientific endeavor.

As Herzfeld's (1987) critique turns on one of the two most prominent cultural traditions of the civilization that produced the discipline of anthropology, mine, with Durkheim, turns in critical part on the other. In addition, while my approach is intended as 'interventionist' (by defining humankind primarily in terms of ethical capacity, it takes a position about the responsibility of taking positions, and by grasping that capacity in terms of the primacy of the other, it offers a general guideline for exercising this responsibility), it also emphatically insists on a relative but critical distinction between theoretical and 'moral' discourse.

As I see it, in its efforts to make the other intelligible, anthropology has tended gradually to erode the otherness of the other. This intellectual evolution seems to have reached a tipping point in much current anthropology. In its effort to deal remedially with the discipline's own unwanted proclivity to 'colonize' the other by exoticizing and eroticizing it, this anthropology has turned sharply inward. And in doing so, it has found that, like the 'other' cultures of anthropology's yesteryear, the professional anthropological enterprise is, far from being a matter of truth, principally a system of beliefs, values, and ideas, in a word, a kind of culture or ideology—only in its case, one with a strong, but secreted, political bent. In effect, anthropology has transformed itself into the other.

There appears to be, however, an exception to this self-transformation, for it seems at least implicit that by discerning and disclosing the discipline's hidden complicity in subjecting the other, the anthropology that has helped to promote the recent reflexive turn has positioned itself to address the disciplinary problem at issue. Moreover, because this problem is seen as essentially political, so, too, the proposed solution is plainly political in nature—social activism. As a result, the anthropology in question might appear to present itself as having transcended the problem altogether. In this light, practitioners of this anthropology look as if they have kept their ethnographic authority pure—that is, their anthropology, precisely because it is openly and pointedly political, tends to present itself as self-transparent and untainted by any need to subject the other.

Coupled with this exception to the discipline's alienation from its integral self is the following consideration. The charge against the older anthropology is typically leveled at the ethnographer in his or her relation to the representative other (primitive, preliterate, traditional, etc.). In other words, it is aimed at the anthropologist in his role 'abroad', as a kind of would-be other. Excluding the experience of female members of the profession, who have themselves been made to feel as a category the relegation to otherness, the charge is not leveled at the anthropologist, in his professional capacity in relation to other anthropologists, when he is at home. It would appear that when the anthropologist is in academic residence, there is little cause for alarm.

The point is that, putting aside for another time the question of the efficacy of the reflexive critique at issue, the principled restriction of the accusation of 'othering' to the relation between the anthropologist and the ethnographic other enables the critic to conceal from her- or himself (if only thinly) the consequences of the critique in respect of his or her own professional relationship vis-à-vis, instead of the discipline's usual 'others', other anthropologists. It generally does not occur to such a critic that his radical appraisal of his colleagues, by depicting them as not simply theoretically wrongheaded but ideologically backward (or worse), may well implicitly project him as their ethico-political superior. To be sure, this failure of reflexivity also marks a generational function whereby the position that is fresh and new, post-colonialist anthropology, is inclined to see itself as enlightened relative to the 'dark ages' of the 'politically naive' anthropology that preceded it. But, tellingly, this generational function displays an expansion of self that plainly runs contrary to the ethico-political claims of the new anthropology.

In the same vein, this sense of superiority is predisposed to consign a great deal of anthropology, including the 'classics', to the dustbin of history.[19] Is it the case, however, that our discipline is so unlike philosophy (to choose an obvious example, even if we grant significant differences) that we need not bother to read and reread these anthropological masters and many others who followed them? After all, a great deal of philosophy, perhaps even the bulk, from the Greeks through Kant and the moderns, is, although not by the surface lights of formal disciplinary boundaries, anthropological in a sense in which we deeply share. Does our discipline really 'advance', theoretically and ethnographically, at a pace so swift that its ancestors, both distant and near, are simply no longer relevant, mere relics worth regarding only to highlight by contrast how far we have come? Does not this sort of scientistic pretension to the accumulation of knowledge run contrary to the political and ethical tenor of modern anthropology, ironically, the very tenor these activist critiques—with their defining focus on value no less, if not more, than on fact—propose to cherish?

These observations about a distinct lack of reflexivity within reflexive anthropology suggest that there is something still secure, even comforting, about *alterizing* ourselves in our ethnographic role as would-be others. In that role we remain still, as it were, at a fairly safe distance from ourselves. Although it is serious and can threaten the anthropological identity in a useful way, the recent charge against the ethnographic authority of the anthropologist does not quite hit home, does not truly kick the self where it lives—in the hallowed halls of academia.[20] If this observation runs true, then an ethnography of an association or department of anthropology would make a salutary piece of epistemological violence. By accessing ourselves where our otherness to ourselves is most immediate and closest to home, where reflexive observation becomes peculiarly threatening to the anthropological self, we stand to alter the terms of our discourse in such a way as to extend our reflexive endeavor 'abroad' to reflect on itself and its own professional as well as intrinsic limitations. Of course, for the very reasons I have just adumbrated, we should not expect to see an ethnographic undertaking of the kind.[21]

I suspect that we have no more reason to think that today's anthropologists are not themselves significantly informed with the 'colonization' of self characterizing the Western episteme than we have to presume that the anthropologists of colonialism's heyday managed to free themselves cleanly from the gravity of colonialist and rationalist presumption and design. While it is true that anthropologists have been duly taken with the argument to the fallacy of autonomous selfhood, if Foucault and others are right about its a priori nature, as well as its epistemic depth and reach in Western self-identity, then our sense of self will scarcely change overnight. It would be a gross disciplinary conceit to think that, because of our theoretical and critical insight into this sense of self, we anthropologists have transcended it. Insofar as we have not, it is bound to show up in our work, including our self-critiques.

In the past several decades, anthropology has been characterized by a driving concern to expose hegemonic power structures that foster oppression and injustice. It is easy to sympathize with this concern, which, as a form of resistance in its own right, has largely proceeded as a monologue of power. But even though the resulting analyses of power can be insightful, they tend to remain, in respect of their work of resistance, critically narrowing and naive. If power alone is at work, if it is the sole operative force, then one cannot help but wonder what legitimates the movement of anthropological resistance and what social forces other than power per se are ethnographically obscured. Are all social conditions reducible to power as such? Does justice too reduce to terms of power? Does the academic discourse of resistance spell yet another would-be or emerging power structure? Without explicit acknowledgment and theorizing of something other than power per se, can there be a meaningful sense of moral inquiry or even, to invoke Durkheim's elementary sociological insight, of moral force and order?

The turn to the discourse of resistance has encouraged a concomitant interest in dissolving the distinction between academic anthropology and social activism. Although the notion of participant observation has long been a shibboleth in ethnographic research, generally it has conveyed earnest observation but token participation. It is only in recent decades that the discipline, in line with twentieth-century philosophy of science, has come fully to realize that there is no observer who is not in some fundamental way participant in what he or she observes. However, this important realization—that there is no such thing as a view from nowhere, or that pure objectivism is chimerical—appears to have issued in an at least tacit conclusion that between anthropological research and social activism there is no difference to speak of. And from this conclusion, it is a mere baby step to reckon, not only that it makes sense to try to choose one's bias in an overt and considered manner, but also that one's research ought to proceed primarily as a function of this bias.

In fact, though, the assumption of simple identity between research and activism is fallacious, for a premise of imperfect distinction does not logically entail a conclusion of total indistinction. What is more, monistic collapse of the distinction at point reveals the very dualism that cultivates the Western sense of self in question. The collapse results from the same logic of reification that holds that wherever two mutually exclusive phenomena co-exist (mind and body, self and other, subject and object, and so on), one of them must be reducible to the other. In other words, this Cartesian logic inherently excludes relative difference. It is, then, a logic of power. And here it is worth reminding ourselves of Agamben's (1998: 86, 105, 107, 122) explication of the Western tradition of governmental sovereignty: he speaks of a "zone of indistinction" by virtue of which the sovereign stands at once within *and* outside the law, and is therefore possessed of unlimited power.

I suggest that this development in anthropology—however well intentioned, and even if it is only an ambiguous trend—is importantly perverse, self-defeating even, for inasmuch as it decides uncritically, without carefully deliberating, the question of the relation between activism and objectivism, it threatens analytical rigor and quality of research and thereby undermines the discipline's unique ability to assist social causes. I must save expansion of this criticism for another place. Here I will only make three quick points. First, although the present work is intended as a contribution to interventionist anthropology, it has also striven to convey that if this anthropology is to prove useful and sound, it needs thoughtfully to maintain a relative but crucial difference between anthropological research and social activism—namely, the difference registered in the fact that, by contrast to social activism, anthropology must also proceed categorically and eminently on a basis of relative objectivity and, hence, reason. Derrida (in Derrida and Kearny 1984: 120) captures the tension I am driving at between, on the one hand, taking a stance on what is just and good and, on the other, rigorously, if also critically, analyzing how things stand: "But the difficulty is to gesture in opposite directions at the same time: on the one hand, to preserve a distance and suspicion with regard to the official political codes governing reality; on the other, to intervene here and now in a practical and *engaged* manner whenever the necessity arises. This position of dual allegiance, in which I personally find myself, is one of perpetual uneasiness. I try where I can to act politically while recognizing that such action remains incommensurate with my intellectual project of deconstruction." But I can also enlist here the support of perhaps the key philosophical figure in anthropology's reflexive turn, Foucault himself (quoted in Gutting 2001: 262): "The project, tactics and goals to be adopted are a matter for those who do the fighting. What the intellectual can do is to provide the instruments of analysis ... But as for saying, 'Here is what you must do!', certainly not."[22] Second, it is crucial to take into account that while resistance and reform can be effective, they always comport with, just as Foucault argued, acute dangers of their own and are never as melioristic as they are hopeful. And third, anthropological Foucauldianism aside, any such anthropology ought to be able to justify itself in terms other than those of sheer power.

CONCLUSION
Emancipatory Selfhood and Value-Rationality

Emancipatory Selfhood

In this book I have argued on empirical, pragmatic, and ethical grounds for a nondualist ontology in which reality is regarded as basically ambiguous as between body and thought. Because it describes reality as precisely neither this nor that, ontology of this kind, strictly speaking, does not qualify as ontology at all—it is deontologized. Under this description of reality, human beings are caught so fast and definitively in the inbetween that they present the ambiguousness of reality in a painfully acute but wonderful form. Of course, if this ontological picture is sound, then everything, not just humans, must project, in one way or another, this indefinite bearing of reality—which in the case of humans takes the form of reflexivity. But without having to conclude (with Descartes) that we cannot think without also thinking that it is man who is thinking,[1] I would argue that humans may be regarded as peculiarly representative of the fundamentally ambiguous nature of reality. This exemplary nature rests with their conduct of choice, which amounts to their self-identifying in terms of conventions that they themselves make and unmake continuously. As a consummate *dynamis* of ontological ambiguity, humans are condemned to construct their own reality. By an act of moral selection, creating their own evolutionary niche, humans in outstanding, if also fundamentally limited, measure create themselves.[2]

The limits imposed by a basically indefinite reality, then, as both Genesis 2 and 3 and the Dinka creation myth narrate, do not so much curtail choice as admit of it. To be sure (another lesson of the Hebrew and Dinka stories), these limits present the primacy of otherness and the Other. As a result, no matter how humans choose, even if their choice is flagrantly self-interested, they necessarily choose for the sake of the Other. That this is so is given in the consideration that all choices, however consequential for the time being, come to the same end in the long run: dissolution into otherness, or mortality. Nevertheless, a founding determination of this pre-eminently ambiguous kind does not obviate choice. On the contrary, it imposes itself in the way of obligation; put another way, it inaugurates an ethical dynamic. It determines not only that choice must be for the sake of the Other, but also that one must choose. Therefore, the obligation can be satisfied if, and only if, one also chooses for the sake of oneself, for choice can be definitive as choice only so long as it emanates from a relatively autonomous self. But since, from one of the two vantage points offered by the structure of ambiguity, self and other are essentially opposed to each other, one's choices are always, to extend Bateson's (1972: 271–278) concept, doubly bound. In effect, one is truly constrained by an ultimately undecidable choice (a 'double bind') between self and other. If the fact that one's choices are in a sense inconsequential in the long run demonstrates the 'lawful' nature of the primacy of the Other, then the consideration that one's choices are always consequential for the time (of) being, proves the authenticity or originary nature of the choice between self and other. In this world, it matters how one chooses.

By omitting to take into account the need to satisfy both sides of the self-other equation, humans can choose in a way that puts the equation itself at risk. Such a choice accelerates the entropic dissolution into sheer otherness. In other words, since what we are talking about is the human equation, our choices can actually put an end to human being. And they can do so, as the example of Nazism (which, although hardly the only shocking example of twentieth-century barbarism, is a master key to modernity's intellectual disillusionment with itself and the Enlightenment project) shows, by defining humankind away as well as by destroying it physically. Such lethal choices are so egregiously irresponsible to the Other, so unbalanced, that they sorely threaten the human equation.

Sheer selflessness, though, appearances notwithstanding, may be construed as a variation on this theme. By failing to care for the possibility of the self as a condition of the self-responsibility granted by the Other, attempts at perfectly comprehensive self-sacrifice also constitute a dismissal of the obligation to the Other. In the idiom of theology, as only the Other can sacrifice itself and still subsist, such attempts bespeak excessive pride. To be viable, as the example of the Akedah shows, sacrifice entails economy.

Obviously, in light of such vital responsibility, one's choices are subject to ethical evaluation. In view of its generative primacy, the obligation to the other is the standard of evaluation. Conformity to this standard may indeed be measured in the economic terms of 'survival value'. But, as is absolutely crucial to understand and as the various Darwinisms, utilitarianisms, materialisms, etc., fail to grasp, what is at stake is not solely physical survival but the survival of otherness as the author of the human equation. As with my interpretation of the Akedah and of the Holocaust, we are talking about the survival of the human being as a person, a creature whose basic identity is founded no less in moral than in natural selection. Put another way, the value of one's choices should be referred to the capacity of those choices to preserve and develop responsible or other-regarding choice. In any particular situation, the good choice is the choice that best ensures such survival by deferring the entropic collapse of the difference made by responsible choice (cf. Jonas 1984).

If the standard of responsible choice obtains accordingly (as an offer, but one that cannot be finally refused), then, notwithstanding the absence of a normative foundation (in the positivist sense of 'foundation'), we are indeed endowed with the ethical wherewithal to make considered judgments as between different ways of living the irresolvable dilemma that constitutes the human condition. In this connection, I have spoken of formulaic modes of coping with this dilemma. The logical constitution of the dilemma defines two limiting modes. In trying to defer the inevitable end of being obliged to somehow satisfy equally vital but incompatible demands, one has got to privilege, in the meantime, in one way or another, either other-regard or self-interest. Whereas mythic rationality promotes a differential emphasis on other-regard, instrumental rationality gives primacy of place to the competing principle.

Judging between these two modes of transcendence, I have taken stock of the relative merits of mythic rationality by pointing to the ethical openness intrinsic to this rationality's primary focus on other-regard. However, it is plain that, by virtue of the naive way in which it takes for granted the overriding discretionary power of the Other, mythic rationality sorely impedes the development of the critical openness associated with self-reflection and properly scientific inquiry. But instrumental rationality, with its master principle of self-interest, is so devoted to the autonomous self that it is inclined to dismiss altogether the ethical openness attaching to the Other. The dualistic boundaries fostered by the idea of the subject-complete-unto-itself, which boundaries produce in turn the scientific idea of unadulterated objectivity, tend to define away—as enchanted, heuristic, irrational, superstructural, epiphenomenal, etc.—the otherness or discretionary power by virtue of which the idea of subjectivity makes sense in the first place.

Undoubtedly, as Habermas (see chap. 6, this volume), in line with critical theory, maintains, mythic rationality's benighted narrowness of vision leaves much to be desired, ethically and otherwise. Evidently, however, for reasons of its aspiration to universalization and its pronounced weakness for *pars pro toto* thinking, instrumental rationality constitutes by far the more urgent threat to the survival of the human equation. Still, no less implicit in this rationality is the promise of an even more acute self-reflection, one so critical as to discern and respect its own foundations in heteronomy. Therefore, instrumental rationality is capacitated to transform itself into an other-regarding axiology, holding out the possibility of a 'progressive' leap of conscience.

Human history exhibits a broad, if vastly uneven and varietal, shift from mythic to modern rationality. I venture that all of the major social theorists of this shift, whether we have in mind Durkheim, Toennies, Spencer, Maine, Weber, Marx, Habermas, Foucault, Voegelin, or someone else, find, at least implicitly, the logical and phenomenological warrant for their accounts in what I have called the double boundedness of being human. This character not only delimits dual modes of transcendence but also marks the duality as itself inherently dynamic—a nondualism. As modes of transcendence, each of these approaches to the double bind constitutes a system of deferral, in a word, a temporality. Hence, I have spoken of short-term and long-term time.

What is important here, however, is that because the ambiguity they constitute is by no means total, because it admits of relative resolution, the two modes of transcendence also define a temporality together. This temporality is developmental. The direction of the shift at point is restricted according to the principle of formal priority: just as, say, office presupposes status differentiation, and official hierarchies presuppose office, so instrumental rationality presupposes mythic rationality.[3] To take a cue from the Dumontian concept of hierarchy, whereas the incompletely differentiated nature of mythic rationality includes the possibility of instrumental rationality, the dualism of the latter rationality excludes the mythic variety as logically impossible. Coupled with the idea of lived contradiction, this order of formal priority implies (but does not entail) a developmental shift from mythic to instrumental rationality.

It is illuminating (if intellectually risky) to speak here of dialectical movement, as long as it is borne in mind that the movement is not inevitable and has no point of culmination (cf. Derrida and Kearney 1984: 112–13). It cannot be brought to completion because the whole implicit in the fact of the dialectic is not absolute—as Derrida might say, the steering mechanism of this whole always has a certain amount of 'play' in it. It is interminable also because the movement never leaves behind entirely the mythic rationality with which it begins. And because the movement, although driven by contradiction, is decided by moral selection, it is not inevitable.

In spite of such selection, though, the direction of the movement is broadly constrained by the order of formal priority. Insofar as development occurs at all, it must go from the mythic to the instrumental. But because the mythic is encompassing, it can never be utterly abandoned. For this reason, it is currently open to humans to bring back the repressed of the mythic, but in conjunction with a self-limiting instrumentalism, that is, an advanced self-consciousness, one raised to the point of grasping its own fundamental limitedness. To the extent that this dynamic human exercise has an object, that object ought to be not overcoming contradiction once and for all but making contradiction situationally livable. Even before utility and sheer physical existence (two 'values' that can be maximized by eliminating contradiction), situational livability is a question of the moral life, the life of responsible and creative choice. In the absence of the possibility of responsible and creative choice, there can be no human existence as such. The reason we should choose situational livability as our object is twofold: first, we have no choice but to make a choice, and, second, the only choice available to us other than livability is accelerated death. This reason reveals, then, not a 'transcendental signified', but a certain existential openness that, as the biblical story of the Creation and the fall implicitly narrates, condemns humans to choice for a living. In other words, the reason or foundation at point is ethics itself.

What renders contradiction particularly unlivable is the overriding dualism to which Western reason has been given. By delineating contradiction as a thing in itself, dualist thought conduces a law of non-contradiction, making life-as-choice or ethical existence virtually unlawful. Taken as an epistemological tool for negotiating the ambiguity of reality more efficiently for instrumental purposes, the law of non-contradiction has much to offer. But once it is taken as a law of practical reason (as it is, famously, in Kant's monumental philosophy), non-contradiction virtually defines away or outlaws the openness of genuine discretionary power, violently and oppressively excluding authentic choice as non-logical. Such an epistemological move constitutes a choice to take the play out of existence.

Hence, at this juncture of human history, bringing the modern consciousness face to face with its own otherness, its own essential openness, must count as emancipatory and progressive. Even resolute deconstructionism—for all its rejection of foundations—cannot deny this without making a patent nonsense of itself (cf. McGowan 1991: 28f., chap. 3). History may have no transcendental resolution, but it need not be an exercise in futility: it can grant the relative goodness of the autonomous self by acknowledging, through the use of creative and responsible choice, the self's infinite indebtedness to the Other. As I argue in chapter 11, even Foucault, in his last years, began to conceive of selfhood along these lines. In connection with this revised, forward-looking sense of self, the discipline of anthropology, in view of its focal concern to address the question of otherness, can play an exceptional part.

Anthropology and Value-Rationality

According to Wittgenstein (1971: 33), "When we watch the life and behavior of human beings all over the earth we see that apart from what we might call animal activities, taking food etc., etc., humans also carry out actions that bear a peculiar character and might be called ritualistic." In making this observation, Wittgenstein proposed that it would be a good way to begin a book on anthropology. In the present case, I expect it is also a good way to end one. Among humans, the so-called animal activities themselves seem inextricably and to a distinguishing degree suffused with the peculiar character Wittgenstein points to, such that even when they purport to be wholly a matter of natural functions—when they are, so to speak, at their most bestial—these activities are never merely functional but always exhibit a facultative aspect. This aspect corresponds to a certain loosening of the ties that bind humans to their determining ground. Selfhood takes up the slack. The self and the distance established by the play in man's relation to his ground are two sides of the same coin. It is as if in the case of humans, the vacuum that nature abhors gets filled with, not nature as such, but second nature—a fresh and mediate ground, which I have considered in the philosophical terms of the synthetic a priori. As second nature, the synthetic a priori is, for all practical purposes, more bodily than facultative. But it is facultative too. It was somehow, if only tacitly, chosen, and therefore, even though its potent embodiment makes it—as described by Bourdieu's 'habitus'—incredibly secure, at bottom it remains open to choice. I have tried here to plumb this dynamic, 'ritualistic' character to which we are given so peculiarly and which I comprehend as ethics.

In connection with this end, this book brings professional anthropology squarely into the philosophical discourse of postmodernity. It does so by addressing directly the pressing and comprehensive problem of ethics and relativism that the anti-foundationalism of postmodern thought both points to and provokes. The book attends squarely to the ontological scaffolding that gives substance to the shibboleths of postmodernism (essentialism, difference, power, hegemony, and the like) and their opposing principles. In so doing, the argument has opened ethics to penetrating insights of the postmodern critique but has refused the development of the absolute ethical vacuum that otherwise follows from the rejection of any and all foundations. Put in the terms of the day, it promotes political commitment and acknowledges the ubiquity of power but nonetheless rejects the political essentialism and reduction to 'power' that currently characterize so much anthropology and social thought.

With my ontological project in mind, I have essayed here the ethical limitations of dualism and the ethical superiority of nondualism for thinking about human beings and their social behavior. Since it denies that there is any absolute essence, nondualist ontology is a contradiction in terms. Whereas dualism depicts reality in terms of discrete things or substances (identities), nondualism projects what there is as ultimately uncertain and ambiguous. Like dualism, nondualism too serves to differentiate the world. But whereas the former cuts with an absolute edge, the latter does so with a relative one: the one trades in immaculate boundaries, the other in boundaries that are fuzzy and permeable to variable degrees. The object of this ontological exercise has been, thus, to upend the fundamental categories through which we, in the West, are accustomed to regard our world and ourselves.

I have made my comparative case about the ethical import of these two perspectives, dualism and nondualism, by conceiving of all human existence in terms of sacrifice. By sacrifice, I mean the human conduct of displacement we speak of as the self-other relation. Because selfhood is unintelligible unless it describes at one and the same time both separation from and dependence on the other, the self-other relation is nothing if not a fundamentally irresolvable behavioral tension of self- and other-sacrifice. I exist as myself only by virtue of differentiation from, and therewith contraction or sacrifice of, the other. Yet by the same token, I cannot continue to exist except by virtue of the continuing existence of the other. In the absence of the other, the other being representative of otherness in general, what is there against which my self can win any definition? But as a self—a being possessed *of* moral consciousness and *by* responsibility—the only way I can ensure the continuing existence of the other is by ceding my place to it: in a word, self-sacrifice. Therefore, irreducibly caught between a rock and a hard place, selfhood is open and incomplete from the start. For insofar as it endures, it is nothing but a definitive nondualism, an aspect of the self-other dynamic.

The trouble is (as I read in the Akedah as well as the Hebrew and Dinka creation stories), once the self comes into existence, given the exhilaration it feels in virtue of its uniquely vital opposition to its originary and limiting ground, it inclines to forget that it exists only at the behest of the latter. In effect, selfhood, whether individual or collective, naturally constitutes a temptation to complete itself by setting out to sever altogether its ties to that ground. This is the defining phenomenological move of dualism. Put another way, seeing itself solely in light of its felt opposition to the ground, the self occludes the fact that without a continuing ground to stand *against*, in the end, it has no ground to stand *on*, and therefore none on which to sustain selfhood. The self can hold itself in relief, which is to say, remain apparent to itself, only as against its originary ground, and for this reason must not lose sight of this ground. More exactly, since this ground is not the kind of thing open to plain seeing, the self must not lose insight into it. In order to keep this ultimately indeterminate foundation in some kind of view, the self is forced to face off against the ground that has apparently supplanted the originary one. But this ground, the one that mediates the originary ground, is none other than the self's current self. In other words, the self has to abnegate itself. In thus making itself other to itself—definitively an act of self-sacrifice or self-emancipation—the self at once reopens the perspective on its originary ground and creates space in which to refashion itself, to make itself anew.

Through intensive analyses of materials ranging from the Hebrew scriptures and the Holocaust to African witchcraft and stories of creation, I have maintained that while dualism critically threatens this truly vital sacrificial tension, nondualism, although dialectically capacitated to take advantage of the very real benefits of dualistic thinking (such as growth of knowledge and developed reflexivity), does not accord with dualism's proclivity for 'final solutions'. On the one hand, as an order of immaculate boundaries and mutual exclusion, dualism promises to resolve totally the tension of self-and-other. In other words, it holds out the idea of a sacrifice that would end the need for sacrifice once and for all. On the other hand, nondualism entertains the tensile nature of the self-other relation continuously, thus projecting human existence as an interminably sacrificial dynamic.

In connection with nondualism's existential logic of sacrifice, I have offered what seems to me an original thesis about the abiding anthropological problem of traditional or atheoretical thought. The alleged disadvantages of such thought, which have served to mark it as 'closed', are indeed substantial when judged in terms of strict rationality. But when they are seen from the perspective of nondualism, these same 'disadvantages' feature the defining openness of ethics. The openness I have in mind is that of self to other. This openness bespeaks a fundamental veracity underlying atheoretical thought, a veracity effectively obscured by the perspective of modernity. In view of this thesis about openness and atheoretical understanding, I have essayed the possibility of a paradigm shift from what I call 'mythic rationality' to rationality that is, paradoxically, at once both relative and universal—a 'value-rationality'. The possibility of such a shift hinges especially on the consideration that modern or strict rationality (including scientific thought), despite its closed nature and its characteristic mystification of atheoretical understanding, continues to share in the openness characterizing the latter. As a science of the other, anthropology marks a place where ethics and rationality are scarcely distinguishable from each other, making anthropology, in the capacious sense of the term, a conduct of inquiry uniquely positioned to think and practice the idea of value-rationality, a discourse meant to re-create our habitus or second nature as, not closed, but essentially open.

NOTES

Acknowledgments

1. These portions were published as, respectively, "Bourdieu and the Logic of Practice: Is All Giving Indian-Giving or Is 'Generalized Materialism' Not Enough," *Sociological Theory* 37, no. 1 (1999): 3–31; "Witchcraft and Selfcraft," *Archives Européennes de Sociologies* 37, no. 1 (1996): 23–46; "Rationality, Hierarchy and Practice: Contradiction as Choice," *Social Anthropology* 1, no. 1B (1993): 101–18; and "Mythic Rationality, Contradiction and Choice among the Dinka," *Social Anthropology* 2, no. 2 (1994): 99–114.

Introduction

1. As if this distinction were not vexatious enough, I need to mention, as one of many examples of additional complexity, Spinoza's philosophical monism. In his metaphysics, mind and body are regarded as two different aspects of one and the same substantive reality. He thus rises above Descartes' dualism, wherein the two substances of thought ('thinking stuff') and corporality ('extended stuff') stand to each other in a relationship of mutual exclusion and the reality of only one of which, *res cogitans*, is logically indubitable. As a result, Spinoza's monism furnishes an answer to the question that Cartesian dualism raised but could not satisfactorily address: if reason is the primary end of God's creation, and man is the sole vessel of this provision, then why did God bother to create bodily life? Still, one might think that in spite (or perhaps because) of its ingenuity, Spinoza's monism is inconsistent with the idea of total oneness. By virtue of its perspectivism, reality is seen as beholden to man as well as to God. As a consequence, like nondualism, and notwithstanding his characterization of the one (all-encompassing) substance as absolute and of the manyness of material being as merely a mode of this infinite absolute rather than a finite substance in its own right, his ontology implicitly admits of basic ambiguity. Or so one might argue. At any rate, my point is that when it is considered from the standpoint of logic proper, unequivocal monism is of a piece with Cartesian dualism—both are decisively conditioned by the idea of a perfect boundary, a boundary that separates but does not connect.

For this brief aside about Spinoza's monism, I have drawn on the analysis of the phenomenologist Hans Jonas (1974: chap. 10). In this connection, I want to add that, in coming to and developing a concept of nondualism, I have been stimulated primarily by my reading of philosophical phenomenology, so much of which begins with a critique of Cartesian dualism. Merleau-Ponty's monumental *Phenomenology of Perception* started me on the way. Within anthropology proper, most exceptionally I was moved along by my own (continuing) phenomenological studies of Nuer reality (as this reality stood at the time Evans-Pritchard worked among them) and Louis Dumont's brilliant and paralogical revision of the notion of hierarchy.

2. As I am claiming only a loose but pervasive hold on anthropology by empiricism, I do not have in mind 'true believers' (few, if any, of which could be found today). The kind of adherence I am concerned with is more in the nature of a subtle and insidious prejudice against theory, where 'theory' continues to be seen in shrill opposition to 'empirical observation'. For example, some years ago, seeking constructive commentary from a distinguished colleague, I sent to him my (then) unpublished reanalysis of a particular ethnographic problem found in Evans-Pritchard's Nuer ethnography. Although he was trained (as was I) in the anthropological tradition of British empiricism, and therefore placed great value (as do I) on intensive field research, I have little doubt that he would reject empiricism as I have defined it for present purposes. Yet he responded to my reanalysis of the Nuer data by suggesting that further fieldwork alone could suffice to resolve the problem. I was taken aback by this response for two reasons. First, given the awkward fact that almost fifty years had gone by since Evans-Pritchard had gathered the relevant data among them, surely the Nuer were no longer the Nuer as Evans-Pritchard had found them. Second, my reanalysis was plainly predicated on the consideration that the data were basically in, and that—as in principle is the end case with all ethnography—the problem was of a nature that what was needed were not more data but a fresh way of looking at them, in this case an ontological way. (The present book—which obviously lays no claim to being ethnography in the standard sense—continues, on a broader scale, this exercise of rethinking perspectives on the basis of ontology.) As I see it, my colleague's response betrayed nothing more than the sort of vague and uncritical empiricist presumption that concerns me here, and that serves needlessly to close off theoretical possibility.

As to empiricistic anathema to ontology, I may as well cite Evans-Pritchard, who, although a gifted theorist, in *Nuer Religion*, a book fairly bursting with ontological implication with regard to specific Nuer notions that are particularly representative in this respect, explicitly refrains from discussing the ontological question (1956: 124; my italics): "I do not discuss this ontological question here beyond saying that were we to suppose that such phenomena are in themselves regarded as God we would misunderstand and misrepresent Nuer religious thought, *which is pre-eminently dualistic*." Although this (tautological) avoidance appears in only one place in the book, it is, in my view, equally applicable to the whole of his analysis. I find the avoidance at once ingenuous and convenient, for it permitted him to impose a dualist ontology he bore with him to Nuerland, all the while supposing that he was deriving it from his empirical ethnographic observations. I cannot do here the close analysis of Evans-Pritchard's great monograph that is necessary to demonstrate this. But as the quotation might suggest, in his fierce concern to show that the Nuer were not hypostasizing the godhead but, rather, were speaking figuratively, he was inclined to pre-empt ontological discussion in favor of presuming what he wished to find out, namely, whether Nuer religion is or is not dualist.

3. Kant's rejection of heteronomy as a principle of moral imperatives is wholesale. His metaphysic of morals is keyed to an absolute distinction between subject and object, self and other, and is predicated on the pure autonomy of the subject's will, 'will' being defined in terms of the universality of (practical) reason as opposed to the instrumentality of desire and the like. The principle of autonomy, Kant writes (1964: 108; original italics),

> is the sole principle of ethics. For analysis finds that the principle of morality must be a categorical imperative, and that this in turn commands nothing more nor less than precisely this autonomy.
>
> If the will seeks the law that is to determine it *anywhere else* than in the fitness of its maxims for its own making of universal law ... the result is always *heteronomy*. In that case the will does not give itself the law, but the object does so ... This relation ... can give rise only to hypothetical imperatives: 'I ought to do something *because I will something else*'. As against this, the moral, and therefore categorical, imperative, says: 'I ought to will thus or thus, although I have not willed something else'. For example, the first says: 'I ought not to lie if I want to maintain my reputation'; while the second says: 'I ought not to lie even if so doing were to bring me not the slightest disgrace'. The second imperative must therefore abstract from all objects to this extent—they should be without any *influence* at all on the will so that practical reason (the will) ... may simply manifest its own sovereign authority as the supreme maker of law.

Of course, heteronomy comes in different forms, some of which (e.g., tyranny, slavery, blind faith, mechanical obedience) may hardly be said to enable autonomy. My usage here is largely due to Levinas's special sense of the other, and is described more fully in chapters 12 and 13.

4. Weber's usages in connection with the notion of rationality are well known. Acknowledging that for the most part concrete cases of action are not easily reducible to only one of these kinds of rationality, he distinguished among instrumental, value, affectual, and traditional rationality (the first mentioned being logical determination, the second being determination by value-as-such, the third by emotion, and the last by habit). All four of the meanings on which he based his distinctions play a role in my thinking in the present work. The difficulty is to unravel the variety of relations that can obtain between any one sort of rationality and the others. I am not prepared to do that in the abstract, except to say that I am making a case for value-rationality as what definitively distinguishes human being, and therefore as what ought to be born in mind when making decisions and conducting ourselves. It is possible that I depart from Weber in suggesting that there is something rational about attributing this primacy to value-rationality, since he regarded all ('absolute') value as, by definition, 'irrational'. What I mean by my attribution is that, rationally speaking, as humans our rational deliberations ultimately always refer to values, that is, that rationality itself is a matter of ethics.

Chapter 1: Anthropology and the Synthetic a Priori

1. The key work here is Kant's *Critique of Pure Reason*. But laying no claim to Kant scholarship, I have relied exclusively on secondary sources of Kant's ideas, especially W. H. Walsh's (1967) substantial entry on this most influential of thinkers in *The Encyclopedia of Philosophy*. I have also found useful Jaspers's (1962) book-length presentation of Kant's ideas, as well as Kenneth Burke's (1969: 185–200) wonderfully clear and concise exegesis of Kant. Mikel Dufrenne's (1966) probing and original phenomenological study of the notion of the a priori, in which he seeks to revise Kant's concept in the direction of what I call nondualism, was consulted as well. In addition, although I came too late to it to allow me to take it into the careful consideration it deserves, Clair Colebrook's (1999: chap. 1) discussion of Kant is distinguished by a lucid, rich, and nuanced reading in relation to the question of dualism that concerns me here. Finally, it is important to bear in mind that my focus in this chapter is not Kant but Wittgenstein and Merleau-Ponty, as the philosophy of each of these two twentieth-century thinkers bears on the idea of the synthetic a priori. Because this idea is due to Kant, I found it necessary to begin my discussion with a brief of his understanding of it.

2. My understanding of Hume's empiricism is, I expect, routine. Deleuze, however, reads Hume's empiricism otherwise, as philosophically revolutionary (Deleuze 1991; Rajchman 2000: chap. 2). Hume's philosophical shift was away from the rational certainty of Descartes to belief and psychological probability. Taking this shift as refounding philosophy on a brand-new image, Deleuze seems to suggest that Hume opened philosophy to nondualism. I expect that Deleuze's reading is arguable but generous. I mention it here because it evokes a certain important parallelism between Kant's idealism and Hume's empiricism. In view of Kant's synthetic a priori and Hume's pragmatic psychology, both men were pointing toward an onto-epistemological 'between'. But because any such middle is always already broken, evidently each man felt constrained to reaffirm the very dualism his novel philosophical turn served to mitigate—Kant by picturing this middle as transcendent, and Hume by seeing it as immanent.

3. In a lucid and intriguing discussion of Kant's a priori, Wyschogrod (1985: 57–61) argues that in view of Kant's *Critique of Judgment*, in which "imagination" is given a key role in the determination of what there is, "historical actualization of forms" and a middle ground between reason and experience are indeed implied.

4. Cioffi (1998) suggests that Wittgenstein's opposing arguments here—that primitive peoples regard their magical acts in expressive rather than instrumental terms *and* that "it is the most natural thing in the world" (Cioffi's words) to think that such acts are instrumentally efficacious—reflect the fact that Wittgenstein got carried away with his rejection of Frazer's sheer instrumentalism. There

can be no question that Wittgenstein's conservatism, like Heidegger's, included a profound distrust of modern technology and its overriding instrumentalism (cf. Monk 1990). However, I suggest that Wittgenstein's tendency to contradict himself in the *Remarks* results not so much from his anti-instrumentalism as from his failure to see that the deepest failure on Frazer's part was his utterly dualistic outlook. Wittgenstein's grasp of the intuitive compellingness of magic assumes precisely nondualism, but he never quite sees it in this way.

5. Ordinarily, we would not be able to make any sense of someone who denied the existence of his own hands. Thus, when (left-sided) hemiplegic patients ignore their paralyses, their failure to recognize their own limbs seems absurd and presents a rare enigma for those who seek to comprehend it (Straus 1967). The fact that such 'anosognosics' have suffered cerebral injury provides causal account but does not make the inability of these patients to recognize their own limbs any the more comprehensible. Such incapacity seems so strange and unlikely that it suggests not a mistaken mental state but an unhinged one. Hence, Wittgenstein states: (1972: § 155): "In certain circumstances a man cannot make a *mistake* ... If Moore were to pronounce the opposite of those propositions which he declares certain, we should not just not share his opinion: we should regard him as demented."

6. On the other hand, if what we have here is a system "in which consequences and premises give each other mutual support" (Wittgenstein 1972: § 142), then in principle the system is open to transformation were the "consequences" themselves to undergo change so strongly felt or striking to the eye that it breaks the mind-lock enjoyed by the "premises." Because the latter ordinarily serve to channel perception, once they are broken, the change in the consequences becomes transparent as such. Alternatively, such a system of mutual support is also vulnerable to direct critique whereby the premises themselves are, through sustained and focused reflection, brought directly into relief and question. Such contemplative deliberation, too, can disrupt the circle of mutual support, leading to a reassessment of the nature of that which surrounds "what stands fast" (ibid.: § 114). History abounds with examples of both paths to onto-epistemological change, which, as one might expect in a system of mutual support, ultimately co-occur. After all, at one time contentions rather than preconceptions, synthetic a priori, although massively resistant to change, are not in fact immutable.

As an instance of this sort of systemic change, take the current socio-political condition of the United States. Americans appear to take for granted that their representative democracy is both exemplary and immutable. In effect, this image of their mode of government constitutes a synthetic a priori. That it does is perhaps understandable in view of America's past, which, speaking comparatively, and despite the many questionable and even destructive acts that characterize it, may be said to be impressive as regards the implementation of democratic values. In this sense, we can say that the truth of America's democracy has been held fast by "what lies around it" (Wittgenstein 1972: § 114). By democratic values I mean, broadly speaking, rule by the people or self-determination, an ideal closely associated with the notion of freedom. But at this particular juncture in time, there is reason to think that the circle of mutual support characterizing this system may be coming unraveled. The suggestive evidence for this is at least twofold. First, the electorate has proven to be more or less evenly divided as to their support of the current administration, its policies and actions, and radically so as to their opinion of the moral character of these policies and actions: a substantial element sees it as patently good, while another element, no less substantial, sees it as not just wrongheaded but downright evil. Second, the discrepancy between what the administration says and what it does, or between premises and consequences, is striking enough—by which I mean that it is excessive in relation to the expected degree of inconsistency—that at least a large element of the population cannot miss it.

For just one example, take the enveloping premise of 'freedom'. President George W. Bush repeatedly brandishes this principle in sweeping legitimation of the administration's actions, but the actions include unadorned, profound, and even secret and illegal assaults on both civil and human rights. This incongruity between premise and consequence may be understood to expose a critical ambiguity in the American premise of freedom (Patterson 2005). One meaning plainly entails such phenomena as civil rights and social justice, while the other promotes the right of the individual to remain unconstrained by interference in the pursuit of especially material success. What appears to be happening under the current administration is that the weight of the balance of these two meanings has swung sharply to that of personal freedom to pursue socio-economic success. In the present context, what is particularly arresting about this shift is that because it tends to eclipse and undercut social justice and civil liberties, principled considerations that have been crucial to the truth of American democracy, it is in fact eroding the latter. If only because it is representative rather than direct democracy, this democratic order is bound to be characterized by a noticeable gap between form and performance. But under the current administration, because of a glaring and methodical failure to represent a near majority of the people, the gap is being grossly amplified. When a formally democratic government fails egregiously on this count, it may constitute a threat more subtle than outright despotism. For while in virtue of its form it can continue to represent itself as a citadel of freedom, it will in fact have become an instrument of oppression. As in the notorious cases of Fascist Italy and Nazi Germany, failed democracy is a proven condition of the emergence of authoritarianism and fascism. To be sure, in neither of these (paradigmatic) cases was the democratic tradition as strong as in the American instance. But then we should not expect that the transformation of American democracy would have to replicate exactly the paradigmatic forms of such regimes. The point I wish to emphasize here, though, is the likelihood that the meaning of American democracy is being altered in such a way that the presumption of the goodness and immutability of this government may be brought to light and exposed as unwarranted, that is, that this premise's days of standing fast may be numbered.

7. The physicalistic presumption of kinship, that is, the failure to grasp that kinship is also a synthetic proposition, has plagued the anthropology of kinship from its beginnings; indeed, in a sense, this failure inaugurated the anthropology of kinship. Focusing on the Nuer ethnography, I have elsewhere analyzed the ontologically synthetic character of kinship (Evens 1989). As I argue there, the position I promote seems even more radical than the pioneering and powerful critiques (associated with such imposing scholars as Rodney Needham and David Schneider), pertaining to the anthropological study of kinship that have appeared in recent decades. Looking outside the discipline, the extraordinary work of Marc Shell (1988, 1993), a Harvard professor of English, does as much if not more than any anthropology proper to 'deconstruct' the anthropology of kinship.

8. The concept "body without organs" is due to Deleuze and Guattari (e.g., 1987: 149ff.).

9. For an elaboration of this argument, about "the end of having ends" as a universal that is determinable only in the particular, see Evens (1995: chap. 10).

10. The anthropological relevance of this usage could scarcely be clearer as when Merleau-Ponty (1968: 115) proposes that "the communication from one constituted culture to another occurs through the wild region wherein they all have originated." Given its originary scientism, anthropology has not much thought about its defining translational endeavor in such terms. A probing exception is Kenneth Read's *The High Valley* (1965), in which he tries to understand how he could have bonded to persons whose cultural practices literally made him sick. In response, Read points to an experiential dynamic that rests beneath cultural difference and makes possible a deep, silent communication between self and other. I suggest that the emotional dynamic Read describes in his beautiful personal account of his relationships with the Gahuku-Gama may well be assimilated to the "wild region" (of our being) about which Merleau-Ponty speaks.

Chapter 2: Blind Faith and the Binding of Isaac—the Akedah

1. As against the "shocking violence" of Kierkegaard's interpretation of the story, Levinas suggests that one might well think that "Abraham's attentiveness to the voice that led him back to the ethical order, in forbidding him to perform a human sacrifice, is the highest point in the story" (1996: 76, 77). In my interpretation, it is obvious that that event is a high point of the story. But whether it might be considered "the highest" point, as if it were unambiguously the basic intentional element of the

story, is not clear to me. Here I have no cause to save the story for its received (sacrosanct) standing, although I do aim to bring out not only what I regard as the malevolent nature of the story, but also what I see as the story's deep wisdom.

2. Lyotard's argument puts one in mind of the Azande witch doctor's apprentice, who during his training is taught how to practice the deception of sucking out a foreign object from a patient's body by concealing the object in his mouth before he begins the cure. But his belief in the truth of this particular practice remains unshaken, as he continues to think that there are still some witch doctors who can effect this cure without resorting to deception (Evans-Pritchard 1937: 229–30). In strictly logical terms, as Hume showed, the apprentice's conclusion cannot be faulted (such witch doctors may exist or come to exist), but precisely because it shows itself thus to be hermetically sealed against any sort of doubt whatsoever, the conclusion should give one serious pause.

3. In his imposing study of the 'religious' character of Derrida's work, John Caputo (1997), following his interpretation of the French master, conceives of 'blind faith' inversely. Since genuine otherness is abiding but by definition beyond the scope of one's 'vision', Caputo sees blind faith as both necessary and good. As I understand it, his deconstructive conception of faith corresponds in part to my existential understanding of the notion in connection with the human condition of fundamental uncertainty. But whereas, in light of the dogmatic and dualistic foundations of the determinable religions, I have no specifically religious ax to grind, Caputo seems keen to save religion as such. He does not do so uncritically. He argues that the effect of bringing into account the deconstructive sense of faith keyed to the human condition of uncertainty is not to "undo a specifically religious faith but to resituate it" outside of dogma ("knowledge and triumphalism") and within fundamental indeterminacy. Let "faith be faith," he enjoins (ibid.: 57). And he is alert to the peril posed by faith when it becomes religious dogmatism (ibid.: 313): "The danger that inheres in the determinate faiths—the 'positive' religions— ... is that they will confuse seeing and believing and forget that the eyes of faith are blind. That is when they become intolerant of other faiths." When seeing and believing are confused, such that the believer, in his or her utter certitude, forgets that faith is blind and forges ahead unthinkingly, blind to the blindness of faith, it is indeed blind faith, *now in my terms*, that manifests itself.

Caputo's is a splendid argument. I confess, however, to finding it difficult to fathom how the determinable religions can be salvaged as "specifically religious" faiths if their dogmatic foundations are removed. It occurs to me to ask whether the differentiation of religion as such does not already stand on all fours with dogmatism, and whether it does not presuppose the dualism and perfectibilism that make blind faith (my usage) and atrocious violence so very likely. I find it more than hard not to see Abraham's murderous commitment in just this light, despite the luminosity of Kierkegaard's shift of emphasis away from the question of belief in God to that of the mode of existence of the believer.

4. In speaking of the Akedah, Derrida (1995: 69) observes parenthetically, "and it is the sacrifice of both of them [Abraham and Isaac]." Here the structural and substantive analogy between, on the one hand, Abraham, Sarah, and Isaac and, on the other, God, Jesus, and Mary is illuminating. According to Marc Shell (1994: 627–28), "Christianity, in deriving its Holy Family (God the father, Mary the mother, and God the son) from the first Jewish family (Abraham, Sarah, and Isaac), presents itself as Judaism's teleological completion." The movement of completion is meant also to apply to the way in which the identity of Abraham and Isaac is defined by reference to neither of the two figures taken individually, but rather to the father-son relationship. The Christological deifying transmutation of this relational identity into the Father-Son consubstantiality is nothing if not a perfecting of it. Throughout my interpretation of the Akedah, I find this idea of the developmental connection between the Akedah and the story of the sacrifice of Jesus singularly illuminating. Of course, though, given the nature of my analysis, I see the connection as generative rather than teleological, the development proceeding according not to a divine plan, but rather to a man-made principle of perfectibilism.

5. Certainly, in his learned and very substantial study of the institutions of ancient Israel, Roland de Vaux (1965: 456) does not doubt that "the Church which Jesus has founded" managed to consummate the Israelite rite of sacrifice:

The way was thus prepared for the New Testament. Jesus did not condemn sacrifice; indeed, he offered himself as a sacrifice; he is the Paschal victim and his sacrifice is the sacrifice of the New Covenant. This is the perfect sacrifice, by reason of the nature and of the dispositions of the victim: he offered himself of his own free will, in an act of obedience. It is perfect also by reason of the manner in which it was performed: it was a total gift, in which the victim returned wholly to God; a communion-sacrifice more intimate than man could ever have suspected; an expiation-sacrifice sufficient to atone for all the sins of the world. And precisely because it was a perfect sacrifice which at one stroke exhausted all the possible aspects of sacrifice, it is unique. The Temple could disappear, and animal sacrifices had to end, for they were merely the imperfect figure, indefinitely repeated, of the sacrifice of Christ who offered himself "once for all" in a "unique offering" for our redemption and our sanctification, as the epistle to the Hebrews repeatedly insists. And the Church which Jesus has founded will continue, until the end of time, to commemorate this perfect sacrifice and to live by its fruits.

This impassioned commentary (from an author who explicitly forewarns [ibid.: 447] against the danger of explaining "the true meaning of Old Testament sacrifice" by reference to "the sacrifice of the New Testament") is used by Vaux to conclude his discussion of Israelite sacrifice. Plainly, he sees the Crucifixion as the perfecting of the Hebrew institution. He counts the aspects of perfection as the voluntary offering of oneself; a total giving, in which nothing is held back; complete communion; and the redemption of all the sins of humankind. And because it is perfect, this sacrifice makes possible the termination of the "Temple" as well as of animal sacrifices, which he pictures as "merely the imperfect figure, indefinitely repeated, of the sacrifice of Christ." He does not mention the aspect of the sacrifice of Jesus that I have featured by contrast to the Akedah (save by vague implication when he tells us that the Church will continue "until the end of time"), namely, the miraculous logic of resurrection, which, to use the Akedah's imagery, allows both for the knife to fall and for the son to live.

6. A good deal hangs on the clause "in his right mind." Needless to say, many fathers do manage to 'sacrifice' their sons. As Freud drove home (and as I will bring to bear on the case of Abraham and Isaac), the father-son relationship is fraught with anxiety. But apart from interpersonal filicide (and patricide), there is the situation of war. For many years now, my wife has expressed the opinion that war would be a far less attractive option were there a policy that the fathers rather than their grown sons serve as the combatants. Needless to say, I am using "right mind" in its normative acceptation to denote the model father, not the actual one.

7. God's demand of perfection on Abraham's part could be seen as a rendering, in a different context, of the same paradox that repeatedly drove poor Augustine to distraction in his *Confessions*: if God, who is omnipotent, created us as imperfect, why then are *we* to blame for evil? Augustine resolved—which resolution bears the name of Christianity—that so long as we fail to embrace Christ, we are indeed to blame. More fully, he proposed that if we acknowledge our inherent imperfection and concomitant need to devote ourselves to the Perfect or Christ, then once we leave the imperfect world of creation (another version of the gift of perfection), we too can be wholly redeemed and attain perfection or eternal life. But of course if we do not accept the blame for the imperfection of our nature (which is not necessarily the same thing as failing to take responsibility for our individual actions), we must then, in a sense, court the antinomian and put to question (as Augustine had to reprimand himself for doing) the very figure of this God who would demand perfection from what he himself made imperfect.

8. Sarnum (1966: 162–63) writes that "Biblical faith is not a posture of passivity. It is not subscription to a doctrine and it bears no catechismic connotations. The existence of God is regarded in the [Hebrew] Bible as being a self-evident proposition, not requiring affirmation. The Hebrew word *emunah* is best approximated by faithfulness, steadfast loyalty and, occasionally, trust. The important thing is that it finds its fullest expression in the realm of action." (Later in this chapter, when I contrast the Akedah to Nuer sacrifice, I describe a sense of faith along these lines.) But according to Sarnum, the expression of faith in this sense is only the "first lesson" of the Akedah. The "second lesson" (the lesson from which Kierkegaard took his cue) is that "the value of an act may lie as much in the inward intention of the doer as in the final execution."

9. Notwithstanding the trenchant point that, on Kierkegaard's (dualistic) reading, the dimension of secrecy is of the essence of Abraham's act (Caputo 1997: 197–201; Derrida 1995: 53ff.). Although Abraham knew what he was about to do, he was in no position to explain it, not even to himself. Had he been able to communicate a reason to anyone who asked, it would then have been implicit that the sacrificial responsibility he was about to discharge was relative rather than absolute, a function of this world instead of the hidden, unfathomable other world of God. But did the Nazis know why they were slaughtering their victims, any more than Abraham knew why he was embarking on his murderous endeavor? The Nazis were only too well aware that by the ethical standards of the rest of the Western world, the death camps were an abomination. After the fact, when brought before the law, they were prone to respond that they were just following orders, orders ultimately lacking all reason save that they were presumed to have issued from the will of the Führer.

What I mainly wish to query here is that although his back would have been against the wall had his son asked him why, Abraham could well have told the inquiring Isaac of his terrible plan. In failing to do so, was he not exhibiting a fear of condemnation similar to that displayed by the Nazis when they sought to conceal their acts from the rest of the world?

10. Derrida and Caputo imply something of the sort, but in connection with the story's exclusion of Sarah's ('the woman's') point of view. Derrida (1995: 75–76) argues: "It is difficult not to be struck by the absence of woman in [the story]. It is a story of father and son, of masculine figures, of hierarchies among men (God the father, Abraham, Isaac; the woman, Sarah, is she to whom nothing is said …) Would the logic of sacrificial responsibility within the implacable universality of the law, of its law, be altered, inflected, attenuated, or displaced, if a woman were to intervene in some consequential manner?" Caputo, carrying on Kierkegaard's system of pseudonyms and crafting a commentary by one Johanna de Silentio (i.e., a commentary from 'the woman's point of view'), answers Derrida's question unequivocally in the affirmative (Caputo 1993: 144): "Johanna is inclined to agree that Abraham was being tested, but she thinks that the great patriarch and father of faith failed the test, that he missed the point, kept on missing the point, and that the only one who has it right in the story is Sarah, the absent mother who is almost never mentioned and certainly not consulted by Abraham. Johanna turns this story on its head by retelling it from the point of view of the violence and sacrifice, by reading it as a story of the end of sacrifice, rather than of how much steely male machismo it takes to be willing to spill blood in the name of God."

I would only add here that although the Akedah is indeed a story "of masculine figures," Isaac's point of view, once he had undergone his agonizing ordeal and suffered near-death at his father's hand, would be, in connection with judging Abraham's decision, no less edifying than Sarah's. Would it not amount to a 'survivor's account'? One leitmotif found in such accounts by those who came through the Nazi death camps is that of the 'living dead'; that is, the survivors often feel themselves to be already deceased, even while they carry on 'normal' lives (e.g., Delbo 1995: 224f., 262f.). This jarring leitmotif may well be implicit in the Talmudic-Midrashic literature, where these writings include commentaries to the effect that Isaac was actually slaughtered and then brought back to life (Spiegel 1993: 129ff.). To be sure, in these commentaries as in the case of Golgotha, the doctrine of redemptive purpose is meant to turn on its head the manner in which such sacrificial ordeals destroy vitality. But the Akedah seems far less successful in this respect. Although it ends on an emphatic note of life, because Isaac is not God, his suffering is not so easily justified as such, a fact well testified to by the plethora of interpretations struggling to do just that. In effect, there remains in the story a certain disconnect between the command to kill and the countermand to let live.

11. My use of the term 'extension' is inspired directly by the biblical scholar Aubrey Johnson's brilliant discussion of the one and the many in the Israelite conception of God (1961; see also Johnson 1964). This little book makes superb anthropological reading. The following quotation gives the flavor of his (patently nondualist) concept of extension (Johnson 1961: 15):

[H]ere we may remind ourselves that in Israelite thought, while man was conceived, not in some analytical fashion as "soul" and "body," but synthetically as a psychical whole and a unit of vital power, this power was found to reach far beyond the contour of the body and to make itself felt through indefinable "extensions" of the personality. Now the same idea is quite clearly present in the conception of the Godhead—notably, in the first place, in this very notion comprehended by the term [*ruach* or spirit]. We have already touched upon the fact that any manifestation of unusual vigour which marked a man out as an exceptionally powerful personality [such as, one would think, Abraham's geriatric potency] ... might be attributed to the influence of the [*ruach*] (as the "Spirit") of Yahweh; but, clearly, such examples must be understood in terms of the "Spirit" as an "Extension" of Yahweh's Personality.

12. In her splendid book, *Abraham on Trial* (1998), Carol Delaney focuses on, in my words, the "patriarchal warrant" of the Akedah. Her book appeared after I had effectively forged my own interpretation. While I regard her analysis as important, I do not think that, had I read it before embarking on mine, it would have made a significant difference to the way I approach the story. I believe I could have benefited substantially from her research, which is nothing short of prodigious. But although I was from the beginning of my interpretive endeavor alert to the patriarchal essence of the story (see my deconstruction of the biblical figure of Eve in Evens 1997), my sights were set on other essential conditions. By analyzing the story's patriarchal designs and foundations in such depth and so insightfully, Delaney has done a major service. She argues (1998: 13) that the Akedah has had wide-ranging malevolent consequences, bearing on the "ways in which the sacrifice and betrayal of children has been institutionalized," especially in connection to warfare and poverty, and that these consequences largely flow from the patently patriarchal assumptions of the story. In her analysis, the story presupposes a one-sided (monogenetic) "theory" of procreation, in which only the male is credited with any real generative power ("seed"). As a result, Delaney (ibid.: 14) argues, the story "exemplifies and legitimates a hierarchical structure of authority, a specific form of family, definitions of gender, and the value of obedience," all of which conditions tend to go unquestioned wherever the story has prevailed theologically—that is, in the Jewish, Christian, and Muslim socio-religious traditions. I find particularly admirable the bold and inclusive way in which she dares to question the taken-for-granted fundamentals of the monotheistic traditions at point, right down to the justification by faith and to the very figure of god (ibid.: 152f., 159).

Delaney's analysis is not without limitations, though. In the end, her exclusive focus on the issue of gender, so remedial in significant respects, tends to reduce the story overmuch. The theme of sacrifice is, after all, hardly confined to the three powerful religious faiths that see themselves as the children of Abraham. I will argue here that sacrifice has a basis in human existence as such and thus exceeds even a matter so utterly pervasive in human affairs as gender. Without an element of selfhood, there can be no humanity, and selfhood, by definition, is a process of displacement—in effect, of sacrifice. If this understanding is sound, then the Akedah and its malevolent aspect can be adequately plumbed neither solely nor primarily in terms of gender. Delaney's analysis risks the implication that if only patriarchy were eliminated, sacrifice would vanish with it. (Despite the substantiality of her book and its argument, it remains more than hard not to question her questioning the fitness of interpreting the story "in the context of theories of sacrifice" [1998: 13].) But the question that always confronts us is, I believe, not how to eliminate sacrifice, but rather who should be given up—and how. The rule of patriarchal presumption helps roundly to explain why women and children are victimized. But bringing this consideration into relief cannot address the existentially (and ethically) pressing question of how to go about choosing the 'gift'. In connection to this question, I maintain that what makes the Akedah so humanly injurious in the first place is, even before patriarchal presumption, absolutism or perfectibilism. Indeed, I would argue that the Akedah's monogeneticism as well as the monotheism to which it (as Delaney perceptively points out) is tightly linked critically presuppose self-perfectibility, and that patriarchy too feeds off this distinctively human faculty. As I seek to demonstrate in chapter 4, with an analysis of the Holocaust, whatever the life at stake, perfectibilism defeats the vital purpose of sacrifice. On my reading of the Akedah, then, as eminent as its patriarchal presumption is, the story is most principally about economy of sacrifice and tacitly exhibits, in addition to the profound malevolence that both Delaney and I bring into relief, a prescription to a distinctly mediative sacrificial economy.

13. In the Jewish tradition, at least one interpreter was not blind to this matter. Isaac Kook (who served as chief rabbi in Palestine in the early 1900s) held that since God's mercy extends to all creatures, the need to kill even the ram was just a stopgap measure, "a concession to human moral weakness," and that the Akedah was simply the initial step in a progressive evolution toward man's realization that God's love extends to all his creatures (Gellman 1994: 116–18).

14. I have elaborated this thesis—about choice, obedience, and the development of selfhood—at length in *Two Kinds of Rationality* (1995).

15. The classic ethnographic text here is Evans-Pritchard's *Nuer Religion* (1956). See also his "The Meaning of Sacrifice among the Nuer" (1954).

16. Citing in support the remark by "Miss Ray Huffman, an American Presbyterian missionary who spent many years among the Nuer," that "'the missionary feels as if he [*sic*] were living in Old Testament times, and in a way this is true,'" Evans-Pritchard maintained that Nuer religion exhibited notions resembling ones characteristic of the Judeo-Christian ethic, what he spoke of as "features that bring to mind the Hebrews of the Old Testament" (1956: vii). More telling in connection with my comparison and contrast between the Akedah and Nuer sacrifice is the last chapter of Evans-Pritchard's book, in which he holds that Nuer religion is based on what is known not to "the senses" but only to "the imagination" and "is ultimately an interior state" (ibid.: 321, 322). With these psycho-epistemological dualisms of concept and imagination, and of interior state and exterior action, Evans-Pritchard assimilates Nuer religion, not, I suspect, to the religion of the Hebrew Bible, but rather to the interpretation of that text arising with the development of Christianity and embedded in the appellation "Old Testament." I would contend that throughout his great book on Nuer religion, Evans-Pritchard is prone to superimpose on the material an Augustinian dualism, allowing him to defeat at a stroke the once standard anthropological thesis of irrationality as well as the Durkheimian reductionism that religion is nothing but society worshipfully regarding itself. Unfortunately, Evans-Pritchard's dualist depiction is a surpassing misunderstanding. Approaching the anthropological question of sacrifice from a structuralist perspective, Luc de Heusch (1985: chap. 1) has carefully shown, in relation to Nuer sacrifice, the Indo-European ethnocentrism of Evans-Pritchard's translation. Given my approach to Judeo-Christianity, though, in which dualism is seen developmentally, as a matter of degrees, I am less concerned here with Indo-European ethnocentrism than with finding and constructing a ground common enough to allow an intelligible rendering of Nuer religion as nondualistic.

17. I borrow my usage of 'stupidity' from philosopher Gilles Deleuze (1994: 150ff.), and discuss it more fully in chapter 4.

18. In this specific connection, one can see a certain parallelism between God's command to Abraham to forgo his power to choose and God's expulsion of Adam and Eve from the Garden. The latter act, expressly purposed to deny the first couple access to the Tree of Life, amounts to a containment of their powers. The Tree of Life, however, is less a source of simple physical renewal than of the power to re-create oneself at *will*—that is, in godlike fashion, by choice.

19. In identifying ourselves as 'individuals', we tend to forget that we flow materially into the rest of the world: our skins are porous and our bodies full of holes. We flow out of ourselves, and 'the outside' seeps in. In this respect, our defining material boundary is less a hermetic barrier that defines an absolute interior and exterior than a fold or a pleat or a curve, by virtue of which the inside and the outside are not only relative but ultimately indeterminate. I take the idea of the fold from Deleuze (1993), who took it from Leibniz.

20. In a fascinating essay, on (in my terms) dualism and the emergence of self-consciousness, Owen Barfield (1977: 235) writes of

the moment at which the flow of the spiritual tide into the individual self was exhausted and the possibility of an outward flow began. This was the moment at which there was consummated that age-long process of contraction of the immaterial qualities of the cosmos into a human center, into an inner world, which had made possible the development of an immaterial language [i.e., language of mental events and states of mind]. This, therefore, was the moment in which his true selfhood, his spiritual selfhood, entered into the body of man. Casting about for a word to denote that moment, what one would he be likely to choose? I think he would be almost obliged to choose the word "incarnation," the entering into the body, the entering into the flesh.

21. From a phenomenological point of view, it is easy to appreciate Derrida's description of the difference between sight and sound. But I cannot agree with his description's exculpatory implication in respect of Abraham (Derrida 1995: 90–91):

> But there is also absolute invisibility, the absolutely non-visible that refers to whatever falls outside of the register of sight, namely, the sonorous, the musical, the vocal or phonic … but also the tactile and odoriferous …
> God sees me, he looks into me in secret, but I don't see him, I don't see him looking at me, even though he looks at me while facing me and not, like an analyst, from behind my back. Since I don't see him looking at me, I can, and must, only hear him. But most often I have to be led to hear or believe him, I hear tell what he says, through the voice of another, another other, a messenger, an angel, a prophet, a messiah or postman, a bearer of tidings, an evangelist, an intermediary who speaks between God and myself.

Levinas, too, in line with his Judaic view of idolatry or irresponsible representing of the essentially unrepresentable, lays great stress on the primacy of voice over vision and on the idea that one can see or face God only through *hearing* his word (see esp. Robbins's excellent discussion [1999]). Of course, I am hardly the only reader to question Abraham's hearing. Both Kant and Buber question the presumption, in the context of the Akedah, that the words Abraham received were God's. But whereas Buber—conceding that Abraham, and only Abraham (since God had addressed him once before), could not have been mistaken in identifying God's voice—criticizes Kierkegaard for using the figure of Abraham in such a way as to promote the possibility that anyone with knightly aspirations might think himself in direct communication with God, Kant rejects even Abraham's auricular presumption on the ground that the murderous words reported in the story are immoral (Gellman 1994: 2ff.).

22. Perhaps we have here the other side of Foucault's (1965) argument about madness and civilization. Abraham's madness is indeed inspired and, as Kierkegaard thematizes, utterly resistant to the rewards and punishments associated with ordinary moral consciousness. But ironically enough, instead of enchantment (to use Weber's term), Abraham's action may be seen to participate, however nascently, in the development of the extreme self-consciousness to which Foucault takes such burning exception. The Protestant 'inwardness' Kierkegaard associates with Abraham's mad 'leap of faith' seems no less incompatible with Foucault than it does with Enlightenment reason.

23. In this connection, see Sass's (1994) fascinating study of Ludwig Wittgenstein and the paranoid schizophrenic, Daniel Paul Schreber. The following quote from Sass's introduction (ibid.: 9) highlights the relevance of his book to my point about the figure of Abraham:

> Wittgenstein's likening of traditional, metaphysical philosophy to madness is more than just a striking metaphor: many of the pathological tendencies of mind, the diseases of intellect, which he diagnoses in his favorite examples of philosophical illusion turn out to correspond with uncanny precision to the experiences of such insane patients as Schreber. Like the solipsist and other metaphysicians discussed by Wittgenstein, Schreber was convinced of both the profundity and the ineffability of his own special vision of reality—which derived, he believed, from some special insight not vouchsafed to the common man. And, like the metaphysics Wittgenstein criticizes, Schreber's metaphysical vision can be shown to be less a revelation of some higher reality than a projection of his own overly convoluted and disengaged stance toward existence.

24. As described here, then, the 'objective world' amounts to a creative process. This process normally flows so readily that it can foster the illusion that we all see the world from exactly the same standpoint—a veritable view from nowhere. This illusion is extremely powerful, not only because it moves us to forget the particularity of our own standpoint, but also because at least for very many

practical purposes it yields a picture impressively true to the visible world. For this reason, I suggest, modern science, which is critically based on this illusion, commands respect. That is to say, science may well be (as anthropological relativism tends to presume) just another standpoint, but its remarkable practical attunement to the visible world makes it an imposingly efficacious one. I address the question of the efficacy of science directly in chapter 7.

25. Erwin Straus (1969: 29) states:

> The drivers on a super-highway guide themselves in accordance with the structure of the road, despite differences of age and sex and of experience and skill. From his own position each grasps the same visible formation, the road and the cars that travel ahead of or toward him. Everyone is also aware of his own relationship to the street as stationary and to the vehicles as in motion. In seeing the visible he apprehends not only the surroundings, but simultaneously himself as the person who sees in his relation to what is seen. To be sure, he does not see himself, but even so his total experience reaches well beyond what is seen ...
>
> The drivers who move from north to south, those who move in the opposite direction, and those on foot who cross the road at right angles, all of them grasp the road and their own positions in perspectives while oriented to the identical order of visible things in their own order.

For my textual notion of the objective world, I have relied wholly on Straus's tremendously rich and penetrating phenomenological exposition. Straus (ibid.) observes that if that world did not exist, then "our highways would be littered with corpses."

26. It is of interest to quote Rodney Needham here, in his careful anthropo-philosophical study of the notion of belief (1972: 188): "The specific argument of the investigation that I have undertaken here is that the notion of belief is not appropriate to an empirical philosophy of mind or to an exact account of human motives and conduct. Belief is not a discriminable experience, it does not constitute a natural resemblance among men, and it does not belong to 'the common behaviour of mankind.'"

27. Walter Kaufmann also argues that Abraham's claim should not be believed, but only if it were being made "today." He accuses Kierkegaard of an anachronism but allows Abraham's claim to go unquestioned as it applies in the time of Genesis (Kaufmann 1960: 178): "If a man today proposed to act as Abraham did, I should not, like Kierkegaard, 'saddle my horse and ride with him'; for I should not believe the man that it was God who had asked him to sacrifice his son. Kierkegaard places the intuitive certainty that we are confronted with God's will above all critical reflection. For him faith is 'everything.' In Genesis it is assumed that Abraham knows God well, that there is no doubt whatever that it is God who speaks to him, and above all that in fact—*ex hypothesi*—it is God ... These conditions cannot simply be taken over." Unsurprisingly, then, while Kaufmann finds that Kierkegaard's reading of the lesson of the story is fanatical and authoritarian, he moves to save the story itself from ethical doubt (ibid.): "[I]t might well be argued that one of the major lessons of the story in Genesis is precisely this: If any man *hereafter* [my italics] should feel called upon to sacrifice his son, he may be sure that God does *not* [Kaufmann's emphasis] want him to do it."

28. I mean, then, to question the figure of God as well as of Abraham in the story. Kaufmann (1960: 179), citing a Talmudic tale, offers a Hebrew conception of God very different from Kierkegaard's:

> There is a story in the Talmud in which some rabbis have an argument about a point of law. One of them performs various miracles to persuade the others that he is right, and when all else fails he exclaims: "If the law is as I think, they shall tell us from heaven." And a loud voice is heard: "What have you against Rabbi Eliezer, for the law is as he says." But the rabbis decide: "We no longer pay attention to voices, for on Mount Sinai already thou hast written into the Torah to decide according to the majority." Later, one of them meets Elijah and asks him what God did in that hour, and Elijah replies: "God smiled and said: My children have won against me, my children have won."
>
> In this story God is the father; but not all fathers are stern, humorless authoritarians like Kierkegaard's father. God is pictured like the proverbial Jewish father: it is as if he had taught his sons to play chess and was delighted and proud that one of them had beaten him for the first time. He has given his children priceless gifts and is pleased when they grow up and learn to use them independently.

This Talmudic conception of the godhead, though, strikes me as inimical not only to a stern Protestant father figure but also to the Akedah's figure of God, at least in certain critical respects. If the God of Abraham were anything like Kaufmann's "proverbial Jewish father," he would have expected Abraham to refuse to comply with the order to kill Isaac.

Chapter 3: Excursus I

1. Even a current grand theory such as René Girard's (e.g., 1977, 1986), which claims (somewhat disingenuously) to have no religious axe to grind and presents sacrifice (somewhat oxymoronically) as a removable fundament of society, takes it as a practice in its own right. In a nutshell, Girard holds that sacrifice both derives from and conceals a basic violence issuing with the desire to be what the other is and have what he has. According to Girard, who echoes here Rousseau in the *Second Discourse*, society itself is rooted in such 'mimetic desire'. As a result, the other, who is both rival and ideal, is subject to victimization in an act of sacrifice that perpetuates the violence while controlling and cloaking it in ritual practice. However, as the New Testament teaches, with its gospel of a sacrifice to end all sacrifice, love can liberate humankind from such envy and scapegoat violence. By showing us that the victim is in fact innocent, says Girard, the Bible demystifies or reveals ritual sacrifice for what it is—mimetic murder.

Arguing from the perspective of close, ethnographic research, anthropologists have been largely dismissive of Girard's theory. For example, Luc de Heusch (1985: 16–17) finds that Girard has constructed his theory on the basis of a dogmatic, ethnocentric "bias" (viz., that violence is the key to sacrifice), while Kapferer (1997: 210–19) contends that Girard "imposes" a functionalist model on exotic materials, thereby neglecting the subtleties and ambiguities of the material. Bruce Chilton (1992), a religious studies scholar, takes Girard more seriously but remains highly critical. Chilton principally objects to Girard's finding that in the end sacrifice is unnecessary. Although Chilton remains focused on sacrifice as a constituent element of religion, his objection to Girard (as well as his informed and thematic comprehension of sacrifice in terms of an existential linkage between "eating" and *eschaton*) strikes me as consistent in certain respects with my picture of sacrifice as the very structure of human existence. Perhaps even closer to my way of thinking is Gillian Rose's (1992: chap. 4) philosophical and intellectually intensive critique. She takes Girard to task for his failure to grasp that not only is there "love" (i.e., social harmony) in violence, but also there is violence in love. "Love is not opposed to violence," she says, citing in illustration the Akedah (as Kierkegaard reads it): "[T]he violence in love—Abraham's exclusive, violent love of Isaac; the love in violence—his willingness to bind Isaac with faith not with resignation" (ibid.: 148). In effect, Rose is criticizing Girard for absolutism. On her reading, Girard eclipses the fact that "the middle" is always already broken. The "broken middle" is Rose's Hegelism for a whole innately divided against itself, which is to say, the self-relation that amounts to human being. Given this concept, her reading of Girard seems to me to proceed on the basis of what I am calling here nondualism, and to accord well with my description of sacrifice as the veritable form of the human dynamic.

2. Of course, although this account of sacrifice and religion makes it tautological why sacrifice is a major focus of religions in general, in itself it cannot explain why this focus is a matter of ritual. To pose the question of the nature of ritual, if sacrifice is the structure of human existence, why is it necessary to ceremonialize it? Girard, as we have seen, provides a functionalist answer to this question. But so do a great many other scholars, without, however, agreeing on what exactly the function is. I would argue, as against functionalist theories, that the only thing that all rites of sacrifice share is their labor to present what cannot be re-presented or said. In which case, whatever instrumental functions it may fulfill, the rite must constitute its own end. Thus, in the case of the Akedah, it is the very essence of the story's terrible pointedness that allegiance to God's command is not simply a question of declaration but must be shown. As the rite waxes economistic, moving toward surrogacy, the more it becomes a matter of re-presentation rather than presentation, and the less it is an accomplishment in its own right. For example, for some sacrificial purposes a Nuer might offer up a cucumber instead of an ox. And although on that occasion he

regards the cucumber as an ox, the reason for the sacrifice will be considerably lesser than when the victim is a proper beast, making the blatant economism of the rite apt. I would conjecture, then, that such rites, by presenting and not just picturing human existence as it ought to be, mediate, with varying degrees of success, the inevitable gap between the ideal and the real—between how things should be and how they tend to be. In effect, they constitute dynamic icons of human practice, and as such are oxymoronically and thus peculiarly representative of the diacritic of human existence, which is to say, the way in which such existence always runs a line between presentation and representation, between act and meaning. In chapter 9, I have more to say along these lines about the nature of ritual. For a recent, thorough, and reflexive discussion of ritual, which also moves away from functionalism toward a practice approach, but keys itself to a Foucauldian concept of power, see Bell (1992).

3. This theme could not be clearer in, for example, Steven Spielberg's 1998 war film, *Saving Private Ryan*. Fulminating against Girard and his thesis about transcending sacrifice, Chilton, though, nails the overall point discursively (1992: 24):

> Girard asserts in particular that sacrifice is a means of dealing with vengeance, and that law is a far more effective means of doing so. Even assuming, for the sake of discussion, that precisely the same social peril lies at the basis of two quite different sorts of institution, how can we possibly know, in an abstract argument such as Girard's, which of the two deals the more effectively with violence? If it is to be a matter of counting corpses, for example, then sacrifice must appear incalculably more benign than nationalism. Nonetheless, Girard finds it natural to speak of "bloody sacrifice" as a matter of course. Why not "bloody patriotism," or "deadly idealism," or "mortal piety"?

And again (ibid.: 25):

> [Girard's theory] only throws into relief the modern dilemma, where it concerns the understanding of sacrifice. The line of demarcation between the ancient and the modern worlds may be drawn at the point where sacrifice is no longer offered. So understood, Christianity and Judaism (for different reasons) are precursors of the modern world; the Roman Empire became modern when it eschewed its ancestral religion in favor of Christianity, and every other culture has been modernized (if it has been) while embracing the notion that sacrifice is at best a waste. Girard has shown us that sacrifice is so alien to modern consciousness that our very attempt to understand it might turn it into a monstrous double that we imagine would threaten our existence as civilized people.

4. Indeed, even what we normally think of as natural disaster may fit here. Take the massive loss of life suffered as a result of the 2004 tsunami in Southeast Asia. When conversing with my son about this terrible event, I remarked that at least the tsunami was, unlike George W. Bush's war in Iraq, a natural rather than man-made disaster. My son pointed out to me—what goes unseen and yet is obvious—that what happened in Southeast Asia exceeds the designation of natural disaster insofar as the scale of loss may be attributed to a lack of adequate technological resources, including, of course, an early tsunami warning system, in the stricken countries. This lack plainly reflects differential (and sacrificial) control over global resources.

5. Later on in the same work, discussing the notion of 'in-visibility', Derrida again highlights the idea of individual responsibility (1995: 91):

> There is no face-to-face exchange of looks between God and myself, between the other and myself. God looks at me and I don't see him and it is on the basis of this gaze that singles me out ... that my responsibility comes into being. Thus is instituted or revealed the "it concerns me" or "it's my lookout" that leads me to say "it is my business, my affair, my responsibility." But not in the sense of a (Kantian) autonomy by means of which I see myself acting in total liberty or according to a law that I make for myself, rather in the heteronomy of an "it's my lookout" ... even when I can't see anything and can take no initiative, there where I cannot preempt by my own initiative whatever is commanding me to make decisions, decisions that will nevertheless be mine and which I alone will have to answer for.

Compare with Emmanuel Levinas, who in speaking of "the I ... which says 'here I am,'" writes (1993: 168–69):

"Each of us is guilty before everyone, for everyone and for each one, and I more than others," writes Dostoyevsky in *The Brothers Karamazov*. The I which says I is not that which singularizes or individuates a concept or a genus. It is I, unique in its genus, who speaks to you in the first person ... This exposedness is not like self-consciousness, the recurrence of the subject to himself, confirming the ego by itself. The recurrence in awakening is something one can describe as a shudder of incarnation through which *giving* takes on meaning, as the primordial dative of the *for another*, in which a subject becomes a heart, a sensibility, and hands which give. But it is thus a position ... already in debt, "for the other" to the point of substitution for the other, altering the immanence of the subject in the depths of its identity.

Chapter 4: Counter-Sacrifice and Instrumental Reason—the Holocaust

1. In recent years, many scholars have found the word 'Holocaust' objectionable as applied to the Nazi genocide, preferring instead to speak of the Shoah (Hebrew for 'destruction'). The English word 'holocaust' derives from the Septuagint, by way of the Vulgate. The original Hebrew is *olah*, although that is only one of several terms in the Hebrew Bible with the meaning of sacrifice. Behind the qualms about using 'holocaust' as the name for what the Nazis did to the Jews are several highly significant considerations. Meaning "whole burnt offering" (OED), the word implies a divinely sanctioned sacrifice (e.g., M. Bernstein 1994: 10, 132n2). Notwithstanding this ready association with positive, sacred motives, the term has in fact a history of being used by perpetrators to justify killings and massacres of different sorts, including pogroms (Agamben 1999: 28–31; Robbins 1999: 133). In addition, when it is capitalized and applied to the Nazi death camps—as in 'the Holocaust'—the term is unfortunate on two counts: first, it suggests that this event was so outside the pale of humanity that ordinary men could not have committed it (a self-avoiding and therewith gravely consequential underestimation); second, used in this way, it suggests that this particular genocide is elevated above all other instances of man-made mass death. I concur with these objections and understand why they have led important thinkers to seek another name for what happened. Nevertheless, precisely because 'holocaust' conveys the idea of sacrifice, I prefer it to 'destruction' or *shoah* (which, as Agamben points out [1999: 31], "often implies the idea of divine punishment"). Given the interpretive position I take here—that the Nazi death camps were a refraction of a constitutive feature of the Judeo-Christian ethic of sacrifice, and that all human behavior (even at its most inhumane) expresses a sacrificial dynamic—the term 'Holocaust' suits my purpose. But it does so in a form that exceeds the standard acceptation. In no way, *as I use it*, is the term meant to suggest that the concentration camps were divinely sanctioned, or that the industrial slaughter that took place in them is intrinsically more grievous than other instances of man-made mass death.

2. The broadest explanatory trouble with 'revisionist' history of the Holocaust is not that it shows that ultimately the fact(s) cannot be grounded absolutely. Rather, what is wrong with such histories is that in effect the 'standards' of truth by which they tend to proceed leave no room for the possibility of asserting anything at all. Were these standards to be applied comprehensively, one would not be able to make any reasonable or sensible claims whatsoever about what happens or has happened anytime, anywhere.

3. To use Primo Levi's evocative expression (1961: 51).

4. The usage is Primo Levi's (1989: 21):

[U]p to the moment of this writing, and notwithstanding the horror of Hiroshima and Nagasaki, the shame of the Gulags, the useless and bloody Vietnam War, the Cambodian self-genocide, the *desaparecidos* of Argentina, and the many atrocious and stupid wars we have seen since, the Nazi concentration camp system still remains a *unicum*, both in its extent and its quality. At no other place or time has one seen a phenomenon so unexpected and so complex: never have so many human lives been extinguished in so short a time, and with so lucid a combination of technological ingenuity, fanaticism, and cruelty. No one wants to absolve the Spanish conquistadors of the massacres perpetrated in the Americas throughout the sixteenth century. It seems they brought about the death of at least sixty million Indios; but they acted on their own, without or against the directives of their government, and they diluted their misdeeds ... over an arc of more than one hundred years, and they were also helped by the epidemics that they inadvertently brought with them.

This passage may have the feel of an effort to place supreme comparative value on the case of the Holocaust, but in fact it does no more than distinguish its unique features.

5. For support in this connection I appeal to Edith Wyschogrod's outstanding phenomenological analysis of man-made mass death, in which she writes (1985: 27–28): "A unique and paradoxical situation is generated by the technological society: a movement toward a single homogeneous culture, global in scale, whose functions are transparent to everyone has emerged along with technique, but no overarching system of meaning has accompanied it, because such meaning cannot derive from the language of utility and quantification." She goes on to submit that the "death-world makes its appearance upon this already demythologized ground as an effort to sacralize [remythologize, that is, revalorize] a world of impoverished symbolic meanings."

6. "Useless cruelty" is Primo Levi's usage (1998: 107). The eminent Holocaust scholar, Lawrence Langer, opens his essay, "Preempting the Holocaust," as follows (1998: 2):

Let me begin with a concrete detail, because I am convinced that all efforts to enter the dismal universe of the Holocaust must start with an unbuffered collision with its starkest crimes. Recently I was watching the testimony of a survivor of the Kovno ghetto. He spoke of the so-called *Kinderaktion*, when the Germans rounded up all the children (and many elderly) and took them to the nearby Ninth Fort for execution. The witness was present in the room when an SS man entered and demanded from a mother the one-year-old infant she was holding in her arms. She refused to surrender it, so he seized the baby by its ankles and tore the body in two before the mother's eyes.

Although the atrocious act Langer cites may be one of the "starkest crimes" of the Holocaust, it is not unrepresentative (which is why, I expect, the act is related in so matter-of-fact a tone). Jerzy Kosinski, in his powerful novel *The Painted Bird* (1976), undertook to imagine—to horrifying effect—the sort of unimaginable acts at point here, and to those critics who deemed exploitative the unrelieved (and near unendurable) brutality conjured up by him, Kosinski answered by recalling the admonition of those of his Eastern European friends who had written to censure him "for watering down historical truth" (ibid.: xxii; see here also Tadeusz Borowski's [1967] 'fictional' masterpiece). Langer, throughout his work, is unrelenting in impressing upon his readers the lesson that the inhumanity of the Holocaust was so staggering, so unprecedented, that it defies meaning in any discourse available to us and is certainly far beyond any attempt to draw from it redeeming value. As he states (1998: 10), "There is nothing to be learned from a baby torn in two." I do not focus here on such individual acts of horror, and I find it hard to overestimate the importance of Langer's argument about a rupture in our meaningful world and the supreme difficulty of comprehending what happened. Nevertheless, my ethical and phenomenological interpretation of the Nazi project seems to me to make intelligible, in a deep but necessarily limited way, how people can come to do such things. The crucial lesson to be learned from a man tearing a baby in two is that a man can choose to do that, that some men in particular have, and that under certain conditions whereby the self comes to see itself, at its most comprehensive (which is to say, on the plane of selfhood in which primordial choices reveal themselves), as dependent on the absolute exclusion of the other, such unconscionable choices can become routine. And from this lesson, one can draw still another: by bearing witness to such acts, as loudly and forthrightly as possible, the conditions favorable to making such choices become harder to institute, if only because, once enunciated, these conditions can no longer be held naively in relation to their murderous implications.

7. In his profound study of testimony and the Nazi death camps, Agamben (1999) argues that the point of the death camps was not to produce death but rather to ensure "infinite survival." By "infinite survival," he means, though, sheer, organic life, that is, "inhuman" or "vegetative" existence (ibid.: 156, and chap. 4; see also note 31, below). One of the primary themes of Primo Levi's *Survival in Auschwitz* (1961) is that of being twice-killed: before people were put to biological death, they were murdered as human beings, that is, their peculiarly human component or, as Agamben calls it, "form of life," was eradicated. Playing on this crucial insight into the double nature of Auschwitz death, and taking the notions of bio-politics and bio-power beyond Foucault, Agamben brings into relief what may well be the most modern (in the sense of technologically puissant) effort to prove one's power over life and death, namely, by ensuring (in what could be seen as a mimetic attempt at resurrection) the survival of the already dead. There can be no doubt that the camps did concretely produce such 'living death', both on-site (the so-called *Musselmann*, or inmate who had in every way given himself up for dead) and beyond (the survivor's chronic experience of him- or herself as already dead). Nevertheless, Agamben's bio-political thesis is not wholly consistent with the express purpose of the camps: Auschwitz was after all an unrivaled site for the extermination of organic life. Later in this chapter, I make use of Levi's penetrating insight about victims being doubly murdered, in support of my argument that the underlying dynamic of the Nazi project was sacrificial.

Wyschogrod (1985) also argues that the death camps disclose the institution of a death-world in place of the life-world. Doubtless, Agamben's "form of life," which refers to the peculiarly human component of life that came under such devastating assault in the death camps, stands with the Husserlian notion of the life-world. Wyschogrod (ibid.: 16ff.) defines the life-world not only in terms of pre-reflective understandings or the synthetic a priori on the basis of which one can make sense of anything at all, but also as necessarily characterized by a project of vitality and futurity, that is, of the normal continuity of existence. If its project is death, even if this death is a question of the living dead, then the life-world can no longer exist as such.

8. It is at least partly for this reason, I surmise, that the literature is so often inclined to proclaim the Holocaust unintelligible. Hitlerism's utter rejection of value qua value and its absolute commitment to death and dissolution evince the very meaning of meaninglessness according to the Western understanding. This meaning can be experienced (as, say, loss of a sense of self, or purposelessness), but, by definition, it cannot be made meaningful, which is to say, it cannot be assigned purpose or value. But this does not mean that the horror of the death camps remains beyond our ability to describe and understand, as if meaninglessness were not an integral component of the meaningful world of the Judeo-Christian ethic. Indeed, to suggest otherwise would be to imply a hallowed unfathomability, thus validating the very godlike identity to which Nazism aspired. I see the meaninglessness of death-camp death as the manifestation of an unrestrained will to power or, what amounts to the same thing, a self-identity defined in immaculately dualist terms, coupled with the unprecedented efficacy of modern technique and rational know-how.

9. There are two key mythological traditions in connection with National Socialism, the Judeo-Christian, which Hitler was so violently bent on overcoming, and the Greek, to which Hitler's desire to establish an 'Aryan' nation was tied directly. Richard Rubenstein (1966), whose analysis I am rethinking in this chapter, seems to be of the opinion that Hitler's need to displace the Judeo-Christian religious heritage took an instrumental precedence over (but of course did not eclipse) the call to Aryanism. In a brilliant argument, however, two imposing French thinkers, Philippe Lacoue-Labarthe and Jean-Luc Nancy (1990), have essayed the significance of the Greek inspiration to Nazism. Their interpretation is too intricate and involved for me to do justice to here. But in essence they argue that National Socialism was itself a myth inspired by the Greek tradition, a tradition that Germany "reads" intimately and well. With the "collapse of Christianity" (ibid.: 299; I presume that the authors have in mind the Reformation and its resulting schism), all of Europe, searching for a political structure to imitate in order to establish national identities, looked backwards to the ancients and the classical model. Germany lacked not only a national identity or "subject" ("a German language could barely be

said to exist and ... in 1750, no 'representative' work of art ... had as yet come to light in that language" [ibid.]), but also, in view of the fact that classicism had already been opulently appropriated by France, ownership of the means of identification. In response, Germans took recourse to a side of Greek mythology different from that informing French neoclassicism. Instead of the Greece of "measure," "clarity," "law," and "the city," Germans appealed primarily to the "mystical Greece," "the archaic, savage Greece of group rituals, of bloody sacrifices and collective intoxications, of the cult of the dead" (ibid.: 301). Taking this Dionysian path, Germany set out to construct, quite consciously (theoretically and philosophically), a new identitarian myth keyed to aesthetics (music, theatre, poetry, allegory, etc., as expressed by Hölderin, Hegel, Schelling, Wagner, Nietzsche, etc.). In doing so, they redefined the very idea of myth to make of Germany's nationalist myth not simply a model but a veritable operator of identity, an "energy" or creative force for effecting identification. In the end, the myth presented itself as self-realizing: by virtue of their "adhesion" to the myth's identitarian dream of creation, Germans produced a political subjectivity—themselves—as a work of art. Paralleling this dialectical presentation of myth as act was a fusing of racial and spiritual identity. This identitarian synthesis of body and soul, both forms of generative power, conveyed the dialectical union of procreation and creation. Hence, the relevant mythical identity or type—Aryan—distinguished itself as, in addition to a soulful or creative spirit, a race, a blood-bound people (*ein Volk*). The soulful aspect of this Aryan identity, whereby life becomes art (and art, life), drew inspiration from Greek myths of the sun and its creative power. The upshot of all this, in Lacoue-Labarthe and Nancy's reading (ibid.: 307), is that the myth of National Socialism identified the Germans as self-creators, and the Jew ("the bastard par excellence") as not simply another type but the "antitype," the type that denies absolute identity.

Lacoue-Labarthe and Nancy's interpretation is analytically rich and ingenious. As illuminating as it is, though, it does not obviate the importance of attending, in connection with the construction of Nazism, also to the Judeo-Christian mythological tradition. In reading their interpretation, I was taken by the varied manner in which it dovetailed with my reading of the connection between National Socialism and the Western biblical tradition. A close comparison (and contrast) would prove fruitful, but as I came late to Lacoue-Labarthe and Nancy's piece, I cannot undertake this task here. I will say, though, considering that we start from two different (though historically indelibly linked) mythological traditions, it is notable that their and my analyses both focus on Nazism as a lived myth, on the corresponding phenomenological question of how myth can realize itself in act, and on the Aryan aspiration to the self-identity of self-creator or, in my biblically informed terms, godlike identity. Finally, to anticipate the productive promise of such a comparison, I might point to Lacoue-Labarthe and Nancy's finding that from the perspective of the Nazi myth, the Jew was the veritable antitype. Given my interpretation based on the Judeo-Christian mythological tradition, this finding, bearing on the Jews as the representative target of the Nazi's program of racial purification, gains acutely telling support. Inasmuch as the Jew epitomized the idea of creation arising from the other rather than from the self, and also stood to Germany, by way of the Judeo-Christianization of that country, as the figure of that other, he presented and represented the absolute denial of the Nazi identification in terms of perfect self-creation.

10. It is worth quoting Kant here (1964: 76):

[U]nless we wish to deny to the concept of morality all truth and all relation to a possible object, we cannot dispute that its law is of such widespread significance as to hold, not merely for men, but for all *rational beings as such*—not merely subject to contingent conditions and exceptions, but *with absolute necessity*. It is therefore clear that no experience can give us occasion to infer even the possibility of such apodeictic laws. For by what right can we make what is perhaps valid only under the contingent conditions of humanity into an object of unlimited reverence as a universal precept for every rational nature? And how could laws for determining *our* will be taken as laws for determining the will of a rational being as such—and only because of this for determining ours—if these laws were merely empirical and did not have their source completely *a priori* in pure, but practical, reason?

11. With reference to Marx's thought about Jews, Zygmunt Bauman (1988: 50) puts it like this: "[T]he kingdom of universality could be attained only at the price of annihilating Judaism: that most particular of particularities; particularity as such." However, arguing that "progress," "emancipation," and "redemption through universality" may be seen to issue from the union of the "utopianism" of Jewish messianism with the "millenarism" of Jewish mysticism (ibid.: 46–49), Bauman points to a profound irony here: the Enlightenment emancipation "meant the renunciation of a specific Jewish particularity: the one and only peculiarity [*sic*] which gave credence to the program of universalization" (ibid.: 50).

12. Nor should Lang be taken as arguing that Kant would have approved of Nazism. It is important to distinguish between "a tradition of thought and the ideology that inscribes itself ... within it" (Lacoue-Labarthe and Nancy 1990: 295). Although Kant, a devout Lutheran, was not free from anti-Semitism, the intentional thrust of his philosophy makes it plain that he would have found the Nazi genocide ethically intolerable. In this connection, Hannah Arendt's (1994: 135–37) discussion of Eichmann's invocation of Kant's philosophy is instructive. On the one hand, Eichmann declared that he had lived his whole life according to the Kantian definition of duty, by which he understood the categorical imperative or the universalizing principle that one ought to will what all men under similar circumstances would find desirable. Plainly, some men, the victims of the Nazis, could hardly find it desirable to live under a system that gave the Eichmanns of the world the right to exterminate them. On the other hand, Eichmann confessed that once he had agreed to carry out the Final Solution, he had indeed ceased to live according to the categorical imperative. Arendt points out, though, that Eichmann had not simply abandoned Kant's principle but had gravely distorted it by reducing it to the prescription, also Kantian, that one ought to go beyond the principle of duty to identify one's will with the source of the law. Whereas for Kant that source is practical reason, in the case of Nazism it was Hitler's will: "Act in such a way that the Führer, if he knew your action, would approve it," is how Hans Frank, the Nazi governor general of occupied Poland, formulated the categorical imperative in the Third Reich. Moreover, as Arendt is quick to clarify, because Kant's moral philosophy is bound up with the faculty of judgment, it patently rules out blind obedience. Nevertheless, Eichmann's abdication of his will in favor of Hitler's, and Frank's Nazification of the categorical imperative—although they constitute perversions of Kant's ethic and in a way stand closer to the biblical ethic of faithful allegiance found in the story of Abraham and Isaac—express a strong Kantian consciousness and share in Kant's fundamental commitment to the standard of the universal.

13. Dumont makes his own (Hegelian) case, but it is useful to cite here Nietzsche, talking about decadence: "The whole no longer lives at all: it is composite, calculated, artificial and artifact." This remark is cited by Wyschogrod (1985: 27) in the context of her characterization of technological society in terms of "the substitution of utility for immediate quality, [and] the transformation of the propertied life-world into units of quantity." In light of Dumont, it is worth noting that Wyschogrod holds that "only mythical thought" can provide the global perspective inherent in genuine holism. Her source for arriving at this conjecture about the unifying force of myth is none other than Lévi-Strauss.

14. The literature on the administration of the Final Solution is replete with the rationale that those carrying out the actual executions were not only doing their duty but making an exceptional self-sacrifice in taking on the horrendous work (see Hilberg 1985: 137). Here's how Heinrich Himmler (who, as SS leader and chief of the German Secret Police, was responsible for the implementation of the Final Solution) expressed it (cited in Bonhoeffer n.d.: 18): "In 'solving the Jewish problem,' disagreeable though this was to the entire people, the followers of Hitler made a great sacrifice, thus doing their patriotic duty for the sake of Germany's future!" Although perverse, this appeal is not surprising in view of the inordinate degree to which Nazi Germany managed to turn its people into functionaries of the state. In *Mein Kamph*, Hitler focuses on just this idea of sacrifice in "the service of the community" to draw a diametrical contrast between Aryan and Jew (1943: 297, 302):

This self-sacrificing will to give one's personal labor and if necessary one's own life for others is most strongly developed in the Aryan. The Aryan is not greatest in his mental qualities as such, but in the extent of his willingness to put all his abilities in the service of the community. In him the instinct of self-preservation has reached the noblest form, since he willingly subordinates his own ego to the life of the community and, if the hour demands, even sacrifices it …

If the Jews were alone in this world, they would stifle in filth and offal; they would try to get ahead of one another in hate-filled struggle and exterminate one another, insofar as the absolute absence of all sense of self-sacrifice, expressing itself in their cowardice, did not turn battle into comedy here too.

So it is absolutely wrong to infer any ideal sense of sacrifice in the Jews from the fact that they stand together in struggle, or, better expressed, in the plundering of their fellow men.

Here again the Jew is led by nothing but the naked egoism of the individual.

The terrible irony of Hitler's description of the Jews in terms that apply so precisely to the cloacal order of the death camps ("filth and offal," "hate-filled struggle," and extermination) that he himself created is truly stunning. In connection with this irony, it is arresting to compare Hitler's characterization of the Jews to Eichmann's (see note 27 below).

15. Bauman's (1988: 55–56) discussion of the rise of racist anti-Semitism has a certain affinity with Dumont's argument. Bauman pictures racism as a reaction to individualism in the following sense. He finds that with the legal emancipation resulting from Enlightenment thought, "the boundary-keeping (and hence segregatory) concerns of most communities could no longer be maintained by means of old religious criteria, which rendered membership ultimately dependent on individual choice." Racism, according to Bauman, filled the need for "another criterion," "one which rendered cultural or religious conversion impotent and subjective self-definition irrelevant."

16. Hitler's dismissal of "the principles of humanity" and reduction of displacement to self-interested combat seem to anticipate, in an intriguing way, the postmodernist's deconstruction of humanism and correlative tendency to construe human relations in terms of power alone. Indeed, the event of the Holocaust, given its staggering impact on the self-image of civilizational modernity, must have contributed critically to the inception of postmodernist thought, as it did to the substance of so much social thought in general. Of course, the key figures associated with postmodern philosophy are anything but fascistic. Nevertheless, it would be fruitful to study intensively the relationship between this conceptuality—which, like the death camps, has thrown into question foundational understandings of Western civilization—and the occurrence of the Holocaust.

17. Dumont's interpretation of Hitlerian racism finds a philosophical parallel in the phenomenological reflections of Emmanuel Levinas. Remarkably, these reflections were first published in 1934, shortly after Hitler came to power. Like Lang, Levinas (1990) starts his thinking here by pointing to the Western promise of absolute freedom from time and history, linking this promise to, among other Western epistemological traditions, the Enlightenment ("French writers of the eighteenth century" as well as "a reason that exorcises physical, psychological, and social matter" [ibid.: 66]). He maintains that, for reasons of intuition and experience, this ahistoricist view of humanity stimulated its own contestation by materialism. Marxism (as Dumont also suggests [1986: e.g., 150–51]) of course is a central doctrine in connection with this reaction. In its wishful projection of an economy based on need and a state withered to the point of extinction, Marx's materialism continues to hold out the promise of freedom. In doing so, however, it can—like the Enlightenment project to which it is in part a reaction—foster a desire for total freedom, thus undermining respect for and commitment to 'truth'. By contrast, to come to Levinas's main point, racist materialism essentializes human being wholly in terms of its material bonds. Basing it thus on a community of blood, racism can restore the principle of 'truth', and in turn resurrect the feeling of sincerity and authenticity that prevailed prior to the thematic emergence of the spirit of freedom. Unfortunately, in doing so, racism converts universality from a principle of value to one of force, thus virtually abolishing the distinctly human aspect of humanity. In essence, as Dumont might say, the expression of difference gets restricted to physical struggle.

18. Foucault's famous development of the idea that knowledge is power is in fundamental ways continuous with the critical theory school.

19. Hitler recorded his anti-Semitism copiously throughout *Mein Kamph*. Here, though, in his private conversations, is what he had to say about Christianity (1973: 7; see also 75ff.):

> The heaviest blow that ever struck humanity was the coming of Christianity. Bolshevism is Christianity's illegitimate child. Both are inventions of the Jews … Christianity was the first creed in the world to exterminate its adversaries in the name of love … Its key-note is intolerance. Without Christianity, we should not have had Islam. The Roman Empire, under Germanic influence, would have developed in the direction of world-domination, and humanity would not have extinguished fifteen centuries of civilization at a single stroke.

20. For an explanatory appeal, much more recent than Rubenstein's, to the idea of sacrifice in relation to the Holocaust, one can look to LaCapra's closely argued essay (1994: chap. 3). There are very substantial differences between his and Rubenstein's respective positions. Whereas LaCapra is dealing in secular historiography, Rubenstein (who is a rabbi as well as a professional historian) is preoccupied with implications and questions of sacred history. But by virtue of their mutual appeal to psychoanalytic theory, their arguments have in common a fundamental emphasis on the relation between scapegoating and self-identifying where the identity at stake is perfectibilist in nature. (It is very surprising, then, that LaCapra fails to cite Rubenstein.) Offering a "model" of the Nazi regime, LaCapra turns insistently to "the role of scapegoating and victimization that involved a secularized 'ritual' or even distorted 'sacrificial' component" (ibid.: 100–101): "I intimate that this role was significant, at least for certain figures such as Hitler, Himmler, and their more fanatical followers—figures who arguably were prime movers in the Nazi *Bewegung* … I am insisting on this component because I think it has recently been underemphasized and, more important, that its problematic combination with more obvious and easily documentable features, such as the role of bureaucracy or hygienic considerations, has tended to be ignored."

LaCapra's "model" is complexly keyed to a psychoanalytic dynamic of repression, phobic anxiety, and scapegoating. In essence, he conjectures that the Jews and other elements of German society—elements that, like the Jews, were "out-groups" but nonetheless on "the inside"—served as scapegoats for getting rid of "the alien other" in a nation-self that had come to see its own identity in terms of sublime purity. LaCapra's focus on the dynamic of self-identifying captures something absolutely critical for understanding how the Nazi regime moved itself to commit acts of such harrowing cruelty and unspeakable crimes. Taken on its pre-predicative plane, self-identity moves people in the nature of the case, simply because it is indistinguishable from that movement; put another way, the movement virtually defines the lived identity of the people in question. In the case of the perpetrators of the Holocaust, speaking generally, the self-identity of the 'prime movers' may well have differed from the other participants, in that whereas the former were wholly taken with what amounts to a godlike image of themselves, the latter inclined to identify themselves (for a variety of reasons, including naiveté, fear, hate, power, stupidity, indifference, convenience, cowardice, etc.) by reference to the self-understanding of the prime movers. However, LaCapra's psychoanalytical model, as Lang (1990: 158–59, and chap. 2) suggests of Rubenstein's and indeed of all psycho-dynamic models, tends to frustrate one of the crucial advantages of seeing the Holocaust in terms of the idea of sacrifice, namely, that of avoiding the obviation of the question of responsibility. By its very nature, sacrifice implicates responsible agency. But notwithstanding its rich intellectual character and intense concern with symbolics, the psychoanalytical framework in effect supposes a deterministic behavioral dynamic and thus makes illusory the idea of such agency. For a non-psychoanalytic but brilliantly incisive interpretation of Hitler's anti-Semitism in terms of ritualistic sacrifice, see Burke's brief exposition of the "dramatistic" logic of scapegoating (1969: 406–8).

21. For my description of the formal nature of ritual sacrifice, I rely here on Evans-Pritchard's Henry Myers Lecture on sacrifice among the Nuer (1954) as well as his account in *Nuer Religion* (1956). For present empirical purposes, though, I have chosen to blur his distinction between "two main theories of sacrifice, the communion theory and the gift theory" (1954: 22; see also 1956: chap. 11).

22. Levi's *Survival in Auschwitz: The Nazi Assault on Humanity* (1961) first appeared in English as *If This Is a Man* (1958), true to the original Italian title, *Se questo è un uomo* (1947).

23. Could the Nazis have envisioned restoring the prelapsarian paradisiacal garden? On 16 July 1941, Hitler boasted in conference that in his newly won territories in the east he would create "a Garden of Eden" (Browning 1992: 10). Although Hitler's mention of the biblical garden might well have been nothing more than a casual usage, when one considers what he did in fact create in the east, the reference also seems more than suggestive. For, as was noted above (note 7, this chapter), Auschwitz amounted to a community of the living dead, a social state of being that, for reasons of its defining inhumanity, in some of the anti-utopian literature has been assimilated to the biblical idea of a garden in which for all practical purposes men existed in principle solely as functions of their Other, without benefit of their own specifically human life, their moral capacity (see, e.g., the epigram to chapter 9, this volume).

24. To suggest that the Nazi project was seen by the Nazis as redemptive is to disable the attribution of the status of sheer evil to that project, and thus, in view of the fact that the Final Solution was as evil as evil can be, to relativize the very idea of evil. In chapter 12, I take up the matter of the relative nature of good and evil, and try to show that that nature does not relieve us of the responsibility of producing good moral reasons for our actions. Nor does it make 'transparent' moral judgments impossible.

25. "The trouble with Eichmann," writes Arendt (1994: 276), "was precisely that so many were like him, and that the many were neither perverted nor sadistic, that they were, and still are, terribly and terrifyingly normal. From the viewpoint of our legal institutions and of our moral standards of judgment, this normality was much more terrifying than all the atrocities put together, for it implied … that this new type of criminal, who is in actual fact *hostis generis humani*, commits his crimes under circumstances that make it well-nigh impossible for him to know or to feel that he is doing wrong." Améry (1980: 25) takes Arendt to task for what might be called misplaced abstractness:

> Many things do indeed happen approximately the way they were anticipated in the imagination: Gestapo men in leather coats, pistol pointed at their victim—that is correct, all right. But then, almost amazingly, it dawns on one that the fellows not only have leather coats and pistols, but also faces; not "Gestapo faces" with twisted noses, hypertrophied chins, pockmarks, and knife scars, as might appear in a book, but rather faces like anyone else's. Plain, ordinary faces. And the enormous perception at a later stage, one that destroys all abstractive imagination, makes clear to us how the plain, ordinary faces finally become Gestapo faces after all, and how evil overlays and exceeds banality. For there is no "banality of evil," and Hannah Arendt … knew the enemy of mankind only from hearsay, saw him only through the glass cage.

I cannot gainsay Améry's cutting phenomenological insight (about the abyssal difference between anticipating the blow and experiencing it), nor, with Lang (1990: 22–23), can I agree with Arendt's definition of banality simply in terms of thoughtlessness or lack of intentionality. Nevertheless, I regard the thrust of Arendt's point as supremely important—that within Nazi Germany, radical evil was normalized. I quote from Arendt again, in a wonderfully astute passage (1994: 150):

> And just as the law in civilized countries assumes that the voice of conscience tells everybody "Thou shalt not kill," … so the law of Hitler's land demanded that the voice of conscience tell everybody: "Thou shalt kill," although the organizers of the massacres knew full well that murder is against the normal desires and inclinations of most people. Evil in the Third Reich had lost the quality by which most people recognize it—the quality of temptation. Many Germans and many Nazis, probably an overwhelming majority of them, must have been tempted *not* to murder, *not* to rob, *not* to let their neighbors go off to their doom … and not to become accomplices in all these crimes by benefiting from them. But, God knows, they had learned how to resist temptation.

For me, the crucial question pertains to the conditions for the normalization of evil, that is, for learning to do evil as a banal act of everyday life and coming to perceive the good as temptation. In this connection, the systematic effort by the Nazis to hide their exterminatory activities makes perfectly clear that they knew only too well how these activities would be taken by the 'outside' world. This implies that they were not really in a position to be perfectly thoughtless in carrying out these activities, that they could not help but take into account a view that, far from regarding the project of extermination as a necessary and millennial good, pictured it as absolutely evil. As a result, the Nazis were forced to try to hide their endeavors not only from others but also, in a certain sense, from themselves, and to justify these endeavors ideologically. A considerable number of devices and measures in connection with this state of things have been isolated and identified in the literature. On the question of how ordinary Germans were moved to participate in the Final Solution, see Browning's (1992) uniquely important study, the final chapter of which provides a closely argued critical look at some of the important responses to this question. My principal argument here bears on the phenomenological role of the sacrificial dynamic and the ideological appropriation of this dynamic of self-construction by the Nazi regime, such that the Hitlerites were moved routinely to butcher others as a condition of their own most basic self-identity—that identity the self cannot imagine itself as existing without.

26. "Useless suffering" is Levinas's concept for suffering that cannot really be made meaningful by reference to theodicy and that has no redemptive value (see Levinas 1998: chap. 8).

27. In his exposition of the logic of Nazi anti-Semitism, Burke (1969: 407) depicts the scapegoat as representing both the "essence" of evil and, since the goal of the sacrifice is "rebirth," a "bad parent." Arendt (1994: 22) tells us that Eichmann "left no doubt that he would have killed his own father if he had received an order to that effect." In an actual sense, he did both kill his 'father' and receive an order to that effect. It is richly provocative here to cite Arendt recounting Eichmann's striking testimony (ibid.: 42):

> The reason he [Eichmann] became so fascinated by the "Jewish question," he explained, was his own "idealism"; these Jews, unlike the assimilationists, whom he always despised, and unlike Orthodox Jews, who bored him, were "idealists," like him. An "idealist," according to Eichmann's notions, was not merely a man who believed in an "idea" or someone who did not steal or accept bribes, though these qualifications were indispensable. An "idealist" was a man who lived for his idea ... and who was prepared to sacrifice for his idea everything and, especially, everybody. When he said in the police examination that he would have sent his own father to his death if that had been required, he did not mean merely to stress the extent to which he was under orders, and ready to obey them; he also meant to show what an "idealist" he had always been. The perfect "idealist," like everybody else, had of course his personal feelings and emotions, but he would never permit them to interfere with his actions if they came into conflict with his "idea."

How remarkable and supremely ironic to find Eichmann describing himself by appealing to Jews as a positive model and avowing, in virtue of this model, that he would have murdered his own father had it been demanded of him. And what is that model if not a description, as found in the Akedah, of the true patriarchal Jew? Like Kierkegaard's Abraham, Eichmann's Eichmann demonstrated that he was a true knight of faith, capable of resisting the tremendous gravity of his "personal feelings and emotions," as well as of all compromise of principle (as glossed in his reference to the "assimilationists," whom he "despised"). And like Abraham, he proved his unswerving devotion in a willingness to sacrifice that which is held most dear in terms of the ethical order, that is, life itself—in Eichmann's case, the lives of millions of Jews, although expressed figuratively by him as the life of his own father. He thus tropes his murderous act of knightly faith as the laying waste of the father by the son, rather than the son by the father. Of course, whereas Eichmann succeeded in killing millions of 'fathers', in the end Abraham is stopped from slaughtering his son, validating the Father's faith as vital rather than lethal.

Put differently, although both Eichmann and Abraham were, to use Eichmann's term, "idealists," the respective ideas for which each "lived" could not be more opposed—for together they describe the difference between, to recall both Lyotard (1990: chap. 3) and Arendt (note 25, above), the moral imperatives of "Thou shalt kill" and "Thou shalt not kill." Moreover, in his rejection of "Orthodox Jews," whom he found "boring," Eichmann was alienating from religion proper the Jewish "idealism" he professed to admire, thus grossly distorting it. In point of fact, the "idea" for which Eichmann "lived" was, in diametrical contrast to the Jewish (Abrahamic) object of devotion, utterly secular. Although it commanded a sacrosanct approach (he would permit nothing "to interfere with his actions" if it "came into conflict with his 'idea'"), Eichmann's "idea" reduced human existence to its bio-material being and mass (in effect, inhuman life), and thus expressed a secularity so total as to belie the very idea of idealism. Nevertheless, in appealing to the Jews as his role model, Eichmann evoked the uncompromisingly principled sacrificialism of the Akedah, bringing into relief a patricidal logic that is deeply rooted in this story of a father setting out to terminate the life of his son and is given added weight in the story of the Crucifixion, where the Son's life is actually taken.

28. In 1964, a German public prosecutor, investigating the culpability of an SS man accused of murdering children, ruled as follows: "The investigations did not prove with the certainty that is demanded of them that the children suffered *unduly* before they died. On the contrary, much can be said for the fact that all the children became unconscious as soon as they received the first injection and were therefore not aware of all that happened to them thereafter. *And so, beyond the destruction of their lives no further harm was done to them; and in particular, they did not have to suffer especially long, either in body or soul.*" Langer cites this legal ruling (1995: 68–69; the italics are his), confessing that for the first time in his 20 years of studying the Holocaust experience, he was reduced by this prosecutor's reasoning "to a stunned and baffled silence," and inquiring about the "kind of thinking that inspires a human being to regard the destruction of lives with such trifling inconsequence." The prosecutor's ruling is consistent with Arendt's (1994: 105–6) observation that the problem for the Nazi regime became to overcome not so much the conscience but rather the animal pity of the killers. (As they had so thoroughly capitulated their own agency to that of the state considered in terms of its self-described legality, Nazi war criminals had a tough time grasping the charges against them.) I cite the ruling in order to suggest that once people are deprived of all their rights, the question of guilt on the part of he who would maltreat them becomes just a matter of animal pity. Consult here also Bauman (1991: 24ff.).

29. One might well ask here, what of the ram in the Akedah? But the biblical story plainly contrives to identify the ram with Isaac, thus bringing it into the realm of sacrificial subjectivity, not objectifying it. Nuer sacrifice does much the same by engraving the horns of their bovine victims into the foreheads of the initiates. As a result, these animals are construable as extensions of humanity and therefore as true donors. By acute contrast, the Nazis strove mightily to desubjectify their victims, thus removing the identitarian warrant for sacrifice.

30. Of course, the Crucifixion provides in Western culture the paradigm of a perfect sacrifice, the intention of which is resurrection. But seen as undertaken by men alone, perfect sacrifice of this kind can only amount to a catastrophic affectation. In the case of the Akedah, apart from a demonstration of faith, the intended consequence is patently unclear. Outside of his own son's death, Abraham does not know what to expect. It is arguable that the demonstration of faith amounts precisely to a resurrection, but of the life of the spirit, and that in this sense the act was indeed meant as life-giving. That is essentially what I have argued in chapter 2, with the added point that because the perfection of the sacrifice stands on all fours with an absolute separation of spiritual from material life, the act reflects an existential intelligence gone terribly awry and, correlatively, an essential malevolence. For a cinematic example of perfect sacrifice bent on utter self-destruction, one might think of Stanley Kubrick's *Dr. Strangelove*, a superb political satire about a nuclear holocaust or doomsday, the basic theme of which could be summed up in Kenneth Burke's revision of an old nursery jingle, which is, even today, only too apposite. Burke substitutes for the original actors ("trees," "axes," and "men") ones that better express his concern "with perfection on a grand scale" (1966: 21–22):

If all the thermo-nuclear warheads
Were one thermo-nuclear warhead
What a great thermo-nuclear warhead that would be.

If all the intercontinental ballistic missiles
Were one intercontinental ballistic missile
What a great intercontinental ballistic missile that would be.

If all the military men
Were one military man
What a great military man he would be.

And if all the land masses
Were one land mass
What a great land mass that would be.

And if the great military man
Took the great thermo-nuclear warhead
And put it into the great intercontinental ballistic missile
And dropped it on the great land mass,

What great PROGRESS that would be!

31. Leaving wholly intact the received acceptation of 'sacrifice', Giorgio Agamben has determinedly expanded the meaning of 'the sacred' in the Western tradition to embrace a representatively negative phenomenon. His *Homo Sacer* (1998) and *Remnants of Auschwitz* (1999) are enormously penetrating and important interpretations of the ethico-political pathology of modern society. Had I read them before I forged my own analysis of the Holocaust and the Akedah, they would have directly informed my thinking. As it is, I want to note his argument here and comment on it in relation to my own. Agamben writes that the idea of life underlying the homicidal victimization that characterizes so modern an occurrence as the Holocaust "is more original than the opposition of the sacrificeable and the unsacrificeable, and gestures toward an idea of sacredness that is no longer absolutely definable through the conceptual pair ... of fitness for sacrifice and immolation, according to ritual forms. In modernity, the principle of the sacredness of life is thus completely emancipated from sacrificial ideology" (1998: 114). Taking his cue from an "enigmatic figure" of archaic Roman law, that of "homo sacer," Agamben argues that the original Western notion of the sacred rests on a conception of a kind of life not fit for sacrifice but open to killing with impunity. This kind of life, excepted on the one hand by divine law and on the other by human law, is called by him "bare life," and he sees it as the categorial key to the determining structure of the very idea of sovereignty in the Western political tradition. What ultimately defines sovereign power in this tradition, he argues, is absolute right over life and death, such that the decision is an expression of the unqualified autonomy of the sovereign, rather than any prior general power (in his discussion, the power of the law, whether divine or human). Sovereignty and bare life, thus, are absolutely integral to each other ("the production of bare life is the originary activity of sovereignty" [ibid.: 83]).

Given that Agamben's thesis about sovereign power takes sacrificeability into account by excluding it, he naturally rejects the term 'Holocaust' as the name for what the Nazis did to the Jews. Nevertheless, my argument has far more in common with his than meets the eye. Let me mention two important aspects in which this is so. The first bears on the consideration that bare life, as that which may be killed but not sacrificed, bespeaks for Agamben "a zone of indistinction." This notion, reiterated throughout his argument, denotes a total collapse of difference, most pointedly between life and politics (1998: 153). In effect, the biological becomes immediately political, and politics becomes immediately biological. Put less abstractly, the exclusion of people from both human and divine law defines them as, relative to sovereign power, no more than, say, lice (so much for the Western canonical definition of humanity in terms of rights, as Agamben is keen to accentuate). Indeed, Agamben invokes here Levinas's penetrating 1934 analysis of National Socialism, in which Levinas implicitly links, as a matter of logic, Hitler's biological politics to Heidegger's ontological deconstruction of the distinction between body and mind. Leaving aside the question of whether or not Heidegger's emphasis on 'facticity' and embodiment dovetails with racialism, it is clear that with his notion of indistinction, Agamben is driving at monism. That is, he is arguing that where no distinction whatsoever, not even a relative one, is made between body and mind, the political pathology on which he dwells will present itself. To come to my point now, what Agamben is in fact invoking when he links this pathology to "indistinction" is ontological dualism, for monism is conceptually coherent only in terms of absolute boundaries, and boundaries of this unambiguous kind betoken dualism. Put another way, monism can emerge only where one of the two principles to a dualism, constrained by the sheer opposition of their relationship, manages to reduce to itself the other. In other words, although Agamben does not put it this way, his argument, like mine, amounts to a critique of ontological dualism. (What I cannot say is whether, in light of his discussion, he would embrace what I have referred to in the present work as nondualism.)

The second point I wish to make, as regards common ground between my argument and Agamben's, has to do with the role I give to the concept of sacrifice. Here the difference between my position and his may appear patent. His organizing concepts are power and politics, whereas mine are religion and ethics; he critically rejects 'sacrifice' as the name for the political pathology characterizing modern life, whereas I roundly embrace it. Yet it is suggestive that when Agamben discusses the origins of the Western idea of sovereignty, he cites as the first mention of "right over life and death" in the history of Roman law "the unconditional authority ... of the *pater* over his sons" (1998: 87). This patriarchal right, he states, is "tightly intertwined" with sovereign power and "seems to define the very model of political power in general" (ibid.: 88). In view of his thesis that the life subject to the sort of power he wishes to elucidate is definitively unsacrificeable, it is not surprising that Agamben does not mention in this context the Akedah. But when it is borne in mind that my interpretation of the biblical story proposes that Isaac's distinctive sacrificeability serves, however irrationally, as a pretense for Abraham to secure his own selfhood, the binding of Isaac begins to look like a gesture toward the sort of sovereignty on which Agamben dwells. It needs also to be borne in mind that whereas Agamben keeps to the standard technical meaning of the term 'sacrifice', my usage is keyed in the first place to existential rather than ritual conduct, and thus transgresses (burrows beneath, as I see it) the standard meaning. My usage, then, describes the quotidian and facultative human dynamic constituted by a selfhood that is at once opposed to and defined by otherness. As a result of this dilemmatic condition, we humans make our way in this world willfully, and our choices, whether they are large or small, witting or naive, at the end of the day cannot but result in the displacement (the sacrifice) of either others or ourselves. Given this unorthodox usage of 'sacrifice' (which in many ways corresponds to ordinary language), my conclusion that the Holocaust is a counter-sacrificial form of sacrifice seems in keeping with Agamben's thesis of 'unsacrificeability'. By projecting the Jews as totally unsuitable as victims with whom to identify, the Nazis were indeed defining them very precisely as unsacrificeable. My usage may even be consistent with Agamben's idea of killing outside the compass of human law. The depiction of the Holocaust as a form of sacrifice appears to remove the killing from the restrictions of human law, while immunizing the killing against divine law by defining that form as a counter-sacrifice.

32. What I have elsewhere called "half-logic" (Evens 1983).

33. The quotation is from Deleuze (1994: 150), whose Nietzschean discussion of the notion of stupidity has inspired my interpretation here of Hitlerism and its logic. Deleuze distinguishes between thought in the sense of "good will" or "common sense," which he says is essentially a matter of repeating or recognizing or representing identity or the Same, and thought that is truly creative, which, he holds, opens identity to difference, spontaneity, invention, and becoming. "Stupidity," "malevolence," and "madness," for Deleuze, disrupt the Same and constitute figures that reveal "true transcendental structures of thought." But he also maintains that such creative figures are perilous, for "turning over the ground is the most dangerous occupation, but also the most tempting in the stupefied moments of an obtuse will" (ibid.: 152). The danger appears to be not simply violence, which is endemic to such thought, but violence unlimited, total destruction. In this connection, it is helpful to cite Deleuze and Guattari's discussion, elsewhere, on the nature of fascism (1987: 230–31):

A bizarre remark by Virilio puts us on the trail: in fascism, the State is far less totalitarian than it is *sui-cidal*. There is in fascism a realized nihilism. Unlike the totalitarian State, which does its utmost to seal all possible lines of flight [i.e., all that lies in between and cannot be fixed and determined], fascism is constructed on an intense line of flight, which it transforms into a line of pure destruction and abolition. It is curious that from the very beginning the Nazis announced to Germany what they were bringing: at once wedding bells and death, including their own death, and the death of the Germans ... Suicide is presented not as a punishment but as the crowning glory of the death of others.

Deleuze and Guattari speak here of the Nazi state as a *"war machine that no longer had war as its object* and would rather annihilate its own servants than stop the destruction."

34. In view of the fact that both Stalin and Pol Pot murdered millions of their own peoples, the assertion that the Nazis were cannibalistic may seem, by comparison, hard to sustain. But my argument follows primarily from a logical rather than evidential thesis: if the self is constitutively dependent on the existence of the other, then any root-and-branch attempt to eradicate otherness will at some point in the course of events necessarily result in acts of self-destruction. To what degree this thesis applies also to regimes such as Stalin's Russia or Pol Pot's Cambodia is a matter for further research. But it should not be forgotten here that in addition to the above consideration about the evident self-destructive tendencies of the Nazis in the face of military defeat, the populations they targeted for extermination—Jews, Gypsies, and the mentally retarded—were in fact, notwithstanding the classificatory otherness imposed on them, in whole or in part Germans.

35. I conjecture that this role is intimately tied to the way in which the Jew came to represent in Western understanding what is ambiguous and uncertain, the outsider and the stranger—in short, the nondual or the Other. In this connection, see Bauman's (1991: chaps. 2 and 3) exceptional sociological discussion of the Jews as the "non-national nation," an identity the glaring ambiguity of which, in the context of modernity, posed a fearsome threat to the very idea of identity, the absolutism of which is perhaps nowhere more evident than in the Nazi ideal of racial (Aryan) identity.

Chapter 5: Bourdieu's Anti-dualism and "Generalized Materialism"

1. When in 1971 I first read Louis Dumont's (1970) great monograph, *Homo Hierarchicus*, I was so impressed that I wrote him a letter of admiration, attaching to it a piece of my own work. Very graciously, Dumont answered. In his response, he remarked that in their thrust my ideas brought to mind the work of his colleague Pierre Bourdieu. As I was then unfamiliar with Bourdieu's thought, I promptly went out to find something by him to read. I located a piece in (as I recall) *Social Research*, one that, however, I was unable to understand. In hindsight, it is curious to me that I found his article impenetrable, for when *Outline of a Theory of Practice* first appeared in English (in 1977), my experience was quite the reverse. Whereas colleagues and students have told me that they found the book difficult going, its powerful and remedial argument about practice seemed abundantly clear to me. So close did I feel to the argument that after the first hundred pages or so, I had to put the book down—it made me feel that there was nothing left to say. But at some point I returned to finish the book, only to discover that I had some deep differences with it, which I develop in this chapter.

2. The interview, conducted over a period of three years and expanded through written exchange, was edited by the interlocutor, Loïc J. D. Wacquant. It makes up the main part of Bourdieu and Wacquant's *An Invitation to Reflexive Sociology* (1992) and incorporates a good deal of the oft-cited "Toward a Reflexive Sociology: A Workshop with Pierre Bourdieu" (Wacquant 1989). The book in which the interview appears contains an incomplete but very useful bibliography of Bourdieu's writings and may be consulted for references to critiques of and works about Bourdieu.

3. My point here coincides with Calhoun's critical commentary (1993: 77–82). He finds that 'modern' social systems "call for a more theoretical kind of understanding" than Bourdieu's notion of practice allows. For in social systems of this kind, a patently theoretical attitude is diagnostically an

integral component of practice. Both his critique and mine point to a failure on Bourdieu's part to see the dialectical importance of theory. But whereas Calhoun is arguing that this failure has hampered Bourdieu's analysis of the shift from tradition to modernity, I am suggesting that the failure gets in the way of Bourdieu's central endeavor to break free from the mind-lock of subject-object dualism. Calhoun ventures that the assumption underlying Bourdieu's inadequate grasp of the importance of theory is not "necessary" to Bourdieu's analysis of the shift from tradition to modernity. The assumption Calhoun is referring to is that of the "stable reproduction of the encompassing field of power." In principle, this assumption of societal conservatism runs contrary to the reflexivity that one might expect to find where a theoretical attitude is the rule. Bourdieu's assumption may not be necessary to his analysis, as Calhoun suggests, but from the perspective of my critique, Bourdieu's theory would look markedly different without it. Resting on the claim that Bourdieu's implicit ontology is not equal to his ontological purpose, my critique will suggest that that assumption discloses a fault and incoherence deep in his sociology.

4. I have not chosen to test my critical claims about Bourdieu's theory by scrutinizing in their connection his numerous substantial empirical studies taken in themselves. I have preferred instead to select certain areas of his theoretical framework that, by virtue of the exemplary way they present the ontological underpinnings of Bourdieu's social thought, can serve as litmus tests of dualism (or nondualism). To be sure, these 'theoretical' areas do not lack for and are inseparable from empirical analyses by Bourdieu. Doubtless, though, close examination of his empirical work proper for its implicit ontology offers another important and highly desirable way to proceed with my critical inquiry. It is not clear to me, however, that such an examination would necessarily be the straightforward and definitive test that an empiricist orientation might lead one to expect. Since facts always require a conceptual screening for their determination (even as *facts*), were one to find that Bourdieu has overcome the problem of dualism in his empirical work but not in his conceptual apparatus, it would imply that he is operating analytically with concepts other than or somehow beyond those constituting his express theoretical framework. In point of fact, one's empirical analyses always implicate such tacit concepts, which is what makes it possible for empirical research to lead to findings that may move one to make changes in one's theory. Nevertheless, my routine readings of, say, Bourdieu's *Distinction* (1984) and *Homo Academicus* (1988) do not lead me to suspect that his ontological presuppositions in these highly empirical studies are other than those exhibited in his more theoretical framework. I find both of these studies to be, while empirical tours de force, seemingly reductionistic. From my critical perspective, the challenge would be to show that *Distinction* leaves room for aesthetic judgments that are illuminating independently of their empirical social causes, and that *Homo Academicus* treats academic capital not only as a different kind of capital but also as something other than capital at all. It does not follow from the actuality of authentic aesthetic judgment and (in contrast to economic worth) value-as-such that empirical research plays no role, or a nugatory one, in social science. Rather, there are fundamental sociological and anthropological perplexities that in the first place do not call for causal analysis and empirical assessment, demanding instead responses that enable and transform empirical explanation.

5. Jenkins (1992: 183) advises that most readers need no longer bother with *Outline*. Although *Outline* has been crucial for my thinking about Bourdieu, *Logic* has furnished me with a neater focus for my critique. Wacquant (1993) argues that because of "fragmented and piecemeal" readings of the corpus of his work, by and large Bourdieu's Anglo-American critics have missed the "systematic nature and main thrust" of Bourdieu's sociology. Given the broad topical scope and great abundance of Bourdieu's writings, plus the character of his endeavor as a research program rather than a theory in the strict sense, Wacquant's point does help explain the strikingly inconsistent contents of Bourdieu criticism taken in all its variety. But of course, depending on one's critical aims, it is not necessary to have read all of Bourdieu in order to produce intelligent critical commentary on some of his work or even on his ideas in general. I confess that although I have read more of Bourdieu's work than I cite here, I have not studied the body of it. My criticisms derive especially from having thought about *Outline* ever since its publication in English translation three decades ago. It remains

a remarkably exciting anthropological landmark. With the English-language publication of *Logic*, I was moved to gather my thoughts together. In light of Wacquant's point, though, it is important to note that in finally crystallizing my ideas here, I have benefited from Wacquant's and Bourdieu's own overviews of the cut and thrust of Bourdieu's "reflexive sociology."

6. One cannot help but be reminded here of Rousseau's (1950: 250–51) deeply cynical discussion, in his *Second Discourse*, of political institutionalization, in which he redefines Hobbes's "state of nature" as really the natural state of society, a lapsarian state induced precisely by convention:

> It is impossible that men should not at length have reflected on so wretched a situation, and on the calamities that overwhelmed them. The rich, in particular, must have felt how much they suffered by a constant state of war, of which they bore all the expense; and in which, though all risked their lives, they alone risked their property ... Destitute of valid reasons to justify and sufficient strength to defend himself, able to crush individuals with ease, but easily crushed himself by a troop of bandits, one against all, and incapable, on account of mutual jealousy, of joining with his equals against numerous enemies united by the common hope of plunder, the rich man, thus urged by necessity, conceived at length the profoundest plan that ever entered the mind of man: this was to employ in his favour the forces of those who attacked him, to make allies of his adversaries, to inspire them with different maxims, and to give them other institutions as favourable to himself as the law of nature was unfavourable.
>
> With this view, after having represented to his neighbours the horror of a situation which armed every man against the rest, and made their possessions as burdensome to them as their wants, and in which no safety could be expected either in riches or in poverty, he readily devised plausible arguments to make them close with his design. "Let us join," said he, "to guard the weak from oppression, to restrain the ambitious, and secure to every man the possession of what belongs to him: let us institute rules of justice and peace, to which all without exception may be obliged to conform; rules that may in some measure make amends for the caprices of fortune, by subjecting equally the powerful and the weak to the observance of reciprocal obligations. Let us, in a word, instead of turning our forces against ourselves, collect them in a supreme power which may govern us by wise laws, protect and defend all the members of the association, repulse their common enemies, and maintain eternal harmony among us."
>
> Far fewer words to this purpose would have been enough to impose on men so barbarous and easily seduced ... All ran headlong to their chains, in hopes of securing their liberty; for they had just wit enough to perceive the advantages of political institutions, without experience enough to enable them to foresee the dangers.

7. In *Homo Academicus*, in an analysis both rich and powerful, Bourdieu (1988: esp. chap. 5) fleshes out this theory of change in connection with the world of the French university and the famous student crisis of May 1968.

8. For example: "[T]he theory of habitus aims at excluding the 'subjects' ... dear to the tradition of philosophies of consciousness without annihilating agents to the benefit of a hypostatized structure, even though these agents are the product of this structure and continually make and remake this structure, which they may even radically transform under definite structural conditions" (in Bourdieu and Wacquant 1992: 140).

9. Elsewhere, obviously perceiving the likelihood of a favorable comparison, Bourdieu (1988: 148–49) takes pains to distinguish his position from cybernetics. He rejects the latter as a kind of "spontaneous physicalism" and holds up the habitus as the key to the conservative entelechy of any social system. My argument, of course, depends on the success of the habitus as a saving concept in this connection. Bourdieu maintains that the habitus is reducible neither to "the subjective teleology of a universe of agents" nor to "the objective teleology of personified collectivities pursuing their own goals." I contend, however, that under close scrutiny the concept fails really to give agency its due, such that the impact of the dualism of subject and object is allowed still to have its way, making the cybernetic picture of Bourdieu's theory a telling likeness.

10. Sahlins's "structure-minded history" and Giddens's "structuration" are no less dialectical than Bourdieu's theory of practice, and indeed (as incongruous as it may seem in the case of Sahlins) project a picture of how socio-culture works that is very like that of Bourdieu's (Giddens 1979; Sahlins 1981, 1985). However, both Sahlins and, I think, although to a lesser extent, Giddens do give pride of sociological place to the side of the dialectical equation that Bourdieu speaks of as "symbolic" (Giddens 1979: 25; Sahlins 1981: 7–8). The crucial issue is, of course, the nature of the articulation between, to quote Sahlins (1981: 72), "the practice of the structure and the structure of the practice." I argue that that articulation is in the first place a matter of neither practice-as-power nor structure, but of ethics.

11. Wacquant sees the difference otherwise, although in terms that suggest we are barking up the same tree. He argues (in Bourdieu and Wacquant 1992: 20) that Merleau-Ponty, grasping practice wholly from the point of view of the "acting agent," failed to allow for the "objective moment" of practice. In favor of Wacquant's interpretation, it must be said that Merleau-Ponty, under the influence of Saussure, eventually came to see a discrepancy in *Phenomenology of Perception* between the chapter on speech and the chapter on the "tacit cogito" (Merleau-Ponty 1968: 176; see also Schmidt 1985: 152). The idea of the tacit cogito still clung, unacceptably for him, to the philosophy of consciousness and subjectivity. However, in his major study of Merleau-Ponty's ontology, M. C. Dillon (1988) argues, to great effect, that the author of *Phenomenology of Perception* did in fact succeed in overcoming dualism. Putting the question of Merleau-Ponty's phenomenological theory aside, I am arguing that the allowance for the 'subjective moment' in Bourdieu's theory is more apparent than real.

12. Inspired by the philosophy of Gilles Deleuze as well as, to a lesser extent, that of Levinas, the literary critic Syed Islam also makes emphatically clear that irreducible otherness does not entail 'othering'. His incisive book (1996) on the ethics of travel enjoys great anthropological relevance.

13. As I documented above in chapter 3, this is the key point in Derrida's (1995) re-reading of Kierkegaard's famous interpretation of the Akedah. Undoubtedly, in developing this point Derrida was deeply influenced by Levinas.

14. In this connection, Charles Taylor's subtle discussion is edifying (1985b: 143–44):

> [I]t comes quite naturally to us to distinguish sharply between scientific study of reality and its accompanying technological spin-off, on one hand, and symbolic activity in which we try to come to terms with the world on the other. This kind of contrast is one that has developed out of our form of life. But exactly for this reason, it is probably going to be unhelpful in understanding people who are very different from us. It certainly would not help to say, for instance, that ritual practices in some primitive society were to be understood simply as symbolic, that is, as being exclusively directed at attunement and not at all at practical control; or that the body of religious beliefs was merely expressive of certain attitudes to the contingencies of life, and not also concerned with giving an account of how things are …
>
> But it is still insufficiently helpful to say something to the effect that ritual practices somehow combine the practical and the symbolic. This may not be flatly untrue, but it is putting the point in ethnocentric language. Somebody might try to combine the two in our civilization, and we could describe his attempt in these terms because we distinguish them clearly. But the point about quite different societies is that the question at least arises whether this distinction has any sense for them.

Distinguishing his approach from Habermas's, Bourdieu (in Bourdieu and Wacquant 1992: 139) makes a point very similar to Taylor's: "[My praxeology] rejects the reductionist and coarse distinction between instrumental and communicative action, a distinction which is completely inoperative in the case of precapitalist societies and never fully accomplished even in the most differentiated societies. To realize that, it suffices to analyze institutions typical of the capitalist world such as business gifts or public relations." In which case, though, would not the magical and religious actions traditionally studied by anthropologists have to have more of a purpose than simply "to say and do something rather than nothing"? Would they not have to display in an ambiguous way a signifying intentionality bearing also on what we call instrumental accomplishment?

15. As Frank Cioffi has pointed out in his book *Wittgenstein on Freud and Frazer* (1998: chap. 6), Wittgenstein's critique of Frazer's *The Golden Bough* offers two opposing views of magic in primitive settings: (1) that primitive peoples certainly know better than to think that their magical acts are instrumentally efficacious, and (2) that it is "the most natural thing in the world" (Cioffi's words) to think that acts of this kind are just that—instrumentally efficacious. In the present volume, I have attended only to the first of these views. The second is very hard to describe but easily illustrated, as when, for example, after characterizing a magical cure as indicating "to an illness that it should leave the patient," Wittgenstein remarks (1979: 6–7e), "If the illness doesn't understand that, then I don't know how one ought to say it." I simply want to note here that this second view of Wittgenstein's—on "the intuitive compellingness of magic" (Cioffi's words)—is in my opinion anthropologically invaluable and has had a major impact on my thinking. Having taught Wittgenstein's "Remarks on Frazer's *Golden Bough*" to undergraduate students for many years, I am confident that my own position concerning nondualism, ethics, and the primacy of otherness has been duly informed by my studied reading of that view.

16. Needless to say, it is hard to think of any scholarship on Weber that does not acknowledge this preoccupation. Schutz (1967), though, is especially worth citing here, as he develops systematically the phenomenological force of Weber's sociology.

17. Implying that Bourdieu is more phenomenological than he thinks, Ostrow (1981) has argued that Merleau-Ponty's philosophy does address the question of "intentionless dynamics" and therefore can treat of Bourdieu's problem of embodied habitus. But Charles Taylor's work, as I read it, suggests that it would be no simple matter to reconcile Bourdieu with phenomenology. Taylor (1985a) has made compellingly clear that practice and lived experience are integrals of each other, such that together they present meaning that is precisely not subjective, but intersubjective. Like Bourdieu's "habitus," Taylor's "intersubjective" reconceptualizes Durkheim's concept of mechanical solidarity to powerful theoretical effect. By strong contrast, however, Taylor's "intersubjective" is tied to a concept of practice in which norms and meanings will not reduce to the material reality of production and reproduction, but bespeak a genuine moral process (ibid.: chap. 1). Taylor himself (1993: chap. 3) has commented quite positively on Bourdieu's social theory. He confines his commentary, though, to elaborating the salutary point that, as an operational concept of embodied knowledge, the habitus marks a critical advance in social science. He does not ask after the conceptual limitations of the habitus in relation to embodiment, nor does he query the avowed materialism of Bourdieu's concept of practice.

18. As Webb puts it in his excellent discussion of Derrida's inordinately difficult text on the gift (1996: 74): "How do you render an account of that which does not balance? The gift is both *alogos*, that is, without reason, and *atopos*, without place ... Even in Mauss's text, his attraction to the potlatch shows the insinuation of madness into any discussion of the gift. In fact, madness could be defined as that which does not return, that is, as the gift." Webb also draws with considerable subtlety the contrast between Derrida and Levinas in connection with the question of giving. The contrast is relevant here, since my thesis about the primacy of ethics is heavily indebted to Levinas. I might add that Webb's (ibid.: 39–41) brief review of Bourdieu's argument about the gift lends firm support to my critique.

19. In their intensive, comparative study of exchange in four societies, Barraud et al. (1994), inspired especially by the work of Louis Dumont, develop systematically an anthropological holism keyed to the idea of a hierarchy of value. In doing so, they offer a valuable discussion on the "fluctuating nature of the distinction between subject and object" (ibid.: 105). In connection with this thesis, they make plain their differences with structuralism (ibid.: 3–4), feeling a need to call on (contrary to Lévi-Strauss's well-known criticism that Mauss took his informants' theories as his own) Mauss's thesis that objects of exchange "convey something of the persons who set them in motion." I suspect, however, that my understanding of the whole as basically ambiguous is not altogether consistent with their holism. For if the whole is ambiguous in the way I maintain, then it defines a hierarchical order that not only admits of relative distinctions internally but also presents itself as finally less than absolute. Put another way, in this sort of holism, the supreme value of the hierarchy can define a whole but no totality, since it itself, regardless of its ideology, must always betray a paradox and therefore,

the most pivotal consideration, a dependence on something other than itself. Accordingly, although it opens on an irreducible intersubjectivity, the view from the whole is no less fundamentally relative and open than the view from the individual constituent of the whole.

20. In discussing research that he was carrying out on "social suffering" (Bourdieu and Wacquant 1992: 201), Bourdieu says that the goal of the study

> is to make an unformulated, repressed discourse emerge by talking with people who are likely to be good "historians" of their own disease because they are situated in sensitive areas of social space ... Armed with full knowledge of the individual's social trajectory and life-context, we proceed by means of very lengthy, highly interactive, in-depth interviews aimed at helping interviewees discover and state the hidden principle of their extreme tragedies or ordinary misfortunes; and at allowing them to rid themselves of this external reality that inhabits and haunts them, possesses them from the inside, and dispossesses them of initiative in their own existence in the manner of the monster in [the film] *Alien*. *Alien* may be seen as a sort of modern myth which offers a good image of what we call *alienation*, that is, this presence of otherness at the very heart of subjectivity.

The passage strikes me as extraordinary, but not because it envisions a society of *lumières*. The liberating goal of Bourdieuian therapy, his "social maieutics," as Wacquant perceptively deems it (Bourdieu and Wacquant 1992: 200), is both admirable and feasible. Rather, the passage is extraordinary because the liberation it describes smacks of a potent dualism. The interviewees are held to free themselves from "alienation." The alienation is understood by Bourdieu in terms of "subjectivity," conceived of as an "inside" space, inhabited by an "external" force, an "otherness." By reference to a horror film, the otherness is pictured as invasive, consuming, and monstrous. These are usual and strong—even mythic (as Bourdieu himself suggests in his characterization of the movie *Alien*)—terms of Western dualism. It is worth recalling here that in his approach to the anthropological problem of magic, ritual, and belief, Bourdieu's object is to resolve the apparent otherness of such thought and practice. He uses the word 'alien' to describe the intentions with which we are wrongly inclined, according to him, to credit such actions. In the passage cited here, about the benefits of socio-analysis, Bourdieu implicitly assimilates the otherness we tend to attribute to magical and religious actions to that which "dispossesses" the self of its integrity and thus imposes limits on self-possession. By doing so, he places himself in the camp of the very enterprise he sets out to overturn—the enterprise of epistemic 'selfcraft' (cf. Evens 1996). This is the enterprise of philosophy in the strict or Platonic sense, according to which the soul (or the one) defines itself through resisting the destructive force of society (or the many). In other words, by giving to otherness and "alienation" here no other role than that of oppression, no positive or vital role, Bourdieu again exhibits a residual attachment to Western ontological dualism and reveals the implicit reductionism of his socio-logic. To bring home the point, I note also the following passage from Bourdieu's *Distinction* (1984: 54):

> To be able to play the games of culture with the playful seriousness which Plato demanded, a seriousness without the 'spirit of seriousness', one has to belong to the ranks of those who have been able ... to maintain for a long time, sometimes a whole lifetime, a child's relation to the world. (All children start life as baby bourgeois, in a relation of magical power over others and, through them, over the world, but they grow out of it sooner or later.) This is clearly seen when, by an accident of social genetics, into the well-policed world of intellectual games there comes one of those people (one thinks of Rousseau or Chernyshevsky [or, possibly, Bourdieu?]) who bring inappropriate stakes and interests into the games of culture; who get so involved in the game that they abandon the margin of neutralizing distance that the *illusio* (belief in the game) demands; who treat intellectual struggles ... as a simple question of right and wrong, life and death. This is why the logic of the game has already assigned them rôles—eccentric or boor—which they will play despite themselves in the eyes of those who know how to stay within the bounds of the intellectual illusion.

Here Bourdieu ties alienation or the "neutralizing distance" of intellectualism (later he speaks of "*schole*, i.e., leisure, distance from urgency and necessity, the absence of vital stakes, and the scholastic institution capable of providing all these" [1984: 476]) to philosophy as Platonic, to the bourgeois perspective, and, making sociology out of Freud's psychoanalytical ontogeny, to magical thinking seen as an infantile approach to the world. But he appears to do so in so radical a tone, with such dualistic bias, as to leave no room for alienation or otherness as a condition of selfhood and human existence. Indeed, I conjecture that in significant part Bourdieu's monumental analysis in *Distinction*, his "social critique of the judgement of taste," draws its stunning power from a misunderstanding that is dualist or totalist in nature—that "neutralizing distance" in itself is what constitutes social differentiation as injustice, rather than the tendency to take and define such distance in absolute instead of relative terms.

21. To be sure, Bourdieu himself makes a similar point about objectivity (Bourdieu and Wacquant 1992: 214): "[Reflexive sociology] compels us to repudiate the absolutist claims of classical objectivity, but without for all that being forced into the arms of relativism; for the conditions of possibility of the scientific 'subject' and of the scientific object are one and the same." Indeed, finding Bourdieu engaged in a Cartesian exercise is disconcerting, if only in view of the plain fact that, by means of the objectification of objectifying, he aims to problematize social scientific objectivity in such a way as to disabuse sociology of its tendency to represent a world that is basically a matter of concrete practical activity—i.e., the social world—as an abstract, rule-governed order. The picture of the social actor as improvisatory and strategic rather than rational and rule-bound stands opposed to Descartes' thesis of a "thinking stuff" through which one can arrive at human nature. It is a picture of, to use the Heideggerian terminology, being-in-the-world rather than of being on the basis of thinking qua thinking. Nevertheless, the emphatic result of the objectification of objectification, in Bourdieu's theory of practice and practice of theory, is, rather than a developed awareness of the limits of social science, a superior objective view of the social world. The trouble here is ontological: despite his focus on practice as essentially fluid and indeterminate, Bourdieu never does see that before it is either objective or subjective, social reality is basically ambiguous. Jenkins's critique offers strong support in this connection. Calling Bourdieu's project of overcoming the dualism of objectivism and subjectivism an "impressive and interesting failure," he concludes (1992: 91) that Bourdieu "remains trapped within an objectivist point of view. Thompson has recently put it like this: 'Bourdieu's view is that both subjectivism and objectivism are inadequate intellectual orientations, but the latter is less inadequate than the former.' I want to go further than this: Bourdieu cannot hope to achieve his theoretical aims without letting go of both ends of the dualism, and this he fails to do. In his sociological heart of hearts he is as committed to an objectivist view of the world as the majority of those whose work he so sternly dismisses." In light of this critical picture, it is not so surprising that, as Jenkins (ibid.: 95) puts it, despite Bourdieu's "rejection of the epistemological [and profoundly Cartesian] arrogance of structuralism, where the social scientist (like mother) knows best, he eventually adopts a similar position" (see also Dreyfus and Rabinow 1993). For a comprehensive critique of Bourdieu's work, Jenkins's book is, if grossly underappreciative and sometimes too simple, clearly written and in important ways critically penetrating (notwithstanding Bourdieu and Wacquant 1992: 169; Wacquant 1989, 1993).

22. To be sure, there is nothing vulgar about Bourdieu's position on this question (1993: 274): "Both habitus and field," he holds (1993: 274), "... are the site of a sort of *conatus*, of a tendency to perpetuate themselves in their being, to reproduce themselves in that which constitutes their existence and their identity ... This I hold against a finalist, utilitarian vision of action which is sometimes attributed to me. It is not true to say that everything that people do or say is aimed at maximizing their social profit; but one may say that they do it to perpetuate or to augment their social being." But in the context of Bourdieu's theory, although "social being" cannot be for him merely a matter of material advantage, there is no reason to interpret it as anything more than symbolic advantage. Certainly, this is the interpretation given by Dreyfus and Rabinow (1993: 40). And as I have argued throughout, Bourdieu's concept of the symbolic remains epiphenomenal and ontologically ill-equipped to do justice to the surpassing reality of the meaningful side of existence.

23. Bourdieu's concept of field, of course, presents a well-developed and admirably concrete notion of social space. A field, he says (Bourdieu and Wacquant 1992: 97), "may be defined as a network, or

a configuration, of objective relations between positions," having its own logic and necessity. For instance, "while the artistic field has constituted itself by rejecting or reversing the law of material profit ..., the economic field has emerged, historically, through the creation of a universe within which ... 'business is business'" (ibid.: 97–98). As I see it, Bourdieu's notion of field, which he regards as "ontologically complicit" with that of "habitus" (ibid.: 273–74), is also ontologically gravid. This is so because it is directly about boundaries, and the boundaries it describes are, by sharp contrast to the immaculate ones of Cartesian reality, essentially fuzzy, shifting, and ever under construction (ibid.: 100; also esp. 97–98n48): "The question of the limits of the field is a very difficult one, if only because it is *always at stake in the field itself* and therefore admits of no *a priori* answer." As the present critique was initially provoked by the notion of the habitus and grew rather naturally to address the questions of otherness and the gift, I have not taken up Bourdieu's concept of the field. There is no question, though, that it demands critical scrutiny in its own right (see, e.g., Calhoun 1993; Jenkins 1992: 84ff.). Were I to address it, I would do so by exploring the difference between ethics and power as keys to understanding social space. Whereas the vital struggle of self and other I describe constitutes a pre-eminently moral space, for Bourdieu the competition over the determination of fields and their boundaries is chiefly a matter of power, and power may be said to constitute the subsuming field of any society. As is implicit throughout this critique, I am inclined to think that so long as one's notion of social space is keyed to power, one cannot finally free oneself from Descartes' dualism. To borrow an image from (and of) another celebrated student of practice, Fox Broadcasting's Homer Simpson, it is like trying to extricate yourself from quicksand by reaching down and pulling yourself out by your own legs and feet.

24. The neat juxtaposition of "what justifies me?" to "what am I?" is due to Diane Moira Duncan (2001: 40) in her comparative discussion of Levinas and Derrida. Levinas (1989: 81) makes the point this way: "One comes not into the world but into question."

25. From Stevens's essay, "The Noble Rider and the Sound of Words" (1942: 31). He essays this idea also in "Imagination and Value" (ibid.) and gives it poetic development in his deeply reflexive "Notes toward a Supreme Fiction" (1955: 380ff.). *Illusio* is Bourdieu's usage (e.g., 1990a: esp. chap. 4; 1984: 250). According to Dreyfus and Rabinow (1993: 41), "Like Heidegger in Division Two of *Being and Time*," Bourdieu holds that "the interestedness of everyday life—that is, the illusion that there are intrinsic meaningful differences—is a motivated cover-up of the basic arbitrariness of human purposes, sedimented in the social field, which Heidegger calls 'fallenness' ... *Illusio* is his [Bourdieu's] name for the self-deception necessary to keep players involved in the game." In their appreciative but penetrating critique, Dreyfus and Rabinow argue that Bourdieu is moved to this position, which they rightly regard as fraught with serious difficulties, by his mistaken understanding that reflexive sociology has given him a truly external or objective perspective on social life. My criticism here dovetails with theirs, although my argument from ethics seems to move in a direction different from their emphasis on the philosophical opposition between natural and human science, that is, between explanatory and interpretive inquiry.

Chapter 6: Habermas's Anti-dualism and "Communicative Rationality"

1. Bourdieu himself describes the difference (Bourdieu and Wacquant 1992: 188–89):

If there exist, *pace* Habermas, no transhistorical universals of communication, there certainly exist forms of social organization of communication that are liable to foster the production of the universal. We cannot rely on moral exhortation to abolish "systematically distorted" communication from sociology. Only a realistic politics of scientific reason can contribute to the transformation of structures of communication ... I believe indeed that science is thoroughly historical without for that matter being relative or reducible to history. There are historical conditions for the genesis and progress of reason in history. When I say that a situation of open conflict ... is to be preferred over a situation of false academic consensus, of "working consensus," as Goffman would put it, it is in the name of a philosophy of history according to which there can be a politics of Reason. I do not think that reason lies in the structure of the mind or of language. It resides, rather, in certain social structures of dialogue and nonviolent communication.

In brief, Bourdieu concludes (ibid.): "Habermas notwithstanding, reason itself has a history: it is not Godgiven, already inscribed in our thinking or language. Habitus (scientific or otherwise) is a transcendental but a *historical transcendental* bound up with the structure of and history of a field."

2. McCarthy (1978: 432n36) notes: "It would be interesting to compare Habermas's argument with Popper's move from 'the logic of inquiry' to the conception of an 'open society'. The differences would be as instructive as the similarities." I agree, but given my purposes here I am struck by the apparently critical influence on Habermas of Horton's anthropological disposition of the famous distinction made by Popper between "open" and "closed" societies. As I suggest later in this volume (chap. 10, note 9), although I have reservations about some of his ideas, Horton's contributions to the anthropological debate on 'traditional thought' have been exceptional.

3. And therefore, in Levinas's philosophy, spills over into yet a third kind: openness to the otherwise than being or the ontologically Other.

4. Chris Roberts (pers. comm.) observes here that the "zygote-cum-embryo," not yet being independently viable, can hardly be considered in terms of the sense of singularity that we ordinarily intend when we speak of a person. In the same connection, he proposes that a single conglomeration of genetic materials cannot be "all that 'singular' either, since to see it this way fundamentally misrepresents the nature of the genes, the great bulk of which need specific environmental triggers in order to become phenotypic." What is more, he goes on, "If we understand the great genetic lottery as making every single fertilization singular in a way that carries all the weight of ethical deliberation, then we've accepted … a genetic determinism that is closely akin to … eugenic-racist thought." My main aim here is to disclose the falsely binary construal of choice in the abortion debate. Roberts's observations, which go to the critical question of what is a person, and with which I have considerable sympathy, complicate but do not vitiate this point.

5. In respect of the fetus, since its soulfulness constitutes a capacity for ethical being, I intend by "homicidal behavior" the killing of a potential person (see note 4 of this chapter). In respect of the mother, the meaning of "homicidal behavior" seems clear: granting a critical link between the development of a woman's self-identity as woman and her unique capacity for reproduction, depriving her of substantial discretionary control over that capacity must constitute a direct assault on her existing personhood and, in this essential connection, on her life. As my earlier chapter on the Holocaust makes plain, this defining sense of human life, above and beyond our bare biological being, cannot be doubted. Indeed, as I have argued, it is in crucial part the same sense of human life that the pro-life movement claims to be at jeopardy in abortion.

6. In an earlier work (Evens 1995), I show how, in the context of generational conflict, the failure to oppose the other and choose for the sake of oneself also deprives the self of any way to demonstrate to itself its own relative autonomy. The point is, as I develop here in chapter 12, when I come to speak of the double bind, developed selfhood depends on running a line between opposition and choice for one's self, and complementarity and choice for the sake of the other.

7. The following observation by Richard Bernstein (1986: 72–73), writing about key claims of Habermas's theory of communicative rationality, seems to me to lend indirect support to what I am suggesting here concerning a certain confusion in Habermas's idea of validity claims:

> The idea of practical truth is intended to be the analogue to the idea of theoretical truth; and both sorts of truth can be redeemed and warranted through appropriate forms of substantive argumentation. When questions concerning the appropriateness and legitimacy of claims to universal normative validity are raised, no matter how these questions and potential conflicts are resolved, the participants are unavoidably committed to the idea that such claims can be resolved by argumentative discourse. However sympathetic one may be to this as a regulative ideal which ought to be approximated, it is not

clear in what sense this is an "unavoidable" or "necessary" presumption that is somehow grounded in the very nature of intersubjectivity.

In his overall discussion (ibid.: 72ff.), Bernstein perhaps runs together two different (but connected) points, the one bearing on this matter of two kinds of truth ("theoretical" and "practical"), and the other pertaining to the question of the supposed universality of the ideal speech situation. Nevertheless, what he has to say about a certain deep-seated ambiguity in Habermas's theory is, although it goes to a very different point, compatible with my argument.

8. Habermas is contending here also with his own Frankfurt School predecessor, Adorno, who posited a fundamental gap between concept and reality, logical consistency and the world (Jay 1992: 263–64).

9. Cf. Dumont (1980: 239): "[I]f the advocates of difference claim for it both equality and recognition, they claim the impossible. Here we are reminded of the American slogan 'separate but equal' which marked the transition from slavery to racism."

10. It is illuminating to trace this essentialism back to Descartes. By virtue of what he construed as the essence beneath our skin—namely, our capacity to reason—we are all equal, identifiable as the same by virtue of our 'I think'. As expressly bodiless, the view is objectivist, a view from nowhere. Abstracting us from the embodied world and reducing us to nothing more than a *cogito*, Descartes objectifies us precisely as subjects, making it possible to identify us as the same, universally, across all difference. In this conception rests the basis of modern Western humanism. In this connection, Kant's notion of freedom remains of a piece with the Cartesian turn. But Kant's notion brings into sharp relief the unresolved bipolarity between freedom as will and freedom as external value, implicit in this understanding of the self. For Kant, autonomy is a question of self-legislation by appeal to the universality of reason. However, so long as Kant's understanding starts with the self, rather than with ambiguity as such, he cannot escape from the essentialism at point (see the related discussion of Kant in chap. 1, this volume). If in the categorical imperative the will of the chooser and external value run contrary to each other, then what we have is, rather than transcendent moral demands, a conflicted self, but a self-contained one nonetheless. If, though, the self is understood as always already other to itself—that is, as constitutionally open to otherness—then selfhood emerges as an open dynamic, in which case, selfhood or the 'I', can appear only in a continuous becoming other.

11. One might be inclined to see this state of affairs as characteristic of political debates under any democratic regime, where the point can become not to win the votes of the opposing side but rather, through high political drama (truth-telling aside), to win those of the uncommitted. I am conjecturing that this quality of debate is especially likely where ontological dualism constitutes the epistemological scaffolding of deliberation.

12. Cf. here Mary Ann Glendon's study (1987), in which she shows that, in stark contrast to American law on abortion, the law of certain modern Western European countries manages to emphasize the value of fetal life and at the same time ensure that women have substantial legal access to abortion. She locates the difference in the influence of Hobbes on American law on the one hand, and of Rousseau on the law of these European countries on the other. Of course, the social thought of both thinkers centers on a principle of individual liberty, but whereas Rousseau acknowledged the possibility of a genuine common good, one that rises above simple self-interest, Hobbes did not. In other words, Glendon suggests that abortion law in the US is informed by individualism more or less uncut by transcending value.

13. Throughout this discussion of second- and third-person language in relation to otherness and equality, I have drawn directly on the work of Levinas (1969: 101):

> The 'communication' of ideas, the reciprocity of dialogue, already hide the profound essence of language. It resides in the irreversibility of the relation between me and the other, in the Mastery of the Master coinciding with his position as other and as exterior. For language can be spoken only if the interlocutor is the commencement of his discourse, if, consequently, he remains beyond the system, if he is not on the same plane as myself. The interlocutor is not a Thou, he is a You; he reveals himself in

his lordship. Thus exteriority coincides with a mastery. My freedom is thus challenged by a Master who can invest it. Truth, the sovereign exercise of freedom, becomes henceforth possible.

And from a later work (Levinas and Kearney 1986: 21–22; see also Levinas 1987: chap. 3):

[B]ecause there are more than two people in the world, we invariably pass from the ethical perspective of alterity to the ontological perspective of totality. There are always at least three persons. This means that we are obliged to ask who the other is, to try to objectively define the undefinable, to compare the incomparable, in an effort to juridically hold different positions together. So that the first type of simultaneity is the simultaneity of equality, the attempt to reconcile and balance the conflicting claims of each person. If there were only two people in the world, there would be no need for law courts because I would always be responsible for and before, the other. As soon as there are three, the ethical relationship with the other becomes political and enters into the totalizing discourse of ontology. We can never completely escape from the language of ontology and politics. Even when we deconstruct ontology we are obliged to use its language.

14. For examples of "language" conceived of in this way, see Merleau-Ponty (1962: pt. 1, chap. 6), who distinguishes between "the word in the speaking" and the "spoken word," and Levinas (1991: 45ff.; see also 1987: chap. 7), who distinguishes between "the said" and "the saying." My argument suggests that in his evolutionist anxiety to mark the advance from "prelinguistic" to linguistic speech and communication, that is, to "propositionally differentiated" or "grammatical" language, Habermas (1987a: 61) tends to divorce language from its bodily and sensible foundations, leaving him, for all his efforts to the contrary, nothing but a concept of language as a third-person phenomenon, of communication as a pragmatic activity, but an activity that is given as a corollary of the logical work of speech.

15. Which is certainly not to say that this kind of rationality is reducible to binarism but only that where it is critically informed by the latter principle, instrumental rationality appears as such—pure and overridingly powerful.

16. Notwithstanding the great academic tradition of exploration of selfhood, psychoanalysis being perhaps the most emblematic in this connection, it is not clear to me that there has been a deliberated probing of selfhood in respect of this particular postmodern representation. Even Foucault's extensive analyses of the self do not, I think, deal with the problem of a self haunted by the logical necessity of seeing itself, no matter how sincere its commitment to sincerity, as self-deceptive. Is this not a post-postmodern problem?

17. In this discussion of the connection between reason and the third party or other others, I am following Levinas's highly original argument (see esp. 1987: chap. 3).

Chapter 7: Technological Efficacy, Mythic Rationality, and Non-contradiction

1. Although I regard mythic rationality as a form of value-rationality, what I have in mind departs from Weber's concept in important ways. Presupposing the standards of instrumental rationality, Weber saw value-rationality as basically inferior (cf. Löwith 1993: chap. 2). In addition, whereas Weber pictured value-rationality as entering in the choice of whether or not to pursue a certain end, I see mythic rationality as functioning to select ends, in the sense of creating them. My phenomenological emphasis on its lived, as opposed to reflective, character also serves to distinguish mythic rationality from Weber's concept.

2. My use of 'instrumental rationality' also gives me pause, since it hardly encompasses the complexity of meaning attached to the idea of rationality in Western thought. My usage is close to that of Horkheimer and Adorno (1998), and I must hope that for my purposes it serves to capture well enough the essence of Western rationality against the backdrop of which my argument may take intelligent shape. For an account of rationality that does do considerable justice to the semantic history and nuances of the idea of rationality in Western thought, see Charles Taylor (1989).

3. *Means without End* is the title of Agamben's (2000) small, stimulating collection of essays about politics. Although it may seem to have nothing to do with what I am calling an end as such, Agamben intends by his expression to subvert "the false alternative between ends and means that paralyzes any ethics and any politics" (ibid.: 116).

4. The assessment of science's instrumental superiority is dependent on the reduction of the mythic perspective to a matter of expedience. It is important not to confuse this kind of assessment with the question of value-as-such. The distinction between what is desired and what is desirable is not clearly drawn in Taylor's argument, although in the body of his work he could not be more alert to the import of a distinction of this sort.

5. Compare here the realist James Brown (1994: 20): "[F]alse premises can yield true conclusions, so truth is not (logically speaking) necessary for [scientific] success," and "truth is neither a necessary nor a sufficient condition for the success of science." Brown also maintains, however (as I, too, go on to do, although in a very different way), that "truth matters to the outcome, though it only matters a little."

6. The question of how to explain the success of science has been much debated in the philosophy of science. My purpose here is defined narrowly with reference to Taylor's (1985b) argument about epistemic gain. I want to raise the possibility that the evident success of science—which is to say, its ability to control, predict, and manipulate nature (to cite what are often conceived of as the standard standards)—is open to understanding that does not necessarily imply that the scientific picture of the world is simply true. Insofar as my brief discussion in this chapter may have something to contribute to the sophisticated philosophical debate on the issue of the success of science, I would invoke my overall thesis about dualism.

Take, for example, Laudan's (1990) small but thorough and clear introduction to this and other issues in the philosophy of science, which is written in the form of a dialogue among representative positions and focuses on the question of science and relativism. His discussion nicely captures the way in which the relativist and non-relativist tend to turn each other's arguments into totalistic ones, such that the latter is made to appear utterly foundationalist and the former absolutist in his relativism (and thus a clever fool). However, because nondualism remains unrepresented in his book, Laudan himself cannot offer any way out of such dualistic ascription.

Nondualism, as I use it, hews to both relativism and foundationalism, allowing the tension between them to remain fundamental yet tempering the opposing positions in such a way that each makes a certain sense. Blind to this possibility, Laudan's (1990: chap. 4) epistemological combatants tend to overlook certain nuances of the question of science and relativism. For instance, they argue over the issue of whether universal standards obtain underneath the cultural variation of standards of success, thus debating the matter of what 'success' can mean. Dualistically pitting empirical effectiveness against magical thought, they do not see that the notion of standard is similarly subject to cultural difference. A standard, of course, is a rule of measurement, a means. But if the distinction between means and ends is made only incompletely (as I argue in chapter 10 is the case for the Azande), then the very ideas of standard and empirical effectiveness lose their ideally clear and distinct definition. Under such epistemological conditions, 'instrumental effect' can still enter into judgments of success, but what it means for something to work can no longer be told by reference to means alone, since instrumentality as such cannot signify.

Another question, related to that about the standards of scientific success, bears on the presumption of the unity of science. Both Kuhn's and Feyerabend's views served to undermine the idea that science constitutes a single unified project. Students of science studies have since developed the thesis that science is in fact not correctly conceived as a project of this kind (Dupré 1993; Galison and Stump 1996). The juxtaposition of scientific to mythic thinking may seem out of keeping with the thesis of the disunity of science, but the contrary is the case. My argument hinges on the difference between the presumption of an objective universe that operates principally according to, if not 'natural' laws, at least reliable and determinable regularity, and the presumption of an enchanted (in Weber's sense of the term) universe that is routinely subject to irregular and uncertain intervention from forces that simply cannot be fixed in objective terms. In other words, the difference made by the dualistic differentiation of a realm of sheer objectivity is what has served to demarcate modern science from mythic thought. (When one considers that falsification relies on rationality proper, and that the latter goes hand in glove with the presumption of objective determination, then even Karl Popper's (1968) famous criterion of demarcation falls in line here.) The thesis that science cannot in fact be summed up in terms of the ontological presumption of "a deterministic, fully law-governed, and potentially fully intelligible structure" (Dupré 1993: 2) follows from looking at science as it is practiced rather than as it presents itself in theory. By maintaining here (and in the next chapter) that, paradoxically, the rationality of mythic thought comprehends rationality proper, I not only relativize the line demarcating science from myth, but I also remove the possibility that science could indeed be a unified project. The hierarchical subsumption of rationality by nondualism entails the shift to the perspective from practice, which in turn implies the disorder of things. More exactly, nondualism projects the relativization of thinghood and thus the mitigation of the positivist foundations on which modern science arose.

7. Popper described and extolled the method of science as a matter of testing theories by trying to falsify them. Once a theory is falsified, Popper held, the scientist is in a position to learn from experience and revise his theory accordingly or construct another that avoids the weaknesses of the failed one. The theory that best withstands such rigorous testing is not, in Popper's view, necessarily or even approximately true but simply preferable. For as he sees it, although a theory can be falsified, there is no proving it true. He spoke of this epistemological process as the method of "conjecture and refutation" (Popper 1965), which amounts, more broadly of course, to learning by trial and error.

Popper himself, given his critique of induction, thought that the success of science could not really be 'explained', since, logically speaking, we cannot conclude from that success the truth of science (1972: 28–29, 203–4). Put loosely, it is not rational (in the strict sense of the term) to infer from the fact that something has always been the case that it must always be the case. I aim here to use Popper's trial-and-error picture of scientific practice to suggest that the success of science can be, if not 'explained' (in the sense of inductively validated), at least made intelligible. And I want to make this suggestion without, however, having to conclude that such success necessarily means that the scientific picture of the world corresponds, for all important purposes, to the world as we find it. As Popper puts it (ibid.: 203–4): "[T]hat the true structural theory of the world (if any), is discoverable by man, or expressible in human language" is "most likely a false assumption."

Chapter 8: Epistemic Efficacy, Mythic Rationality, and Non-contradiction

1. The argument is Wittgenstein's, on what it means to make a mistake; see Wittgenstein's (1979) stunning critique of Sir James Frazer's *The Golden Bough*. Unfortunately, in propounding his penetrating insight—that the expressive nature of magic means that Frazer's picture of magic as physics must be mistaken—Wittgenstein so exaggerates the difference between these two ways of going about things that he removes from magical practices all instrumental intentionality. He thus establishes a dualism (in this volume, see chap. 1, note 4, and chap. 5, note 15). The irony is that Wittgenstein's (1979) critique is, at bottom, directed at Frazer's dualism. Frazer's pejorative account of magic and religion depends on the observation that these practices fail to keep apart the real from the ideal. By construing magic and religion in terms of expression, however, Wittgenstein appears to have in mind an essential form of human practice the sense of which depends precisely on a fundamental lack of differentiation between the real and the ideal. This, I take it, is why he finds that there is a certain truth in saying "man is a ceremonious animal"—as if 'ideal behavior' were as natural to human beings as "animal activities, taking food, &c., &c." (ibid.: 7e).

2. In a certain sense, the work is precisely not geared to recompense, but obtains for its own sake. Hence, it never comes exactly to rest in a thing or a product; it resists definition as a totality. In the words of Emmanuel Levinas (1987: 91–93), on whose work I am drawing here: "A work conceived

radically is a movement of the Same towards the Other which never returns to the Same." Although they are based on a deep and complex philosophy, these words encapsulate much of what I have in mind by 'mythic rationality'. It helps here to invoke also Giorgio Agamben. Although he speaks of "means without end," he means, I believe, much the same as do I in conceiving of ends as 'works'. "Politics," Agamben says (2000: 117; see also 56–57), "is the sphere neither of an end in itself nor of means subordinated to an end; rather, it is the sphere of a pure mediality without end intended as the field of human action and of human thought."

3. Using Hegel and Marx as whipping boys, and along these lines, Popper (1965) makes a driving case against logical indifference to contradiction.

4. In anthropology, the intellectual debates between Dumont and Marriott on the nature of Indian society and between Dumont and Needham on Dumont's concept of hierarchy bear on this matter. With exemplary analytical rigor and ethnographic sensitivity, Marriott (e.g., 1976), rejecting what he calls Dumont's dualism, expressly argues that Indian thought is best regarded as monist. By 'monism', however, he has in mind a view of a world in which boundaries exist but are regarded as fluid. It is also curious that Marriott seems to think that by avoiding the dualities of Western thought and embracing transactional analysis, he is beginning his ethnography from the perspective of Indian society. I do not see that the difference between his and Dumont's approach can be explained by referring to Dumont's as ethnocentric and his as ethno-sociological. Rather, the difference has to do with the contrast between 'hierarchy' and 'transaction' as organizing analytical concepts, and between the kinds of holism respectively implicated by a kind of systems theory, on the one hand, and a kind of structuralism, on the other.

Needham's critique (1987), although logically refined and meticulous, tends to miss the forest for the trees. He focuses on the logical incoherencies, imprecisions, and anomalies of Dumont's usages. But, speaking broadly, it is not so hard to see what Dumont is driving at with his notion of hierarchical encompassment (certainly, Marriott gets it). After all, the kind of paradoxical structure Dumont intends to describe by 'hierarchy' has one of its anthropological representations in Evans-Pritchard's first book on the Nuer. Although I remain impressed by Needham's close investigation of the concept of opposition, I am not convinced that the question of translation raised by the sort of (apparently) logically anomalous structure that Dumont has in mind can be treated satisfactorily with Needham's innovative approach, what he calls "a kind of empirical philosophy" (ibid.: 3). As I aim to show in the present essay, Dumont's concept may be construed to promise to put an end to the exhausting theoretical oscillation—the perpetual-motion epistemic of Western thought—between empiricism and intellectualism.

5. In his lecture "Anti Anti-Relativism," Geertz (1984) suggests that anti-relativists tendentiously picture all relativisms as absolute, and argues that relativism does not in fact lead to the frightening litany of bad ends implicit in absolute relativism. However, for all his imposing 'rhetor-work', he does not show that anthropological relativisms are not in fact absolutist; nor does he show what a non-absolutist relativism would look like. It is not so clear to me that anthropology has succeeded in avoiding the bad ends—"subjectivism, nihilism, incoherence, Machiavellianism, ethical idiocy, esthetic blindness, and so on" (ibid.: 263)—that flow logically from absolute relativism. But even if it has, it would not necessarily follow that the relativisms so far produced in anthropology are not absolutist in inclination. In this connection, it is important to bear in mind that, like anthropological holism, anthropological relativism tends to be held naively, as a kind of fundamentalist dogma, and is generally not well worked out as regards its ethical or, for that matter, deep theoretical implications. At any rate, to take Geertz's point, it would also be a mistake to define all anti-relativisms as absolutist. While the present work might be thought to assume an anti-relativist position of a kind, it does not embrace a foundationalism—at least not one that admits of interpretation in terms of an admonishment to stay at home (cf. ibid.: 276). Put another way, my anti-relativism is itself relativized, such that it is basically indistinguishable from relativized relativism.

6. The phrase is due to Evans-Pritchard (1937) in his great study of the Azande.

7. In practice theory proper, the original site of this deconstruction of the usual distinction between theory and practice is the Marx of *The German Ideology* (in Kamenka 1983: 175): "Division of labour only becomes truly such from the moment when a division of material and mental labour appears. From this moment onwards consciousness *can* really flatter itself that it is something other than consciousness of existing practice, that it is *really* conceiving something without conceiving something *real*; from now on consciousness is in a position to emancipate itself from the world and to proceed to the formation of 'pure' theory, theology, philosophy, ethics, etc." From the perspective of phenomenology, it is as if theory were something other than an embodied mode of human practice.

8. Since this kind of selection may or may not proceed according to reason, it has little or nothing to do with Kant's notion of moral choice. What is imperative about moral choice, as I use the term here, is not that it follows from reason but that we have no choice but to practice it.

9. Jung and Lacan are notable exceptions. Whatever Jung exactly intended by the 'collective unconscious', though, I certainly am not entertaining anything like a mental realm wherein archetypal images dwell as autonomous agents. Despite its difference from Freud's notion, Jung's 'unconscious' remains firmly anchored to the Cartesian distinction of an inner and outer world. Lacan's equation of the unconscious with the intersubjectivity of language, and hence with the Other, is certainly closer to what I have in mind (cf. Dews 1987: 81ff.). The highly structuralist character of Lacan's notion gives me pause, though, for reasons Derrida has expounded (cf. Norris 1987: 116–17). Obviously, my usage of the unconscious here is as yet undeveloped.

10. Because of its title (as well as its content), I have cited here Michael Polanyi's book, *The Tacit Dimension*. But as I set out in chapter 1, the essence of the idea of tacit knowledge runs throughout both Wittgenstein's and Merleau-Ponty's thinking about the synthetic a priori. It is also worth noting Heidegger's (1978: 99–105) distinction between the "present to hand" and the "ready to hand," in which the former is linked to explicit, differentiated, or theoretical knowledge of things, while the latter pertains to the undifferentiated knowledge that bears on things immediately in relation to practice (the sort of knowledge that is displayed about, say, a doorknob, when one routinely turns it to open the door). Heidegger's (ibid.) concept of "being-in-the-world" pictures this latter kind of knowing as our primary mode. Analytic philosophers talk of this kind of knowing as 'knowing how' in contrast to 'knowing that'.

11. The inspiration here is Merleau-Ponty (1962: 194): "We must therefore recognize as an ultimate fact this open and indefinite power of giving significance—that is, both of apprehending and conveying a meaning—by which man transcends himself towards a new form of behaviour, or towards other people, or towards his own thought, through his body and his speech." And Heidegger (1982: 299): "The Dasein itself oversteps in its being and thus is exactly *not the immanent*." The citation from Heidegger anticipates the additional meaning I go on to give 'transcendence' here. For a collection of case studies in the tradition of the Manchester School, stimulated by this notion of transcendence, see Evens and Peacock (1990).

12. Chris Roberts (pers. comm.) reminds me that this argument about the positivity of the negative is in fact, famously, Hegel's. Indeed, negation is a critical component of the Hegelian dialectic. Here is a brief example in which Hegel (1977: 51) distinguishes his idea of "*determinate* nothingness" (nothingness "that has *content*") from the "skepticism which only ever sees pure nothingness": "The skepticism that ends up with the bare abstraction of nothingness or emptiness cannot get any further from there, but must wait to see whether something new comes along and what it is, in order to throw it too into the same empty abyss. But when, on the other hand, the result is conceived as it is in truth, namely, as a *determinate* negation, a new form has thereby immediately arisen, and in the negation the transition is made through which the progress through the complete series of forms comes about itself." Hegel sees this work of negation in the constitution of the specifically human, as in his famous master-slave dialectic, wherein the master, by consuming it, makes absolutely nothing of what the slave produces for him, but the slave, using the determinate nothingness of imagination, alters positive reality and thus, along with the concrete product of his labor, produces himself (his self) as that which is relatively distinct from the external world.

In his reading of Emersonian perfectionism, Stanley Cavell seems to turn the point in relation to the idea of "democratic morality" (1990: 124–25; emphasis added):

> [Authentic democracy] means living as an example of human partiality, that is to say, of whatever Moral Perfectionism knows as the human individual, one who is not everything but is open to the further self, in oneself and in others, which means holding oneself in knowledge of the need for change; which means, being one who lives in promise, as a … representative human, which in turn means expecting oneself to be … intelligible as an inhabitant now also of a further realm … and to show oneself prepared to recognize others as belonging there … This is not a particular moral demand, but the condition of democratic morality; it is what that dimension of representativeness of democracy comes to which is not delegatable … So that conformity is not a mere lack of community, but its parody, learning and teaching the wrong thing of and to one another. The price of liberty is our subjection to eternal vigilance.

13. Wittgenstein (1979: 4e, 7e) may have alluded to something of the kind: "The description of a wish is, *eo ipso*, the description of its fulfillment. And magic does give representation to a wish; it expresses a wish." He added (ibid.: 7e): "In magical healing one indicates to an illness that it should leave the patient. After the description of any such magical cure we'd like to add: If the illness doesn't understand that, then I don't know how one ought to say it." The principle here seems consistent with some sort of ontological gradualism, wherein neither the empirical nor the normative can be found without a measure, however small, of each other's character (cf. Evens 1983: 127–28). Under an ontology of this kind, medicine not only has ethics but is always ethical procedure before it is anything else. This understanding puts in a fresh light the 'magical healing' that is Dinka medicine.

Chapter 9: Contradiction and Choice among the Dinka and in Genesis

1. In this connection, it is important to see that the change of anthropological perspective from theory to practice not only transfigures logical indifference into choice but also redefines the very idea of choice. The same holds for other key notions of my argument—'nature' and 'supernature' as well as 'self' and 'other'. In each case, redefinition takes the radical form of a shift away from both dualism and monism. Thus, as it bears on the Dinka, 'nature' is far more than natural, the 'self' is far less than self-contained, and 'choice', although still discretionary or creative, is far less than witting, individual, and free. As my focus in this chapter is the theoretical transfiguring of logical indifference into choice, these ontological redefinitions are deployed here only on behalf of that focus. However, it is important that the reader remain alert to them, even if they are not foregrounded. Throughout this chapter, I have found it edifying to enlist the support of Lienhardt's interpretations, which, like my own, have a strong phenomenological bent. It is especially my ontological aim—to develop for anthropological purposes a nondualist ontology—that distinguishes what I do here from Lienhardt's sensitive account.

2. My usage of the term 'participation', in ontological counterpoint to empiricism's presupposition of the wholly detached observer, seems plain enough here. Of course, the anthropological idea of participation is due to Lévy-Bruhl, whose brilliantly insightful work was so ill-received in anthropology that it was woefully neglected. Indeed, Lévy-Bruhl (1975) himself felt compelled by critical opinion to recant some of his own ideas, in my view, not always to advantage. In his sophisticated study of belief, which he dedicates to the memory of Lévy-Bruhl (and of Wittgenstein), Rodney Needham (1972) has helped considerably to set the record straight. Cazeneuve's little book (1972), an appreciation and a collection of extracts from Lévy-Bruhl's work, is a very useful introduction to this most anthropology-minded of French philosophers. For a forceful adaptation of Lévy-Bruhl's concept of participation, to the end of reinterpreting the history of Western consciousness, see Owen Barfield's iconoclastic *Saving the Appearances* (1965).

3. Here Lienhardt's (1985) essay on African representations of the self should be consulted. He plainly asserts that there obtains among the Dinka and other African peoples a strong sense of private or individual self, and that "one can lay too much one-sided stress on the collectivist orientation of

African ideas of the person" (ibid.: 145). But he also argues that this private self is difficult for us to describe and translate, in view of, if I follow him correctly, the "absence, among ... the Dinka, of the mind-body dichotomy" (ibid.: 150–51). However, evidently failing to see that the dualism of metaphor and letter is logically tied to that of mind and body, Lienhardt seems to think that the way in which the Dinka refer to the body to define human characteristics is simply metaphorical (ibid.: 149–50).

4. In his case study of his own people, Deng (1972) uses the distinction freely.

5. Durkheim (1915: 26–27), whom Lienhardt cites here, had already securely captured this insight:

> Moreover, the idea of the supernatural, as we understand it, dates only from to-day; in fact, it presupposes the contrary idea, of which it is the negation; but this idea is not at all primitive. In order to say that certain things are supernatural, it is necessary to have the sentiment that a *natural order of things* exists, that is to say, that the phenomena of the universe are bound together by necessary relations, called laws. When this principle has once been admitted, all that is contrary to these laws must necessarily appear to be outside of nature, and consequently, of reason; for what is natural in this sense of the word, is also rational, these necessary relations only expressing the manner in which things are logically related. But this idea of universal determinism is of recent origin; even the greatest thinkers of classical antiquity never succeeded in becoming fully conscious of it. It is a conquest of the positive sciences; it is the postulate upon which they repose and which they have proved by their progress. Now as long as this was lacking or insufficiently established, the most marvellous events contained nothing which did not appear perfectly conceivable. So long as men did not know the immutability and the inflexibility of the order of things, and so long as they saw there the work of contingent wills, they found it natural that either these wills or others could modify them arbitrarily. That is why the miraculous interventions which the ancients attributed to their gods were not to their eyes miracles in the modern acceptation of the term.

6. Compare with Evans-Pritchard's discussion in *Nuer Religion* (1956: 7–9, 156). Also, a hierarchical admixture of creativity and procreativity is an idea of foundational importance to Christianity, in relation, of course, to the nature of Christ's birth. Here Peter Brown (1988: 444) talks about the stress placed by late antique Christians on the cult of the Virgin and the continuity of Christ's flesh with human flesh:

> In the conception, the birth, and the nurturing of Christ, every human physiological process had been respected, except for the hot human act of male procreation and the wrenching-open of the womb at childbirth. To a late antique sensibility, the miraculous quality of the virgin birth shimmered all the more hypnotically because the two violent and indispensable links of a normal human process had been excised. The *pudo aureus* of Mary spoke of the resilience of a human body from which the disorder introduced into it by Adam's fall had been expunged. Virgins of the church bore bodies analogous to that of Mary: unshaken by intercourse and childbirth, here was a body "that has the marks of sex without its dire constraint."

By contrast to the Dinka, however, here only the procreative aspect is taken for granted, while the creative aspect is featured as so exceptional as to be "miraculous." Brown's wonderful study shows that the world of late-antique Christianity is internally diverse and rich in ideas, including apparently nondualistic doctrines of body and soul (see, e.g., ibid.: 235f.). Nevertheless, the comparison to the Dinka seems to point straight to the way in which Christianity is founded on ontological dualism.

7. In Evens (1984), I show how the same lived logic of hierarchical encompassment allows the Nuer to uphold their principle of agnation by, in our terms, violating it.

8. Here is where Max Gluckman's functionalism fails. If ritual constitutes its own end, then it is not reducible to a function of social structure. Even Victor Turner's determined (Manchester School) advance in connection with the question of ritual does not quite do the trick. While its performativism is rich and powerful, Turner's understanding of ritual continues to rely pre-eminently on representation rather than presentation. In this reliance on the symbolic, a leading element of Durkheim's sociologism, the theory remains only a step away from structural functionalism and

thus fails to capture what is most diagnostic about ritual: the way in which it takes itself as its own end. So does, I suggest, Geertz's aestheticism (1973a), which features the expressive aspect of ritual, emphasizes the concomitant emotionality of the participants, and calls for interpretation instead of explanation. Kapferer (1997, n.d.), however, drawing on Kant's *Critique of Judgment* to develop a sophisticated, thought-provoking phenomenological notion of the aesthetic, directs his inquiry squarely to the question of the ontological aspect of ritual efficacy. The result is impressive and gets beyond the attribution of ritual efficacy to emotionality (a thesis that seems still to reflect a trace of nineteenth-century anthropological evolutionism). But given my Levinasian persuasion (and relying primarily on secondary sources of Kant's eminently difficult philosophy), I suspect that despite Kapferer's directly ontological concern for the question of efficacy, Kantianism cannot do the trick. Here I rely primarily on Catherine Chalier's (2002) wonderfully lucid comparative study of Kant and Levinas. In his turn to beauty and the sublime, Kant thought he was pointing to something (God as revealed in "the starry heaven above me") that exceeds the subjective and synthesizes the particular with the universal, drawing man out of his interested self to a disinterested respect for moral personhood. Nevertheless, as with Durkheim's sociological version of this Kantian argument, the position seems still to fall short of cogency. In fact, although Durkheim did not try to shake himself loose from Descartes' dualism, his replacement of Kant's "starry heaven" with the social order may do more to move us beyond the philosophical tradition of reflective consciousness. But Kant (and even Durkheim) failed to think outside, to escape the potent gravity, of Cartesian dualism. Contemplation of the heavens, although it may indeed awaken wonder, cannot directly compromise one's moral sense of self-containment as can that of being solicited by another person or, in Levinas's terms, a "face." Such solicitation implicates a moral universe the reality of which is at once ideal and, in view of its 'face-to-face' this-worldliness, also quite real. It is on the basis of this essentially ambiguous reality, conveyed in the ambiguity of the self-other relationship, that ritual enjoys its efficacy. In this light, it appears that Kant's appeal to beauty as a symbol of God's universe does not truly take for granted the reality and priority of the exterior and the other. If this conjecture is sound, then, although it taps into the power of sensibility, the invocation of the beautiful cannot ultimately grasp the ontic force of ritual efficacy—or at least there is good reason to doubt that it can.

9. This generalization holds true, I believe, from nineteenth-century anthropological evolutionism to twentieth-century anthropological tropology. But of course there are significant exceptions, one of which I cite in the note immediately preceding this one. Tambiah (1985a, 1985b), relying on linguistic philosophy, is another, not to mention Lévi-Strauss (1963b) in his analytically masterful intellectualist piece, "The Effectiveness of Symbols."

10. I owe this insight to Chris Roberts (pers. comm.), who arrived at it in mind of Wittgenstein's (1979: 9ff.) notion of a "perspicuous presentation," a picture that leads to understanding something by facilitating the seeing of connections between that something and other things, including especially whoever is looking to understand it. For a superlative realization of this sort of anthropological reflexivity, see Kenneth Read's *The High Valley* (1965), in which he relates how, by contrast to his theoretical aims, his unavoidable affective participation with the Gahuku Gama radically transformed his self-understanding. His being in and of their social world (i.e., his 'being there') made him dangerously ill, producing a bodily experience of self-becoming through which he found himself *in* his other and altered his anthropological understanding by seeing the truth in the Gahuku Gama understanding of themselves and the world.

11. In his marvelous interpretation of Velasquez's brilliant painting, *Las Meninas*, Foucault (1970: 3–16) develops this point superbly. In chapter 11, I discuss Foucault's interpretation.

Chapter 10: Contradiction in Azande Oracular Practice

1. The 'writing ethnography' thinkers (see Clifford 1982; Crapanzano 1979) have done anthropology a decided service by salvaging Leenhardt's work from the relative obscurity to which it had been

consigned by the linguistic (structuralist and anti-phenomenological) deconstruction of the idea of primitive mentality. Leenhardt's account of a genuine otherness that is irreducible to metaphorical language is distinguished by its remarkably open ontological sensibility.

2. In at least four other places, I have argued forthrightly against the universal anthropological application of the opposition between the metaphorical and the literal, but on ontological rather than simply epistemological grounds (Evens 1983, 1989, 1993, 1995).

3. Although it suits my purpose here to rely on Evans-Pritchard's ethnography, of course his picture of the Azande (1937) is not unproblematic, as Geertz's (1983) critique of Evans-Pritchard highlights. However, notwithstanding the important contribution of the school of anthropological thought focused on ethnography as writing, there is something much too easy about Geertz's argument. To maintain that Evans-Pritchard's famous clarity of style betrays a mighty socio-centric conceit appears to court the admonishment that in addition to being an intrinsically interpretive exercise, ethnographic translation should also be unclear. Surely, the relevant objective is to 'clarify'—that is, make intelligible for the reader—the apparently radical other, even if clarification entails the *altera*-tion of its own conditions. It is not obvious that clarification of this kind necessarily demands, by contrast to directness, elegance, and limpidity of style, a "shaded," "unflattened," and "tendentious" manner of expression—qualities that, as Geertz says (1983: 74), well characterize his own brilliant and rhetorically imposing style. At any rate, although Evans-Pritchard could not have simply escaped the colonial mentality of his time and culture, and although of course there is something telling about the relationship between Evans-Pritchard's ethnographic authority and his ethnographic style, it is by no means transparent to me that he did simply presume there is nothing about the Azande that is new under the British sun. Indeed, the penetrating, interpretive sensibility of *Witchcraft, Oracles and Magic* (not to mention the corpus of his work)—as measured by the degree to which the book begins to question Western categories of thought (such as 'non-contradiction')—stands as compelling testimony that he did not. This is one reason why I find Geertz's critique too easy, and perhaps even, despite his outright declaration of admiration for Evans-Pritchard (Geertz 1983: 70), a bit mean.

Of course, numerous others have pointed to flaws in Evans-Pritchard's analysis. In her introduction to the abridged edition of Evans-Pritchard's book, Gillies (1976) suggests that Evans-Pritchard, still under the spell of functionalism, gave Azande society a misleading homeostatic cast. Gluckman himself was fond of observing that Evans-Pritchard failed to analyze satisfactorily Azande thought and practice in relation to their social organization. He and others (see Gluckman 1965: chap. 6) did supply analyses of this kind for other peoples. In her compact appreciation of Evans-Pritchard's work, Mary Douglas (1980: chap. 5) does a neat job of teasing out of the monograph on the Azande how their witchcraft ideas depend on their political institutions.

Any definition of the situation will be the more imposing for having behind it institutional relations of power. But as especially Foucault and Bourdieu have thought through, knowledge, considered as practice rather than sheer thinking stuff, has its own ways of making power. In his study of terror and healing in Colombia, Taussig (1987: 463–64) has argued that it is precisely this sort of power that Evans-Pritchard, in his account of Zande witchcraft, failed to discern. Like Geertz, Taussig is a bit too quick and easy with Evans-Pritchard's explanatory analysis, overlooking the phenomenological and praxiological implications of Evans-Pritchard's wonderfully precocious and powerful theses about "ideas imprisoned in action" and about the inverse relation between the notions of contradiction and situation. But my argument about the Azande finds a striking parallel in Taussig's observation that "coincidence and sorcery pose questions concerning one's life's environment, opening out the world as much as closing it in," and that it is therefore "woefully mistaken" to call this a "'closed system'" (1987: 465). Indeed, Taussig's broad thesis about the terrible healing power of shamanic, "epistemic murk" is of a piece with my understanding here—that we need to learn from, as well as about, the other. However, whereas for Taussig basic ambiguity or uncertainty is primarily a question of epistemology and power (cf. Surin 1993), for me it is at bottom a matter of ontology and ethics. In her deeply felt and moving book on the violence of hunger and suffering in Brazil, Nancy

Scheper-Hughes (1992: 21) has thought to ask about, in respect of Evans-Pritchard's study, the connection between witchcraft and ethics.

4. Given the patently contrived circumstances of the ethnomethodological example, the use of it as a prop for my argument is bound to give some readers misgivings. It is important, then, to note just why it is suitable here. I was drawn to the example many years ago by its stunning likeness to the proceedings of the Zande poison oracle. The issue here is not whether the example is odd and artificial (it is, by definition), but rather, given this condition, what argumentative purpose it is meant to serve. In line with the basic intentions of McHugh's (1968) ethnomethodological exercise, the exceptional nature of the example—designed as it is to obstruct the actor's taken-for-granted social world—serves to disclose expectancies of ordinary interaction that are fundamental but so routine and familiar that they normally go unnoticed. The expectancy I want to bring into relief, in relation to Zande witchcraft and the poison oracle, is the critical manner in which much Western social interaction is produced and maintained by the individual's sense of him- or herself as morally self-contained.

It needs to be borne in mind, then, that what is crucial to my argument is not the ethnographic verisimilitude of the example but the thesis of a certain practice pertaining to selfhood in the West. This thesis does not stand or fall with the example. The practice I have in mind, which I call here 'selfcraft', when taken broadly scarcely stands in need of documentation. Its existence as a diagnostic feature of Western thought and action is attested to by the philosophical corpus of discourse in the West, from Augustine's penitentially self-searching *Confessions* to Foucault's impassioned and sustained interrogation, in one work after another, of the self thus fashioned. Indeed, the notion of selfcraft obviously resonates with Foucault's (1988) "technologies of the self," practices he traces back to late antiquity. The example from McHugh is not adduced to demonstrate the thesis of selfcraft, but rather to furnish a perspicuous picture, an iconic model, of one extant way selfcraft can work—a job for which it is eminently suited by virtue of its outlandishly extreme constitution.

That said, however, it would be a mere disciplinary conceit to conclude that simply because it was generated artificially, the example is of no ethnographic value. On the contrary, what it lacks in ethnographic richness and intensity, it makes up for in ethnographic depth, as one might expect from McHugh's purpose of uncovering presuppositions of everyday interaction. Hence, while I do not wish to suggest that the example may be taken to represent all psychotherapeutic interaction, I would contend that the particular picture of selfcraft that the example projects is diagnostic of a great deal of modernity, including much psychotherapy, if thinkers such as Lacan (1981), Foucault (1965), and Deleuze and Guattari (1977) have anything to say about the matter.

5. We learned long ago, from Kenneth Read's (1955) remarkable essay on the Gahuku-Gama, that the Kantian individual is not a universal. Although Read does not suggest there that Western thought can take a lesson from the Gahuku-Gama about the nature of discretion, it is tempting to read his *The High Valley* (1965), another landmarking work, as an attempt on his part to see just what can be learned from these people about what it means to be a human being.

6. There is no room here to argue this point. I can, however, bare the bones of the argument I have in mind by quoting a Heideggerian Derrida on the subject of the intrinsic connection of the dualism of 'metaphor' and 'letter' with 'Western philosophy as metaphysics', as well as on the implicitly repressive character of this connection (Derrida 1978: 27; see also Bruzina 1978; Derrida 1982): "Metaphor in general, the passage from one existent to another, or from one signified meaning to another, authorized by the initial [dualistic] *submission* of Being to the existent, the [dualistic] *analogical* displacement of Being, is the essential weight which anchors discourse in metaphysics, irremediably repressing discourse into its metaphysical state."

7. Needless to say, I am not making an argument on behalf of Popper's theory of rationality, for which countless strong critiques exist (e.g., Feyerabend 1974). I employ it here, not because I believe it can satisfactorily demarcate science from metaphysics, but because it is very helpful in bringing out what Evans-Pritchard (1937) found wrong with the oracular thought of the Azande. As I will come to in the text, my own candidate for such a line of demarcation is not rationality per se but the

phenomenological emergence of a *rule* of rationality. A line of this kind is indeed consequential, but no more than any rule can it fix a separate mentality.

8. Since writing this chapter, I have discovered that David Zeitlyn (1990), in an ethnomethodological analysis of Mambila 'spider' divination, has also drawn the parallel to McHugh's experiment, employing the work of McHugh's teacher, the founder of ethnomethodology, Harold Garfinkel. However, by contrast to my phenomenology, which is, I expect, heterodox and concerned with ontology, Zeitlyn's essay constitutes an exercise in 'conversational analysis'. I should add that Zeitlyn misread an earlier essay of mine (Evens 1983). He cited it as an example of the anthropological recommendation to construe the sort of thinking in question here—thinking that customarily exhibits indifference to contradiction—as non-standard logic (Zeitlyn 1990: 665n13). To the contrary, though, that essay plainly constitutes a carefully considered repudiation of 'the other logic' thesis in anthropology and accords with the present chapter's phenomenological and situationalist turn toward nondualism and a concept of practice.

9. Of course, under these circumstances, the 'general case', no more than the 'particular case', can amount to the inductivist's notion. The blurring of the distinction between the particular and the general must impede the differentiation of generality as it does that of particularity. In this connection, Leenhardt's (1979: chap. 2) discussion of the lack of 'perspective' in Canaque art makes for an interesting comparison. Leenhardt contends that the Melanesian artist's "vision unfolds in only two dimensions." "He has not separated out the third dimension: he is unaware of depth," writes Leenhardt, who then goes on to observe that that this state of aesthetic perception is paralleled among the Canaque by a lack of "the expression of generality in language" (ibid.: 11, 12). Thus, just as the Melanesian artist can depict the trunk of the human body only by graphically unrolling it, like a "triptych," so he can designate the body's trunk in his language only by naming the parts. He has no "generic term" for it (ibid.: 12).

I suspect that the lack of generality to which Leenhardt points is another aspect of what I have in mind by 'the presumption of generality'. I would argue that when the third dimension is perfectly taken for granted rather than cognitively 'separated out', the universal connectivity it implicitly guarantees impairs the development of depth in artistic expression. Where everything is presumptively connected to everything else by virtue of the third, nothing can appear in the round, since under such an epistemological condition nothing (no-thing) can be self-contained. It is only when the third dimension is differentiated as such (that is, separated out), so that mediation or thirdness is expressly predicated rather than naively presumed, that a bodily thing can be grasped as a thing. A thing-in-itself supposes a medium that intervenes between it and everything else. But to say that mediation (the third) is simply presumed is to say, precisely, that it is not mediacy but *im*mediacy that prevails. Of course, it needs to be borne in mind here that perspective in art is a scientific convention that developed in the fifteenth century, and that perception is not a direct ontological disclosure but always depends on what Gombrich (1961: chap. 8) calls the "beholder's share."

10. In all fairness to the student, he did. As we saw, once he grew suspicious, he tested with some of his questions the veracity of the therapeutic definition of the situation. But in terms of logic, he did so inexpertly. For example, instead of "Do you say no regardless?" he might have asked "Do you ever say yes?" In this case, the therapist's reply of no would have left the student with no logical pretext for avoiding the conclusion that the definition of the situation was not as advertised. Of course, this does not guarantee that the student would have so concluded, but the possibility points to a significant difference between the oracular situation and psychotherapy proper.

Both psychotherapy and oracular practice involve expectations of expertise, but the degree to which this is so and the nature of the expertise differ between the two cases. The oracle presents itself as primarily a prophetic mode of inquiry. By contrast, the psychotherapist is a professional expert who specializes in bringing to the surface for his or her clients the truths of their particular psychological make-up, where 'truth' is keyed technically and ultimately to logical logic and is, therefore, in principle inapplicable to prophetic, as distinct from predictive, statements. This is a difference that makes a difference (one that correlates with, as I go on to argue in this chapter, the emergence of the idea of pure theory, an idea on the basis of which it appears possible to decide, if not truth, at least falsity in absolute terms). No doubt the calculated lack in the pseudo-therapeutic interaction of much that we might normally regard as professional psychotherapeutic expertise gives the event its appearance of something like an Azande oracular consultation—at bottom, a signally irrational or prophetic practice. But in the present context, the advantage of this example is precisely that it brings into relief elements of psychotherapy that, even if normally of small measure, tend to be concealed by the presumptive primacy of professional specialization and rational practice. That is, precisely because of its artificial and extreme nature, the example delineates forcefully the exceptional power of the definition of the situation to ensure its own validity.

11. *Pace* Horton, for whom the shift is idiomatic and epistemological rather than ontological. His discussions of the sort of problem that concerns me here are rich and studied (see, e.g., Horton 1970, 1982). My key point about the phenomenological liberation of theory from practice finds much to go on in Horton's (1982: 246) account of the consequences of the "divorce of secondary theory [by which he means 'theoretical discourse' as opposed to 'everyday discourse' or 'primary theory'] from practical life." Moreover, I have some sympathy for his bold argument that when it comes to the domain of "human social life," by contrast to that of "non-living things," the "traditionalist" enjoys a certain superiority over the "modernist" (ibid.: 249). Nevertheless, the differences between Horton's ('intellectualist') approach and mine are, I suspect, profound, centering as they do on the difference between cognitivism and phenomenology and between epistemology and ontology.

12. Cf. Sartre's critique of Kantian idealism, in which Sartre (1956: 225ff.) argues that Kant's affirmation of the other runs contrary to the essential solipsism of the Kantian thesis of pure subjectivity.

13. Although Anthony Giddens does not allow Philip Rieff's thesis about the rise of therapy as a function of secularization and of the moral vacuum created by the weakening of traditional religion to go unqualified, and although he is keen to explore the advantages of the modern sense of self, he certainly focuses on the aspect of therapy featured here (Giddens 1991: 180): "Therapeutic endeavours ... take place against the background of sequestration of experience and the internally referential systems of modernity. It is not surprising that many—not all—therapies are oriented primarily towards control. They interpret the reflexive project of the self in terms of self-determination alone, thus confirming, and even accentuating, the separation of the lifespan from extrinsic moral considerations." In other words, therapy tends to arise with and create social environments in which people, by virtue of a highly exclusive self-identity, are very well insulated from the discretionary power of, and uncertainty presented by, the other.

14. Cf. Ashis Nandy's (1989) witty but scathing critique of the commoditization of the game of cricket in modern India and, therewith, of the country's course toward modernization and nationalization. In it, Nandy speaks of the "increasingly less self-critical moral culture of the modern sector in non-modern societies" and observes that both cricket and astrology—each somehow centered in a sense of uncertainty—have the capacity to reaffirm "the existence of a moral universe" (ibid.: 102–3): "Astrology in this part of the world shows all the signs of being not only a reading of the vicissitudes of fate but also an insight into the morality of one's own thoughts and actions, in fact into one's own moral self. At this plane, astrology becomes, however self-contradictory this may sound, a mirror as well as a critique. You see in it not so much your future as your past and your present."

15. The possibility of such an advance may be seen in relation to the obvious consideration that the fundamentally discretionary nature of witchcraft does not save particular others from being targeted for alienation (as witches, of course). Indeed, as has been well documented, between the fifteenth and seventeenth centuries, whole categories of people in Europe (including lepers, Jews, and 'witches') were subjected to savage torture and capital punishment because they were held to be morally responsible for contingent misfortunes (see, e.g., Ginzburg 1991). On the one hand, by sealing off and certifying the self ontologically and epistemologically, selfcraft tends to totalize the process of the alienation of the other and thus the principle of moral discretion as well. A self-identical self leaves no room at

all for authentic otherness and therefore, inasmuch as otherness is a necessary condition of the practice of moral selection, none for genuine moral selection either. On the other hand, by promulgating self-reflection, as I will develop in the next few chapters, selfcraft makes conceivable the opening up of such ultimately suicidal behavior to critical viewing. For a philosophically magisterial argument in this direction, see Taylor (1989, 1991). For a strong, thoughtful, and well-informed Habermasian account, see McGowan (1991). For a critically reserved but positive sociological slant, see Giddens (1991).

16. Gluckman and another late, great social anthropologist, Sir Edmund Leach, regarded each other with, so to speak, a sorcerous professional respect (cf. Kuper 1983: chap. 6).

Chapter 11: Epistemic and Ethical Gain

1. Foucault studied with two existential phenomenologists, Sartre and Merleau-Ponty. In this connection, it is worth noting that *The Visible and the Invisible* is the title of one of Merleau-Ponty's books and *The Prose of the World* (the second chapter of Foucault's *The Order of Things*) is the title of another.

2. In her excellent essay, Foti (1996: 2), also thinking by contrast of Merleau-Ponty, argues that Foucault "is not fully attentive to the materiality of painting and to its resistance to discursive appropriation but remains, strangely, bound to a Cartesian understanding of vision and painting." Her criticism is especially interesting in light of Foucault's debt to Merleau-Ponty. Merleau-Ponty privileged vision as he did the body, but the sense of vision was that belonging to bodily participation (as if the eye were a tactile organ) rather than, as with Cartesianism, spectating. He was intellectually preoccupied with escaping the philosophy of consciousness, an ambition Foucault plainly shared. But in result, Merleau-Ponty does not exactly eliminate the 'I think'; rather, he settles on the understanding that the body itself thinks and perceives, thus rendering reality basically ambiguous as between substance and thought. It is not clear to me that Foucault took to heart this ontologically scandalous move. Although Foucault accepted Merleau-Ponty's argument against Husserl, to grasp transcendental consciousness as basically embodied, he seems not to have agreed that this argument addresses the dualism of the empirical and the transcendental. On the contrary, it would appear that as far as he was concerned, Merleau-Ponty's phenomenology had simply embraced the empirical over the transcendental. Foucault (1970: 321) asserts: "It is doing no more ... than fulfilling with greater care the hasty demands laid down when the attempt was made to make the empirical, in man, stand for the transcendental." About Foucault's argument here, Gutting (2001: 273–74), working from chapter 9 of *The Order of Things*, writes:

> This is not a very satisfactory critique, since Foucault gives no reason for his claim that the world of lived experience is simply the empirical world. Here he seems to be ignoring his own recognition, before the statement of this criticism, of the irreducible ambiguity of lived experience, which he describes as "a specific yet ambiguous stratum, concrete enough for it to be possible to apply to it a meticulous and descriptive language, yet sufficiently removed from the positivity of things for it to be possible, from that starting-point, to escape from that naiveté, to contest it and seek foundations for it." Why, we wonder, if lived experience in fact has this "mixed" nature, does Foucault insist that phenomenological description is always "empirical despite itself"?

In this light, one might well ask if Foucault was being fair to Merleau-Ponty and the kind of phenomenology he proffered. It is hard to believe that Foucault failed to understand that Merleau-Ponty was making an ontological argument according to which reality is neither transcendental nor empirical but basically ambiguous between the two. Could Foucault really have been so hoodwinked by the representative materialism of the stock Western acceptation of the notion of body as to miss that that dualist notion is precisely what Merleau-Ponty's pivotal usage, "the body," was meant to explode? Despite its debt to Nietzsche and the latter's concept of power, Foucault's project is profoundly phenomenological, especially when this term is taken to refer to the existential variety of phenomenology, the sort associated particularly with Merleau-Ponty, Sartre, and Heidegger. His critical intellectual and liberationist concern to disclose or 'dig up' key a priori notions is obviously akin to phenomenology's essential ends of 'bracketing' and 'reduction', and to its 'archaeological' concept of sedimentation, each of which pertains analytically to reflexivity. And his focused concern with constructions on and of the body, even if this concern is thickly lined with the question of power, is basically continuous with Merleau-Ponty's (1964a: 166) phenomenologically innovative turn to the body as "the *vinculum* of the self and things." Perhaps in his need to distinguish himself from the phenomenological project, Foucault felt compelled to picture that project not simply as part of the modern age's preoccupation of man and his doubles, but as one form of the folly of the dualist ambition to reduce this "empirico-transcendental doublet"—"of what belongs to the order of positivity *and* what belongs to the order of foundations" or "that being whose thought is constantly interwoven with the unthought"—to "the Same" (Foucault 1970: 318, 340, 350).

3. I have modified Wittgenstein's critical phenomenological insight and lesson solely by adding, to suit my topic more exactly, the prefix 'auto' to 'investigation'.

4. Foucault sums up his own work as "a history of the different modes by which, in our culture, human beings are made subjects" (1983: 208; see also Foucault 1988: 146).

5. It is worth noting that in this quotation Berger, Berger, and Kellner speak of the "discovery" of human dignity and rights. But this word is loaded, as it suggests that dignity and rights are given by dint of nature. Although it is the case that we as social beings cannot escape making primordial choices as to whether they should prevail, it is plain that dignity and rights are humanly constructed entitlements.

6. Of course, the thrust of Foucault's position is that these ideals are illusory, even delusory. The implication is that precisely because their goodness seems undeniable, the ideals, by serving as so many smokescreens of legitimacy, enable conduct that runs wholly contrary to what they plainly enjoin. For example, as I cite later in this chapter, Giorgio Agamben (2000), expressly influenced by Foucault and Hannah Arendt, has argued that the concept of human rights, on which our representations of the political subject have been based since the time of the French Revolution, is demonstrably a sham and should be abandoned in favor of a concept that is truer to the singularity of a human being. Filling in where Foucault left off, Agamben (ibid.: 24) suggests that we replace, as our guiding principle, "the *ius* (right) of the citizen" with the "*refugium* (refuge) of the singular." Underlying this recommendation is his thesis that human rights have inevitably been determined as a function of the nation-state, effectively leaving many human beings—the deracinated, the stateless, the refugee—without any rights at all. Technically, *refugium* entails a sense of selfhood and of extra-territorialized statehood substantially different from that associated with *ius*. Despite the material significance of this difference, though, one cannot but suspect that Agamben's provocative recommendation is perfectly in keeping with the ethical meliorism, its direction and sensibility, that rests at the heart of the modern ideals that so concern Taylor.

7. Durkheim's (1960) thesis of "the duality of our nature" remains instructive here. In his argument about "the duality of structure," Giddens (1979: 80ff.) has corrected for the outright dualism that infects Durkheim's notion.

8. Foucault (1984a: 42–43) responded to this kind of criticism by arguing that it is—since it supposes that one "has to be 'for' or 'against' the Enlightenment"—a form of Enlightenment "blackmail." In his probing and balanced account, Richard Bernstein (1992: chap. 5) seems to find that in the end Foucault does not succeed in defending himself against the relevant charge. I suspect it is too easy for anthropologists to be oblivious of this difficulty in Foucault's work. Perhaps they are more likely than most to be so inclined to renounce as totally colonialist the entire Western tradition of thought, that the emergence of their own critique on the scene becomes perfectly incomprehensible. To intellectually ambitious scholars in a discipline singularly dedicated to overcoming ethnocentrism, the radical content of Foucault's assault on Western thought must constitute a powerful attraction. (In an early appreciation, Foucault singled out ethnology and psychoanalysis as self-subverting "counter-sciences" [1970: 373ff.].) Ironically, this attraction to Foucault can lead too readily to uncritical devotion to his ideas. This irony is not surprising in light of the consideration that Foucault's assault on totalism in Western thought has itself, although perhaps not the substance, at least the feel of, as Taylor's criticisms insinuate, a totalistic bent, so that the assault inclines somewhat to teach by example that which it rails against—dogmatism.

9. On the other hand, this difference between Foucault and Taylor is very substantial. In his well-known essay, "What Is Enlightenment," wherein he refuses to be intellectually threatened into an either-or position on Enlightenment rationalism, Foucault (1984a: 43) asserts that "we do not break free of this blackmail by introducing 'dialectical' nuances while seeking to determine what good and bad elements there may have been in the Enlightenment." The question arises, then, whether Taylor's argument about a slide between domination and free agency and about the ambivalence of the modern self does not amount to just such an introduction of dialectical nuances bearing on the good and bad elements in the Enlightenment. In this connection, there appears to obtain a fundamental difference between Foucault's pessimistic activism and Taylor's pious concern for the good qua good. A major burden of Foucault's argument is that power is not simply proscriptive but also, and critically, positive and productive. As I read it, his ethics might be described in terms of the idea of using power against itself to combat one "main danger" after another (Foucault 1984b: 343). But Taylor's focus on the good as such suggests that he would regard as reductionist an ethics the essence of which is a matter of power. Of course, one might well ask whether power deployed against itself is still sensibly construable as power, and if not, then how it should be construed.

10. Again, however, the question of unfairness to Foucault arises here. Given his grasp of human life as quintessentially a matter of history, Foucault (1984a: 46) was of course acutely aware that his viewpoint too was bound to a particular historical context: "This means that the historical ontology of ourselves must turn away from all projects that claim to be global or radical. In fact we know from experience that the claim to escape from the system of contemporary reality so as to produce the overall programs of another society, of another way of thinking, another culture, another vision of the world, has led only to the return of the most dangerous traditions." Perhaps what is at stake in Taylor's criticisms is the sense in which Foucault's grasp of the good as a continuous practice of overcoming the bad, the dangerous, might itself be counted as 'foundationalist'. That is, is it not plausible that Foucault understood his pessimistic activism as culture- and history-bound, and that for him it constituted or served as a foundation of sorts? Even so, apropos of Taylor's point, it still leaves dangling the issue of identifying the criteria according to which the dangers that are the targets of one's activism are to be determined.

11. Although it is intriguing to search Eastern thought for a key inspiration of Foucault (Schaub 1989), the determination of such an inspiration cannot obviate the logical need to acknowledge a basis for his critique in Western thought. If there is an Oriental subtext to Foucault's ideas, it necessarily presupposes a receptivity in his Occidental text, one that opened him to definition by his Other.

12. As it remains unelaborated, it is difficult to know what to make of Foucault's aestheticism. In a very useful discussion, McGowan (1992: 138ff.) shows how Foucault's ideas of self-creating or self-inventing, of freedom from socio-political constraint, and of ethics, considered as how one practices freedom, hang together. More recently, Loesberg (2005: chap. 3) argues, along these lines but much more intensively, that Foucault's overall project is essentially aesthetic. According to Loesberg, at the same time that it is inclined to construe aesthetics as just another form of social domination, post-modernism also relies on conceptual understandings that have their source in the deep sense of aesthetics that Kant lays out in his third *Critique*—the sense in which, because they show purposiveness but in themselves serve no ultimate, practical purpose, beauty and the sublime inspire an ideal of a "*moral* author" and a God-designed universe, thereby providing a warrant for moral autonomy as a human condition (ibid.: 53–54, 148–49; see also Pippin 1989: 73ff.; Solomon 1988: 42–43). Loesberg (2005: 150) is not claiming that Foucault was a Kantian but that—in view of Foucault's correlative emphases on self-fashioning as the good life, on meaning as constructed in human practice, and on the sense in which such meaning presents a kind of fiction, and notwithstanding his Nietzschean and postmodern intellectual outlook—there is a basic and distinct continuity between Foucault's aestheticism and Kant's.

13. Although he also finds it wonderful, Popper (1972: 204; see also ibid.: 23, 98–99) presents a somewhat different picture of regularity in the world:

If the picture of the world which modern science draws comes anywhere near to the truth—in other words, if we have anything like 'scientific knowledge'—then the conditions obtaining almost everywhere in the universe make the discovery of structural laws of the kind we are seeking—and thus the attainment of 'scientific knowledge'—almost impossible. For almost all regions of the universe are filled by chaotic radiation, and almost all the rest by matter in a similar chaotic state. In spite of this, science has been miraculously successful in proceeding towards what I have suggested should be regarded as its aim. This strange fact cannot, I think, be explained without proving too much.

In addressing in the text the question of why science works, I have offered no explanation in terms of positive knowledge, and, therefore, I have not, I hope, tried to prove "too much." Indeed, taking my cue from Popper's (1972: 24–25) evolutionary approach to the growth of knowledge, I have simply argued that science is a way of making the method of trial-and-error elimination very efficient.

14. For an exception, see Stoller and Olkes's (1987) study of sorcery among the Songhay of Niger. Hans Peter Duerr's (1985) study, *Dreamtime*, strongly Wittgensteinian in its inspiration, provides a powerful philosophical discussion of the matter at hand. Duerr is not a professional anthropologist, but his phenomenological argument, keyed to intensive and fascinating ethnographic archival research, is exceptionally provocative in the present connection.

15. It is tempting to say here, in the most literal sense, that Western civilization has lost its mind. Such a proposition is in keeping with, say, Bateson's (1972) ecological critique, in which he argues that the Western consciousness has become blind to its own vital dependence on the relational whole. The proposition also fits well with the intellectual celebrities of postmodernism, who see reason as playing itself out in mad totalitarian regimes, whether collective or personal. The madness in question has to do with reason's alienation from, by exclusion of, its own basis in the non-rational. In a similar connection, psychoanalysis takes on a fresh significance: the so-called unconscious can be discovered and recovered only if it is first lost. Of course, since it grasped the unconscious ontologically as part of the subject, orthodox psychoanalysis could not really bring Western civilization to its senses. Thus, in taking Freud's notion of the unconscious beyond Oedipus to the structure of language, Lacan (1981: 47) tells us that in order to understand the Freudian concept, one must start with "the subject of Cartesian origin."

16. I have shown (Evens 1989b) that among the Nuer, where traditionally the principle of agnation reigns supreme, various routine behaviors that were logically out of keeping with it were not necessarily regarded so by the people themselves. Focusing on such discrepancies between principle and practice, anthropologists were led to conclude, despite the Nuer's patent self-understanding, that these people were not truly agnatic. In my view, though, given a nondualist sense of reality, both 'principle' and 'conformity' would have had a meaning for the Nuer critically different from that given to these notions in modern Western discourse. To take a current example, as one might expect where principle and practice are understood dualistically, Americans and the media compulsively measure the success of the US administration's war in Iraq. I suggest, though, that one reason why the administration has been able to get away with interpreting as success what is empirically a transparent military disaster is because the known or principled 'blueprint' for the war was forged on the anvil of ideological conviction rather than rationality. Therefore, there are few details in the overall plan of action against which the reality on the ground can be measured with reason, which is to say, according to settled rules that describe with any real precision the empirical meaning of success.

17. For a superbly intelligent discussion of the vexed relation between the Western political principles of liberty and equality, see Dahrendorf (1968: chap. 7).

18. Unless, of course, one is still willing to maintain that in itself skin color correlates with intelligence, or that (equally contrary to the preponderance of reason) their history of discriminatorily limited opportunity has nothing to do with the fact that many blacks do not pursue higher education as a pathway to a better life.

19. In his exchange with Derrida, Foucault (1979) offers a substantial discussion of Descartes' *Meditations*.

20. In *Forget Foucault*, Baudrillard (1987: 35) sees his compatriot as having entered into "a strange complicity with cybernetics." Earlier in this volume, in chapter 5, I argued for a certain complicity between Bourdieu and cybernetic theory. The complicity has to do with the ways in which both Foucault and Bourdieu tackle the problem of subjectivity.

21. Relevant here is Eve Sedgwick's (1992: 582) essay on addiction in general, in which, taking her cue from Foucault's "account of the invention of *the homosexual*," she depicts the figure of the addict as a modern discursive construct.

22. As one who constantly sought to take the perspective of a 'subaltern', and whose entire enterprise was emphatically based on his status as an 'outsider' (but one who is simultaneously on the inside), Foucault fit neatly with the rise, over the last three decades or so, of reflexive and post-colonial anthropology. Because his work is roundly informed with a broad and developed concept of power, it is especially socio-political in character. In addition, because he tied power singularly to discourse, his thought has a strong culturological bent. It is likely that these features help explain his more or less mesmeric impact on recent anthropology.

Chapter 12: Transcending Dualism and Amplifying Choice

1. I would argue that when it goes unqualified by fundamental openness to the other, the self defined as its own work of art amounts to a form of idolatry. Even though such a self can never be pinned down ontologically, it is valued primarily for its own sake. In this way, the otherness of the self is reduced to the self, and the self to an idol, a kind of artful evasion. Thus, too, the essentialism that the idea of the self-fashioning self is meant to dispel is reintroduced through aestheticism. Indeed, the concept of essentialism, so dear to the postmodernist critique, bears close comparison to the idea of idolatry in ancient Judaism, in which the hollow image of the indescribable is taken instead for what it is intended to describe. For a balanced and profound critique of the possibility of idolatrous aestheticism, a critique ultimately keyed to the importance of introducing the perspective of the relation with the other, see Levinas's (1987) "Reality and Its Shadow." For a brilliant, iconoclastic study of the evolution of Western consciousness in relation to idolatrous thinking, a study whose focus on 'participatory' understanding has much to offer in relation to the present exercise, see Barfield's *Saving the Appearances* (1965).

Still, I must take care not to draw too stark a contrast between ethics and aesthetics. Chris Roberts (pers. comm.) has reminded me of the consideration that the literature on the aesthetic has a rich history and by no means reduces to a call for 'art for art's sake'. Kant's aestheticism entails the understanding that God in a sense reveals Himself in the beautiful and the sublime, moving the subject to a disinterested, moral attitude toward the other. In his *Aesthetic Education of Mankind*, Schiller, a fervent disciple of Kant, enthusiastically prescribes artistic endeavor as the means to develop moral character. Although Nietzsche was hardly an admirer of Kant (but the most decisive influence on Foucault), the ideal of the aesthetic—the importance of living one's life as a work of art by virtue of the sight of the beautiful—veritably amounted to Nietzsche's own ethics. Theories of this kind reveal that aestheticism is not only about the creativity of the self but also about the perception of the beautiful—that is, it speaks to the importance of being open to otherness and the exterior world. The Greek word *aisthesis* means sensation or perception or even perceptiveness. In this light, Roberts's suggestion that my project is importantly congruent with a certain emphasis on the aesthetic is correct, especially when one considers the great influence that Merleau-Ponty's philosophy of perception—the aestheticism of which is explicit (as in, e.g., Merleau-Ponty 1964b: chap. 5)—has exercised on my thinking. Indeed, this insight about aesthetics has helped me understand why I have been disposed to construe Levinas's ethics in substantial extension of Merleau-Ponty's phenomenology in particular. The thesis that the body is not in the first place a thing but rather the final horizon of perception pictures the self as, from the outset, other to itself—a self-other relationship in which self and other, interior and exterior, body and mind, etc., are 'ontologically' continuous with each other—and therewith artlessly implicates the sense of ethics Levinas propounds and develops, an ethics keyed to other-dependence. Still, although it may allow for an aesthetic component, for reasons I set out above (see chap. 9, note 8, this volume), the Levinasian thesis of the primacy of ethics does not allow for the equation, much less reduction, of ethics to aesthetics.

2. Wittgenstein (1979: 8e) ponders: "But why does Frazer use the word 'ghost'? He evidently understands this superstition well enough, since he uses a familiar superstitious word to describe it." He goes on to observe, "nothing shows our kinship to those savages better than the fact that Frazer has at hand a word as familiar to us as 'ghost' or 'shade' to describe their views," and "What is queer in this is not limited to the expressions 'ghost' and 'shade', and too little is made of the fact that we include the words 'soul' and 'spirit' in our own civilized vocabulary. Compared with this, the fact that we do not believe our soul eats and drinks is a minor detail" (ibid.: 10e). Wittgenstein's point applies equally to the modern descendants of Frazer, that is, to present-day anthropologists, who, although it would be impossible to locate even one who regards Frazer's idea of intellectual backwardness as anything less than backward itself, continue to try to explain away (as linguistic indirection, such as symbol, metaphor, etc.) the existential fundamentality of religious force. By and large, the depth of Wittgenstein's critique has escaped the comprehension of modern anthropology.

3. Habermas's (1987b) critique of deconstructionism bears scrutiny here. My point about the capacity of modernity to transcend itself seems consistent with his argument that the deconstructionist critique is not so radical as to escape its roots in Enlightenment thought (see also McGowan 1991).

4. I have drawn the term 'eccentrism' from Plessner's (1970) study of laughing and crying, in which, predicating human bodily existence as a fundamentally ambiguous relation, he finds that "the human position can be understood as eccentric. Just as the world and my own body are revealed to me and can be controlled by me, only insofar as they appear in relation to me as a central 'I', so, on the other hand, they retain their ascendancy over their subjection in this perspective as an order indifferent to me and including me in a nexus of mutual neighborhoods" (ibid.: 36). As applied to anthropology, Plessner's concept of human bodily existence as constitutionally acentered suggests that the ethnographer cannot observe other peoples without being defined by them herself. Elsewhere, I have spoken of this ethnographic relation in hermeneutic terms of "reciprocal translation" (Evens 1983). Gadamer's (1975) notion of "fusion of horizons" and his critique of the dogma of the disinterested hermeneutic investigator are important here.

5. For a scholar who was profoundly critical of postmodernism but who, with exceptional intellectual learning and sophistication, drives home in work after work that ethics is necessarily a question of having to choose between alternatives that are precisely not finally reconcilable, see the work of Gillian Rose (e.g., 1992, 1996).

6. This idea of a selfhood commanded by otherness is difficult. In coming to it, I have been guided most directly by the Talmudically informed philosophy of Emmanuel Levinas (e.g., 1969, 1991). But the notion of subjectivity as otherness involuted was stimulated by a Jewish tradition of thought other than Talmudism, to wit, Lurianic Kabbalah. In considering how it is that if God is everywhere, there can be anything that is not God, the sixteenth-century Jewish mystic, Issac Luria, answered with the idea of 'contraction' or 'withdrawal' (*Tsimtsum*).

> God was compelled to make room for the world by, as it were, abandoning a region within Himself, a kind of mystical primordial space from which He withdrew in order to return to it in the act of creation and revelation. The first act of *En-Sof*, the Infinite Being, is therefore not a step outside but a step inside, a movement of recoil, of falling back upon oneself, of withdrawing into oneself. Instead of emanation we have the opposite, contraction. The God who revealed himself in firm contours was superseded by one who descended deeper into the recesses of His own Being, who concentrated Himself into Himself, and had done so from the very beginning of creation. (Scholem 1941: 260–61)

Obviously, Luria's 'Gnostic' thesis makes a stunningly ingenious solution to the enigma of 'creation out of nothing'. More to the point, the divine contraction, as described by Luria, constitutes a limiting act: in limiting itself, the Other delimits its own other, which is to say, the creaturely or finite self. The "mystical primordial space" of this self, the space created by the imposition of these limits, is what I have called a space of choice. As it is constituted by creative withdrawal, it is creative space; it remains encompassed by the Creator in an order of 'chiasm' (Scholem 1941: 262). It is instructive to consult here also Harold Bloom (e.g., 1975, 1982), who has adapted Luria's Kabbalah as a literary critical glass through which to read poetry, not so much darkly as creatively. For an intriguing parallel in theoretical physics to Luria's doctrine, see David Bohm's (1980) work on the universe as an implicate order. I should also add here, following Susan Handelman's (1991: 259) brilliant interpretation, that although Levinas does not draw his inspiration from Jewish mysticism, his theory of self-and-other seems well in keeping with the idea of the *Tsimtsum*.

Regarding the sense in which God may have been diminished by such self-contraction, I find myself drawn to Hans Jonas's (1996: 134, chap. 6) profound rewriting of "the concept of God after Auschwitz":

> In the beginning, for unknowable reasons, the ground of being, or the Divine, chose to give itself over to the chance and risk and endless variety of becoming ... [I]n order that the world might be, and be for itself, God renounced his being, divesting himself of his deity—to receive it back from the odyssey of time weighted with the chance harvest of unforeseeable temporal experience: transfigured or possibly even disfigured by it. In such self-forfeiture of divine integrity for the sake of unprejudiced becoming, no other foreknowledge can be admitted than that of *possibilities*, which cosmic being offers in its own terms: to these, God committed his cause in effacing himself for the world.

Speaking here of a "*myth* of my own invention" (ibid.: 134), Jonas begins thus to revise, for our age of atrocity, the received story of Genesis. What is more, his revision strongly intimates that the idea of self-contraction as primordially creative is another way of talking about the profoundly paradoxical dynamic of selfhood, wherein, in order to create and re-create itself, the self needs continually to relinquish itself. In other words, the notion of the *Tsimtsum* may be seen to furnish a marvelous, mystical account of selfhood or creation as a phenomenon of sacrifice.

7. In phenomenology, the concept of 'authenticity' is associated especially with Jean-Paul Sartre, who understood it in terms of living one's life in recognition of oneself as nothing but a free agent. Because my usage also stresses the importance of the human being as a responsible agent, it is, I suppose, not unrelated to Sartre's usage. However, my emphasis on the Merleauian ontological thesis of basic ambiguity and uncertainty, as well as on the Levinasian notion of the primacy of the other and of ethics as first philosophy, distinguishes my usage from Sartre's by giving to 'authenticity' an ontological rather than epistemological significance and an essentially moral character. In a lucid discussion, Taylor (1991) develops at length a concept of authenticity as a matter of the good or desirable rather than the desired—what he calls a moral ideal.

8. In *Fear and Trembling*, what Kierkegaard (1985) pictures as paradox may be described in terms of the double bind. God issues conflicting decrees to Abraham concerning Isaac: according to these, the figure of Isaac registers at one and the same time the vital promise of humankind as well as a lethal debt that must be paid out in full. Kierkegaard sees Abraham's transcendence of this dilemma in terms of a leap of faith. Insofar as Abraham's response produces a vital solution and gains time, it does indeed transcend the bind. But as an act of transcendence, the response is less than true, for it addresses only one horn of the dilemma. It directly engages the indebtedness but not the promise of the generations; it is God who meets the latter. In fact, Abraham's response is absolutist. Considered in its own right, apart from God's intervention, it does not really transcend the dilemma. There is no human ingenuity in Abraham's choice, as may be found, say, in the serpent's wise and demonstrably transcendental counsel to Eve in the story of the first couple. A truly transcendental answer on Abraham's part might have been to reject God's murderous commandment by rejecting any god, as a god, who would have recourse to such an order. Such an answer would compare favorably to the solution offered by Bateson (1972: 303–4) to an epistemically incarcerative Zen *koan*.

9. It is helpful here to consult Sass's (1994) discussion of solipsism, as well as Nieli's (1987: 118–23).

10. As noted in Wilden (1972: chap. 5). My reading here of Bateson owes much to Wilden's highly intelligent discussion. Outside of the idea that, by contrast to contradiction, paradox is endemic to being human, it is not very clear to me what Bateson had in mind by the distinction between the two logical forms. Wilden (1972: 121) explicates the distinction in terms of Bateson's idea of levels of learning, characterizing paradoxical double binds as involving the fourth or 'higher' level of learning, the level of 'meta-rules' and 'therapeutic efficacy'. Undoubtedly, this level of learning connects up to the use of double binds (*koans*) in Zen Buddhism to teach transcendence, an example that Bateson (1972: 303–4) mentions in his analysis of the double bind.

11. On ritual, see my earlier discussions in chapters 5, 8 and 9 in this volume. In the context of social science, it has been common to speak of this mode of transcendence and its counterpart in terms of, on the one hand, 'synchrony' and 'structure', and, on the other, 'diachrony' and 'agency'. These terms, however, as has been the case in fact, incline to dichotomize cleanly, whereas I have sought to distinguish the two modes of time or transcendence in terms of significant but consequentially incomplete difference.

12. As I have not studied the literature on wisdom, my usage here is meant to be suggestive only. I hit on the concept of wisdom, knowing that there is a field of study devoted to the wisdom literature of ancient Israel. Were I to explore this concept further, I would want to consult not only that field of study but also Aristotle's notion of *phronesis* (in the *Nichomachean Ethics*), which refers to a kind of practical reasoning that helps one to decide the good situationally.

13. Gluckman's (1963: chap. 7) rich thesis about the "reasonable man" in Barotse law comes to mind here. Basically, Gluckman argues that, whether among the Barotse or elsewhere, the operation of the law is bound to appeal to a concept of the reasonable person: "The reasonable man occupies this central position because he is the means by which abstract legal rules are focused on to the varied circumstances of life" (ibid.: 179). That is to say, the reasonable person is determined by reference to how a person should behave under the law, given that person's particular circumstances. Arriving at what it is reasonable to do in any particular set of circumstances entails bringing into account, says Gluckman, not only "many facets of Barotse life which are not ostensibly part of the law," but also change and uncertainty. Clearly, then, the notion of 'reasonable' here is not reducible to some kind of formal judicial calculation, but critically includes a sense of circumstantial and situational balance.

Chapter 13: Excursus II

1. As readers of Derrida will know, 'dissemination' is one of his specialized usages. Although his meaning is itself ingeniously disseminative, roughly, folding together 'sememe' and 'semen', it conveys a hither-thither proliferation of the meanings of notions and ideas.

2. In a brief discussion of "Bartleby the Scrivener," Derrida (1995: 74–76) takes up directly the notion of 'preference', pointing out that Melville's usage of this idea in his story (Bartleby is given to respond, time and again, "I prefer not to …") marks "a response without response" and yet does not lack for a certain content. Here, though, Derrida does distinguish between a 'preference' and a 'decision', noting that whatever one's preference, one may always decide to do otherwise. Plainly, such a distinction leaves room for acknowledgment of a difference between what is desired and what is deemed desirable.

3. Gillian Rose (1996: 11, 70) makes a like point in observing that Derrida is "[d]esperate for … ethics," but because deconstruction emphatically focuses only on the downside of things, he places us between "the desire for presence and the acceptance of absence," between utopia and nihilation. Quoting Derrida modifying Descartes' gloss on the basically real (the 'I think') to read "I mourn, therefore I am," Rose (ibid.: 11–12) informs us that, by contrast, the title of her book, *Mourning Becomes the Law*, signifies an affirmation "that the reassessment of reason … can complete its mourning" by acknowledging "the creative involvement of action in the configurations of power and law: it does not find itself unequivocally in a closed circuit which exclusively confers logic and power." Hegelian as she is, she aims to put back the "material" element in what she sees as Derrida's Hegelian/Heideggerian dialecticism (ibid.: 65–69). Although I find her attack on Derrida (and, more generally, postmodernism)

too cut-and-dried, Rose is barking up a very real tree, and I can easily see how and why she arrived at it. I might add that in connection with the problem at hand, that is, the lack of secure foundations, her argument is imposing—a veritable powerhouse of philosophical drive and acuity.

4. Here's how Richard Bernstein makes the point (1992: 191): "Derrida knows all too well that there is no ethics or politics—or even meta-ethics or meta-politics without 'taking a position.' But few have written more persuasively and imaginatively than he has about all the snares and traps that await us in 'taking a position' ... But even if we learn this lesson over and over again, we are still left with the unanswered question: *how can we 'warrant' (in any sense of the term) the ethical-political 'positions' we do take?* This is *the* question that Derrida never satisfactorily answers."

5. In his erudite study, Snell (1982: chap. 8) traces the development of the Greek idea of ethics, from the pre-Socratics to Socrates. Although Socrates upped the philosophical ante by asking what makes any particular virtue good, that is, by asking after the general rather than the particular good, and although he failed to provide an apt answer to his question, he nonetheless presumed that there is some such fixed and universal good—that knowledge and the true can be immaculately distinguished from mere opinion and the apparent.

6. I am claiming that by our very nature we have no choice but to be free, a fundamental sense of freedom that holds even under political conditions that effectively deprive us of freedom. Rousseau's (1950: 3, 17, 18, 106) point is that since once we have departed from the state of nature (in which we are indeed "born free") the "general" rather than the "particular" will is the only means to ensure freedom, a state based on the social contract should have the authority to compel the general will: "In order that the social compact may not be an empty formula, it tacitly includes the undertaking, which alone can give force to the rest, that whoever refuses to obey the general will shall be compelled to do so by the whole body. This means nothing less than that he will be forced to be free." Seeing as Rousseau also argues that force is an "act of necessity, not of will" (ibid.: 6), it is no wonder that—despite his famous argument that because one enters into the social contract voluntarily, the resulting civil union reconciles one's freedom with one's subjugation to the state—Rousseau has been seen by some as a key originator of totalitarian democracy (for an excellent example, see Talmon 1970: 38–50).

7. Deleuze points out that while Kant substituted for "the substantial self" a "self profoundly fractured by a line of time," he still failed to renounce his implicit presupposition of identity or, as Deleuze calls it, "recognition"—that is, Descartes' 'I think' (Deleuze 1994: 135, 136). Deleuze himself distinguishes between the "I," the "Self," and the "individual," and argues that the last, which "is far from indivisible" and has its "lack of ground in a difference of difference" (ibid.: 257, 258), serves to disrupt "the matter of the Self as well as the form of the I" (ibid.) and lies "beyond" them. Whereas the I and the Self must be replaced, writes Deleuze, invoking Nietzsche directly, "individuation itself" is irreplaceable (ibid.: 258). I expect that Deleuze's concept of individuation is comparable to Derrida's (1995: 41) of "singularity."

8. Others, of course, are peculiarly representative of otherness. It is important to realize, though, that such others may constitute selves in their own right. On the other hand, bearing in mind the existence of non-human creatures, they need not. In addition, one can think of otherness in terms of the absolute other—what is Wholly Other or otherwise than being or infinitely other, and thus utterly inassimilable to the self.

9. In my earlier discussion of the Akedah (chap. 2, this volume), it was my goal to show that, notwithstanding the evident intention of the redactors and many exegetes, the story can be read otherwise: as an account in which Abraham's faithful obedience to what he takes to be God's command amounts to, for all of Abraham's sincerity and conviction, a deeply self-aggrandizing act.

10. Hence, Heidegger (1978: div. 2; chap. 1) focused on death as the locus of choice that does most to bring into relief one's authentic self, which is to say, one's singular identity as a chooser. In this, however, Heidegger not only tied himself to a crucial content of Nazism (the deployment of death as the means to self-realization) but also was terribly wrong, for, and here I follow Levinas's refutation of Heidegger (in Hand 1989: 1:3), one's death is never exactly one's own. Rather, it issues finally from the other and hence serves to mark the heteronomy rather than autonomy of our selfhood.

11. Note, by contrast, the Greeks' use of 'moderation' as a call to virtue (Snell 1982: 162f.): *"Sophrosyne*, moderation, is the knowledge which governs our health and well-being, and thus our happiness; it is an appreciation of organic nature with a bent toward the practical. In its own domain it has a function similar to the calculation of profit, which we might call a practical appreciation of definite quantities, i.e. of dead objects and their mathematically constant relations. In the case of *sophrosyne* also knowledge is the court of appeal before which morality must render its account."

12. In connection with this crucial thesis about openness to the future, Derrida (1995: 88ff.) brings into play a notion of "secrecy," as in "God sees me, he looks into me in secret, but I don't see him. I don't see him looking at me, even though he looks at me while facing me and not, like an analyst, from behind my back." What Derrida wants to get across is a sense of secrecy that "is incommensurable with knowing" (ibid.). Caputo's (1997: 101–16) discussion of Derrida's concept is rich.

Chapter 14: Anthropology and the Generative Primacy of Moral Order

1. No one should take Voegelin's distinction, analogous to so many bygone anthropological constructions that tend to belittle the 'primitive', as suggesting that some social orders are in fact unchanging. It is important to keep in mind that, as forms of consciousness, both 'order' and 'history' refer to how the structure of reality is experienced and not directly to historical process per se. In other words, the classifying of a society as primarily attuned to a cosmic order (instead of to itself as its own fashioner), such that this society's paradigmatic narrative of reality is cosmological, does not mean that things there are unchanging in the light of objective history—even should one prefer, as Voegelin did, not to apply the term 'history' to the process of change in such societies.

2. Cf. Kenneth Burke's (1970) brilliant and powerful "logological" interpretation of the first three chapters of Genesis, in which he argues that the story performs a shift of temporalities, from a tautological cycle to a narrative linear progression.

3. Cf. Bauman's (1988: 50) discussion of Judaism, emancipation, and universality, in which he finds that "[t]he idea of redemption through universality was as much at home in Jewish history as the idea of progress," and that Jewish particularity is the "one and only" that gives "credence to the program of universalization."

4. In another place (Evens 1997), I have developed at length this interpretation of the figure of Eve, showing also, in a fuller and more substantial way, what it means to say that something like the feminine principle can serve as a non-foundational foundation.

5. In this connection, see Hartman and Budick's (1986) collection on the resemblance between Midrashic interpretation and modern literary criticism. One might also wish to consider here the question of whether deconstruction is simply a perverse and clever way of undermining any text, or if, rather, it is the case that strong texts manage to question themselves by inviting strong readings. Indeed, in light of texts that greatly exhibit this magical quality of self-deconstruction, one might also wonder about the possibility of building strong institutions in much the same way, so that they incline to invite, instead of resist, self-questioning.

6. In my description of the nature of philosophy as a mode of consciousness, I have been guided especially by Voegelin's (1956, 1957a, 1957b) monumental historical account of the development of the "symbolisms" of revelatory Hebrew thought, on the one hand, and philosophical Greek thought, on the other; by Bruno Snell's (1982) brilliant study of the Greeks' "discovery of the mind"; and by Boman's (1960) classic analysis of the difference between Greek and Hebrew thought.

7. In their penetrating analysis of Israeli state ceremonies, Don Handelman and Eliahu Katz bring out the profound way in which "Jewish time" is a matter of "Becoming" (in D. Handelman 1990: 224): "As important for our purposes was the idea that the movement of time, and the fixing of times, be imbued with the moral valuation of the human condition. Then Becoming is in the first instance (and in the last) a moral problem; and therefore that time, the medium of 'becoming', is necessarily the moral ordering of existence. Put otherwise, the pulsation of Jewish time was and is the encoding

of the impulsion of moral order." They speak of how this "rhythm of time—pulsating and climactic, morally encoded, lineally moving from low to high, holding within itself impulsions from fragmentation to unification—shares much in common with the progressive visions of secular zionism" (ibid.: 231). Yet, if I read them right, they also suggest that Israeli nationalism and the state, having been predicated on the staged progression of "exile, leading to return, culminating in redemption," manifest a certain tension in connection with Jewish time. By projecting "the achievement of utopia," this "onto-logic of Becoming," although profoundly Jewish, "denies" or threatens Jewish cultural time with "circular inevitability" (ibid.: 224ff.).

8. Evans-Pritchard (1940) coined the term as a description of the Nuer, among whom order is kept as a function of a segmentary social structure in conjunction with a principle of self-help. It would be enormously instructive to do a comparative analysis of the Nuer and the kibbutz, in respect of the democratic principle. Although the kibbutz has painstakingly organized itself as a radical democracy, there is far more democracy, in the sense of absence of authority of one person over another, among the Nuer. However, the difference depends precisely on the fact that a 'person' is not the same among the Nuer as in the kibbutz. The absence of the person, in the sense of the Kantian individual, among the Nuer makes usefully problematical the application of the notion of democracy to the Nuer. Presumably, Derrida's "democracy yet to come" would be something like Nuer democracy, but with postmodern individuals/selves as the constituents.

9. Although the idea of respect as a prime directive of anthropological research flows naturally from my argument, I first saw the idea in a highly original work by Lee Schlesinger, which has gone unpublished. His idea impressed me profoundly. The gist of his argument was a call to clean the anthropological slate of presuppositions save respect, the sole relation owing to the other when one begins one's research. For a very astute phenomenological account of and prescription for the ethics of research, see Liberman (1999).

10. My thinking on anthropological translation has been colored here especially by Levinas's philosophy of sacrifice and the other. I want also to comment, however, on Walter Benjamin's (1968) essay on translation (cf. also S. Handelman 1991: 29ff.). As Benjamin sees it, a good translation aims at imparting, not the sense of the original, as if what is at stake were simply information, but rather what remains when the information is stripped away—an ultimately untranslatable significance or a pure language, which, I venture, corresponds to what I have been calling, in Levinasian terms, the saying. "[A] translation," writes Benjamin (1968: 78), "instead of resembling the meaning of the original, must lovingly and in detail incorporate the original's mode of signification, thus making both the original and the translation recognizable as fragments of a greater language." As to what this means in more practical terms, Benjamin (ibid.: 80–81) quotes Rudolf Pannwitz: "Our translations ... proceed from a wrong premise. They want to turn Hindi, Greek, English into German instead of turning German into Hindi, Greek, English. Our translators have a far greater reverence for the usage of their own language than for the spirit of the foreign works ... The basic error of the translator is that he preserves the state in which his own language happens to be instead of allowing his language to be powerfully affected by the foreign tongue."

Even more down to earth in connection with translation in this sense is Duerr (1985: 129), who tells us that "We may even have to howl with the werewolves to understand how they howl," and distinguishes between "understanding" and "translation" as follows:

> To understand is not the same as to translate if, taken with a pinch of salt, we mean by translation a transposing of a meaning from one medium to another ... To understand often means that instead of recognizing what is strange as if it were familiar ... we learn how a word is used in a strange context, how it functions in an unfamiliar environment ... At times we will have to howl with the wolves, and that means that we will have to forget some things that are familiar, especially those things that prevent us from understanding strange contents. This in no way suggests that we will forget everything for all times, as implied by a consistent relativism. The anthropologist returns home changed but he is not going to be an entirely different person, for in that case, it would not be he who had gained the insight.

Duerr's account of translation is more experiential than linguistic. He plainly argues for the transformation of the translator, and yet, by relativizing relativism, manages to retain the idea of agency in the account.

In a less eccentric theoretical style, Calhoun (1991: 252–58) has also suggested that "translation *per se*" is conceptually inadequate as a description of the anthropologist's work. He proposes instead the idea of a "richer, more complex discourse" in connection with this work. As the work amounts to "coming to terms with incommensurable practices," it must be conceived of, says Calhoun (ibid.), in the dynamic terms of "understanding" arrived at through change on the part of both the "informant" and the "anthropologist." Apropos of Calhoun's passing mention of the Nuer in connection with this sort of ethnographic work, see also my article on the 'logic' of the Nuer incest prohibition (Evens 1983). There, aiming at 'reciprocal translation' and an 'interpretive helix', I explicitly set out to 'translate' the Nuer incest prohibition—not as a signification plain and simple, but as a form of existence—and I do so methodically by allowing the Nuer practice to alter fundamentally the Western idea of logic.

11. Although I am both expounding and calling for this standard of ethnographic authority, at its strongest moments all anthropology already serves to demonstrate it. Allow me to cite, though, just two monographs that strike me as exemplary in this regard: in *Do Kamo*, Maurice Leenhardt (1979) gives a mind-turning phenomenological account of the otherness of Canaque reality, and Kenneth Read (1965), in his introspective *The High Valley*, undergoes a profound self-transformation in virtue of what he learns about embodiment from the Gahuku-Gama.

12. In view of the singularly Greek character of philosophy, it seems curious that, taking his cue throughout from the romanticism of Greek nationalism and theoretical anthropology, Herzfeld tends to ignore the profound rationalism of these two discourses. His emphasis fits well, though, with his presupposition of the strongly political nature of his subject matter, a nature which implies that if reason is not really reason, then it must amount to rhetorical power play.

13. Certainly, the messianic elements of Judaism and Christianity do not allow for a clean demarcation between the two religions. But if only because in Judaism the messiah is, chronically, still to come, the difference between the two messianisms is profound, epochal even. Here Gershom Scholem makes this point, identifying correlative differences, ones that—suitably enough in connection with the present work's discussions of dualism, selfhood, and bodily existence—bear on the ideas of self and history.

> The magnitude of the Messianic idea corresponds to the endless powerlessness in Jewish history during all the centuries of exile, when it was unprepared to come forward onto the plane of world history. There's something preliminary, something provisional about Jewish history; hence its inability to give of itself entirely. For the Messianic idea is not only consolation and hope. Every attempt to realize it tears open the abysses which lead each of its manifestations *ad absurdum*. There is something grand about living in hope, but at the same time there is something profoundly unreal about it. It diminishes the singular worth of the individual, and he can never fulfill himself, because the incompleteness of his endeavors eliminates precisely what constitutes its highest value. Thus in Judaism the Messianic idea has compelled a *life lived in deferment*, in which nothing can be done definitively, nothing can be irrevocably accomplished. One may say, perhaps, the Messianic idea is the real anti-existentialist idea. Precisely understood, there is nothing concrete which can be accomplished by the unredeemed. This makes for the greatness of Messianism, but also for its constitutional weakness. Jewish so-called *Existenz* possesses a tension that never finds true release; it never burns itself out. And when in our history it does discharge, then it is foolishly decried (or, one might say, unmasked) as "pseudo-Messianism." (Scholem 1971: 35)

> A totally different concept of redemption determines the attitude to Messianism in Judaism and in Christianity … Judaism, in all of its forms and manifestations, has always maintained a concept of redemption as an event which takes place publicly, on the stage of history and within the community. It is an occurrence which takes place in the visible world and which cannot be conceived apart from such a visible appearance. In contrast, Christianity conceives of redemption as an event in the spiritual and unseen realm, an event which is reflected in the soul, in the private world of each individual, and which effects an inner transformation which need not correspond to anything outside. Even the *civitas dei*

of Augustine, which within the confines of Christian dogmatics and in the interest of the Church has made the most far-reaching attempt both to retain and to reinterpret the Jewish categories of redemption, is a community of the mysteriously redeemed within an unredeemed world. (ibid.: 1)

14. Cf. here Gillian Rose's (1993: chap. 2) highly intelligent and informed discussion.

15. Here is another side to Eilberg-Schwartz's (1990) exercise to construct an anthropology of Judaism. As a professional student of religious studies, he is concerned to overcome the routine ethnocentric bias of his discipline and bring anthropological comparison fully to bear on the study of Israelite religion and ancient Judaism. His success is impressive. Here, though, I simply take for granted the applicability of anthropology to the study of Jews and Judaism, and focus instead on what anthropology can learn not only about but also from Judaism. The very feature that perhaps has most encouraged scholars of religion to construe Judaism as absolutely distinct from so-called primitive religions—namely, Judaism's projection of human life as above all an ethical journey—gives me reason to rethink anthropology. Although Durkheim, as Eilberg-Schwartz points out (ibid.: 19), explicitly formulated his theory of religion by reference to the Australian Aborigines, whose religion he ethnocentrically regarded as the most simple and primitive, the French master nevertheless informed anthropology implicitly with a profoundly Jewish perspective. I have in mind, of course, the ontological thesis, positively central to Durkheim's sociological project, that society is a moral system.

16. The prescription of other-responsiveness can no more prevent some contemporary Jews from summarily disregarding just claims of Palestinians than it could prevent the ancient Hebrews from attacking the Canaanites. But this consideration proves the prescription neither wrong nor worthless, for the power of the prescription rests on what is 'better', not on what is more powerful. Perhaps even more to the point is the consideration of religious monotheism itself, which inherently admonishes responsiveness to the Other's otherness while it breeds intolerance of other others. I have in mind not only others who follow a different maker, but also, as in Kierkegaard's reading of the Akedah (where creaturely morality is subordinated to faith), the otherness of humankind in relation to any absolute figure of God.

17. Strenski's (1997) study of Durkheim is informative and useful but, even so, unconvincing. His (ibid.: 2, 149, chap. 1) principal thesis—that there is nothing "essentially" Jewish in Durkheim's sociology—strikes me as problematic for the following reasons. Although I cannot speak here to the existing attempts to understand Durkheim's work by reference to his Jewish upbringing and education, it simply is not the case that every such attempt need constitute an exercise in 'essentialism'. Strenski (ibid.: chaps. 2–3) makes a forceful (Durkheimian) argument for the formative influence of French nationalism and modernism on Durkheim's thought. But the fact of such influence scarcely means that in forging his sociology Durkheim may not also have been critically informed by his Jewish rearing, which no doubt must have included certain characteristically Hebraic understandings of the nature of human social life. It does not necessarily follow from the reality of such understandings that, as essentialism would imply, Judaism is unchanging and everywhere the same. It has been a burden of my book to bring home the exceptional phenomenological significance and staying power of meanings that are received as so fundamental, so presumptively certain, that they serve to anchor various forms of life even as they are historically contingent and subject to change. Take, for example, Strenski's (ibid.: chap. 6) interesting argument about Durkheim's theory of sacrifice. In brief, he asserts (ibid.: 156–57) that Durkheim's is "the modified gift theory" of sacrifice first set out by Hubert and Mauss. Strenski uses the qualifier "modified" because the theory holds (ibid.: 157) that "perfection of self-giving" serves only as an "asymptotic ideal," to be compromised by the use of a surrogate victim. Such a compromise is of course in the interest of the individual ('the self'), which leads Strenski to believe (ibid.) that Durkheim resorted to it "because of his profoundly liberal bourgeois worldview and social location," which is to say, because of his "individualist values." The argument is more subtle and credible than my adumbration of it may suggest. But what I wish to bring out is that the sort of 'values' Strenski attributes to Durkheim typically run deep, so deep that they inform the self-identities on which socio-political worldviews rest. In the present case, Durkheim's gift theory of sacrifice fits not only a bourgeois worldview but also a critical understanding of the individual as

constitutionally doubly bound, a paradoxical understanding that is, in its diagnostic focus on moral rather than rational choice, peculiarly and emphatically Hebraic. For reasons of its phenomeno-onto-logical depth and comprehensiveness in Western thought, I believe that, without taking into account this understanding, it would be hard to explicate at heart Durkheim's notion of society as a moral system, an anomalous notion in relation to his aim of founding sociology as a positive science. In other works (Evens 1982a, 1982b), I have more to say in this vein.

18. I have italicized 'explicitly' because, owing to its characteristic aim of translating otherness, all anthropology is innately reflexive and comparative.

19. In his compact critique of what he calls the 'postmodernist mood' of much current anthropol-ogy (a critique in which he bemoans the Foucauldian fetishism of "power" in today's anthropology), Marshall Sahlins (2002: 26), with his characteristic wit, comments as follows:

> I don't know about Britain, but in America many graduate students in Anthropology are totally uninterested in other times and places. They say we should study our own current problems, all other ethnography being impossible anyhow, as it is just our "construction of the other."
>
> So if they get their way, and this becomes the principle of anthropological research, fifty years hence no one will pay the slightest attention to the work they're doing now. Maybe they're onto something.

20. Of course, Bourdieu's (1988) grand study of the French academic world, *Homo Academicus*, must be counted here. The self-designated 'ex-historian' Sande Cohen (1993), in his *Academia and the Luster of Capital*, provides a powerful critique of the 'high university'. In the third chapter in par-ticular, detailing a case of a grievance filed by a faculty member (Cohen served on the grievance com-mittee), as well as his own tenure case, Cohen fairly skewers the institutional process, leading him to arrive at conclusions of the following kind (ibid.: 35): "There isn't a faculty in the United States that offers resistance to its Officer Corps and bureaucratic 'center' (e.g., legislature)," and "we can say that this Officer Corps ensures that the university will not be contaminated by acts of reading that under-mine its own consistency." For a book-length historical (and notorious) case study of an iniquitous dismissal of a faculty member at Rutgers University, see Oshinsky, McCormick, and Horn (1989).

21. In connection with reflexive memory slippage, whereby self-criticism fails to reflect on the political implications of its own endeavor, I might also mention another reflexive possibility pertain-ing to the anthropologist in academic residence. Many of us are either familiar with or have observed first-hand departmental conduct that constructs others out of fellow members who seriously ques-tion the institution's or discipline's professional integrity, identity, and authority. These members are commonly labeled 'difficult', 'irrational', 'unrealistic', 'troublemakers', 'loose cannons', 'whistleblowers', and the like. Important here is not the accuracy of these labels in any particular instance, but rather the process of power they betray. Of course, this sort of thing is hardly confined to the institutional setting of the discipline of anthropology. But if our discipline is to be truly reflexive, then it must be prepared to analyze conduct of this kind in the departmental and organizational settings of the profession. These days, few anthropologists would hesitate to conclude that other social and episte-mological orders run on a basis of power (we have become exquisitely expert in our ability to uncover power at work in social orders), including now the order composed by the ethnographic relation. But few also are inclined to admit, if only to themselves, the open secret that their own professional orders at home may be similarly characterized.

When I began my field research in Kibbutz Timem, a few members of the community asked me, disapprovingly, if it was my intention to treat them like 'guinea pigs'. Once I thought about it, I replied that I intended to treat them in the only way open to me to treat any human being (including myself): as a 'subject-object'. This response was significantly imprecise, however, for the polarity of subject and object admits of degrees of direction as between the two poles, and given that my primary goal in being there was ethnographic research, these apprehensive and inquiring members had a substantial point. But there was more to the question than that of over-objectifying other human beings, for members also wanted to know, in a related vein of inquiry, if I was after their 'dirty laundry'. Can there be any doubt that we, as anthropologists, have similar apprehensions about being scrutinized ethnographically, apprehensions compounded by our self-identification as experts on the nature of society and its operation? Indeed, do we not readily understand the concerns of Timem's members about objectification and scandal precisely because we have experienced them at home?

22. "[Foucault's] history of madness," writes Gutting (2001: 262), "although taken up by Laing and others in the anti-psychiatry movement, was not intended as a call to abolish asylums or for any other specific reforms in society's treatment of the mad. In Foucault's view, decisions about how to deal with political and social problems are the province of those immediately involved in and familiar with them. Disengaged intellectual analysis is important but only as a background suggesting possibilities, not as a normative summons to action."

Conclusion

1. The allusion is to Foucault's (1970: 342–43) feverish denunciation of philosophical anthropology as based on the "sovereignty of the 'I think'": "To all those who still wish to talk about man, about his reign or his liberation, to all those who still ask themselves questions about what man is in his essence, to all those who wish to take him as their starting-point in their attempts to reach the truth, to all those who, on the other hand, refer all knowledge back to the truths of man himself, to all those who refuse to formalize without anthropologizing, who refuse to mythologize without demystifying, who refuse to think without immediately thinking that it is man who is thinking, to all those warped and twisted forms of reflection we can answer only with a philosophical laugh." In another place, I have questioned the usual acceptation of 'thinking', on the grounds that that acceptation reflects body-mind dualism (Evens 1983: 130n12).

2. In an extremely evocative analysis, Popper (1972: chap. 7) argues that this is how evolution works in general.

3. I am drawing here directly on M. G. Smith's (1960: 299f.) powerful study, *Government in Zazzau*, in which he develops the idea of formal priority as a conceptual tool for understanding the "structure of a process." Here, in short, is the relevant argument (ibid.: 302): "[T]he subsequent concepts in a logically successive series assume but are not directly entailed by those which precede them. The process by which subsequent concepts of such a series are developed from antecedent ones is eductive and 'evolutionary' rather than deductive or deterministic. These latter categories give explicit expression to possibilities latent in those which precede them. Conversely these earlier categories are implicit in those which follow after; but consistency rather than necessity governs the development of the subsequent concepts."

References

Agamben, Giorgio. 1998. *Homo Sacer: Sovereign Power and Bare Life*. Trans. Daniel Heller-Roazen. Stanford, CA: Stanford University Press.

_____. 1999. *Remnants of Auschwitz: The Witness and the Archive*. Trans. Daniel Heller-Roazen. NY: Zone Books.

_____. 2000. *Means without End: Notes on Politics*. Trans. Vincenzo Binetti and Cesare Casarino. Minneapolis: University of Minnesota Press.

Akiga. 1939. *Akiga's Story: The Tiv Tribe as Seen by One of Its Members*. Trans. and annot. Rupert East. Oxford: Oxford University Press, for the International Institute of African Language and Cultures.

Alpert, Harry. 1961. *Emile Durkheim and His Sociology*. New York: Russell & Russell.

Améry, Jean. 1980. *At the Mind's Limits*. Trans. Sidney Rosenfeld and Stella P. Rosenfeld. Bloomington: Indiana University Press.

Arendt, Hannah. 1994. *Eichmann in Jerusalem: A Report on the Banality of Evil*. New York: Penguin Books.

Arnold, Matthew. 1925. *Culture and Anarchy*. Ed. William S. Knickerbocker. New York: Macmillan.

Barfield, Owen. 1965. *Saving the Appearances: A Study in Idolatry*. New York: Harcourt, Brace & World.

_____. 1977. *The Rediscovery of Meaning, and Other Essays*. Middletown, CT: Wesleyan University Press.

Barraud, Cécile, Daniel de Coppet, and André Iteanu. 1994. *Of Relations and the Dead: Four Societies Viewed from the Angle of Their Exchanges*. Trans. Stephen J. Suffern. Oxford: Berg.

Bateson, Gregory. 1972. *Steps to an Ecology of Mind*. New York: Ballantine Books.

Baudrillard, Jean. 1987. *Forget Foucault*. New York: Semiotext(e).

Bauman, Zygmunt. 1988. "Exit Visas and Entry Tickets: Paradoxes of Jewish Assimilation." *Telos*, no. 44: 45–77.

_____. 1991. *Modernity and the Holocaust*. Ithaca, NY: Cornell University Press.

Beidelman, T. O. 1981. "The Nuer Concept of *Thek* and the Meaning of Sin: Explanation, Translation, and Social Structure." *History of Religions* 21, no. 2: 126–55.

Beiser, Frederick C. 1987. *The Fate of Reason: German Philosophy from Kant to Fichte*. Cambridge, MA: Harvard University Press.

Bell, Catherine. 1992. *Ritual Theory, Ritual Practice*. New York: Oxford University Press.

Benjamin, Walter. 1968. *Illuminations*. Ed. Hannah Arendt; trans. Harry Zohn. New York: Schocken Books.

Berger, Peter, Brigitte Berger, and Hansfried Kellner. 1973. *The Homeless Mind*. New York: Vintage Books.

Bernstein, Michael André. 1994. *Foregone Conclusions: Against Apocalyptic History*. Berkeley and Los Angeles: University of California Press.

Bernstein, Richard J. 1986. *Philosophical Profiles*. Philadelphia: University of Pennsylvania Press.

_____. 1987. "Serious Play: The Ethical-Political Horizon of Jacques Derrida." *Journal of Speculative Philosophy* 1, no. 2: 93–117.

_____. 1992. *The New Constellation: The Ethical-Political Horizons of Modernity/Postmodernity*. Cambridge, MA: MIT Press.

Bloch, Maurice. 1992. *Prey into Hunter: The Politics of Religious Experience.* Lewis Henry Morgan Lectures. Cambridge: Cambridge University Press.

Bloom, Allan. 1987. *The Closing of the American Mind.* New York: Simon and Schuster.

Bloom, Harold. 1975. *A Map of Misreading.* New York: Oxford University Press.

_____. 1976. *Wallace Stevens: The Poems of Our Climate.* Ithaca, NY: Cornell University Press.

_____. 1982. *The Breaking of the Vessels.* Chicago: University of Chicago Press.

Bohm, David. 1980. *Wholeness and the Implicate Order.* London: Routledge and Kegan Paul.

Boman, Thorleif. 1960. *Hebrew Thought Compared with Greek.* Trans. Jules L. Moreau. New York: W.W. Norton.

Bonhoeffer, Emmi. n.d. *Auschwitz Trials: Letters from an Eyewitness.* Trans. Ursula Strechow. Richmond, VA: John Knox Press.

Borowski, Tadeusz. 1967. *This Way for the Gas, Ladies and Gentlemen.* Trans. Barbara Vedder. New York: Penguin Books.

Bourdieu, Pierre. 1977. *Outline of a Theory of Practice.* Trans. Richard Nice. Cambridge: Cambridge University Press.

_____. 1984. *Distinction: A Social Critique of the Judgement of Taste.* Trans. Richard Nice. Cambridge, MA: Harvard University Press.

_____. 1988. *Homo Academicus.* Trans. Peter Collier. Stanford, CA: Stanford University Press.

_____. 1990a. *The Logic of Practice.* Trans. Richard Nice. Stanford, CA: Stanford University Press.

_____. 1990b. *In Other Words: Essays Towards a Reflexive Sociology.* Trans. Matthew Adamson. Stanford, CA: Stanford University Press.

_____. 1993. "Concluding Remarks: For a Sociogenetic Understanding of Intellectual Works." In *Bourdieu: Critical Perspectives,* ed. Craig Calhoun, Edward LiPuma, and Moishe Postone, 263–75. Cambridge: Polity Press.

Bourdieu, Pierre, and Loïc J. D. Wacquant. 1992. *An Invitation to Reflexive Sociology.* Chicago: Chicago University Press.

Bowes, Alison M. 1989. *Kibbutz Goshen: An Israeli Commune.* Prospect Heights, IL: Waveland Press.

Brown, James Robert. 1994. *Smoke and Mirrors: How Science Reflects Reality.* London: Routledge.

Brown, Peter. 1988. *The Body and Society: Men, Women, and Sexual Renunciation in Early Christianity.* New York: Columbia University Press.

Browning, Christopher R. 1992. *Ordinary Men: Reserve Police Battalion 101 and the Final Solution in Poland.* New York: HarperCollins.

Bruzina, Ronald. 1978. "Heidegger on the Metaphor and Philosophy." In *Heidegger and Modern Philosophy,* ed. Michael Murray, 184–200. New Haven, CT: Yale University Press.

Burke, Kenneth. 1966. *Language as Symbolic Action.* Berkeley: University of California Press.

_____. 1969. *A Grammar of Motives.* Berkeley: University of California Press.

_____. 1970. *The Rhetoric of Religion.* Berkeley: University of California Press.

Burridge, Kenelm. 1969. *New Heaven, New Earth: A Study of Millenarian Activities.* Oxford: Basil Blackwell.

Calhoun, Craig. 1991. "Culture, History, and the Problem of Specificity in Social Theory." In *Postmodernism and Social Theory,* ed. Steven Seidman and David Wagner, 244–88. Cambridge, MA and Oxford, UK: Basil Blackwell.

_____. 1993. "Habitus, Field, and Capital: The Question of Historical Specificity." In *Bourdieu: Critical Perspectives,* ed. Craig Calhoun, Edward LiPuma, and Moishe Postone, 61–88. Cambridge: Polity Press.

Caputo, John D. 1987. *Radical Hermeneutics.* Bloomington: Indiana University Press.

_____. 1993. *Against Ethics.* Bloomington: Indiana University Press.

_____. 1997. *The Prayers and Tears of Jacques Derrida: Religion without Religion.* Bloomington: Indiana University Press.

Cavell, Stanley. 1990. *Conditions Handsome and Unhandsome: The Constitution of Emersonian Perfectionism.* Chicago: University of Chicago Press.

Cazeneuve, Jean. 1972. *Lucien Lévy-Bruhl.* Trans. Peter Rivière. NY: Harper Torchbooks.

Chalier, Catherine. 2002. *What Ought I to Do? Morality in Kant and Levinas.* Trans. Jane Marie Todd. Ithaca, NY: Cornell University Press.

Chilton, Bruce. 1992. *The Temple of Jesus*. University Park: Pennsylvania State University Press.

Cioffi, Frank. 1998. *Wittgenstein on Freud and Frazer*. Cambridge: Cambridge University Press.

Clifford, James. 1982. *Person and Myth: Maurice Leenhardt in the Melanesian World*. Berkeley: University of California Press.

Cohen, Erik. 1976. "The Social Transformation of the Kibbutz." In *Social Change: Conjectures, Explorations, Diagnosis*, ed. George K. Zollschan and Walter Hirsch, 703–42. Cambridge: Schenkman.

Cohen, Richard A. 1986. "Introduction." In *Face to Face with Levinas*, ed. Richard A. Cohen, 1–10. Albany: State University of New York Press.

Cohen, Sande. 1993. *Academia and the Luster of Capital*. Minneapolis: University of Minnesota Press.

Colebrook, Claire. 1999. *Ethics and Representation: From Kant to Post-structuralism*. Edinburgh: Edinburgh University Press.

Crapanzano, Vincent. 1979. "Preface." In *Do Kamo*, Maurice Leenhardt. Trans. Basia Miller Gulati, vii–xxv. Chicago: University of Chicago Press.

Dahrendorf, Ralf. 1968. *Essays in the Theory of Society*. London: Routledge and Kegan Paul.

Darrouzet, Christopher. 1990. "Sorcery Salvation and the Politics of Death in Lowland New Guinea Society: A Case Study of a Modernizing Culture and Consciousness." In *Transcendence in Society: Case Studies*, ed. T. M. S. Evens and James L. Peacock, 9–59. Comparative Social Research, Supplement 1. Greenwich: JAI Press.

Delaney, Carol, 1998. *Abraham on Trial: The Social Legacy of Biblical Myth*. Princeton, NJ: Princeton University Press.

Delbo, Charlotte. 1995. *Auschwitz and After*. Trans. Rosette C. Lamont. New Haven, CT: Yale University Press.

Deleuze, Gilles. 1991. *Empiricism and Subjectivity: An Essay on Hume's Theory of Human Nature*. Trans. Constantin V. Boundas. New York: Columbia University Press.

_____. 1993. *The Fold: Leibniz and the Baroque*. Trans. Tom Conley. Minneapolis: University of Minnesota Press.

_____. 1994. *Difference and Repetition*. Trans. Paul Patton. New York: Columbia University Press.

Deleuze, Gilles, and Félix Guattari. 1977. *Anti-Oedipus: Capitalism and Schizophrenia*. Trans. Robert Hurley, Mark Seem, and Helen R. Lane. New York: Viking Press.

_____. 1987. *A Thousand Plateaus*. Trans. Brian Massumi. Minneapolis: University of Minnesota Press.

De Man, Paul. 1979. *Allegories of Reading*. New Haven, CT: Yale University Press.

Deng, Francis M. 1972. *The Dinka of the Sudan*. New York: Holt, Rinehart and Winston.

Derrida, Jacques. 1978. "Force and Signification." In *Writing and Difference*, trans. Allan Bass, 3–30. Chicago: University of Chicago Press.

_____. 1982. "White Mythology: Metaphor in the Text of Philosophy." In *Margins of Philosophy*, trans. Allan Bass, 207–71. Chicago: University of Chicago Press.

_____. 1992. *Given Time: 1. Counterfeit Money*. Trans. Peggy Kamuf. Chicago: Chicago University Press.

_____. 1995. *The Gift of Death*. Trans. David Wills. Chicago: University of Chicago Press.

Derrida, Jacques, and Richard Kearney. 1984. "Dialogue with Jacques Derrida." In *Dialogues with Contemporary Continental Thinkers*, ed. Richard Kearney, 105–26. Manchester: Manchester University Press.

Dews, Peter. 1987. *Logics of Disintegration*. London: Verso.

Dillon, M. C. 1988. *Merleau-Ponty's Ontology*. Bloomington: Indiana University Press.

Douglas, Mary. 1980. *Edward Evans-Pritchard*. Harmondsworth: Penguin Books.

Dreyfus, Hubert, and Paul Rabinow. 1993. "Can There be a Science of Existential Structure and Social Meaning?" In *Bourdieu: Critical Perspectives*, ed. Craig Calhoun, Edward LiPuma, and Moishe Postone, 35–44. Cambridge: Polity Press.

Duerr, Hans Peter. 1985. *Dreamtime: Concerning the Boundary between Wilderness and Civilization*. Trans. Felicitas Goodman. Oxford: Basil Blackwell.

Dufrenne, Mikel. 1966. *The Notion of the a Priori*. Trans. Edward S. Casey. Evanston, IL: Northwestern University Press.

Dumont, Louis. 1970. *Homo Hierarchicus*. Trans. Mark Sainsbury. Chicago: Chicago University Press.

_____. 1977. *From Mandeville to Marx: The Genesis and Triumph of Economic Ideology.* Chicago: University of Chicago Press.

_____. 1980. "On Value." Radcliffe-Brown Lecture in Social Anthropology. *Proceedings of the British Academy* 66, 208–41. Oxford: Oxford University Press.

_____. 1986. *Essays on Individualism: Modern Ideology in Anthropological Perspective.* Chicago: University of Chicago Press.

Duncan, Diane Moira. 2001. *The Pre-Text of Ethics: On Derrida and Levinas.* New York: Peter Lang.

Dupré, John. 1993. *The Disorder of Things.* Cambridge, MA: Harvard University Press.

Durkheim, Emile. 1915. *The Elementary Forms of the Religious Life.* Trans. Joseph Ward Swain. London: George Allen & Unwin.

_____. 1960. "The Dualism of Human Nature and Its Social Conditions." In *Emile Durkheim, 1858–1917,* ed. Kurt H. Wolff, 325–40. Columbus: Ohio State University Press.

Edwards, James C. 1982. *Ethics without Philosophy: Wittgenstein and the Moral Life.* Tampa: University Presses of Florida.

Eilberg-Schwartz, Howard. 1990. *The Savage in Judaism.* Bloomington: Indiana University Press.

Elster, Jon. 1983. *Sour Grapes: Studies in the Subversion of Rationality.* Cambridge: Cambridge University Press.

Evans-Pritchard, E. E. 1937. *Witchcraft, Oracles and Magic among the Azande.* Oxford: Clarendon Press.

_____. 1940. *The Nuer.* Oxford: Oxford University Press.

_____. 1954. "The Meaning of Sacrifice among the Nuer." Henry Myers Lecture. *Journal of the Royal Anthropological Institute* 84, pt. 1 (January–June): 21–33.

_____. 1956. *Nuer Religion.* Oxford: Clarendon Press.

_____. 1965. *Theories of Primitive Religion.* Oxford: Clarendon Press.

Evens, T. M. S. 1982a. "On the Social Anthropology of Religion." *The Journal of Religion* 62, no. 4: 376–91.

_____. 1982b. "Two Concepts of Society as a Moral System: Evans-Pritchard's Heterodoxy." *Man* (n.s.) 17: 205–18.

_____. 1983. "Mind, Logic and the Efficacy of the Nuer Incest Prohibition." *Man* (n.s.) 18: 111–33.

_____. 1984. "Nuer Hierarchy." In *Différence, Valeurs, Hiérarchie: Textes Offerts à Louis Dumont,* ed. Jean-Claude Galey, 319–34. Paris: Editions de l'Ecole des Hautes Etudes en Sciences Sociales.

_____. 1985. "The Paradox of Nuer Feud and the Leopard-Skin Chief: A Creative Solution to the Prisoner's Dilemma." *American Ethnologist* 12, no. 1: 84–102.

_____. 1989a. "The Nuer Incest Prohibition and the Nature of Kinship: Alterlogical Reckoning." *Cultural Anthropology* 4, no. 4: 323–46.

_____. 1989b. "An Illusory Illusion: Nuer Agnation and First Principles." In *Culture,* ed. Craig Calhoun, 301–18. *Comparative Social Research: A Research Annual.* Vol. 11. Greenwich, CT: JAI Press.

_____. 1993. "Rationality, Hierarchy and Practice: Contradiction as Choice." *Social Anthropology* 1, no. 1B: 101–18.

_____. 1994. "Mythic Rationality, Contradiction and Choice among the Dinka." *Social Anthropology* 2, no. 2: 99–114.

_____. 1995. *Two Kinds of Rationality.* Minneapolis: University of Minnesota Press.

_____. 1996. "Witchcraft and Selfcraft." *Archives Européennes de Sociologie* 37, no. 1: 23–46.

_____. 1997. "Ethics and the Feminine Principle in the Second and Third Chapters of Genesis." In *The Ethnography of Moralities,* ed. Signe Howell, 203–28. London: Routledge.

_____. 1999. "Bourdieu and the Logic of Practice: Is All Giving Indian-Giving or Is 'Generalized Materialism' Not Enough." *Sociological Theory* 37, no. 1: 3–31.

Evens, T. M. S., and James L. Peacock. 1990. "Introduction." In *Transcendence in Society: Case Studies,* ed. T. M. S. Evens and James L. Peacock, 1–7. Comparative Social Research. Supplement 1. Greenwich, CT: JAI Press.

Feenberg, Andrew. 1986. *Lukacs, Marx and the Sources of Critical Theory.* New York: Oxford University Press.

Ferry, Luc, and Alain Renaut. 1990. *French Philosophy of the Sixties: An Essay on Antihumanism.* Trans. Mary Schnackenberg Cattani. Amherst: University of Massachusetts Press.

Feyerabend, P. K. 1974. "Popper's Objective Knowledge." *Inquiry* 17: 475–507.

————. 1978. *Against Method*. London: Verso.

Foti, Veronique M. 1996. "Representation Represented: Foucault, Velazquez, Descartes." *Postmodern Culture* 7, no. 1: 1–41.

Foucault, Michel. 1965. *Madness and Civilization*. Trans. Richard Howard. New York: Random House.

————. 1970. *The Order of Things: An Archaeology of the Human Sciences*. London: Tavistock Publications.

————. 1979. "My Body, This Paper, This Fire." Trans. Geoff Bennington. *Oxford Literary Review* 4, no. 1: 9–28. (Originally published in French as an appendix to the 1972 French edition of Foucault's *Madness and Civilization*.)

————. 1983. "The Subject and Power." In *Michel Foucault: Beyond Structuralism and Hermeneutics*, ed. Hubert Dreyfus and Paul Rabinow, 208–26. Chicago: Chicago University Press.

————. 1984a. "What Is Enlightenment." In *Foucault Reader*, ed. Paul Rabinow, 32–50. New York: Pantheon Books.

————. 1984b. "On the Genealogy of Ethics: An Overview of Work in Progress." In *Foucault Reader*, ed. Paul Rabinow, 340–72. New York: Pantheon Books.

————. 1988. "The Political Technology of Individuals." In *Technologies of the Self*, ed. Luther H. Martin, Huck Gutman, and Patrick H. Hutton, 16–49. Amherst: University of Massachusetts Press.

Friedlander, Saul. 1992. *Probing the Limits of Representation: Nazism and the "Final Solution."* Cambridge, MA: Harvard University Press.

Gadamer, Hans-Georg. 1975. *Truth and Method*. Trans. G. Barden and J. Cumming. New York: Seabury.

Galison, Peter, and David J. Stump, eds. 1996. *The Disunity of Science*. Palo Alto, CA: Stanford University Press.

Geertz, Clifford. 1973a. "Deep Play: Notes on the Balinese Cockfight." In *The Interpretation of Cultures*, 412–53. London: Hutchinson.

————. 1973b. "Thick Description: Toward an Interpretive Theory of Culture." In *The Interpretation of Cultures*, 3–30. London: Hutchinson.

————. 1983. "Slide Show: Evans-Pritchard's African Transparencies." *Raritan* 3, no. 2: 62–80.

————. 1984. "Distinguished Lecture: Anti Anti-Relativism." *American Anthropologist* 86, no. 2: 263–78.

Gellman, Jerome I. 1994. *The Fear, the Trembling, and the Fire: Kierkegaard and Hasidic Masters on the Binding of Isaac*. Lanham, MD: University Press of America.

Geuss, Raymond. 2001. *History and Illusion in Politics*. Cambridge: Cambridge University Press.

Giddens, Anthony. 1979. *Central Problems in Social Theory*. Berkeley: University of California Press.

————. 1991. *Modernity and Self-Identity*. Stanford, CA: Stanford University Press.

Gier, Nicholas F. 1981. *Wittgenstein and Phenomenology*. Albany: State University of New York Press.

Gillies, Eva. 1976. "Introduction." In E. E. Evans-Pritchard, *Witchcraft, Oracles and Magic among the Azande*, abridged ed., vii–xxxiii. Oxford: Clarendon Press.

Ginzburg, Carlo. 1991. *Ecstasies: Deciphering the Witches' Sabbath*. Trans. Raymond Rosenthal. New York: Penguin Books.

Girard, René. 1977. *Violence and the Sacred*. Trans. P. Gregory. Baltimore: Johns Hopkins University Press.

————. 1986. *The Scapegoat*. Trans. Y. Freccero. Baltimore, MD: Johns Hopkins University Press.

Glendon, Mary Ann. 1987. *Abortion and Divorce in Western Law*. Cambridge, MA: Harvard University Press.

Gluckman, Max. 1963. "The Reasonable Man in Barotse Law." In *Order and Rebellion in Tribal Africa: Collected Essays*, 178–206. London: Cohen & West.

————. 1965. *Politics, Law and Ritual in Tribal Society*. Oxford: Basil Blackwell.

Gombrich, E. H. 1961. *Art and Illusion*. 2nd ed. Princeton, NJ: Bollingen Series.

Gutting, Gary. 2001. *French Philosophy in the Twentieth Century*. Cambridge: Cambridge University Press.

Habermas, Jürgen. 1984. *The Theory of Communicative Action*. Vol. 1. Trans. Thomas McCarthy. Boston: Beacon Press.

————. 1987a. *The Theory of Communicative Action*. Vol. 2. Trans. Thomas McCarthy. Boston: Beacon Press.

————. 1987b. *The Philosophical Discourse of Modernity*. Trans. Frederick Lawrence. Cambridge, MA: MIT Press.

_____. 1989. *The New Conservatism*. Trans. Shierry Weber Nicholsen. Cambridge, MA: MIT Press.

_____. 1990. *Moral Consciousness and Comunicative Action*. Trans. Christian Lenhardt and Shierry Weber Nicholsen. Cambridge, MA: MIT Press.

_____. 1992. *Postmetaphysical Thinking*. Trans. William Mark Hohengarten. Cambridge, MA: MIT Press.

Hall, Harrison. 1979. "The *a Priori* and the Empirical in Merleau-Ponty's *Phenomenology of Perception*." *Philosophy Today* 23: 304–9.

Hand, Seán, ed. 1989. *The Levinas Reader*. Oxford: Blackwell.

Handelman, Don. 1990. *Models and Mirrors: Towards an Anthropology of Public Events*. Cambridge: Cambridge University Press.

Handelman, Susan A. 1991. *Fragments of Redemption: Jewish Thought and Literary Theory in Benjamin, Scholem, and Levinas*. Bloomington: Indiana University Press.

Hartman, Geoffrey H., and Sanford Budick, eds. 1986. *Midrash and Literature*. New Haven, CT: Yale University Press.

Harvey, David. 1989. *The Condition of Postmodernity*. Oxford: Basil Blackwell.

Hegel, G. W. F. 1977. *Phenomenology of Spirit*. Trans. A. V. Miller. Oxford: Oxford University Press.

Heidegger, Martin. 1978. *Being and Time*. Trans. John Macquarrie and Edward Robinson. Oxford: Basil Blackwell.

_____. 1982. *The Basic Problems of Phenomenology*. Trans. A. Hofstadter. Bloomington: Indiana University Press.

Herzfeld, Michael. 1987. *Anthropology Through the Looking-Glass: Critical Ethnography in the Margins of Europe*. Cambridge: Cambridge University Press.

Heusch, Luc de. 1985. *Sacrifice in Africa*. Trans. Linda O'Brien and Alice Morton. Bloomington: Indiana University Press.

Hilberg, Raul. 1985. *The Destruction of the European Jews*. Student ed. New York: Holmes & Meier.

Hirsch, David H. 1991. *The Deconstruction of Literature: Criticism after Auschwitz*. Hanover, NH: University Press of New England-Brown University Press.

Hitler, Adolf. 1943. *Mein Kamph*. Trans. Ralph Manheim. Sentry ed. Boston: Houghton Mifflin.

_____. 1973. *Hitler's Table Talk 1941–1944: His Private Conversations*. 2nd ed. Trans. Norman Cameron and R. H. Stevens. London: Weidenfeld and Nicolson.

Hollis, Martin, and Steven Lukes, eds. 1982. *Rationality and Relativism*. Cambridge, MA: MIT Press.

Honneth, Axel. 1991. *The Critique of Power*. Trans. Kenneth Baynes. Cambridge, MA: MIT Press.

Horkheimer, Max, and Theodor W. Adorno. 1998. *Dialectic of Enlightenment*. Trans. John Cumming. New York: Continuum.

Horton, Robin. 1967. "African Traditional Thought and Western Science." Pts. 1 and 2. *Africa* 37: 50–71, 155–87.

_____. 1970. "African Traditional Thought and Western Science." In *Rationality*, ed. Bryan R. Wilson, 131–71. Oxford: Basil Blackwell.

_____. 1982. "Tradition and Modernity Revisited." In *Rationality and Relativism*, ed. Martin Hollis and Steven Lukes, 201–60. Cambridge, MA: MIT Press.

Hubert, Henri, and Marcel Mauss. 1964. *Sacrifice: Its Nature and Function*. Trans. W. D. Halls. London: Cohen & West.

Husserl, Edmund. 1970. *The Crisis of European Sciences and Transcendental Phenomenology*. Trans. David Carr. Evanston, IL: Northwestern University Press.

Islam, Syed Manzurul. 1996. *The Ethics of Travel: From Marco Polo to Kafka*. Manchester: Manchester University Press.

Jaspers, Karl. 1962. *Kant*. Ed. Hannah Arendt, trans. Ralph Mannheim. New York: Harcourt, Brace and World.

Jay, Martin. 1992. "The Debate over Performative Contradiction: Habermas versus the Poststructuralists." In *Philosophical Interventions in the Unfinished Project of Enlightenment*, ed. Axel Honneth et al., 261–79. Cambridge, MA: MIT Press.

Jenkins, Richard. 1992. *Pierre Bourdieu*. London: Routledge.

Johnson, Aubrey R. 1961. *The One and the Many in the Israelite Conception of God.* 2nd ed. Cardiff: University of Wales Press.

_____. 1964. *The Vitality of the Individual in the Thought of Ancient Israel.* 2nd ed. Cardiff: University of Wales Press.

Jonas, Hans. 1966. *The Phenomenon of Life.* Chicago: University of Chicago Press.

_____. 1974. "Spinoza and the Theory of Organism." In *Philosophical Essays: From Ancient Creed to Technological Man,* 206–23. Englewood Cliffs, NJ: Prentice-Hall.

_____. 1984. *The Imperative of Responsibility.* Chicago: University of Chicago Press.

_____. 1996. *Mortality and Morality: A Search for the Good after Auschwitz.* Evanston, IL: Northwestern University Press.

Kamenka, Eugene, ed. 1983. *The Portable Karl Marx.* New York: Viking Penguin.

Kant, Emmanuel. 1963. *Introduction to Logic.* Trans. T. K. Abbott. London: Vision Press.

_____. 1964. *Groundwork of the Metaphysic of Morals.* Trans. J. J. Paton. New York: Harper Torchbooks.

Kapferer, Bruce. 1997. *The Feast of the Sorcerer.* Chicago: University of Chicago Press.

_____. n.d. "The Dynamics of Ritual Formation as a Practical/Technical Intervention." Unpub. ms.

Kaufmann, Walter. 1960. *From Shakespeare to Existentialism.* Garden City, NY: Doubleday, Anchor Books.

Kierkegaard, Søren. 1985. *Fear and Trembling.* Trans. Alastair Hannay. London and New York: Penguin Books.

Klagge, James C., and Alfred Nordmann. 1993. *Ludgwig Wittgenstein: Philosophical Occasions 1912–1951.* Indianapolis, IN: Hackett Publishing.

Kosinski, Jerzy. 1976. *The Painted Bird.* New York: Grove Press.

Koyre, Alexandre. 1957. *From the Closed World to the Infinite Universe.* Baltimore, MD: Johns Hopkins University Press.

Kripke, Saul A. 1980. *Naming and Necessity.* Cambridge, MA: Harvard University Press.

Kuhn, Thomas S. 1970. *The Structure of Scientific Revolutions.* 2nd ed., enlarged. Chicago: University of Chicago Press.

Kuper, Adam. 1983. *Anthropology and Anthropologists: The Modern British School.* Rev. ed. London and New York: Routledge.

Lacan, Jacques. 1981. *The Four Fundamental Concepts of Psycho-Analysis.* Trans. Alan Sheridan. New York: W.W. Norton.

LaCapra, Dominick. 1994. *Representing the Holocaust: History, Theory, Trauma.* Ithaca, NY: Cornell University Press.

Lacoue-Labarthe, Phillipe, and Jean-Luc Nancy. 1990. "The Nazi Myth." *Critical Inquiry* 16, no. 2: 291–312.

Lang, Berel. 1990. *Act and Idea in the Nazi Genocide.* Chicago: University of Chicago Press.

Langer, Lawrence L. 1991. *Holocaust Testimonies.* New Haven, CT: Yale University Press.

_____. 1995. *Admitting the Holocaust.* New York: Oxford University Press.

_____. 1998. *Preempting the Holocaust.* New Haven, CT: Yale University Press.

Laudan, Larry. 1990. *Science and Relativism: Some Key Controversies in the Philosophy of Science.* Chicago: University of Chicago Press.

Leenhardt, Maurice. 1979. *Do Kamo: Person and Myth in the Melanesian World.* Trans. Basia Miller Gulati. Chicago: University of Chicago Press.

Lerner, Gerda. 1986. *The Creation of Patriarchy.* Oxford: Oxford University Press.

Levi, Primo. 1961. *Survival in Auschwitz: The Nazi Assault on Humanity.* Trans. Stuart Woolf. New York: Collier Books.

_____. 1989. *The Drowned and the Saved.* Trans. Raymond Rosenthal. New York: Vintage International.

Levinas, Emmanuel. 1957. "Lévy-Bruhl et la Philosophie Contemporaine." *Revue Philosophique* 147: 556–69.

_____. 1969. *Totality and Infinity.* Trans. Alphonso Lingis. Pittsburgh, PA: Duquesne University Press.

_____. 1986. "The Trace of the Other." In *Deconstruction in Context,* trans. Alphonso Lingis; ed. Mark C. Taylor, 345–59. Chicago: University of Chicago Press.

_____. 1987. *Collected Philosophical Papers.* Trans. Alphonso Lingis. Dordrecht: Martinus Nijhoff.

_____. 1989. "Ethics as First Philosophy." In *The Levinas Reader,* ed. Sean Hand, 75–87. Oxford: Blackwell.

_____. 1990. "Reflections on the Philosophy of Hitlerism." Trans. Sean Hand. *Critical Inquiry* 17, no. 1: 62–71.

_____. 1991. *Otherwise Than Being or Beyond Essence*. Trans. Alphonso Lingis. Dordrecht: Kluwer.

_____. 1996. *Proper Names*. Trans. Michael B. Smith. Standford, CA: Stanford University Press.

_____. 1998. *Entre Nous: Thinking of the Other*. Trans. Michael B. Smith and Barbara Harshav. New York: Columbia University Press.

Levinas, Emmanuel, and Richard Kearney. 1986. "Dialogue with Emmanuel Levinas." In *Face to Face with Levinas*, ed. Richard A. Cohen, 13–34. Albany: State University of New York Press.

Lévi-Strauss, C. 1963a. *Totemism*. Trans. Rodney Needham. Harmondsworth: Penguin Books.

_____. 1963b. *Structural Anthropology*. Trans. Claire Jacobson and Brooke Grundfest Schoeph. New York: Basic Books.

Lévy-Bruhl, Lucien. 1975. *The Notebooks on Primitive Mentality*. Trans. Peter Rivière. Oxford: Basil Blackwell.

Liberman, Kenneth. 1999. "From Walkabout to Meditation: Craft and Ethics in Field Inquiry." *Qualitative Inquiry* 5, no. 1: 47–63.

Lienhardt, Godfrey. 1961. *Divinity and Experience: The Religion of the Dinka*. Oxford: Clarendon Press.

_____. 1973. "Morality and Happiness among the Dinka." In *Religion and Morality*, ed. Gene Outka and John P. Reeder, Jr., 108–22. Garden City, NY: Anchor Books.

_____. 1985. "Self: Public, Private. Some African Representations." In *The Category of the Person*, ed. Michael Carrithers, Steven Collins, and Steven Lukes, 141–55. Cambridge: Cambridge University Press.

Lloyd, G. E. R. 1990. *Demystifying Mentalities*. Cambridge: Cambridge University Press.

Loesberg, Jonathan. 2005. *A Return to Aesthetics: Autonomy, Indifference, and Postmodernism*. Stanford, CA: Stanford University Press.

Löwith, Karl. 1993. *Max Weber and Karl Marx*. Trans. Hans Fantel. London: Routledge.

Lukacs, Georg. 1971. *History and Class Consciousness*. Trans. Rodney Livingstone. London: Merlin Press.

Lukes, Steven. 1973. *Emile Durkheim: His Life and Works*. Harmondsworth: Penguin Books.

Lyotard, Jean-François. 1988. *The Differend*. Trans. Georges Van Den Abeele. Minneapolis: University of Minnesota Press.

_____. 1990. *Heidegger and "the jews."* Trans. Andreas Michel and Mark S. Roberts. Minneapolis: University of Minnesota Press.

Malcolm, Norman. 1994. *Wittgenstein: A Religious Point of View?* Ed. and respondent Peter Winch. Ithaca, NY: Cornell University Press.

Marriott, McKim. 1976. "Hindu Transactions: Diversity without Dualism." In *Transaction and Meaning: Directions in the Anthropology of Exchange and Symbolic Behavior*. ASA Essays in Social Anthropology, 1. Ed. Bruce Kapferer, 109–42. Philadelphia: Institute for the Study of Human Issues.

McCarthy, Thomas. 1978. *The Critical Theory of Jürgen Habermas*. Cambridge, MA: MIT Press.

McGowan, John. 1991. *Postmodernism and Its Critics*. Ithaca, NY: Cornell University Press.

McHugh, Peter. 1968. *Defining the Situation*. Indianapolis and New York: Bobbs-Merrill.

Merleau-Ponty, Maurice 1962. *Phenomenology of Perception*. Trans. Colin Smith. London: Routledge and Kegan Paul.

_____. 1964a. *Signs*. Trans. Richard C. McCleary. Evanston, IL: Northwestern University Press.

_____. 1964b. *The Primacy of Perception*. Trans. James M. Edie. Evanston, IL: Northwestern University Press.

_____. 1968. *The Visible and the Invisible*. Trans. Alphonso Lingis. Evanston, IL: Northwestern University Press.

Monk, Ray. 1990. *Ludwig Wittgenstein: The Duty of Genius*. New York: Penguin Books.

Nandy, Ashis. 1989. *The Tao of Cricket: On Games of Destiny and the Destiny of Games*. New Delhi: Penguin Books.

Needham, Rodney. 1972. *Belief, Language, and Experience*. Chicago: University of Chicago Press.

_____. 1987. *Counterpoints*. Berkeley: University of California Press.

Nieli, Russell. 1987. *Wittgenstein: From Mysticism to Ordinary Language*. New York: State University of New York Press.

Norris, Christopher. 1987. *Derrida*. Cambridge, MA: Harvard University Press.

_____. 1993. *The Truth about Postmodernism*. Oxford: Blackwell.

Obeyesekere, Gananath. 1992. *The Apotheosis of Captain Cook: European Mythmaking in the Pacific*. Princeton, NJ: Princeton University Press.

Oshinsky, David M., Richard P. McCormick, and Daniel Horn. 1989. *The Case of the Nazi Professor*. New Brunswick, NJ: Rutgers University Press.

Ostrow, James M. 1981. "Culture as a Fundamental Dimension of Experience: A Discussion of Pierre Bourdieu's Theory of Human Habitus." *Human Studies* 4: 279–97.

Pagels, Elaine. 1988. *Adam, Eve, and the Serpent*. New York: Random House.

Passmore, John. 1970. *The Perfectibility of Man*. New York: Scribner & Sons.

Patterson, Orlando. 2005. "The Speech Misheard Round the World." Op. ed., *New York Times*, 22 January.

Pecora, Vincent P. 1992. "Habermas, Enlightenment, and Antisemitism." In *Probing the Limits of Representation*, ed. Saul Friedlander, 155–70. Cambridge, MA: Harvard University Press.

Philmus, Robert M. 1974. "Wells and Borges and the Labyrinths of Time." *Science Fiction Studies* 1, no. 4: 1–13. http://www.depauw.edu/sfs/backissues/4/philmus4art.htm.

Pippin, Robert B. 1989. *Hegel's Idealism: The Satisfactions of Self-Consciousness*. Cambridge: Cambridge University Press.

Plessner, Helmuth. 1970. *Laughing and Crying: A Study of the Limits of Human Behavior*. Trans. James Spencer Churchill and Marjorie Grene. Evanston, IL: Northwestern University Press.

Polanyi, Michael. 1967. *The Tacit Dimension*. Garden City, NY: Anchor Books.

Popper, Karl. 1962. *The Open Society and Its Enemies*. Vols. 1 and 2. London: Routledge and Kegan Paul.

_____. 1965. *Conjectures and Refutations*. 2nd ed. London: Routledge and Kegan Paul.

_____. 1968. *The Logic of Scientific Discovery*. Rev. ed. London: Hutchinson.

_____. 1970. "Normal Science and Its Dangers." In *Criticism and the Growth of Knowledge*, ed. Imre Lakatos and Alan Musgrave, 51–58. Cambridge: Cambridge University Press.

_____. 1972. *Objective Knowledge*. Oxford: Clarendon Press.

_____. 1974. "Replies to My Critics." In *The Philosophy of Karl Popper*, book 2, the Library of Living Philosophers, vol. 14, ed. P. A. Schilpp, part 3. La Salle, IL: Open Court.

Quine, W. V. O. 1953. "Two Dogmas of Empiricism." In *From a Logical Point of View*. New York: Harper Torchbooks.

Rad, Gerhard von. 1972a. *Genesis: A Commentary*. Rev. ed. Trans. John H. Marks. Philadelphia: Westminster Press.

_____. 1972b. *Wisdom in Israel*. Nashville, TN: Abingdon Press.

Rajchman, John. 2000. *The Deleuze Connections*. Cambridge: MIT Press.

Rashi. 1995. *Commentary on the Torah*. Vol. 1: *Bereishis/Genesis*. Sapirstein ed. Trans. Yisrael Isser Zvi Herczeg. Brooklyn, NY: Mesorah Publications.

Rawls, John. 1955. "Two Concepts of Rules." *Philosophical Review* 64: 3–32.

Read, Kenneth E. 1955. "Morality and the Concept of the Person among the Gahuku-Gama." *Oceania* 25, no. 4: 233–82.

_____. 1965. *The High Valley*. New York: Columbia University Press.

Remmling, Gunter W. 1987. "Discrimination, Persecution, Theft, and Murder Under Color of Law: The Totalitarian Corruption of the German Legal System, 1933–1945." In *Genocide and the Modern Age: Etiology and Case Studies of Mass Death*, ed. Isidor Wallimann and Michael N. Dobkowski, 185–201. New York: Greenwood Press.

Robbins, Jill. 1991. *Prodigal Son/Elder Brother: Interpretation and Alterity in Augustine, Petrarch, Kafka, Levinas*. Chicago: University of Chicago Press.

_____. 1999. *Altered Reading: Levinas and Literature*. Chicago: University of Chicago Press.

Rose, Gillian. 1992. *The Broken Middle*. Oxford: Blackwell.

_____. 1993. *Judaism and Modernity*. Oxford: Blackwell.

_____. 1996. *Mourning Becomes the Law*. Cambridge: Cambridge University Press.

Rotman, Brian. 1987. *Signifying Nothing: The Semiotics of Zero*. New York: St. Martins Press.

Rousseau, Jean-Jacques. 1950. *The Contract and Discourses*. Trans. G. D. H. Cole. New York: E.P. Dutton.

_____. 1966. *On the Origin of Language*. Trans. John H. Moran and Alexander Gode. Chicago: University of Chicago Press.

_____. 1992. *Discourse on the Origin of Inequality*. Trans. Donald A. Cress. Indianapolis, IN: Hackett.

Rubenstein, Richard L. 1966. *After Auschwitz*. Indianapolis, IN: Bobbs-Merrill.

Sahlins, Marshall. 1981. *Historical Metaphors and Mythical Realities*. ASAO Special Publication No. 1. Ann Arbor: University of Michigan Press.

_____. 1985. *Islands of History*. Chicago: University of Chicago Press.

_____. 1995. *How Natives Think: About Captain Cook, For Example*. Chicago: University of Chicago Press

_____. 2002. *Waiting for Foucault, Still*. 3rd ed. Chicago: Prickly Paradigm Press.

Sarnum, Nahum M. 1966. *Understanding Genesis*. New York: Schocken Books.

Sartre, Jean-Paul. 1956. *Being and Nothingness*. Trans. Hazel E. Barnes. New York: Philosophical Library.

Sass, Louis A. 1994. *The Paradoxes of Delusion*. Ithaca, NY: Cornell University Press.

Schaub, Uta Liebmann. 1989. "Foucault's Oriental Subtext." *PMLA* 104, no. 3: 306–17.

Scheper-Hughes, Nancy. 1992. *Death without Weeping*. Berkeley: University of California Press.

Schmidt, James. 1985. *Maurice Merleau-Ponty: Between Phenomenology and Structuralism*. New York: St. Martins Press.

Scholem, Gershom G. 1941. *Major Trends in Jewish Mysticism*. New York: Schocken Books.

Schutz, Alfred. 1967. *The Phenomenology of the Social World*. Trans. G. Walsh and F. Lehnert. Evanston, IL: Northwestern University Press.

Sedgwick, Eve Kosofsky. 1992. "Epidemics of the Will." In *Incorporations*, ed. Jonathan Crary and Sanford Kwinter, 582–95. New York: Zone.

Shell, Marc. 1988. *The End of Kinship*. Baltimore, MD: Johns Hopkins University Press.

_____. 1993. *Children of the Earth*. New York: Oxford University Press.

_____. 1994. "The Want of Incest in the Human Family: Or, Kin and Kind in Christian Thought." *Journal of the American Academy of Religion* 62: 625–50.

Shulman, David. 1993. *The Hungry God: Hindu Tales of Filicide and Devotion*. Chicago: University of Chicago Press.

Smith, M. G. 1960 *Government in Zazzau, 1800–1950*. International African Institute. Oxford: Oxford University Press.

Smith, Steven G. 1986. "Reason as One for Another: Moral and Theoretical Argument." In *Face to Face with Levinas*, ed. Richard A. Cohen, 53–72. Albany: State University of New York Press.

Snell, Bruno. 1982. *The Discovery of the Mind*. Trans. T. G. Rosenmeyer. New York: Dover Publications.

Solomon, Robert C. 1988. *Continental Philosophy since 1750: The Rise and Fall of the Self*. Oxford: Oxford University Press.

Sperber, Dan. 1985. *On Anthropological Knowledge*. Paris and Cambridge: Maison des Sciences de l'Homme and Cambridge University Press.

Spiegel, Shalom. 1993. *The Last Trial*. Trans. Judah Goldin. Woodstock, VT: Jewish Lights Publishing.

Spiro, Melford E. 1979. *Gender and Culture: Kibbutz Women Revisited*. Durham, NC: Duke University Press.

Stevens, Wallace. 1942. *The Necessary Angel: Essays on Reality and the Imagination*. New York: Vintage Books.

_____. 1955. *The Collected Poems of Wallace Stevens*. London: Faber and Faber.

Stoller, Paul, and Cheryl Olkes. 1987. *In Sorcery's Shadow: A Memoir of Apprenticeship among the Songhay of Niger*. Chicago: University of Chicago Press.

Straus, Erwin W. 1966. *Phenomenological Psychology*. New York: Basic Books.

_____. 1967. "On Anosognosia." In *The Phenomenology of Will and Action*, ed. Erwin W. Straus and Richard M. Griffith, 1–83. Pittsburgh, PA: Duquesne University Press.

_____. 1969. "Psychiatry and Philosophy." In Erwin W. Straus, Maurice Natanson, and Henri Ey, *Psychiatry and Philosophy*, trans. Erling Eng and Stephen C. Kennedy; ed. Maurice Natanson, 103–38. New York: Springer-Verlag.

Strenski, Ivan. 1997. *Durkheim and the Jews of France*. Chicago: University of Chicago Press.

Surin, Kenneth. 1993. "Transform the World, Change Life: Michael Taussig's Poetics of Destruction and Revelation." *South Atlantic Quarterly* 92, no. 2: 261–94.

Talmon, J. L. 1970. *The Origins of Totalitarian Democracy*. London: Sphere Books.

Talmon-Garber, Yonina. 1965. "Sex-Role Differentiation in an Equalitarian Society." In *Life in Society*, ed. Thomas E. Lasswell, John H. Burma, and Sidney H. Aronson, 144–55. Chicago: Scott, Foresman.

Tambiah, Stanley J. 1985a. "Form and Meaning of Magical Acts." In *Culture, Thought and Social Action*, 60–86. Cambridge, MA: Harvard University Press.

_____. 1985b. "A Performative Approach to Ritual." In *Culture, Thought and Social Action*, 123–66. Cambridge, MA: Harvard University Press.

_____. 1990. *Magic, Science, Religion, and the Scope of Rationality*. Lewis Henry Morgan Lectures. Cambridge: Cambridge University Press.

Taussig, Michael. 1987. *Shamanism, Colonialism, and the Wild Man*. Chicago: Chicago University Press.

Taylor, Charles. 1979. *Hegel and the Modern Society*. Cambridge: Cambridge University Press.

_____. 1985a. *Human Agency and Language: Philosophical Papers*. Vol. 1. Cambridge: Cambridge University Press.

_____. 1985b. *Philosophy and the Human Sciences: Philosophical Papers*. Vol. 2. Cambridge: Cambridge University Press.

_____. 1989. *Sources of the Self: The Making of Modern Identity*. Cambridge, MA: Harvard University Press.

_____. 1991. *The Ethics of Authenticity*. Cambridge, MA: Harvard University Press.

_____. 1993. "To Follow a Rule ..." In *Bourdieu: Critical Perspectives*, ed. Craig Calhoun, Edward Lipuma, and Moishe Postone, 45–60. Cambridge: Polity Press.

Thomson, Judith Jarvis. 1971. "A Defense of Abortion." *Philosophy and Public Affairs* 1, no. 1: 47–66.

Tiger, Lionel, and Joseph Shepher. 1975. *Women in the Kibbutz*. New York: Harcourt, Brace and Jovanovich.

Tugendhat, Ernst. 1986. *Self-Consciousness and Self-Determination*. Trans. Paul Stern. Cambridge, MA: MIT Press.

Vaux, Roland de. 1965. *Ancient Israel: Its Life and Institutions*. Trans. John McHugh. London: Darton, Longman & Todd.

Voegelin, Eric. 1956. *Order and History*. Vol. 1: *Israel and Revelation*. Baton Rouge: Louisiana State University Press.

_____. 1957a. *Order and History*. Vol. 2: *The World of the Polis*. Baton Rouge: Louisiana State University Press.

_____. 1957b. *Order and History*. Vol. 3: *Plato and Aristotle*. Baton Rouge: Louisiana State University Press.

Wacquant, Loïc J. D. 1989. "Towards a Reflexive Sociology: A Workshop with Pierre Bourdieu." *Sociological Theory* 7, no. 1: 26–63.

_____. 1993. "Bourdieu in America: Notes on the Transatlantic Importation of Social Theory." In *Bourdieu: Critical Perspectives*, ed. Craig Calhoun, Edward LiPuma, and Moishe Postone, 235–62. Cambridge: Polity Press.

Walsh, W. H. 1967. "Kant, Immanuel." In *The Encyclopedia of Philosophy* 3: 305–24. New York: Macmillan.

Walzer, Michael. 1985. *Exodus and Revolution*. New York: Basic Books.

_____. 2004. *Arguing about War*. New Haven, CT: Yale University Press.

Webb, Stephen H. 1996. *The Gifting God: A Trinitarian Ethics of Excess*. Oxford: Oxford University Press.

Wilden, Anthony. 1972. *System and Structure: Essays in Communication and Exchange*. London: Tavistock.

Wilson, Bryan R., ed. 1970. *Rationality*. Oxford: Basil Blackwell.

Wisdom, John. 1969. *Philosophy and Psycho-analysis*. Berkeley: University of California Press.

Wittgenstein, Ludwig. 1971. "Remarks on Frazer's *Golden Bough*." Trans. A. C. Miles and Rush Rhees. *The Human World*, no. 3 (May): 18–41.

_____. 1972. *On Certainty*. Ed. G. E. M. Anscombe and G. H. von Wright; trans. Denis Paul and G. E. M. Anscombe. New York: Harper Torch Books.

_____. 1979. "Remarks on Frazer's *Golden Bough*." With German text, trans. A. C. Miles, rev. Rush Rhees. Bilingual edition. Cross Hill Cottage Gringley-on-the-Hill: Brynmill Press.

_____. 1993. "Remarks on Frazer's *Golden Bough*." Trans. John Beversluis. In *Ludwig Wittgenstein: Philosophical Occasions 1912–1951*, ed. James Klagge and Alfred Nordmann, 119–55. Indianapolis, IN, and Cambridge: Hackett.

Wyschogrod, Edith. 1985. *Spirit in Ashes: Hegel, Heidegger, and Man-Made Mass Death*. New Haven, CT: Yale University Press.

Yeo, Michael. 1992. "Perceiving/Reading the Other: Ethical Dimensions." In *Merleau-Ponty: Hermeneutics and Postmodernism*, ed. Thomas W. Busch and Shaun Gallagher, 37–52. Albany: State University of New York Press.

Zeitlyn, David. 1990. "Professor Garfinkel Visits the Soothsayers: Ethnomethodology and Mambila Divination." *Man* (n.s.) 25: 654–66.

Zengotita, Thomas de. 1989. "On Wittgenstein's *Remarks on Frazer's Golden Bough*." *Cultural Anthropology* 4, no. 4: 390–98.

INDEX

abortion debate. *See* choice

activism. *See* anthropology: relation to social activism

addiction, 239, 353n21

Adorno, Theodor, 336n8. *See also* Horkheimer, Max, and Theodor Adorno

aestheticism, 14, 229, 242, 261, 344n8, 347n9, 353–54n1. *See also* Foucault; Geertz

affect, 24–25, 35, 194, 303n4 (chap. 1), 344n10

Agamben, Giorgio, 84, 233, 238, 256, 274, 293, 317n7, 315n1, 325–26n31, 338n3, 340n2, 350n6

  "bare life," 325n31

  "form of life," 317n7

agency, x, xxii, 6, 8, 11, 14, 66, 78, 110, 113–18, 124, 152, 169, 173–74, 321n20, 137–38, 152, 179, 183, 211–12, 227, 231, 246–47, 252–53, 264, 329n9, 338n3, 340n2, 350n6, 360n10

  autonomous, 135, 225, 239, 246

  creative, 115–16, 137–38

  "means without end." *See* means

  Means without End, 338n3

  moral, 152, 201, 211–13, 248

  self-conscious, 174

  subjective, 183

  unconscious, 114–15, 129

Akedah (Abraham's sacrifice of Isaac), 10–11, 48–75, 77, 79, 80, 100, 127, 129, 216, 257–59, 264–65, 270, 272, 282–84, 295, 299, 305n1, 307n4, 307n8, 308n10, 309–10nn12–13, 311nn21–22, 312nn27–28, 313nn1–2, 323n27, 324n29–30, 330n13, 355n8, 357n9, 361n16

  said vs. saying, 71

  sound vs. sight, 70, 311n21

  unholy desire, 53, 55

  See also Bible

Akiga, 198

alcoholism, 239, 241, 250

  as disease of selfhood, 239

alienation, 158, 182, 187, 332–33n20

  of the other, 348n15

  self-alienation, 266

ambiguity, ix–xii, xv, xx–xxi, xxiii, 1, 3, 5–7, 11, 14, 21–22, 25, 29, 32–34, 42–46, 48, 58, 67–68, 74, 82, 93, 110, 117, 120, 122, 127, 129–30, 134–36, 138, 144, 147, 152, 159, 164–65, 167, 179–87, 190, 192, 196, 210–212, 216, 220, 222–23, 225, 235, 237–38, 241–43, 246–50, 254, 256, 266–70, 277–78, 280, 283–84, 289, 293–97, 299, 304n6, 326n31, 327n35, 330n14, 331n19, 333n21, 336n7, 336n10, 344n8, 345n3, 349n2, 354n2, 354n4, 355n7

  of the body, 34, 117

  and final resolution, 10, 12, 35

  of the individual, 212

  ontological, 16, 42, 67, 110, 117, 120, 127, 130, 138, 143–44, 165, 177–78, 183, 269, 289, 301n1 (intro.), 355n7

  of the other, 179, 181

  of the self, 134, 136, 138, 179, 181, 227–28

  of time, 184–85

  See also uncertainty

Améry, Jean, 96, 322n25

anosognosia, 304n5

anthropology, 1–5, 8, 10–12, 14–15, 18, 20–23, 36, 43–46, 119, 125, 151–52, 163, 167, 176, 188, 195–96, 198, 201–2, 210, 216, 224, 240, 244–45, 251, 280–81, 283–93, 298, 300, 340n4, 342n1, 344n1, 354n2, 359n8, 362n21

  a priori, 20–21

  Bourdieu's impact on, 111, 118, 125

  empirical research, x, 3–4

  as ethics, x, xv, 8, 10, 11, 216, 280

  hermeneutic turn, 4

and holism. *See* holism
of kinship, 305n7
ontological presuppositions, x, xv–xvi, 3–5
and otherness, x, 119, 151, 224, 240, 280, 284,
286–92, 300
politicization of, 4, 288, 290–91
post-colonialist, 119, 291, 353n21
problem of magico-religious thought or
actions, 3, 18, 22–23, 118–19, 151, 166,
188, 330n14
problem of primitive mentality, xi, 22, 120,
151, 166–67, 205, 213, 231, 300
problem of rationality, 8, 11, 14, 172, 176,
198–99, 201
problem of ritual, 194, 196
as science, xvi, 4–5, 224, 240, 244, 287
relation to social activism, 290–93
symbolic, 151, 164, 191, 198–99, 280
theory, 107–8, 287–88
translation, xii–xv
See also ethnography; reflexivity; structural-
functionalism; structuralism
anti-Semitism, 10, 321n20, 323n27
a posteriori, 18, 22, 32
a priori, 18, 22, 32, 121, 156, 216, 234, 248, 271, 292
synthetic, 5, 18–21, 22, 25–32, 35, 39–40, 42,
44–45, 50, 105, 171, 216, 244, 247, 261,
278, 298, 304n6, 341n10
Arendt, Hannah, 9, 319n12, 323–24nn27–28
banality of evil, 97, 322n25
Aristotle, 89
Arnold, Matthew, 282
Augustine of Hippo, Saint, 24, 136, 288, 307n7,
346n4, 361n13
Confessions, 24, 307n7, 346n4
Auschwitz, 96, 322n23
authority, 2, 56, 64–65, 67, 118, 122, 141, 183–84,
200, 243–44, 250, 286–87, 309n12
authoritarianism, 57, 146, 227, 243, 305n6
ethnographic, 287, 290–91, 345n3, 360n11
moral, 239, 247
patriarchal, 75
political, 112
revelatory, 64–65
temporal, 2
autonomy, xxi, 6, 69, 74, 87, 112, 114, 121, 123,
136, 147, 190–91, 226, 231, 240, 243, 246,
248–499, 275, 302–3n3, 314n5
moral, 87, 351n12
subjectivity/selfhood, 127, 170, 142–44, 175–
77, 181, 225–26, 231–32, 236, 277, 285,
292, 295–97, 302–3n3, 335n6, 357n10
See also agency; choice

Azande, 152, 197, 200–205, 209, 212–13, 306n2,
345n3
mystical premises of thought, 197, 201, 205–6,
209, 211
and pseudo-psychotherapy, 197–98, 201, 206,
210, 347n10
Witchcraft, Oracles, and Magic, 345n3
witchcraft and oracle, 197–98, 200–206, 208,
210–13, 346n4, 346n7, 348n10
See also psychology; selfcraft

Bacon, Francis (philosopher), 4, 92
Barfield, Owen, 310–11n20, 342n2
Saving the Appearances, 342n2, 353n1
Bateson, Gregory, 239, 249–50, 352n15, 356n10
Baudrillard, Jean, 353n20
Forget Foucault, 353n20
Bauman, Zygmunt, 89, 319n11, 320n15, 327n35,
358n3
belief, notion of, 24–26, 31, 50, 54, 63–64, 72, 164,
202–4, 215, 221, 243–44, 246, 248, 250,
254, 262, 267, 276, 312n26
Benjamin, Walter, 359n10
Berger, Peter (Brigitte Berger and Hansfried Kell-
ner), 226–228, 231, 350n5
Bernstein, Richard, 335–36n7
on Derrida, 357n4, 357n4
on Foucault, 350n8
on Habermas, 146, 335–36n7
Bible, 52, 57, 97, 190, 230, 246, 268, 288, 307n8,
310n16, 313n1
Adam and Eve, 62, 96, 106, 310n18
'the fall', 288, 297
Genesis, 17, 22, 48, 55, 56, 66, 81, 96, 152, 170,
175, 177–78, 184, 189–91, 215, 221, 243–
44, 246, 248, 250, 254, 262, 267, 276–80,
283, 285, 288, 294, 297, 299, 355n6, 358n2
Gospel of Matthew. *See* Derrida, Jacques
Exodus, 283
New Testament, 307n5, 313n1
See also Akedah; choice: Genesis paradoxes of;
creativity of the self: in Bible; life: Tree of Life
binarism. *See* dualism
Bloch, Maurice, 199
Prey into Hunter, 199
Bloom, Harold, 355n6
body, 24–25, 33, 38, 111–12, 115–18, 279–80,
305n8, 360n13
bodily language, 24–25, 117–18
"the body," 111–12, 115–18
body without organs, 33, 38, 305n8
See also consciousness: bodily
Bohm, David, 355n6
Borges, 217–18

boundaries, xx, 2, 6–7, 67–68, 93, 104, 108,
    230–31, 233, 241–42, 268, 283, 299, 301n1
    (intro.), 334n23
    fluid. *See* dualism
    immaculate. *See* dualism
Bourdieu, Pierre, xx, 107–30, 203, 210, 225, 228,
    252, 259, 327n1–2, 328–29n4–5, 329n7–9,
    330n10, 330n14, 331n17, 332–34n20–23,
    334n25, 334–35n1, 345n3, 353n20
    capital, 112–13, 116, 121, 125–27, 328n4
    capital, academic, 126, 328n4
    capital, symbolic, 112, 115–16, 121, 125, 127,
        129, 333n22
    criticism of, 108–10, 113
    Distinction, 328n4, 332–33n20
    "generalized materialism," 112
    the gift, 124–25
    on Habermas, 334–35n1
    habitus, 111–15, 118, 122, 124, 131, 252, 298, 300,
        329n8–9, 331n17, 333–34n22–23, 335n1
    Homo Academicus, 328n4, 329n7, 362n20
    illusio and misrecognition, 112, 116, 124, 125,
        126, 129, 259, 332n20, 334n25
    "immanent law," 117
    Jenkins's critique of, 328n5, 333n21, 334n23
    Lévi-Strauss, critique of, 124
    The Logic of Practice, 111, 328–29n5
    on magico-religious actions, 119–20
    negentropy, 116
    Outline of a Theory of Practice, 111, 124, 327n1,
        328n5
    power, xxiii
    practice, theory of, 124, 126–27, 327–28n3,
        330n10
    relations of domination, 112
    social change, 113–114
    "theoretical talk," 109
    See also anthropology: Bourdieu's impact on;
        capitalism: accumulation; Calhoun, Craig:
        on Bourdieu; practice: Bourdieu's logic of;
        practice: Bourdieu's theory of
'bracketing'. *See* phenomenology
Brown, James Robert, 338n5
Brown, Peter, 343n6
Buber, Martin, 311n21
Burke, Kenneth, 20, 323n27, 324n30, 358n2

Calhoun, Craig, 360n10
    on Bourdieu, 327–28n3
Canaque, 68, 233, 347n9, 360n11
cannibalism, 94, 103, 327n34
capitalism, 112, 149, 236, 330n14
    accumulation, 112, 126
    capital. *See* Bourdieu, Pierre

free market ideology, 7, 237, 258
Caputo, John, 70, 258, 306n3, 308n10
    Against Ethics, 258
causality, x, 6, 18, 111, 201, 277, 328n4
cause and effect, 6
Cavell, Stanley, 342n12
Cazeneuve, Jean, 342n2
Chabon, Michael, 47
Chalier, Catherine, 344n8
Chilton, Bruce, 313n1, 314n3
choice, xxii–xxiii, 6–7, 26, 51, 60–62, 66, 69, 74,
    135, 138, 154, 160, 166, 169–71, 173–74,
    176–80, 182, 186–87, 189–90, 197, 200,
    212, 215–16, 223, 231, 241, 243, 246–56,
    258–65, 268–69, 273, 276, 278, 294–95,
    297–98, 310n14, 316n6, 335n4, 335n6,
    342n1, 357n10
    abortion debate, 7, 135–36, 140–41, 335n4–5,
        336n12
    autonomous, 174, 243, 275
    capacity for, 179, 246, 255, 280
    choice as such, 6, 174, 278
    to choose, 61, 169, 188, 190, 231, 243, 250, 256,
        262–63, 265–66, 277–78, 295
    conscious, 231, 239, 273
    and consumerism, 7
    creativity of, 60, 66, 130, 169, 171, 216, 251,
        261, 263, 297
    Enlightenment paradoxes of, 136
    freedom of, 242, 261
    Genesis paradoxes of, 177
    (in)/authentic, 137, 197, 215, 249, 253, 260,
        295, 297
    instrumental. *See* instrumentality
    Judith Jarvis Thomson on, 141
    life-as-choice, 297
    livability. *See* practice: and livability
    moral accounting. *See* morality
    moral, 142, 164, 198, 263, 341n8, 341n8
    and not-choice. *See* dualism: choice/not-
        choice
    primordial, 6–7, 10, 27, 39, 49, 85, 102, 105,
        107, 115, 136, 169, 174, 229, 273, 278
    radical, 189, 191
    rational, 152, 162, 169, 273
    responsible, 216, 254, 265, 277, 284, 295, 297
    unconscious/subconscious, 170
    See also uncertainty: of choice
Christ. *See* Jesus Christ
Christianity, 95–96, 98, 225, 229, 250–51, 259,
    321n19, 343n6, 360–61n13
Cioffi, Frank, 303n4 (chap. 1), 331n15
    Wittgenstein on Freud and Frazer, 331n15

civilization, 84, 94–95, 258–59
closure. *See* openness
Cohen, Sande, 362n20
    Academia and the Luster of Capital, 362n20
conflict
    forms of, xi, 7–8
    generational, 170–71, 229–30, 253, 274–75,
        277, 335n6
connectivity, 35, 191, 221, 267–68, 347n9
Conrad, Joseph, 247
consciousness, xiv, 13, 20–21, 29, 30, 33–36, 39, 41,
        69–70, 106, 109, 111–12, 115, 117, 126–27,
        130, 162, 179, 184, 218, 223, 230–33,
        244–45, 276, 283, 285, 296, 330n11, 342n2,
        352n15, 353n1, 358n1
    bodily, 117, 130
    conscious choice. *See* choice
    consciousness-raising, 126, 248
    instrumental, 275
    moral, 94, 105–6, 129, 145, 236–37, 299
    mythic, 246, 281
    non-mythic, 276
    self-consciousness, 29, 33–34, 40–42, 54, 61,
        66, 69, 72, 74, 92, 126, 217–18, 220–22,
        228, 232–33, 239, 242–43, 246, 248, 261–
        62, 276, 283, 297, 310n20, 311n22
    theories of, 11, 20–21, 33–34, 40–42, 69,
        111–2, 117, 126, 329n8
constraint, 113
contempt, xv, 26
contradiction, xii, 14, 44–45, 67, 70, 87, 89, 92, 98,
        114, 126, 132, 137–40, 143–44, 151–52,
        157, 162, 164–65, 167, 171–72, 174–75,
        177, 180–82, 184, 186–87, 189, 192, 197,
        200, 202–4, 209–10, 215, 240, 241, 250–51,
        275, 277, 297, 299
    and ethics, 139
    law of non-contradiction, xix–xx, 6, 45,
        138–40, 143–44, 151–4, 162–64, 167–68,
        175–76, 186, 189, 197, 211, 215, 297
    lived, 180, 239, 297
    performative, 138–139, 144, 179, 189
    rule of thought, 241
    tolerance of, 163, 165, 171–73, 175–76
    See also Habermas, Jürgen: performative
        contradiction
creativity of the self, x, xiii, xxi, 6–8, 11–13, 25–27,
        41, 50, 106, 117, 134, 136–8, 190–91, 221,
        223, 230, 245–46, 250–51, 262, 275, 280,
        284, 343n6, 351n12
    in Bible, 53, 55–57, 60–61, 65–67, 177
    'body creative' and embodiment of culture,
        117–18,

creative capacity, 7, 136, 161, 173, 191, 193
    pro-creativity, 67, 68, 185, 276, 280, 309n12,
        318n9, 343n6
    See also agency: creative; choice: creativity of;
        self: self-fashioning
critical theory, 128, 239–40, 245, 320n18
cultural relativism, 21
culture, 3, 5, 8, 16, 21, 34, 80, 83, 117, 119, 129,
        284–85, 290, 305n10
    theoretical cultures, 157, 161
    See also anthropology; ethnography
cybernetic theory, 116, 329n9, 353n20

Darwinism, 90, 91
death, 48, 49–50, 55, 59, 62, 74, 75, 85, 100, 183,
        249, 258, 267–69, 276, 295, 297
    'living dead', 308n10, 317n7, 322n23
death camps. *See* Nazism: Nazi death camps
Delaney, Carol, 309n12
Delbo, Charlotte, 83
Deleuze, Gilles, 303n2, 305n8, 310n17, 310n19,
        326n33, 357n7
democracy, 92, 94, 170, 231, 236, 247, 252–53, 263,
        274–75, 283, 304–5n6, 336n11, 342n12,
        357n6, 359n8
    American, 304–5n6
    democratic morality, 342n12
    democratic participation, 252–53, 274–75
    kibbutz, 252–53, 274–75, 359n8
    and the Nuer, 359n8
Derrida, Jacques, 2, 9, 79–81, 124–25, 128, 142,
        216, 242, 247, 257–60, 262, 264–65, 269–
        72, 277, 279, 282–83, 297, 306n3, 306n4,
        308n10, 311n21, 314n5, 330n13, 341n9,
        346n6, 356n1–3, 357n4, 358n12
    différance, 242
    ethical suspension, 264–65
    Given Time, 124
    on the Gospel of Matthew, 259, 270, 272
    on the human condition, 258, 262, 265
    on Kierkegaard, 49, 77–79, 257–58
    on Mauss, 124
    Stephen Webb on, 331n18
    universalizing, 78, 258–59
    See also gift
Descartes, René, 11, 20, 32, 55–56, 108, 119, 190,
        217, 219, 232, 234, 236, 238, 294, 301n1
        (intro.), 336n10
    cogito, xii, 6, 19–20, 33, 68, 93–94, 119, 127,
        223, 232, 236, 238, 336n10
    doubt, xi–xii
    dualism, 14, 93, 108, 119, 344n8
    mathesis, 219, 230

determinism, 86, 116, 136, 140, 177, 183, 211, 235, 321n20. *See also* dualism: determinacy versus self-fashioning
dialectical theory and process, 35, 91–92, 111, 113–14, 191, 193
Dickenson, Emily, 101
Dillon, M. C., 330n11
Dinka, 152, 165–66, 172–75, 177–89, 197, 243, 342n13, 342n1, 342–43n3
   Divinity, 165, 173–74, 179–80, 183–89
   natural-supernatural dualism, 177, 179–80, 182, 184–85, 187
   and nondualism, 173, 177
   origin myth, 152, 187, 278, 294, 299
   rationality of, 180
   and religion, 178, 180, 186, 189, 284
   sense of self and other, 179, 181, 186–88, 342n2
   and time, 182–88
   tolerance of contradiction, 165–66, 172, 178, 184, 187
discretion, xxii–xiii, 3
displacement, 10, 68, 73, 78, 98
double bind, 59–60, 62, 126, 249, 251, 253, 261–62, 265, 275–78, 295–96, 355n8, 356n10
   original sin as, 250
   See also Bateson, Gregory
doubt, xi–xii, 29–30
Douglas, Mary, 345n3
Dreyfus (and Rabinow), 333n22, 334n25
dualism (and binarism), xx, 1–2, 19–20, 64, 67–68, 71, 74, 84, 86, 93, 102, 107–8, 110–11, 113, 115, 119–20, 126–27, 131–32, 138, 141–42, 146, 149, 151, 156, 159, 187–88, 190–91, 194, 196, 199–02, 204–5, 210–212, 215–16, 219, 221–23, 225, 230, 232, 234–4–2, 249, 266–68, 271, 277, 284, 287–88, 293, 296–300, 301n1 (intro.), 310n16, 310n20, 326n31, 328n4, 340n4, 330n11, 332–33n20, 335n4, 337n15, 338n6, 339n1, 342n1, 346n6, 349n2, 360n13
   choice/not-choice, 189–91
   determinacy versus self-fashioning, 177
   epistemology, 108, 110, 142
   fluid boundaries, 67, 86, 156, 166, 186, 242, 246, 289, 340n4
   good-evil, 189–90, 246, 257, 260, 263
   ideal-real, 46, 172–73, 175, 191, 195, 199–200, 277, 314n2, 339n1
   immaculate boundaries, 6, 14, 29, 50, 67–68, 86, 93, 104, 120, 134, 136, 147–48, 156, 159, 167–68, 191, 222, 231–32, 238, 242, 246–47, 257, 267, 299–300, 317n8, 334n23, 357n5

inside-outside, 9, 20, 29, 51, 192–93, 218–19, 233, 267, 283–85, 310n19, 341n9
   material-immaterial, 71, 110, 130, 166
   mind-body, 12, 94, 111, 119, 127–28, 138, 171, 173, 191, 193, 195–96, 199, 229, 236, 293, 301n1 (intro.), 325n31, 343n3, 353n1, 363n1
   monism, xx, 1–2, 115, 165, 242, 267, 289, 301n1 (intro.), 326n31, 340n4, 342n1
   natural-supernatural. *See* Dinka
   onto-epistemological, 238, 336n11, 343n6
   overcoming, 216
   physical-metaphysical, 159, 165, 171
   pluralism, 2
   scientific perspective, 108
   self-other, xii–xv, 7, 37, 41–42, 58, 128, 134, 136, 140, 142–45, 148, 177, 179, 182, 188, 191, 193, 195, 197, 202, 216, 220–21, 223, 228–32, 237–40, 242–46, 248–50, 253–56, 259, 261–68, 270, 275, 282–85, 288–89, 295, 299–300, 334n23, 335n6, 336n10, 342n1, 344n8, 353n1, 357n8
   spirit-body, 233, 267, 279
   spirit-matter, 48, 54, 56, 63–64, 66–68, 122, 138, 171
   subject-object, x, xix, 1–2, 9, 20, 29, 35, 44–45, 108, 110, 115, 127–28, 131, 133, 138, 147, 191, 222–23, 230, 242, 251, 281, 293, 302n3, 328n3, 329n9, 331n19, 332n20, 362n21
   theory-practice. *See* practice: relation to theory
   totalism, 165, 200, 249
   true-false, 169, 246
   visible-invisible, 171–72
   witchcraft-selfcraft, 211
   See also logic: dualist or binary; nondualism; representation
Duerr, Hans Peter, 352n14, 359n10, 360n10
   Dreamtime, 352n14
Dufrenne, Mikel, 303n1
Dumont, Louis, xx, 89–94, 122, 319n13, 320n17, 327n1, 331n19, 336n9, 340n4
   hierarchy, 90, 191, 301n1 (intro.), 331n19, 340n4
   Homo Hierarchicus, 327n1
Durkheim, Emile, x, 24, 107, 118, 127, 130, 144, 178, 192, 289–90, 331n17, 343n5, 344n8, 350n7, 361n15, 361–62n17
   "mechanical solidarity," 113
   society as moral system, 289, 361n15, 362n17

egalitarianism, 91, 226–27, 231, 271
Eichmann, Adolf, 115, 319n12, 320n14, 323n27
Eilberg-Schwartz, Howard, 361n15

Einstein, Albert, 184–85

empiricism, 3–5, 19–23, 28, 31–33, 41, 155, 172, 174, 176, 209, 230, 235, 274, 302n2, 340n4
  philosophy of. *See* philosophy

enchantment of the world. *See* rationality

ends, xxii–xxiii, 13–14, 39, 74, 85, 93, 101–2, 128, 154, 156, 164, 166, 169, 171, 177, 184, 186, 212, 235, 237, 269, 274, 338n3
  end of having ends, 39–40, 42, 274, 305n9
  See also Agamben, Giorgio; means

Enlightenment, 21, 50, 87–89, 91, 92, 132, 139, 146, 149, 216, 270, 295, 320n17, 350n8, 351n9

equality, 91, 94, 140, 143, 236, 279–80, 336n9, 336–37n13, 336n13
  inequality, 112, 236

ethics, xxi–xxiii, 8, 27, 39, 42, 43, 61, 69, 79–80, 110, 119, 123–24, 129, 131, 133, 139, 142, 146–47, 152, 160–61, 164, 176, 182, 215–16, 220, 225–28, 240, 242–43, 245, 248–49, 253–56, 258–65, 267, 269–72, 274–77, 279–80, 283, 286, 289–90, 295–300, 330n10, 334n23, 342n13, 346n3, 350n6, 351n9, 351n12, 353–54n1, 354n3, 357n5, 359n9
  anthropology as. *See* anthropology
  ethical evaluation, 27, 79, 259, 295
  ethnical nature of human experience, 176
  ethos, xxi
  heteronomy, xxi, 6, 11, 14, 68–69, 106, 181, 249, 276, 296, 302–303n3, 314n5, 357n10
  human nature as, 256
  hyper-ethical, 257–58, 260
  philosophy and. *See* philosophy
  primacy of, 331n18, 354n1
  versus rationality, 132, 137
  See also morality

ethnocentrism, 165, 245, 280, 310n16, 340n4, 350n8, 361n15

ethnography, xiii–xv, 3–5, 13, 46, 120, 152, 158, 165, 180, 199, 286–87, 290, 344n1
  ethnographic other, 119, 151
  ethnographic self, xv, 9
  ontology, 3–4
  participant observation, 292
  translation, 45, 285–86, 305n10, 340n4, 345n3, 354n4, 359–60n10, 362n18
  as writing, 287, 344–45n1, 345n3

Evans-Pritchard, Edward Evan, xx, 76–77, 199, 200–205, 209–10, 224, 288–89, 301n1 (intro.), 302n2, 310nn15–16, 321n21, 340n4, 340n6, 343n6, 345n3, 346n7, 359n8
  "if I were a horse" fallacy, 24, 224
  See also Nuer

Evens, T. M. S., 155, 273–74, 358n4
  Two Kinds of Rationality, 155, 273–74

evil, 97, 103, 189–90, 322nn24–25

evil eye, 37, 196

evolutionism, 21, 84, 114–15

extension (of personality), 57, 308n11

faith, 49–51, 54, 63–64, 72, 74, 307n8
  blind, 50–51, 54–55, 62, 64, 69, 75, 306n3
  community of the faithful, 72–73
  instrumental, 65
  test of, 49, 61, 65

falsifiability. *See* science

fascism, 146, 305n6, 326–27n33

Feyerabend, P. K., 175, 338n6

Final Solution, 101, 323n25

finitude, 48, 69, 106

Foti, Veronique, 349n2

Foucault, Michel, 9, 104, 215, 217–19, 221–22, 224–33, 235, 238–40, 242–43, 249, 260, 292–93, 298, 311n22, 320n18, 337n16, 344n11, 345n3, 346n4, 349–50n1–2, 350n4, 350n6, 350n8, 351n9–12, 352n19, 353n20–22, 363n1
  aestheticism, 347n12
  doubt, xii
  Madness and Civilization, 229
  on Merleau-Ponty, 349n2
  on the modern self, 137, 225–30, 240, 243
  The Order of Things, 217, 349n2
  power, xxiii, 4–5, 225–29
  on Velasquez's *Las Meninas*, 217–22, 238, 344n11

foundations, 3, 18, 26, 35, 45, 74. *See also* ground

Frank, Hans, 319n12

Frazer, J. G., 22–24, 27, 303n4 (chap. 1)
  Beltane May Day, 27–28
  The Golden Bough, 22, 43
  See also Wittgenstein: critique of Frazer

freedom, 39, 90–91, 140, 142, 233, 236, 304n6, 320n17, 357n6
  liberty, 236, 336n12, 342n12, 352n17
  negative, xxiii

Freud, Sigmund, 94–95, 98, 127, 307n6
  notion of the unconscious, 352n15
  primal scene, 95

functionalism, 313nn1–2

futurity, 60, 105

Garden of Eden, 96, 322n23

Geertz, Clifford, 199, 278
  aestheticism, 344n8
  "Anti Anti-Relativism," 340n5
  critique of Evans-Pritchard, 199, 345n3
  "hermeneutics," 199

gender, 6, 279–80, 309n12
generation, 51, 170–71, 253, 273–77, 279–80,
      283–84, 289, 291, 355n8
   primacy of, 67, 145, 289
genocide. *See* murder
geometry, 19, 32
gestalt, 25–26, 28, 35
gesticulation, 24–25, 33
Geuss, Raymond, 234
Giddens, Anthony, 330n10, 348n13, 350n7
   "structuration," 330n10
Gier, Nicholas F., 31
gift, 58, 62, 98–99, 110, 127–28, 309n12
   of death, 48, 54, 78, 80
   perfect, 48
   of perfection, 52, 54
   perfectly imperfect, 48
Gillies, Eva, 345n3
Girard, René, 313n1, 314n3
Glendon, Mary Ann, 336n12
Gluckman, Max, 200–201, 212, 343n8, 345n3,
      349n2, 356n13
Goldhagen, Daniel Jonah, 10
Gombrich, E. H., 347n9
good, xxi–xxiii, 13–14, 39, 156, 189–90, 193, 216,
      226–28, 254, 256, 260–61, 263, 265, 268–
      71, 276, 281, 297, 322n25, 336n12
   hypergood, 40, 42, 269, 272
   of life, 74–75
Greek tradition, 11, 15, 119, 216, 229–30, 282, 291,
      317–18n9, 357n5, 358n6, 360n12
   ethos, xxi
   Greek ethnography, 287–90
ground, 30–31, 32, 44–45, 64, 69–70, 97
   common ground, xiii, xv, 7, 74
   groundlessness, 13, 30–31, 44–45, 256, 263
Guattari, Félix, 305n8, 326n33
guilt, 51–52, 95, 99
Gutting, Gary, 349n2, 363n22
   on Foucault, 349n2, 363n22

Habermas, Jürgen, 9, 131–34, 136–40, 143–49, 225,
      296, 330n14, 335–36n6–7, 354n3
   communicative rationality, 131–33, 137–38,
      145, 147–48, 335n7
   as discussed by Martin Jay, 138, 143
   ethics, 131, 133–34, 146, 149
   on Holocaust, 146
   on Horkheimer and Adorno, 146
   Horton's influence on, 132, 335n2
   ideal speech situation, 133, 139, 143, 336n7
   on immaculate differentiation between subject
      and object, 147–48
   instrumental rationality. *See* instrumentality

   on language, 132, 139, 143–44, 337n14
   on moral consciousness, 145
   mythic thought, 131–33, 146, 296
   openness/closure, 133–34, 136, 335n2
   performative contradiction, xx, 138–39, 144
   Piaget's influence on, 133
   regarding Bourdieu, 131–33
   regarding Durkheim, 144–45
   on self and other, 134, 140, 144–45
   three worlds (subjective, objective, normative),
      133–34, 137, 139, 147
   See also contradiction; other: primacy of
Hamann, Johann Georg, 21
Hamlet, 61
Handelman, Don, and Eliahu Katz, 358n7
Handelman, Susan, 355n6
Hebrew tradition, xxi, 9, 216, 230, 238, 282,
      288–89, 358n6
Hegel, 35, 50, 90–91
   "dialectic," 191, 341n12
   Phenomenology of Spirit, 90
Heidegger, Martin, 193, 304n4, 325n31, 341n10–
      11, 357n10
   on Kant, 192
hermeneutics, 4, 14
Herzfeld, Michael, 287–90, 360n12
heteronomy. *See* ethics; Kant; Levinas
Heusch, Luc de, 310n16, 313n1
hierarchy, xx, 67, 90, 301n1 (intro.)
Hilberg, Raul, 84
Himmler, Heinrich, 319n14
Hitler, Adolf, 49, 54, 82, 90–91, 102–3, 319n14,
      320n16, 321nn19–20, 322n23. *See also*
      Nazism
Hitlerism, 89–90, 103
Hobbes, Thomas, 90, 336n12
   "state of nature," 329n6
holism, 6, 30, 35, 89–90, 127, 268, 319n13, 340n4
   anthropological, 331n19, 340n5
Holocaust, 9–10, 12, 49–50, 77, 84, 88, 93–99, 101,
      105, 146, 149, 224, 239, 247, 260, 265–66,
      270–71, 295, 299, 315n1–2, 316n4, 316n6,
      317n8, 320n16, 321n20, 324n28, 325n31
   as "*unicum*," 84, 97, 315n4
   See also inhumanity
Horkheimer, Max, and Theodor Adorno, 4–5, 47,
      92, 337n2
   Dialectic of Enlightenment, 92
Horton, Robin, 132–33, 348n11. *See also*
      Habermas, Jürgen
Hubert, Henri, 76–77
human condition, xi, 1, 3, 58, 93, 101, 129, 142,
      149, 162, 175, 180, 188, 194, 216, 250–51,

258, 261–62, 275, 277–78, 280, 296, 306n3, 351n12, 358n7
  as ethics, xxii, 9, 258, 265, 280
human existence, 193–94
human nature, 8, 10, 42, 87, 89, 101, 110, 237, 256, 333n21
  groundlessness of, 256
human rights, 79, 88, 99, 226, 228, 231, 233–238, 324n28, 304n6, 350n6
Hume, David, 18, 19, 20, 209–10, 303n2
Husserl, Edmund, 244, 349n2

idealism, 19–20, 26, 92–93, 115
identity, 51–52, 56, 85, 94, 95, 120–21, 136, 138, 140, 170, 188, 230, 237, 249, 257, 263, 267–68, 281–83, 287, 289, 292, 295, 298, 357n7
  as 'human', 105
  law of, 163, 165
  sacrificial, 52, 53, 62–63, 81, 95–96, 98–100
  self-identity, ix, 6, 8, 11, 85–86, 88, 102, 105, 123, 136, 170, 211–12, 229–32, 253, 275, 292, 294, 321n20, 324n29
ideology, 89–92
incarnation, 68, 97, 232, 311n20, 315
indebtedness to the other. *See* self
individual, 55, 67–68, 71, 89–94, 101, 140, 170, 192–93, 211–12, 237–38, 243, 252, 279, 310n19
  individualism, 89–93, 98, 228–29, 236, 336n12
  naturalistic individualism, 212
  relation to social context, 145, 198, 212
inhumanity, 105, 146, 316n6, 322n23
instinct, 42, 54, 95, 172–75, 250
instrumentality, xxii, 102, 303n4 (chap. 1)
  failure of instrumentalism, 195
  instrumental choice, 212
  instrumental rationality, 12–13, 84–85, 102, 131, 133, 137, 147, 151–57, 160–61, 163, 166–67, 247, 274, 276, 296–97, 337n15, 337n1–2
  instrumental reason, 83, 92, 102, 156
  instrumentalism, 93–94, 121, 153–61, 164–65, 186, 191, 230, 237, 243, 248–49, 251
  logic of, 166–67, 273
  See also consciousness: instrumental
intellectualism, 2, 28, 33, 83, 108–9, 340n4, 332n20
  intellect, 281
intelligibility, xii–xiii, 1, 3, 7, 46, 49, 74, 121, 139, 154, 164–65, 178, 224–25, 238, 273, 285, 287, 290, 299, 317n8, 316n6, 339n7, 345n3
  common ground, xiii, xv, 7, 74
  meaninglessness, 85, 317n8
intersubjectivity. *See* subjective
invisible, 69–72, 105, 130, 166, 191, 195, 218–19, 221, 238, 311n21

  as condition of the visible, 219
  See also Merleau-Ponty, Maurice; other
Islam, Syed, 330n12

Jenkins, Richard. *See* Bourdieu, Pierre
Jesus Christ, 48, 51, 56, 64, 68, 95, 97–98, 259, 306–7nn4–5
  Crucifixion, 97, 100, 324n30
Johnson, Aubrey, 308n11
Jonas, Hans, 1, 301n1 (intro.), 355n6
Judaism, 95, 259, 280, 290, 306n4, 314n3, 353n1, 358n3, 360n13, 361n15, 361n17
  Jewish mysticism, 319n11, 355n6
  "Jewish time," 358–59n7
  Jews, 49, 88–90, 95, 98–99, 103–5, 259, 270, 282, 288, 315n1, 318n9, 319n11, 319–20n14, 321n20, 323–24n27, 327n35, 361n15–16
Jung, Karl, 341n9
  'collective unconscious', 341n9

Kapferer, Bruce, 313n1, 344n8
Kant, Immanuel, 18–21, 22, 26, 32, 87–94, 192, 201, 211, 219, 225, 234, 236, 281–82, 297, 303nn1–3, 311n21, 318n10, 319n12, 336n10, 351n12, 353n1, 357n7
  autonomy, xxi, 87, 91, 302n3, 336n10
  categorical imperative, 87, 93, 319n12
  Critique of Judgment, 344n8
  heteronomy, 302n3
  "imagination," 303n3 (chap. 1)
  "inner sense," 192
  "Kantian individual," 92–93, 201, 243, 359n8
  metaphysic of morals, 6, 302n2
  synthetic a priori, 18–21
Kaufmann, Walter, 312nn27–28
kibbutz, xv, 8, 152, 155, 170–71, 229–30, 252, 273–77, 279–80, 359n8
  female principle in, 278–280
Kierkegaard, Søren, 49, 50–51, 53–54, 64–65, 70, 71, 72, 74–75, 77–78, 257–58, 308n9, 312nn27–28, 323n27, 330n13, 355n8, 361n16
  Fear and Trembling, 49, 355n8
kinship, 305n7
knowledge, xii, 4, 18, 29, 34, 170, 203, 235, 245–46, 281, 289–90, 345n3, 352n13
  analytic, 219
  politics of, 245
  "progressive," 231
  scientific. *See* science
  synthetic, 219
  tacit, 2, 170, 341n10
Kook, Isaac, 310n13
Kosinski, Jerzy, 316n6

Kripke, Saul, 22
Kuhn, Thomas, 175, 223, 338n6
    'paradigm', 223
    The Structure of Scientific Revolutions, 223

Lacan, Jacques, 37, 341n9, 352n15
LaCapra, Dominick, 321n20
Lacoue-Labarthe, Philippe, 317n9
Lang, Berel, 87–94, 101, 103, 105, 322n25, 324n28
Langer, Lawrence, 50, 316n6
language, 23, 31–33, 117–18, 132–33, 143, 337n14.
        See also Habermas, Jürgen: on language
Las Meninas. See Foucault, Michel
Laudan, Larry, 338n6
law, 54, 57, 79, 94–95, 138, 145, 197, 204, 236, 258–
        59, 264, 271, 293, 302n3, 308n10, 312n28,
        314n3, 318n10, 322n25, 325–26n31,
        336n12, 337n13, 343n5, 356n13, 356n3
    of excluded middle, 6, 163
    of identity. *See* identity
    moral, 87, 225, 236–37
    natural, 40, 120, 180, 232, 329n6, 338n6
    of non-contradiction. *See* contradiction
    "reasonable man," 356n13
    thought, laws of, 163
    universal, 204, 302n3
Leenhardt, Maurice, 68, 232–33, 344–45n1, 347n9
    Do Kamo, 198, 232, 360n11
Leibniz, Gottfried Wilhelm, 117, 310n19
Levi, Primo, 315nn3–4, 316–17nn6–7, 322n22
Levinas, Emmanuel, xx–xxiii, 9, 10, 43, 119, 122,
        172, 202, 216, 243, 245, 261, 264, 277,
        282–83, 305n1, 311n21, 315n5, 320n17,
        325n31, 330n13, 331n18, 334n24, 335n3,
        336n13, 337n17, 339–40n2, 353n1, 354n6,
        355n7, 359n10
    *author*itarian anarchy, 243
    heteronomy, xxi, 303n3 (intro.)
    and language, 337n14
    "Reality and Its Shadow," 353n1
    primacy of ethics, xxii–xxiii, 9
    "useless suffering," 323n26
Lévi-Strauss, Claude, 115, 118, 122, 154, 199–200,
        319n13
Lévy-Bruhl, Lucien, 191, 342n2
Lienhardt, Godfrey, 165, 178, 180, 183, 186–88,
        342n1, 342n3
life, 7, 48, 50, 52, 53, 57, 58–60, 62, 65, 74, 76,
        90, 85, 100, 102, 112, 129–30, 135–36,
        138, 141–42, 193, 221, 233, 238, 241, 245,
        266–73, 276, 297, 301n1 (intro.), 317n7,
        322n23, 325n31, 335n2, 335n5
    art of, 218, 228, 230, 318n9, 353n1
    "bare life." *See* Agamben, Giorgio

eternal, 95, 259, 307n7
    and ethics, 271, 323n27, 361n15
    "form of life." *See* Agamben, Giorgio
    life-giving/constituting, 99–100, 129, 324n30
    life-world, 317n7
    and logic, 162, 164–65
    moral, 297, 322n23
    power over life and death, 53, 55, 74–75, 85,
        96, 234, 317n7, 325–26n31
    temporizing, 191, 251
    Tree of Life, 53, 62, 96, 106310n18
Lloyd, G. E. R., 198
Loesberg, Jonathan, 351n12
    on Foucault, 351n12
logic, xx, 2, 149, 164, 172–73, 177, 181–82, 203–5,
        212, 215, 218, 234, 278, 281, 360n10
    of ambiguity, 7
    bodily, 113
    of calculation, 163
    dualist or binary, 132, 134, 143, 159, 163, 293
    "half-logic," 199, 326n32
    and identity, 6, 137
    as lived, 102
    metalogic, 215
    of necessity, 241
    non-contradiction, xx, 6, 45
    paralogic, 6, 29, 110, 216
    of practice, 174
    pre-logical mentality, 200
    propositional, 133, 137
    of reification, 293
    rule of, 203
    transcendental, 19, 20, 21
    See also rationality; reason
logos. *See* rationality
Lukacs, Georg, 190
Luria, Isaac, 354n6
Lyotard, Jean-François, 9, 49–50, 54, 104–5
    "the jews," 104–5
    on the primally repressed, 105

madness, 71–74, 102, 311n22, 326n33
    schizophrenia, 49, 71, 311n23
magic, 22–25, 43–46, 59–60, 123, 196, 231, 234,
        304n4
    magico-religious thought, 3, 18, 119, 146, 151,
        166–67, 193
    See also myth: mythic thought; anthropology:
        problem of magico-religious thought
malevolence, 65, 71, 74–75, 102, 326n33
Malinowski, Bronislaw, 23, 166
Manchester School, xx, 188, 341n11, 343n8, 341n11
Marriott, McKim, 340n4
Marx, Karl, 319n11, 320n17, 341n7

materialism, 26, 92–93, 108, 110, 112, 115, 320n17

Mauss, Marcel, 76–77, 124–25, 127, 331n19, 361n17

    The Gift, 125

McGowen, John, 351n12

    on Foucault, 351n12

McHugh, Peter, 201, 206, 211–12

    pseudo-psychotherapeutic experiment, 201, 206–212, 346n4, 347n8

    See also Azande

means

    means-ends continuum, 274

    "means without end," 156, 195, 274, 340n2

    See also Agamben, Giorgio; ends

medicine, 174, 342n13

Merleau-Ponty, Maurice, xx, 32–46, 115, 117–18, 219, 248, 278, 330n11, 331n17, 337n14, 341n10–11, 349–50n2, 353n1

    body-subject, 33, 35, 44, 280

    flesh, 35, 38

    "flesh of the world," 35, 38, 39

    Fundierung (founding), 32–33, 34

    the intertwining, 34–35, 37, 40

    the invisible, 41–42, 219

    language-as-expression, 33

    mirror-image, 36–37

    Phenomenology of Perception, 32, 301n1 (intro.), 330n11

    reversibility, 34, 37, 38

    the sensible and the sentient, 38–41

    tacit *cogito*, 33–34, 41, 44, 219, 330n11

    "unknown law," 117

    the visible, 36–37, 41, 219

    The Visible and the Invisible, 34, 41, 349n1

    wild being, 45

method of doubt, xi–xii, 30

Midrash, 69

modernity xix–xx, 4, 8–9, 13, 140, 144, 181, 184–85, 191, 198, 206, 213, 215–16, 219, 222, 227, 230, 233, 238, 240, 243–48, 254, 275, 295, 300, 325n31, 327n35, 328n3, 354n3, 346n4, 348n14, 354n3

    and ethics or values, 213, 215–16, 227, 234

    modern self/identity, 11, 90, 04, 120, 123, 137, 139, 158, 215–16, 224–31, 238–40, 242–46, 348n43, 351n9

    modern thought, 11, 84, 91, 133, 170, 173, 203, 215, 221, 297

    modern world/era, 7, 120, 149, 211, 219, 221, 227, 238, 314n3, 350n2

    See also science: modern; self: selfcraft

monism. *See* dualism

monotheism, 2, 51, 309n12

Moore, G. E., 29, 304n5

morality, xxi–xxii, 79, 101, 103, 145, 211–12, 231, 236, 239, 242, 249, 252–53, 255, 257–59, 277, 284, 294–95, 348n14

    democratic. *See* democracy

    moral accounting, 198, 201, 211–13

    moral being, 223, 230, 275, 277

    moral capacity, 189, 222–23, 249, 280, 322n23

    moral certainty, 265

    moral law. *See* law

    moral selection, xxii, 6, 8, 117, 122, 162, 169–75, 177, 183, 212, 295, 297

    moral space, 171, 187, 238, 334n23

    moralism, xxi, 3, 80, 262

    See also agency: moral; consciousness: moral; human condition; natural selection; practice

motivation, ix, x, 10, 53–54, 102

murder, 9–10, 49, 52, 55, 59, 84, 94–96, 98–99

    deicide, 95, 98

    filicide, 98

    genocide, 10, 12, 88, 101, 103, 216, 241

    homicide, 7, 10, 12, 55, 77

    infanticide, 53, 61

    sociocide, 84

    suicide, 12, 55, 83

    See also Holocaust

myth, 24–25, 129, 166, 199, 215, 239, 243–45, 276, 317n9, 319n13

    creation, 188

    Greek mythic tradition, 317n9

    Judeo-Christian mythic tradition, 48, 85–86, 105, 317n9

    mediative primacy of mythic perspective, 163

    mythic rationality, 12–13, 144, 151–52, 154–55, 160, 162–68, 215–16, 223, 274, 276, 296–97, 300, 337n1

    mythic thought, 132, 146, 149, 151, 156, 163, 165, 167, 215, 221–22, 231, 233, 274, 338–39n4

    mythos, 132, 151, 235

    nondualism of. *See* nondualism

    normativism of, 146, 156

    openness of. *See* openness

    of rationality, 146

    pre-scientific thought, 132, 155–58

    See also Bible: Genesis; Dinka: origin myth

mysticism, 43, 205–6, 211. *See also* Judaism: Jewish mysticism

Nancy, Jean-Luc, 317n9

Nandy, Ashis, 348n14

nationalism, 88, 90, 314n3

natural law. *See* law

natural selection, xxii, 6, 117, 152, 162, 169–70, 295

Nazism, 16, 87–90, 99, 105, 146, 265–66, 270, 295, 317–18n8–9, 319n12, 357n10

Nazism (*cont.*)
    Aryanism, 90, 317n9, 319n14
    National Socialism, 10, 88–90, 317n9
    Nazi death camps, 50, 54, 94–96, 101–2, 104,
        272, 308m9, 308n10, 317n7
    Nazi Germany, 10, 12, 260, 263
    Nazis, 10, 49, 54, 308n9
    and Poles, 104
    See also Auschwitz; Hitler, Adolf
Needham, Rodney, 305n7, 312n26, 340n4, 342n2
negation, 38–39, 40, 106
Nietzsche, Friedrich Wilhelm, 230, 270–71,
        319n13, 353n1
    critique of rationality, xxii
    "dogma of immaculate perception," 230
    eternal return, xii
    Genealogy of Morals, 271
    power, xxiii, 5
nihilism, 86, 260, 270, 274, 327n33
non-contradiction. *See* contradiction: law of non-
        contradiction
nondualism, xi, xx, 1–2, 19, 29, 42, 64, 110, 115,
        121, 151, 154, 156, 162–65, 167, 172, 177,
        179, 181, 193, 195–96, 216, 270, 289, 294,
        296, 298–300, 313n1
    of mythic rationality, 164, 167, 175
    of theory and practice, 177
    See also dualism
normative, 155, 162, 186, 206, 295, 335n7, 342n13
    normativism, 133, 137, 139, 145, 161
    'norming', 145
    norms, 52, 74, 145, 331n17
    and myth. *See* myth: normativism of
    rationality, 153, 162
    See also Habermas, Jürgen: three worlds (subjec-
        tive, objective, normative); science: scientific
        rationality; Wittgenstein, Ludwig: norms of
        description; worlds: normative world
Nuer, 8, 62–65, 252, 301n1 (intro.), 340n4, 343n7,
        352n16, 359n8, 360n10
    gar ('the cutting'), 62
    incest prohibition, 22, 360n10
    Nuer Religion, 199, 302n2, 310n14, 343n6
    religion, 284, 310nn15–16
    ritual sacrifice, 62–63, 65, 66, 272, 313n2,
        321n21, 324n29
    thek ('respect'), 64

obedience, 48, 60–61, 64, 66, 310n14, 319n12
Obeyesekere, Gananath, 199–200
    The Apotheosis of Captain Cook, 199
    critique of Marshall Sahlins, 199
object. *See* dualism: subject-object
objective, 118, 187, 190, 223

objectification, 108, 112, 239, 246
objectifying, 120, 122, 127
    thought, 44, 50, 243
objectivity, 4, 126, 293, 339n6
    relative objectivity, 4
    truth, 172–73, 178, 281, 287
    See also Habermas, Jürgen: three worlds
        (subjective, objective, normative); science:
        scientific thought; worlds: objective world
obligation, 8, 77–80, 104, 142, 257–62, 264–66,
        271, 295
Odysseus, myth of, 282
ontology, xx, 17–18, 42–43, 64, 86, 91–92, 104, 108,
        110, 171–72, 174, 196, 201, 211, 223, 289,
        294, 326n31
    ontological conversion, 3
    See also ambiguity: ontological
openness, 11, 67, 70, 124, 128, 132–37, 139, 142,
        144, 152, 183, 198, 201, 204–5, 221–22,
        227, 229, 231–33, 238–39, 242–45, 252,
        255, 260, 272, 289, 296, 298, 300, 335n2,
        358n12
    of body, 117
    of choice, 134–35, 255
    versus closedness or closed thinking, 132, 215,
        221–25, 232–33, 238, 244, 300
    of communication, 143
    epistemological, 224
    and ethics, xiv, 6, 12, 137, 152, 296, 300
    of faith, 50
    to future, 169
    of human existence, 139, 297
    Karl Popper's critique of dogmatism, 132
    and mythic rationality, 216, 221–23, 230–33
    to the other, 134, 142, 148–49, 169, 215, 229,
        231–32, 242–46, 274, 280, 282, 335n3, 353n1
    primordial, 244, 246
    and scientific rationality, 215, 221–24, 230–33
    of the world, 222
    See also ambiguity
Ostrow, James, 331n17
other, x, xx–xxi, 27, 140, 183, 186, 193, 195, 216,
        223–24, 230, 232, 237, 239–40, 245–46,
        249–50, 254, 259–60, 264–68, 270, 275,
        281–282, 284–91, 295, 299, 345n3
    an-other, xxi, 55, 58–59, 86, 183, 248, 261–62,
        270, 282, 284
    authenticity of, 119, 284, 355n8
    ethnographic. *See* ethnography
    exoticization of, 289
    invisible, 70–71, 105
    "the Other," xx–xxi, 119, 135, 183–84, 188, 231,
        249, 251, 257, 271–72, 275–76, 279–83,

286, 289, 294–96, 298, 340n2, 341n7, 351n11, 355n6, 361n16

otherness, xx–xxi, 1, 3, 7–10, 12–13, 43, 50, 56, 58–60, 68–75, 77, 90–91, 94–97, 101–2, 104, 110, 118–19, 121, 123–24, 141, 145, 151, 187, 193, 198, 200–201, 212, 215–16, 247, 254, 256, 259, 268, 276, 279, 281–82, 284–85, 287–90, 292, 295–99, 330n12, 332–33n20, 336n13, 345n1, 353n1, 354n6, 357n8, 361n16, 362n18

otherness of the self, 9, 12–13, 140, 282, 287

other-regard, 8–10, 12–13, 97, 101, 239, 247–52, 254, 260, 264–65, 275, 295–96

primacy of, 57, 69, 119, 137, 144–45, 149, 152, 195, 202, 216, 243, 247, 254, 256, 259, 268, 276, 280, 285, 294, 295, 355n7

radical, 122–23, 287, 345n3

responsibility to, 267

wholly, xii, 78, 98, 100, 248, 257, 260, 262, 265–66, 268, 357n8

See also ethnography; self

Owen, Wilfred, 47

paganism, 52, 99

Pannwitz, Rudolf, 359n10

'participation', 71, 127, 140, 143–45, 168, 179, 191, 194, 196, 342n2, 349n2

democratic. *See* democracy

participant observation. *See* ethnography

See also Lévy-Bruhl, Lucien

particularism, 87–89, 92, 93, 319n11

patriarchal warrant, 57, 309n12

patriarchy, 70–71, 75, 97, 170

perception, 4, 22, 25, 33–36, 40, 41, 63, 113

blind spot of, 35, 41, 68, 69, 70, 80, 278, 280

development of, 36–37

religious, 178

as touch, 34–35

visual, 35–36

perfectibilism, 85, 91, 100, 105, 216, 275, 279, 306nn3–4, 309n12

self-perfectibility, 56, 66, 85, 100–101, 309n12, 321n20

perfection, 52, 55, 57, 66, 67, 96, 103, 307n7

perfectionism, 96–97, 100, 105

perspective, 71–72

in Canaque art, 347n9

mediative primacy of mythic perspective. *See* myth

particularistic, 71–72

scientific. *See* dualism

phenomenology, xx, 2–3, 33, 171, 178–79, 184–86, 191, 193, 212, 235, 237, 244, 251, 270, 280,

301n1 (intro.), 331n17, 337n1, 341n7, 347n8, 349–50n2–3, 353n1, 355n7

'bracketing', 244–45, 350n2

and experience, 178–79, 184, 186

phenomenological epoché, 3

philosophy, 17–18, 44, 50, 87, 281–83, 291, 303n2, 312n26, 332n20, 355n7, 357n5, 358n6

of/as consciousness, 11, 127, 144, 329n8, 330n11, 344n8, 349n2, 358n6

of empiricism, 312n26, 340n4

and ethics, 42, 281, 283, 334n25, 341n7, 355n7

of science, 158, 281, 292, 338n6

Plato, 18–19, 32, 281

The Republic, 281

Plessner, Helmuth, 354n4

'eccentrism', 354n4

Pol Pot, 327n34

Polanyi, Michael, 175, 341n10

The Tacit Dimension, 341n10

Popper, Karl, 9, 132, 159, 168, 206, 223–24, 227, 231, 243, 335n2, 339n6, 340n3, 351–52n13, 363n2

"critical rationalism," 224

"reinforced dogma," 109, 221

theory of rationality, 346n7

positivism, 144, 191, 230

post-colonialist studies, 4

postmodernism, xxi, 17, 51, 62, 138–39, 144, 147, 191, 200, 245, 247, 254, 282, 298, 320n16, 351n12, 352n15

critique of modernity, 8

critique of rationality, xxii, 274

critique of rhetoric of choice, 177

Sahlins's critique of, 330n10

post-structuralism, 14, 240

power, xxiii, 4–5, 8, 92, 107–8, 110, 113, 125–26, 129, 147, 149, 225–28, 267, 271–72, 292–93, 297–98, 328n3, 334n23, 345n3, 351n9

anti-value, 110

empiricism, 4–5

masquerading as ethics, xxiii, 147

negative, xxiii

over life and death, 53, 85, 96

positive, xxiii

and structure of the state, 229

and what is right, xxiii

practice, ix, xiii, xix, 3, 5, 7, 9, 14–15, 19, 22–24, 27, 29–31, 33–35, 41–44, 85–86, 107–24, 126–27, 129–30, 138, 154, 162, 168–69, 171–74, 176–78, 180, 182–83, 186, 188, 193–95, 197–98, 201, 210, 212, 230, 235, 237, 241, 330n11, 345n3

Bourdieu's logic of, 111, 118, 130, 174

practice (*cont.*)
Bourdieu's theory of, 16, 107–17, 119–22, 124, 26–27, 130–31, 176, 330n10, 333n21, 327n1
contradiction in, 240
as creative, 169
epistemological power of, 211
and ethics, ix, x, 8, 107, 110, 129–30, 275
as fundamentally social, 169
as its own objective, 177
and livability, 209, 297
as meaningful action, 168
as moral selection, 169, 172–73
and/as power, 107, 110, 129, 330n10
relation to theory, 14, 24–25, 168–69, 188, 203, 209–12, 235, 288, 341n7, 342n1, 348n11
ritual, 191
uncertainty of, 183
See also Bourdieu
pragmatism, 22, 127, 130, 144, 166, 200, 277, 283, 294, 303n2
pragmatics of language, 132–34, 137–38, 143, 337n14
pre-scientific thought. *See* myth
primitivism, 12, 22, 25, 36, 44, 119, 152, 164, 166–67, 205, 215, 224, 237, 254, 287, 330n14, 331n15, 358n1
primitive mentality, 11, 22, 120, 167, 215, 233, 345n1
See also anthropology: problem of primitive mentality; religion: primitive
production, 108, 112
reproduction, 112–13
psychology, 199
modern psychotherapy, 152, 201, 206–7, 212
pseudo-psychotherapy. *See* Azande; McHugh, Peter
psychoanalytic interpretation, 37, 94–95, 321n20, 337n16

Quine, W. V. O., 22

racism, 90–91, 236, 320n15, 320n17
Rad, Gerhard von, 48
Rashi (Rabbi Shlomo Yitzchaki), 17
rational choice theory, 113, 152, 162, 169, 223, 251
rationality, 11–14, 45, 85–86, 119, 131, 151–52, 154–55, 157, 164, 166–68, 175–76, 199, 202–3, 210, 215, 221, 224, 230, 244, 254–55, 274, 276, 280, 296, 300, 303n4 (intro.), 337n2
communicative. *See* Habermas, Jürgen
(dis)/(re)enchantment of the world, 126, 149, 201, 216, 221, 224
epistemological primacy of, 151
instrumental. *See* instrumentality

as logic, 149
logos, 44, 119, 121, 132, 137, 151, 154, 200, 235, 254, 281
mythic. *See* myth
mythos. See myth
normative. *See* normative: rationality
rational determination, 142, 235
rationalism, 224, 240–41, 270, 351n9
rationalization, 16, 55, 63, 245
scientific. *See* science: scientific rationality
value-rationality, 13, 131, 153–54, 174, 216, 274, 276, 300, 303n4 (intro.), 337n1
and violence, 11, 13
See also choice: rational; Dinka: rationality of; logic; reason
Read, Kenneth, 305n10, 344n10, 346n5, 360n11
The High Valley, 344n10, 346n5, 360n11
reality, 3–6, 27, 31, 63, 103–4, 108–110, 116, 118–19, 121–22, 129, 132–33, 144, 152, 159, 165, 171–73, 178–80, 182, 185–86, 188, 190, 193–96, 198, 204, 218–20, 222–23, 235, 263–64, 283, 289, 293–94, 297–98, 301n1 (intro.), 311n23, 344n8, 349n2, 352n16, 358n1
bodily, 219
creating, 228
positive or negative, 171–72, 341n12
social, 109, 116, 129, 333n21
social determination of, 178
Western, 199
See also worlds
reason, 2–3, 5, 7–8, 10–11, 13–16, 18–22, 24–25, 34, 50, 64–65, 69, 87, 156, 164, 167–68, 199, 215, 223–24, 234–37, 239, 241, 297, 336n10, 356n3
demarcation from magic, 200
instrumental. *See* instrumentality: instrumental reason
intellectual, 200
intersubjective, 245
presupposition of, xii–xiii
pure, 19, 20, 21
self-responsible, 87, 93
truth of, 32–33
universal, 87–88, 90–91
See also logic; rationality
recognition, 25
reductionism, xiii, xvi, 7, 75, 108, 113, 115
reflexivity, x–xii, xv, 12–13, 15, 39, 61, 81, 105, 109, 115, 119, 121–22, 127, 179, 194–95, 218–21, 232, 238, 262, 265, 267, 286–87, 290–94, 328n3, 334n25, 344n10, 348n13, 350n2, 353n22, 362n18, 362n21

relativism, 21, 27, 29, 81, 139, 144, 149, 152, 155,
    165–66, 172, 202, 230, 245, 260, 266,
    271–72, 298, 312n24, 322n24, 333n21,
    338–39n6, 340n5
  absolute, 266, 269, 286, 340n5
  anti-relativism, 340n5
  of the law of non-contradiction, 168, 197
  of mythic rationality, 162, 165
  of rationality, 154
  relativizing, 215, 272, 359–60n10
religion, 22–25, 43, 77, 244
  ancient, 77
  divinity, 72, 136
  magico-religious thought. *See* magic
  modern, 77
  primitive, 77, 166, 361n15
  religious intentionality, 84, 103
  See also myth
Renaissance, 219, 221, 238
representation, 102, 111, 114–15, 120, 125, 133,
    163, 169, 172, 182, 199, 206, 209, 219–22,
    224, 238
  infinite regress, 218, 220
  paradoxes of, 177, 217–18, 220
  representational truth, 223
  Western notions of, 219
resistance, 134, 138, 171–73, 176–79, 183, 187, 192,
    229, 231, 242, 244–45, 248, 292–93
  filial, 230
responsibility, xii, 3, 8–9, 78, 80–81, 86, 103,
    114–15, 142, 144, 186, 189, 226, 247–48,
    257, 261–66, 271, 278, 283, 295, 297, 299,
    314n5, 321n20
  Derrida on, 142, 144
  to other. *See* other
  responsible choice, 277
  self-responsibility. *See* self
Rieff, Philip, 348n13
risk, 64, 65–66
ritual, 101, 120–21, 123, 164, 188–96, 199, 254,
    298, 313n1–2, 314n2, 330n14, 343–44n8.
    See also practice: ritual; sacrifice: as ritual
    or rite; transcendence: ritual
Roberts, Christopher, 335n4, 341n12, 344n10,
    353n1
Rose, Gillian, 313n1, 354n5, 356–57n3, 361n14
  on Derrida, 356–57n3
  Mourning Becomes the Law, 356n3
Rousseau, Jean-Jacques, 14, 56, 91, 101, 120, 163,
    194–95, 261, 313n1, 329n6, 336n12
  'general will', 275, 357n6
  on Hobbes, 329n6
  Second Discourse, 329n6

Rubenstein, Richard, 94–95, 101, 103–5, 317n9,
    321n20
rules, 31, 111, 115
  of thumb, 254
Russell and Whitehead, 218

sacrifice, 10–11, 48, 52, 58, 65–66, 73, 76–82, 85–86,
    94–102, 105, 128, 186, 188–89, 193–95, 206,
    210, 233, 247, 249, 257–62, 270–72, 287,
    295, 299–300, 306n5, 309n12, 313n1, 314n3,
    315n1, 321nn20–21, 325n31, 355n6, 359n10
  animal, 51, 52–53, 307n5
  anti-sacrifice, 58, 99
  communion, 95, 98
  counter-sacrifice, 48, 99–100
  Durkheim's theory of, 361n17
  economy of, 48–49, 51–58, 100, 260, 270, 296,
    309n12
  holocaust, 55, 58, 59, 73, 95–96, 315n1
  of Jesus, 48, 51, 64, 306–7nn4–5
  and natural disaster, 314n4
  and the other, 299, 359n10
  perfect, 57–59, 97–98, 100, 307n5, 324n30
  perfectly imperfect, 100
  as ritual or rite, 13, 52, 62–63, 77, 96, 99–100,
    313n1–2, 321n20–21, 325n31
  self-sacrifice, 55, 61, 64, 68, 80–81, 249, 289,
    295, 299, 319n14
  sinister aspect of, 27–28
  of spirit for matter, 48, 65
  as structure of human existence, 77, 80, 101,
    326n31
  substitution in, 52, 53, 58, 59, 63, 95
  surrogate or imperfect, 51–63, 95–96, 81,
    98–100, 362n17
  'survivor's account', 308n10
  'woman's point of view', 308n10
Sahlins, Marshall, 199–200, 330n10
  on Descartes, 217
  on Obeyesekere, 200
  on postmodernism. *See* postmodernism
  "structure-minded history," 330n10
Sarnum, Nahum M., 307n8
Sartre, Jean-Paul, 348n12, 355n7
  on Kantian idealism, 348n12
Sass, Louis A., 311n23
  solipsism, 355n9
Saussure, Ferdinand de, 114, 330n11
scapegoating, 321n20, 323n27
Scheler, Max, 20
Scheper-Hughes, Nancy, 345–46n3
Schiller, Friedrich von, 353n1
  Aesthetic Education of Mankind, 353n1
Schneider, David, 305n7

Schutz, Alfred, 331n16
science, 71–72, 108, 126–27, 151–52, 155–61, 168,
        175, 190, 223–24, 230–32, 235, 281, 291–
        92, 296, 300, 312n24, 334n1, 338–39n6-7
    contrasted with pre-scientific or mythic
        thought, 23, 43, 132–33, 156, 197, 200–201,
        203, 206, 215, 222, 338–39n6
    falsifiability of, 206, 210
    modern, xvi, 134–37, 139, 155–60, 175, 206,
        312n24, 339n6, 352n13
    ontology of "objectivity," x–xi, 33, 42, 71–72,
        110–11, 116, 159–60
    openness of. *See* openness
    and paradigms. *See* Kuhn, Thomas
    philosophy of. *See* philosophy
    as practice, 158
    primacy/presumed superiority of, 155, 163,
        167, 338n4
    scientific knowledge, 230–31
    scientific rationality, 155, 205–6, 210, 215, 222,
        224, 227, 286
    scientific thought, 215, 223
    and technology, 5, 84, 92, 123, 151–52, 157–58,
        160, 225, 304n4
    See also instrumentality; logic; medicine;
        modernity; objective: thought
second nature, xv, 6, 85
secrecy, 308n9
Sedgwick, Eve, 353n21
self, ix–xv, xxi, 1–3, 7–14, 20, 36–38, 41–42, 48–49,
        52, 58–60, 65–66, 68, 70–73, 77, 80, 87–88,
        93–95, 97, 100–104, 119, 123, 128–29,
        136–37, 140, 142–43, 145, 147–48, 179,
        187–90, 192–93, 220, 22–23, 225, 227,
        229–32, 239, 242–44, 249–50, 256, 264–68,
        270, 275, 281–82, 284–85, 289–91, 295,
        297–99, 336n10, 353n1
    ambiguity of the/uncertainty of the. *See* ambi-
        guity; uncertainty
    anthropological, 286–87, 292
    authentic, 229, 357n10
    belatedness of, 40, 56, 69, 73, 97, 105, 119, 178,
        183, 261, 265, 267–68, 276, 283
    essential, 230
    ethnographic. *See* ethnography
    humanity of, 226–28
    indebtedness to the other, vii, xx, 12, 51, 57,
        59, 96–97, 99, 105, 123, 128, 246, 249, 254,
        261–62, 266, 355n8
    monadic self/individualism, 247–48
    Occidental/Western, 3, 9, 105, 202, 280, 292–
        93
    passive, 192–93

    positive, 228–29
    postmodern, 246
    rational, 223
    reduction to, 281
    resistance to the other, 179
    Self, 68, 94, 96, 102, 190, 244, 266, 357n7
    self-aggrandizement, 48–49, 266, 272, 287,
        357n9
    self-confession, 229
    self-consciousness. *See* consciousness
    selfcraft, 198, 209, 211–13, 231–32, 332n20,
        346n4, 348–49n15
    self-criticism, 134, 222–23, 277, 362n21
    self-deconstruction, xv, 216, 358n5
    self-definition, 61, 66–67, 71, 93, 128
    self-destruction, 58, 83–84, 92, 103–4, 188,
        239, 241, 260, 324n30, 327n34
    self-determination, 149, 190–91, 238, 269,
        304n6, 348n13
    self-discipline, 239
    self-fashioning (and self-construction), 26,
        102, 130, 169, 177–79, 229–31, 242, 245–
        46, 248–49, 279, 351n12, 353n1
    selfhood, xii, xix, 3, 10–14, 41, 50–51, 61, 65–
        66, 86, 94, 97, 100–101, 119, 134–35, 142,
        147, 152, 169, 178, 190, 192, 195, 215, 220,
        228, 239, 243–44, 248, 262, 264–67, 282,
        285, 298, 310n14, 311n20, 333n20, 335n6,
        337n16, 346n4, 354–55n6, 360n13
    self-identification, 8, 10, 85, 102, 141, 268,
        363n21
    self-identity. *See* identity
    self-interest, 8, 10, 237, 247, 249–52, 264–65,
        279, 296, 336n12
    selflessness, 55, 99, 101, 129, 247, 265–66, 270,
        272, 295
    self-mediation, xxiii, 128
    self-objectification, 127, 130
    self-other. *See* dualism
    self-reflection, 53, 116, 193, 296, 349n15
    self-regard, 272
    self-responsibility, xxi, 80, 87, 93, 101, 129, 220,
        253–54, 295
    self-transcendence. *See* transcendence
    sense of, 2, 9, 10, 61, 66, 77, 139, 179, 222, 240,
        254, 292–93, 298, 317n8, 348n13, 350n8
    temporal nature of, 192
    'true', 226, 229
    See also agency; creativity of the self; ethnogra-
        phy: ethnographic self; openness; other
Shell, Marc, 305n7, 306n4
singularity, 59, 68, 78–79, 13, 142, 148, 257, 259,
        262, 335n4, 350n6, 357n7

situationalism, 143, 167, 252–53, 255, 262, 297, 347n8

skepticism, 19, 20, 29

Smith, M. G., 363n3
   Government in Zazzau, 363n3

Smith, Robertson, 77

Snell, Bruno, 357n5

sociology, 107–9, 111

Socrates, 357n5

sovereignty, 2, 51, 89, 96, 114, 232–34, 293, 302n3, 325–26n31, 337n13, 363n1

space, 32–33, 79, 128, 155, 170–71, 183, 187, 204, 218, 220, 239, 242, 332n20, 333–34n23, 354n6
   moral. *See* morality
   primordial, 354–55n6
   space-time, 170, 242, 268

Sperber, Dan, 198–99
   "semi-proposition," 199

Spiegel, Shalom, 51, 52

Spielberg, Steven, 314n3

Spinoza, Baruch, 301n1 (intro.)

spirit-matter. *See* dualism

spirituality, 24–25

Stalin, Joseph, 327n34

Stevens, Wallace, 129, 334n25
   "The Noble Rider and the Sound of Words," 334n25

Straus, Erwin, 304n5, 312n25

Strenski, Ivan, 361n17

structural-functionalism, 14, 111

structuralism, 14, 111, 115–16, 199, 331n19

'stupidity', 65, 73, 85, 102, 310n17, 326n33

subject, 19–20, 41, 133–35, 170, 183, 191, 223, 230–32, 238, 242, 246–48, 250, 276–78, 283, 315n5, 336n10

subject-object. *See* dualism

subjective, 5–6, 19, 71–72, 115, 129, 133–34, 136–39, 144–45, 172–73, 178, 180, 183, 223, 243, 331n17, 333n21, 344n8
   agency. *See* agency
   deliberation, 173
   (de)subjectification, 93, 102, 221
   intersubjectivity, 170, 245, 331n17, 332n19
   subjectivity, 5, 10–11, 20, 41, 44, 53–54, 71, 74, 94, 112, 116, 127, 136, 170, 182, 187, 190, 227–30, 242, 244–46, 248, 261, 296, 318n9, 324n29, 330n11, 332n20, 348n12, 353n20, 354n6
   subjectivization, 232, 248
   truth, 172, 178
   See also Habermas, Jürgen: three worlds (subjective, objective, normative)

supernatural/enchanted worlds. *See* worlds

symbol, 23, 46, 59, 63, 108, 112, 116, 118, 121, 125–27, 129, 164, 191, 198–99, 280, 316n5, 321n20, 330n10, 330n14, 33n22, 344n8–9

"symbolic capital." *See* Bourdieu, Pierre

symbolic anthropology. *See* anthropology

synthetic a priori. *See* a priori

Talmon-Garber, Yonina, 279

Taussig, Michael, 345n3

Taylor, Charles, 155–61, 164, 225–28, 231, 233, 238, 330n14, 331n17, 337n2, 338n4, 338n6, 350n6, 351n9–10, 355n7
   on Foucault, 225–28, 233, 350n8
   on rationality, 155–61

technology. *See* science

time, 33, 44, 59–61, 84, 89, 94, 116, 123–25, 128, 143, 145, 191–95, 210, 242, 251, 256, 258, 261, 263, 269, 272, 275–76, 296, 356n11, 357n7, 358–59n7
   and the Dinka. *See* Dinka
   homogeneous, 183
   "Jewish time." *See* Judaism
   long-term, 3, 160–61, 183, 185, 195, 251, 296
   sempiternal, 251, 276
   short-term, 160–61, 183, 251, 296
   temporality, 33, 122, 182–85, 210, 251, 276, 296, 358n2
   time (of) being 59, 261, 263, 272, 295
   See also space: space-time

Tiv, 198

totalism, 165, 225, 230

totalitarianism, 89, 92, 225, 327n33

totality, 35, 58, 68

transcendence, 40, 67, 121, 124, 127, 130, 171–74, 192, 229, 232, 250–51, 255, 267, 270, 296, 341n11, 356n10–11
   ritual, 251
   self-transcendence, 41, 171, 192, 245, 284

translation. *See* ethnography

Tree of Life, 53, 96, 106, 310n18

Trobrianders, 23

truth, 18, 21, 32–33, 35, 108, 119, 163–64, 166, 169, 171–74, 178, 187–88, 202, 209, 219, 226, 228, 230, 234, 241, 281, 338n5, 347n10, 352n13
   objective. *See* objective
   subjective. *See* subjective

Turner, Victor, 343n8

uncertainty, 3, 11, 39, 50, 60, 112–14, 116, 123, 128, 134, 136–37, 143, 145, 159–60, 168–69, 183–84, 187, 190, 195, 210–12, 216, 246, 249, 255, 260–61, 268, 272, 280,

situationalism, 143, 167, 252–53, 255, 262, 297, 347n8
skepticism, 19, 20, 29
Smith, M. G., 363n3
   Government in Zazzau, 363n3
Smith, Robertson, 77
Snell, Bruno, 357n5
sociology, 107–9, 111
Socrates, 357n5
sovereignty, 2, 51, 89, 96, 114, 232–34, 293, 302n3, 325–26n31, 337n13, 363n1
space, 32–33, 79, 128, 155, 170–71, 183, 187, 204, 218, 220, 239, 242, 332n20, 333–34n23, 354n6
   moral. *See* morality
   primordial, 354–55n6
   space-time, 170, 242, 268
Sperber, Dan, 198–99
   "semi-proposition," 199
Spiegel, Shalom, 51, 52
Spielberg, Steven, 314n3
Spinoza, Baruch, 301n1 (intro.)
spirit-matter. *See* dualism
spirituality, 24–25
Stalin, Joseph, 327n34
Stevens, Wallace, 129, 334n25
   "The Noble Rider and the Sound of Words," 334n25
Straus, Erwin, 304n5, 312n25
Strenski, Ivan, 361n17
structural-functionalism, 14, 111
structuralism, 14, 111, 115–16, 199, 331n19
'stupidity', 65, 73, 85, 102, 310n17, 326n33
subject, 19–20, 41, 133–35, 170, 183, 191, 223, 230–32, 238, 242, 246–48, 250, 276–78, 283, 315n5, 336n10
subject-object. *See* dualism
subjective, 5–6, 19, 71–72, 115, 129, 133–34, 136–39, 144–45, 172–73, 178, 180, 183, 223, 243, 331n17, 333n21, 344n8
   agency. *See* agency
   deliberation, 173
   (de)subjectification, 93, 102, 221
   intersubjectivity, 170, 245, 331n17, 332n19
   subjectivity, 5, 10–11, 20, 41, 44, 53–54, 71, 74, 94, 112, 116, 127, 136, 170, 182, 187, 190, 227–30, 242, 244–46, 248, 261, 296, 318n9, 324n29, 330n11, 332n20, 348n12, 353n20, 354n6
   subjectivization, 232, 248
   truth, 172, 178
   See also Habermas, Jürgen: three worlds (subjective, objective, normative)

supernatural/enchanted worlds. *See* worlds
symbol, 23, 46, 59, 63, 108, 112, 116, 118, 121, 125–27, 129, 164, 191, 198–99, 280, 316n5, 321n20, 330n10, 330n14, 33n22, 344n8–9
   "symbolic capital." *See* Bourdieu, Pierre
symbolic anthropology. *See* anthropology
synthetic a priori. *See* a priori

Talmon-Garber, Yonina, 279
Taussig, Michael, 345n3
Taylor, Charles, 155–61, 164, 225–28, 231, 233, 238, 330n14, 331n17, 337n2, 338n4, 338n6, 350n6, 351n9–10, 355n7
   on Foucault, 225–28, 233, 350n8
   on rationality, 155–61
technology. *See* science
time, 33, 44, 59–61, 84, 89, 94, 116, 123–25, 128, 143, 145, 191–95, 210, 242, 251, 256, 258, 261, 263, 269, 272, 275–76, 296, 356n11, 357n7, 358–59n7
   and the Dinka. *See* Dinka
   homogeneous, 183
   "Jewish time." *See* Judaism
   long-term, 3, 160–61, 183, 185, 195, 251, 296
   sempiternal, 251, 276
   short-term, 160–61, 183, 251, 296
   temporality, 33, 122, 182–85, 210, 251, 276, 296, 358n2
   time (of) being 59, 261, 263, 272, 295
   See also space: space-time
Tiv, 198
totalism, 165, 225, 230
totalitarianism, 89, 92, 225, 327n33
totality, 35, 58, 68
transcendence, 40, 67, 121, 124, 127, 130, 171–74, 192, 229, 232, 250–51, 255, 267, 270, 296, 341n11, 356n10–11
   ritual, 251
   self-transcendence, 41, 171, 192, 245, 284
translation. *See* ethnography
Tree of Life, 53, 96, 106, 310n18
Trobrianders, 23
truth, 18, 21, 32–33, 35, 108, 119, 163–64, 166, 169, 171–74, 178, 187–88, 202, 209, 219, 226, 228, 230, 234, 241, 281, 338n5, 347n10, 352n13
   objective. *See* objective
   subjective. *See* subjective
Turner, Victor, 343n8

uncertainty, 3, 11, 39, 50, 60, 112–14, 116, 123, 128, 134, 136–37, 143, 145, 159–60, 168–69, 183–84, 187, 190, 195, 210–12, 216, 246, 249, 255, 260–61, 268, 272, 280,

uncertainty (*cont.*)
    282–84, 299, 306n3, 327n35, 339n6, 345n3,
        348n13–14, 355n7, 356n13
    of choice, 11, 160, 246
    of the future, 160
    of the other, 113, 280, 282, 327n35, 348n13
    of the self, 50, 134, 136, 211, 268
    See also ambiguity
universality, 18, 19, 20–21, 24–25, 28, 39, 40,
        87–90, 92, 93, 102, 277, 319n11
    universal law. *See* law
    universalism, 237
utility, 14, 84, 92–93, 156, 164, 222–23, 316n5,
    319n13

value, xxiii–xiv, 13, 38–39, 40, 108, 110, 163, 167,
        174, 188, 197, 222–23, 233–36, 256, 258,
        291, 297
    freedom, xxiv
    hierarchy of, 197, 331n19
    instrumentality, xxiv, 84, 92
    survival, 250–51, 295
    of Value, 13
    value-as-such, xxiii–xiv, 83, 85, 235, 328n4
    value-rationality. *See* rationality
Vaux, Roland de, 306n5
Velásquez. *See* Foucault, Michel
Vico, 288, 289
    "etymology," 288
violence, 7, 11, 13, 49, 73, 313n1, 314n3
visible, 69, 71–72, 122, 130, 166, 191, 211, 218–21,
        238, 312n24–25, 360n13. *See also* Merleau-
        Ponty, Maurice: the visible
Voegelin, Eric, 276, 280, 358n1, 358n6

Wacquant, Loïc J. D., 108–10, 126, 327n2, 328n5,
        330n11, 332n20, 327n2, 329n5
    on Bourdieu, 126
    An Invitation to Reflexive Sociology, 327n2
Webb, Stephen. *See* Derrida, Jacques
Weber, Max, 13, 118, 121, 331n16, 337n1
    enchantment, xi, 311n22
    'practical reason', 200
    rationality, 13, 153, 303n4 (intro.)
Weil, Jiří, 83
Western onto-epistemological tradition, 2–3, 9,
        121, 132–34, 170, 183, 190, 192, 198–200,
        202, 225, 228–29, 237–38, 246, 258, 264,
        282–83, 289, 292–93, 297, 299, 337n2,
        340n4
Wilden, Anthony, 356n11
will, 39, 45, 48, 102, 136, 302n3, 318n10, 336n10,
        345n3, 350n8, 351n11m 352n16
wisdom, 254–56, 281, 356n12

Wittgenstein, Ludwig, 22–32, 35, 42–46, 76, 115,
        119–20, 123, 127, 129–30, 164, 166, 193,
        298, 303–4nn4–6, 311n23, 331n15, 339n1,
        341n10, 342n13, 344n10, 350n3, 354n2
    critique of Frazer, 331n15, 339n1, 354n2
    empirical propositions, 31
    ethics, 26–27
    grammatical rules, 31–32
    instrumental and expressive acts, 23–24
    loss of problem, 200
    norms of description, 31, 32
    On Certainty, 29–31
    "perspicuous presentation," 344n10
    recognition, experience of, 25
    scaffolding of thought, 31, 32
    Weltbild (world picture), 30
women's studies, 4
worlds, 6–7, 182, 190, 222, 224, 299
    an-'other' world, 224
    common world, 72–73
    creating of, 231, 250, 260–61
    cultural world, 6
    detachment from, 230
    existential world, practical engagement with,
        255
    modern world, 7, 226
    normative world, 75, 145
    object/material world, 232
    objective world, 71–72, 74, 179, 222, 311–
        12nn24–25, 338n6
    openness. *See* openness: of the world
    oracular world, 202
    primary world, 75
    rational world, 241
    real world, 167, 171. *See also* reality
    supernatural/enchanted worlds, 181, 222
    uncertain world, 211–12
    virtual world, 213
Wyschograd, Edith, 303n3 (chap. 1), 316n5, 317n7,
    319n13

Zeitlyn, David, 347n8